An Unamuno source book

MIGUEL DE UNAMUNO (1864-1936)

An Unamuno source book

A catalogue of readings and acquisitions with an
introductory essay on Unamuno's dialectical enquiry

MARIO J. VALDÉS and MARÍA ELENA DE VALDÉS

University of Toronto Press

© University of Toronto Press 1973
Toronto and Buffalo
Printed in Canada
ISBN 0-8020-5268-1
Microfiche ISBN 0-8020-0168-8
LC 76-185742

And when, one day, grown conscious of age
While pondering an eolith
We turned a human page ...
                    (E.J. Pratt)

With gratitude to our parents

Consuelo Cuenca Vda. de Molins
Juanita San Martín de Valdés
Mario Valdés Salinas

To the memory of
Teótimo Molins Urbano

Contents

Illustrations

Frontispiece: Miguel de Unamuno (1864-1936)

Illustrations following page xxxviii:

Card from Unamuno's catalogue.

Notes found in G.W.F. Hegel's *Wissenschaft der Logik*, U-1260.

Reading notes from Concepción Sáiz y Otero and Urbano González Serrano, *Cartas ¿Pedagógicas? Ensayos de psicología pedagógica*, U-148.

Reading notes from William Hazlitt's *Table-Talk. Essays on Men and Manners*, U-459.

Reading notes from Alberto Nin Frias, *Nuevos ensayos de crítica literaria y filosófica*, U-1159.

Reading notes from Pindar's *Pindari Carmina cum fragmentis selectis*, U-350.

Preface

Our purpose in this book is limited to two pre-critical functions: to provide the scholar with an accurate source book of Unamuno's readings, and to examine Unamuno's process of intellectual and aesthetic assimilation. The principal motivation from the outset was our interest in providing source material for the future use of scholars in Unamuno studies. Through examination of Unamuno's marginal notes in the process of this research, however, we became aware of a particular system of enquiry employed by Unamuno. This system is expounded in the introduction, which begins with a description of the marginalia. An outline of Unamuno's process of enquiry then follows, and the introduction concludes with an assessment of Unamuno's theory of knowledge.

Unamuno's library in Salamanca has been a continuing source of valuable material for scholars, and the spirit of co-operation and the accessibility which have characterized this institution undoubtedly will be carried on after the recent purchase (1968) of the collection by the National Government of Spain. We believe, however, that the scholarly community at large can gain much insight into the possibilities of Unamuno research from an authoritative and organized catalogue of Unamuno's readings. Unamuno criticism (e.g., Julián Marías, *Unamuno*, 1943, p. 35; Carlos Clavería, *Temas de Unamuno*, 1953, p. 123) has long been insistent on the radical independence of Unamuno and his unorthodox use of sources, but this generalization (to which we also subscribe) does not lessen the importance of his sources. On the contrary, we believe it makes it imperative that we know the full dimensions of Unamuno's intellectual stimulation. Consequently, once again, we find ourselves repeating the near truism that originality – even the late romantic conception of it – has never precluded the assimilation of the specific material of others.

The need of this research tool has been made even more urgent by the loss of Professor Manuel García Blanco. This dedicated scholar brought to light hundreds of invaluable observations on the multiple facets of Unamuno's readings. The loss to Unamuno criticism of this generous and able man cannot be overcome, but it is in the hope of maintaining the tradition of accessibility that we have accelerated the completion of this source book, which has been our principal project since 1964. The entire academic year of 1966-7 was devoted to the examination of García Blanco's papers in order to make this catalogue as complete as possible.

The library as it now exists in Salamanca has 5700 books; about two-thirds of the estimated collection Unamuno acquired before his exile in 1924. This is not the place to delve into the reasons for the loss of these books. One must be thankful that such a large part of the collection has been safeguarded.

The card catalogue of the University of Salamanca library has approximately 3000 entries for the more than 5000 Unamuno books in the present collection, and the author's card catalogue in the 'Casa Rectoral,' which houses the collection, is equally lacking and in general is unreliable in its title and publication information. Therefore, the first phase of this project was to compile an accurate and complete catalogue of the present collection. Together with this basic catalogue a record of annotations was kept as we examined every book in the 'Casa Rectoral' during 1964 and 1965.

The second phase was initiated by the discovery of a personal card catalogue kept by Unamuno between 1900 and 1917. This consists of 4000 cards written in Unamuno's own script with a personal system of classification of his library. Spanish works were filed in chronological order, and foreign books by topic. When this private catalogue was collated with the present collection, we added more than 2000 entries to the bibliography of readings. This was the first direct indication of the number of lost books. Since Unamuno was not a librarian, and the catalogue was for his personal use, the notations were often inadequate for our identification of the books. Consequently, the next step was to find complete information for each of the books not in the collection today. To this end, we found the catalogue of the British Museum Library most useful. A careful search has turned up almost all of the entries from the Unamuno card file. Only the most esoteric titles remain incomplete.

The Unamuno family further informed us that Unamuno read and often marked books while visiting various members of the family. At the same time we examined the unpublished dissertation of Emile Martel, 'Libros y lecturas francesas de Miguel de Unamuno,' which listed the majority of the books read by Unamuno during the imposed confinement in his home before his death. We were able to examine all of the books owned by the family and to collect the information on annotations.

At this point in the project, we had accumulated a catalogue of 8000 entries, which, in our opinion, could be established without a doubt as having been the property of or as having been read by Unamuno. However, with disturbing frequency, we found that books which Unamuno commented upon at length in his writings were missing from our catalogue. We decided to remedy this deficiency, if only nominally, by compiling a list of all the books and authors mentioned by Unamuno in the *Obras completas* (hereafter cited as *OC*). The resulting list of books and authors forms a separate and complementary index of readings not accounted for in the catalogue.

Had Unamuno not been involved in the most cataclysmic eruption of Spanish history there is little doubt that this project would have been realized long since by his own students in Salamanca, for even a cursory review of his writings points to the advantages of a compilation of his sources. The full ramifications of this catalogue cannot be anticipated by us; it remains for the scholar to take up the challenge which we pass on – to cope with the colossal temerity of a man who made every subject he encountered his personal domain.

MJV
MEV

Acknowledgments

We wish to express our gratitude to the Canada Council, the Humanities and Social Sciences Committee of the University of Toronto, and the University of Toronto Library for the various grants they have awarded us from 1964 to 1969 to enable us to complete this source book.

We also thank Professor Hans Eric Keller, Ohio State University, for reading the manuscript of the bibliography, and Professor S.P. Rosenbaum, University of Toronto, for reading the introductory study.

The encouragement of members of the Department of Italian and Hispanic Studies, especially Professor G.L. Stagg and Professor J.H. Parker, has been of the greatest significance in the organization and completion of this research project.

We also wish to acknowledge the assistance afforded the compilation of this catalogue by the unpublished dissertation, 'Libros y lecturas francesas de Miguel de Unamuno,' Universidad de Salamanca (1964), by Emile Martel. And we thank Professor Demetrius Basdekis of State University of New York for his generous assistance in completing the appendix to the catalogue of readings. This project was made possible through the warm friendship and assistance of Felisa de Unamuno.

This book has been published with the help of grants from the Humanities Research Council of Canada, using funds provided by the Canada Council, and from the Publications Fund of the University of Toronto Press.

Introduction

by Mario J.Valdés

Miguel de Unamuno (1864-1936) has been an enigmatic writer for his critics because of various significant factors: the lack of complete and accurate texts, his unorthodox use of established terminology, and, not least of all his radical disregard of traditional professional methodology in all of his endeavours. It is usual, therefore, to find commentaries that dismiss his works as the paradoxical musings of a mystic and statements that assess his philosophical contribution as the interesting but superficial expression of an unregenerate obstructionist.[1] It is, however, almost a complete waste of time to enter into this debate since no one – detractor or admirer – has undertaken a thorough examination of his methodology. It is to this end that I direct this introduction. I shall not seek to justify or condemn Unamuno's modus operandi but rather present it in as concise a manner as possible. My procedure shall be to outline the unpublished sources of my observations, make a general statement about Unamuno's methodology, and then suggest some of the implications of this statement.

THE MARGINALIA

During the last five years I have examined Unamuno's private library in Salamanca and the thousands of notes he left. I have become convinced that his questioning attitude was highly disciplined and consistent and that a well-defined method of enquiry was behind the highly personal expression of this

---

1 Cf. Susanne K. Langer, *Feeling and Form* (New York, 1953), p. 351: 'Unamuno's feelings are strong and natural; his aphorisms are often poetic and memorable. With his philosophical assertions, however, one cannot take issue, because he prides himself on being inconsistent, on the ground that 'life is irrational,' 'truth is not logical,' etc. Consistency of statements he regards as a mark of their falsity. Like some exasperating ladies, who claim 'a woman's right to be inconsistent,' he cannot, therefore, be worsted in argument, but – also like them – he cannot be taken seriously.'

philosopher-poet. The initial observations of Unamuno's reading habits present him as a careful reader of thousands of books and, most important, as an intellectually and physically active reader. He marked, commented, annotated, and indexed as he read. These external clues indicate an active participation on the part of the reader with his reading, which is certainly not uncommon among critical readers. This is a man responding to ideas as one normally would respond to physical stimulus. Unamuno constructed a dialogue with his reading. Each time the text presented him with the singular opinion of an author, it was a personal challenge to him. At this point it is pertinent to pause and outline some fundamental aspects about language.

The structured expressions of language have been traditionally classified as discourse, lyric song and dialogue.[2] This classification is sufficiently developed in the studies of Cassirer, Kayser, Nicol, and Staiger to warrant the application I shall use in this study.[3] Let us use the term 'discourse' as an expression through a rational structure dependent on syntax, and, in general, performing the function of exposition. It is dominated by the ideals of clarity and consistency. In contrast, let us present lyric song as a construction dependent upon the associative structure of metaphor and dedicated to the general function of the poet's self-manifestation. The level of meaning here is intuitional rather than rational. Thus, the lyric can be said to be dominated by the necessity of externalizing the poet's associative context. Finally, I shall use the term 'dialogue' to express a dialectic structure of language. The basic function is in this case one of stimulation; it is on an intentional level of expression. The direction of language is one of reciprocal exchange. The dialectic structure fulfils the need of enquiry.

I stress the point that Unamuno appears to encounter in the author and his words more than just the ideas expressed in the content of the reading. If I have misread the evidence, my hypothesis does not apply. On the other hand, if my observations are valid, I think the following argument will lead to a greater understanding of the foremost literary figure of twentieth-century Spain.

Let us take first, as examples of Unamuno's methodology, the *Pensées* of Pascal (Unamuno library [hereafter U]-1506), an edition of Herbert Spencer's essays (U-2548-50), and Melville's *Moby Dick* (U-5208). We have the edition of the *Pensées* with Unamuno's notations as well as another edition he must

---

2 See Wolfgang Kayser, 'La estructura del género,' *Interpretación y análisis de la obra literaria* (Madrid, 1954), pp. 529-622, and also the corresponding bibliography, pp. 665-9.

3 For a brief review of the work of Cassirer and Staiger see Kayser, pp. 536-8. For the principal statement of each see Ernst Cassirer, *Philosophie der symbolischen Formen I: Die Sprache* (Berlin, 1923); and Emil Staiger, *Grundbegriffe der Poetik* (Zurich, 1946). The most pertinent commentary by Eduardo Nicol is in *Metafísica de la expresión* (México, 1957), pp. 297-313.

have read only in part.[4] There are numerous references to Pascal and to this
book in particular scattered throughout Unamuno's writings. We are fortunate
that the most extensive commentary, 'La foi de Pascal' (*Agonía del cristianismo*), is also an important statement on how he read this book.

Because Pascal's writing is relatively attuned to Unamuno's 'agonistic'
vision, there is an effective transformation of the discursive prose of each
pensée into a dynamic pattern of oppositions that is as much Unamuno's as it
is Pascal's. Unamuno's reading notes of the *Pensées* develop a sense of polarity
that is unmistakably Pascal's and is intrinsic to the ideas presented in the text.
However, Unamuno's method of reading the *Pensées* is in itself productive of
polarity. The key to understanding these notations is to read them in terms
of Unamuno's search for the inner conflict of the idea represented. Unamuno
cuts away whatever discursive trappings Pascal gives the language in an attempt
to isolate the elements of struggle. The *Pensées* that elicited the longest commentary are characteristically those that stress the inherent strife of existence.
Let us look into some representative examples and Unamuno's ensuing marginal notes. Only the lines marked off by Unamuno are reproduced in these
excerpts.

72 Man's disproportion. Limited as we are in every way; this state which
holds the means between two extremes is present in all our impotence. Our
senses perceive no extreme. Too much sound deafens us; too much light daz-
zles us; ... In short, extremes are for us as though they were not, and we are
not within their notice. They escape us, or we them.

This is our true state; this is what makes us incapable of certain knowledge
and of absolute ignorance. We sail within a vast sphere, ever drifting in uncer-
tainty, driven from end to end. When we think to attach ourselves to any
point and to fasten to it, it wavers and leaves us; and if we follow it, it eludes
our grasp, slips past us, and vanishes forever. Nothing stays for us. This is our
natural condition, and yet most contrary to our inclination; we burn with desire to find solid ground and an ultimate sure foundation whereon to build a
tower reaching to the infinite. But our whole ground work cracks and the
earth opens to abysses.

Let us therefore not look for certainty and stability. Our reason is always
deceived by fickle shadows; nothing can fix the finite between the two Infinites, which both enclose and fly from it. ...

---

4   It is most significant that although Unamuno owned an 1847 edition of the *Pensées*,
    the edition that is annotated dates from 1913, the year after the publication of *Del
    sentimiento trágico* where Pascal is only mentioned in passing (*OC*, XVI, 241) and
    eleven years before the French publication of *La agonía del cristianismo*, where Pas-
    cal is given an entire chapter.

Man, for instance, is related to all he knows. He needs a place wherein to abide, time through which to live, motion in order to live, elements to compose him, warmth and food to nourish him, air to breathe. He sees light; he feels bodies; in short, he is in a dependent alliance with everything. To know man, then, it is necessary to know how it happens that he needs air to live, and to know the air, we must know how it is thus related to the life of man, etc. Flame cannot exist without air; therefore to understand the one, we must understand the other.

... we are composed of two opposite natures, different in kind, soul and body. For it is impossible that our rational part should be other than spiritual, and if anyone maintain that we are simply corporeal, this would far more exclude us from the knowledge of things, there being nothing so inconceivable as to say that matter knows itself. It is impossible to imagine how it should know itself.

78 Descartes useless and uncertain.

125 *Contraries.* Man is naturally credulous and incredulous, timid and rash.

126 Description of man: dependency, desire of independence, need.

127 Condition of man: inconstancy, weariness, unrest.

129 Our nature consists in motion; complete rest in death.

131 *Weariness.* Nothing is so insufferable to man as to be completely at rest, without passions, without business, without diversion, without study. He then feels his nothingness, his forlornness, his insufficiency, his dependence, his weakness, his emptiness. There will immediately arise from the depth of his heart weariness, gloom, sadness, fretfulness, vexation, despair.

139 Diversion ... I have discovered that all the unhappiness of men arises from one single fact, that they cannot stay quietly in their own chamber. ...

As men who naturally understand their own condition avoid nothing so much as rest, so there is nothing they leave undone in seeking turmoil. ...

344 Instinct and reason, marks of two natures.

394 All the principles of skeptics, stoics, atheists, etc. are true. But their conclusions are false, because the opposite principles are also true.

395 Instinct, Reason. We have an incapacity of proof, insurmountable by all dogmatism. We have an idea of truth, invincible to all skepticism.

396 Two things instruct man about his whole nature; instinct and experience.

412 There is internal war in man between reason and the passions. If he had only reason without passions ... If he had only passions without reason. But having both, he cannot be without strife, being unable to be at peace with the one without being at war with the other. Thus, he is always divided against, and opposed to himself.

I shall not develop or enumerate comments of a topical nature made by Unamuno. Rather, I have selected the comments that best exemplify his process of enquiry. [Translations mine.]

The initial comments he writes in response to *Pensée* 72 acknowledge some basic similarities between Pascal and himself; 'dialectic, polemic'; 'only rest for man in death'; 'synthesis aberration of reason'; 'the contrary is contained in every proposition'; 'the eternal dualism of struggle'; 'to question is to reach for the real'; 'to think one knows is to deceive oneself.' After these general remarks, Unamuno begins to build an outline of the *Pensées*. He finds four encounters in this book.[5] All four are concerned with aspects of the inner strife characteristic of the self. The key words are *persona* and *yo*, which I have translated as 'person' and 'individual.' The four polarities, briefly stated, are: (1) the person's social mask opposed by the individual's private consciousness; (2) the collective action of the person in society countered by the radical loneliness of the individual; (3) the social commitment of the person in conflict with the private goals of the individual; and (4) the person's command and use of his rational faculties to enable him to operate safely within the social group contradicted by the individual's irrational need for belief in a structure beyond empirical perception. Each of the four is a pair of contraries that defines reality as a continuous process of struggle. I shall return to the further discussion of the ontological implications, but let us proceed with the notes as methodology.

These polar forces are distinguishable but not separable, for their meaning is inherent in their being opposite. The first set of polarities is the fundamental source for this interpretation of Pascal and the starting point for the other three: the struggle between the social aspect of the self and the individual aspect. Since language is communal,[6] the social *persona* is continuously imposed by language on the individual, i.e., the myself (*yo*). The role of the individual, on the other hand, is to challenge and undermine the validity of the posture taken by the *persona*. In this conflict, Unamuno finds the basis for the second pair of oppositions: the collective action of the social self (*persona*), which is set implicitly in the use of language, is seen as a constant striving to offset and overcome the radical isolation of the individual aspect (*yo*). The major thrust of this individualistic aspect of the self is to oppose the *persona* from the isolated situation of the my-self and thus to counter social action with contem-

---

5 Unamuno followed his usual practice of marginal annotation, but in this book he also wrote some commentary on the backs of official notices from the municipal government of Salamanca. These notes are placed as place-markers in the book, obviously as reminders of the passage that elicited the commentary.

6 The conflicting claims for language as expression and language as communication, described by F.E. Sparshott, *The Structure of Aesthetics* (Toronto, 1963), pp. 426-30, are the basis for Unamuno's reading of the *Pensées*. For a complete statement of language as an existential dialectic see E. Nicol, *Metafísica de la expresión*, pp. 308-9.

plation and self-examination. Unamuno distinguishes a third Pascalian polarity: the willed reaction of the self to the external world; this set of contradictory forces consists of the *persona*'s commitment to the social group versus the individual's conception of life as private. In Unamuno's words, the *persona* belongs to his world and is dedicated to the scale of values of the social group to which he belongs, but the individual *yo* in contrast, dominates his universe as the centre and first cause of all values. Finally, the fourth polarity is the relentless force of the irrational need for belief in some structure beyond the self, which challenges and opposes the equally inexorable power of reason to create a system. The polarity here identified by Unamuno is only too well known to modern existentialist psychology. The self's search for security in a threatening and alien world is described by Unamuno as 'the emotive need for faith,' faith in someone or something that will bring a promise of order and continuity for the self. The rational explanation of causal relations does not satisfy this need and is disrupted and opposed by the irrationality of the individual. The self reverts to rational explanation as long as the security of the group suffices, but the awareness of the insufficiency of reason recurs again and again. All four polarities are contradictory facets of the self, real only by their opposition to one another.

Unamuno's last notes on the *Pensées* are the following: 'conflict between demands required by society and the defense of one's individuality. Concept of harmony seeds of fanaticism. Man is caught between two infinites; composed of irreconcilable opposites; he lives in insatiable turmoil.' Unamuno's notes do not sum up these observations, but we have been supplied sufficient material to go the rest of the way. The two radical sides of the self are the social mask (*persona*) and the private consciousness (*yo*): social participation opposed by solitude, commitment to the world opposed by affirmation as dominance of the universe, sentiment opposed by contemplation, rational order opposed by irrational need. But all of these contradictions are joined in the possibility of annihilation of the self.

Of course one can also see that Unamuno's reading of the *Pensées* takes full advantage of certain similarities in style, and subject matter, but it is of the greatest importance to understand that this interpretation is set in a dialectic pattern. Although Pascal is concerned with the inner conflict within his own experience, it is Unamuno's transformation of Pascal's words into the dialectic that makes the *Pensées* such an overwhelming endorsement of the Unamunian vision.

Let us turn now to a writer whose temper and manner were not so congenial to Unamuno. Herbert Spencer's *Essays: Scientific, Political and Speculative* faced Unamuno with prose that had to be assaulted, dismembered, and partially destroyed before it could be changed from a discursive exposition of a system to a dialectic quest. Unamuno read the three volumes of this collection of essays with great interest, underlining and marking words and paragraphs throughout. This collection was first published in 1891 and Unamuno's translation of a one-volume selection came out in 1895 with the title *De las leyes en general.*

Although Unamuno must have considered Spencer's philosophy on many occasions, as his references to the British writer indicate, the reading and translation of this material probably mark the high point in interest and dedication, since it culminates years of intensive enquiry into this synthetic system of thought. Unamuno's published remarks about Spencer's philosophy are increasingly antagonistic, beginning with *En torno al casticismo* in 1895.

The three volumes of Spencer's *Essays: Scientific, Political and Speculative* contain two types of Unamunian notations: the interest markings along the margin calling attention to specific points made in the discourse, and numerous translations into Spanish. The interest markings always by-pass Spencer's long and involved clarifications, which define and qualify the mechanistic language. Unamuno stresses the implied subject-object dichotomy he finds throughout. He links Spencer's two classes of experience, the vivid and the faint, to the same opposing necessity that sets ego against non-ego or self against non-self. In this manner Unamuno isolates the dialectic elements in Spencer and establishes conflict as the source and sustaining force of reality which Spencer called 'persistence in consciousness.' By concentrating on the elements of inner conflict, Unamuno points out that the synthetic terms, such as 'an unknowable power of persistence' used to describe reality, are rational platforms needed to uphold the system. Thus, it is understandable that the words Unamuno translates with insistence are these very terms of mechanistic synthesis. Spencer's consistent habit of expressing notions implying flux and change, such as space, time, matter, motion, and force, in words of static abstraction is the most obvious objection Unamuno has to his writings.

Unamuno's reading notes of Spencer are extremely valuable as an illustration of the reader in open battle with the language of rational synthesis, the principal adversary of this methodology. Unamuno characterizes the reader as striving to rediscover the structure of the writer's world in the same way that an archaeologist searches for the way of life of another age. The writer's truth is his point of view engulfed in polarities of conflict, but it must be searched for under countless layers of rational sedimentation. Unamuno writes: 'The error of metaphysics is that fundamental questions are always asked as if they were so many problems to be solved.' This initial error, he contends, only leads the system builders to construct pre-fabricated platforms in order 'to ascend to the sought integration or synthesis,' that is, the solution, which is implied, a priori, by the question. Unamuno thus conceives of philosophical enquiry as a creative re-enactment of the conflict and never as an offering of solutions to problems. From these notes, then, we have drawn forth a general outline of an ontology, for in this philosophy methodology can never be completely separated from its ontological foundations.

Unamuno's search for the inner conflict in the two works discussed has in each case drawn out the underlying dynamism of oppositions. In Pascal, Kierkegaard, William James, Bergson, and others like them,[7] Unamuno found prose bristling with the sense of the dialectic, which he sought as essential for dialogue. However, in Spencer, Kant, Spinoza, and others of a rational orientation, the situation varied, as with Herbert Spencer, the language and the structural organization of the material is aimed at resolving conflict, at creating a synthesis of disparate elements. Thus, in these cases, Unamuno's quest is one of seeking out the polarity, which to him is at the root of consciousness and thus underlies the discourse of the writer. Most contemporary commentators will agree with Unamuno's interpretation that Spencer has all the antecedents of a vitalistic philosophy, the language notwithstanding.

Let us now assess the first indications of method as well as the ontological implications we have thus far uncovered in the reading notes. The dialogue encounter between reader and author was in Unamuno's approach a creative re-enactment of the process that went into the writing itself. We can characterize the method as an ontological transcendence that attempts to reach for the very ground of reality in the writer. It follows, I believe, that language or for that matter any form of communication supposes in the listener this creative re-enactment of what has been received. Thus, Unamuno is saying language leads us to an idea that is not 'mine alone' but rather the unique result of exchange. And, consequently, the written word is in a precarious situation, since there is always the possibility, and some would say the probability, that the inherent conflict of exchange will be lost if the reader remains aloof from the reading and does not assert himself. The words of such a reading are nothing more than an empty gesture. This dialogue of challenge and encounter is Unamuno's method of searching for the reality beyond the written words, which is to say that his is a methodology of hermeneutics. Ontologically, reality is seen as a condition of conflict between opposing forces. On the level of human existence, reality becomes the conflict within our point of view, beginning with the self as the subject of enquiry. I shall return to these ideas in more detail in the next section.

7   A list of Unamuno's most read authors would include such diverse writers as St Augustine, Dante, Blake, Amiel, Sénancour, Leopardi, Antero de Quental, and, of course, the authors of the Bible. The common feature in all is the inherent use of contraries. Unamuno's search for these kindred spirits led him over an enormous range of literatures and languages, e.g., his study of Danish in 1900 in order to read Kierkegaard. The fourteen volumes of the collected works of Kierkegaard published in Copenhagen between 1901 and 1906 by A.B. Drachmann and J.L. Heiberg was purchased volume by volume by Unamuno as they were published. Only volumes five and eight are not marked and annotated with occasional extensive commentary.

In the writings discussed so far, the expression of thought or opinion was directed from the writer to the reader. Consequently, Unamuno's dialogue-reading had only to draw out the elements of conflict that uncover the inner personality of the writer. However, there are other than writer-to-reader relationships to consider. For example, although the literary creation brings forth the talent and the vision of the writer, it also has a unique aesthetic value that is independent of the man who created it. Therefore, if Unamuno is to have a dialogue, he must take part as one of the opposing forces against the shifting and sometimes subtle combination of the literary voice of the work and the presence of the author. The fictional character, the character-narrator, or simply the narrative voice, for example, is to Unamuno an intermediary between the writer and the reader. Unamuno dismisses as naïveté any attempt to trace the personality or behaviour of the character back to the biographical circumstances of the author. 'The writer creates as he writes; ideas come into being as he makes the effort to exteriorize what was merely a notion before writing' (*OC*, xi, 937). Consequently, the fictional character has his own realm of reality independent of his creator and it is only through the reconstruction of the implicit or explicit dialectical exchange between the narrative voices and the author that the reader can transcend the intermediary reality and experience author-presence.[8]

Unamuno's readings of Herman Melville's *Moby Dick* (U-5208) exemplify his search for the dialectic in prose fiction. Unamuno read the novel at three times during his exile in France and made a total of 383 markings and commentaries in the book as he read and reread it. These marks and Unamuno's scrap-paper commentaries can be put in the following categories: (1) metaphors of reality, (2) metaphors of man's predicament, (3) biblical references, (4) regional language, (5) references to Hispanic persons or places. The most frequently underlined passages are from the first two categories, and all of the commentary is in response to them.

The metaphors of reality are the divine loom and the sea. Both were quite familiar to Unamuno, who had used them extensively in his own fiction.[9] A typical passage is at the end of *Moby Dick*'s ninety-third chapter: 'He saw

8   Author-presence in Unamuno's own novels has been treated by several commentators, the most extensive study being Ricardo Gullón's *Autobiografías de Unamuno* (Madrid, 1964).
9   For a representative example of Unamuno's use of the loom metaphor see *Niebla* (*OC*, II, 837): 'Mira, Orfeo, las lizas, mira la urdimbre, mira cómo la trama va y viene con la lanzadera, mira cómo juegan las primideras; pero, dime, ¿dónde está el enjullo, a que se arrolla la tela de nuestra existencia, dónde?' My own translation: 'Look at the threads, Orfeo; look at the warp; and see how the thread of the woof goes back and forth with the throw of the shuttle; and watch the play of the treadle as it goes up and down; but, tell me, where is the warp rod upon which is rolled up the fabric of our existence – where?' This passage comes after a long meditative monologue on

God's foot upon the treadle of the loom, and spoke it; and therefore ship-mates called him mad.' Another good example of how Unamuno marked the novel is mid-way through chapter 102: 'Nay – the shuttle flies – the figures float from forth the loom; the freshet-rushing carpet for ever slides away. The weaver-god, he weaves, and by that weaving is he deafened, that he hears no mortal voice; and by that humming, we, too, who look on the loom are deaf-ened; and only when we escape it shall we hear the thousand voices that speak through it. For even so it is in all material factories. The spoken words that are inaudible among the flying spindles; those same words are plainly heard without the walls, bursting from the opened casements. Thereby have villain-ies been detected. Ah, mortal! Then, be heedful; for so, in all this din of the great world's loom, thy subtlest thinkings may be overheard afar.' Unamuno writes: 'life/ceaseless creation,' 'the novel itself woven by the meditative mind of its narrator.'

The underlined passages of the sea metaphor are numerous in the text. (Chapter 1): 'But that same image, we ourselves see in all rivers and oceans. It is the image of the ungraspable phantom of life and this is the key to it all.' (Chapter 3): 'It's the breaking-up of the ice bound stream of time.' (Chapter 72): 'The unsounded ocean you gasp in, is Life.' (Chapter 135): 'And the great shroud of the sea rolled on as it rolled five thousand years ago.' Unamuno's comments are very near to his own use of this metaphor as this sampling indi-cates: 'All is doubt, all is flux the sea'; 'man searches for meaning in the enig-matic waters'; and, finally, 'The eternal vision of the sea, the eternal sea, the sea that witnessed the birth of history.'

Now let us turn to the dominant feature of Unamuno's annotations: the metaphorical and symbolic expression of man's predicament. (Chapter 44): 'God help thee, old man, thy thoughts have created a creature in thee; and he whose intense thinking thus makes him a Prometheus; a vulture feeds upon that heart for ever; that vulture the very creature he creates.' Unamuno's com-ments focus on Ahab's struggle against the white whale as a struggle 'to give meaning to man's presence. Fed by an irrational fear that nothing awaits man beyond death he must prove that man's will matters and that in spite of the indifferent God-nature there was meaning to life – "non-resignation" [*irresig-nación*] to death.'

Unamuno found in this book an extraordinary storehouse of his own most vital images. Thus, it was a discovery of a kindred spirit who saw life itself as a struggle cut off only by death. That Unamuno felt close to Melville is fur-ther evidenced by a short poem he wrote on a scrap of paper on 5 March 1929, and then rewrote in his poetic diary:

the diverse contributing elements which make up one's life pattern. Interested readers will find Unamuno's sea metaphor fully treated in my *Death in the Literature of Una-muno* (Urbana: University of Illinois Press, 1964).

Melville, tu Moby Dick, tu ballena blanca,
vive en el Tormes de Salamanca
¿Cómo sube de la mar?
Baja de Gredos por el agua
en una chispa toda la fragua,
todo y entero Dios en cada lugar.

                           5-III-1929

Melville, thy Moby Dick, thy white whale,
lives in Salamanca's Tormes.
How does it come up from the sea?
It descends from Gredos through the water
In a spark the entire forge
All and complete God in each place.

Unamuno did not approach a specific text as a novel, poem, essay, or drama in the conventional usage of these terms; his focal point was a consideration of the author's situation in the text rather than the historical categories of genre. The structure of the text is to Unamuno a construction of fundamental polarities, which are more or less hidden, more or less revealed by the linguistic instruments used. Style to Unamuno is not only self-expression but a translucent presentation of the inherent conflict in the author's point of view. Consequently, the more the language tends to cover up the author's reality (i.e., the conflict of polarities) the less it is style and the more it becomes a defensive and protective gesturing. Unamuno's unorthodox usage of 'poet,' 'poetry,' 'novel,' and 'drama' can be better appreciated in the light of his understanding of language and style. All writers, be they philosophers, literary critics, or novelists, are poets to the extent that they succeed in expressing themselves, that is, to the degree they are able to invest their written words with the reality of their own speech. The instruments of communication must therefore reveal the subject who is actually speaking. The writer who is able to attain such a unification of self and written language is a poet.

In his notes on St Augustine, Unamuno characterizes a book as a novel if it presents a quest for self-discovery for the three viable participants: narrator, character, and reader. Drama is less clearly defined in the reading notes. There are numerous commentaries on *King Lear* and *Hamlet* of a specific nature but there also appears the following observation: 'Drama is the open confrontation of the *yo* and the other.'[10] The contraries are, of course, similar to the polarities he found in Pascal; however, he is now writing of the embodiment of the conflict in the form of an encounter in dialogue between the private aspect of the self and his opponent, which may be his own public image or

10 Unamuno's dramatic theory is put into practice in many of his dramatic writings, but the most explicit representation is *El otro* (*The Other One*) (*OC*, XII, pp. 800-63).

alter ego. There are also numerous indications that Unamuno considered the theatrical presentation of a work as pantomime, which had the possibility of transcending itself from spectacle into drama only to the degree that the presentation of the words could involve the spectator in the conflict of the protagonist.

Unamuno read extensively in the areas of political economy and history. His markings and commentary in these books are consistent to an extraordinary degree in underscoring man's existential situation. The underlying idea is a Heraclitean view of reality as change and the corollary generalization that man's attempt to understand reality is both limited to an abstraction of it and pragmatically valid, since it enables man to cope with chaos. Unamuno explains the pragmatic validity of rational abstraction by insisting that the functional value of reason is greatest when man is aware that it is a tool he is using for his own interests. Unamuno castigates the writer who attempts to substitute the rational organization of reality for reality itself. Reason and rational thought thus become the means of the individual's conquest of reality. He writes in book after book that nothing is more fearful than the loss of order, that nothing is more to be dreaded than meaningless chaos; but in his *Tragic Sense of Life* rational man emerges from fear of the unknown only to plunge into the alienation of his rational labyrinth.

A representative example of Unamuno's marginal commentary in this area can be found in Leopold von Ranke's *Weltgeschichte* (U-4107-14). The eight volumes of this study have marginal notations of differing degrees of metaphysical extension. Let us begin with some of the generalizations and proceed to the more specific observations.

Unamuno wrote in volume one an extended commentary on the inevitable plunge toward self-destruction taken by an empire that loses the limitation of its own identity and adopts a world-view. Unamuno writes that rational organization is the only way man can control the forces of the social conglomeration. The loss of control comes when the rational structure is insufficient to cope with the diversity it is trying to assimilate. The result is a return to the primordial chaos from which man has sought to escape.

Unamuno added the following general commentaries, which I believe are indicative of his thought on history and on the role of philosophy in the study of history. 'History is not the sum of the events that are commonly called historical; these are never seen together; they are layers of sedimentation one covering over the other. History as a re-created past is a human idea with every affirmation being the reverse side of a negation. The study of History gives me a sense of order that is situated within my perspective of intuitions and logical system.' History as a comprehensible reality begins with understanding, which is to say re-creation. Unmistakably, the first duty of a philosophy of history must be the recognition that the living present of the historian is the situation from which the past is re-created. There are very few true historians, for the historian must be able to relive the reality of the past without losing his own present reality.

Volume one also provokes statements such as 'there is no finality' and 'reality is change; only reason is final' (page 9). In volume two, scores of passages are underlined and various commentaries state approval of and expand on the historian's words. For example, on page 410, he writes that a sense of independence in man is necessary before there can be a cultural expression of any note. Another noteworthy example is in volume seven, page 13, where Unamuno underlines and then translates to Spanish the statement 'to struggle is the nature of man,' a phrase familiar to any reader of Unamuno. In the context of the book the connotation is certainly physical, but Unamuno's implication is just as clearly metaphysical. Finally, for an example of a specific notation by Unamuno, we can turn to volume two, page 247, where he writes: 'the populism of Mario/to serve the proletariat and the Italic people/consequence of the wars/of the last great war and the Russian Revolution which follows it.'

Students of Unamuno have been surprised by the number of scientific books he used and the attention with which they were studied. They range from medicine and psychology to chemistry and geology. Unamuno wrote comments in some of these books, but mostly he marked and underlined. These markings are not the usual underlining of key passages, but rather an intricate outline of the basic propositions and suppositions presented by the writer. Although Unamuno did not write much about scientific matters, he often found the need to interject exemplary material from the sciences. When he does, as in 'La juventud "intelectual" española' of 1896 (*OC*, III, 461), it is with the authority of uncommon familiarity.[11]

The books of the scientist-philosophers, they being the broadest in application, most frequently elicited response from Unamuno. For example, although there are seven books on physiology in the collection, the only one with written commentary is the essay by Claude Bernard on experimental medicine (U-548).

11 Text: 'Es lo que necesita nuestra juventud intelectual, si es que aún hay para ella remedio: ser metarritmizada; una sacudida en las más íntimas y entrañables palpitaciones de su ser. Ni reforma ni revolución bastan. Necesita la conciencia colectiva de nuestro pueblo una crisis que produzca lo que en psicología patológica se llama cambio de personalidad; un derrumbarse el viejo "yo" para que se alce sobre sus ruinas y nutrido de ellas el "yo" nuevo, sobre la base de continuidad de las funciones sociales meramente fisiológicas.' Unamuno's footnote: 'Para los que conozcan cualquier buen trabajo acerca de la filosofía química moderna, verbigracia, el de Lotario Meyer (en francés, *Les théories modernes de la chimie et leur application à la mécanique chimique*), resultará lo sugestivo que deseo cuanto acabo de escribir acerca de la metarritmisis; y para los que conozcan la psicología fisiológica moderna, lo que indico acerca del cambio de personalidad sobre la base de continuidad fisiológica, puede verse *Les maladies de la personalité* de Th. Ribot.' (*OC*, III, 462).

The list of Unamuno's scientific readings is almost a catalogue of research areas: besides the seven books on physiology there are two books on scientific methodology, two on botany, two on astronomy, four on meteorology and geography of Spain, one on geology, six on chemistry, five on general principles of biology and evolution, three on zoology, one on embryology, eleven on psychology and its various specializations and five more on experimental psychology, and, finally, eleven books on physics; sixty in all. The major scientists of the late nineteenth century are well represented in the readings; we find notable figures like Haeckel, Le Bon, Roule, Freud, Latze, Mach, Ostwald, Poincaré, Robat, Wundt, Uexküll, and Vuillemin. Besides the well-known writers there are many manuals, handbooks, and monographs in French, German, and Spanish, which complete the sixty volumes of this relatively unknown part of the Unamuno readings.[12]

Chemistry was of exceptional interest to Unamuno; all six books in the collection are marked throughout and the two general manuals are full of commentary. The most extraordinary aspect about the chemistry readings is the life-long duration that they evidence. Three date from his early years (before 1899, when he was 35); one was sent by the author in 1912 when Unamuno was 48; and the remaining two, both heavily marked, are from 1921 (57 years) and 1932 (year of purchase), read and annotated when he was 68 years of age. Unamuno's earliest readings in chemistry are from French publications: P.E. Marcelin Berthelot, *La synthèse chimique* (1891) (U-1818), and Lothar Meyer, *Les théories modernes de la chimie et leur application à la mécanique chimique* (1887-1889) (U-82). The last book from this discipline is Eduardo Vitoria's *Manual de química moderna* (1929) (U-2248).

Now let us turn to some of the ontological and epistemological implications of Unamuno's method of enquiry. I believe that the basis of Unamuno's reading attitude is an encounter of passionate intensity, that the idea and its author take possession of the reader, drawing out of himself the thoughts and imagery by which the idea is expressed and defended and then provoking contradiction in a fierce intimate struggle. What Unamuno writes down as marginalia represents the cryptic record of both dialectic investigation and a per-

---

12 See the following authors of works on applied or theoretical scientific subjects: José Maria Albiñana Sanz, Fernando Alsina, Pedro Ara, Alfaro Araoz, Domingo Barnés, Claude Bernard, Marcelin Berthelot, Gaston Bonnies, Blas Cabrera, José Carracido, Miguel Correa Oliver, Juan Dantin Cereceda, Yves Delage, Victor Delfino, Mathias Duval, Sigmund Freud, Patrick Geddes, Archibald Geikie, José Gogorza, Ernst Haeckel, Enrique Herrero Ducloux, Enrique Iglesias y Ejarque, José Ingenieros, M.I. Jamin, Fleeming Jenkin, Gonzalo Lafora, Gustave Lebon, Hermann Lotze, Eduardo Lozano y Ponce de León, Ernst Mach, Juan Marina y Muñoz, M. Márquez Sterlin, Emmanuel Martonne, Victor Mercante, Lothar Meyer, José Mouriz Riesgo, Prentice Mulford, I. Orchansky, W. Ostwald, Lucien Poincaré, Théodule Ribot, Charles Richet, L. Rodrigo Lavin, Louis Roule, Jakob Uexküll, Eduardo Victoria, Paul Vuillemin, Wilhelm Wundt.

sonal struggle. Consequently, to understand these notes one must attempt to reconstruct the struggle in oneself.

THE METHOD OF DIALECTIC ENQUIRY

In 1914 Unamuno wrote in his novel *Niebla* a heated dialogue in which the narrative voice answers the fictional character's question about existence: 'In entering this discussion I am merely satisfying a private need of my own. Apart from discussion and contradiction, I am never alive; and when there is no one outside of me to question and contradict me I invent someone to do it within me. My monologues are dialogues.'[13] This seemingly facile remark is one of many clear statements that form an extensive philosophical position and that point to a consistent philosophical structure for our present observations. The specific and limited consideration before us is the method of enquiry used by Unamuno.

Unamuno's system of enquiry is a dialectical method cast in a dualistic epistemology, and the theory of reality on which it is based is also dialectical. Let us be clear first about the use of this terminology. Historically, Unamuno's dialectical ontology is a direct descendant of Hegel's dialectical idealism, but the dialectical method of enquiry in its primary aspects is as old as human thought. In this essay I am concerned exclusively with thinking as it is manifested through the readings and annotations of Unamuno.

Thus, enquiry for Unamuno was thinking in terms of opposites and of the contradictory force that makes them opposites. Let us call the contradictory propositions 'opposites' and the force of opposition 'negation.' Opposites are distinguishable throughout Unamuno's notations on the basis of three essential properties: each opposite has a correlative relation to its partner, each opposite is mutually exclusive of its partner, and each opposite is in conflict with its partner. All three characteristics must be present in each pair of opposites in order to produce the Unamunian enquiry.

Besides fundamental opposites such as good and evil, positive and negative, or form and content, which have always been focal points of human thought, we must distinguish the creation of opposites in new areas. Such a pair of opposites is the myself and the social self, which we observed in the notations of the *Pensées*. I shall use this pair of opposites in order to demonstrate the fundamental characteristics of the method and also to provide the material for a discussion of negation.

The correlative nature of the opposites must be insisted upon. Without society, and, specifically, the self in society (the social self), the isolated or

13 The translation is my own. The Spanish text follows: '... yo necesito discutir, sin discusión no vivo y sin contradicción, y cuando no hay fuera de mí quien me discuta y contradiga, invento dentro de mí quien lo haga. Mis monólogos son diálogos' (*OC*, II, 977).

withdrawn myself would be meaningless. The inverse is also true. Consequently, the bipolar arrangement is chained together by its very nature, and one polar position cannot exist without the other.

The pairs of opposites are also dichotomous; each one is mutually exclusive of the other. The essential factor here is the elimination of any third possibilities. Thus, we are not dealing with ordinary opposites anymore, for although we can say that what is good cannot be bad, and what is bad cannot be good, there is nothing to stop us from considering a given object as neither bad nor good. Unamuno's methodology of opposites must exhaust the possibilities for the subject under examination. In the case of the self, the dichotomy is complete. There is no room for a third position besides the outgoing social participation and the ingoing personal examination; it is an either/or proposition.

Contradiction means conflict, and this is the most important and basic characteristic of the opposites. We must keep in mind the qualifications we have already given to the Unamunian concept of opposites: the correlative relation to each other and the dichotomous division of the subject. It follows logically that merely contradictory terms need not be in conflict. For example, hot and cold are certainly exclusive of each other, but they are not exhaustive of the range of temperature; thus they are not in conflict, because they do not meet in the same subject. The myself and the social self, however, are in conflict, because they meet in contradiction of each other within the same subject, in this case Miguel de Unamuno. They are opposite, correlative, dichotomous, and the only two possibilities for this proposition of the self. To sum up, we can say that opposites are contradictory only when we attribute both opposites to the same thing and cannot avoid doing so.

Now we must consider the most crucial aspect of Unamuno's dialectic enquiry: what does it produce beyond sheer dynamics? The answer is simple to state, but involved to explain in depth because it is built upon a radical ontological premise. Unamuno is not stating that either one of the opposites is true at any given moment, but rather that they are both true, and that they are true only when they are present together. This seems to be paradoxical doubletalk, and unfortunately many commentators have dismissed it as being just that. But if we persevere in our analysis, we soon begin to realize that in Unamuno's philosophy reality is synonymous with struggle; or in other words, the condition of being-in-struggle is the description of that which is real, and anything else is mental abstraction. The dialectic method thus sees the opposites of the social self and the myself in conflict and related because they are the only two possibilities for the man.

Undoubtedly the most serious challenge we can thrust at this Unamunian methodology is to ask whether there is a basis of relationship between pairs of opposites or whether reality is an ultimately unknowable, irrational, chance occurrence of struggling polarities. Of course, this is the same problem Fichte and Hegel encountered with dialectic. Unamuno's focus, however, is not idealistic and is not concerned with the metaphysical absolute, which can give unity to the real. He is trying to approximate as closely as possible the source of the reality (struggle) for the particulars that have been encountered. For example, the (hypothetical) person without both social self and individual self could not be considered as having any validity in terms of the real, for the meaning of the individual self is derived only from its contrast to the social self.

The essence of the process of enquiry itself is negation. At the core of Unamuno's concept of negation is the being of another or, in other words, the idea of the human encounter with another. It is clear that negation can be approached from various viewpoints: it is a process or an operation of contradicting (*this is* negated by *this is not*); it is the result of the operation (i.e., the *is not*); and it is the relation that is maintained by the contradiction (i.e., the struggle). All of these viewpoints are valid aspects of negation but each in turn warrants further clarification: (1) The operation of negation is in Unamuno's methodology the means of discovering the implicit tension that underlies all reality. (2) The result of negation is not an isolated entity such as non-being or death; it is rather a state of reciprocal tension made manifest by the pair of opposites that has emerged. (3) The relation that comes into view because of negation is an insight into the reality of the subject. In conclusion, Unamuno's enquiry is based on negation as a means of reducing appearances to essential characteristics of reality through the cognitive discovery of direct encounter.

Negation looms large in this method of enquiry as a dynamic power driving absolute positions and ideas toward a relativistic position. For example, let us consider the absolute concept of God as the creator guaranteeing personal immortality. The thrust of negation forces the concept into a relativistic position that sees man as the creator of his own project and God as man's desire for immortality. And negation just as emphatically forces relativist positions toward the absolute. For example (Unamuno's example), let us take the position that action is in itself amoral and that morality exists as a singular and personal interpretation of action. Negation contradicts, in this case, by forcing the proposition into a concrete situation. Man's killing of man is not an act that can be separated from the personal interpretation, since it is the destruction of morality itself, i.e., the continuing possibility of personal judgments; therefore, Unamuno would argue that the act can never be separated from the person and all actions are moral actions.

In general, this negating position transforms the writing from an external gesture on the part of the author into a personal experience for the reader. This experience is a type of knowledge I want to refer to as cognitive discovery to distinguish it from learned knowledge.[14] This negation is not a lightly conceived formula of opposition; I believe that it was the natural development of Unamuno's learning process and that a careful study of the formative readings of his youth can demonstrate how this intellectual disposition grew and evolved. Within the scope of the present study, I can state that, to Unamuno, having the will to know means essentially to question, doubt, and enquire. By now it must be obvious that this probing can never be pre-formed; it must be in response to the immediate phenomena. Almost axiomatic to this enquiry of encounter is, primarily, the observation that it can clarify and strengthen the investigator's position which is always based on a previously attained conscious disposition susceptible to transformation. Secondly, but of equal importance, the dialectically inclined reader must be well informed about the material being challenged, so that the assimilation at the outset of the encounter can be effective. Thirdly, the experience of continuous encounters of this kind not only sharpens the weapons of battle, but also places the reader's fundamental position under constant scrutiny and prevents it from becoming a personal dogma.

The term 'cognitive discovery' perhaps needs further clarification. It is not the learning of facts or definitions, but rather the knowledge acquired by an intellectual encounter through communication. Facts, definitions, and meanings are only the tools employed to further the encounter; it is the exchange itself that forces Unamuno to discover himself through the other. Of necessity, this is accomplished within the personal combat zone of the mind where the other's thoughts have been introduced into opposition. Clearly the separation that may have been present at the outset between reader and author is transformed into an intimate dialectic struggle in the reader. Through this transformation and struggle it is the reader himself who is moved into a new position of knowing. Although the dialectic structure of this process suggests that the new grounds of awareness achieved by the self may be a form of synthesis, this is not the case. Synthesis has been ruled out by the very definition

14 The prime importance of this distinction is to place emphasis on the hermeneutic aspect of Unamuno's enquiry. Although the text has a primary autonomy because it is the constant base from which the interpretation is to be made, the situation and intentions of the author are remote and, consequently, of secondary importance. The interpretation is the reading experience, and it is in Unamuno's methodology not only an imaginative attempt to confront the author but also a quite open re-creation of the author's presence and ideas as tempered and altered by the dominant force of the reader's personality. It is not that the historical purpose, intention, and absolute meaning of the writer do not have importance; it is, to put it directly, that the historical writer does not exist in the text. Only the writer's words survive and they serve to provoke Unamuno to renewed self-discovery.

For a slightly different discussion of the cognitive discovery of encounter see Hans U. von Balthasar, 'Man creates meaning in encounter,' pp. 395-402 in Roland Houde and Joseph Mullally, *Philosophy of Knowledge* (Chicago, 1960).

of reality as struggle, the premise upon which the methodology rests. The new ground of knowledge is not a synthesis or a compromise agreement of two points of view; it is exclusively the self-discovery brought about by opposition through a verbalization or search for verbalization of personal insights.

Whatever the focal point, Unamuno's epistemological position appears to be dualistic in these commentaries – dualistic, but not in the Platonic manner, for Unamuno's notes suggest an acquisition of knowledge that is limited by time. Memory is established as the basis of the self's knowing. Each man begins anew 'the eternal struggle to be all and one at the same time,' the process of cognitive discovery.[15] The knowledge others have gained is not transmitted directly to the self; it must be assimilated by the reader and exposed to the fierce scrutiny of his inner struggle before it is his own.

The ontological and epistemological position that I have outlined is certainly not unique. It is a demonstration of the method used by Unamuno and the implications of that method, which are in complete agreement with his diverse writings on the mind and the knowing process. Perhaps we could best characterize Unamuno's way of reading as a dialectical method that changes the reader's ideas by forcing him to battle with the author's structural presence. It is also a methodology that is in itself a direct expression of the ontology of being as struggle.

In this introduction I have treated a few of the many problems that Unamuno's philosophy poses. All are in need of a fuller study in order to establish a basis for philosophical discussion. However, in view of the limited ends of this study and as an introduction to that more complete examination, here is a summary of the key aspects of this kind of enquiry:

1 Enquiry is essentially the process of experiencing something other than the self.

2 All writers put themselves into their writings to a greater or lesser degree. The truly great men have put themselves into their works so completely that those works could not have been written by anyone else.

3 The written work is different from its author, but it is very precisely an essence of himself. Thus, the author actualizes himself in his writing. The principal point to be made here is that the reality of the writing is lost if it is taken in abstraction from its author. This is not a simplistic argument for biographical or historical interpretation of literary or philosophical texts, but rather the proposition that the reality of the written work is the dialectic tension that comes into being as the reader encounters the author and the work.

---

15 This comment appears in the back cover of volume one of the Tauchnitz edition of Spinoza's works (U-492-4), but the thought is found frequently in Unamuno's essays. See, for example, *Del sentimiento trágico de la vida* ... (*OC*, XVI, p. 166): '... quiero ser yo y sin dejar de serlo, ser además los otros.'

4 The re-creation of the dialectic tension in the work is an encounter of the first magnitude with the reality of another. This is, of course, not an operation on a pre-existent substance. It is a genuine discovery of reality.

5 This discovery is a creative encounter, for it creates a fuller realization of the reader's own self. Thus, Unamuno's philosophical cornerstone is that to become other than one's self is to become more completely one's self.

6 Whereas *given* knowledge presupposes the existence of independent objects, *creative* knowledge is a direct encounter with reality; therefore, it is a superior form of experience. Of course, given knowledge, i.e., knowledge of things, etc., is a necessary preliminary to creative knowledge, i.e., the discovery of reality.

7 The effectiveness of Unamuno's enquiry rests on the premise that *every* statement has its implicit opposite that is contradictory and that the truth of the statement lies, not in the statement itself, but in its correlative relation to its opposite.

8 The idea of separateness for any proposition is synonymous to dogma, and is completely rejected. Both parts of the opposition must be entertained together for they are the two sides of the same reality: struggle.

9 The goal of creative knowledge is a fuller attainment of one's self; therefore, the emphasis is on the activity of enquiry itself, for, as has been suggested above, the desired result is not the acquisition of given knowledge, but the assimilation of another's dialectic struggle into one's own dialectic reality. Thus, an ontology follows from the method.

10 No idea is simple and beyond analysis; rather, every idea is inherently complex and inconsistent because it contains a latent opposite. No idea is true in itself, for each idea expressed implies other ideas incompatible to it. Consequently, the moving force of dialectical enquiry is contradiction, and since contradiction is also the moving force in existence, it follows that Unamuno's method of enquiry is a philosophical progression from confused to clear ideas and that reality presents itself existentially in diverse ways.

UNAMUNO: DIALECTIC THINKER

The dialectic encounter and the pattern of thinking that proceeds from it are probably fundamental to the development of intellectual activity in the western world. It is within this framework that I have sought to reconstruct Unamuno's process of enquiry.

Perhaps the most decisive and acknowledged influence on Unamuno was Hegel's *Phenomenology of the Spirit* (1807), specifically the chapter on self-consciousness, and the preface, which he translated into Spanish shortly before 1891. Until very recently one would have had to consider Unamuno's commentary on Hegel and his adaptation of the dialectic method as idiosyncratic. Certainly, his interpretation was one with which the specialists strongly differed. However, since the Findlay re-examination of Hegel in 1958 and the Kaufman reinterpretation of 1965, Unamuno's interpretation has suddenly, dramatically and belatedly, acquired respectability.[16] Unamuno's dialectic methodology takes him very near to the biblical hermeneutics of the radical French, German, and English theologians he so admired, men like F.C. Baur who shared his Hegelian affinity, J.K.L. Giesler, A. Harnack, and Edwin Hatch, whose works on early church history are rich in interpretation of original sources, and J.E. Renan, A. Réville, A. Ritschl. F. Schleirmacher, and D.F. Strauss, whose interpretation of Christ and his mission corresponded so closely to Unamuno's.

For a better understanding of Unamuno's dialectic method, we should note his insistence on realism, whether it be the metaphysical view of reality as process or his dualistic theory of knowledge. Unamuno's literary illustration of the dialectic is best exemplified in his novel *Niebla* (1914) [English translation, *Mist* (1928)]. There is an ironical reversal of the roles of creator and fictional creation at the point (chapter 31) where the fictional character becomes autonomous, i.e., self-reliant, because he realizes his existence depends on his own work, which is his presence in the mind of the reader. The creator then becomes dependent on his fictional character for his continued re-creation. Not only is the concept of the reversal of the roles of author and character clearly Hegelian, but Unamuno also expresses his understanding of its ontological basis in his reading notes. As early as 1895 Unamuno saw Kant's logical method as an attempt to mitigate the essential incompatibility that raged within him and wrote this commentary in the *Kritik der reinen Vernunft*: 'Only the autonomous self [subject] can engage in dialogue with others [and relate to his objects].' I believe 'to engage in dialogue' is used here to mean 'to perceive existence.' It follows, therefore, that if Unamuno is to claim an awareness of reality for his fictional character, he must create an autonomous fictional character.

In general, the Unamunian dialectic produces (a) challenge, (b) contradiction, and (c) transcendence. In a limited number of reading encounters with like-minded authors, the first two steps are not initiated by the reader (Unamuno), since they are already present in the text; he merely re-creates them. But in most readings, Unamuno provides the challenge and the search for opposition. Since only ideas in conflict are real, the three steps of the dialectic enquiry are the necessary stages of rendering meaning to the ideas.

16 In my study of Hegel's 'Phenomenology,' I am indebted to J.N. Findley's *Hegel, A Re-examination* (London, 1958), especially chapter 4 (pp. 83-9); and to Walter Kaufmann's *Hegel: A Reinterpretation* (New York, 1965). I have found interesting similarities to Unamuno's reading of Hegel in G.L. Kline's discussion of J.P. Sartre's interpretation of Hegel's 'Phenomenology.' See 'The Existentialist Rediscovery of Hegel and Marx' in E.N. Lee and Maurice Mandelbaum, *Phenomenology and Existentialism* (Baltimore, 1967), pp. 113-38.

Unamuno was thus developing a philosophy of 'being' recast in neo-Hegelian terms of being-in-struggle, an ethics of existential concern for the tragedy of man, and, in his later years, an aesthetics patterned on the self-realizing dialogue between author and reader. What I wish to emphasize here is that the dialectic methodology and epistemological dualism are at the roots of the philosopher's enquiry.[17]

Unamuno's commentary on Hegel's dialectic can serve as a summation of his philosophical position: 'The opposites of dialectic exist together and their only possible union is the process of existence itself' (U-1260). By turning his focus from *how* do we know to *what* do we know, Unamuno established the interdependent perspectives we have been outlining as (1) the process itself, (2) the existential situation of the self, and (3) the aesthetic survival of man. The answer to the problem of knowledge is that we know only by becoming aware of the essential structure of reality, which is the ever-changing conflict, be it of matter or mind, past or present. The reality of an object lies in its particular process, that is, in its mode of change.

I hope to have argued effectively that Unamuno's methodology as demonstrated in his reading notes has the same structure as the theory of existence that can be found in his published essays.

17 See my *Death in the Literature of Unamuno* (Urbana, 1964), pp. 4-36.

Guide to the catalogue

We wish to emphasize once again that this listing of the readings of Unamuno is as complete as we have been able to make it, but absolute completeness is impossible in this case. Among the books which Unamuno owned, there are of course some that he did not read; this can be ascertained in the case of those whose pages are still unopened. There are two principal sources for the reading matter that is not part of the current Unamuno library: the books owned by his family, especially his son Fernando and his son-in-law José Ma. Quiroga Pla, which have the unmistakable Unamunian annotations, and secondly a cabinet of file cards and notes kept by Unamuno from 1900 to 1917 wherein he recorded the books and papers he used.

In order to maintain a uniform format throughout the catalogue, we have chosen to follow the catalogue of the British Museum. This procedure was selected because most of the entries in Unamuno's personal file were found in the published catalogue of this library.

The system of superscript and marginal notation used so extensively in the majority of the books examined was developed by Unamuno at a very early date, probably during his student days, for there is but scant variation. Unamuno kept a very accurate record of his reading in the book itself. The text is marked throughout and an index of the markings is found on the back cover or adjacent blank pages. Unamuno employed the same system of annotation and markings with rigorous uniformity throughout the most productive years of his life. A vertical line along the margin indicated general interest in the content. A single or a double cross in the margin signified interest in the precise statement made in the text and often this meant that a commentary by Unamuno would follow. On rare occasions the commentary was written at the bottom of the page itself, but more often it was inserted in a form of noun-verb shorthand in the index along with the page number of the textual reference. The crosses are also indicative of special features of interest. In some cases, it is the usage of a word or phrase that he has singled out for comment: in these philological encounters the page number is inserted in a separate index listing at the bottom of one of the back-cover pages. On occasion Unamuno would write letters to the authors, who usually had sent the book to him, and he would point out what he considered to be the errata of the book; this information came directly from the listing compiled while he read the book. This feature is most frequent in the numerous books he received from Hispanic America.

Also kept in a special index are all references by a foreigner to Spain or the Spanish people; this is especially evident in the French and English books. In some books these are the only markings. In the more scholarly books there is usually a place on the back cover index for the listing of pages where further references are given.

The question of when a book was read or reread is partially answered by three notations that are found in some of the books: (a) the date of purchase or of dedication by the author or friend is on the inside front page, e.g., Everett W. Olmsted sent Walt Whitman's *Leaves of Grass* on 30 April 1906; (b) the date of reading can sometimes be ascertained from the index of markings, e.g., Melville's *Moby Dick* was read at three times from 23 February 1929 to December 1930; and (c) in the English books the bookseller's invoice was frequently used as a marker in the reading.

The appendices to the catalogue contain all books and authors and journals and newspapers mentioned by Unamuno in his collected writings but that are not otherwise listed. The appendices complement the catalogue in providing a complete guide to Unamuno's sources. Thus, there is no duplication of entries – only items missing from the catalogue have been listed. The new edition of the complete works will have a complete index, which we are preparing.

Owing to the fragmentary nature of some of the references to books and authors in Unamuno's writings, a number of entries have not been traced to a specific publication; in such cases the reader will find the fragmentary item together with the volume and page where Unamuno first mentions it.

Symbols used in the catalogue

Following is the list of symbols used in the catalogue. The symbols give the pertinent information on source, annotations, catalogue number, and general usage whenever we have been able to ascertain it:

B   markings indicating bibliographical references for the subject being treated.

C   direct commentary by Unamuno in response to the content.

D   indicates that the book was signed by the author, editor or translator with a written dedication to Unamuno.

I   markings along the margins and after specific lines and words denoting general interest in the content.

L   markings indicating interest in language, i.e., the etymological or morphological implications of the usage found in the text.

n/n   indicates the books that are in the Unamuno library but have no number because they have been added only recently to the collection from the family holdings or were recovered from Hendaya after the Library had catalogued the holdings.

n/o   indicates a book from the Unamuno library which has not been opened, i.e., the pages are still uncut.

OC   abbreviation for *Obras completas* (Barcelona: Vergara, 1958), followed by volume and page information, is used in the appendices to indicate the source of the fragmentary information.

QP   the letters *QP* indicate a book that was read by Unamuno and marked but which belonged to his son-in-law Quiroga Pla, and is not part of the library.

T   translation to Spanish of specific words or, on occasion, entire lines.

U-   the letter *U* followed by a number indicates that the book is in the Unamuno library and the number by which it can be found there.

Uc   indicates that the entry is taken from Unamuno's personal catalogue of readings; it does not form part of the library and therefore was not accessible for examination.

*   an asterisk following any of the annotation symbols, i.e., B, C, I, L, T, signifies an extensive usage throughout the book:

Juan González Olmedilla

La llave de oro. / Poesías

ded

Madrid
Imprenta Helénica. Pasaje de la Alhambra, 3
1914

Card from Unamuno's catalogue.

han vuelto los vencejos;
las cosas naturales vuelven siempre,
las hojas a los árboles,
a las cumbres las nieves.
Han vuelto los vencejos; lo que no es arte vuelve
naturaleza no es sino constancia vuelta constante
por cima de las leyes.
los vencejos han vuelto,
¿es como todo vuelve?
todo lo que brotara al sol desnudo
de la inexausta fuente,
todo lo que no fue de algún designio
producto endeble.
Han vuelto los vencejos;
augusto ritmo, única ley perenne!
el año es una estrofa
del canto permanente!
Todo vuelve, no dudes, todo vuelve;
vuelve la vida,
vuelve la muerte!
Cuanto tiene raíces en la tierra
al fin y al cabo vuelve!
Han vuelto los vencejos
y al pecho aquellas mismas ansias vuelven!
Ahora comprenderás lo que en la vida
significa esto (quiere decir el) siempre!
Siempre es la vuelta
quiere decir la vuelta, el ritmo,
la canción de la mar en la rompiente;
si la ola se retira
ha de volver, pues es de lo que vuelve.
Vuelve todo lo que es natura
si ya tan sólo se pierde
lo que es negocio, huero de los hombres,
sus artificios, invenciones, leyes.
Han vuelto los vencejos;
como ellos vuelven siempre.
con su alegre chillar el aire agitan
y el cielo con su ... ir y volver
al caer de la tarde
cobrar vida parece.
No se posan ... quieren ...
... ... las alas,
criaturas celestes

Notes found in G.W.F. Hegel's *Wissenschaft der Logik* (Berlin 1841), U-1260.

Con ritmo de saeta, ritmo yámbico
los versos vivos de su vuelo dejan
chillando la alegría
de sentirse vivientes.
Han vuelto los vencejos, siempre,
los del año pasado, los de siempre,
los mismos de la vieja ...
los del año que viene, siempre,
los que vieron volar nuestros abuelos
encima de sus frentes
y exciencia de las suyas nuestros nietos
verán también volar, negros y leves.
Han vuelto los vencejos,
serán flores de la ... que no mueren
... ¿quién muertos los ha visto? —
heraldos de la vida, amantes fieles
del largo ... de la miel dorada
... de la ... de siempre mensajeros celestes
han vuelto los ... de siempre
Vencejos inmortales, también volar, negros y leves.
alados hijos de natura fuerte — leve
heraldos de cosechas y (de) alegrías
mensajeros celestes, pasan nuestro cielo
bienvenidos seáis a nuestros techos
heraldos de la vida, campos – casas – torres
vosotros, los de siempre
del largo ... de la ... dorada
siega de oro
han vuelto los de siempre.
Vencejos inmortales
alados hijos de natura fuerte
bienvenidos seáis a nuestras casas – torres
heraldos del estrecha y de vendimia
alegría
mensajeros celestes,
bienvenidos seáis a nuestros campos, casas, torres
vosotros, los de siempre!

Cartas... ¿pedagógicas? etc.

Prólogo de Posada

Verdaderas cartas, un artificio. La libertad
que en tales, el vaivén, el ir y venir.

Diferencia entre el mirar y el ver, la recep-
tividad, igual para todos, y la espontaneidad
peculiar en cada uno.

"Nuestros pedagogos no se han formado en la
observación directa del niño español, sino en el
estudio de los más eminentes escritores extranjeros."

"No hay más que un sólo mirar" (una sola realidad)   U.

Notas doctas, de autoridad.

Toda la pedagogía en excitar y dirigir la atención.
Pero ¡ojo! Hermosa carta, pag 109 á 111.
Recalca Urbano sobre los peligros del moderno
uso psicológico en la atención 112

La Pedagogía nacional, la Meca (115)

De dos, de un hombre viril y de una
mujer, ésta corrige á aquel, más perfecto.
La atención y el interés. (Éste depende de aquella)
Contra las lecciones de cosas U (de realidad)
La atención no es planta de estufa 122
La línea media, contra los originalismos 133
La , Sensibilidad é intelecto (139 á 140)
(Son lo mismo, lo mismo instrucción y educación)
Hermoso párrafo sobre el dolor, 141 Educa-
ción por el placer "El placer no impone deberes, con-
cede derechos gratuitam." "dice D" C. 145
Magnífico la señorita 158

Reading notes from Concepción Sáiz y Otero and Urbano González Serrano,
Cartas ¿Pedagógicas? Ensayos de psicologia pedagógica (Madrid 1895), U-148

Defectos.

. no sólo la máxima y la mínima, la *isoterma*

La educación la primera función social, capital personal. Unirnos con el porvenir.

Hazlitt.

Table-talk. To die is only to be as we were before we were born 440 — 441 – 442 — no young man ever thinks he shall die 443 — If I had lived indeed, I should not care to die 444 (cf. Observation

___

Elogio á Clarín (muy merecido) 4; 5 (muy bien!)
(Escribe como un español y escribe bien, lo
que quiere decir...) Entusiasmo por el Ariel
de Rodó; discípulo de éste. "El noble abolengo
castellano" de Rodó 13, "Criticar es perdonar" 18
(Pero antes se castiga) Elogio de Valera 22. Contra
el modernismo imitativo americano 23. Balfour
y el restablec.to de la razón práctica 29
Chocano 43 sigs no es poeta del amor 46. Chocano y clamor 49 — Spencer 59 sigs 66. No 1-
Hume, Berkeley, Stuart Mill, Darwin superiores
á Spencer; éste no un metafísico, sino un Sto
Tomás, un concinador. (El juicio homogeneo quizá
vivo y Ardigó) (Es la fil. de los aficionados
á filosofía; y el enciclopedismo moderno) Spencer es, en rigor, un pre-kantiano; jamás enten-
dió á lo hondo el problema del conocimiento.
Avenarius, Mach. El juicio del autor sobre
Spencer bien — Nuñez de Arce, con motivo
de su muerte. — Menendez Pelayo, ser a lagrado
á él desde América. Es un elogio caluroso —
Una novela de Altamira: — (Lo nuevo, valor
de lo nuevo 125. Solo progreso es otro. La ref
ción. No hay otro yo." Si, había un autor
de ideas y agregas una, habrá 1.000.001 y un mun
do más perfecto. Con cuerpos nuevos más
El con .) Reflejo de Rodó. El afrancesamien
to de Prada 130-131

Reading notes from Alberto Nin Frias, *Nuevos ensayos de crítica literaria y filosófica* (Montevideo 1905), U-1159

Reading notes from Pindar's *Pindari Carmina cum fragmentis selectis*
(Leipzig 1908), U-350

Catalogue

Abasolo, Jenaro. *La personalidad política y la América del porvenir.* Santiago de Chile. Universitaria. 1907. Pp. xiii, 574. U-3002

Abel, Adam. *Das geht zu weit.* München. Stangl. 1926. Pp. 92. U-5449 C

– *Das Leben nach dem Tode.* München. Stangl. 1927. Pp. 47. U-5393

– *Von Gott.* München. Stangl. 1927. Pp. 33. U-5404 C

– *Das Dritte Reich.* München. Stangl. 1927. Pp. 183. U-5403 I

– *Der Dritte Bund.* München. Stangl. n.d. Pp. 28. U-5461

Abeledo, Amaranto. *Campaña anticlerical.* La Plata. La Nueva. 1909. Uc

– *Lecciones de la historia.* Buenos Aires. Alvarez. 1935. Pp. 30. U-2862 D

Abellá, Juan Carlos. *Andén.* Montevideo. Palacio del Libro. 1929. Pp. 131. U-5566 D

Abentofail. See Abu Bakr Ibn al-Tufail

Abreu Gómez, Ermilo. *Humanidades.* México. Imp. Comercio. 1923. Pp. 95. U-3390 D

Abu Bakr Ibn al-Tufail. *El filósofo autodidacto de Abentofail.* Tr. Francisco Pons Boigues. Pról. Menéndez y Pelayo. Zaragoza. Comas. 1900. Pp. lvi, 250. U-4617

Abul-Bagi. See Babuglia, Antonio

Acebal, Francisco. *De buena cepa.* Madrid. Rodríguez Serra. n.d. Uc

– *Huella de almas.* Madrid. La Lectura. 1901. Uc

– *Dolorosa.* Madrid. V. Suárez. 1904. Pp. 285. U-2734

Acevedo Díaz, Eduardo. *Ismael.* Montevideo. Barreiro y Ramos. 1894. Pp. 392. U-2287

– *Nativa.* Montevideo. Barreiro y Ramos. 1894. Pp. 515. U-3512 n/o

– *Grito de gloria.* Montevideo. Barreiro y Ramos. 1894. Pp. 436. U-3670

– *Soledad.* Montevideo. Barreiro y Ramos. 1894. Pp. 177. U-3524

– *Notas y apuntes. Contribución al estudio de la historia económica y financiera de la Rep. Oriental del Uruguay.* 2 vols. Montevideo. El Siglo Ilustrado. 1903. U-4093-4 n/o

– *La enseñanza universitaria en 1904.* Montevideo. El Siglo Ilustrado. 1905. Uc

– *La enseñanza universitaria en 1905.* Montevideo. El Siglo Ilustrado. 1906. Uc

– *Minés.* Buenos Aires. Daroqui. 1907. Pp. iv, 259. U-3359

Acevedo Díaz, Eduardo, hijo. *Los nuestros.* Buenos Aires. Martín García. 1910. Uc

Acosta, Crispo (Lauxar, pseud.). *Motivos de crítica hispanoamericanos.* Montevideo. Mercurio. 1914. Pp. 444. U-3800 D

Acta Medica Ibero-Americana. Barcelona, I, 12 (1935). n/n

Adams, Henry Brooks. *Mont-Saint-Michel and Chartres.* Introd. R. Adams Cram. Boston. Houghton Mifflin. 1913. Pp. xiv, 401. U-1183 I*

— *The Education of Henry Adams. An Autobiography.* London. Constable.
    1919. Pp. viii, 519. U-667 I* C* T

Adler, Paul. *Elohim.* Dresden. Hellerauer. 1914. Pp. 104. U-3721

Adlercreutz, Francisco de. *La cartera del Coronel Conde Adlercreutz.* Introd.
    y notas C. Parra-Pérez. Paris. Excelsior. 1928. Pp. 226. U-5293 I

Adrados, Santiago. *Dolencias políticas y sociales.* Madrid. Minuesa. 1925.
    Pp. 282. U-2161 n/o

Adts, N. *Los progresos del arte de la guerra.* Tr. Antonio Tovar. Madrid.
    Fortanet. 1881. Pp. 196. U-4674

Aeschylus. *Aeschyli Tragoediae.* Ex recensione R. Porsoni passim reficta
    G. Dindorfio. Editio secunda. Lipsiae. Taubner. 1850. Pp. 282. U-1508
    I* T* L

— *Agamemnón, Las coéforas, Las euménides, Los siete sobre Tebas,*
    Prometeo encadenado. Tr. en verso castellano J.R. Salas. Santiago de Chile.
    Cervantes. 1904. Pp. 639. U-756 I*

— *Aeschyli.* Tome I. *Les suppliantes. Les perses. Les sept contre Thèbes.*
    Prométhée enchaîné. Tr. Paul Mazon. Paris. Les Belles Lettres. 1920.
    Pp. xxxv, 199. U-4332 I* C

Agelet i Garriga, Jaume. *La tarda oberta.* Windsor. Oxley. 1927. Pp. 109.
    U-360 D

— *Els fanals del meu sant.* Haarlem. Enschedé en Zonen. 1935. Pp. 79.
    U-2934 D

Agostinho, José. *A mulher em Portugal.* Porto. Figueirinhas. 1908. Pp. 255.
    U-3284 D

— *Definicoes.* Porto. Figueirinhas. n.d. Pp. 62. U-2435

Agramont, Jacome d'. *Regiment de preservació a epidemia o pestilencia e*
    mortaldats. Amb entraments Enrich Arderiu y Joseph M. Roca. Lleyda.
    Pages. 1910. Pp. xvi, 37. U-5705

A Aguia. Pôrto (Jul-agosto 1923). n/n

Aguilar, Gilberto F. *Diez cuentos.* México. 1936. Pp. 170. U-1888 n/o D

Aguiló, Mossen Joan. *Poesíes.* Palma. Guasp. 1903. Pp. 15. U-4438

— *L'Angel de Nazareth.* Reus. Felanitx. 1910. Pp. 124. U-3886

Aguiló y Fuster, Marian. *Llibre de la mort.* Barcelona. Verdaguer. 1898.
    Pp. xv, 286. U-2707 D

— *Fochs Follets.* Barcelona. Giró. 1909. Pp. 178. U-3962 D

Aguirre, Constantino. *Pecado lírico.* Buenos Aires. Rosso. 1923. Pp. 108.
    U-3985 n/o D

Aguirre Achá, José. *Platonia.* La Paz. Imp. Eléctrica. 1923. Pp. iv, 435.
    U-2534 D

Aguirre Morales, Augusto. *La Medusa.* Lima. Rosay. 1916. Pp. 98. U-3334 D

Aita, Antonio. *Notas al margen de la poesía argentina.* Buenos Aires. Nosotros.
    1929. Pp. 14. U-4980 D

El Ajedrez español. Madrid (1934). Año I: 1-3; II: 5-9, 11. n/n

Aladern, Joseph. *Sacramental.* Estudi critich P. Gener. Reus. Ferrando. 1891. Pp. 118. U-3726 D

- *Odas paganas.* Barcelona. Catalana. 1903. Pp. 79. U-3115 D
- *Visita de D. Quixot de la Mancha a la Barcelona actual.* Barcelona. Catalana. 1905. Pp. 24. U-3136 D
- *Homenatge a la memoria d'en Cosme Vidal.* Barcelona. Anglada. 1921. Pp. 63. U-1694 D

Alarcón, Pedro Antonio de. *La alpujarra.* Madrid. Rivadeneyra. 1912. Pp. xvi, 450. U-1147 B I* L

Alarcón Capilla, Antonio. *Galdós y su obra.* Pról. A. González Blanco. Madrid. Matheu. [1922]. Pp. 91. U-2096 I

Alas, Leopoldo (Clarín, pseud.). *Obras completas.* Tomo I. *Galdós.* Madrid. Renacimiento. 1912. Pp. 366. U-921. Tomo II. *Su único hijo.* Madrid. Renacimiento. 1913. Pp. 371. n/n I

Alas Pumariño, Ramón de las. *La hermana Esther.* Madrid. Pueyo. 1923. Pp. xii, 266. U-3875 D

Alaux, Th. *Librito explicativo de los cuadros auxiliares Delmas para la enseñanza práctica de las lenguas vivas.* Bordeaux. Delmas. 1927. Pp. 112. U-5119

Albatrelli, Paolo. *I conquistatori.* Roma. Politica Moderna. 1925. Pp. 456. U-5350 I

Alberdi, Juan Bautista. *Obras completas.* 7 vols. Buenos Aires. La Tribuna Nacional. 1886. U-1653-9

- *Escritos póstumos.* Buenos Aires. Imp. Europea, Moreno y Defensa. 1895. Tomos I, III, VI-XVI. U-1867-80 n/o
- *Las bases.* Buenos Aires. La Facultad. 1915. Pp. 327. U-2787
- *Pensamientos de Alberdi.* Estudio prelimilar M. Escalada. Buenos Aires. Imp. Alberdi. 1902. Pp. lxviii, 406. U-3094

Albert, Salvador. *Les hores que tornen.* Pròl. Lluis Via. Barcelona. Ilustración Catalana. n.d. Pp. 110. U-2865 D

Alberti, Rafael. *La amante. Canciones* (1925). Madrid. Plutarco. 1929. Pp. 95. U-5695

Albiñana Monpó, José. *Gramática latina elemental.* Valencia. Ferrandis. n.d. Pp. xiii, 60. U-5547

Albiñana Sanz, José María. *Concepto actual de la filosofía médica y su valor en el desarrollo de la medicina.* Pról. F. Molina. Pontejos. Madrid. 1912. Pp. viii, 269. U-3439

Albornoz, Alvaro de. *No tiras, lanzas.* Madrid. Suárez. 1903. Uc

- *Individualismo y socialismo.* Barcelona. Henrich. 1908. Uc

Album de la guerra. Los aliados en 1917. Barcelona. Publicación del Comité de Periodistas Catalanes para la Propaganda Aliadófila. [1917]. Pp. 114. U-3562

Alcalá, Pedro de. *Arte para ligeramĕte saber la lĕgua arauiga.* New York.
   Hispanic Society of America. 1928. Ff. 38. U-1204
Alcalá Galiano y Osma, Alvaro. *Impresiones de arte.* Pról. Condesa de Pardo
   Bazán. Madrid. Suárez. 1910. Pp. xxiii, 312. U-2696 D
— *Del ideal y de la vida.* Madrid. Imp. Artística. 1912. Pp. xxiv, 338.
   U-3100 D
— *La verdad sobre la guerra. Origen y aspectos del conflicto europeo.* Madrid.
   Fortanet. 1915. Pp. 67. U-3218 D
— *España ante el conflicto europeo (1914-15).* Madrid. Fortanet. 1916.
   Pp. 276. U-1610 D
— *Conferencias y ensayos.* Madrid. Pueyo. 1919. Pp. 266. U-2047 D
— *Figuras excepcionales.* Madrid. Renacimiento. [1922]. Pp. 294. U-303 D
Alcalá Zamora, Niceto. *El derecho y sus colindancias en el teatro de Don Juan
   Ruíz de Alarcón.* Madrid. Tip. de Archivos. 1934. Pp. 85. U-2237 D
— *Reflexiones sobre las leyes de Indias.* Madrid. Tip. de Archivos. 1935.
   Pp. 94. U-2232 D
Alcázar Molina, Cayetano. *El espíritu corporativo de la posta española.* Madrid.
   Alcoy. 1920. Pp. 118. U-2705 D
— *Los hombres del despotismo ilustrado en España – El conde de Floridablanca,
   su vida y su obra.* Madrid. Instituto de Estudios Históricos. 1934. Pp. 174.
   U-4191
— *La responsabilidad en la historica de España. Memoria.* Madrid. Rivadeneyra.
   1923. Pp. 31. U-5667 D
Alcover y Maspons, Joan. *Poemas y harmonías.* Palma. Tous. 1894. Pp. 138.
   U-4428 D
— *Meteoros.* Barcelona. Gili. 1901. Pp. 249. U-2754.
Aldao, Carlos A. *A través del mundo.* Buenos Aires. Biedma. 1907. Pp. 408.
   U-4148
— *Errores de la constitución nacional.* Buenos Aires. Gurfinkel. 1928.
   Pp. 341. U-4953 D
Aldao, Martín C. *Escenas y perfiles.* Buenos Aires. Moen. 1903. Pp. 197.
   U-4990 D
— *La novela de Torcuato Méndez.* Madrid. Suárez. 1912. Uc D
— *Las confidencias de un expatriado voluntario.* Roma. Cuggiani. 1926.
   Pp. 230. U-4992
— *Las dos Españas de una dama argentina.* Roma. Cuggiani. 1927. Pp. 234.
   U-5603
— *Reflejos de Italia.* Roma. Cuggiani. 1927. Pp. 297. U-4991
Aldao de Díaz, Elvira. *Reminiscencias sobre Aristóbulo del Valle.* Buenos Aires.
   Peuser. 1928. Pp. 271. U-2009
Alemán, Mateo. *Vida y hechos del pícaro Guzmán de Alfarache.* Paris. Baudry.
   1847. Pp. xii, 482. U-3043. Madrid. Renacimiento. 1913. la parte. Pp. 375.
   n/n I

Alemán, Pedro Tomás. *Legislación social.* Alicante. Reus. 1912. Uc

Alemán Bolaños, Gustavo. *Centro y Sud-América.* Pról. A. Alvarez. Santiago de Chile. Universitaria. 1915. Pp. 96. U-2767 n/o D

Aleramo, Sibilla, pseud. [i.e., Rina Faccio]. *Una mujer.* Tr. José Prat. Valencia. Sempere. n.d. Uc D

Alfar. La Coruña (Agosto-sept. 1927). n/n

Alfieri, Vittorio. *Le tragedie di V. Alfieri.* Scelte e illustrate Michele Scherillo. Milano. Hoepli. 1912. Pp. lxxvi, 370. U-3930 I

– *La vita, le rime e altri scritti minori.* A cura M. Scherillo. Milano. Hoepli. 1917. Pp. lxxv, 482. U-5338 I*

Alfonso X. *Primera crónica general. Estoria de España que mandó componer Alfonso el Sabio y se continuaba bajo Sancho IV en 1289.* Publicada R. Menéndez Pidal. (NBAE, 5). Madrid. Bailly-Ballière. 1906. Pp. iv, 776. U-40 I* C

Alfonso, José A. *Educación.* Santiago de Chile. Universitaria. 1912. Pp. 343. U-3867 n/o

– *Discurso académico.* Santiago de Chile. Universidad. 1930. Pp. 54. U-4964 D

Algazel. See Muhammad ibn Muhammad, al-Ghazzali

Les Allemands destructeurs de cathédrales et de trésors du passé. Paris. Hachette. 1915. Pp. 78, pl. 13. U-1187

Allende Salazar, Angel. *Biblioteca del bascófilo.* Madrid. Tello. 1887. Pp. 483. U-731

Almada, Amadeo. *Vidas y obras. Estudios de crítica.* Montevideo. Cervantes. 1912. Pp. 208. U-3149 D

Almafuerte, pseud. See Palacios, Pedro Bonifacio

Almanac de la Poesía. Barcelona. Altés. 1914-16, 1919-21, 1923. Ff. 25 each. U-4448, U-4039, U-4599, U-5564, U-5555, U-4601, U-4600, U-4558

Almanach dels noucentistes. Barcelona. Horta. 1911. Ff. 45. U-3556

Almeida Garrett, João Baptista da Silva Leitão, viscount. *Frei Luiz de Sousa.* Lisboa. Empreza da Historia de Portugal. 1902. Pp. 197. U-531 I

– *Viagens na minha terra.* 2 vols. Porto. Ferreira dos Santos. n.d. U-4270-1 I

Alomar, Gabriel. *El futurisme.* Barcelona. L'Avenç. 1905. Pp. 73. U-2167 I* C* L

Alonso, Amado. *El problema de la lengua en América.* Madrid. Espasa-Calpe. 1935. Pp. 208. U-5628 I C D

– *Góngora y la literatura contemporánea.* Santander. Boletín de la Biblioteca Menéndez y Pelayo. 1932. Pp. 39. U-4941 D

– 'El hidalgo Camilote y el hidalgo Don Quijote,' *Revista de Filología Española,* xx (1933), 391-7. U-1716 D

Alonso Cortés, Narciso. *Arbol añoso.* Valladolid. Viuda de Montero. 1914. Pp. 89. U-4680 n/o

– *Gramática elemental de la lengua castellana.* Valladolid. Aguado. 1931.

Alonso Garrote, Santiago. *El dialecto vulgar leonés.* Astorga. López. 1909.
Pp. 271. U-2575 [Bound with *El antecristo* by Martínez Sacristán]

Alonso Getino, Fr. Luis G. *La autonomía universitaria y la vida de Fray Luis de León.* Salamanca. Noticiero Salmantino. 1904. Pp. 173. U-3740

Alonso Ortega, Canuto. *Gramática teórico-práctica de la lengua griega.* Valladolid. Lezcano y Roldán. 1853. Pp. 212, xlvii. U-2147 I

Alonso Rodríguez, P.V. *Tratado de la oración.* Madrid. Asilo de la Santísima Trinidad. 1907. Pp. 233. U-4439

Alonso Terrón, A. *El pan gratis.* Granada. El Pueblo. 1908. Pp. 208. U-2679 n/o D

Alsina, Ferran. *Nuevas orientaciones científicas.* Barcelona. Henrich. 1904. Uc

Altamira y Crevea, Rafael. *La enseñanza de la historia.* Madrid. Fortanet. 1891. Pp. 278. U-2230

− *Cuestiones hispano-americanas.* Madrid. Rodríguez Serra. 1900. Pp. 96. Uc

− *Psicología del pueblo español.* Madrid. Fé. 1902. Pp. 209. Uc

− *Psicología y literatura.* Barcelona. Henrich. 1905. Pp. 254. Uc

− *Reposo.* Barcelona. Henrich. 1903. Pp. 320. U-2133

− *Historia de España y de la civilización española.* Barcelona. Gili. 1906. Tomo III. Pp. 749. U-4338 I

Altolaguirre, Manuel. *Las islas invitadas y otros poemas.* Málaga. Sur. 1926. Ff. 24. U-5575 D

− *Ejemplo.* Málaga. Sur. 1927. Pp. 51. U-5569 D

Altozanos, Augusto de, pseud. [i.e., Francisco Pujols]. *El nuevo Pascual o la prostitución.* Barcelona. La Neotipia. 1906. Pp. 268. U-4710

Alvares, Joao. *Chrónica do Infante Santo D. Fernando.* Edição crítica Mendes dos Remédios. Coimbra. Amado. 1911. Pp. xxiv, 183. U-132 I

Alvares Pereira, Nuno. *Chrónica do Condestabre de Portugal Dom Nuno Alvares Pereira.* Com revisao, pref., e notas Mendes dos Remédios. Coimbra. Amado. 1911. Pp. xlvi, 234. U-2721 I L B

Alvarez, Agustín. *La transformación de las razas en América.* Barcelona. Granada y Cía. [1915]. Pp. 187. U-2146

− *La creación del mundo moral.* Madrid. Suárez. 1913. Uc

Alvarez, José S. (Fray Mocho, pseud.). *Un viaje al país de los matreros.* Buenos Aires. Ivaldi-Checchi. 1897. Pp. 171. (2 copies) U-2360 n/o. U-2370 I D [Bound with Escalpelo]

− *En el mar austral.* Buenos Aires. Ivaldi-Checchi. 1898. Pp. 262. U-4478 D

− *Cuentos de Fray Mocho.* Buenos Aires. Caras y Caretas. 1906. Pp. vii, 200. U-2401 D

Alvarez, Juan. *Ensayo sobre la historia de Santa Fe.* Buenos Aires. Malena. 1910. Pp. 414. U-3752 D

− *Estudio sobre la desigualdad y la paz.* Buenos Aires. Coop. Edit. Buenos Aires. 1927. Pp. 185. U-5674 D

Alvarez, Ramiro. *Schidlof's Taal-Methode Spaansch.* Amsterdam. Meulenhoff.
[1910]. Pp. xxxix, 296. U-3794 n/o D
Alvarez Conzi, Francisco. *Reflexiones y efusiones.* Madrid. Zabala. 1914.
Pp. 107, 20. U-3412 I* C D
Alvarez Puente, Manuel R. *Almas perdidas.* Madrid. Hernando. 1917. Pp. 385.
U-2908 n/o D
Alves Martins, António. *Mulher de Bênção.* Pôrto. Renascença Portuguesa.
1923. Pp. 109. U-545 n/o
Alzola y Minondo, Pablo. *El arte industrial en España.* Bilbao. Casa de
Misericordia. 1892. Pp. xi, 550. U-3777 D
– *Colección de discursos y artículos.* Bilbao. Casa de Misericordia. 1896. Uc
– *La política económica mundial y nuestra reforma arancelaria.* Bilbao.
Casa de Misericordia. 1906. Pp. 393. U-1859 D
– *Régimen económico-administrativo, antiguo y moderno de Vizcaya y de
Guipúzcoa.* Bilbao. Casa de Misericordia. 1910. Pp. 430. U-2464 D
Amadeo, Octavio R. *Política.* Buenos Aires. Mendesky. 1916. Pp. 231.
U-2405 D
– *Vidas argentinas.* Buenos Aires. La Facultad. 1934. Pp. 324. (2 copies)
U-3033. U-4310 D
Amador, Fernan Félix de. *El libro de horas.* Paris. Gauthièr. 1910. Pp. 186.
U-4273 D
Amador de los Ríos, Rodrigo. *Murcia y Albacete. España, sus monumentos
y artes.* Barcelona. Cortezo. 1889. Pp. 790. U-668
Amaral, Eloy do. *Bocage. Fragmentos de um estudo autobiographico.*
Figueira. Lusitana. 1912. Pp. 40. U-776 D
Amauta. Lima, xix (1928). n/n
Ambris, Alceste de. *Amendola.* Toulouse. Exoria Libr. 1927. Pp. 55. U-5341 I
Ambrogi, Arturo. *Marginales de la vida.* San Salvador. Nacional. 1912.
Pp. 266. U-2226
– *Sensaciones del Japón y de la China.* San Salvador. 1915. Uc
– *El libro del trópico.* San Salvador. Nacional. 1915. Pp. 238. U-565
– *El segundo libro del trópico.* San Salvador. Nacional. [1916]. Pp. 186.
U-248
Ambrosetti, Juan B. *Exploraciones arqueológicas en la Pampa Grande
(Provincia de Salta).* Buenos Aires. Lajouane. 1906. Pp. 197. U-2495
Ambruzzi, Lucillo. *Sulla breccia. Questioni di educazione.* Torino. Grato
Scioldo. 1891. Uc
– *Verso l'aurora.* Torino. Grato Scioldo. 1908. Pp. 372. U-3178 D
– *La diffusione della lingua castigliana.* Torino. Tip. Nazionale. 1909.
Pp. 16. U-5356 D
– 'Rassegna iberica,' *Rassegna Nazionale.* Torino (Giugnio 1934). Pp. 12.
U-5363 I D
Ameghino, Florentino. *Mi credo.* Tortosa. Monclús. n.d. Pp. 79. U-4725

Amengual, Bartolomé. *Estudio sobre la organización corporativa oficial de los comerciantes e industriales.* Barcelona. Guinart. n.d. Uc

American Church Monthly. New Brunswick (May 1921). n/n

Amézaga, Carlos Germán. *Cactus.* Lima. Bacigalupi. 1891. Pp. v, 172. U-1982 D

– *Poetas mexicanos.* Buenos Aires. Coni. 1896. Pp. 414. U-3626 D

Amiel, Henri-Frédéric. *Fragments d'un journal intime.* Précédés d'une étude E. Scherer. 2 vols. Genève. Georg et Co. 1908. U-885-6 I* C*. Edition nouvelle conforme au texte original augmentée de fragments inédits et précédée d'une introd. Bernard Bouvier. 3 vols. Paris. Crès. [1922]. U-1352-4 I* C*

Amunátegui Reyes, Miguel Luis. *Don Manuel de Salas.* 3 vols. Santiago de Chile. Nacional. 1895. U-801-3

– *Mis pasatiempos.* Santiago de Chile. Cervantes. 1905. Pp. 167. U-1646 D

Anales de la Universidad de Valencia (1921-2). n/n

Anales del Instituto de León. Estudio-Cultura. León (Mayo 1920). n/n

Anasagasti, Teodoro de. *Enseñanza de la arquitectura.* Madrid. Rivadeneyra. [1923]. Pp. 307. U-2220

Anasagasti, Victorio de. *El secreto de Belmonte.* Madrid. Sáez. 1915. Pp. 137. (2 copies) U-185 D. U-884

Ancel, Jacques. *Peuples et nations des Balkans.* Paris. Colin. 1926. Pp. 220, 8. U-5231 I

Andersson, Theodore. *Carlos María Ocantos y su obra.* Tr. Francisco Aguilera. Madrid. Soc. Gral. Española. n.d. Pp. 210. U-3049

Andrade Coello, Alejandro. *Nociones de literatura general.* n.p. n.d. Pp. xxi, 526. U-3641 [Cover missing]

André, Eloy Luis. *El histrionismo español. Ensayo de psicología política.* Barcelona. Henrich. 1906. Pp. 250. (2 copies) U-1600, U-3467 D

– *Etica española. Problemas de moral contemporánea.* Madrid. Hernández. 1910. Pp. 304. U-1794 n/o D

– *La mentalidad alemana.* Madrid. Jorro. 1914. Pp. xv, 567. U-4158

– *Ensayo sobre psicología artística.* Pp. 71. U-3530 [Typescript]

André, Marius. *Cantares. Poésies espagnoles avec une traduction française par l'auteur.* Paris. Le Livre Libre. 1930. Pp. 80. U-387

Andrenio. See Gómez de Baquero, Eduardo

Andrews, Capitán J. *Viaje de Buenos Aires a Potosí y Arica en los años 1825 y 1826.* Tr. Carlos A. Aldao. Buenos Aires. Vaccaro. 1920. Pp. 260. U-4194

– *Las provincias del norte en 1825.* Tr. J.A. Saente. Pról. J. Heller. Buenos Aires. Coni. 1915. Pp. 96. U-1664

Andrich, Emilio German. *Ió, Fermín y Juan Valdez.* Buenos Aires. Pesce. 1934. Pp. 99. U-3471 D

Andújar y Solana, Manuel. *Patria y 'Sea Power.'* Pról. L. Saralegui y Medina. Ferrol. Pita. 1901. Pp. xxiii, 172. U-2520 n/o

Angell, Norman. *La grande ilusión.* Paris. Nelson. [1913]. Pp. 372. U-480 C

Angellier, Auguste Jean. *Dans la lumière antique. Le livre des dialogues.* 2 vols. Paris. Hachette. 1905-6. U-1948-9

— *Dans la lumière antique. Les épisodes.* 2 vols. Paris. Hachette. 1908-9. U-1394, U-1950

Angelus, Silesius. See Scheffler, Johann

Angiolini, Alfredo. *De los delitos culposos.* Tr. José Buixó. Barcelona. Henrich. 1905. Uc

Anguilli, Andrés. *La filosofía y la escuela.* Tr. M. Domenge y Mir. Barcelona. Henrich. 1906. Uc

Anguita, Bernabé. *Lejanías.* Valparaiso. Gillet. 1904. Uc

Annalas della Societá Retoromantscha. XXIII. Annada. Samedan. Engadin Press. 1909. Pp. 322. U-2465

Annalen der Philosophie. Leipzig (1929). n/n

Annunzio, Gabriele d'. *Di Gabriele d'Annunzio l'orazione e la canzone in morte di Giosuè Carducci.* Milano. Fratelli Treves. 1907. Pp. 48. U-735

— *Aspects de l'inconnu. Nocturne.* Tr. André Doderet. Paris. Calmann-Lévy. 1917. Pp. 318. U-3073 n/o

— *La torche sous le boisseau.* Tr. André Doderet. Paris. Calmann-Lévy. 1928. Pp. 193. U-1960 n/o

Antecedentes de política económica en el Río de la Plata. 2 vols. Madrid. Rivadeneyra. 1915. (2 copies) U-2959-62 n/o

Anthologia Graeca. Epigrammatum Palatina cum Planudea. Ed. Hugo Stadtmueller. 3 vols. Lipsiae. Teubner. 1894-1906. U-342-4 I* T L

Anthologia Lyrica, sive Lyricorum Graecorum veterum Praeter Pindarum. Reliquiae Potiores. Post Theodorum Bergkium quartum ed. E. Hiller. Lipsiae. Teubner. 1913. Pp. lxxvi, 387. U-352 I* L

Anthologie des philosophes français contemporains. Paris. Sagittaire. 1931. Pp. 533. U-3608 I* C

Antich, José. *Andrógino.* Barcelona. Henrich. 1904. Pp. 311. U-2639 I D

— *Egoísmo y altruísmo.* Barcelona. Henrich. 1906. Uc

Antieuropa. Roma (1 marzo 1930). n/n

Antiga, Juan. *Escritos sociales y reflexiones médicas.* Madrid. Espasa-Calpe. 1927. Pp. 348. U-5124

Antola, Carlos G. *El colectivismo agrario de Rivadavia.* Pról. A.L. Palacios. Buenos Aires. Salita. 1919. Pp. vi, 174. U-558 n/o D

Antologia catalana. Barcelona. Els Clássics Catalans. 1932. Pp. 112. U-5712

Antología de poetas líricos castellanos. Romances viejos castellanos. Introd. y notas Fernando José Wolf y Conrado Hofmann. 2a ed., corr. y adicionada M. Menéndez y Pelayo. 3 vols. Madrid. Hernando. 1899. U-2368

Antología del centenario. *Estudio documentado de la literatura mexicana durante el primer siglo de independencia.* 2 vols. México. Sánchez. 1910.
U-4211-12

Antología hispano-americana. Buenos Aires. Peuser. 1906. Pp. xxii, 250.
U-1743

Antología. Pintura vasca 1909-1919. Bilbao. Amigos del País. 1919.
Pp. 278. n/n

Antón, Enrique de. *Suspiros.* Buenos Aires. Contreras. 1929. Pp. 63.
U-5537 n/o D

Antón, Francisco. *Estudio sobre el coro de la catedral de Zamora.* Zamora.
Tip. de San José. 1904. Pp. 151. U-5050 D

Antón del Olmet, Fernando de. *Queralt, hombre de mundo.* Madrid. Marzo.
1905. Pp. 368. U-283 D

Antuña, José G. *Litterae.* Paris. Fabre. 1926. Pp. 249. U-4996 D

— *Palabra. Conferencias y discursos, 1915-1927.* Paris. Ed. Paris-América.
1927. Pp. 242. U-5619 D

— *Petrarca, Laura y el Renacimiento.* Montevideo. Barreiro y Ramos. 1929.
Pp. 54. U-5620 D

Anuario estadístico de la ciudad de Barcelona, XII (1913), 49-634, pl. 6.
U-5741

Aponte, Adolfo. *Canciones remotas.* Zaragoza. Casañal. 1910. Pp. 247.
U-4814 D

— *Paisajes de almas.* Madrid. 1913. Pp. 168. Uc D

Aponte, José Manuel. *La revolución del Acre (1902-1903).* La Paz. El
Comercio de Bolivia. 1903. Uc

— *Tradiciones bolivianas.* La Paz. Velarde. 1909. Uc

Apraiz, Angel de. *La casa y la vida en la antigua Salamanca.* Salamanca.
Calatrava. 1917. Pp. 47. U-2506 D

Ara, Pedro. *La enseñanza de la anatomía.* Madrid. Museo Anatómico Español.
1934. Pp. 48, pl. 13. U-4972 D

— *Razón y alcurnia de la conservación artificial de la forma y de la fisonomía
humanas.* Discurso recepción. Academia Nacional de Medicina y contestación Prof. L. de la Peña y Díaz. Madrid. Góngora. 1936. Pp. 47. U-5777 D

Aragão, Maximiano d'. *Vizeu. Apontamentos historicos.* Vizeu. Popular.
1894. Uc

— *Grao-Vasco ou Vasco Fernandez.* Vizeu. Popular. 1900. Pp. 140. U-1647 D

Aragon y Escacena, José. *Entre brumas.* Pról. R. Goy de Silva. Astorga. Sierra.
1921. Pp. 169, xv. U-3050 n/o D

Arámburu, Ricardo H. *El presidente Alvear.* Paris. Ed. Franco-Ibero-Americana.
n.d. Pp. 205. U-2057 D

Aramburu y Machado, Mariano. *Doctrinas jurídicas.* Habana. Cuba Intelectual.
1916. Uc D

Arana, Vicente de. *Leyendas del norte.* Pról. Fermín Herrán. Vitoria. Ilustración. 1890. Pp. xxii, 454. U-3465

Aranda, Valentín, Alfonso Barea, y Antonio J. Onieva. *Hacia la escuela hispánica.* Madrid. Magisterio Español. 1936. Pp. 229. U-2252 n/o D

Aranzadi y Unamuno, Telésforo, José M. de Barandiarán, y Enrique de Eguren. *Exploraciones de la Caverna de Santimamiñe.* 2 vols. Bilbao. Dip. de Vizcaya. 1925-31. U-3541, U-5747

Araoz Alfaro. *La meningitis cerebro-espinal epidémica.* Buenos Aires. Coni. 1910. Uc

Araoz de la Madrid, Gregorio. *Memorias.* Compiladas con cartapról. Adolfo Carranza. 2 vols. Buenos Aires. Kraft. 1895. U-737-8

Aravena, Héctor de. *Páginas españolas. Glosas al viaje y al arte.* Santiago de Chile. Ariel. 1929. Pp. 120. U-5602 D

Arboleda, Gustavo. *El periodismo en el Ecuador.* Guayaquil. El Grito del Pueblo. 1909. Pp. 238. U-4418

Archiv für des Studium der neueren Sprachen und Literaturen. (25 numbers 1889-99). n/n

Archivum Romanicum. Genève (1927). n/n

Arcia, Juan E. *Vestigios.* Caracas. Herrera Irigoyen. 1901. Uc D

Arderiu, Clementina. *Cançons i elegíes.* Barcelona. Publ. de la Revista. 1916. Pp. 72. U-2334

Arderíus, Joaquín. *Los príncipes iguales.* Madrid. Argis. 1928. Pp. 239. U-5613 C D

Arenillas, Ignacio. *Una verdad por España.* Salamanca. Comercial Salmantina. 1934. Pp. 222. U-2015 D

Arese'tar Emeteri. *Txindor.* Donostiyan. Leizaola'ren Irarkolan. 1928. Pp. 158. U-5715

Argamasilla de la Cerda, Joaquín. *La explosión de la mentira.* Madrid. Imp. F. de Sales. 1917. Pp. 257. U-282 n/o

Argensola, Die Brüder. See Leonardo y Argensola

Argerich, Juan Antonio. *Artículos y discursos.* Buenos Aires. Coni. 1906. Pp. 320. U-4181 D

– *Artículos y discursos. Segunda serie.* Buenos Aires. Coni. 1906. Pp. 350. U-4170

Arguedas, Alcides. *Pueblo enfermo. Contribución a la psicología de los pueblos hispano-americanos.* Carta-pról. R. de Maeztu. Barcelona. Tasso. 1909. Pp. 255. U-424 C* I. 2a ed. 1910. Pp. 263. U-2432 D

– *Raza de bronce.* La Paz. Gonzáles y Medina. 1919. Pp. 373. U-3751 I* L D

– *Historia de Bolivia. La fundación de la república.* La Paz. Colegio Don Bosco. 1920. Pp. xviii, 442. U-3790 I* L* C D

– *Historia general de Bolivia. El proceso de la nacionalidad. 1809-1921.* La Paz. Arnó. 1922. Pp. xi, 579. U-4216 I* C D

- *La danza de las sombras.* Barcelona. López Robert. 1934. Pp. 424.
  U-4300 I L* D
- *Vida criolla.* Paris. Ollendorff. Uc D

Argüello, Santiago. *De tierra ... cálida.* León (Nicaragua). 1900. Uc D
- *Lecciones de literatura española.* 2 vols. León (Nicaragua). Gurdian. 1903.
  U-3773-4 I D. Guatemala. Tip. Nacional. 1936. Tomo I. Pp. 324. U-3757 D
- *El poema de la locura.* León (Nicaragua). Gurdian. 1904. Pp. 105.
  U-4197 D
- *Viaje al país de la decadencia.* Barcelona. Maucci. 1904. Pp. 253. U-3277
- *Ocaso.* León (Nicaragua). Gurdian. 1906. Pp. 135. U-3734 D
- *Ojo y alma.* Pref. Vargas Vila. París. Bouret. 1908. Pp. 176. U-3208
- *Mi mensaje a la juventud y otras orientaciones.* Con palabras de Rubén
  Darío. México. Herrero. 1928. Pp. 262. U-4879 D. 2a ed. Guatemala.
  Nacional. 1935. Pp. 320. U-300 n/o D
- *Poesías escogidas y poesías nuevas.* Guatemala. Nacional. 1935. Pp. 312.
  U-3745 n/o D
- *Modernismo y modernistas.* 2 vols. Guatemala. Nacional. 1935. U-2751-2 D

Arias Trujillo, Bernardo. *Risaralda.* Manizales. Zapata. n.d. Pp. 256. U-3357 D

Arintero, Fr. Juan T. González de. *La evolución y la filosofía cristiana.*
  Madrid. Gregorio del Amo. 1898. Uc

Ariosto, Ludovico. *L'Orlando furioso di Ariosto.* Note e discorso proemiale
  Giacinto Casella. Firenze. Barbèra. 1913. Pp. xlvi, 1016. U-2273

Aristophanes. *Aristophanis comoediae.* 2 vols. Lipsiae. Teubner. 1825.
  U-1563-4 I* C* T* L
- *Scenes From the Clouds.* Rugby ed. A. Sidgwich. London. Rivingtons.
  1884. Ff. 32. U-4722 T L
- *Morceaux choisis.* Nouvelle éd., avec des notices, des analyses, et des notes
  en français C. Poyard. Paris. Hachette. 1897. Pp. 340. U-4465 I

Aristotle. *Aristotelis politica.* Post. Fr. Susemihlium recognovit Otto Immisch.
  Lipsiae. Teubner. 1909. Pp. xxxix, 352. U-351 I* C* T
- *Constitution d'Athènes.* Tr. G. Mathieu et B. Haussoullier. Paris. Les
  Belles Lettres. 1922. Pp. xxxi, 101. U-3738 I

Armada y Losada, Juan (Marqués de Figueroa). *Gondar y Forteza.* Madrid.
  Tello. 1900. Pp. 259. U-4425 D

Armas y Cárdenas, José de. *El Quijote y su época.* Madrid. Renacimiento.
  1915. Pp. 267. U-193

Armendáriz, Julián de. *Comedia famosa de Las Burlas Veras.* Ed. with introd.
  S.L. Millard Rosenberg. Philadelphia. University of Pennsylvania. 1917.
  Pp. 206, pl. 3. U-5186 I

The Army and Religion. Pref. the Bishop of Winchester. London. Macmillan.
  1919. Pp. xxxi, 455. U-2037 I*

Arnold, Matthew. *Essays in Criticism.* Leipzig. Tauchnitz. 1892. Pp. 264.
  U-4771 I

- *Poetical Works of Arnold*. London. Macmillan. 1903. Pp. xii, 510.
  U-3796 T I*
A[rolas], Juan. *La sílfide del acueducto*. Valencia. Jaime Martínez. 1837.
  Pp. 230. U-4416
Aróztegui, Abdón. *La revolución oriental de 1870*. 2 vols. Buenos Aires.
  Lajouane. 1889. U-2485-6
- *Un sueño dantesco*. Buenos Aires. La Anticuaria. 1896. Pp. 393. U-2989
- *Ensayos dramáticos*. Buenos Aires. Real y Prado. 1896. Pp. xvii, 390,
  pl. 4. U-2154
Arpas cubanas. Poetas contemporáneos. Pról. Conde Kostia. La Habana.
  Rambla y Bouza. 1904. Pp. xi, 436. U-2190 D
Arreaza Calatrava. *Cantos de la carne y del reino interior*. Madrid. 1911. Uc
- *Odas la triste y otros poemas*. Buenos Aires. Michaud. n.d. Pp. 267.
  U-2323 D
Arreguine, Víctor. *Estudios sociales*. Buenos Aires. 1899. Uc D
- *En qué consiste la superioridad de los latinos sobre los anglosajones*.
  Buenos Aires. La Enseñanza Argentina. 1900. Pp. 117. U-2876
- *Tardes de estío*. Pról. Antonino Lamberti. Buenos Aires. 1906. Pp. 148.
  U-1531 D
Arriaga, Emiliano de. *Lexicón bilbaíno*. Bilbao. Amorrortu. 1896. Pp. 317.
  U-5067 I L*
- *Chiplis-Chaplas*. Bilbao. Amorrortu. 1899. Pp. 334. U-4010 D
- *La pastelería*. Bilbao. Martín y Amilibia. 1908. Pp. 283. U-876 I
- *Revoladas de un chimbo*. Pról. M. de Unamuno. Bilbao. Aldama. 1920.
  Pp. xv, 247. (2 copies) U-3031, U-3677
- *Compilación de varios artículos literarios*. Bilbao. Arechalde y Celorrio.
  1920. Pp. 270. U-3959
Arrieta, Rafael Alberto. *Alma y momento*. La Plata. Sesé. 1910. Pp. 98.
  U-3248 D
- *El espejo de la fuente*. Buenos Aires. Nosotros. 1912. Uc
Arroyo, César E. *México en 1935. El presidente Vasconcelos*. Paris. Le Livre
  Libre. 1929. Pp. 58. U-5584 D
- *Galdós*. Madrid. Soc. Gral. Española de Librería. 1930. Pp. 104. U-4989 D
Arroyo de Aldama, José. *El sistema constitucional en las diferentes formas
  de gobierno*. Madrid. Fortanet. 1901. Pp. 320. U-3768
Arsamasseva, Margarita E. *Lobos*. Buenos Aires. El Inca. 1926. Pp. 131. U-5528 D
Art Studies. Medieval, Renaissance, and Modern. Ed. members of the Depts. of
  the Fine Arts at Harvard and Princeton Universities. Vol. I. An extra num-
  ber of the *American Journal of Archaeology*. Princeton University Press.
  1923. Pp. 106, pl. 29. U-5
L'Art tchécoslovaque de l'antiquité à nos jours. Texte MM. V. Birnbaum, A.
  Matejcek, J. Schrávil, Z. Wirth. Praha. Vesmir. 1929. Pp. 39; photos. 134,
  pl. 51. U-3

Artagão, Mário de. *Feras à solta.* Lisboa. Edit. Portuguesa. 1936. Pp. 43.
U-5734 D
Arteaga Alemparte, Justo. *Los constituyentes de 1870.* Bosquejo crítico
Roberto Huneeus. Santiago de Chile. Bibl. Escritores de Chile. 1910.
Pp. lxii, 470. U-2605
Artigas y Ferrando, Miguel. *Menéndez y Pelayo.* Madrid. Voluntad. 1927.
Pp. 310. U-4866 I D
Artola Tomas, Bernat. *Elegies.* Castelló de la Plana. Armengot. 1928. Pp. 108.
(2 copies) U-2793, U-5492 D
— *Terra (1930-1934).* Castelló de la Plana. Soc. Castellonenca de Cultura.
1935. Pp. xiv, 147. U-3389 C D
Arús Colomer, Joan. *Sonets.* Sabadell. Sanllent. 1915. Pp. 81. U-3747 D
Arxius de l'Institut de Ciències. Any I, no. 1. Barcelona. Institut d'Estudis
Catalans. Uc
Arzadun y Zavala, Juan. *Poesía.* Pról. M. de Unamuno. Bilbao. Bibl.
Bascongada. 1897. Pp. xi, 163. Uc
— *Albores de la independencia argentina.* Madrid. Eduardo Arias. 1910.
Pp. 135. (2 copies) U-5515, U-5023
— *Fin de condena.* Madrid. Soc. Autores Españoles. 1912. Pp. 63. U-2033 D
— *Cuentos militares.* Bilbao. Edic. Vizcaina. [1903]. Pp. 139. U-4685 D
Ascasubi, Hilario. *Santos Vega o los mellizos de la flor.* Buenos Aires. Peuser.
1893. Uc
Asenjo del Río, Rufino. *Influencia del anarquismo.* Pról. Carlos Piccinini.
Buenos Aires. Fernández. 1908. Pp. xvi, 175. U-2365 n/o D
Ashton, Sir Arthur, Bolland Leigh, and Basil Gray. *Chinese Art.* London.
Kegan Paul. 1935. Pp. xi, 111. U-1145. Introd. Laurence Binyon.
London. Faber and Faber. 1935. Pp. 397. U-4826
Asín Palacios, Miguel. *Algazel. Dogmática, moral, ascética.* Pról. Menéndez y
Pelayo. Zaragoza. Comas. 1901. Pp. xxxix, 912. U-4615
— *Los precedentes musulmanes de Pari de Pascal.* Santander. Bibl. Menéndez
y Pelayo. 1920. Pp. 64. U-4118
Assen Dzivgov, Georges. *Poètes bulgares.* Sofia. Coll. le Livre Bulgare. [1927].
Pp. 215. U-5286
Assolant, Alfred. *Scènes de la vie des Etats-Unis.* Paris. Charpentier. 1873. Uc
Astarloa y Aguirre, Pablo Pedro de. *Apología de la lengua bascongada.*
Madrid. Ortega. 1803. Pp. xxiv, 452. U-4274
Astigarra y Ugarte, Luis de. *Diccionario manual bascongado y castellano.*
Tolosa. López. 1881. Pp. 89. U-5623 [Incomplete]
Astor, Antonio. *El despotismo del oro.* Barcelona. Presa. n.d. Uc
Astorquiza, Eleodoro. *Literatura francesa.* Concepción. Imp. Inglesa Westcott.
1907. Uc
Astrov, Vladimir. *Dostojewskij und Holzapfel.* München. Psychokosmos Verlag.
1927. Pp. 115. U-5396 D

— *Rudolf Maria Holzapfel, der Schöpfer des Panideals: ein neues Leben.* Mit
  einem Vorwort von Romain Rolland. Jena. Diederich. 1928. Pp. xxii, 73.
  (2 copies) U-5442-3
Asturaro, Alfonso. *El materialismo histórico y la sociología general.* Tr. y pról.
  José Buixó. Barcelona. Henrich. 1906. Uc
Asturias, Miguel Angel. *Rayito de estrella.* Paris. 1929. Ff. 12. U-5520 D
— *Leyendas de Guatemala.* Madrid. Oriente. 1930. Pp. 207. U-5604 D
Atangana, Carlos. *Paz, humanidad y justicia.* Madrid. Edit. Hispano-Africana.
  1910. Pp. 15. U-3707
Ateneo. Madrid (Abril, jun. 1907). n/n
Ateneo. Valladolid (Abril 1915). n/n
Ateneo de Santiago de Chile. *Veladas del Ateneo.* Santiago. 1906. Pp. 207.
  U-3122
Ateneo Puertorriqueño. San Juan, ii, 1 (1936). n/n
Athayde, Tristäo de, pseud. [i.e., Alceu Amoroso Lima]. *Affonso Arinos.*
  Porto. Renascença Portuguesa. 1922. Pp. 197. U-1460 I* T* L D
Atlantic Monthly (August 1925). n/n
Atlas of Ancient Classical Geography. London. Dent. [1910]. Pp. xxxvii, 93.
  U-5177
Attwood, E.L. *El moderno buque de guerra.* Tr. Juan de Goitia. Barcelona.
  Guinart. 1913. Uc
Aub, Max. *Narciso.* Barcelona. Altés. 1928. Pp. 124. U-4948 D
Aubin Rieu-Vernet, José. *¿La inferioridad de la ciencia francesa?* Pról.
  L. Torres y Quevedo. Madrid. La Razón. 1918. Uc
Auclair, Marcelle. *Transparence.* Pról. Paulino Alfonso. Santiago. Universitaria.
  1919. Pp. 95. U-2854 D
Audiencia de Charcas. Publ. dirigida Roberto Levillier. Pról. Adolfo Bonilla y
  San Martín. Madrid. Bibl. del Congreso Argentino. 1918. U-2975
Audisio, Gabriel. *Jeunesse de la Méditerranée.* Paris. Gallimard. 1935.
  Pp. 284. U-3449 D
Augustine, Saint, Bishop of Hippo. *Confessionum libri tredecim.* Paris.
  Chernoviz. 1889. Uc
— *Meditationes.* Paris. Chernoviz. 1902. Pp. 444. U-4567 I
Aulino, Pedro. *Los ciegos.* Buenos Aires. Porter. 1929. Pp. 106. U-5483 D
Aurelius Antoninus, Marcus (called the Philosopher). *Commentarii.* Ed.
  I. Stich. Lipsiae. Teubner. 1903. Pp. xxii, 218. U-4488 T L*
Aurora de Chile. 1812-1813. Reimpresión paleográfica a plana y renglón.
  Introd. Julio Vicuña Cifuentes. Santiago de Chile. Cervantes. 1903. Uc
Aurousseau, Marcel. *Highway into Spain.* London. Davies. 1930. Pp. 686.
  U-1738 L* I*
Ausonius, Decimus Magnus. *Obres.* Vol. i. Text i tr. Carles Riba i Anton
  Navarro. Barcelona. Ed. Catalana. 1924. Pp. xvii, 116. U-5700
Austen, Jane. *Emma.* London. Dent. 1911. Pp. 395. U-1051 I

- *Mansfield Park.* Introd. R.B. Johnson. London. Dent. 1913. Pp. viii, 396.
  U-1052 I C
- *Pride and Prejudice.* Introd. R.B. Johnson. London. Dent. 1913. Pp. viii,
  336. U-1053 I*
- *Sense and Sensibility.* Introd. R.B. Johnson. London. Dent. 1913.
  Pp. xii, 308. U-1054 I*
- *Northanger Abbey* and *Persuasion.* Introd. R.B. Johnson. London. Dent.
  1913. Pp. 216. U-1055 I* C
Autobiografías y memorias. Coleccionadas e ilustr. Manuel Serrano y Sanz.
  (NBAE, 2). Madrid. Bailly-Baillière. 1905. U-37 I* L
Aveline, Claude. *Songes ornés.* Paris. Cochraux. 1925. Pp. 30. U-5250 D
Avellaneda, Nicolás. *Estudio sobre las leyes de tierras públicas.* Buenos Aires.
  La Facultad. 1915. Pp. viii, 292. U-1142 I
- *Discursos. I. Oraciones líricas.* Buenos Aires. Bibl. Argentina. 1928.
  Pp. 388. U-4873
- *Diez ensayos.* Buenos Aires. Bibl. Argentina. 1928. Pp. 353. U-4875 I
Avenarius, Richard. *Kritik der Reinen Erfahrung.* Leipzig. Fues's Verlag.
  1888. Pp. xxii, 528. U-1254 C*
L'Avenir de la culture. Paris. Société des Nations. [1933]. Pp. 326. U-5253
L'Avens. Literari - artistich - cientifich. Revista illustrada. Julio
  1883-novembre 1892. 3 vols. Uc
Avila, Julio Enrique. *El vigía sin luz.* San Salvador. Cuscatlania. 1927. Pp. 141.
  (2 copies) U-4882, U-5065 D
- *El mundo de mi jardín.* San Salvador. La República. [1927]. Pp. 158.
  U-5061 I C D
Avilés Ramirez, Eduardo. *Simbad. Hombres, piedras y paisajes.* Paris. Excelsior.
  1928. Pp. 295. U-5474 D
Ayarragaray, Lucas. *La anarquía argentina y el caudillismo.* Buenos Aires.
  Lajouane. 1904. Pp. vii, 353. U-2531 I D
- *Estudios históricos y políticos.* Buenos Aires. Didot. 1907. Uc D
- *La iglesia en América y la dominación española.* Buenos Aires. Lajouane.
  1920. Pp. 321. U-4104 D
Aymerich, Juan. *Joyeles.* Córdoba. La Industrial. 1907. Pp. 125, v. U-3425 D
Ayuntamiento de Barcelona. Negociado de estadística, padrón, y elecciones.
  Anuario estadístico de la ciudad de Barcelona, IV (1905), V (1906),
  VI (1907), VII (1908). Uc
- *Informe sobre el proyecto de ley autorizando al gobierno para conceder
  el establecimiento de zonas francas.* Barcelona. Elzeviriana. 1915. Pp. 585.
  U-1234 n/o
Ayuntamiento de Salamanca. *Reglamento interior.* Salamanca. Almaraz. 1913.
  Pp. 32. U-4559
Ayuso, Manuel Hilario. *El principio objetivo de certidumbre.* Madrid. La
  Enseñanza. 1920. Pp. 86. U-5663

- *El hedonismo oxomense.* Madrid. Tip. Rev. de Arch., Bibl. y Museos. 1927. Pp. 7. U-5771

Azaña y Diaz, Manuel. *Valera en Italia.* Madrid. Paez-Bolsa. 1929. Pp. 241. U-5028 D

- *El jardín de los frailes.* [Book lost in Hendaye]

Azarola Gil, Luis Enrique. *La sociedad uruguaya y sus problemas.* Paris. Ollendorff. 1911. Pp. 155. U-2706 D

Azcarate, G. de. *Concepto de la sociología y un estudio sobre los deberes de la riqueza.* Barcelona. Henrich. 1904. Uc

Azcoitia, Xavier de. *Defensa de la obra de los vascos. Cavernícolas, cavernícolas!* Bilbao. Imp. Mayli. 1931. Pp. 62. U-5652 D

Azeglio (Taparelli, Marchese d'), Massimo. *Niccolò de' Lapi.* Firenze. Le Monnier. 1891. Pp. 594. U-1451 I T

- *Mis recuerdos.* Tr. Eustaquio Echauri. 3 vols. Madrid. Colec. Universal. 1919. n/n I*

Azevedo Coutinho. *Guia do viajante em Braga.* Braga. Cruz. 1905. Pp. viii, 95. U-266

Azevedo Tojal, Pedro de. *Foguetário.* Pref. e revisto Mendes dos Remédios. Coimbra. Amado. 1904. Pp. xxv, 64. U-2292

Azkúe, Resurrección María de. *Gramática eúskara.* Bilbao. Astuy. 1891. Pp. 401. (2 copies) U-33. U-1209 D

- *Lenengo Irakurgaie beinda betiko.* Bilbao. Casa de Misericordia. 1893. Pp. iv, 128. (2 copies) U-2255-6

Aznar Embid, Severino. *Las grandes instituciones del catolicismo.* Madrid. López del Horno. 1912. Pp. 413. U-276

Azzati, Félix. *El primer pensamiento.* Valencia. Sempere. n.d. Pp. 206. U-3469 D

Babuglia, Antonio. *Harmonías y rebencazos.* Buenos Aires. La Semana Médica. 1905. Uc

- *Reincidencias.* Buenos Aires. La Semana Médica. 1909. Pp. 255. U-2229 C D

Bacchylides. *Bacchylidis carmina* cum fragmentis ed. Fridericus Blass. Editionem quartam curavit G. Suess. Lipsiae. Teubner. 1912. Pp. lxxxii, 154. U-4471 I* T

Backhouse, E., y C. Taylor. *Historia de la iglesia primitiva hasta la muerte de Constantino.* Tr. F. Albricias. Alicante. Reus. 1896. Pp. ix, 354. U-1811

Bacon, Francis. *Franscisci Baconi Novum organum scientiarum.* Wirceburgi. Stanel. 1779. Pp. 386. U-3897

- *The Essays or Counsels Civill and Morall.* Introd. O. Smeaton. London. Dent. 1907. Pp. xxxvi, 199. U-1002 I

Baeza, Alejandro E. *El libro de los pobres viejos.* Santiago. Universitaria. 1915. Pp. 103. Uc D

Baeza, Ricardo. *La isla de los santos. Itinerario en Irlanda.* Madrid. Renacimiento. [1930]. Pp. 310. U-3719 D

— *Clasicismo y romanticismo.* Madrid. Cia. Ibero-Americana de Publ. n.d. Pp. 60. U-5078 D

Bagehot, Walter. *Literary Studies.* Introd. G. Sampson. 2 vols. London. Dent. 1916. U-1086-7 I* C

Bagger, Carl. *Min Broders Levnet.* Kφbenhavn. Schubotheske. 1899. Pp. 268. U-4645 T

Bagot, Richard. *Gl'Italiano d'oggi.* Tr. G.M. Palliccia. Bari. Laterza. 1912. Pp. 199. U-2955 I* C*

— *Los italianos de hoy.* Tr. Juda L. Taltabull. Pról. M. de Unamuno. Barcelona. Libr. Félix y Susanna. 1913. Uc

Baie, Eugène. *Le siècle des gueux (histoire de la sensibilité flamande sous la renaissance).* 2 vols. Bruxelles. Dewarichet. 1928-32. U-5297-8 C* I*

Bailly, Anatole. *Dictionnaire grec-français.* Paris. Hachette. 1895. Pp. xxxii, 2227. n/n

Bain, Alexandre. *Logique déductive et inductive.* Tr. Gabriel Compayré. 2 vols. Paris. Baillière. 1881. U-2602-3 C

Baires, Carlos. *Teoría del amor.* Buenos Aires. Alsina. 1911. Pp. 536. U-904 D

Balbín de Unquera, Antonio. *Andrés Bello, su época y sus obras.* Madrid. Hernández. 1910. Pp. 324. U-2469

Balbo, Cesare. *Della storia d'Italia.* A cura di Fausto Nicolini. 2 vols. Bari. Laterza. 1913. U-1826-7 B* C* I*

Balcazar y Sabariegos, José. *Memorias de un estudiante de Salamanca.* Con un pensamiento inédito, a modo de pról. M. de Unamuno. Madrid. Prieto. 1935. Pp. 314. U-906 D

Baldrich, J. Amadeo. *Historia de la guerra del Brasil.* Buenos Aires. La Harlem. 1905. Pp. xii, 639. U-727 D

Balfour, Arthur James. *The Foundations of Belief.* London. Longmans Green. 1901. Pp. xxxvi, 399. U-1306

Ball, Hugo. *Die Flucht aus der Zeit.* München. Duncker. 1927. Pp. 330. U-5383 I* C*

Ballagas, Emilio. *Pasión y muerte del futurismo.* Habana. Molina. 1935. Pp. 23. U-4122 D

Ballesteros, Mercedes. *Tienda de nieve.* n.p. [1932]. Ff. 14. U-2217 D

B[allve], A. *La penitenciaría nacional de Buenos Aires.* Buenos Aires. Tall. Penitenciaría Nacional. 1907. Uc D .

Balmes, Jaime. *El protestantismo comparado con el catolicismo en sus relaciones con la civilización europea.* 2 vols. Paris. Bouret. 1849. U-194-5 I* C*

— *Curso de filosofía elemental.* Paris. Bouret. 1849. Pp. 644. U-189 I
— *Filosofía fundamental.* 2 vols. Paris. Bouret. 1851. U-190-1 I*
— *El criterio.* Paris. Bouret. 1851. Pp. 354. U-192 I*
— *Cartas a un escéptico en materia de religión.* Paris. Bouret. 1853. Pp. 319. U-193

Balparda, Gregorio de. *Don Martín de los Heros y el progresismo vascongado de su tiempo.* Bordeaux. Feret. 1925. Pp. 47. U-5758
— *Historia crítica de Vizcaya y de sus fueros. II. El primer fuero de Vizcaya, el de los señores.* Bilbao. Mayli. 1933-4. Pp. 559. U-4143 n/o

Balseiro, José A. *El vigía. Ensayos.* Madrid. Hernández Catá. [1928]. Pp. 401. U-5059 I* C* D
— 'Valle Inclán, la novela y la política,' *Hispania,* xv, 5-6 (1932), 437-64. U-5686 D

Balzac, Honoré de. *Scènes de la vie de province. Le lys dans la vallée.* Paris. Calmann-Lévy. 1881. Pp. 310. U-495 I

Bambill, Eduardo B. *Cuestiones constitucionales.* Bahía Blanca. Proyecciones. 1910. Pp. 382. U-2228 D

Banchs, Enrique. *El cascabel del halcón.* Buenos Aires. Edit. Argentina. 1909. Uc D

Baráibar y Zumárraga, Federico. *Vocabulario de palabras usadas en Alava.* Madrid. Ratés. 1903. Pp. 325. U-793 n/o D

Barata da Rocha, Alfredo. *Névoa de Flandres.* Porto. Renascença Portuguesa. 1924. Pp. 134. U-1901 n/o

Barbagelata, Hugo D. *Páginas sudamericanas.* Barcelona. Sopena. 1909. Pp. 240. U-2420 D
— *Bolívar y San Martín.* Pról. Rubén Darío. Paris. Landais. 1911. Pp. 91. U-3201 D
— *Artigas y la revolución americana.* Pról. J. Enrique Rodó. Paris. Excelsior. 1930. Pp. 319. U-772 D

Barbellion, W.N.P. *Journal d'un homme déçu.* Préf. H.G. Wells. Tr. Jean Duren. Paris. Payot. 1930. Pp. 429. QP-1 I

Barber, Edwin Atlee. *Mexican Maiolica in the Collection of the Hispanic Society of America.* New York. Hispanic Society of America. 1915. Pp. 60. U-134
— *Spanish Maiolica in the Collection of the Hispanic Society of America.* New York. Hispanic Society of America. 1915. Uc
— *Spanish Porcelains and Terra Cottas in the Collection of the Hispanic Society of America.* New York. Hispanic Society of America. 1915. Pp. 42, pl. 10. U-3683
— *Hispano-Moresque Pottery.* New York. Hispanic Society of America. 1915. Pp. 278, pl. 88. U-2298

Barbey D'Aurevilly, Julio. *La hechizada.* Tr. R. Sánchez de Ocaña. Madrid.
Universal. 1920. Pp. 303. U-4441

Barbier, Henri Auguste. *Iambes et poèmes.* Paris. Dentu. 1883. Pp. 291.
U-3314

Barbusse, Henri. *Le feu. Journal d'une escouade.* Paris. Flammarion. 1916.
Pp. 378. U-1391 I*

— *Voici ce qu'on a fait de la Géorgie.* Paris. Flammarion. 1929. Pp. 318.
U-5312 I C

— *Zola.* Paris. Gallimard. 1932. Pp. 296. U-1994 D

Barcenilla, José. *Poesías epigramáticas.* Salamanca. Oliva. 1848. Pp. 159.
U-4479

Barchou de Penhoën, Auguste Théodore Hilaire, Baron. *Histoire de la philosophie allemande depuis Leibnitz jusqu'à Hegel.* 2 vols. Paris. Charpentier.
1836. U-1843-4

Barclay, Robert. *An Apology for the True Christian Divinity.* Glasgow.
Barclay Murdoch. 1886. Pp. viii, 435. U-3890 I

Barco Centenera, Martín del. *La Argentina. Poema histórico.* Estudio Juan
María Gutiérrez. Apuntes bio-bibliográficos E. Peña. Buenos Aires. Peuser.
1912. Pp. lii, 270. U-1779

Barcón Olesa, J. *La educación en la campaña.* Buenos Aires. Perrotti. 1916.
Pp. 220. U-1108 D

Barcos, Julio R. *Cómo educa el estado a tu hijo.* Buenos Aires. Acción. 1928.
Pp. 272. U-5096 D

— *Política para intelectuales.* Buenos Aires. 1931. Pp. 175. U-626 n/o D

Bardón, Emilio. *Memoria acerca de la concentración parcelaria.* León.
Diputación Provincial. 1910. Pp. 47. U-2575 [Bound with A. Martínez
Sacristán]

Bardón, Lázaro. *Lectiones graecae, sive manu-ductio hispanae juventutis in
linguam graecam.* Madrid. De manu auctoris, typis et praelo ipsius. 1859.
Pp. 510. U-4024 T* L C I

Bares, Manuel A. *Delenda est Germania!* Buenos Aires. Estrach. 1916. Pp. 369.
U-4401 D

Bargiela, Camilo. *Luciérnagas.* Madrid. Poveda. 1900. Pp. 78, xxv. U-4562

Barja, César. *Otoñal.* Brattleboro. The Vermont Printing Co. 1922. Pp. 60.
U-3209 D

— *Libros y autores contemporáneos.* New York. Stechert. 1935. Pp. 493,
vii. U-2674 D

Barlocco, Jacobo Reinaldo. *Más allá de la felicidad.* Montevideo. Gaceta
Comercial. 1935. Pp. 62. U-2031 D

Barnés, Domingo. *Fuentes para el estudio de la patología.* Madrid. Tip.
Rev. de Arch., Bibl. y Museos. 1917. Uc

Barnich, G. *Essai de politique positive basée sur l'énergétique sociale de Solvay.* Bruxelles. Lebègue. 1919. Pp. 413. U-1710

Baroja, Pío. *Vidas sombrías.* Madrid. Marzo. 1900. Pp. 160. U-3974 I D
- *La casa de Aizgorri.* Bilbao. Bibl. Vascongada de Fermín Herrán. 1900. Pp. 227. U-3671 D
- *Silvestre Paradox.* Madrid. Rodríguez Serra. 1901. Pp. 284. n/n D
- *El escuadrón del brigante.* Madrid. Renacimiento. 1913. Uc
- *Jarmark Glupców.* Tr. Edward Boyé. Warszawa. Towarzystwo Wydawnicze Rój. 1928. Pp. 280. U-5548

Barra, Eduardo de la. *Literatura arcaica.* Valparaiso. n.d. Uc

Barrantes Castro, Pedro. *Maldición.* Lima. Novela Peruana. 1923. Pp. 59. U-1542 n/o D
- *Cumbrera del mundo.* Pról. Clemente Palma. Lima. Ed. Perú Actual. 1935. Pp. 197. U-3212 n/o D

Barrau, Th. H. *Os deveres dos filhos.* Tr. Joao de Deus. Lisboa. Nacional. 1903. Pp. 149. U-4304

Barreda, Ernesto Mario. *Talismanes.* Madrid. Marzo. 1908. Pp. 111. U-2042 n/o D
- *La canción de un hombre que pasa.* Buenos Aires. Nosotros. 1911. Pp. 92. U-3135 D

Barreda, Luis. *Valle del norte.* Pról. Ricardo León. Madrid. Gómez Fuentenebro. 1911. Pp. 107. U-3963 D
- *Roto casi el navío.* Madrid. Gómez Fuentenebro. 1915. Pp. 152. U-415 D

Barrenechea, Mariano Antonio. *Un pensador francés. Remy de Gourmont.* Buenos Aires. Nosotros. 1910. Pp. 86. U-3461 D
- *Ensayo sobre Federico Nietzsche.* Buenos Aires. Nosotros. 1915. Pp. 197. U-1708 D

Barrès, Auguste Maurice. *Colette Baudoche.* Paris. Juven. 1909. Pp. vii, 258. U-2416
- *La grande pitié des églises de France.* Paris. Emile-Paul. 1914. Pp. 419. U-1150 D
- *Greco ou le secret de Tolède.* Paris. Plon. 1923. Pp. 185. U-3225

Barret, C., et E. Blese. See Prince, John Dyneley

Barreto, Simón. *Picas y laudes.* San José de Costa Rica. Moderna. 1913. Uc D

Barrie, Sir James Matthew. *The Little Minister.* London. Cassell. 1905. Pp. 375. U-1418 T D

Barriobero y Herrán, E. *La francmasonería.* Madrid. Galo Sáez. 1935. Pp. 332. U-3871 I* D

Barros, João de. *Vida vitoriosa. Poemas escolhidos (1904-1917).* Paris. Aillaud-Bertrand. [1919]. Pp. 163. U-3367 D

Barros, Juan. *El zapato chino.* Santiago de Chile. Imp. Barcelona. 1913. Pp. 162. U-2864 D

Barros Arana, Diego. *El Dr D. Rodolfo Amando Philippi, su vida i sus obras.*
Santiago de Chile. Cervantes. 1904. Pp. vii, 248. U-1218

Barth, Karl. *Die Lehre vom Worte Gottes. Prolegomena zur christlichen
Dogmatik.* München. Kaiser. 1927. Pp. xii, 473. U-5432 I*

Barthe y Barthe, Andrés. *Las grandes propiedades rústicas en España.* Madrid.
Ratés. 1912. Pp. 80. U-4085

Bartolomé y Cossio, Manuel. *De su jornada. Fragmentos de trabajos viejos,
nuevos, variados y dispersos.* Madrid. La Lectura. 1929. Pp. 334.
U-3927 D

Baruzi, Jean. *Leibniz et l'organisation religieuse de la terre.* Paris. Alcan.
1907. Pp. 524. U-1781 I* C* D

El bascuence en 120 lecciones. Bilbao. La Propaganda. 1896. Pp. 147. U-1891

Basmadjian, K.J. *Histoire moderne des Arméniens depuis la chute du royaume
jusqu'à nos jours (1375-1916).* Préf. J. de Morgan. Paris. Gamber. 1917.
Pp. viii, 174. U-878 L

Bassi, Angel C. *La escuela experimental de Esquina.* 1a parte. La Plata. Sesé,
Larrañaga. 1905. Uc

Basso Maglio, V. *La expresión heróica.* [Montevideo]. Alfar. n.d. Pp. 70.
U-5120 D

Basterra, Félix B. *El crepúsculo de los gauchos. Estado actual de la República
Argentina.* Paris. Grave. 1903. Pp. 141. U-3876 I* C* D

— *Leyendas de la humildad.* Montevideo. García. 1904. Pp. 107. U-3299
n/o D

Basterra, Ramón de. *Los navíos de la ilustración.* Caracas. Bolívar. 1925.
Pp. 307. U-4977 I* C* L* D

Basto, Cláudio. *Foi Eça de Queirós um plagiador?* Porto. Maranus. 1924.
Pp. 277. U-2902 n/o D

Bataillon, Marcel. 'Mona. Etude etymologique,' extrait du *Centenaire de la
Faculté des Lettres d'Alger, 1831-1931.* 1932. Pp. 14. U-5263 D

Batiz. *Italia.* Paris. 1908. Uc D

— *Contribución a los estudios sociales.* Paris. 1908. Uc D

Bátiz, Adolfo. *Mis confesiones. Libro negro.* Paris. Americana. 1908. Pp. 184.
U-636 n/o D

Batres Jáuregui, Antonio. *Los indios. Su historia y su civilización.* Guatemala.
La Unión. 1894. Pp. xii, 216. U-1201 D

— *El castellano en América.* Guatemala. La República. 1904. Pp. 285.
U-2698 D

Batres Montúfar, José. *Poesías.* Ed. y notas Adrián Recinos. Madrid. Helénica.
1924. Pp. xxxvi, 208. U-5016

Baudelaire, Charles. *Les fleurs du mal.* Précédées d'une notice Théophile
Gautier. Paris. Calmann-Lévy. n.d. Pp. 411. U-3837 I

Bayo, Ciro. *El peregrino entretenido.* Madrid. Bailly-Baillière. 1910. Pp. 240.
    U-258 D
 — *Vocabulario criollo-español sud-americano.* Madrid. Hernando. 1910.
    Pp. 254. U-99 I
 — *La colombiada.* Madrid. Suárez. 1912. Pp. viii, 174. U-2847 D
 — *Poesía popular hispano-americana.* Madrid. Suárez. 1913. Uc
 — *Examen de próceres americanos.* Madrid. Pueyo. 1916. Pp. 412. U-372 D
Bazalgette, León. *A quoi tient l'infériorité française.* Paris. Fischbacher.
    1900. Pp. 304. U-260 I D
 — *Walt Whitman, l'homme et son oeuvre.* Paris. Mercure de France. 1908.
    Pp. xi, 513. U-808 I C D
Bazán de Cámara, Rosa. *Rezos de silencio (Poemas en prosa).* Buenos Aires.
    Ff. 67. U-706 [Typescript]
Béarn, Andrée. *Les mendiants d'impossible.* Toulouse. 1910. Uc D
 — *Jean Darette.* Paris. Figuiere. 1912. Uc D
Beato Sala, Isidro. *Higiene barata.* Salamanca. Calatrava. 1915. Pp. 157.
    U-2267 D
Beaumarchais, Pierre Augustin Caron de. *El barbero de Sevilla.* Tr. I. de
    Alberti y E. López Alarcón. Madrid. Universal. 1919. Pp. 148. n/n I
Beccar Varela, Adrián. *San Isidro.* Buenos Aires. 1906. Uc D
Beccari, Gilberto. *L'Italia nagli scrittori stranieri. Impressioni italiane di
    scrittori spagnoli (1860-1910).* Lanciano. Carabba. Uc
Becerra, Ricardo. *Ensayo histórico documentado de la vida de D. Francisco
    de Miranda.* Tomo II. Caracas. Colón. 1896. Pp. 553. U-27
Bécquer, Gustavo Adolfo Dominguez. *Legends, Tales and Poems.* Ed.,
    introd., notes, and vocabulary E.W. Olmsted. Boston. Ginn. [1907].
    Pp. lxvii, 288. U-2732
Bédarida, Henri. *Théophile Gautier et l'Italie.* Paris. Boivin. 1934. Pp. 92.
    U-5287 D
Beddoes, Thomas Lovell. *The Poems of Thomas Lovell Beddoes.* Ed. and
    introd. Ramsay Colles. London. Routledge. [1907]. Pp. xxvii, 460.
    U-447 I*
Bédier, Joseph. *Sur l'oeuvre de Gaston Paris.* Paris. Cahiers de la Quinzaine.
    1904. Pp. 107. U-631
 — *Le roman de Tristan et Iseut. Renouvelé.* Préf. Gaston Paris. Paris. Piazza.
    [1900]. Pp. 284. U-588
Beirão, Mário. *Cintra.* Porto. Renascença Portuguesa. 1912. Pp. 13. U-3438 D
 — *O Ultimo Lusiada.* Porto. Renascença Portuguesa. 1913. Pp. 120.
    U-3317 D
 — *Ausente.* Porto. Renascença Portuguesa. 1915. Pp. 122. U-3111 D
Belascoain Sayós, Marcial. *Teatro realista.* Buenos Aires. Ferrari. n.d. Pp. 246.
    U-5062

Belda, Joaquín. *El pícaro oficio.* Madrid. Renacimiento. 1914. Uc D

Belgrano, Mario. *Belgrano.* Buenos Aires. Pesce. 1927. Pp. 328. U-5742

Belin Sarmiento, Augusto. *El joven Sarmiento.* Saint-Cloud. Belin. 1929.
Pp. 121. U-5597 I D

— *Sarmiento anecdótico.* Saint-Cloud. Belin. 1929. Pp. xvii, 335. U-5763 D

Bell, Aubrey F.G. *Gil Vicente.* Coimbra. Universidad. 1915. Pp. 37. U-2238 D

— *Portuguese Literature.* Oxford. Clarendon Press. 1922. Pp. 375. U-3012

— *Spanish Galicia.* London. John Lane. 1922. Pp. ix, 200. U-3618

— *Luis de León. A Study of the Spanish Renaissance.* Oxford. Clarendon
Press. 1925. Pp. 394. U-2596 I

Bellán, José Pedro. *El pecado de Alejandra Leonard.* Montevideo. Agencia
Gral. de Librería. 1926. Pp. 271. U-5484 D

Bello, Andrés. *Gramática de la lengua castellana.* Notas e índice Rufino José
Cuervo. Paris. Roger y Chernoviz. 1908. Pp. ix, 366, 160. U-1288

Bello, Luís. *Viaje por las escuelas de España.* Madrid. Magisterio Español.
1926. Pp. 317. U-5659 D

Beltramo, Fernando. *Introducción a la estética de la intuición pura.* Soriano,
Uruguay. Galán. [1915]. Pp. 35. U-1603 D

Beltrán, Washington. *Cuestiones sociológicas. Lucha contra la criminalidad
infantil.* Pról. José Irureta Goyena. Montevideo. Barreiro y Ramos. 1910.
Pp. 232. U-2277 D

Benavente, Jacinto. *Gente conocida.* Madrid. Asilo de Huérfanos. 1896.
Pp. 217. U-2396 D

— *Teatro rápido.* Barcelona. Antonio López. n.d. Pp. 155. U-4649

Benavento, Gaspar L. *Tierra maldita.* Buenos Aires. Claridad. 1929. Pp. 101.
U-5089 D

Benavides Olazábal, F. *En el mundo de la filosofía y de la guerra.* Buenos
Aires. 1915. Uc D

Benavides Ponce, R. *Florilegio.* Caracas. Herrera Irigoyen. 1900. Uc D

Benavides Santos, Arturo. *Futuro próximo del mundo.* Buenos Aires. 1915.
Pp. 72. U-3710 D

Benedetti, Giacopone de' da Todi. *Laude di frate Jacopone da Todi secondo
la stampa fiorentina del 1490.* A cura di G. Ferri. Bari. Laterza. 1915.
Pp. 316, 12. U-1825 B* L T I*

Benejam, Juan. *Vida nueva.* Madrid. Suárez. 1908. Uc

Benezes, Elias. *O Manolis Lekas Ki' Alla Diigimata.* Athens. Kalergi. 1928.
Pp. 139. U-4885 I D

Benvenuto, Carlos. *Congreciones.* Montevideo. La Cruz del Sur. 1929. Pp. 162.
U-5145 D

Béranger, Pierre Jean de. *Oeuvres complètes.* Paris. Perrotin. 1835. U-4074

Berchet, Giovanni. *Opere.* A cura di Egidio Bellorini. 2 vols. Bari. Laterza.
1911. U-1822-3 I

Berdeguer, A. Elviro. *Los partidos políticos.* Pról. D.A. Valdivieso. Epíl.
T. Costa. Salamanca. Bajo. 1916. Pp. 139, 25. U-4368 D
Berdyaev, Nikolaus. *Der Sinn der Geschichte.* Einleitung der Grafen Hermann
Keyserling. Darmstadt. Reichl. 1925. Pp. 307. U-5445 T I* C*
Berenson, B. *Les peintres italiens de la Renaissance.* Tr. Louis Gillet. Paris.
Gallimard. 1935. Pp. 349. QP-2 I
Bergamín José. *El cohete y la estrella.* Madrid. Indice. 1923. Pp. 85.
U-5588 C D
– *Tres escenas en ángulo recto (1924).* Madrid. Ascasíbar. 1925. Pp. 41.
U-4981
– *Caracteres (I-XXX).* Málaga. Sur. 1926. Pp. 40. U-5562 D
– *La cabeza a pájaros.* Madrid. Cruz y Raya. 1934. Pp. 151. U-5074 D
Bergier, Nicolas Sylvestre. *Les éléments primitifs des langues, découverts par
la comparaison de racines de l'hébreu avec celles du grec, du latin et du
français.* Paris. Brocas & Humblot. 1764. Pp. iv, 354. U-1524
Bergson, Henri. *Essai sur les données immédiates de la conscience.* Paris.
Alcan. 1889. Pp. viii, 182. U-1778 I C
– *Matière et mémoire. Essai sur la relation du corps à l'esprit.* Paris. Alcan.
1903. Pp. 279. U-864
– *L'Evolution créatrice.* Paris. Alcan. 1907. Pp. viii, 403. U-865 I C
– *Choix de texte.* Avec étude du système philosophique par René Guillouin.
Paris. Michaud. 1910. Pp. 222. U-1978 I
– *L'Energie spirituelle; essais et conférences.* Paris. Alcan. 1919. Pp. 227.
U-2234 I
Bérillon, Edgar. *La psychologie de la race allemande.* Paris. Maloine. 1917.
Pp. 64. U-830
Berisso, Emilio. *La amarra invisible.* Buenos Aires. Moen. 1915. Uc D
– *A la vera de mi senda.* Buenos Aires. Moen. 1915. Uc D
– *Con las alas rotas.* Buenos Aires. Otero y García. 1917. Pp. 205.
U-1476 n/o D
Berisso, Luis. *El pensamiento de América.* Pról. V. Pérez Petit. Buenos Aires.
Lajouane. 1898. Pp. xxi, 418. U-3575 D
Berkeley, George. *A New Theory of Vision and Other Selected Philosophical
Writings.* London. Dent. n.d. Pp. xxiv, 303. U-1073
Bermúdez de Castro, Luis. *Bobes o el león de los llanos.* Madrid. Espasa-Calpe.
1934. Pp. 203. U-2651 C
Bernácer, Germán. *Sociedad y felicidad.* Madrid. Beltrán. 1916. Pp. 582.
U-4174 D
Bernafeld, Simeón. *Historia de los judíos desde los principios hasta nuestros
días.* Compuesta por vía del Dr gran Rabino de Belgrado. Vol. I. Belgrado.
1891. Pp. 265. U-2551 T [Spanish language in Hebrew characters]
Bernal, Emilia. *Exaltación.* Madrid. Hernández. 1928. Pp. 142. U-268 D

Bernaldo de Quirós, Constancio. *Alrededor del delito y de la pena*. Madrid. Rodríguez Serra. 1904. Pp. 181. U-3089 D
— *Criminología de los delitos de sangre en España*. Madrid. Internacional. 1906. Uc
— y José Ma Llanas Aguilaniedo. *La mala vida en Madrid*. Madrid. Rodríguez Serra. 1901. Uc
Bernales, Adonis. *Anthologia ton Kyprion Poeton. 1878-1934*. Chypre. 1934. Pp. 109. U-5752 D
Bernanos, Georges. *La grande peur des bien-pensants*. Paris. Grasset. 1931. Pp. 458. QP-3 I
Bernard, Claude. *Introducción al estudio de la medicina experimental*. Tr. A. Espina y Capo. Madrid. E. Teodoro. 1880. Pp. 445. U-548
Bernard, Saint, Abbé de Clairvaux. *Sancti Bernardi Abbatis de consideratione ad Eugenium papam. Libri V*. Paris. Jouby et Roger. 1878. Pp. xi, 332. U-4574 I C
Bernárdez, Francisco Luis. *Bazar*. Madrid. Rivadeneyra. 1922. Pp. 47. U-684 D
— *Kindergarten*. Madrid. Rivadeneyra. 1923. Pp. 94. U-4261 D
Bernárdez, Manuel. *De Buenos Aires al Iguazu*. Buenos Aires. La Nación. 1901. Pp. 128. U-1191
— *La nación en marcha*. Buenos Aires. Ortega y Radaelli. 1904. Pp. 294. U-2499
— *El Brasil. Su vida, su trabajo, su futuro*. Buenos Aires. Ortega y Radaelli. 1908. Pp. xxxv, 284. U-2213
Bernstein, Max. *Coeur-Dame*. Leipzig. Reclam. n.d. Pp. 40. U-4523
Bertaux, Emile. *Exposición retrospectiva del arte. 1908*. Introd. Mariano de Pano y Ruata. Pról. Paula Moreno. Zaragoza. La Editorial Escar. 1910. Pp. 358. U-3558
— *Donatello*. Paris. Plon. n.d. Uc
Berthelot, Pierre Eugène Marcelin. *La synthèse chimique*. Paris. Alcan. 1891. Pp. viii, 294. U-1810
Bertotto, José Guillermo. *El coraje de callar*. Rosario. 1921. Pp. 153. U-3464 D
Bertran i Pijoan, Lluís. *En el limit d'or*. Barcelona. Altés. n.d. Pp. 80. U-669 n/o D
Bertrand, Hilda. *Les pas dans les pas*. Paris. Desclée. [1933]. Pp. 198. U-3678 D
Besteiro, Julián. *Marxismo y antimarxismo*. Madrid. Gráf. Socialista. [1935]. Pp. xii, 280. U-137 n/o
Beter, Clara. *Versos de una*. Buenos Aires. Claridad. n.d. Pp. 64. U-5586 D
Beucler, André. *La vie de Ivan le Terrible*. Paris. Gallimard. 1931. Pp. 298. QP-4 I

Beyerlein, Franz Adam. *Jena oder Sedan?* Berlin. Vita. [1903]. Pp. 737.
U-1802
Beyle, Marie Henri (Stendhal, pseud.). *De l'amour.* Paris. Calmann-Lévy.
1856. Pp. xxiii, 371. U-3327 I C
— *Le Rouge et le Noir. Chronique du XIXe. siècle.* 2 vols. Paris. Calmann-
Lévy. n.d. U-3339-40 I*. Ed. complète revue et corrigée. Paris. Garnier.
n.d. Pp. 512. QP-5 I
— *Racine et Shakespeare. Etudes sur le romantisme.* Paris. Calmann-Lévy.
n.d. Pp. 324. QP-6 I*
— *La chartreuse de Parme.* Paris. Calmann-Lévy. n.d. Pp. 450. U-1393 I*
Bianco, José. *Recortes.* Córdoba. La Minerva. 1900. Pp. 240. U-3381 D
— *Negociaciones internacionales.* Buenos Aires. Coni. 1904. Pp. 251.
U-2208 D
— *Los problemas del analfabetismo.* Buenos Aires. Mendesky. 1909. Uc
— *La propiedad inmobiliaria.* Buenos Aires. Landreau. 1909. Pp. 442.
U-3025 n/o D
— *Orientaciones.* Pról. y notas. P. de San Martín. Buenos Aires. Mendesky.
1910. Pp. 509. U-2189 n/o
Bible. Old Testament. *Biblia Hebraica.* Ad optimas editiones. Inprimis
Everardi van der Hooght. Ex recensione Aug. Hahnii expressa. Praefatus
est Ern. Fr. Car. Rosenmüller. Lipsiae. Tauchnitz. 1838. Pp. vi, 1036.
U-1522 I
— *El Antiguo Testamento que contiene los Libros Canónicos del Pueblo
Hebreo.* Versión de Casiodoro de Reina en 1569. Madrid. Depósito de
la Soc. Bíblica. [1905]. Pp. 1141. U-26
— *El Gènesi.* Versió segons els textos originals i amb anotació de Mn.
Frederic Clascar. Barcelona. 1915. Pp. 476. U-98
— *Biblia Hebraica.* Ed. Rud. Kittel. Stuttgart. 1934. Ff. 24. U-2284
— *El Libro de Job.* Versión directa del hebreo e introd. F.J. Caminero, y
advertencia preliminar Menéndez y Pelayo. Santander. Joannes, Ep.
Santanderien. 1923. Pp. 216. U-883 I* C
— *Biblia Sacra.* Vulgata editio. Tornaci Nerviorum, topis Soc. Sancti Joannis
Evangelistae. n.p. Desclée Lefebbrée et Soc. 1901. n/n
Bible. New Testament. *Novum Testamentum.* Textus Graecus. Latinae
Vulgatae quem ex antiquis codicibus et scriptis restauravit J.N. Jager.
Parisiis. Didot. [1842]. Pp. 557. U-198 T* C* I* L
— *Jesu Christi Domini Nostri. Novum Testamentum Latine.* Interprete,
Theodoro Beza. Berolini. Societatis Bibliophilorum Britannice et
Externae. 1868. Pp. 493+124. U-4569
— *Nuevo Testamento de Nuestro Señor Jesu-cristo.* Versión de Casiodoro de
Reyna. Los Angeles. Los Angeles Bible Institute. 1905. Pp. 436, xiv.
U-4584

— *El Nuevo Testamento de Nuestro Señor Jesucristo.* Madrid. Soc. Bíblica.
    1908. Pp. 427. U-4071
— *Das Neue Testament unseres Herrn und Heilandes Jesu Christi*, nach der
    deutschen Uebersetzung D. Mart. Luth. Berlin. Britische und Ausländische
    Bibelgesellschaft. 1911. Pp. 123. U-4459
Bible. Gospels. *Escrituras del Nuevo Pacto.* Tr. del original griego. Edimburgo.
    Tomás Constable. 1870. Pp. 543. U-482
— *Jesu Cristoren Evanjelioa Juanen Araura.* Londres. 1883. Pp. 93. (2 copies)
    U-5353-4
Biblioteca de Autores Españoles (Nueva). Dirigida hasta el tomo xx por
    M. Menéndez y Pelayo. Madrid. Bailly-Baillière. 1905-18. U-36-57
    [Each volume listed under author or title]
Biblioteca de las tradiciones populares españolas. Director, Antonio Machado
    y Alvarez. 5 vols. Sevilla. Guichot. 1883-6. U-4384-5, U-5093-4, U-5139.
    U-5139 I
Bibliotheca Publica Municipal do Porto a Patuleia. *Catalogo dos documentos
    manuscriptos que pertenceram a José da Silva Passos.* Porto. Imp.
    Portugueza. 1909. Pp. 595. U-1189 n/o
Bie, Oscar. *Was ist Moderne Kunst?* Wittenberg. Bard. Marquardt. n.d. Pp. 63.
    U-4433 B
Biedma, José Juan. *Crónica histórica del Río Negro de Patagones (1774-
    1834).* Buenos Aires. Canter. 1905. Pp. 688. U-3001 D [Incomplete]
Biest, Edmundo van der. *Los ojos verdes.* Málaga. Zambrana. 1923. Pp. 124.
    U-2748 D
Bilbao, Enrique. *Vizcaya ante el siglo XX.* Pról. Pablo de Alzola. Tomo I.
    Bilbao. Cardenal. 1901. Pp. 134. U-3640 D
Bilbao, Francisco. *Obras completas.* Ed. y introd. Pedro Pablo Figueroa.
    4 vols. Santiago de Chile. El Correo. 1897-8. U-1637. U-1638-40 n/o
Bilbao, Luis G. *Las confesiones de Federico Muga.* Madrid. Clásica Española.
    1917. Pp. 160. U-1113 D
Bilbao, Manuel. *Buenos Aires, desde su fundación hasta nuestros días.*
    Buenos Aires. Alsina. 1902. Pp. xiii, 664. U-858 D
Billia, Michelangelo. *Le ceneri di Lovanio e la filosofia di Tamerlano.* Milano.
    Editrice Milanese. 1916. Pp. 85. U-5366
Bilychnis. Roma (Feb.-marzo 1924). n/n
Bion. *Theocriti, Bionis et Moschi Idyllia.* Recensuit C.H. Weise. Lipsiae.
    Tauchnitz. 1843. Uc
Bittel, Emil. *Die Entstehung der Bibel.* Leipzig. Reclam. n.d. Pp. 224.
    U-4540
Blake, William. *The Poetical Works of William Blake.* Ed., introd., and textual
    notes John Sampson. Oxford. University Press. 1914. Pp. lvi, 453.
    U-5225 I* C* L*

– *Poems of William Blake.* Ed. W.B. Yeats. London. Routledge. [1905].
   Pp. xlix, 277. U-448 I* B
Blanco, José Félix. *Documentos para la historia de la vida pública del liberta-
   dor de Colombia, Perú y Bolivia.* Publicadas por disposición del General
   Guzmán Blanco. Puestos por orden cronólogico y con adiciones y notas
   por el General J.F. Blanco. 14 vols. Caracas. La Opinión Nacional. 1875-7.
   U-10-23
Blanco Fombona, Horacio. *Crímenes del imperialismo norteamericano.*
   México. Churubusco. [1929]. Pp. 144. U-5129 D
Blanco Fombona, Rufino. *Trovadores y trovas.* Pról. M. Díaz-Rodríguez.
   Caracas. Herrera Irigoyen. 1899. Pp. xxxiii, 178. U-4490
– *Cuentos de poeta.* Maracaibo. Americana. 1900. Pp. xiii, 214. U-2796 I D
– *Cuentos americanos.* Paris. Garnier. 1913. Pp. xxiii, 264. Uc. *Contes
   américains.* Paris. Richard. 1903. Pp. 230. Uc D
– *Pequeña opera lírica.* Madrid. Fé. 1904. Uc
– *El hombre de hierro.* Caracas. Americana. 1907. Pp. 338. U-4164 D
– *Letras y letrados de Hispano-América.* Paris. Ollendorff. 1908. Pp. xxvi,
   309. U-3838 D
– *La evolución política y social de Hispano-América.* Madrid. Rodríguez.
   1911. Pp. xxiv, 156. U-1924 D
– *La lámpara de Aladino.* Madrid. Renacimiento. 1915. Pp. 590. U-3270 D
– *Grandes escritores de América. (Siglo XIX).* Madrid. Renacimiento. 1917.
   Pp. 343. U-1125 D
– *El hombre de oro.* Madrid. América. 1916. Pp. xiii, 412. U-3835 I L D
– *Cantos de la prisión y del destierro.* Paris. Ollendorff. n.d. Uc
Blanco Torres, Roberto. *Orballo da media noite.* Cruña. Nos. 1929. Pp. 83.
   U-5717 D
Blas y Ubide, Juan. *El licenciado de Escobar.* Madrid. Fé. 1905. Uc D
Blasco Ibáñez, Vicente. *La catedral.* Valencia. Sempere. 1903. Uc D
– *Los argonautas.* Valencia. Prometeo. 1914. Pp. 597. n/n D
– *Los cuatro jinetes del apocalipsis.* Valencia. Prometeo. 1916. Uc
– *Cañas y barro.* Valencia. Sempere. 1902. Pp. 312. n/n D
– *La bodega.* Valencia. Sempere. 1905. Pp. 452. Uc D
– *Mare nostrum.* Valencia. Prometeo. 1915. Pp. 597. Uc .
– *Cuentos valencianos.* Valencia. Sempere. 1903. Pp. 216. U-5085
Blastos, Petros. *E Elliniki ke Merikes alles Paralliles Diglossies.* Athens. Estia.
   1935. Pp. 254. U-2906 I* C* T*
Blavatsky, Helena Petrovna. *La voz del silencio.* Tr. F. Montoliu. Barcelona.
   Bibl. Orientalista. 1907. Uc
Blest Gana, Alberto. *Los trasplantados.* 2 vols. Paris. Garnier. 1904. U-3337-8 I*
Bloy, Léon. *La femme pauvre.* Paris. Mercure de France. 1913. Pp. 393.
   U-1929 I* C* L

Blum, Jean. *J.-A. Starck et la querelle du crypto-catholicisme en Allemagne.*
Paris. Alcan. 1912. Pp. xvi, 195. U-1299 D
— *Le litre et l'amphore.* Paris. Messein. 1924. Pp. 239. U-5249
— *La vie et l'oeuvre de J.G. Hamann le 'Mage du Nord' 1730-1788.* Paris.
Alcan. 1912. Pp. xxii, 704. U-304 I*
Blunno, Domingo Alberto. *Bouquet de rimas.* Buenos Aires. Porter. 1925.
Pp. 108. U-5136
Boades, Bernat. *Libre dels Feyts Darmes de Catalunya.* Barcelona. Verdaguer.
1873. Pp. xliv, 463. U-3976
Bobadilla, Emilio. *Al través de mis nervios.* Barcelona. Henrich. 1903. Uc
— *A fuego lento.* Barcelona. Henrich. 1903. Pp. 315. U-2454 I* C
— *Sintiéndome vivir.* Madrid. Suárez. 1906. Pp. 301. U-639 D
— *Viajando por España.* Madrid. Tello. 1912. Pp. 300. U-4387 n/o D
— *En pos de la paz.* Madrid. Pueyo. 1917. Uc
Bobia Berdayes de Carbó, América. *Ofertorio.* Matanzas. Estrada. 1928.
Pp. 90. U-4971 D
Boccaccio, Giovanni. *Il Decamerone.* Preceduto da uno studio Adolfo Bartoli.
2 vols. Milano. Editoriale Italiano. 1928. U-154-5 I C
Bodhabhikshu, Brâhmâcharin. See *Jagadisa-chandra Chattopadhyaya*
Boedo, Fernando. *El contraquijote.* Madrid. Soc. Edit. de España. 1916.
Pp. 325. U-1120
Boehl de Faber, Cecilia. *Un servilón y un liberalito.* Ed., introd., notes, and
vocabulary Carlos Bransby. Boston. Heath. 1909. Pp. xii, 171. U-4470
Böhme, Jacob. *Aurora oder die Morgenröthe.* Amsterdam. [1620]. Pp. 360.
U-4473
Bohlmann, Gerhard. *Die silberne Jungfrau.* Leipzig. Reclam. [1932]. Pp. 392.
U-3497 T
Boissier, Marie L.A. Gaston. *La fin du paganisme.* 2 vols. Paris. Hachette.
1898. U-916-17 I
— *La religion romaine d'Auguste aux Antonins.* 2 vols. Paris. Hachette.
1906. U-949-50 I
Boletín del Archivo Nacional. Caracas, II, 8 (dic. 1924). n/n
Bolinder, Gustaf. *Det Tropiska snöfjällets Indianer.* Stockholm. Bonniers.
1916. Pp. 240. U-5699 T D
Bolívar. Literatura y Ciencias. Intercambio hispano-americano, núm. 1.
Manizales, Colombia. 1923. Pp. 50. U-5490
Bolívar, Simón. *La vida y correspondencia general del Libertador.* Precede la
vida de Bolívar escrita por Felipe Larrazábal. 2 vols. New York. Cassard.
1883. U-708-9 I*
— *Cartas del Libertador.* Publicadas por orden del Gen. Guzmán Blanco.
Caracas. Gobierno Nacional. 1887-8. Uc

- *Cartas de Bolívar. (1799-1822).* Pról. J. Enrique Rodó y notas R. Blanco-Fombona. Paris. Michaud. 1913. Pp. 459. U-3074 I* C L B
- *Discursos y proclamas.* Compilados, anotados, prologados, y publicados R. Blanco-Fombona. Paris. Garnier. 1922. Pp. xlvii, 302. U-1337 I*
- *Simón Bolívar, Libertador de la América del Sur por los más grandes escritores americanos.* Pról. M. de Unamuno. Madrid. Renacimiento. 1914. Pp. xvi, 542. (3 copies) U-1330, U-3917. U-3459 n/o
- *Cartas de Simón Bolívar, 1823-24-25.* Notas R. Blanco-Fombona. Madrid. América. 1921. Pp. xv, 427. U-2221 I
- *Discurso en el Congreso de Angostura.* San José de Costa Rica. García Monge. 1922. Pp. 130. U-4449
- *Commémoration du centenaire de la mort du Libérateur Simon Bolivar le 17 décembre 1930.* La Haya. Légation du Vénézuela. 1930. Pp. 59. U-2224
- *Choix de lettres, discours et proclamations.* Tr. Charles V. Aubrun. Paris. Institut International de Coop. Intellectuelle. 1934. Pp. 333. U-2139 n/o

Bollo, Sarah. *Diálogos de las luces perdidas.* Pról. Juana de Ibarbourou. Montevideo. Barreiro y Ramos. 1927. Pp. 122. U-5017 D

Bonafoux, Luis. *Casi críticas.* Paris. Ollendorff. 1910. Pp. 311. U-379
- *Melancolía.* Paris. Ollendorff. n.d. Pp. 389. U-2781

Bonilla y San Martín, Adolfo. *El mito de psyquis.* Barcelona. Henrich. 1908. Pp. 339. U-3755

Bonn, Moritz Julius. *Amerika und sein problem.* München. Meyer & Jessen. 1925. Pp. 175. U-5388 I
- *Die Krisis der Europäischen Demokratie.* München. Meyer & Jessen. 1925. Pp. 154. U-5407 I C

Bonnard, Abel. *Les familiers.* Paris. Société Française d'Imprimerie et de Librairie. 1906. Pp. 260. U-3849

Bonnefon, Charles. *Dialogue sur la vie et sur la mort.* Paris. Fischbacher. 1911. Pp. xiii, 115. U-3099 I* C D

Bonnier, Gaston. *Le monde végétal.* Paris. Bibliothèque de Philosophie Scientifique. 1918. Pp. 392. U-4008 I* C B*

Bonsor, George Edward. *The Archaeological Expedition Along the Guadalquivir 1889-1901.* Tr. Clara L. Penney. New York. The Hispanic Society of America. 1931. Pp. 86, pl. 41. U-1
- *An Archaeological Sketch-book of the Roman Necropolis at Carmona.* Tr. Clara L. Penney. New York. The Hispanic Society of America. 1931. Pp. 159, pl. 88. U-2

Böök, Emil. *Joannes Ludivicus Vives.* Helsingfors. 1887. Pp. 214. U-2270 T

Bopp, Franz. *Grammaire comparée des langues Indo-Européenes.* Tr. et introd. Michel Bréal. 5 vols. Paris. Nationale. 1874-8. U-66-70

Borges, Jorge Luis. *Fervor de Buenos Aires.* n.p. 1923. Pp. 30. U-5707 D
- *Discusión.* Buenos Aires. Gleizer. 1932. Pp. 161. U-2152 D
- *Las Kenningar.* Buenos Aires. Colombo. 1933. Pp. 26. U-1713 D
- *Historia universal de la infamia.* Buenos Aires. Col. Megáfono. 1935.
  Pp. 139. U-5508 D
Borges Grainha, M. *A Instrucção secundaria.* Lisboa. Universal. 1905.
  Pp. xv, 389. U-2630 D
Bórquez Solar, Antonio. *Dilectos decires.* Paris. Ollendorff. n.d. Uc
Borrás, J. *Sistema científico luliano.* Palma de Mallorca. Tous. 1916. Pp. 29.
  U-4813
Borrow, George. *Lavengro: the Scholar, the Gipsy, the Priest.* Introd. Thomas
  Seccombe. London. Dent. 1907. Pp. xxvi, 547. U-976 I* C
- *Wild Wales: The People, Language and Scenery.* Introd. Th. Watts-Dunton.
  London. Dent. 1907. Pp. xxiii, 617. U-980 I* T
- *The Romany Rye.* London. Dent. 1907. Pp. xiv, 392. U-979 I*
- *La Biblia en España.* Tr. Manuel Azaña. 3 vols. Madrid. Jiménez-Fraud.
  1920-1. U-4487 C
- *The Bible in Spain.* Introd. Edward Thomas. London. Dent. [1906].
  Pp. xiv, 510. U-977 I
- *The Zincali. An Account of the Gypsies of Spain.* Introd. Edward Thomas.
  London. Dent. [1914]. Pp. xiv, 251. U-978 I
Bosanquet, Bernard. *Psychology of the Moral Self.* London. MacMillan. 1904.
  Pp. viii, 132. U-289 I
- *The Principle of Individuality and Value.* London. MacMillan. 1912.
  Pp. xxxvii, 409. U-95 B I
- *The Value and Destiny of the Individual.* London. MacMillan. 1913.
  Pp. xxxii, 331. U-96 I
Boselli, Carlo. *Nuovo dizionario tascabile spagnuolo-italiano e italiano-*
  spagnuolo. II. Italiano-spagnuolo. Milano. Fratelli Treves. 1917. Pp. xviii,
  416. n/n
Bossuet, Fénelon. Le quiétisme. Souvenirs de la crypte de St Augustin. 2 vols.
  Paris. Lecoffre. 1912. U-3419-20
Boswell, James. *The Life of Samuel Johnson.* 2 vols. London. Dent. 1909.
  U-1079-80 I*
- *The Journal of a Tour to the Hebrides with Samuel Johnson, Ll.D.*
  London. Dent. n.d. Pp. xxv, 414. U-1048 I*
Botero Saldarriaga, Roberto. *Sangre conquistadora.* Medellín, Colombia.
  Botero-Soto [1911]. Pp. 122. U-2813 D
Boti, Regino E. *Arabescos mentales.* Barcelona. Tobella. 1913. Pp. 310. n/n D
Botto, António. *Baionetas da morte.* n.p. [1936]. Pp. 32. U-5719 D
Bougaud, Em. *Historia de Santa Juana Francisca Premiot.* Tr. por una
  religiosa del segundo Monasterio de la Visitación de esta Corte. 2 vols.
  Madrid. Aguado. 1880. U-1281-2

Bouillier, Francisque. *De la conscience en psychologie et en morale*. Paris. Germer-Baillière. 1872. Pp. vii, 206. U-1518
— *Du plaisir et de la douleur*. Paris. Hachette. 1885. Pp. xiii, 365. U-1154
Bouillon, Léon. *L'Eglise apostolique et les juifs philosophes jusqu'à Philon*. Orthez. 1913. Pp. 448. U-4219
Boulanger, André. *Orphée. Rapports de l'orphisme et du christianisme*. Paris. Rider. 1925. Pp. 171. U-5319 I
Bourgade la Dardye, E. de. *Le Paraguay*. Paris. Plon et Nourrit. 1889. Pp. 460. U-374
Bousset, Wilhelm. *Jesus*. Halle. Schwetschke. 1904. Pp. 103. U-2128 I
Boutroux, Etienne E.M. *Pascal*. Paris. Hachette. 1903. Pp. 205. U-299 B* I
— *De la contingence des lois de la nature*. Paris. Alcan. 1905. Pp. 170. U-199
— *Science et religion dans la philosophie contemporaine*. Paris. Flammarion. 1908. Pp. 400. U-3458 I B
Bouvier, René. *L'Espagne de Quevedo. Voyages au Monde Caduc avec le chevalier des Tenailles*. Paris. Droz. 1936. Pp. 226. U-5325 I* C* D
Bové, Salvador. *Santo Tomás de Aquino y el descenso del entendimiento*. Palma de Mallorca. Guasp. 1911. Pp. xii, 828. U-305 D
Bóveda, Xavier. *Los motivos eternos*. Buenos Aires. Juan Roldán. 1927. Pp. 165. U-5054 D
— *Tierra nativa*. Buenos Aires. La Facultad. 1928. Pp. 197. U-4987 n/o D
— *La esencia de lo español y otros temas*. Buenos Aires. Cabaut. 1929. Pp. 160. U-5140 D
— *Tertulias literarias*. Buenos Aires. Libr. del Colegio. 1935. Pp. 172. U-5084 D [Incomplete]
Boyd, Ernest. *Studies From Ten Literatures*. New York. Scribner's. 1925. Pp. viii, 333. U-5367 I
Boza, Luis Roberto. *El Cilicio*. n.p. Franklin. 1911. Pp. 234. U-3261 n/o D
Braga, Erasmo. *Religião e Razão*. S. Paulo. Campinas. [1916]. Pp. 21. U-1921
Brandão, Raúl. *Humus*. Porto. Renascença Portuguesa. [1917]. Pp. 334. U-2434 I L D
— *1817. A conspiração de Gomes Freire*. Porto. Renascença Portuguesa. [1917]. Pp. 319. U-2912 I D
— *Teatro. I. O gebo e a sombra. O rei imaginario. O doido e a morte*. Porto. Renascença Portuguesa. 1923. Pp. 164. U-3295
— e Joaquim Pereira Teixeira de Vasconcellos. *Jesus Cristo em Lisboa*. Paris. Aillaud e Bertrand. n.d. Pp. 120. U-5735 I* D
Brandau, V. *Carácteres mentales de la mujer según la sociología contemporánea*. Santiago de Chile. 1908. Uc
Brandes, Georg. *Henrik Ibsen*. Kφbenhavn. Hegel. 1898. Pp. 183. U-2112 T* C
— *Essais choisis. Renan. Taine. Nietzsche. Heine. Kielland. Ibsen*. Tr. S. Garling. Préf. Henri Albert. Paris. Mercure de France. 1914. Pp. 317. QP-7 I

Bratli, Carl. *Filip II af Spanien.* København. Lybeckers. 1909. Pp. 283.
U-2259 I* D

— *Norsk-Dansk-Spansk Ordbog.* Med et forord Phil. Kr. Nyrop. København.
Aschehoug. 1916. Pp. 517. U-1298 D

Brea, Antonio. *Campaña del Norte de 1873 a 1876.* Barcelona. Biblioteca
Popular Carlista. 1897. Pp. 524. U-1715

Bremond, Marie J.F.R.I. Henri. *Prière et poésie.* Paris. Grasset. 1926.
Pp. xv, 221. QP-8 I

Brenes Argüello, Carlota. *Música sencilla.* San José, C.R. Alsina. 1928. Ff. 91.
U-5115 D

Brenes Mesén, Roberto. *Hacia nuevos umbrales.* San José, C.R. Alsina.
1913. Uc D

Briceno-Iragorry, Mario. *Horas.* Caracas. Mercantil. 1921. Pp. 194. U-2439 D

— *Motivos.* Caracas. Mercantil. 1922. Pp. 77. U-3513 D

Brighenti, Eliseo. *Dizionario greco moderno-italiano e italiano-greco moderno.*
Parte I. Greco moderno-italiano. Milano. Hoepli. 1927. Pp. xvi, 696. n/n

Bright, John. *Selected Speeches of the Rt. Hon. John Bright on Public*
Questions. Introd. J. Sturge. London. Dent. 1910. Pp. xii, 271.
U-1046 I* T

Brinkmann, Friedrich. *Die Metaphern.* Bonn. Marcus. 1878. Pp. 600. U-4227

Briones Luco, Ramón. *Origen y desarrollo del matrimonio y el divorcio en la*
familia humana. Santiago de Chile. La Ilustración. 1910. Uc D

Brizeux, Julien Auguste. *Marie. Les Bretons. La fleur d'or. Primel et Nola.*
Paris. Michaud. n.d. Pp. 128. U-522 I B

Brøndsted, Holger Valdemar. *Juan de la Cruz. Et forsøgiiden Religiøse Tankes*
Historie. København. Gyldendalske. 1932. Pp. 325. U-1769 I* C* B T

Brontë, Charlotte. *Jane Eyre. An Autobiography.* London. Nelson. 1906.
Pp. 517. U-5150 I

Brontë, Emily Jane. *Wuthering Heights.* Introd. Currer Bell. London. Dent.
1912. Pp. xxviii, 371. U-1075 I* T

Brooke, Rupert. *1914 & other Poems.* London. Sidgwick, Jackson. 1917.
Pp. 63. U-2038 I*

Brooks, Phillips. *Sermons Preached in English Churches.* London. MacMillan.
1900. Pp. 311. U-288 B*

— *The Mystery of Iniquity and Other Sermons.* London. MacMillan. 1900.
Pp. vii, 362. U-290 I*

Brossa, Jaume. *Els sepulcres blancs.* Barcelona. L'Avenç. 1900. Pp. 118.
U-2877 D

Browne, Robert W. *History of Rome.* London. Longman, Brown, Green.
1859. Pp. viii, 146. U-4570

Browne, Thomas. *The Religio Medici and Other Writings of Sir T. Browne.*
Introd. C.H. Herford. London. Dent. 1912. Pp. xvi, 296. U-1059 I*

Browning, Elizabeth Barrett. *The Poetical Works of Elizabeth Barrett Browning.* London. Smith, Elder. 1906. Pp. xxi, 667. U-1328 I* T B

Browning, Robert. *Bells and Pomegranates.* London. Ward, Lock. 1896. Pp. xiv, 326. U-3856

— *The Poetical Works of Robert Browning.* 2 vols. London. Smith, Elder. 1905. U-1339-40 I* T

Brugmann, Carl. *Griechische Grammatik.* München. Beck'sche Verlagsbuchhandlung. 1900. Pp. xix, 632. U-666

Brull, Mariano. *La casa del silencio.* Introd. P. Henríquez Ureña. Madrid. García y Galo Sáez. 1916. Pp. xii, 177. U-2731

Brunet, Jaime. *Música di cámera.* Madrid. Perlado, Paez. 1915. Uc D

Brunet, Pierre Gustave. *Anciens proverbes, basques et gascons* remis au jour par Pierre Gustave Brunet. Bayonne. Cazals. 1873. Pp. 29. U-4299

Brunetti, Carlo Mario. *Chi sono i Cavalieri.* Genova. Peyré. 1923. Pp. 173. U-3750 D

Brunhes, Antoine Joseph Bernard. *La dégradation de l'énergie.* Paris. Flammarion. 1912. Pp. 394. U-617 B* I* C*

Brunner, Constantin. *Vom Einsiedler Constantin Brunner. Mein leben und Schaffen.* Potsdam. Kiepenheuer. 1924. Pp. 151. U-5462 I* C* B

Bruno. See Pereira de Sampaio, José

Bruno, Giordano. *Opere italiane.* 3 vols. Bari. Laterza. 1907. U-1813-15 I* C B

Bryce, James. *South America. Observations and Impressions.* London. MacMillan. 1912. Pp. xxiv, 611. U-1849 I*

Buen y del Cos, Odón de. *Historia natural.* 2 vols. Barcelona. Soler. 1897. Uc

Buendía, Rogelio. *La rueda de color.* Huelva. Muñoz. 1923. U-723 D

Buendía Manzano, R. *El poema de mis sueños.* Madrid. Pueyo. n.d. Uc D

Bueno, Manuel. *Viviendo. Cuentos é historias.* Pról. J. Verdes Montenegro. Bilbao. Müller y Zavaleta. [1896]. Pp. xv, 204. U-503 D

— *Corazón adentro.* Madrid. Sáenz Jubera. 1906. Pp. 328. U-2344 D

— *El sabor del pecado.* Barcelona. Araluce. 1935. Pp. 376. U-3789 I D

— *A ras de tierra.* Valencia. Sempere. n.d. Uc D

Bulletin de Dialectologie Romane, II (avril-juin 1909). U-4853

Bulletin of Spanish Studies, I, 1 (1923). U-781

Bullon y Fernández, Eloy. *Alfonso de Castro y la ciencia penal.* Madrid. Hernández. 1900. Pp. 138. U-1325 n/o D

Bulnes, Francisco. *Las grandes mentiras de nuestra historia: la nación y el ejército en las guerras extranjeras.* Paris. Bouret. 1904. Pp. 924. U-2572 I*

Búlnes, Gonzalo. *Guerra del Pacífico de Antofagasta a Tarapacá.* Valparaiso. Universo. 1911. Pp. 747. U-2970

Bulwer, Edward George Earle Lytton. *The Last Days of Pompeii.* Leipzig. Tauchnitz. 1879. Pp. xii, 444. U-510 T*

Bunge, Augusto. *Las conquistas de la higiene social. Informe.* Buenos Aires.
    Penitenciaria Nacional. 1910. Uc D
Bunge, Carlos Octavio. *El espíritu de la educación.* Buenos Aires. Penitenciaría
    Nacional. 1901. Pp. 383. U-717 I C L*
— *Principios de psicología individual y social.* Pról. Luis Simarro. Madrid.
    Jorro. 1903. Pp. xiv, 240. U-1349 D
— *Nuestra América. Ensayo de psicología social.* Buenos Aires. Abeledo.
    1905. Pp. xxx, 376. U-1805 I D
— *Teoría del derecho. Principios de sociología jurídica.* Buenos Aires.
    Marana. 1905. Pp. xxxi, 388. U-1162 I D
— *El derecho. Ensayo de una teoría científica de la ética en su fase jurídica.*
    Buenos Aires. Abeledo. 1907. Uc D
— *Casos del derecho penal. Dictámenes.* Buenos Aires. Moen. 1911. Pp. lv,
    440. U-4836 D
— *Nuestra patria.* Buenos Aires. Estrada. 1910. Pp. 471. U-1780 D
— *Historia del derecho argentino.* Tomo I. Buenos Aires. Facultad de Derecho
    y Ciencias Sociales. 1912. Pp. xxxv, 330. U-3538 D
— *El sabio y la horca.* Madrid. Espasa-Calpe. 1926. Pp. 292. U-5595
— *Sarmiento. Estudio Biográfico y crítica.* Madrid. Espasa-Calpe. 1926.
    Pp. 206. U-5516 I C
— *Juicios sobre su personalidad y su obra.* Madrid. Espasa-Calpe. n.d.
    Pp. 125. U-5684
— *Le droit, c'est la force.* Tr. Emile Desplanque. Paris. Schleicher. n.d.
    Pp. xxvii, 476. U-4272 D
Bunge de Gálvez, Delfina. *Simplemen.* Paris. Lemerre. 1911. Pp. 222. U-4747 D
Bunyan, John. *The Pilgrim's Progress From This World To That Which Is To*
    Come. Leipzig. Tauchnitz. 1855. Pp. xviii, 364. U-4775 I B*
Buonaiuti, Ernesto. *Apologia dello spiritualismo.* Roma. Formiggini. 1926.
    Pp. 66. U-5351
— *Le modernisme catholique.* Tr. René Monnot. Paris. Rieder. 1927.
    Pp. 204. U-5322 I B
Buonarroti, Michel Angelo. *Poesie.* Pref. G. Amendola. Lanciano. Carabba.
    1911. Pp. 158. U-2914 I*
Burckhardt, Jacob. *Die Kultur der Renaissance in Italien.* 2 vols. Leipzig.
    Seeman. 1899. U-836-7 I* T. Wien. Phaidon-Verlag. n.d. Pp. 702. U-5444
Bureau, Noël. *Ruptures.* Paris. Rythme et Synthèse. 1925. Pp. 134. U-5304 D
Bureau des Longitudes. *Annuaire pour l'an 1877.* Paris. Gauthier-Villars. Uc
Burghi, Juan. *Madre-Tierra.* Buenos Aires. Index. 1921. Pp. 93. U-2941 n/o D
Burgos, Fausto. *Hojas caídas.* La Plata. 1915. Uc
Burgos y Mazo, Manuel de. *El verano de 1919 en gobernación.* Cuenca. Pinós.
    [1921]. Pp. 628. U-2215 I
Burguette, Ricardo. *Mi rebeldía.* Madrid. Fé. 1904. Pp. 328. U-3354 D

- *Preparación de las tropas para la guerra.* Madrid. Fé. 1905. Pp. 153. U-3177
- *Dinamismo espiritualista.* Madrid. Fé. 1905. Pp. 206. U-3242
- *La ciencia del valor.* Madrid. Sáenz de Jubera. 1907. Pp. ix, 243. U-2759 D
- *Rectificaciones históricas. De Guadelete a Covadonga.* Madrid. Sáenz de Jubera. 1915. Pp. 321. U-2760
- *Morbo nacional.* Madrid. Fé. 1906. Pp. 215. U-2758 D
Burke, Right Hon. Edmund. *The Works of the Rt. Hon. Edmund Burke.* Introd. William Willis. 6 vols. Oxford. University Press. [1906]. U-433-8. IV-VI I*
Burns, Robert. *The Poetical Works of Robert Burns.* London. Warne. 1892. Pp. xxvi, 614. U-202 I* C T*
Busaniche, José Luis. *Estanislao López y el federalismo del litoral.* Buenos Aires. Cervantes. 1927. Pp. 287. (2 copies) U-4916. U-5053 I B D
Bustamante, P. *Peregrina.* Buenos Aires. Peuser. 1905. Pp. 263. U-2826 D
Bustamante y Ballivián, Enrique. *Elogios: poemas paganos y místicos.* Lima. La Revista. 1910. Pp. 88. U-2175 D
- *La evocadora. Divagación ideológica.* Lima. Penitenciaría. 1913. Pp. 96. U-3253 D
- *Arias de silencio.* Lima. [1916]. Pp. 88. U-406 D
Bustos, Zenón. *Anales de la Universidad Nacional de Córdoba. Segundo período (1778-1795).* Córdoba. Domenici. 1902. Pp. xiv, 983. U-4822 n/o
Butler, (Bishop) Joseph. *The Analogy of Religion.* Introd. R. Bayne. London. Dent. 1906. Pp. xxxii, 280. U-1058 I
Butler, Samuel. *Erewhon Revisited. Twenty Years Later.* London. Fifield. 1910. Pp. 338. U-3498 I
- *Erewhon or Over the Range.* London. Fifield. 1913. Pp. xviii, 323. U-1311 I
- *The Note-Books of Samuel Butler.* Sel., ed. Henry Festing Jones. London. Fifield. 1912. Pp. xii, 438. U-4790 I C
- *The Way of All Flesh.* London. Fifield. 1919. Pp. 420. U-4791 I* C
Butlleti de l'associació protectora de l'ensenyanca catalana, III, 1 (1919). n/n
Butti, Enrico A. *Encantamiento.* Tr. Miguel Domenge Mir. Barcelona. Henrich. n.d. Pp. 297. U-2281
Buylla, Adolfo, Adolfo Posada, y Luis Morote. *El Instituto del Trabajo.* Madrid. Fé. 1902. Pp. clxvii, 342. U-1833 I
- y G. Alegre. *Memorias acerca de la información agraria en ambas Castillas.* Madrid. Minuesa de los Ríos. 1904. Uc
- *Economía por Newmann,* et al. Versión española del alemán precedida de un estudio sobre 'El concepto de la economía y el caracter de su ciencia.' Madrid. La España Moderna. Uc
Buzzi, Paolo. *L'Esilio.* Tomos I, III. Milano. Edizioni di Poesia. 1905-6. U-4412-13 D

Byne, Arthur, and Mildred Stapley. *Rejería of the Spanish Renaissance.*
New York. The Hispanic Society of America. 1914. Pp. vii, 101. U-3565

Byron, George Gordon. *The Poetical Works of Lord Byron.* Ed. with a
memoir by Ernest Hartley Coleridge. London. Murray. 1905. Pp. lxxii,
1048. U-3063 I* C* L

Caballero Audaz. See Carretero Novillo, José María

Caballero, Carlos. *El proscrito.* Valencia. Prometeo. n.d. Uc D

Cabanillas Enríquez, Ramón. *Vento Mareiro.* Santiago de Cuba. 1913. Pp. 199.
U-2680 D

Cabot y Rovira, Joaquim. *De fora casa. Narracions de viatge.* Barcelona.
Verdaguer. 1898. Pp. 208. U-2878 D

Cabral, Luis D. *Defensas militares.* Buenos Aires. Alsina. 1905. Pp. xv, 376.
U-2517 n/o D

Cabral de Moncada, [Luis]. 'O problema metodológico na ciencia de história
do direito português,' *Anuario de Historia del Derecho Español* (1933).
Pp. 29. U-2493 D

Cabrera, Alonson de, Fr. *Sermones.* Discurso preliminar Miguel Mir. (NBAE, 3).
Madrid. Bailly-Baillière. 1906. Pp. xxxii, 712. U-38 I* L* C*

Cabrera, Blas. *¿Qué es la electricidad?* Madrid. Publ. de la Residencia de
Estudiantes. 1917. Pp. 181. U-2123

Cabrera, Lydia. *Contes nègres de Cuba.* Tr. F. de Miomandre. Paris.
Gallimard. 1936. Pp. 251. U-3925

Cabrera y Bosch, Raimundo. *Mis buenos tiempos. Memorias de un estudiante.*
Paris. Ollendorff. n.d. Pp. xxiii, 273. U-3181

Caccia, José. *Nuevo diccionario italiano-español y español-italiano.* Paris.
Garnier. n.d. Pp. xvi, 528 + xvi, 333. n/n

Cáceres, Esther de. *Las insulas extrañas.* Santiago del Estero. Col. La Brasa.
1929. Ff. xx. U-5504 D

− *Los cielos.* Montevideo. Imp. Uruguaya. 1935. Pp. 82. U-1342 n/o D

Cáceres, Zoila Aurora (Evangelina, pseud.). *Mujeres de ayer y de hoy.* Pról.
L. Bonafoux. Paris. Garnier. [1909]. Pp. xiv, 345. U-3587 D

− *Oasis de arte.* Pról. Rubén Darío. Paris. Garnier. 1911. Pp. xi, 413. U-642 D

− *La ciudad del sol.* Pról. E. Gómez Carrillo. Lima. Libr. Francesa
Científica. 1927. Pp. 199. U-5125 n/o D

Cadalso, José de. *Cartas marruecas.* Ed. y pról. J. Martínez Ruiz. Madrid.
Calleja. 1917. Pp. 321. U-4417 I* C

Cadilla de Martínez, María. *Cazadora en el alba y otros poemas.* Madrid.
Bolaños y Aguilar. 1933. Pp. 81. U-2308

− *La mística de Unamuno y otros ensayos.* Madrid. Bolaños y Aguilar.
1934. Pp. 110. U-373 D

Cádiz, Beato Diego José de. See Diego José, de Cádiz

Caine, Sir Thomas Henry Hall. *The Christian. A Story.* London. Heinemann.
1897. Pp. 452. U-3887 I* T
Calabritto, Giovanni. *I romanzi picareschi di Mateo Alemán e Vicente Espínel.*
Valletta. Malta. 1929. Pp. 225. U-1107 D
Calamita, Carlos. *Los inútiles.* Madrid. Fé. 1910. Pp. 154. U-3262 D
Calandrelli, Alcides. *Cuestiones de derecho internacional privado.* Madrid.
Suárez. 1913. Pp. 396. U-4821 D
Calasanctio a Llevaneras, José. *Compendium theologiae dogmaticae beate
Marie Virgini dicatum.* Barcinone. Immaculatae Conceptionis. 1882.
Pp. 332, 451. U-4656
Calcaño, Julio. *Tres poetas pesimistas del siglo XIX ... (Lord Byron, Shelley,
Leopardi). Estudio critico.* Caracas. Universidad. 1907. Pp. 322.
U-2467 n/o D
– *Poesías.* 2 vols. Caracas. Tip. del Comercio. 1915. Uc
Caldera R., Rafael. *Andrés Bello. Ensayo.* Caracas. Parra León. 1935. Pp. 167.
U-835 D
Calderón, Alfredo. *Nonadas.* Bilbao. Müller y Zavaleta. 1896. Pp. 318. U-4165
– *De mis campañas.* Barcelona. Henrich. 1899. Pp. 322. U-2668 D
– *Palabras.* Barcelona. Henrich. 1905. Pp. 310. U-1835 D
– *A punta de pluma.* Barcelona. Libr. Española. [1902]. Pp. 186. Uc D
Calderón, B. *Fomento de la ganadería.* Madrid. Bailly-Baillière. 1906. Uc D
Calderón de la Barca, Pedro. *Teatro de Calderón de la Barca.* Estudio y
apuntes García-Ramón. 4 vols. Paris. Garnier. 1882-3. U-203-6. U-203 I
– *La vita è sogno.* Tr. Gherardo Marone. Napoli. L'Editrice Italiana. 1920.
Pp. 174. U-2050
– *Comedias religiosas. I. La devoción de la cruz y El mágico prodigioso.*
Pról. y ed. A. Valbuena Prat. Madrid. Espasa Calpe. 1930. Pp. 344.
(CC, 106). U-5692 I* L
– *Autos y loas.* Valencia. Clásicos Españoles. n.d. Pp. 215. U-5488
*Calendar of Letters, Despatches and State Papers, Relating to the Negotia-
tions Between England and Spain.* Ed. M.A.S. Hume and Royall Tyler.
Hereford. The Hereford Times Ltd. 1912. Pp. xiii, 603. U-716
Calle e Yturrino, Esteban. *Rimas, sonetos y madrigales.* Pról. y epíl. Salvador
Sellés. Alicante. Muñoz. 1915. Pp. 133. U-2860 n/o D
Calleja, Rafael. *Voz y voto.* Madrid. Historia Nueva. 1929. Pp. 285. U-5058 D
Calosso, Umberto. *L'Anarchia di Vittorio Alfieri.* Bari. Laterza. 1924. Pp. 211.
U-5349 I* C
Calot, F. *Traitement rationnel du mal de Pott à l'usage des praticiens.* Paris.
Doin. 1906. Pp. 116. U-685
Calzada, Rafael. *Rasgos biográficos de José Segundo Decoud.* Buenos Aires.
1913. Pp. 152. Uc D

— *Narraciones.* Pról. Salvador Rueda. Buenos Aires. Robles y Cía. 1914.
Pp. 284. Uc D

Camacho Beneytez, Manuel. *Poemas líricos.* Pról. Angela Barco. Madrid. Fé.
1911. Pp. 175. U-3877 D

— *Modulaciones.* Pról. Consuelo Alvarez. Madrid. Pueyo. 1914. Pp. 207.
U-315 D

Camara, João da. *Media noche.* Tr. J. Nombela y Campos. Madrid. La Ultima
Moda. 1907. Pp. xiv, 118. U-4591

Cámara de Diputados de la Provincia de Buenos Aires. *Justicia provincial.*
La Plata. 1916. Pp. ccclxxxi, 317. U-1188

Cambours Ocampo, Arturo. *Max, la maravilla del mundo.* Buenos Aires.
Tor. [1935]. Pp. 108. (2 copies) U-382, U-3125 n/o D

Camões, Luiz Vaz de. *Os Lusiadas de Luiz de Camões.* Critica litteraria
Paulino de Souza. Paris. Guillard, Aillaud. 1865. Pp. 536. U-475 I*

— *Obras completas de Luiz de Camões. I. Parnaso. Sonetos.* Porto.
Imprenta Portugueza. 1873. Pp. 220. U-4500

— *Os Lusiadas.* Edição para as escolas. Revista, prefaciada, e annotada
Mendes dos Remedios. Coimbra. Amado. 1903. Pp. xiv, 340. U-3166 L

— *Antologia portuguêsa. Camões lírico. I. Redondilhas. V. Canções.* 2 vols.
Paris. Aillaud e Bertrand. 1923. U-4399, U-5729

Camón Aznar, José. *El héroe.* Pról. M. de Unamuno. Madrid. Artes Gráficas
Municipales. 1934. Pp. 165. U-3667 D

Camón y Humanes, Francisco C. *Crédito y fomento de la producción
nacional agrícola.* Madrid. Mateu. 1916. Pp. 159. U-3797 D

Camp, Jean. *Minouche au pays du Cid.* Carcassonne. Jordy. [1925]. Pp. 62.
U-5782 I* C D

— *Sancho.* Paris. Editions des Portiques. 1933. Pp. 234. U-419 D. Typescript
copy. Pp. 172. U-3532

Campa, Gustavo E. *Críticas musicales.* Proemio F. Pedrell. Paris. Ollendorff.
1911. Pp. xii, 352. U-3230 n/o

Campagne's Schoolwoordenboek der Fransche en Nederlandsche Talen.
Amsterdam. Campagne & Zoon. Uc

Campión, Arturo. *Ensayo acerca de lus leyes fonéticas de la lengua euskara.*
San Sebastián. Baroja. 1883. Pp. 68. U-3702

— *Euskariana. I: Historia a través de la leyenda. II: Fantasía y realidad.*
2 vols. Bilbao. Biblioteca Bascongada. 1896-9. U-2075-6

— *Discursos políticos y literarios.* Pamplona. Erice y García. 1907. Pp. 315.
U-3644 D

— *La bella Easo.* Pról. F. Gascue. 2 vols. Pamplona. Erice y García. 1909.
U-3505-6

— y P. Broussain. *Informe de los señores académicos ... a la Academia de la
Lengua Vasca sobre unificación del Euskera.* Bilbao. Ave-María. 1920.
Pp. 20. U-1549

Campo, Angel de. *Cuentos de Angel de Campo.* Con nota Luis G. Urbina.
México. Cultura. 1916. Pp. 59. U-4493
Campo, Cupertino del. *El romance de un médico.* Buenos Aires. Menéndez.
1904. Uc D
— *Vibraciones y reflejos.* Buenos Aires. Rodríguez Giles. 1908. Uc D
Campo, Estanislao del. *Fausto, impresiones del gaucho Anastasio el Pollo en
la representación de esta ópera.* Barcelona. Progreso. n.d. Pp. 62. U-2212
Campoamor, Ramón. *Obras poéticas completas.* 2 vols. Barcelona. Tasso.
1900. U-2393-4. U-2394 I
Campos, Agostinho de. *Universidade e educação.* Coimbra. Ediçoes Estudos.
1936. Pp. 29. U-5733 I D
Campos Ortega, Lino Ramón. *Fugaces.* Oaxaca, México. Márquez. 1910.
Pp. 108. (2 copies) U-5577, U-5071 D
— *Nocturnales.* Oaxaca, México. La Universal. 1923. Pp. 210. U-5021
— *El lirio y la noche.* Oaxaca, México. La Universal. 1925. Pp. 99. (2 copies)
U-5582 D. U-5583
— *Boceto histórico sobre el ahuehuete de El Tule.* Oaxaca, México. Tall.
Imprenta del Gobierno del Estado. 1927. Pp. 127. (2 copies) U-5531,
U-5535 D
— *Perspectiva.* Oaxaca, México. Vázquez. [1927]. Pp. 120. (2 copies)
U-5005, U-5645 n/o D
Canales, Nemesio. *La leyenda benaventina.* Buenos Aires. Editorial Martín
Fierro. 1922. Pp. 127. U-5589 n/o
Canals, Salvador. *Los sucesos de España en 1909.* 2 vols. Madrid. Imp.
Alemana. 1910-11. U-1256-7 I*
Cancio, Jesús. *Romancero del mar.* Santander. Aldus. 1930. Pp. 111.
U-3956 D
Cancionero castellano del siglo XV. Ordenado R. Foulché-Delbosc. 2 vols.
(NBAE, 19, 22). Madrid. Bailly-Baillière. 1912-15. U-54, U-56 I
Cancionero de Coimbra. Escolhidas Affonso Lopes Vieira. Coimbra. Amado.
1918. Pp. 146. U-518
Candamo, Bernaldo G. de. *Estrofas.* Pról. M. de Unamuno. Madrid. Faure.
1900. Uc
Candler, Edmund. *The Unveiling of Lhasa.* London. Thomas Nelson. 1905.
Pp. 375. U-231 I* C B T
Cané, Luis. *Romancero del Río de la Plata.* Buenos Aires. Porter. 1936.
Pp. 95. U-730 D
Cané, Miguel. *Notas e impresiones.* Buenos Aires. Moen. 1901. Pp. x, 397.
U-3365 D
— *Juvenilia.* Buenos Aires. Moen. 1901. Pp. 191. U-521 D
— *Prosa ligera.* Buenos Aires. Moen. 1903. Pp. 264. U-2415 I D
Canel, Eva. *Por la justicia y por España.* Buenos Aires. Robles. 1909. Pp. 744.
U-3064

Cañellas, Francisco. *La vida que pasa*. Pról. Andrés Alcalá Galiano. Valencia.
Sempere. Uc D
Cankar, Ivan. *The Bailiff Yerney and his Rights*. Tr. S. Yeras and H.C. Sewell
Grant. Introd. J. Lavrin. London. Rodker. 1930. Pp. xiii, 114. U-5214
Cannizzaro, Tommaso. *Vox Rerum*. Per l'autore di Quies [i.e., T. Cannizzaro].
Messina. Tipi dell'autore. 1900. Pp. xxiv, 840. U-3238 D
Cansinos-Asséns, Rafael. *La nueva literatura. (1898-1900-1916)*. 2 vols.
Madrid. Sanz Calleja. 1914-27. U-3853-4 n/o D
Cantar de mio Cid. Texto, gramática, y vocabulario R. Menéndez Pidal. 2 vols.
Madrid. Bailly-Baillière. 1908. Uc
Canti popolari serbi e croati. Tr. e annotati Pietro Kasandric. Milano. Fratelli
Treves. 1914. Pp. xv, 271. U-5711 I*
Cantilo, José Luis. *Don Juan de Garay*. Buenos Aires. Brédahl. 1904. Uc D
Cantilo, José María. *Los desorbitados*. Buenos Aires. Roldán. 1916. Pp. 295.
U-402 D
Capdevila, Arturo. *Jardines solos*. Córdoba. Imp. Argentina. 1911. Pp. 122.
U-2875 D
– *Melpómene*. Córdoba. Beltrán y Rossi. 1912. Pp. 163. U-2909 D
– *Dharma. Influencia del oriente en el derecho de Roma*. Córdoba. Beltrán
y Rossi. 1914. Pp. 272, vii. U-1865 n/o D
– *La sulamita*. Buenos Aires. Nosotros. 1916. Pp. 121. U-3131 D
– *El cantar de los cantares*. Buenos Aires. Atlántida. 1919. Pp. 175.
U-2354 D
– *Los hijos del sol*. Buenos Aires. Agencia Gral. de Libr. y Publ. 1923.
Pp. 278. U-4840 I* C* L D
– *Babel y el castellano*. Buenos Aires. Cabaut. 1928. Pp. 189. U-4911 D
– *Rivadavia y el españolismo liberal de la revolución argentina*. Buenos Aires.
El Ateneo. 1931. Pp. 268. U-2138 I D
Capecelatro, Alfonso. *Vida de San Felipe Neri*. Tr. Jaime Collell. Barcelona.
Tip. de la Hormiga de Oro. 1895. Pp. xii, 568. U-25
Capello, F. *'Alla Citta' di Ferrara.' Note alla ode di Giosué Carducci*. Buenos
Aires. [1905]. Pp. 28. U-740
Capo, J.M. See Márquez (Ex Coronel) y Capo, J.M.
Capuana, Luigi. *Jacinta*. Tr. M. Domenge Mir. Barcelona. Henrich. 1907. Uc
Carabaño, R.M. *Canto a la batalla de Ayacucho*. San Juan, P.R. Imp.
Venezuela. 1925. Pp. vi, 60. U-4933 D
Caras y caretas. Buenos Aires (28 Dic. 1929, 27 Mayo 1933). n/n
Cárbia, Rómulo D. *La leyenda del sol*. Barcelona. Maucci. n.d. Pp. 125.
U-3431
Carbonara, Francesco (Cilly, pseud.). *Batavia*. Campobasso. Edizioni Psiche.
1929. Pp. 120. U-3661 I* C D
– *Ore pagane*. Bruxelles. Edizioni Psiche. 1932. Pp. 99. U-538 n/o D
Carbonell, Diego. *Psicopatología de Bolívar*. Paris. Libr. Franco-Española.

- *En torno a la ciencia.* Caracas. Vargas. 1929. Pp. 198. U-5642 n/o D
- *1830.* Paris. Le Livre Libre. 1931. Pp. xxix, 239. U-2378 n/o D
- *De biología trascendental.* Bogotá. El Gráfico. 1935. Pp. 142. U-4218 n/o D
- *Por los senderos de la biología.* Buenos Aires. Michaud. n.d. Uc D

Carbonell, Miguel Angel. *Hombres de nuestra América.* Pról. Ismael Clark. Habana. La Prueba. 1915. Pp. 278. U-4809 D

Cardaberaz, Agustin. *Ondo iltcen icasteco.* Iruñean. Antonio Castilla. 1765. Pp. 110. U-465

Cardamatis, Jean P. *L'Egopathie.* Paris. Baillière. 1934. Pp. 110. U-2371 n/o D

Cardona, Rafael. *El sentido trágico del Quijote.* San José. C.R. El Convivio. 1928. Pp. 153. U-5106 D

Carducci, Giosuè. *Poesie di Giosuè Carducci (1850-1900).* Bologna. Zanichelli. 1902. Pp. 1075. U-2688 I* C
- *Prose di Giosuè Carducci (1859-1903).* Bologna. Zanichelli. 1905. Pp. 1485. U-3167 I* L
- *Da un carteggio inedito di Giosuè Carducci.* Pref. A. Messeri. Bologna. Zanichelli. 1907. Pp. 179. U-2957

Carlo, Miguel di. *Ataúdes.* Pról. Juan José Soiza Reilly. Buenos Aires. Tommasi. n.d. Pp. 173. U-2080 D

Carlyle, Thomas. *The French Revolution: A History.* 3 vols. Leipzig. Tauchnitz. 1851. U-4762-4. U-4764 B I*
- *Sartor resartus. Heroes and Hero-Worship* and *Past and Present.* London. Routledge. 1888. Pp. 192, 222. U-557 T*
- *Scottish & Other Miscellanies.* Introd. J.R. Lowell. London. Dent. [1915]. Pp. xi, 339. U-5175 I* C*
- *Past and Present.* Chicago. The Henneberry Co. n.d. Pp. 418. U-270
- *English and Other Critical Essays.* London. Dent. [1915]. Pp. 341. U-5181 I* C*
- *Sartor resartus. Vida y opiniones del señor Tanfelsdröckh.* Tr. González Blanco. 2 vols. Barcelona. Henrich. 1905. Uc
- *Los héroes. El culto de los héroes y lo heróico en la historia.* Tr. P. Umbert. 2 vols. Barcelona. Henrich. 1907. Uc

Carmen. Revista de poesía. Gijón-Santander (Junio 1928). n/n

Carmona Nenclares, F. *La prosa literaria del novecientos.* 2 vols. Madrid. Sáez. 1929. U-5087, U-5644 D

Carner, Josep. *L'Idili dels nyanyons.* Barcelona. Cunill. 1903. Pp. 46. U-4411 D
- *Els fruits saborosos.* Barcelona. 1906. Ff. 24. U-4860 D
- *La malvestat d'Oriana.* Barcelona. 1910. Pp. 182. U-3999 D
- *Verger de les galanies.* Barcelona. Giró. 1911. Pp. 78. U-2936 D
- *Les monjoies.* Barcelona. Gili. 1912. Pp. 82. U-2330 D

- *Auques i ventalls.* Barcelona. Galve. 1914. Pp. xii, 80. U-3879 D
- *La paraula en el vent.* Barcelona. Giró. 1914. Pp. xv, 94. U-2295 D

Carossa, Hans. *Eine Kindheit.* Leipzig. Infel. 1929. Pp. 166. U-5410

Carpenter, Edward. *Después de la civilización.* Tr. J. Molina y Vedía.
Buenos Aires. Imp. Argentina. 1929. Pp. 110. U-5587

Carpintero, Heliodoro. *Eco y voz.* Madrid. El Magisterio Español. 1934.
Pp. 92. n/n I

Carracido, José Rodríguez. *Compendio de química orgánica.* Barcelona. Soler.
n.d. Uc

Carranque de Ríos, A. *La vida difícil.* Madrid. Espasa Calpe. 1935. Pp. 257.
U-2306 D

Carranza, Adolfo P. *Leyendas nacionales.* Buenos Aires. Checchi. 1894. Pp. 99.
U-4021 n/o
- *Patricias argentinas.* Buenos Aires. Monqaut y Vasquez Millán. 1901.
Pp. 133. U-3350
- *San Martín.* Buenos Aires. Rosas. 1905. Uc D
- *Argentinas.* Buenos Aires. Mendesky. 1913. Uc

Carranza, Adolfo S. *¿Alberdi fué traidor?* Tucumán. Taller Graf.
Penitenciaría. 1920. Pp. 43. U-2502

Carrasco Albano, Alejandro. *Portales.* Santiago de Chile. Moderna. 1900.
Pp. 173. U-1278 I D

Carrasco y Jelves, Rosendo. *Otoñales.* Santiago de Chile. Esmeralda. 1903.
Pp. 198. U-2518 n/o D

Carrasquilla, Tomás. *La Marquesa de Yolombó.* Medellín. Cano. 1928.
Pp. 398. U-5108

Carrel, Alexis. *L'Homme, cet inconnu.* Paris. Plon. 1935. Pp. viii, 400. QP-9 I

Carrera, Ismaele Mario. *I canti di Laèrte Appulo.* Varese. Giornale di Poesia.
1923. Pp. 60. U-4678 n/o D

Carrera y Jústiz, Francisco. *Introducción a la historia de las instituciones
locales de Cuba.* 2 vols. Habana. La Moderna Poesía. 1905. U-3696-7 D
- *Estudios políticos-sociales. Orientaciones necesarias. Cuba y Panamá.*
Habana. La Moderna Poesía. 1911. Pp. xix, 435. Uc D

Carreras, Ricardo. *Doña 'Abulia.'* Barcelona. Henrich. 1904. Pp. 304.
U-2131 D

Carretero, Luis. *La cuestión regional de Castilla la Vieja.* Pról. S. Aragón.
Epíl. J. Ruano de la Sota. Segovia. San Martín. 1918. Pp. xi, 446.
U-5550 I D

Carretero, Manuel. *El triunfo de la vida. Diálogos novelescos.* Madrid. Pueyo.
n.d. Uc D
- *La espuma de Venus.* Barcelona. Antonio López. n.d. Uc

Carretero Nieva, Luis. *Las comunidades castellanas en la historia y su estado
actual.* Pról. Marqués de Lozoya. Segovia. Lozano. 1922. Pp. 49. U-5755

Carretero Novillo, José María (El Caballero Audaz, pseud.). *El novelista que vendió a su patria*. Madrid. Renacimiento. [1924]. Pp. 135. U-4883

Carriazo, Juan de M. 'Los herejes de Durango,' *Memoria XXXV* (sesión 28), 35-69. U-5770 D

Carriegos, Ramón C. *El idioma argentino*. Buenos Aires. Monteverde. 1904. Pp. 146. U-2798 I* D

Carrillo Ruedas, Armando. *Gotas de opio. 1907-1909*. Santiago de Chile. Cervantes. 1910. Pp. 109. U-3410 D

Carrión, Benjamín. *Los creadores de la nueva América*. Pról. Gabriela Mistral. Madrid. Soc. Gral. Española de Librería. 1928. Pp. 217. U-5648 D

— *El desencanto de Miguel García*. Madrid. Soc. Gral. Española de Librería. [1929]. Pp. 216, xviii. U-5594 D

Cartey, Guido Anatolio. *Cadenas rotas*. Buenos Aires. Progreso. 1905. Pp. 133. U-2740

Carton, Paul. *La vie sage. Commentaires sur les vers d'or des pythagoriciens*. Paris. Maloine. n.d. Pp. 208. U-5246 I D

Carvalho, Elysio. *Príncipes del espíritu americano*. Tr. y pról. César A. Comet. Madrid. Editorial América. n.d. Pp. 257. U-4624 D

Carvalho, Joaquim de. *A evolução espiritual de Antero*. Lisboa. Seara Nova. 1929. Pp. 109. U-2372 I* D

Casais Monteiro, Adolfo. *Confusão. Poemas*. Coimbra. Presança. 1929. Pp. 70. U-5718 T D

Casal, Julio J. *Regrets. Poesía*. Madrid. Imp. Art. Española. 1910. Uc D

— *Allá lejos ... Poesías*. Madrid. Helénica. 1912. Pp. 109. U-3648 D

— *Cielos y llanuras. Poesías*. Madrid. Hispano-Alemana. 1914. Pp. 115. U-3146 D

— *Nuevos horizontes*. Madrid. Pueyo. 1916. Pp. 196. U-3675 D

— *Huerto maternal. Poesías*. Madrid. Pueyo. 1919. Pp. 64. U-3455 D

— *Arbol*. La Coruña. Moret. 1925. Pp. 66. U-5554 D

Casanova, Mariano. *Obras oratorias*. Santiago de Chile. Cervantes. 1891. Uc

Casanova, Sofía. *Fugaces*. La Coruña. Andrés Martínez. 1898. Uc D

— *El cancionero de la dicha*. Madrid. Velasco. 1911. Uc D

Casanueva, Arturo. *Temas americanos. 5 Gritos*. Santander. La Atalaya. 1927. Pp. 43. U-5556

Casas, Fray Bartolomé de las. *Historiadores de Indias. I. Apologética historia de las Indias*. Ed. M. Serrano y Sanz. (NBAE, 13). Madrid. Bailly-Baillière. 1909. Pp. vii, 704. U-48

Casasus, Joaquín D. *Cayo Valerio Catulo, su vida y sus obras*. Pról. V. Salado Alvarez. México. Escalante. 1904. Pp. 389. U-2479 D

— *En honor de los muertos*. 2a parte. México. Escalante. 1913. Pp. 56. U-4130

Cascales y Muñoz, José. *El problema político al inaugurarse el siglo XX. El régimen parlamentario y el funcionarismo.* Pról. J. Canalejas y Méndez. Madrid. Suárez. 1902. Pp. xlv, 215. U-1110 D
— *Los Estados Unidos y el Japón.* Madrid. Moderna. 1908. Uc D
— *Los conflictos del proletariado.* Madrid. 1913. Uc
— *D. José de Espronceda, su época, su vida y sus obras.* Madrid. Hispania. 1914. Uc D
— *Sociología contemporánea. El apostolado moderno. Estudio histórico-crítico de el socialismo y el anarquismo hasta terminar el siglo XIX.* Barcelona. F. Granada. 1909. Pp. 357. U-146 D
— *Democracia colectivista. Lecciones de sociología.* Madrid. Sociedad Española de Librería. 1915. Pp. 102. U-1969 n/o D
Cascella, Armando. *La tierra de los papagayos.* Buenos Aires. Gleizer. 1927. Pp. 149. U-5694 D
Cases-Carbó, Joaquim. *Poesies Franciscano-Maragallianes.* Pròl. en francès Josep Baches. Barcelona. Llibr. Catalònia. 1934. Pp. xv, 171. U-2720 D
— *33 poesies hispàniques-internationals-intimes.* Barcelona. Llibr. Catalònia. 1936. Pp. 192. U-3222 n/o D
Casimiro, Augusto. *A evocação da vida.* Coimbra. Amado. 1912. Pp. 69. U-1682 D
Casona, Alejandro, pseud. [i.e., Alejandro Rodríguez Alvarez]. *La flauta del sapo. Poemas.* Valle de Arán. 1930. Pp. 66. U-4625 D
Cassou, Jean. *Panorama de la littérature espagnole contemporaine.* Paris. Kra. [1929]. Pp. 213. U-1943 I D. Ed. remaniée et augmentée. 1931. Pp. 192. U-5313 I D
— *Les nuits de Musset.* Paris. Emile-Paul. 1930. Pp. 213. U-3600 D
— *Comme une grande image. Roman.* Paris. Emile-Paul. 1931. Pp. 271. U-252 D
— *Grandeur et infamie de Tolstoï.* Paris. Grasset. 1932. Pp. 271. U-5316 I* C D
— *Souvenirs de la terre. Roman.* Paris. Corrêa. 1933. Pp. 189. U-5317 I* D
— *De l'Etoile au Jardin des Plantes.* Paris. Gallimard. 1935. Pp. 270. U-3447 D
— *Pour la poésie.* Paris. Corrêa. [1935]. Pp. 316. U-1733 I* D
Castañeda Aragón, G. *Máscaras de bronce.* Magdalena, Colombia. Magollón. 1916. Uc
Castelao, Alfonso. *Segundo libro de cousas.* Cruña. Nós. 1929. Pp. 55. U-5736 D
— *Cincoenta homes por dez reás.* Cruña. Nós. 1931. Pp. 52. U-5738 D
— *Os deus de sempre. Novela.* Santiago. Nós. 1934. Pp. 271. U-1397 I* L D
Castelar, Emilio. *Historia de un corazón.* Madrid. López. 1874. Pp. 279. U-4910

– *Correspondencia de Emilio Castelar.* Compilada Adolfo Calzado. Madrid. Rivadeneyra. 1908. Pp. viii, 439. U-664 I*

– *Recuerdos de Elda o Las fiestas de mi pueblo.* Elda. Moderna. 1932. Pp. 25. U-2173 C*

Castellá, Condesa del. *Poema del cisne y la princesa. Sonetos.* Madrid. Hernando. 1911. Uc D

Castellano, B. *Caminando.* Buenos Aires. Mercatali. 1923. Pp. 128. U-5518 D

Castellanos, Daniel. *Luz de otros soles. Anacreonte.* Pról. G. Marañon. Madrid. Rivadeneyra. 1936. Pp. 257. U-4172 D

Castellanos, Jesús. *De tierra adentro. Cuentos.* Habana. Cuba y América. 1906. Pp. vi, 202. U-3733 D

– *La conjura. Novela.* Madrid. Revista de Archivos. 1908. Pp. 310. U-2169

– *Los optimistas. Lecturas y opiniones, crítica de arte.* Habana. Avisador Comercial. 1914. Pp. 431. U-3754

Castellanos, Joaquín. *Labor dispersa.* Lausanne. Payot. 1909. Pp. 544. U-2207 D

– *El limbo. Poema dramatizado por Dharma.* Buenos Aires. Pellerano. 1914. Pp. 280. U-654 n/o D

– *Acción y pensamiento.* Buenos Aires. Pellerano. 1917. Pp. 452. U-2547 I* C D

– *Poemas viejos y nuevos.* Buenos Aires. Menéndez. 1926. Pp. 539. (2 copies) U-4982, U-5002

Castello Branco, Camillo. *Eusébio Macário.* Porto. Chardron. 1897. Uc

– *Sentimentalismo e historia.* Porto. Chardron. 1897. Pp. 286. U-3320

– *A mulher fatal. Romance.* Lisboa. Pereira. 1902. Pp. 212. U-3517 I

– *Novellas do Minho.* 3 vols. Lisboa. Pereira. 1903. U-3518-20. Vol. ii, I*. Vol. iii, I [U-5727, another copy of vol. iii]

– *Coisas espantosas. Romance.* Lisboa. Pereira. 1904. Pp. 225. U-2930

– *Obras de Camillo Castello Branco.* 7 vols. Lisboa. Pereira. 1902-7. U-2346-52 I* L B T

– *Scenas innocentes da comédia humana.* Lisboa. Pereira. 1908. Pp. 246. U-2931 I

– *Camillo inédito.* Pref. e anotaçoes Visconde de Villa-Moura. Pôrto. Renascença Portuguesa. 1913. Pp. 152. U-1917

Castelnuovo, Elias. *Teatro.* Buenos Aires. El Inca. 1929. Pp. 174. U-5482 D

Castillejo, Cristóbal de. *'Diálogo de mugeres. (1544).* Wieder abgedruckt von Ludwig Pfandl,' extrait de la *Revue Hispanique*, lii (1921). Pp. 67. U-2501

Castillo, Ricardo del, pseud. [i.e., Darío Rubio]. *Los llamados mexicanismos de la Academia Española.* México. Franco-Mexicana. 1917. Pp. 191. U-2266

Castillo Nájera, Francisco. *Un siglo de poesía belga.* Pról. J.J. Tablada. Madrid.
    Aguilar. 1931. Pp. xliv, 548. U-695 n/o D
    — *El gavilán. Corrido grande.* Paris. Estrella. 1934. Pp. 89. U-732
Castro, Alfonso. *Abismos sociales.* Medellin. Imp. Editorial. 1912. Pp. 103.
    U-4706 D
Castro, Américo. 'Más sobre Boquirrubio,' *Revista Filología Española,* VI
    (1919), 290-8. U-4929 D
Castro, Ernesto L. *Entre las sombras.* Buenos Aires. El Inca. 1928. Pp. 138.
    U-5532 D
Castro, Eugênio de. *Sagramor. Poema.* Coimbra. Amado. 1895. Pp. 126.
    U-1762 D
    — *O rei galaor. Poema dramatico.* Coimbra. Amado. 1897. Pp. 77. U-2884
    — *Belkiss, reina de Sabá, de Ascum y de Hymiar.* Tr. y crítica Luis Berisso.
    Discurso preliminar Leopoldo Lugones. Buenos Aires. Lajouane. 1899.
    Pp. xxxviii, 208. U-3620
    — *Constança. Poema.* Coimbra. Amado. 1900. Pp. 80. (2 copies) U-3382,
    U-3394 D. Tr. castellana F. Maldonado, pról. M. de Unamuno. Madrid.
    Revista de Archivos. 1913. Pp. 100. U-3393
    — *Poesias escolhidas. (1889-1900).* Paris. Aillaud. 1902. Pp. xxx, 231.
    U-1473 I D
    — *A sombra do quadrante.* Coimbra. Amado. 1906. Pp. 88. U-520 D
    — *O anel de Polycrates. Poema dramatico.* Coimbra. Amado. 1907. Pp. 130.
    U-525 D
    — *A fonte do Satyro e outros poemas.* Coimbra. Amado. 1908. Pp. 110.
    U-519 D
    — *O filho prodigo. Poema biblico.* Porto. Magalhães & Moniz. 1910. Pp. 37.
    U-553 D
    — *O cavaleiro das maos irresistíveis. Conto em verso.* Coimbra. Amado. 1916.
    Pp. 87. U-4696 D
    — *Canções deste negra vida.* Lisboa. Lumen. 1922. Pp. 120. U-3571 D
    — *A tentação de São Macário.* Lisboa. Lumen. 1922. Pp. 58. U-3403 D
    — *Obras completas. I. Oaristos. Horas.* Tr. castellana y ensayo J. González
    Olmedilla. Madrid. Castilla. 1922. Pp. xlii, 156. U-2858
    — *A mantilha de Madronhos. Impressoes e recordaçoes de Espanha.* Lisboa.
    Lumen. 1923. Pp. 112. U-4023 D
Castro, Guillen de. *Las mocedades del Cid.* Bonn. Weber. 1878. Uc
Castro, Horacio de. *Don Juan de Lanuza. Justicia Mayor de Aragón.* Madrid.
    Ed. Nuestra Raza. 1935. Pp. 183. U-1389 D
Castro, Mafalda de. *Botoes de rosa. Primeiros versos.* Coimbra. Lumen. 1923.
    Pp. 45. U-539 D
Castro, Rasalía de. *Obras completas. II. Cantares gallegos. III. Follas novas.*
    IV. El caballero de las botas azules. Madrid. Pueyo. 1909-11. U-1122-4.
    U-1122 I

Catalá, Víctor. *Solitut. Novela.* Barcelona. Joventut. 1905. Pp. 364.
U-1931 I T. *Soledad.* Tr. F.J. Garriga. Barcelona. Montaner y Simon.
1907. Pp. 381. U-679 C*
Catarineu, Ricardo J. *Madrigales y elegías.* Madrid. Renacimiento. 1913.
Pp. 214. U-3306 D
Catasús, Trinitat. *De l'hort i de la costa. Poesíes.* Sitges. El Eco. 1915. Pp. 150.
U-2251 D
— *Poemes del temps.* Barcelona. Altés. 1919. Pp. 121. U-3645 D
Caterina de Siena, Santa. *Libro della Divina Dottrina.* A cura di Matilde
Fiorilli. Bari. Laterza. 1912. Pp. 474. U-1824 I*
Cather, Willa. *A Lost Lady.* Leipzig. Tauchnitz. 1927. Pp. 263. U-5166 I L T
Catolicismo y protestantismo. Pastoral del Exmo. Sr Arzobispo de Montevideo.
Montevideo. Martínez. 1902. Pp. xxxii, 333. U-2837
Catullus, C. Valerius. *Catulli, Tibulli et Propertii Carmina* ad Praestantium
Librorum lectiones accurate recensuit C.H. Weise. Lipsiae. Tauchnitz.
1843. Pp. 272. U-4589 T*
— *Las poesías de Cayo Valerio Catulo.* Tr. Joaquín D. Casasus. México.
Escalante. 1905. Pp. 388. U-1717 I
Cavacchioli, Enrico. *Le ranocchie turchine.* Col manifesto del futurismo di
F.T. Marinetti. Milano. Edizioni di Poesia. 1909. Pp. 209. U-2697 D
Caváco, Carlos. *¡Ciego de amor!* Buenos Aires. Gadola. n.d. Pp. 60. U-5576 D
Caveda, José. *Poesías selectas en dialecto asturiano.* Oviedo. Brid. 1887.
Pp. 317. Uc
Ceballos, José G. *La nacionalización del poder naval y el concurso para la
escuadra.* Madrid. Perales y Martínez. 1908. Uc
Cecchi, Emilio. *La poesia di Giovanni Pascoli. Saggio critico.* Napoli.
Ricciardi. 1912. Pp. 151. U-2915
Cejador y Frauca, Julio. *Gramática griega según el sistema histórico-comparado.*
Barcelona. Henrich. 1900. Uc
— *Los gérmenes del lenguaje. Estudio fisiológico y psicológico de las voces
del lenguaje como base para la investigación de sus orígenes.* Bilbao. Soc.
Bilbaina de Artes Gráficas. 1902. Pp. vii, 504. U-4312 D
— *Embriogenia del lenguaje. Su estructura y formación.* Madrid. Hernández.
1904. Pp. xii, 575. U-899
— *Oro y oropel. Novela.* Madrid. Hernando. 1911. Uc D
Celedon, Anibal. *Cuestiones lingüísticas.* Santiago. Universitaria. [1907].
Pp. 189. U-3786
Cellini, Benvenuto. *La vita di Benvenuto Cellini scritta da lui medesimo
restituita esattamente alla lezione originale, con osservazioni filologiche e
brevi note dichiarative ad uso dei non Toscani.* Per cura di B. Bianchi.
Firenze. Le Monnier. 1903. Pp. viii, 626. U-532 I* B
— *La vita di Benvenuto Cellini* ad uso delle scuole, con note storiche, di lingua e
di stile, per cura di Orazio Bacci. Firenze. Sansoni. 1908. Pp. 203. U-2956 n/o

Cena, Giovanni. *Gli ammonitori. Romanzo.* Roma. Nuova Antologia. 1904.
Pp. 215. U-2102 D
— *Homo.* Con una composizione originale Leonardo Bistolfi. Roma. Nuova
Antologia. n.d. Pp. 136. U-3943 D
El centenario de la Batalla de Las Piedras (1811-1911). Montevideo. El Siglo
Ilustrado. 1912. Pp. 224. U-2516
Centenario de la reconquista de Ubeda, VII. 1234-1934. Programa guía oficial
de festejos. Feria de S. Miguel. 1934. Ff. 34. U-1631
Centenario de la Universidad de Buenos Aires. 1821-1921. Buenos Aires.
Rosso. 1921. Pp. 142. U-1645
Cento, V. *Religione e morale nel pensiero di Giovanni Gentile.* Roma.
Quaderni di Bilychnis. 1923. Pp. 92. U-682 n/o
The Century Magazine, civ, 4 (August 1922). U-820
Cerrejón, Simón. *Anticlericalismo del 'Quijote.'* Madrid. La Itálica. [1916].
Pp. 100. U-2889 D
Cervantes Saavedra, Miguel de. *El ingenioso hidalgo Don Quijote de la Mancha.*
4 vols. 4a ed. corregida por la Real Academia Española. Madrid. 1819.
U-2657-60 I C. Ed. reducida y compulsada D. Eduardo Vicenti. Madrid.
Hernández. 1905. Pp. 468. U-5105 n/o. Ed. y notas F. Rodríguez Marín.
8 vols. Madrid. La Lectura. 1911. (cc, 4, 6, 8, 10, 13, 16, 19, 22).
U-922-9 I C
— *Don Quijote. Den Skarpsindige adelsmand Don Quijote av la Mancha.*
Oversat fra Spansk av Nils Kyaer og Magnus Grφnvold. 2 vols. Kristiania.
Cammermeyer. 1916. U-712-13 T
— *The Visionary Gentleman Don Quijote de la Mancha.* Tr. Robinson Smith.
2 vols. New York. Hispanic Society of America. 1932. U-698-9
— *Novelas ejemplares.* 2 vols. Madrid. Saiz. 1883. U-3344-5 I*
— *Poesías de Cervantes.* Compiladas y prol. Ricardo Rojas. Buenos Aires.
Coni. 1916. Pp. cii, 530. U-910 I
— *Rinconete and Cortadillo.* Tr. Mariano J. Lorente. Pref. R.B. Cunninghame
Graham. Boston. Four Seas Co. 1917. Pp. 152. U-2723
— *Trabajos de Persiles y Segismunda.* 2 vols. Madrid. Universal. 1920. n/n I*C L
A Cervantes en su tercer centenario. Buenos Aires. Homenaje del Instituto
Argentino de Artes Gráficas. 1916. Ff. 14. U-2491
Cervera, Manuel M. *Historia de la ciudad y provincia de Santa Fé (1573-1853).*
2 vols. Santa Fe. La Unión. 1907. U-4144-5 n/o D
Cervesato, Arnaldo. *Primavera di idee nella vita moderna.* Bari. Laterza. 1904.
Pp. 271. U-4317
— *Piccolo libro degli eroi d'occidente.* Roma. La Nuova Parola. 1907. Pp. 164.
U-3909 D
César (Caius Julius Caesar). *Commentaires sur la guerre des Gaules. Livres
I-IV.* Expliqués littéralement, tr. en français, et annotés E. Sommer. Paris.
Hachette. n.d. Pp. 387. OP-10 I*

Cesareo, G.A. *Conversazioni letterarie.* Catania. Giannotta. 1899. Pp. 187.
U-1544

Césped, M. *Símbolos profanos.* Buenos Aires. Mercatali. 1924. Pp. 116.
U-5762 D

Cestero, Tulio M. *El jardín de los sueños.* Santo Domingo. La Cuna de
América. 1904. Pp. 84. U-2766 D

— *Citerea.* Madrid. Rodríguez Serra. 1907. Pp. 94. U-4576 n/o D

— *Ciudad romántica. Escenas de Santo Domingo de Guzmán la primada.*
Paris. Ollendorff. [1911]. Pp. 212 U-3298 n/o

— *Hombres y piedras. Al margen del Baedeker.* Pról. Rubén Darío. Madrid.
Soc. Española de Librería. [1915]. Pp. 304. U-3096

— *Rubén Darío. El hombre y el poeta.* Habana. Bibl. del Heraldo de Cuba.
1916. Pp. 19. U-3730 D

Cetineo, Ante. *Laste nad uvalom.* Split. Izdanje Korablje. 1935. Pp. 62.
U-2661 D

Chaboseau, A. *Les Serbes, Croates et Slovènes.* Paris. Bossard. 1919. Pp. 110.
U-3379

Chabret, Antonio. *Sagunto. Su historia y sus monumentos.* 2 vols. Barcelona.
Ramírez. 1888. U-691-2 n/o D

Chabrillon, Andrés. *A la luz de una sombra.* Poesías. n.p. n.d. Uc

Chacon Trejos, Gonzalo. *Maquiavelo: maquiavelismo del presidente Ricardo
Jiménez. A-maquiavelismo del presidente Alfredo González.* San José de
Costa Rica. Trejos. 1935. Pp. 64. U-5480

Chadwick, French Ensor. *Causes of the Civil War, 1859-1861.* New York.
Harper. 1906. Pp. xiv, 372. U-4818 I C

Chagas, João. *Cartas políticas.* Lisboa. Bayard. [1909]. Pp. 320. U-1812 I D

Chalas, Antonios. *Ta satyrika gymnasmata tou Kosta Palama ke e sokratike
paradosis.* Istambul. Beyoglu. 1933. Pp. 272. U-2260

Chamberlain, Basil Hall. *Things Japanese, Being Notes on Various Subjects
Connected with Japan.* London. Murray. 1905. Pp. iv, 552. U-4186 I* C B*

Chamberlain, John. *El atraso de España.* Tr. Cazalla. Valencia. Sempere.
[c.1909]. Pp. 298. U-3197 D

Chambon, Henry de. *Origines et histoire de la Lettonie.* Préf. M. Noulens.
Paris. Mercure Universel. 1933. Pp. xii, 221. U-1807

Chamisso de Boncourt, Adelbert von. *Gedichte von Adelbert von Chamisso.*
Mit biographischer Einleitung von Otto S. Lachmann. Leipzig. Reclam.
n.d. Pp. xvi, 431. U-4577 T

— *Peter Schlemihl's wundersame Geschichte.* Leipzig. Reclam. n.d. Pp. 72.
U-4555 T*

Champsaur y Sicilia. *Nueva religiosidad.* Laguna de Tenerife. Curbelo. 1913.
Uc D

— *Mi muerta.* Laguna de Tenerife. Curbelo. 1914. Uc D

Channing, William Ellery. *The Complete Works of W.E. Channing. Including The Perfect Life.* London. Christian Life. 1884. Pp. 637, xxi. U-5772 I

Charnwood, Godfrey Rathbone Benson. *Abraham Lincoln.* New York. Henry Holt. 1917. Pp. vi, 482. U-5188 I* C

Chase, Gilbert. *Cities and Souls. Poems of Spain.* Chartres. Durand. 1929. Pp. 124. (4 copies) U-605, U-3602, U-5153, U-5154 D

Chassang, A. *Nouveau dictionnaire grec-français.* Paris. Garnier. 1889. Pp. xii, 126 + 1168

Chaverra, Gaspar. *Rara Avis ... Novela.* Medellín. Restrepo. 1911. Uc

Chaves Arias, Luis. *Las cajas rurales de crédito del sistema Raiffeisen.* (Conferencia). Zamora. José. 1906. Uc D

Chávez y Aliaga, Nazario. *Parábolas del Ande.* Cajamarca. 'El Perú.' 1928. Ff. 63. U-5757

Chénier, André. *Oeuvres poétiques ...* Paris. Dentu. 1884. Pp. xii, 304. U-515

Chesterton, Gilbert Keith. *Letters to an Old Garibaldian.* London. Methuen. 1915. Pp. 48. U-559 I

– *Ortodoxia.* Tr. A. Reyes. Madrid. Calleja. 1917. Pp. 315. U-4333

– *Dickens.* Tr. Achille Laurent et L. Martin-Dupont. Paris. Gallimard. 1927. Pp. 212. QP-11 I

Chevalier, Jacques. *La notion du nécessaire chez Aristote et ses prédécesseurs particulièrement chez Platon.* Paris. Alcan. 1915. Pp. 304. U-1262 C* B D

– *Etude critique du dialogue pseudo-platonicien l'Axiochous sur la mort et l'immortalité de l'âme.* Paris. Alcan. 1915. Pp. 144. U-847 D

– *Descartes.* Paris. Plon-Nourrit. 1921. Pp. vii, 362. U-2089 C* I* D

– *Pascal.* Paris. Plon-Nourrit [1922]. Pp. viii, 386. U-3720 I C B D

– 'Les deux conceptions de la morale,' extrait du *Bulletin de l'Académie des Sciences morales et politiques* (1922). Pp. 19. U-3075 D

– *Essai sur la formation de la nationalité et les réveils religieux au pays de Galles, des origines à la fin du 6ième siècle.* Paris. Alcan. 1923. Pp. xxxviii, 439. U-2990 I C D

– *Bergson.* Paris. Plon-Nourrit [1926]. Pp. xii, 317. U-5277 I C

– *La forêt. Tronçais en Bourbonnais.* Paris. Chronique des Lettres Françaises. 1930. Pp. 122. U-4119

Chiappelli, Alessandro. *El socialismo y el pensamiento moderno.* Tr. M. Domenge Mir. 2 vols. Barcelona. Henrich. 1905. Uc

– *Voces de nuestro tiempo. Ensayos sociales.* Tr. M. Domenge Mir. 2 vols. Barcelona. Henrich. 1908. Uc

– *Amore, morte ed immortalitá.* Milano. Albrighi, Segati. 1913. Pp. 184. U-3942 D

Chiesa, Eugenio. *La situation politique financière et économique en Italie.* Paris. Ed. de la Concentrazione Antifascista. 1929. Pp. 45. U-5251

Chirveches, Armando. *Flor del trópico.* Paris. Excelsior. 1926. Pp. 189. U-4891 D

— *A la vera del mar. Novela.* Paris. Ed. Paris-América. 1926. Pp. 225.
U-5673 D

Choromanski, Michel. *Médecine et jalousie. Roman.* Tr. le comte Jacques de
France de Tersant et Joseph-André Teslar. Paris. Société Française
d'Editions Littéraires et Techniques. 1934. Pp. 266. U-5314 I

Christ, E. *Héroes españoles de la fe. Cuadros de la reforma.* Madrid. Libr.
Nacional y Extranjera. n.d. Pp. 340. U-281

Christ in Us. A Book of Verse. Oxford. 1935. Pp. 46. U-4155

Chuang-Tzu. *Wisdom of the East. Musings of a Chinese Mystic. Selections
from the Philosophy of Chuang-Tzu.* Introd. Lionel Giles. London.
Murray. [1927]. Pp. 112. U-369 I* C

Chueco, Manuel C. *La república Argentina en su primer centenario.* 2 vols.
Buenos Aires. Cía. Sud-Americana de Billetes de Banco. 1910.
U-3527-8 D

— *Solidaridad. Novela.* Buenos Aires. Martín García. 1912. Uc D

Church, R.W. *The Oxford Movement. Twelve years 1833-1845.* London.
MacMillan. 1909. Pp. xv, 416. U-370 I*

Cibils, José. *Ondas de luz.* Santa Fé. El Nuevo Día. 1909. Uc D

Ciccotti, E. *El ocaso de la esclavitud en el mundo antiguo.* Tr. Domenge Mir.
Barcelona. Henrich. 1907. Uc

Ciccotti, Francesco. *Re Vittorio e il Fascismo.* Toulouse. Exoria. n.d. Pp. 110.
U-5348 I*

Cicéronis, M.T. *De officiis ad Marcum filium Libri tres.* Ed. classique publiée
avec des sommaires et des notes en français H. Marchand. Paris. Hachette.
n.d. Pp. 202. QP-12 I

Las cien mejores poesías españolas. Pref. y selección Fernando Maristany.
Barcelona. Cervantes. 1921. Pp. 200 n/n D

Ciencia social. Revista de sociología, artes y letras. 1 (oct. 1895) a 9 (junio
1896). Uc

Ciges Aparicio, M. *El libro de la crueldad. Del cuartel y de la guerra.* Madrid.
Rodríguez. [1906]. Pp. 423. U-4461

— *El libro de la vida doliente. Del hospital.* Madrid. n.d. Uc

Cilly. See Carbonara, Francesco

Cimbali, G. *El derecho del más fuerte.* Tr. J. Buixó Monserda. 2 vols.
Barcelona. Henrich. 1906. Uc

Cione, Otto Miguel. *Lauracha. La vida en la estancia. Novela.* Buenos Aires.
Checchi. 1906. Uc D

Cirot, Georges. *Etudes sur l'historiographie espagnole. Mariana, historien.*
Bordeaux. Feret. 1905. Pp. xiv, 481. U-665 D

— *Les histoires générales d'Espagne entre Alphonse X et Philippe II.*
Bordeaux. Feret. 1904. Pp. xi, 180. U-694 D

Clar Margarit, María Francisca (Halma Angélico, pseud.). *La nieta de Fedra.*
Pról. Alejandro Bher. Madrid. Velasco. 1929. Pp. 201. U-5122 D

— Santas que pecaron. Psicología del pecado de amor en la mujer. Madrid.
    Aguilar. 1935. Pp. 265. U-254 I* D
Clare, Dardo E. Relación Chaqueña. Durazno, Uruguay. La Aurora. 1926.
    Pp. 91. U-5102 D
Claudel, Paul Louis Charles Marie. L'annonce faite à Marie. Mystère en quatre
    actes et un prologue. Paris. Nouvelle Revue Française. 1913. Pp. 210.
    U-1372 I*
— Cinq grandes odes. Paris. Nouvelle Revue Française. 1913. Pp. 204.
    U-1373 I T
Clausen, Jul., og Paul Levin. Dansk Litteraturhistorie. København.
    Salmonsen. 1894. Pp. 234. U-4294
Clavijero, Francisco Javier. Historia antigua de Méjico sacada de los mejores
    historiadores españoles. Escrita en italiano. Tr. Francisco Pablo Vázquez.
    México. Navarro. 1853. Pp. x, 439, v. U-1193
Clemens, Alexandrinus. Herausgegeben von der Kirchenväter-commission der
    Königl. Preussischen Akademie der Wissenschaften von Dr Otto Stählin.
    3 vols. Leipzig. Hinrichs'sche. 1905-9. Die griechischen christlichen
    Schriftsteller des ersten drei Jahrhunderte. U-1289-91 I* C* T*
Clemente Romeo, Esteban. Fronda latina. Lisboa. Lumen. 1922. Pp. 302.
    U-592 n/o D
— Jardín lírico. Devocionario de amor. Bilbao. Ed. Vasca. 1923. Pp. xi, 222.
    U-3305 D
El clero argentino de 1810 a 1830. 2 vols. Buenos Aires. Museo Histórico
    Nacional. 1907. U-4295-6
Clifton, E.C., et Adrien Grimaux. Nouveau dictionnaire anglais-français et
    français-anglais. Paris. Garnier. n.d. Pp. xiv, 1062. n/n
Closa, Cándido. Haciendas locales. Tarrasa. La Industrial. n.d. Pp. 74.
    U-1602 D
Clouard, Henri. La destinée tragique de Gérard de Nerval. Paris. Grasset.
    1929. Pp. xii, 254. U-405 I D
Club Alpino Español. Memoria 1911-1912. U-2500
Cobbett, William. Rural Rides. Introd. Edward Thomas. 2 vols. London. Dent.
    [1912]. U-967-8 I*
Cobos, Pablo de A. Estampas de aldea. Literatura para los niños. Madrid.
    Escuelas de España. 1935. Pp. 138. U-4635 D
Cochrane, Thomas, 10th Earl of Dundonald. Memorias de Lord Cochrane.
    Madrid. Ed. América. [1916]. Pp. 301. U-3021
Cocteau, Jean. Le rappel à l'ordre. Le coq et l'arlequin. Carte blanche, etc.
    Paris. Stock. 1926. Pp. 296. U-5303
Codera, Francisco. Estudios críticos de historia árabe española. Zaragoza.
    Uriarte. 1903. Pp. xvi, 372. U-4618
Codex Iuris Canonici. Pii x Pontificis Maximi iussu digestus Benedicti Papae
    xv. Romae. Vaticanis. 1917. Pp. xxxii, 870. U-1327

Coelho, António José de Castro de Azevedo Fernandes. *A Senhora do Socorro de São Felix da Marinha. Versos.* Porto. 1917. Pp. 14. U-1707 D

Coelho de Carvalho, Joaquim José. *O grande doutor. Psicose do Fausto.* Lisboa. Lucas. 1926. Pp. 391. U-5740 D

Coelho Lisboa, Rosalina. *O desencantado encantamento.* Sao Paulo. Compañia Editora Nacional. 1927. Pp. 189. U-5723 D

Cogliolo, Pietro. *Storia del Diritto Privato Romano.* 2 vols. Firenze. Barbèra. 1889. U-1424-5

– *Filosofia del Diritto Privato.* Firenze. Barbèra. 1891. Pp. 226. U-1540

Cohen, Gustave. *Le théâtre en France au moyen âge. I. Théâtre religieux.* Paris. Rieder. [1928]. Pp. 75, pl. 59. U-5252

Cohen, Hermann. *System der Philosophie. I. Logik der reinen Erkenntniss.* Berlin. Cassirer. 1902. Pp. xvii, 520. U-1259 I* C*

Coimbra, Leonardo. *O criacionismo.* Pôrto. Renascença Portuguesa. 1912. Pp. 311. U-1755 D

– *O pensamento criacionista.* Pôrto. Renascença Portuguesa. [1912]. Pp. 220. U-3319 D

– *A morte.* Conferência. Pôrto. Renascença Portuguesa. 1913. Pp. 114. U-3318 D

– *A alegria, a dôr e a graça.* Pôrto. Renascença Portuguesa. 1916. Pp. 325. U-479 D

– *A luta pela imortalidade.* Pôrto. Renascença Portuguesa. 1918. Pp. 267. U-2020 D

– *Adoração. Cânticos de amor.* Pôrto. Renascença Portuguesa. [1921]. Pp. 116. U-2403 D

– *A Rússia de hoje e o homem de sempre.* Pôrto. Tavares Martins. 1935. Pp. 484. U-2012 D

Colajanni, N. *Razas superiores y razas inferiores o latinas y anglo-sajonas.* Versión española y pról. José Buixó Monserdá. 3 vols. Barcelona. Henrich. 1904. Uc

Colecção de manuscriptos ineditos agora dados a estampa. III. Fastigimia Thomé Pinheiro da Veiga. Pôrto. Bibliotheca Publica Municipal do Porto. 1911. Pp. 374. U-4141 I

Colección de entremeses, Loas, Bailes, Jácaras y Mojigangas desde fines del siglo XVI a mediados del siglo XVIII. Ed. y estudio preliminar E. Cotarelo y Mori. 2 vols. (NBAE, 17-18). Madrid. Bailly-Baillière. 1911. U-52-3

Colección de poesías castellanas anteriores al siglo XV. 2 vols. Madrid. A. de Sancha. 1780-2. U-162-3 I

Coleridge, Samuel Taylor. *Confessions of an Inquiring Spirit, to Which Are Added Miscellaneous Essays From 'The Friend.'* London-Paris. Cassell. 1892. Uc

— *The Poetical Works of S.T. Coleridge.* Reprinted from the early editions.
   London. F. Warne & Co. 1893. Pp. xxi, 680. U-167 I* C* T
— *Biographia Literaria.* Introd. Arthur Symons. London. Dent. 1906.
   Pp. xv, 334. U-1064 I*
— *Coleridge's Essays and Lectures on Shakespeare and some other Old Poets
   and Dramatists.* London. Dent. [1907]. Pp. xvi, 479. U-1022 I
Coll, Pedro-Emilio. *El castillo de Elsinor.* Caracas. Herrera Irigoyen. 1901.
   Pp. 129. U-3175 I D
— *La escondida senda. Años de aprendizaje de Simón Bolívar,* etc. Madrid.
   Espasa Calpe. 1927. Pp. 140. U-5043 C D
Colle, Elio M.A. *El drama del Paraguay.* Buenos Aires. Col. Claridad. [1936].
   Pp. 157. U-2765 n/o D
Collin-d'Ambly, François, and F. Trémery. *Nouveau manuel complet
   d'arithméque.* Paris. Roret. 1845. Pp. 331 + 90. U-4594
Colmo, Alfredo. *Principios sociólogicos.* Buenos Aires. Biedma. 1905. Uc D
— *Sobre didáctica del derecho civil.* Liverpool. Birchall. 1913. Pp. 135.
   U-3679 D
— *La cultura jurídica y la Facultad de Derecho.* Buenos Aires. Otero. 1915.
   Uc D
— *Los países de la América latina.* Madrid. Reus. 1915. Uc
— *Bases de organización universitaria en los países americanos.* Buenos Aires.
   Revista de Filosofía. 1917. Pp. 120. U-2998 D
— *La justicia.* Precedida de una nota biográfica sobre el autor por Agustín
   Rivero Astengo. Buenos Aires. Rosso. 1936. Pp. 189. U-3705
Coloma, Luis. *Pequeñeces.* Bilbao. El Mensajero del Corazón de Jesús. 1921.
   Pp. 605. U-401
— *Cuentos para niños.* Bilbao. El Mensajero del Corazón de Jesús. n.d.
   Pp. 120. U-596
Colominas, J.V. See Vallmitjana, Julio
Colorado, Vicente. *Besos y mordiscos.* Madrid. Fortanet. 1887. Pp. 277.
   U-2861
— *Francisca de Rímini. Obra dramática. El acta. Comedia.* Madrid. Fé. 1897.
   Pp. 211. U-3383
— *Teatro.* Carta Pedro Antonio de Alarcón y crítica Manuel Cañete. Madrid.
   Fé. 1897. Pp. 223. U-3370
Comes y Sorribes, José. *Aires de Fora.* Conferencia. Lleyda. Pagés. 1909.
   Pp. 16. U-4325
Comisión Consultiva para la transformación del impuesto de Consumos.
   Documentos y trabajos. Madrid. Minuesa de los Ríos. 1908. Uc
Comisión extra-parlamentaria para la transformación del impuesto de
   consumos. *Dictamen de la ponencia.* Madrid. Minuesa de los Ríos. 1906.
   Uc

Comisión provincial de la Cruz Roja de Barcelona. *Oro y plata.* Barcelona.
Cunill. 1912. Pp. vii, 296. U-2036 n/o
Compte y Riqué, Enriqueta. *Lecciones de mi escuela.* Montevideo. Nacional
Colorada. 1933. Pp. 240. U-5037 D
— *Estudio y trabajo.* Impresión realizada como homenaje a la gran maestra.
Montevideo. Nacional Colorada. 1933. Pp. 470. U-4950 D
Conangla Fontanilles, J. *Elegía de la guerra. Poesías. Impresions de la guerra
de Cuba.* Pref. Joan Maragall. Barcelona. Tip. Catalana. 1904. Pp. 110.
U-285 n/o D
Concha, José Vicente. *Tratado del derecho penal y comentarios al código
penal colombiano.* Paris. Ollendorff. Uc
Conde y Luque, Rafael. *Oficios del derecho internacional privado.* Madrid.
Alvarez. 1901. Pp. vii, 577. U-2581
Congregational Quarterly. (July 1925). n/n
Congreso de Estudios Vascos, Oñate, 1918. Bilbao. Rochelet. 1918. Ff. 16.
U-3932
Congreso General de Enseñanza pública de 1902. *Actas y Trabajos.* Santiago
de Chile. Imp. Barcelona. 1904. Pp. 700. U-3534
Conkling, Alfred R. *El gobierno municipal.* Tr. F. Carrera y Justiz. Pról.
Pablo Desvernine. New York. Appleton. 1900. Pp. lxii, 243. U-1941.
Constant de Rebecque, Benjamin. *Adolphe.* Introd. Paul Bourget. Paris.
Crès-Dent. [1914]. Pp. xix, 180. QP-13 I
Constitución de la República de Guatemala. Guatemala, C.A. Secretaría
de Gobernación y Justicia. 1928. Pp. 104. U-2851
Constitución política de la República de Centroamérica. Guatemala. Imp.
Nacional La Instrucción. [1921]. Pp. 118. U-2447
Constituciones Baiulie Mirabeti. Ed. Galo Sánchez. Madrid. Residencia de
Estudiantes. 1915. Pp. xix, 44. U-4137
Contadino, Fausto. *Virgia evangélica spirito della follìa. Poemi e canti di
passione.* Torino. Il Pensiero Contemporaneo. 1924. Pp. 366. U-1253 n/o
Contreras, Francisco. *Los modernos.* Paris. Ollendorff. 1909. Pp. xvi, 290.
U-1972 D
— *Romances de hoy.* Paris. Garnier. n.d. Uc
Cook, Sir Edward Tyas. *Por qué está en guerra la Gran Bretaña. Causas y
cuestiones en disputa.* Expuestas en forma breve. Edimburgo. Nelson.
n.d. Pp. 19. U-5578
Cordeiro, José. *Farrapos.* Lisboa. Silva. 1908. Pp. 114. U-1863 D
Cordero, Juan Luis. *Mi torre de Babel. Poesías.* Cáceres. El Noticiero.
1908. Uc D
— *La tragedia del héroe. Poemas.* Pasajes. [1915]. Pp. 86. (2 copies)
U-1608, U-2805 D
— *Mi patria y mi dama.* Poesías. Barcelona. Maucci. Uc

Corneille, Pierre. *Théâtre de Corneille.* Paris. Hachette. n.d. Pp. 353. U-357
Cornejo, Mariano H. *Sociología general.* Pról. José Echegaray. 2 vols. Madrid.
    Hernández. 1908-10. U-4146-7 D
Corominas, Pere. *Les presons imaginàries.* Barcelona. L'Avenç. 1899. Pp. xx,
    242. U-3938 D
—   *Las prisiones imaginarias.* Madrid. Rodríguez Serra. 1900. Pp. 217.
    U-3312 D
—   *La vida austera.* Barcelona. L'Avenç. 1908. Pp. 359. U-2717 D. Tr. G.
    Martínez Sierra. Madrid. Renacimiento. 1916. Pp. 415. U-3901 D
—   *Les hores d'amor serenes.* Barcelona. L'Avenç. 1912. Pp. 190. U-3060 D
—   *Método para elevar las pensiones.* Barcelona. 1914. Uc D
—   *El sentimiento de la riqueza en Castilla.* Madrid. Residencia de
    Estudiantes. 1917. Pp. 251. n/n I D
—   *Cartes d'un visionari.* Barcelona. López. 1921. Pp. 297. U-3372 I* C D
Corral, Andrés. *Extracto de las dos causas formadas por la Inquisición de
    Valladolid contra el Maestro Francisco de las Brozas.* Transcripción y
    notas preliminares Miguel de la Pinta Llorente. Madrid. Monasterio de
    El Escorial. 1934. Pp. 105. U-4177 I
Correa Calderón, Evaristo. *El milano y la rosa. Novela.* Lugo. Ronsel. 1924.
    Pp. 94. U-5570 D
—   *Notas para un magisterio idealista.* Lugo. Castro. 1927. Pp. 54. U-5607 D
—   *Intuición del romanticismo. Conferencia.* Almería. Moya. 1936. Pp. 67.
    U-5679
Correa Luna, Carlos. *Don Baltasar de Arandia.* Buenos Aires. Coni. 1915. Uc
Correa Oliver, Miguel. *Tratado elemental de meteoreología.* 2 vols. Madrid.
    García. 1909. U-762-3
Correa Robín. *Voces del ambato.* Poesías. Catamarca. 'El debate.' 1909. Uc D
Corredor la Torre, Jorge. *L'Eglise romaine dans l'Amérique latine.* Paris.
    Giard et Briere. 1910. Pp. 442. U-320 D
Correia de Campos. *Mundo novo que surge.* Pôrto. Imprensa Portuguesa.
    1935. Pp. vii, 319. U-1122 D
Correia de Oliveira, António. *Raiz. 1898-1903.* Coimbra. Amado. [1903].
    Pp. 234. U-845 D
—   *Auto do fim do dia.* Paris. Aillaud. 1900. Pp. 71. U-4598 D
—   *Allivio de tristes.* Paris. Aillaud. 1901. Pp. 74. U-4597 n/o D
—   *Cantigas.* Lisboa. Ferin. 1902. Ff. 17. U-5732 n/o D
—   *Ara.* Lisboa. Ferreira & Oliveira. 1904. Pp. 153. U-2904 D
—   *Parábolas.* Lisboa. Ferreira & Oliveira. 1905. Pp. 190. U-4316
—   *Tentações de Sam Frei Gil.* Lisboa. Ferreira & Oliveira. 1907. Pp. 173.
    U-2091 D
—   *O Pinheiro exilado.* Lisboa. Ferreira. 1907. Pp. 20. U-1648 D
—   *Elogio dos sentidos.* Porto. Magalhães & Moniz. 1908. Pp. 136. U-786 D

– *Auto das quatro estações.* Lisboa. Cernadas. 1911. Pp. 210. U-3247 D
– *Dizêres do pôvo.* Emposende. Silva Vieira. [1911]. Pp. 148. U-4571 D
– *A Criação. I. Vida e historia da arvore.* Viana. Modelo. 1913. Pp. 218.
   U-2056 D
– *Alma religiosa.* Porto. Magalhães & Moniz. n.d. Pp. 238. U-4652 D
Correspondance. Paris (15 sept. 1913). n/n
Correspondencia de la ciudad de Buenos Aires con los reyes de España.
   Reunida en el Archivo de Indias, coordinada, y publicada Roberto
   Levillier. 3 vols. Buenos Aires. Bibl. del Congreso Argentino. 1915.
   (2 copies of vol. I) U-2971-4
*Correspondencia de los oficiales reales de Hacienda del Río de la Plata con
   los reyes de España.* Reunida en el Archivo de Indias de Sevilla, coordinada,
   y publicada Roberto Levillier. Madrid. Rivadeneyra. 1915. (2 copies vol. I)
   U-4201-2 n/o
Cortes, Manuel Ll. *Almas esclavas: Novela.* 1931. Pp. 248. U-1471 D
   [Typescript].
Cortesão, Jaime. *Cancioneiro popular.* Porto. Renascença Portuguesa. 1914.
   Pp. 186. U-2373
Corthis, André. *Pèlerinages en Espagne.* Paris. Fasquelle. 1930. Pp. 207.
   U-3499 D
Cortines y Murube, F. *De Andalucía. Rimas.* Sevilla. Izquierdo. 1908. Uc D
– *Nuevas rimas.* Madrid. Suárez. 1911. Pp. 227. U-1470 D
Cortón, Antonio. *Espronceda.* Madrid. Colec. Autores Célebres. 1906.
   Pp. 315. U-945 C D
– *El fantasma del separatismo. Escenas de la vida barcelonesa.* Valencia.
   Sempere. n.d. Pp. ix, 253. U-3196 D
Corvaglia, Luigi. *S. Teresa e Aldonzo.* Commedia in quattro atti. Bologna.
   Cappelli. 1931. Pp. 134. U-2496
Cossío, José Ma. de. *Epístolas para amigos.* Valladolid. Montero. 1920.
   Pp. 107. U-4715
– *La obra literaria de Pereda, su historia y su crítica.* Santander. Martínez.
   1934. Pp. 408. n/n I* C D
Cossío, Manuel B. See Bartolomé y Cossío, Manuel
Cosson, Alfredo. *Trozos selectos de literatura y método de composición
   literaria.* 3 vols. Buenos Aires. Rivadavia. 1912. U-1763-5
Costa, Giovanni. *Diocleziano.* Roma. Formiggini. 1920. Pp. 77.
   U-1548 I* C* D
Costa, Julio A. *El presidente.* [Buenos Aires]. Rossó. [1913]. Pp. 170.
   U-2427
Costa Alvarez, Arturo. *El castellano en la Argentina.* La Plata. San Vicente de
   Paul. 1928. Pp. 350. U-4944 C* L* D

Costa Figueiras, José. *La risa de Dios. Novela.* Pról. Francisco de la Escalera.
     Buenos Aires. Virgilio Guerra. 1913. Uc D
Costa y Llobera, Miquel. *Tradicions y fantasías.* Barcelona. Edició Catalunya.
     [1903]. Pp. 202. U-4489
Costa y Martínez, Joaquín. *Colectivismo agrario en España. Partes I y II,
     doctrinas y hechos.* Madrid. San Francisco de Sales. 1898. Pp. 606.
     U-4133
 − *Reconstitución y europización de España.* Madrid. 1900. Pp. xxvi, 366. Uc
 − *Oligarquía y caciquismo como la actual forma de gobierno en España:
     urgencia y modo de cambiarla.* Madrid. Hernández. 1903. Uc
Coster, A. 'Une description inédite de la demeure de Don Vincencio Juan de
     Lastanosa,' extrait de la *Revue Hispanique*, xxvi (1912), pp. 49.
     U-1703 D
 − 'Baltasar Gracián (1601-1658),' extrait de la *Revue Hispanique,* xxix
     (1913), 347-754. U-1249 I* C
 − 'Corneille, a-t-il connu *El Héroe* de Baltasar Gracián?' extrait de la
     Revue Hispanique, xlvi (1919), 569-72. U-2508 D
 − 'A propos d'un manuscrit des poésies de Luis de León,' extrait de la
     Revue Hispanique, xlvi (1919), 573-82. U-2509 D
 − 'Notes pour une édition des poésies de Luis de León,' extrait de la
     Revue Hispanique, xlvi (1919), 193-248. U-683 D
 − *Luis de León. 1528-1591.* New York. *Revue Hispanique,* liii (1921), liv
     (1922). U-4200 I* D
 − *Album de Luis de Leon.* Chartres. Lester. 1923. Pl. 6. U-2492 D
Coster, Dirk. *Wege zum leben.* Aphorismen ... Einleitung von Emil Lucka.
     Wien. König. [1923]. Pp. 288. U-5405 D
Cotarelo y Mori, Emilio. *Don Francisco de Rojas Zorrilla.* Noticias biográficas
     y bibliográficas. Madrid. Rev. de Archivos. 1911. Pp. 311. U-947
Cotta, Juan Manuel. *Laureles.* Pról. Ramón Melgar. Buenos Aires. Ivaldi &
     Checchi. 1913. Pp. 96. U-571 D
 − *Arpegios. Poesías.* La Plata. Olivieri y Domínguez. 1918. Pp. 167.
     U-2772 D
 − *Poemas heroicos.* Buenos Aires. Moen. 1923. Pp. 80. U-4880 D
 − *Briznas, surcos y evocaciones. Poesías.* Buenos Aires. Tor. [1924]. Pp. 156.
     U-5664 D
Couchoud, Paul-Louis. *Sages et poètes d'Asie.* Préf. Anatole France. Paris.
     Calmann-Lévy. 1923. Pp. 229. U-5276 I* C D
 − *Le mystère de Jésus.* Paris. Rieder. 1924. Pp. 186. U-5323 I
 − 'La première édition de Saint Paul,' *Revue de l'histoire des Religions.*
     Paris (1926). U-5264 D
Coudenhove-Kalergi, R.N. *Héros ou saint.* Tr. M. Beaufils. Paris. Rieder.
     1929. Pp. 226. U-5309

Couperus, Louis. *De Stille kracht.* 2 vols. Amsterdam. Veen. [1900].
U-2135-6 I* T

Courier, Paul-Louis. *Lettres et pamphlets.* Paris. Vanier. 1876. Pp. 320.
U-2027 I* C*

— *Lettere dall' Italia (1799-1812).* Tr., pref., e note Giovanni Rabizzani.
Lanciano. Carabba. 1910. Pp. 144. U-2103 n/o

Cournot, Antoine-Augustin. *Traité de l'enchaînement des idées fondamen-
tales dans les sciences et dans l'histoire.* Avertissement L. Lévy-Bruhl.
Paris. Hachette. 1911. Pp. xviii, 712. U-1795 I*

— *Essai sur les fondements de nos connaissances et sur les caractères de la
critique philosophique.* Paris. Hachette. 1912. Pp. vii, 614. U-1788 I

Cowper, William. *The Poetical Works of William Cowper.* Ed. with notes and
biographical introd. William Benham. London. MacMillan. 1889.
Pp. lxxiii, 536. U-150 I* C* T

Craik, George Lillie. *Manual of English Literature.* London. Dent. [1909].
Pp. xii, 356. U-1023

Crashaw, Richard. *The Poems of Richard Crashaw.* Ed. J.R. Tutin. Introd.
Canon Beeching. London. Routledge. [1905]. Pp. lv, 301. U-450

Crespo y Martínez, Gilberto. *En México y Cuba. Datos para varios estudios.*
Habana. Avisador Comercial. 1905. Pp. 224. U-1355 D

Crexells, Juan. *Assaigs de Joan Crexells.* Ed. J. Estelrich y C. Riba. Barcelona.
Libreria Catalonia. 1933. Pp. 215. U-4367

Criminología argentina. Reseña bibliográfica. Precedida de un estudio sobre
el problema penal argentino por el Dr Eusebio Gómez. Buenos Aires.
Libr. Europea. 1912. Pp. lviii, 286. U-4204 n/o

Crisógono de Jesús Sacramentado, Fray. *San Juan de la Cruz, su obra
científica y su obra literaria.* 2 vols. Madrid. Edit. Mensajero de Santa
Teresa y S. Juan de la Cruz. 1929. U-870-1 D

— *La escuela mística carmelitana.* Madrid. Edit. Mensajero de Santa Teresa
y S. Juan de la Cruz. 1930. Pp. 456. U-869 I* C* D

— *Compendio de ascética y mística.* Madrid. Edit. Mensajero de Santa Teresa
y S. Juan de la Cruz. 1933. Pp. 389. n/n I*

Cristianesimo e critica. Ed. dalla Direzione della Scuola Teologica Battista
di Roma. Torino. Biblioteca di Studi Religiosi, no. 1. 1912. Pp. xii, 102.
U-240

Criterion. A quarterly review. London (April 1923). U-4234

Crítica política. Roma (25 April 1924). n/n

Croce, Benedetto. *Filosofia dello spirito.* 4 vols. Bari. Laterza. 1909-17.
U-1621-4 I* C B

— *Saggi filosofici.* 3 vols. Bari. Laterza. 1910-13. U-1625-7 I C

— *Breviario di estetica. Quattro lezioni.* Bari. Laterza. 1913. Pp. 127.
(2 copies) U-3046-7

— *La Spagna nella vita italiana durante la Rinascenza.* Bari. Laterza. 1917.
    Pp. 291. U-1628 I B
— *Contributo alla critica di me stesso.* Napoli. 1918. Pp. 89. U-238 D
— 'Inizio periodi e carattere della Storia dell'estetica,' estratto degli *Atti
    dell'Accademia Pontaniana,* XLVI (1916). U-1698
— 'Ludovico Ariosto,' estrato della *Critica.* Bari (1918). U-1723 D
— 'Due note di estetica,' estratto degli *Atti dell'Accademia Pontaniana,*
    XLVIII (1918). U-4084
— *Storia d'Italia dal 1871 al 1915.* Bari. Laterza. 1928. Pp. viii, 354.
    U-5355 I* C B*
— *Opere di Benedetto Croce.* (Catalogue). Bari. Laterza. 1935. Pp. 28.
    U-5365 B
Crociere barbare. Napoli (15 March 1917). n/n
Croiset, Alfred, et Maurice Croiset. *Manuel d'histoire de la littérature grecque
    à l'usage des lycées et collèges.* Paris. Fontemoing. [1900]. Pp. iv, 844.
    U-207
Croiset, Jean. *Réflexions chrétiennes sur divers sujets de morale.* Tome II.
    Paris. Boudet. 1752. Pp. 435. U-4397
Cromwell, Oliver. *Letters and Speeches.* With elucidations by Thomas
    Carlyle. 4 vols. London. Chapman and Hall. 1850. U-4793-6 I* C* T
Crónica silense. Ed. Francisco Santos Coco. Madrid. Rivadeneyra. 1919.
    Pp. xliv, 111. U-3056
Crónicas del Gran Capitán por Antonio Rodríguez Villa. (NBAE, 10).
    Madrid. Bailly-Baillière. 1908. Pp. 612. U-45 I* L
Cruchaga Santa María, Angel. *Job.* Poema. [Santiago de Chile]. Grimm &
    Kern. 1922. Pp. 75. U-487 D
Cruz, Pedro N. *Pláticas literarias. 1886-1889.* Santiago de Chile. Cervantes.
    1889. Pp. 404. U-585 C
Cruz Olóriz, Juan de la. *De espaldas al ayer.* Bilbao. Edit. Vizcaína. 1925.
    Pp. 83. U-5610 D
— *Vade-Mecum del contribuyente vizcaíno.* Bilbao. Grijelmo. 1926.
    Pp. 163. U-5669
Cruz y Raya. Madrid (Núm. 14, mayo 1934; núm. 39, junio 1936). n/n
Cuadernos de la Facultad de Filosofía y Letras. Madrid. Universidad Central.
    (Dic.-enero 1935-6). n/n
Cuadernos socialistas de trabajo. Bilbao (Enero 1927). n/n
Cuadri, Guillermo. *El agregáo. Versos gauchescos.* Minas. Monfort Doria.
    1926. Pp. 127. U-5624 I D
Cuba contemporánea. La Habana. (Junio, julio 1926). n/n
Cubí, Manuel. *Vida del Beato Don Juan de Ribera.* Barcelona. Pla. 1912.
    Pp. 444. U-1286

Cuentistas aragoneses. Antología. Pról. J. García Mercadal. Madrid. Suárez. 1910. Pp. xvi, 236. U-2007

Cuero y Pita-Pizarro, Luis. *La hija de Fedra. Novela.* Madrid. Gaceta Administrativa. 1909. Uc D

Cuervo, Rufino José. *Apuntaciones críticas sobre el lenguaje bogotano.* Paris. 1914. Uc

Cuervo Arango y Rodríguez Trelles, Fr. Justo. *Biografía de Fray Luis de Granada con unos artículos literarios donde se demuestra que el venerable Padre, y no San Pedro de Alcántara, es el verdadero y único autor del 'Libro de la Oración.'* Madrid. G. del Amo. 1895. Pp. 278. U-909 I

Cuervo Márquez, Emilio. *Phineés. Tragedia de los tiempos de Cristo.* Bogotá. La Luz. 1909. Pp. 301. U-2923 D

Cuesta, Teodoro. *Poesías asturianas.* Pról. A. Pidal y Mon. Oviedo. Pardo, Gusano y Cía. 1895. Pp. xiv, 292. U-2271

Cueto, Juan. *Los límites de España y de las Españas.* Conferencia. Madrid. Clásica Española. 1928. Pp. 24. U-5665 D

– *De mi ideario.* Madrid. Clásica Española. n.d. Pp. 146. U-2655 D

Cullen, Countee. *Caroling Dusk. An Anthology of Verse by Negro Poets.* New York. Harper. 1927. Pp. xxii, 237. U-5191 I*

Cultura Venezolana. Caracas (Agosto 1929). n/n

Cundall, Frank. *The Darien Venture.* New York. Hispanic Society of America. 1926. Pp. ix, 155. U-1413

Cuneo, Niccolò. *Le Mexique et la question religieuse.* Turin. Bocca. 1931. Pp. xiv, 263. U-2750 D

– *Il Granducato dei Poverelli.* Genova. Marsano. 1932. Pp. 171. U-873 D

– *Spagna cattolica e rivoluzionaria.* Milano. Gilardi e Noto. 1934. Pp. 352. U-3221 C D

Cúneo-Vidal, Rómulo. *España. Impresiones de un sudamericano.* Paris. Garnier. 1890. Pp. vi, 258. U-3084

Cunha, Augusto, y Antonio Ferro. *Missal de Trovas.* Lisboa. Ferreira. 1914. Pp. 38. U-2082 D

Cuoco, Vincenzo. *Saggio storico sulla rivoluzione napoletana del 1799.* Seguito dal Rapporto al cittadino Carnot di Franceso Lomonaco. A cura di Fausto Nicolini. Bari. Laterza. 1913. Pp. 395. U-1819 I*

Cuquerella Alonso, Félix. *Del amor.* Pról. Emilia Pardo Bazán. Ferrol. El Correo Gallego. 1905. Pp. 99. U-563 D

Curet, Francisco. *El arte dramático en el resurgir de Cataluña.* Barcelona. Minerva. 1926. Pp. 406. U-3567 I D

Curros Enríquez, M. *Aires d'a miña terra.* Madrid. La Ilustración Gallega y Asturiana. 1881. Uc

Curtius, Georg. *Grammatica della lingua greca.* Versione italiana riveduta sull'ultima edizione originale da Giusseppe Müller. Torino. Loescher. 1872. Uc

- *Gramática griega elemental.* Tr. Enrique Soms y Castelín. Pról. M.
  Menéndez y Pelayo. Madrid. Fé. 1887. Pp. xxii, 434. U-5510 I* C*
- *Griechische Schulgrammatik.* Altenburg. Stephan Geibel & Comp. 1875.
  Pp. 226. U-4167 [Cover missing]
- *Das Verbum der griechischen Sprache.* 2 vols. Leipzig. Hirzel. 1873-6.
  U-1817-18 I* C*
- *Grundzüge der griechischen Etymologie.* Leipzig. Teubner. 1879. Pp. xvi,
  858. U-1673 C L T

Curtius Rufus (Quintus). *De rebus Alexandri Magni Historia,* ab Academia
    Latina Matritensi editur in lucem, etc. Madrid. Gabriel Ramírez. 1761.
    Pp. 591. U-4430

Cusano, Nicolò. *Della Dotta Ignoranza.* Libri Tres. Testo latino con note di
    Paolo Rotta. Bari. Laterza. 1913. Pp. xliv, 189. U-3715 I

Custine, Delphine de. *Delphine de Custine. Belle amie de Miranda. Lettres
    inédites.* Introd. et notes C. Parra-Pérez. Paris. Excelsior. 1927. Pp. 95.
    U-5292

Cuveiro Piñol, Juan. *Diccionario gallego.* Barcelona. Ramírez. 1876. Pp. 334.
    U-1857

Cuyas, Arturo. *Nuevo diccionario español-inglés e inglés-español.* Barcelona.
    Bosch. 1911. Pp. vii, 585 + xiv, 618. n/n

Cvijié, Jovan. *La péninsule balkanique. Géographie humaine.* Paris. Colin.
    1918. Pp. 528 + 31 maps. U-688 I*

D., J.N. *Les opérations de l'esprit de Dieu.* Nouvelle édition. Tr. entièrement
    revue. Vevey. Guignard. 1900. Pp. 164. U-296
- *Episcopacy: What Ground is there in Scripture or in History for
  Accounting It an Institution of God?* London. Morrish. n.d. Pp. 23.
  U-4476

D'Acosta, Diógenes, y Martín T. Irisarri. *Liras hermanas. Ecos de una vida*
    por Diógenes D'Acosta. *Páginas del corazón* por Martín T. Irisarri.
    Montevideo. El Arte. 1911. Pp. 152. U-3187 D

Dagnino, Vicente. *El correjimiento de Arica. 1535-1784.* Arica. La Epoca.
    1909. Uc D

Daireaux, Godofredo. *Tipos y paisajes criollos.* III serie. Buenos Aires.
    Prudent y Moetzel. 1903. Pp. 324. U-2424
- *El hombre dijo a la oveja ... Fábulas argentinas.* Buenos Aires. La Nación.
  1905. Pp. 213. U-4623 D

Dalsace, Lionel. *Deuda fatal.* Tr. Sánchez Pujol. Madrid. Pueyo. n.d. Uc

Dana, Richard Henry. *Two Years Before the Mast. A Personal Narrative.*
    Boston. Houghton Mifflin. [1911]. Pp. xiii, 553. U-5189 I* C T

Danesi, Achille Giulio. *Alla Sardegna: Carme.* Clagiari. Sarda. 1913. Pp. 55.
    U-764 D

Dantas, Julio. *La cortina verde. Drama en cuatro actos.* Tr. Ribera Rovira.
    Barcelona. Teatro Mundial. 1915. Pp. 56. U-1996

Dante Alighieri. *La Divina Commedia.* Spiegazioni Giovanni Boccacio. Paris.
    Didot. 1853. Pp. xxxvi, 432. U-1521 I* T
— *La Comedia de Dant Allighier.* Tr. de rims vulgars toscans en rims vulgars
    catalans N'Andreu Febrer Dala á luz con ilustr. crítico-literarias C. Vidal
    y Valenciano. Barcelona. Verdaguer. 1878. Pp. xxii, 596. U-4405 I T
— *Divina Commedia di Dante Alighieri.* Note per cura di Eugenio Camerini.
    Milano. Sonzogno. 1881. Pp. 430. U-2792 C. Comento Pietro Fraticelli.
    Firenze. Barbèra. 1907. Pp. 623, cxlv. U-2893
Dantín Cereceda, Juan. *Resumen fisiográfico de la península ibérica.* Madrid.
    Instituto Nacional de Ciencias Naturales. 1912. Pp. 275. U-2468 I C
— *Ensayo acerca de las regiones naturales de España.* Madrid. Cosano. 1922.
    Pp. xv, 386. U-4210 D
Danville, Gaston. *La psicología del amor.* Tr. Magda Schjoeksy. Barcelona.
    Carbonell y Esteva. 1908. Uc
Darby, J.N. *De la présence et de l'action du Saint-Esprit dans l'église.*
    Valence. Marc Aurel. 1844. Pp. viii, 184. U-267
Darío, Rubén. See García Sarmiento, Félix Rubén
Darmesteter, Arsène. *Cours de grammaire historique de la langue française.*
    Publiée par les soins de M. Léopold Sudre. Paris. Delagrave. 189 .-7.
    Pp. xi, 203 + vi, 189 + ix, 237 + vi, 169. U-149
Daverio de Bonavita, Láyly. *Párrafos del amor dichoso.* Montevideo.
    Instrucción Pública. 1928. Pp. 101. U-4908
Dedeu, Martin. *Nuestros hombres de la Argentina. Dr Rafael Calzada.*
    Buenos Aires. Robles. 1913. Pp. 125. U-1109 D
Defoe, Daniel. *Robinson Crusoe.* London. Dent. 1914. Pp. x, 453. U-1003 I*
Dehmel, R. *Zwanzig Gedichte* mit einem Geleitbrief von W. Schäfer. Berlin.
    Schuster & Loeffler. 1897. Pp. 87. U-4006 T
Dekker, E.D., the Elder (Multatuli, pseud.). *Vorstenschool.* Amsterdam.
    Nederlandsche Bibliotheek. 1907. Pp. 159. U-1449 T
Delage, Yves, et M. Goldsmith. *Les théories de l'évolution.* Paris.
    Flammarion. 1916. Pp. 383. U-2736 I* C* B
Delaisi, Francis. *Les contradictions du monde moderne.* Paris. Payot. 1925.
    Pp. 560. U-5289
Deledda, Grazia. *Elias Portolu. Romanzo.* Torino. Editrice Nazionale. 1903.
    Pp. 235. U-2101 I* T
— *Nostalgia. Novela.* Tr. Domenge Mir. Barcelona. Henrich. 1905. Uc
— *Cenizas.* Barcelona. Henrich. 1906. Uc
Deleito y Piñuela, José. *El sentimiento de tristeza en la literatura*
    contemporánea. Barcelona. Minerva. [1923]. Pp. 446. U-3984
Delfino, Víctor. *El alcoholismo y sus efectos en el individuo, la familia y la*
    sociedad. Pról. J. Scosaria. Barcelona. F. Granada. 1907. Uc D
— *Anuario científico e industrial.* Pról. Comas Solá. Barcelona. F. Granada.
    1909. Uc

– *Fisiología e higiene de la voz.* 2 vols. Buenos Aires. Maucci. 1909.
U-4371-2
– *Las rutas del infinito.* Pról. J. Comas Solá. Barcelona. Feliu y Susanna.
1911. Pp. viii, 432. U-3434 D
– *Atomos y astros.* Valencia. Sempere. n.d. Uc D
Delgado, Eleuterio. *Organización de la hacienda.* Apuntes E. Gómez de
Baquero. Madrid. Hernández. 1904. Pp. xv, 301. U-1907 n/o
Delgado, José Maria. *El relicario. Poesías.* Montevideo. Mercatali. 1919.
Pp. 277. U-1358 D
Delgado, Juan B. *París y otros poemas.* México. Escalante. 1919. Pp. 119.
U-4496
Delgado, Luis Humberto. *Vida de Rodó.* Lima. American Express Ltd. 1932.
Pp. 162. U-5019
Delgado,Fito, C. *Versos del emigrante. Poemas.* Buenos Aires. Ricordi. 1926.
Pp. 81. U-4939 D
Delicado, Francisco. *Retrato de la lozana andaluza.* Madrid. Rodríguez Serra.
n.d. Uc
Deligne, Gaston F. *Galaripsos.* Santo Domingo. La Cuna de América. 1908.
Pp. 216. U-3665 n/o D
Delitzsch, Friedrich. *Babel und Bibel.* Erster Vortrag. Leipzig. Hinrichs'sche.
1905. Pp. 82. U-3706
Dell, Floyd. *This Mad Ideal.* Leipzig. Tauchnitz. 1925. Pp. 270.
U-5167 I B* T
Dellepiane, Antonio. *Estudios de filosofía jurídica y social.* [Buenos Aires].
Abeledo. 1907. Pp. 236 U-2157
Demolder, Eugène. *L'Espagne en auto. Impressions de voyage.* Paris. Mercure
de France. 1906. Pp. 290. U-1152
Demolins, Edmundo. *En qué consiste la superioridad de los anglo-sajones.*
Tr., pról., y notas S. Alba y Bonifaz. Madrid. Suárez. 1899. Pp. cxxx, 350.
U-2191 I
Demosthenes. *Demosthenis orationes.* E recensione Guilielmi Dindorfil.
Editio quarta correctior curante F. Blass. 3 vols. Lipsiae. Teubner. 1908.
U-323-5 I* L*
Denifle, Heinrich Seuse. *Das geistliche Leben. Blumenlese aus den deutschen
Mystikern und Gottesfreunden des 14 Jahrhunderts.* Graz. Mofer. 1895.
Pp. xii, 651. U-485 I C T
Denis, Ernest. *La grande Serbie.* Paris. Delagrave. 1915. Pp. xiii, 336. U-3980
Dennett, Edward. *The Name Above Every Name. Being Papers on the
Excellency, Exaltation, and Supremacy of Christ.* London. Rouse. 1896.
Pp. 116. U-4672
Dennye Litteratur. Kφbenhavn (Nov. 1925). n/n
Depta, Max Victor. *Lope de Vega.* Breslau. Ostdeutsche Verlagsanstalt. 1927.
Pp. iv, 343. U-5456

De Quincey, Thomas. *The Confessions of an English Opium-Eater.* Introd.
G. Douglas. London. Dent. [1907]. Pp. xvi, 274. U-1067 I* T
— *The English Mail-Coach and Other Essays.* Introd. J.H. Burton. London.
Dent. [1912]. Pp. xvi, 339. U-1062 I*
— *Reminiscences of the English Lake Poets.* London. Dent. [1907].
Pp. xi, 335. U-1061 I
Descartes, René. *Oeuvres de Descartes.* Introd. M.J. Simon. Paris. Charpentier.
1844. Pp. lxi, 596. U-590 C
— *Obras filosóficas de Descartes.* Tr. e introd. Manuel de la Revilla. 2 vols.
Madrid. Perojo. [1878]. U-860 C
Deschamps, Enrique. *La República Dominicana. Directorio y guía general.*
Barcelona. Cunill. [1913]. Pp. 383 + 336. U-1213 D
Desclot, Bernat. *Crónica del Rey en Pere e dels seus antecessors passats.*
Prefaci sobre els cronistes catalans J. Coroleu. Barcelona. La Renaixensa.
1885. Pp. xxiii, 383. U-2588
Desdevises du Dezert, Georges. *L'Espagne de l'ancien régime. La richesse et la
civilisation.* Paris. Société Française d'Imprimerie et de Librairie. 1904.
Pp. xxxii, 422. U-1671 I* D
— *L'Inquisition aux Indes espagnoles à la fin du dix-huitième siècle.* New
York. *Revue Hispanique,* xxx (1914). Pp. 118. U-4101 D
— *La Louisiane à la fin du XVIIIe siècle.* Paris. Société de l'Histoire des
Colonies Françaises. [1914]. Pp. 30. U-1761
— *Une race de proie. La famille des Hohenzollern.* Clermont-Ferrand. Impr.
de G. Mont-Louis. 1915. Pp. 53. U-662 I D
Dessus, Luis Felipe. *Flores y balas. Estados de alma.* Guayana, P.R. Tip.
Guayamesa. 1916. Uc D
De Stem. Arnhem (1 juni 1926). n/n
Deulofeu de Cadorniga, José Ma. *La odisea de Anselmo Garcés.* Madrid. Imp.
Artística Española. 1912. Uc D
Deus, João de. *Pedagogia. A cartilha maternal e o apostolado.* Lisboa.
Bertrand. [1881]. Pp. xx, 258. U-2643
— *Pedagogia. A cartilha maternal e a crítica.* Lisboa. Bertrand. 1897.
Pp. xxiii, 367. U-1988
— *Campo de flôres.* Lisboa. Nacional. 1897. Pp. xxxviii, 484. U-2646 I* C T D
— *Prosas. Narrativas singelas. Cartas. Prólogos e criticas.* Coordenadas
Theóphilo Braga. Lisboa. Bertrand. 1898. Pp. xii, 734. U-2774
— *A cartilha maternal ou arte de leitura.* Lisboa. Nacional. 1903. Pp. 139.
U-3285
— *Guia pratico e theórico da cartilha maternal ou arte de leitura.* Lisboa.
Nacional. 1906. Pp. 160. U-2686 D
— *Arte de escripta.* Lisboa. Nacional. 1903. Uc
— *Prosódia portugueza. Estudio prévio da orthographia coordenado por
João de Deus Ramos.* Coimbra. Amado. 1909. Pp. 95. U-5724 n/o

Devaux, André. *Armand Godoy, poète catholique*. Paris. Au Sans Pareil.
1936. Pp. 210. U-3746 n/o
Dewey, John. *The Philosophy of John Dewey*. Selected and ed. J. Ratner.
New York. Holt. [1928]. Pp. xii, 560. U-5198 I* C
Diario de las sesiones de la Asamblea Constituyente de 1879. Reimpreso por
acuerdo de la Comisión de Régimen Interior de la Asamblea Constituyente
de 1927. Preámbulo del ex-representante Rafael Montúfar. Guatemala.
Nacional. 1927. Pp. 189. U-2494 n/o
Díaz, Leopoldo. *Traducciones*. Buenos Aires. Pablo e Coni. 1897. Pp. 206.
U-1940 D
— *Las sombras de Hellas. Les ombres d'Hellas*. Tr. en vers français F. Raisin.
Préf. Remy de Gourmont. Genève. Eggimann. 1902. Pp. 211. U-2666 D
— *Atlántida conquistada. L'Atlantide conquise. Poème en sonnets*. Tr. F.
Raisin. Genève. Atar. 1906. Pp. 379. U-3992 D
Díaz, Luis M. *Sonetos i canciones*. Buenos Aires. 1913. Uc D
Díaz-Caneja, Juan. *Cumbres palentinas. Impresiones*. Madrid. Ibérica. 1915.
Pp. 126. U-4035
— *Verde y azul*. Novela. Con un poema de Enrique de Mesa. Madrid.
Rivadeneyra. 1927. Pp. 243. U-5003 D
Díaz Cisneros, César. *La liga de las naciones y la actitud argentina*. Buenos
Aires. Mercatali. 1921. Pp. 207. U-1351 n/o D
Díaz Dufoo, Carlos. *Robinsón mexicano*. México. Ballescá. n.d. Pp. 264.
U-3117 D
Díaz-Jiménez y Molleda, Eloy. *Juan del Encina en León*. Madrid. Suárez.
1909. Pp. 40. U-4126 n/o D
Díaz Meza, Aurelio. *Bajo la selva*. Santiago de Chile. Meza. 1914. Uc D
Díaz de Molina, Alfredo. *¡Ja, ja, ja!* Buenos Aires. El Inca. 1925. Pp. 181.
U-5112 D
Díaz Morales, José (alias Zaz). *'Gulliver' en el país de la calderilla*. Pról. M.
de Unamuno. Madrid. Agencia Gral. de Librería y Artes Gráficas. 1936.
Pp. 270. n/n D
Díaz Muñoz, Pedro. *Compendio de antropología y pedagogía*. Salamanca.
Núñez. 1902. Pp. 556. U-1674 n/o D
Díaz Plaja, Guillermo. *Visiones contemporáneas de España*. Barcelona. Bosch.
1935. Pp. 285. U-4999 D
Díaz Rodríguez, Manuel. *Sensaciones de viaje*. Paris. Garnier. 1896. Uc D
— *Confidencias de psiquís*. Caracas. El Cojo. 1896. Uc
— *De mis romerías*. Caracas. El Cojo. 1898. Pp. 130. U-2797
— *Cuentos de color*. Caracas. Herrera Irigoyen. 1899. Pp. 213. U-2162 D
— *Idolos rotos*. Paris. Garnier. 1901. Pp. 349. U-2926 I D
— *Sangre patricia*. Caracas. Herrera Irigoyen. 1902. Pp. 233. U-1141 I* D.
Madrid. Sociedad Española de Librería. n.d. Pp. 296. U-3597

- *Camino de perfección. Apuntaciones para una biografía espiritual de Don Perfecto.* Paris. Soc. de Ediciones Literarias. n.d. Uc

Díaz Romero, Eugenio. *Raza que muere. Poema dramático.* Buenos Aires. Brédahl. 1905. Pp. 287. U-1991 C* D

Díaz Usandivaras, Julio. *Jazmín del país.* Buenos Aires. Ruiz. [1923]. Pp. 121. U-3255 D

Dickens, Charles. *The Posthumous Papers of the Pickwick Club.* 2 vols. Leipzig. Tauchnitz. 1842. U-4760-1 I

- *The Life and Adventures of Martin Chuzzlewit.* Introd. G.K. Chesterton. London. Dent. [1907]. Pp. xv, 803. U-1040 I*

- *Vie et Aventures de Martin Chuzzlewit.* Tr. sous la direction de P. Lorain. Paris. Hachette. 1900. Pp. 476. U-3967 I

- *Barnaby Rudge, a Tale of the Riots.* Introd. W. Jerrold. London. Dent. 1906. Pp. xiv, 633. U-1035

- *The Old Curiosity Shop.* Introd. G.K. Chesterton. London. Dent. [1907]. Pp. xvi, 541. U-1028 I T

- *American Notes and Pictures from Italy.* Introd. G.K. Chesterton. London. Dent. [1907]. Pp. xxii, 430. U-1060

- *Great Expectations.* Introd. G.K. Chesterton. London. Dent. [1907]. Pp. xiii, 453. U-1034 I

- *Our Mutual Friend.* Introd. G.K. Chesterton. London. Dent. n.d. Pp. xx, 779. U-1037

- *Bleak House.* Introd. G.K. Chesterton. London. Dent. [1907]. Pp. xxiv, 838. U-1039 I

- *The Life and Adventures of Nicholas Nickleby.* Introd. G.K. Chesterton. London. Dent. [1907]. Pp. xxx, 843. U-1036 I. London. Collins' Press. n.d. Pp. 846. n/n I* C

- *Sketches by Boz Illustrative of Every-Day Life, Every-Day People.* Introd. G.K. Chesterton. London. Dent. [1907]. Pp. xvi, 616. U-1027 I

- *Dombey and Son.* Introd. G.K. Chesterton. London. Dent. n.d. Pp. xxiv, 814. U-1033 I*

- *Little Dorrit.* Introd. G.K. Chesterton. London. Dent. [1907]. Pp. xiv, 784. U-1038

- *The Personal History of David Copperfield.* Introd. G.K. Chesterton. London. Dent. Pp. xviii, 823. (2 copies) U-1031-2 I*

- *A Tale of Two Cities.* Introd. W. Jerrold. London. Dent. 1908. Pp. xii, 375. U-1030

- *Hard Times.* Introd. G.K. Chesterton. London. Dent. n.d. Pp. xvi, 363. U-5183 I* T

- *A Child's History of England.* Introd. G.K. Chesterton. London. Dent. n.d. Pp. xx, 396. U-1029

- *Christmas Books.* Introd. G.K. Chesterton. London. Dent. Uc

— *Oliver Twist.* Introd. G.K. Chesterton. London. Dent. Uc

Dickinson, G. Lowes. *A Modern Symposium.* London. Dent. 1912. Pp. 159.
    U-4712 I

— *The Magic Flute. A Fantasia.* London. George Allen & Unwin. 1920.
    Pp. 128. U-361 I* C*

Diego, Gerardo. *Imagen. Poemas, 1918-1921.* Madrid. Gráf. Ambos Mundos.
    1922. Pp. 124. U-5640 D

— *Soria. Galería de estampas y efusiones.* Valladolid. Montero. 1923. Pp. 72.
    U-5489 D

— *Versos humanos.* Madrid. Sáenz. 1925. Pp. 200. U-5580 D

— *Viacrucis. Verso.* Santander. Aldus. 1931. Ff. 28. U-4132

Diego José, de Cádiz. *Cartas de conciencia que el B. Diego J. Cádiz dirigió a
    su director espiritual D. Juan José Alcover é Higueras.* Anotadas P. Diego
    de Valencia. Pról.-censura F. Muñoz Pabón. Sevilla. La Divina Pastora.
    1904. Pp. viii, 586. U-2819

Dieste, Eduardo. *Los místicos.* Montevideo. Renacimiento. 1915. Pp. 233.
    U-578 D

— *Buscón poeta.* Montevideo. Bertani. Uc

Dieste, Rafael. *La vieja piel del mundo.* Madrid. Signo. 1936. Pp. 160.
    U-3251 D

Díez-Canedo, Enrique. *La visita del sol.* Madrid. Pueyo. 1907. Pp. 152.
    U-3107 D

— *Algunos versos.* Madrid. La Lectura. 1924. Pp. 143. U-5072 D

— *Epigramas americanos.* Madrid. Espasa-Calpe. 1928. Pp. 42. U-5026 D

— *Unidad y diversidad de las letras hispánicas.* Discurso leído por el autor
    en el acto de su recepción académica el 1 de diciembre de 1935. Contesta-
    ción T. Navarro Tomás. Madrid. Tip. de Archivos. 1935. Pp. 57. U-4121

— *Imágenes. Versiones poéticas.* Paris. Ollendorff. n.d. Pp. 260. U-3466 D

Diez Maestros. Conferencias 'Plan Cultural.' Radio Prieto. Buenos Aires.
    Tall. Gráf. Argentinos. 1935. Pp. 185. U-3392

Díez Mateo, Félix. *El pequeño académico. Diccionario español escolar
    etimológico.* n.p. n.d. Pp. xiv, 217. U-5133 D

Díez de Medina, Angel. *Cantos de juventud.* Buenos Aires. Tragant. 1908.
    Pp. 144. U-2400 n/o D

Díez de Medina, Eduardo. *Estrofas nómadas.* La Paz, Bolivia. Imp. Velarde.
    1908. Pp. xxi, 121. U-3701 n/o

Dillon, Emile Joseph. *Mexico on the Verge.* London. Hutchinson. [1922].
    Pp. viii, 328. U-2536 I C

Dinis, Julio, pseud. [i.e., Joaquim Guilherme Gomes Coelho]. *As pupilas de
    Senhor Reitor. Chronica de aldeia.* Lisboa. n.d. Pp. 273. U-2673

Diputación de Barcelona. *Guia de les institucions científiques i d'ensenyança.*
    Barcelona. Publicacions del Consell de Pedagogia. 1916. Pp. 359. U-2789 I

Dirección General de Estadística de la Provincia de Buenos Aires.
El periodismo en la Provincia de Buenos Aires. Año 1907. Publicado bajo
la dirección de Carlos P. Salas. La Plata. Taller de Impresiones Oficiales.
1908. Pp. viii, 243. U-3698

Dirección general del Instituto Geográfico y Estadístico. *Coordenadas
geográficas de puntos comprendidos en la zona de la totalidad del eclipse
de sol del 30 de agosto de 1905.* Madrid. 1905. Uc

Divorcio. Debates en la Cámara de Diputados. República Argentina.
Publicación oficial. Buenos Aires. Tip. El Comercio. 1902. Pp. vi, 736.
U-1344

*Documentos para la historia de la vida pública del libertador de Colombia,
Perú y Bolivia.* Publicadas por disposición del General Guzmán Blanco.
Puestos por orden cronólogico y con adiciones y notas ... por el General
José Felix Blanco. 14 vols. Caracas. La Opinión Nacional. 1875-7. U-10-23

Dodgson, E.S. *Le verbe basque trouvé et défini dans l'épître de St Jacques.*
Chalon-sur-Saone. Marceau. 1899. Pp. 40. U-5268 n/o

— *The Verb in the Second Book in Gipuskoan Bask.* Hertford. Stephen
Austin. 1901. Pp. 44. U-2615

Domenech y Montaner, Luis. *Poblet.* Barcelona. J. Thomas. [1916]. Pp. 42,
pl. 48. U-4436

Domingo, Marcelino. *Teatro. Flores de Almendro. Táctica nueva.* Tortosa.
Querol. 1906. Pp. 251. U-4394 D

— *Temas.* Tortosa. Monclús Balagué. 1916. Pp. 313. U-3888 D

Domínguez, María Alicia. *Crepúsculos de oro. Poesías.* Buenos Aires. Tor.
[1926]. Pp. 159. U-5693 D

— *Idolos de bronce. Cuentos.* Buenos Aires. Tor. [1926]. Pp. 158. U-5042 D

Domínguez Berrueta, Juan. *La canción de la sombra. Un cuento y una
filosofía.* Salamanca. Calatrava. 1910. Pp. 129. U-4711 D

— *Santa Teresa de Jesús y San Juan de la Cruz. Bocetos psicológicos.*
Madrid. Beltrán. 1915. Pp. 69. U-1942 D

— *Salamanca. Guía sentimental.* Salamanca. Calatrava. 1916. Pp. 115.
U-3369 D

Dominici, Pedro César. *La tristeza voluptuosa.* Madrid. Bernardo Rodríguez.
1899. Uc D

— *El triunfo del ideal.* Paris. Bouret. 1901. Pp. 130. U-3185 I

— *De Lutecia. Arte y crítica.* Paris. Ollendorff. 1907. Pp. iv, 348.
U-3839 n/o D

Don Segundo Sombra. Revista de Letras, Crítica y Arte. Núm. 2. La Plata
(Enero 1929). n/n

Donoso, Armando. *Los nuevos. La joven literatura chilena.* Valencia.
Sempere. [1912]. Pp. xxiii, 236. U-2764 D

– *Menéndez Pelayo y su obra.* Santiago de Chile. Imp. Universitaria. 1913.
   Pp. 112. Uc
– *Bilbao y su tiempo.* Santiago de Chile. Zig-zag. 1913. Pp. 206. U-2151 D
– *La senda clara.* Pról. Leopoldo Lugones. Buenos Aires. Cooperativa
   Editorial Ltda. 1919. Pp. 257. U-2389 D
– *La otra América.* Madrid. Calpe. 1925. Pp. 270. U-5033 I* C* D
Donoso Cortés, Juan. *Ensayo sobre el catolicismo, el liberalismo y el
   socialismo.* Barcelona. 1851. Pp. iv, 412. U-616 I*
Dorado, Pedro. *Nuevos derroteros penales.* Barcelona. Henrich. 1905. Uc
Dorado Montero, Pedro. *El positivismo en la ciencia jurídica y social
   italiana. la parte. El derecho penal.* Madrid. Revista de Legislación. 1891.
   Pp. 343. U-868 I
Dordević, Tihomir R. *Macedonia.* London. George Allen & Unwin. 1913.
   Pp. xvi, 283. U-116 I
Dos Santos Moraes, Leonardo. *Maria Jesus.* [Salamanca]. Minerva. 1929.
   Pp. 92. U-5647 D
Dossi, Carlo. *Opere di Carlo Dossi.* Milano. Fratelli Treves. 1910. Pp. xxiv,
   359. U-3482 I* T
Dostoïeffsky, Fedor. *Letters from the Underworld.* Tr. and introd. C.J.
   Hogarth. London. Dent. [1913]. Pp. ix, 308. U-1077 I*
– *The Brothers Karamazov.* Tr. Constance Garnet. London. Heinemann.
   [1919]. Pp. xii, 838. U-1329 I*
– *Los hermanos Karamazov.* Tr. Alfonso Nadal. 4 vols. Madrid. Publ. Atenea.
   1927. n/n I* C L
– *The Idiot.* London. Dent. [1914]. Pp. vii, 605. U-1047 I*
– *Poor Folk* and *The Gambler.* Introd. C.J. Hogarth. London. Dent. [1915].
   Pp. x, 307. U-1076 I*
– *Schuld und Sühne.* Tr. Hans Moser. Leipzig. Reclam. n.d. Pp. 703.
   U-4046 I T
– *Les possédés* suivis de *La confession de Stavroguine.* Seule tr., intégrale et
   conforme au texte russe Jean Chuzeville. 2 vols. Paris. Bossard. 1925.
   QP-14-15 I
– *Mémoires écrits dans un souterrain. Zapiski iz Podpolia 1864.* Tr. Henri
   Mongault et Marc Laval. Paris. Bossard. 1926. Pp. 244. QP-16 I
– *Journal d'un écrivain. Dnievnik picatelia 1873-1876-1877.* Tr. Jean
   Chuzeville. 3 vols. Paris. Bossard. 1927. QP-17-19 I
Dostor, G. *Eléments de la théorie des déterminants.* Paris. Gauthier-Villars.
   1877. Pp. xxxi, 352. U-3763
Dotti, Victor M. *Los alambradores.* Montevideo. Albatros. 1929. Pp. 106.
   U-5036 n/o D
Douél, Martial. *L'Héroïque misère de Miguel de Cervantes esclave barbaresque
   (Alger 1575-1580).* Paris. Editions de la Vraie France. 1930. Pp. 269.
   U-390 D

Dowden, Edward. *The Life of Robert Browning.* London. Dent. [1915].
Pp. 404. U-5180 I

Drachmann, Holger. *Forskrevet.* København. Nordisk-Forlag. 1908. Pp. 479.
U-819 I L T*

— *Es war einmal.* Uebersetzung von M. von Borch. Leipzig. Reclam. n.d.
Pp. 79. U-4548

Drago, Luis María. *La doctrina Drago.* Colección de documentos.
Advertencia preliminar S. Pérez Triana, introd. W.T. Stead. Londres.
Wertheimer, Lea. 1908. Pp. lxxx, 257. U-2134

Driesch, Hans. *Il vitalismo. Storia e dottrina.* Tr. Mario Stenta. Milano.
Remo Sandron. n.d. Pp. xxiii, 428. U-1771

Droulers, Charles, et Léon Bocquet. *Les poètes de la Flandre française et
l'Espagne.* Paris. Crées. 1917. Pp. 101. U-1119 D

Duarte, Félix. *Azul y armiño. Poesías.* Pról. César Luis de León. n.p. Hermes.
n.d. Pp. 160. U-5511 D

Dublé Urrutia, Diego. *Del mar a la montaña.* Santiago de Chile. Imp.
Barcelona. 1903. Pp. xiv, 136. U-2310 I D

Du Bos, Charles. *Extraits d'un journal 1908-1928.* Paris. Corrêa. 1931.
Pp. 468. QP-20 I

— *Approximations.* Paris. Corrêa. 1932. Pp. 326. QP-21 I

Dünwald, Willi. *Der missverstandene Nazarener.* München. Muller. 1927.
Pp. 241. U-5374 I

Dufresne, Jean. *Kleines Lehrbuch des Schachspiels.* Leipzig. Reclam. n.d. Uc

— *Das Buch der Schachmeisterpartien.* Leipzig. Reclam. n.d. Uc

Dugour, Antoine Jeudy. *Histoire d'Olivier Cromwell.* Paris. Bureaux de la
Publication. 1866. Pp. 190. U-4606

Duhamel, Georges. *Vida de los mártires. 1914-1916.* Madrid. Calleja. 1921.
Pp. 246. n/n I* C

— *Les plaisirs et les jeux.* Paris. Mercure de France. 1923. Pp. 274. U-3138 D

— *Scènes de la vie future.* Paris. Mercure de France. 1930. Pp. 248.
U-5234 I D

— *Géographie cordiale de l'Europe.* Paris. Mercure de France. 1931. Pp. 279.
U-253 D

— *Querelles de famille.* Paris. Mercure de France. 1932. Pp. 247.
U-3851 n/o D

Dumas (fils), Alexandre. *La question du divorce.* Paris. Calmann-Lévy. 1882.
Pp. 417. U-643

Dumur, Louis. *Les deux Suisse (1914-1917).* Paris. Bossard. 1918. Pp. 371.
U-2222

Duncker, Max. *Geschichte der Arier in der alten Zeit.* Leipzig. Duncker und
Humblot. 1867. Pp. xii, 962. U-3821

Dunn, Joseph. *A Grammar of the Portuguese Language.* Washington, DC.
National Capital Press. 1928. Pp. xi, 669. U-1412

Dupuy de Lôme, Roberto. *Femina Tea Room. Comedia.* Buenos Aires. 1913.
Pp. 77. U-2437 D

Durá, Francisco. *Naturalización y expulsión de extranjeros.* Buenos Aires.
Coni. 1911. Uc D

Durán, Alfonso. *Hojas del corazón y páginas del alma.* Buenos Aires. Molinari.
1913. Pp. 197. U-3657 D

Durán y Tortajada, Miquel. *Himmes & Poemes.* Sabadell. Valencia. 1916.
Pp. 90. U-2937 D

Durán y Ventosa, Lluís. *Regionalisme y federalisme.* Pròl. Enrich Prat de la
Riba. Barcelona. Puig. 1905. Pp. xxxiv, 339. U-3040 I*

Durbán Orozco, José. *Tardes grises.* Madrid. Fernando Fé. 1900. Uc D

Duval, Mathias, et Paul Constantin. *Anatomie et physiologie animales.* Paris.
Baillière. 1894. Uc

Dyroff, Adolfo. *El concepto de la existencia.* Tr. Andrés González Blanco.
Barcelona. Henrich. 1906. Uc

Earle, Homer Price. *An Essay by Homer Price Earle. Alonso Quijano & Don
Quijote. Comments on the Novel of Cervantes.* Los Angeles. Smith. 1932.
Pp. 19. U-2513

Eça de Queiroz, José Maria. *A cidade e as serras.* Pôrto. Chardron. 1903.
Pp. 384. U-1959 I* C B

– *Cartas de Inglaterra.* Pôrto. Chardron. 1905. Pp. 242. U-3432

– *A reliquia.* Pôrto. Chardron. 1915. Pp. 419. U-3995 I*

– *Os Maias. Episodios da vida romantica.* 2 vols. Pôrto. Moderna. n.d.
U-367-8 I L

Echebarría, Ezequiel de. *Etimologías vascongadas o sea ensayo sobre la
interpretación y reconstrucción del vocabulario vascongado.* Durango.
Soloaga. 1899. Pp. viii, 238. U-4269

Echegaray, Aristóbulo. *24 poemas para una muchacha querida.* Buenos Aires.
Editorial Hoy. 1928. Pp. 31. U-5498 D

Echegaray, Bonifacio de. *El proceso de la Zamacolada.* Bilbao. Cultura Vasca.
1921. Pp. 63. U-2512 D

– *Aspectos jurídicos de la Zamacolada. Régimen y gobierno del Puerto de la
Paz. Conferencia.* Bilbao. Grijelmo. 1921. Pp. 35. U-4322

Echegaray, Carmelo de. *Las provincias vascongadas a fines de la edad media.
Ensayo histórico.* San Sebastián. Jornet. 1895. Pp. 496. U-4837

Echevarría, Estéban de. *Obras completas de don Estéban de Echevarría.*
5 vols. Buenos Aires. Imp. de Mayo. 1870-4. U-100-4

– *Dogma socialista.* Noticia preliminar Ricardo Rojas. Buenos Aires. La
Facultad. 1915. Pp. vi, 303. U-3581 I*

Echevarría, Mariano de. *Bilbao ante el bloqueo y bombardeo de 1873-1874.*
Bilbao. J.F. Mayor. 1874. Pp. vi, 185. (2 copies) U-5702-3

Echevarría Rotaeche, José de. *España sin pulso. Un viaje a los Estados Unidos narrados en dos conferencias.* Bilbao. Rochelt. 1916. Pp. 45. U-2395

Echevarría y Reyes, Aníbal. *Voces usadas en Chile.* Santiago. Elzeviriana. 1900. Pp. xxii, 246. (2 copies) U-3274, U-3915 n/o

Echeverría de Larraín, Inés. *Hacia el Oriente. Recuerdos de una peregrinación a la Tierra Santa.* n.p. Cervantes. n.d. Pp. xiii, 500. U-3596

Eckermann, Johann Peter. *Conversaciones con Goethe.* Tr. J. Pérez Bances. 3 vols. Madrid. Colec. Universal. 1920. n/n I*

Economical and Social Progress of the Republic of Chile. Santiago de Chile. Imp. Barcelona. 1906. Pp. 342. U-4103

Ecos literarios, religiosos, históricos y artísticos. Revista. Bilbao. 9 oct. 1897 a 29 sept. 1898. Uc

Edwards Bello, Joaquín. *El chileno en Madrid.* Santiago de Chile. Nascimento. 1928. Pp. 294. U-4988 I* D

Egaña, Pedro de. *Breves apuntes en defensa de las libertades vascongadas.* Bilbao. Dalmas. 1870. Pp. 170. U-3691 n/o

Eguiguren, Luis Antonio. *La holgazanería en el Perú.* Lima. Moreno. 1915. Pp. 109. U-4677 D

Eguilaz y Yanguas, Leopoldo. *Glosario etimológico de las palabras españolas de origen oriental.* Granada. La Lealtad. 1886. Pp. xxiv, 591. U-1251

Eichthal, Gustave d'. *Les Evangiles.* 2 vols. Paris. Hachette. 1863. U-2477-8

Eisner, Paul. *Die Tschechen.* Herausgegeben von Paul Eisner. München. Piper. 1928. Pp. 442. U-2099

Eldgast, Harald. *Ausgewählte Stücke aus der lettischen Literatur. 1. Sammlung. Harald Eldgast.* Berechtigte Uebertragung aus dem Lettischen von Senta Maurin. Riga. Lettalnd-Bücherei 3. 1924. Pp. 140. U-1448

Elementos para el estudio del problema de Cataluña. Madrid. Artes Gráficas Mateu. 1918. Pp. 115. U-1862

Elephantina, Silovan de. *La ciencia sondeando el misterio.* Habana. Rambla. 1927. Pp. 288. U-5031 D

Elflein, Ada M. *Leyendas argentinas.* Buenos Aires. Cabaut. 1909. Uc D

Eliot, George. *Scenes of Clerical Life.* 2 vols. Leipzig. Tauchnitz. 1859. U-4748-9 I*

— *Adam Bede.* 2 vols. Leipzig. Tauchnitz. 1859. Uc

— *The Mill on the Floss.* 2 vols. Leipzig. Tauchnitz. 1860. U-4750-1 I* T

— *Silas Marner: the Weaver of Raveloe.* Leipzig. Tauchnitz. 1861. Pp. 297. U-4752 I T

Ellis, Henry Havelock. *Man and Woman. A Study of Human Secondary Sexual Characters.* London. Walter Scott. 1899. Pp. xiv, 409. U-1312 I* C B*

— *The Soul of Spain.* London. Constable. 1908. Pp. viii, 420. U-4138 D

Emerson, R.W. *La confiança en sí mateix. L'amistat.* Tr. introd. Cebriá
   Montoliu. Barcelona. L'Avenç. 1904. Pp. 115. U-4455 B D
— *Essays.* 2 vols. New York. Hurst. n.d. U-1444-5
— *Poems.* New York. Hurst. n.d. Pp. 165. U-1443
— *English Traits.* New York. Hurst. n.d. Pp. iv, 234. U-1441 I*
— *Representative Men. Seven Lectures.* New York. Hurst. n.d. Pp. 211.
   U-1442
Eminescu, Mihail. *Poezii.* Bucaresti. Cultura Nationala. [1924]. Pp. 246.
   U-5331 D
Encina, Juan del. *El aucto del Repelón.* Publicado con un estudio crítico-
   biográfico, glosario, y notas A. Alvarez de la Villa. Paris. Ollendorff.
   1910. Pp. 336. U-911
Engel, Georg. *Der Hexenkessel.* Berlin. Verlag des Bibliographischen Bureaus.
   1894. Pp. 87. U-3614
Engelhardt, J.G.V. *Richard von St Victor und Johannes Ruysbroec.*
   Erlangen. Palm'sche Verlagsbuchhandlung. 1838. Pp. xiv, 400. U-3859
English Prose, Narrative, Descriptive and Dramatic. Compiled H.A. Treble.
   Oxford. University Press. [1928]. Pp. xi, 510. U-5147
The Englishwoman. Ed. Elisina Grant Richards. 4 vols. London. 1909-10.
   U-87-90
Epictetus. *Epictète manuel.* Texte grec précédé d'une introd., accompagné
   de notes, et suivi d'un lexique des mots techniques Charles Thurot. Paris.
   Hachette. 1892. Pp. 71. U-4659 T
Ercilla y Zuñiga, Alonso de. *La Araucana.* 4 vols. Paris. Cormon y Blanc.
   1824. U-4063-6. U-4066 I. Edición del centenario. Biografía de José
   Toribio Medina. 3 vols. Santiago de Chile. Elzeveriana. 1910-17.
   U-3559-61
Ernst, Fritz. *Die Zukunft der Historie.* Aarau. Sauerlaender. 1921. Pp. 22.
   U-1740 D
Errázuriz, Isidoro. *Obras de Isidoro Errázuriz.* Discursos parlamentarios.
   Introd. y estudio preliminar Luis Orrego Luco. 2 vols. Santiago de Chile.
   Imp. Barcelona. 1910. U-2607-8
Errázuriz Urmeneta, Rafael. *Roma.* 2 vols. Santiago de Chile. Imp. Barcelona.
   1904-6. U-714-15
Escalante, Amós de. *Poesías de D. Amós de Escalante.* Edición póstuma.
   Estudio crítico D.M. Menéndez y Pelayo. Madrid. Tello. 1907. Pp. cxxiii,
   229. U-2747 I
— *Costas y montañas. Diario de un caminante.* Madrid. Renacimiento.
   [1921]. Pp. 429. U-637 I* L
Escalante, Eduardo. *Colección completa de las obras dramáticas de D. Eduardo
   Escalante.* Pról. Teodoro Llorente. 3 vols. Valencia. Domenech. n.d.
   U-1236-8 I* L

Escalpelo, pseud. *El senado de 1890.* Buenos Aires. Escary. 1891. Pp. 252.
U-2370 [Bound with José S. Alvarez]

Escholier, Raymond. *La vie glorieuse de Victor Hugo.* Paris. Plon. 1928.
Pp. v, 412. QP-22 I

Escobio, Félix R. *Temas.* Buenos Aires. Rosso. 1918. Pp. 18. U-3426 D

— *Lecciones populares de historia de la civilización. La civilización en
Grecia.* Buenos Aires. Peuser. 1928. Pp. 205. U-5685 D

Escofet, José. *La reina.* México. Paz. 1907. Uc D

Escritores místicos españoles. Ed. Miguel Mir. Tomo I. Hernando de Talavera,
Alejo Venegas, Francisco de Osuna, Alonso de Madrid. (NBAE, 16).
Madrid. Bailly-Baillière. 1911. Pp. xxxii, 660. U-51 I* L*

Escuelas de España. Segovia (Oct. 1929). n/n

Esercicios de S. Ignacio. n.p. n.d. Pp. 120. n/n

Esparbès, Georges d'. *El tumulto. Canto republicano.* Tr. E. Diez-Canedo.
Paris. Sociedad de Ediciones Literarias y Artísticas. n.d. Pp. 271.
U-1839 n/o

Esperabé de Arteaga, Enrique. *Historia pragmática e interna de la Universidad
de Salamanca. I. La Universidad de Salamanca y los Reyes.* Salamanca.
Francisco Nuñez. 1914. Uc

Espina, Antonio. *El nuevo diantre.* Madrid. Espasa-Calpe. 1934. Pp. 201.
U-3629 D

Espina, Concha. *Ruecas de marfil.* Madrid. Renacimiento. 1917. Pp. 239.
U-3783 D

— *El príncipe del cantar ... Novelas y cuentos.* Toulouse. Maurin. 1929.
Pp. 215. U-611

Espinosa, Eloi B. *Orientación del código penal peruano de 1924.* Lima.
Penitenciaria Central. 1929. Pp. 113. U-5524 D

Espinosa Medrano, Juan de. *Apologético en favor de D. Luis de Góngora.*
Reimpreso Ventura García Calderón. New York. Extrait de la *Revue
Hispanique,* LXV (1925), pp. 146. U-4965 D

Espinoza, Enrique. *Geografía descriptiva de la República de Chile.* Santiago
de Chile. Imp. Barcelona. 1897. Pp. 493. U-719 I*

Del espíritu de los vascos. Palabras preliminares J. Ortega y Gasset. Bilbao.
Editorial Vasca. 1920. Pp. 179. U-1143

Esplugas, Miguel de. *San Francisco de Sales. Psicología Espíritu. Máximas.*
Edición castellana. Barcelona. Libr. Salesiana. 1906. Pp. xv, 223.
U-306 n/o

— *Maragall. Notes íntimes.* Barcelona. Gili. 1912. Pp. 92. U-2587

Espoz y Mina, Condesa de. See Vega de Mina, Juana

*Estadística de la administración de justicia en lo criminal durante el año de
1901 en la península e islas adyacentes,* publicada por el Ministerio de
Gracia y Justicia. Madrid. 'Gaceta de Madrid.' 1907. Uc

Estébanez Calderón, Serafín. *Escenas andaluzas*. Madrid. Pérez Dubrull. 1883.
Pp. 386. U-1562

Estelrich y Artigues, Joan. *Fenix o l'esperit de Renaixença*. Barcelona.
Biblioteca Catalana d'Autors Independients. 1934. Pp. 259. (2 copies)
U-223, U-222 I D

– *Al servei dels ideals*. Barcelona. Llibr. Catalonia. 1934. Pp. 178. U-2422 D

Estelrich y Perelló, Juan Luis. *Páginas mallorquinas*. Palma de Mallorca.
Tous. 1912. Pp. vii, 305. U-3588 D

Estrada, Dardo. *Historia y bibliografía de la imprenta en Montevideo.*
1810-1865. Montevideo. Cervantes. 1912. Pp. 318. U-1210

– *Fuentes documentales para la historia colonial.* Conferencia. Discurso
preliminar Dr Gustavo Gallinal. Montevideo. Renacimiento. 1918. Pp. 39.
U-4321 n/o

Estrada, Genaro. *Algunos papeles para la historia de las bellas artes en México.*
México. 1935. Pp. 89. U-1711

Estrada, José Manuel. *Lecciones sobre la historia de la República Argentina.*
2 vols. Buenos Aires. Igón. 1896. U-2593-4

– *La política liberal bajo la tiranía de Rosas.* Buenos Aires. Igón. 1898.
Pp. 371. U-4162. Bibl. Argentina. 1927. Pp. 345. U-4868

– *El génesis de nuestra raza. El catolicismo y la democracia. Los comuneros
del Paraguay.* Noticia biográfica del autor por J.M. Garro. Buenos Aires.
Igón. 1899. Pp. civ, 565. U-4161 n/o

– *Fragmentos históricos.* Buenos Aires. Cabaut. 1901. Pp. xi, 626. U-4163

– *Curso de derecho constitucional.* 3 vols. Buenos Aires. Cabaut. 1901-2.
U-3765-7 n/o

– *Miscelánea. Estudios y artículos varios.* Buenos Aires. Cía. Sud-Americana
de Billetes de Banco. 1903. Pp. 584. U-4241

Estrada y Ayala, Aurora. *Como el incienso*. Guayaquil. Imp. Municipal. 1925.
Pp. 78. U-5493 D

Estrella Gutiérrez, Fermín. *Un film europeo*. Buenos Aires. Imp. Futura.
1930. Pp. 25. U-2489 n/o D

El estudiante. Madrid. Año I, núm. 2 (1925); año II, núm. 10 (1926). n/n

Etchegoyen, Gaston. 'Etude sur *Le roman de Sainte Thérèse* par Edmond
Cazal,' *Bulletin Hispanique*, XXIII, 4 (1921). Pp. 19. U-5257 D

– *L'Amour divin. Essai sur les sources de Sainte Thérèse*. Bordeaux. Feret.
1923. Pp. 380. U-1676

Etkin, Alberto M. *Primaveral. Poesías líricas*. Buenos Aires. Tor. 1929.
Pp. 217. U-5519 D

Ettiffal, Oderfla. *El pensamiento humano*. San Sebastian. Martín, Mena y
Cía. 1907. Pp. 158. U-3398 n/o

Eucken, Rudolf. *Hauptprobleme der Religionsphilosophie der Gegenwart.*
Berlin. Reuther & Reichard. 1909. Pp. viii, 172. U-3830 I

– *Die Lebensanschauungen der grossen Denker.* Leipzig. Veit. 1909. Pp. 530.
U-1787 I
– *Der Wahrheitsgehalt der Religion.* Leipzig. Veit. 1912. Pp. xiv, 422.
U-1731 I
Eugui, Fray García de. *Crónica general de España.* Ed. del ms. de El
Escorial por G. Eyzaguirre Rouse. Chile. Anales Universidad. 1907-8.
Pp. 304. U-2504
Euripides. *Euripidis Tragoediae.* Cum fragmentis ad optimorum librorum
fidem recognovit Augusutus Witzschel. 2 vols. Lipsiae. Tauchnitz. 1841.
U-4054-5 I* C T*
Europe. Revue mensuelle. Paris (Oct. 1925, fev., mai, juillet, sept. 1926). n/n
Euskalzale. Euskerazko albistari edergarriduna. Bigarren urteko liburua 1898.
Bilbon. Euskalzalen Moldagintzan. 1899. Pp. ii, 424. U-4
Euzkeltzale-Bazkuna. Clave de ejercicios. Bilbao. Editorial Vasca. 1918. Pp. 22.
U-2257
Euzkeltzale-Bazkuna. Método gradual para aprender el Euzkera. Bilbao.
Editorial Vasca. 1918. Pp. xii, 116. U-2258
Evangelina. See Caceres, Zoila Aurora
El evangelio en triunfo o historia de un filósofo desengañado. México.
Navarro. 1852. Pp. x, 284. U-1192
Excursión a Toledo. Madrid. Publ. de la Comisaría Regia del Turismo y
Cultura Artística. n.d. Pp. 16. U-5746
Exposition universelle et internationale de San Francisco. La science française.
2 vols. Paris. Ministère de l'Instruction Publique et des Beaux-Arts. 1915.
U-848-9
Fabela, Isidro. *La tristeza del amo.* Pról. Francisco Villaespesa. [Madrid]. Tip.
Artística. [1916]. Pp. 168. U-3323 D
– *Arengas revolucionarias. Discursos y artículos políticos.* Madrid. Tip.
Artística. 1916. Pp. 139. U-2105 D
Faber, Frederick William. *Bethlehem.* London. Burns & Oates. [1886].
Pp. xii, 500. U-2052 I T
Fabo del Corazón de María, Fr. Pedro. *Rufino José Cuervo y la lengua
castellana.* 3 vols. Bogotá. Arboleda & Valencia. 1912. U-1897-9
Fabra, Nilo. *Interior.* Madrid. Tip. Revista Archivos. 1905. Uc D
Fabra, Pompeyo. 'Le Catalan, dans la grammaire des langues romances de
W. Meyer-Lübke et dans le Grundriss der rom. philologie,' *Revue
Hispanique,* xvii (1907). Pp. 45. U-5262
Fabre, Ferdinand. *L'Abbé Tigrane. Candidat à la Papauté.* Paris. Charpentier.
1905. Pp. 107. U-1930
Fabricio, León. *El hipódromo.* Buenos Aires. Ivaldi & Checchi. 1909. Uc D
Fagetti, Juan A. *Pueblo chico.* Paysandú, Uruguay. Diario Moderno. n.d.
Ff. 32. U-5626 D

Falcao Espalter, Mario. *Del pensamiento a la pluma.* Barcelona. Gili. 1914.
   Pp. 352. Uc
Falchi, Persio. *Le novelle del demonio.* Firenze. Ferrante Gonnelli. n.d.
   Pp. 175. U-3240 D
Falcón César. *El pueblo sin Dios.* Madrid. Historia Nueva. 1928. Pp. 248.
   U-5691 I D
Fara-Musio, Giuseppe. *Il crocifisso.* Cagliari. Ledda. 1924. Pp. 10. U-5360 D
Faria, Carlos. *1.000$000 Reis.* Porto. Alcino Aranha. [1909]. Pp. 271.
   U-1683 D
 — *Un conto de reis.* Porto. Aranha. n.d. Uc D
Farinelli, Arturo. *Francesco Petrarca. Discorso.* Capodistria. Cobol e Priora.
   1905. Pp. 24. U-5357 D
 — *Il romanticismo in Germania.* Bari. Laterza. 1911. Uc
 — *Hebbel e i suoi drammi.* Bari. Laterza. 1912. Pp. ix, 276. U-2669 I D
 — *La vita è un sogno.* 2 vols. Torino. Bocca. 1916. U-3066-7 I D
 — *Michelangelo e Dante e altri brevi saggi.* Torino. Bocca. 1918. Pp. viii, 455.
   U-3472 D
 — *Viajes por España y Portugal desde la Edad Media hasta el siglo XX.*
   Divagaciones bibliográficas. Madrid. Centro de Estudios Históricos. 1920.
   Pp. 511. U-677
 — *Viajes por España y Portugal. Suplemento al volumen de las divagaciones*
   bibliográficas. Madrid. Centro de Estudios Históricos. 1930. Pp. 564.
   U-1200
 — 'La Spagna nella vita italiana durante la rinascenza,' *Giorn. stor. della*
   letterat. italiana, LXXI (1918), 243-302. U-3026 D
 — 'Fuga in Spagna a Vent' Anni,' *Nuova Antologia,* XIII (1935). U-5358 D
Fariña Núñez, Eloy. *Las vértebras de Pan. Cuentos.* Buenos Aires. Bibl.
   Selecta Americana. 1914. Uc
Fariña Núñez, Porfirio. *El maestro de Sarmiento, Ignacio Fermín Rodríguez.*
   Buenos Aires. Talleres Gráf. Argentinos. 1931. Pp. 30. U-2997 D
Farnell, Ida. *Spanish Prose and Poetry Old and New with Translated Speci-*
   mens. Oxford. Clarendon Press. 1920. Pp. 185. U-4154
Faro, I (1908-9). n/n
Farrand, Max. *The Development of the United States from Colonies to a*
   World Power. Pref. Viscount Bryce. London. T.C. & E.C. Jack. 1919.
   Pp. xii, 311. U-3029 I* B
Farrère, Claude. *Las temporeras.* Tr. M. García Rueda. Paris. Ollendorff.
   n.d. Uc
Fastenrath, Johann. *La Walhalla y las glorias de Alemania.* Pról. M.R. Blanco-
   Belmonte. Madrid. Rivadeneyra. 1910. Uc
Faure, Elie. *Les constructeurs.* Paris. Crès. 1914. Pp. xxviii, 267. U-3727 I D
 — *La conquête.* Paris. Crès. 1917. Pp. 274. U-1158 D

— *La sainte face.* Paris. Crès. 1917. Pp. 335. U-1953 I* D
— *La roue.* Paris. Crès. 1919. Pp. 271. U-3110 I* D
— *La danse sur le feu et l'eau.* Paris. Crès. [1920]. Pp. 209. U-417 I* C* B D
Favorables. Paris. Poema. Núms. 1, 2 (1926). U-5679-80
Febres Cordero, Tulio. *D. Quijote en América.* Mérida, Venezuela. El Lápiz. 1906. Pp. viii, 348. U-2164 D
Federación Vasca de Alpinismo. *Anuario 1930.* Bilbao. Verdes y Achirica. 1931. Pp. 190. U-4825
La Fédération Balkanique (février 1928). n/n
Feinmann, Enrique. *La ciencia del niño. Nociones de puericultura e higiene infantil.* Pról. Genaro Sisto. Buenos Aires. Cabaut. 1915. Pp. 214. U-3884 D
Felipe, León. See León-Felipe
Feliu y Vegués, Francisco. *Algunos trabajos matemáticos.* Pról. S. Mundi y Giró. Barcelona. Seix. [1905]. Pp. xiii, 221. (2 copies) U-2664, U-3028 D
Fernán, Luis. *Alma mía.* Pról. A. Meyer Arana. Epíl. V. French Matheu. Buenos Aires. Bibl. Miniatura Argentina. 1905. Pp. 109. U-4034 D
Fernandes Thomás, Pedro. *Velhas canções e romances populares portuguêses.* Introd. A. Arroyo. Coimbra. F. Amado. 1913. Pp. lii, 191. U-2203 D
Fernández, Agapito. *Los golfos de antaño.* Barcelona. La Neotipia. 1913. Pp. 156. U-3436 D
Fernández Ardavín, Luis. *Meditaciones y otros poemas.* Pról. E. Díez Canedo. Madrid. 1914. Uc
— *La eterna inquietud. Versos.* Con 'Nuestro Ardavín, forjador' de Miguel de Unamuno. Madrid. Rivadeneyra. 1922. Pp. 215. U-5475 D
Fernández-Cancela, José. *Cómo nació la familia.* Madrid. La Nación Militar. 1909. Pp. 131. U-3631 D
Fernández de Navarrete, Martín. *Vida de Miguel de Cervantes Saavedra.* Madrid. R. Academia Española. 1819. Pp. 643. U-2656
Fernández García, Alejandro. *Oro de alquimia.* Caracas. Herrera Irigoyen. 1900. Pp. xiv, 69. U-1395 D
Fernández Guardia, Ricardo. *Cuentos ticos.* San José de Costa Rica. Libr. Española. 1901. Pp. 317. U-2448 D
Fernández Pesquero, Javier. *Redención.* Santiago de Chile. Imp. del Comercio. 1905. Pp. 213. U-3127
— *El amor y la fe en la patria.* Santiago de Chile. El Globo. 1906. Pp. 14. U-2944
Fernández Shaw, Carlos. *Poesía del mar.* Madrid. Hernando. 1910. Uc D
— *La patria grande.* Pról. T. Llorente. Madrid. Hernando. 1911. Pp. 160. U-2850 D
Fernández Torres, Eleuterio. *Historia de Tordesillas.* Valladolid. Martín Sanchez. 1914. Pp. 375. U-4193 n/o

Fernández Vaamonde, Emilio. *Dulces y amargas. Poesías cortas.* Madrid. Odriózola. 1896. Uc D
- *Diálogos. Poesías.* Madrid. F. Fé. 1898. Pp. 77. U-3577 D
Ferrari Oyhanarte, Elisa. *Cepeda. 23 de octubre de 1859.* Buenos Aires. Coni. 1909. Pp. xvi, 402. U-1265 D
Ferrater Mora, José. *Cóctel de verdad.* Madrid. Ediciones Literatura. 1935. Pp. 190. U-5008 C D
Ferraz y Turmo, Vicente. *Margari o el 31 de agosto.* Madrid. F. Fé. 1913. Uc
Ferreira Borjas, B. *Misceláneas.* Buenos Aires. Imp. Evangélica. 1910. Pp. x, 279. U-3913 D
Ferreira Monteiro, Antonio. *Noites de Narciso.* Porto. Renascença Portuguesa. [1916]. Pp. 110. U-547 D
Ferreiro, Alfredo Mario. *El hombre que se comió un autobús.* Montevideo. Peña. 1927. Pp. 97. U-5014 D
Ferrer, Eduardo. *Rumores del camino y orquideas de mi sierra.* Cartagena, Colombia. Diario de la Costa. 1929. Pp. 47. U-4938 D
Ferrer de Valdecebro, Fr. Andrés. *Govierno general, moral, y político hallado en las aves más generosas, y nobles.* Madrid. Villa-Diego. 1683. Pp. 432. U-3717
Ferrería, José P. *Evolución civil y organización agraria de Asturias. Apuntes para la historia política del Principado.* Rosario, Argentina. n.d. Pp. xii, 207. U-2540 D
Ferro, Antonio. *Oliveira Salazar. El hombre y su obra.* Próls. Oliveira Salazar y Eugenio d'Ors. Madrid. Fax. 1935. Pp. xx, 238. U-1343 D
Feyjóo y Montenegro, Fr. Benito Jerónimo. *Teatro crítico universal.* Selec., pról., y notas A. Millares Carlo. Madrid. La Lectura. 1923. Pp. 335. U-951 I* B
Fialho d'Almeida, José Valentim. *A Esquina. Jornal d'um vagabundo.* Coimbra. F. Amado. 1903. Pp. xxvii, 213. U-2274
- *Barbear, pentear.* Lisboa. Teixeira. 1910. Pp. 273. U-3291 I* L
Fiallo, Fabio. *Primavera sentimental.* Caracas. Irigoyen. 1902. Pp. 101. U-2728 D
- *Cuentos frágiles.* New York. Braeunlich. 1908. Uc
Fielding, Henry. *The History of the Adventures of Joseph Andrews and His Friend Mr Abraham Adams.* Introd. G. Saintsbury. London. Dent. [1910]. Pp. lii, 387. U-1016 I* C
- *The History of Tom Jones. A Foundling.* Introd. G. Saintsbury. 2 vols. London. Dent. n.d. U-1014-15 I*
Fierens-Gevaert, H. *Nuevos estudios acerca del arte contemporáneo.* Tr. L.Ma. Cabello y Lapiedra. Madrid. F. Fé. 1904. Pp. viii, 231. U-1116
Fierros, Franciso F. *La casa de Dios.* Santo Domingo. El Independiente. [1930]. Pp. 85. U-5561 D

Figueiredo, Anthero de. *Doida de amor*. Lisboa. Ferreira. 1910. Pp. 207.
U-2379 I* C D
— *Dom Pedro e Dona Inês. O grande desvario*. Lisboa. Aillaud e Bertrand.
1914. Pp. 328. U-3325 I* C D
— *Leonor Teles, flor de altura*. Lisboa. Aillaud e Bertrand. 1916. Pp. 412.
U-3081 D
— *Antologia portuguesa*. Introd. Agostinho de Campos. Lisboa. Aillaud e
Bertrand. 1923. Pp. xcv, 262. U-3609 n/o
Figueiredo, Fidelino de. *Estudos de litteratura. Artigos varios*. Lisboa.
Teixeira. 1917. Pp. 247. U-1798
— *Historia da litteratura clássica (1502-1580)*. Lisboa. Teixeira. 1917.
Pp. x, 432. U-1789 D
— *Critica do exilio*. Lisboa. Libr. Clássica. 1930. Pp. 269. U-1979 D
— *Donjuanisme et anti-donjuanisme en Portugal*. Coimbra. Institut Français
en Portugal. 1933. Pp. 43. n/n D
— 'O dever dos intellectuaes,' *Las Ciencias*, II, 2 (1935). n/n
Figuera, P. Gaspar de la. *Suma espiritual*. Madrid. Apostolado de la Prensa.
1903. Pp. 330. U-4686
Figueroa, Pedro Pablo. *Historia de Francisco Bilbao, su vida y sus obras.
Estudio analítico*. Santiago de Chile. El Correo. 1898. Pp. ix, 253.
U-1692 n/o
Figueroa y Torres, Alvaro de (Conde de Romanones). *El ejército y la política.
Apuntes sobre la organización militar y el presupuesto de la guerra*.
Madrid. Renacimiento. 1920. Pp. 270. U-310 I
— *Amadeo de Saboya, el rey efímero*. Madrid. Espasa-Calpe. 1935. Pp. 257.
U-2652 I* D
Filartigas, Juan M. *En el Uruguay*. Montevideo. Peña. 1928. Pp. 85. U-5551
[Pages in decay]
Filosofia della fede. Appunti. Roma. Tip. dell'Unione Coop. Editrice.
[1906]. Pp. 88. U-241 n/o
Fingerit, Marcos. *Canciones mínimas y nocturnos de hogar*. Buenos Aires.
Tor. 1926. Pp. 78. U-5598 D
Finlay, George. *History of the Byzantine Empire. From DCCXVI to MLVII*.
London. Dent. 1906. Pp. xiv, 432. U-992 I* C*
— *Greece Under the Romans*. London. Dent. [1907]. Pp. viii, 469. U-1063 I
Finot, Jean. *La philosophie de la longévité*. Paris. Reinwald. n.d. Uc
Firmery, J. *Goethe*. Madrid. Autores Célebres. [1904]. Pp. 237. U-3256
Fiske, John. *El destino del hombre*. Tr. de la 25o ed. inglesa y prol.
F. de Río Urruti. Barcelona. Henrich. 1905. Uc
Fite, Warner. *Moral Philosophy. The Critical View of Life*. New York.
Dial Press. 1925. Pp. ix, 320. (2 copies) U-2994, U-5197 I* C*
— *The Living Mind*. New York. Dial Press. 1930. Pp. 317. U-1864 I D

- *The Platonic Legend.* London. Scribner's. 1934. Pp. viii, 331.
    U-4290 I* C D
Fitzmaurice-Kelly, James, et al. 'La vida del Buscón,' *Revue Hispanique,* XLIII
    (1918). U-2991
Fix, H.C. *Manual de estrategia.* Tr. D.A. Hernández Pérez. Madrid. Fortanet.
    1881. Uc
Flaubert, Gustave. *Oeuvres complètes de Gustave Flaubert.* 18 vols. Paris.
    Conard. 1910. U-1579-96 I C
- *Madame Bovary.* Paris. Charpentier. 1885. Uc
Fletcher, John Gould. *Parables.* London. Kegan Paul. 1925. Pp. xii, 143.
    U-5224 I* T D
Fleury, Abad Claudio. *Catecismo histórico.* Madrid. Amarita. 1825. Pp. 176 n/n
Flitch, J.E. Crawford. *Mediterranean Moods.* London. Richards. 1911. Pp. 323.
    U-1747 D
- *A Little Journey in Spain. Notes of a Goya Pilgrimage.* London. Richards.
    1914. Pp. 304. U-1791 I D
Florence, Jean, pseud. See Blum, Jean
Florez, Julio. *Fronda lírica. Poemas.* Madrid. Balgañón y Moreno. 1908. Uc D
Florián, Carlos. *Los moros de Granada.* Pról. Dr Perier. Versión de P. Mora
    Albenca. Madrid. F. Fé. 1897. Pp. 163. U-3150 n/o
Florian-Parmentier, Ernest. *Camille Spiess et sa psycho-synthèse.* Paris.
    Fauconnier. 1928. Pp. 35. U-5273
Florilegio de poesías castellanas del siglo XIX. Introd., notas biográficas y
    críticas Juan Valera. 2 vols. Madrid. F. Fé. 1902. U-4620-1
Floro Costa, Angel. *Rasgos biográficos del Doctor Juan Carlos Gómez.*
    Montevideo. El Siglo Ilustrado. 1905. Pp. vii, 100. U-3330
Foemina. (Mme Bulteau). *L'âme des Anglais.* Paris. Grasset. 1911. Uc
Foerster, Paul. *Spanische Sprachlehre.* 2 vols. Berlin. Weidmannsche
    Buchhandlung. 1880. U-2472-3 I* C L*
Fogazzaro, Antonio. *Daniels Cortis. Romanzo.* Torino. Casanova. 1891.
    Pp. 177. U-156 I T
Fola Igúrbide, José. *Origen del mal.* Barcelona. Artis. 1912. Pp. 201.
    U-1326 D
- *Teoría del arte.* Barcelona. Cosmopolita. n.d. Uc
Folklore argentino. Proyecto del vocal Dr J.P. Ramos. Buenos Aires. Consejo
    Nacional de Educación. 1921. Pp. 32. U-3010
Fondane, Benjamin. *Rimbaud: le voyou.* Paris. Denoël et Steele. 1933.
    Pp. 251. U-3451 I* C* D
Fonseca, Faustino da, e Joaquim Leitao. *Os filhos de Ignez de Castro.*
    Romance historico. Lisboa. Tavares Cardoso. 1905. Pp. 406. U-1307 D
Ford, Henry. *El judío internacional. Un problema del mundo.* Tr. Bruno
    Wenzel y readaptada L. Brunet. Leipzig. Hammer Verlag. 1930. Pp. 432.
    U-3756

Ford, Julia Ellsworth. 'Opium and the British Policy,' reprinted from *Unity* (2 March 1925). U-5212

Forel, Auguste Henri. *Der Weg zur Kultur.* Leipzig. Anzengruber. [1924]. Pp. 163. U-5371

Forero Franco, Guillermo. *La parroquia.* New York. 1911. Uc D

Forjaz de Sampayo, Albino María Pereira. *Palabras cínicas.* Lisboa. Fluminense. 1913. Pp. 143. U-3322 D

— *Lisboa trágica. Aspectos da cidade.* Lisboa. Fluminense. 1914. Pp. 221. U-3283 D

Fornell, J. '"El Comte Arnau" d'en Maragall. La saba popular, l'estètica, la ideologia,' Extret del *Butlletí de l'Ateneu Barcelonès,* XI-XII (1917). U-769 D

Forthuny, Pascal. *Isabel ou Le poignard d'argent. La tragédie des deux Espagnes.* Paris. Sansot. 1911. Pp. 300. U-3975 I* C* D

Fortún, Fernando. *Reliquias.* Madrid. Clásica Española. 1914. Pp. 171. U-1390 I

Forum. Kφbenhavn (1931). n/n

Fosa, Salvador de la. *El ojo clínico.* Buenos Aires. Peuser. 1915. Pp. xix, 189. U-4403

Foscolo, Niccolò Ugo. *Ultime lettere di Jacopo Ortis e discorso sul testo della Commedia di Dante.* Milano. Sonzogno. 1877. Pp. 387. U-3418 I* L*

— *Prose.* A cura di Vittorio Cian. 2 vols. Bari. Laterza. 1912. U-1820-1 I* C

— *Poesie.* Note a cura di A. Donati. Milano. Albrighi, Segati. 1927. Pp. xvi, 262. U-3944 I C T

Fouillée, Alfred. *Critique des systèmes de morale contemporains.* Paris. Baillière. 1883. Pp. xv, 408. U-841

Fradryssa, G.V. *Roman Catholicism Capitulating Before Protestantism.* Mobile, Alabama. Southern Publishing Co. 1908. Pp. xvi, 359. U-1335

France, Anatole. *Les opinions de M. Jérôme Coignard.* Paris. Calmann-Lévy. 1893. Pp. 290. U-3979 I*

— *El jardín de Epicuro.* Tr. M. Ciges Aparicio. Barcelona. Henrich. 1904. Uc

— *La rebelión de los ángeles.* Tr. Luis Ruiz Contreras. Madrid. 1914. Uc

Franceson, C.F. *Nuevo diccionario portátil de las lenguas española y alemana.* Tomo I. *Español-alemán.* Leipzig. Fleischer. [1829]. Pp. xi, 854. n/n

— *Nuevo diccionario de las lenguas española y alemana.* Tomo I. *Español-alemán.* Leipzig. Fleischer. n.d. Pp. viii, 853. U-4590

Francis of Assisi, Saint. *I fioretti di S. Francesco.* Testo di lingua secondo la lezione adottata dal P.A. Cesari. Milano. Guigoni. 1893. Pp. 216. U-473

— *I Fioretti del glorioso messere Santo Francesco e de suoi frati.* A cura di G.L. Passerini. Firenze. Sansoni. [1903]. Pp. xxvi, 342. U-474 I

— *Floretes de Sant Francesch.* Versió catalana J. Carner. Pròl. R.P. R.Ma. de Manresa. Barcelona. Gili. 1909. Pp. xxxi, 213. U-3378 n/o

Francisco de Sales, Saint. *Philotea.* Tolosan. Robert. 1749. Pp. 569. U-4432
– *Práctica del amor de Dios.* Tr. F. Cuvillas Donyague. Madrid. Villaver.
    1883. Pp. xlviii, 493. U-188
– *Introduction à la vie dévote du bienhaureux François de Sales.* Paris.
    Société Générale de Librairie Catholique. n.d. Pp. xx, 591. U-4565
Franco, Verónica. *Terze rime e sonetti.* Pref. e bibliografia a cura di G.
    Beccari. Lanciano. Carabbi. 1912. Pp. 144. U-3219 D
Francos Rodríguez, José. *El teatro en España.* Madrid. B. Rodríguez. 1909.
    Uc D
Frank, Waldo. *Our America.* New York. Boni and Liveright. [1919]. Pp. xi,
    232. U-1331 I* B
– *The Re-discovery of America. An Introduction to a Philosophy of*
    American Life. New York. Scribner's. 1929. Pp. 353. U-5216 I* C T B D
– *In America hispana.* New York. Instituto de las Españas. 1930. Pp. xi,
    292. U-1886
Franklin, Benjamin. *The Autobiography of Benjamin Franklin.* London.
    Hutchinson. 1903. Pp. 380. U-1089
Franss-Opaliinae, Didac, pseud. [i.e., Diego Ruiz]. *La vida d'en Pepet.*
    Barcelona. Horta. 1920. Pp. 78. U-3912 D
– *Mentre la llum arriba.* Barcelona. L'Aveli Artis. 1921. Pp. 79. U-4603
Frases chilenas. Paris. 1919. Pp. 73. U-4410
Fred, W. *Madrid. Die Kunst.* Herausgegeben von Ricard Muther. Wittenberg.
    Bard, Marquardt. 1906. Pp. 62. U-4434
Fredro, Jan Aleksander. *Seine einzige Tochter.* Nach dem polnischen des
    F.A.F. von Wilhelm Lange. Leipzig. Philipp Reclam. 1882. Pp. 48. U-4554
Freeman, Edward A. *The Growth of the English Constitution. From the*
    Earliest Times. Leipzig. Tauchnitz. 1872. Pp. 287. U-4773
Fregones, Arnoldo. *Odas singulares.* Buenos Aires. Athenas. 1911. Pp. 102.
    U-397 n/o D
Freire, João Paulo. *Fogos-Fátuos.* Porto. Renasçença Portuguesa. 1923.
    Pp. 173. U-2342 n/o
Frenssen, Gustav. *Das Leben des Heilands.* Berlin, Leipzig. Fischer und
    Wittig. 1907. Pp. 109. U-560 I T
– *Der Untergang von Anna Hollmann.* Berlin. Grotesche Verlagsbuchhandlg.
    1911. Pp. 198. U-1957 I T
Freud, Sigmund. *Obras completas del profesor Sigmund Freud. I. Psicopato-*
    logía de la vida cotidiana. Tr. Luis López-Ballesteros y de Torres. Pról.
    J. Ortega y Gasset. Madrid. Bibl. Nueva. 1922. Pp. 265. U-4220 I C
Freytag, Gustav. *Soll und Haben.* 2 vols. Leipzig. Hirzel. 1878. U-3950-1 T
– *Graf Waldemar.* Leipzig. Hirzel. 1887. Pp. 88. U-3695
Fría Lagoni, Mauro. *Concha Espina y sus críticos.* Toulouse. Maurin. 1929.
    Pp. 416. U-613

Friedmann, Fritz. *L'Empereur Guillaume II et la Révolution par en haut. L'Affaire Kotze.* Paris. Ollendorff. 1896. Uc

Fromentin, Eugène. *Dominique.* Paris. Plon-Nourrit. 1901. Pp. 315. U-1926 I*

Froude, J.A. *Froude's History of England.* Introds. W. Llewelyn Williams. 10 vols. London. Dent. 1909-12. U-981-90 I* C

— *Short Studies on Great Subjects.* Vol. I. *Essays in Literature and History.* Introd. Hilaire Belloc. London. Dent. 1908. Pp. xxiii, 326. U-991 I*

Fuente, Eulogio R. de la. *Toda la sed. Confesiones del Barón de Novimy.* Buenos Aires. 1914. Uc D

Fuente Arrimadas, Nicolás de la. *Fisiografía e historia del Barco de Avila.* 2 vols. Avila. Senén Martín. 1925-6. U-1294-5

Fuenzalida Grandon, Alejandro. *La evolución social de Chile (1541-1810).* Santiago de Chile. Imp. Barcelona. 1906. Pp. xi, 416. U-1199 D

Fueros leoneses de Zamora, Salamanca, Ledesma y Alba de Tormes. Ed. y estudio Américo Castro y F. de Onís. Madrid. Centro de Estudios Históricos. 1916. Pp. 339. U-726 I C

Fueros, privilegios, franquezas, y libertades del M.N. y M.L. Señorio de Vizcaya. Bilbao. Egusquiza. 1761. Ff. 383. U-1164

Fulda, Ludwig. *Der Talísman.* Stuttgart. Gotta'schen Buchhandlung. 1893. Pp. 147. U-3616 T

— *Die wilde Jagd.* Leipzig. Philipp Reclam. [1893]. Pp. 96. U-4539

— *Die Aufrichtigen.* Leipzig. Philipp Reclam. [1883]. Pp. 45. U-4528

Gabelentz, Georg von der. *Die Verwandtschaft des Baskischen mit den Berbersprachen Nord-Africas.* Herausgegeben. Dr A.C. Graf von der Schulenberg. Braunschweig. Sattler. 1894. Pp. v, 286. U-821 T

Gabriel, José. *Martorell. Monografía de arte.* Buenos Aires. Santi. 1926. Pp. 14, pl. 11. U-4962 D

Gabriel y Galán, José María. *Castellanas.* Salamanca. Núñez. 1902. Pp. xxiv, 120. U-2903 D

— *Extremeñas.* Salamanca. Calón. 1904. Pp. 61. U-5069 n/o

— *Campesinas.* Salamanca. Calón. 1904. Pp. 124. U-2894 C

— *Obras completas.* 2 vols. Madrid. F. Fé. 1917. U-1439-40

Gabulli, Plorio A. *Flores enfermas. Poesías.* Montevideo. Monteverde. 1934. Pp. 154. U-5116 D

Gache, Roberto. *La delincuencia precoz.* Buenos Aires. Lajouane. 1916. Pp. 295. U-3013

Gaffarot, Eduardo. *Comentarios a civilización y barbarie.* Buenos Aires. Europea. 1905. Pp. 242. U-743 C

Gago Rabanal, Elías. *Estudios de arqueología protohistórica y etnografía de los astores lancienses (hoy leoneses).* León. Miñón. 1902. Pp. vi, 114. U-1834

— *Arquebiología, estudio retrospectivo de la provincia de León.* León. Miñón.
　1910. Pp. viii, 124. U-850 n/o
Galbis y Rodríguez, José. *Memorias del Instituto Geográfico y Estadístico.*
　Tomo XIII. Madrid. 1905. Uc
Galilei, Galileo. *Il pensiero di Galileo Galilei.* Frammenti filosofici scelti e
　ordinati da Giovanni Papini. Lanciano. Carabba. 1909. Pp. 117. U-3572
Gallego y Burín, Antonio. *Ganivet.* Granada. Imp. de P. Ventura Traverset.
　1921. Pp. 45. U-3161
Gallegos, Rómulo. *Doña Bárbara.* Barcelona. Araluce. 1930. Pp. 395.
　U-2183 D
— *Cantaclaro.* Barcelona. Araluce. 1934. Pp. 365. U-3946 I* L* D
Gallinal, Gustavo. *Tierra española.* Barcelona. Tasso. 1914. Pp. 159. U-2077 D
Galsworthy, John. *The White Monkey.* Leipzig. Tauchnitz. 1924. Pp. 302.
　U-5162 I* L* T
— *The Silver Spoon.* Leipzig. Tauchnitz. 1927. Pp. 310. U-5163 I* L*
Galton, Francis. *Inquiries into Human Faculty and Its Development.* London.
　Dent. [1907]. Pp. xviii, 261. U-1088 I*
Gálvez, Manuel. *El enigma interior. Poemas.* Buenos Aires. 1907. Uc D
— *La maestra normal.* Buenos Aires. Nosotros. 1914. Uc D
— *Sendero de humildad.* Buenos Aires. Moen. 1909. Pp. 185. U-1983 D
— *El diario de Gabriel Quiroga.* Buenos Aires. Moen. 1910. Uc D
— *El solar de la raza.* Buenos Aires. Nosotros. 1913. Pp. 286. U-159 D
— *Nacha Regules.* Buenos Aires. Pax. 1919. Pp. 325. U-3272 I* L D
— *Humaitá.* Buenos Aires. La Facultad. 1929. Pp. 318. U-5064 I D
Gálvez y López, Pedro Luís de. *Existencias atormentadas.* Madrid. Mestre.
　1908. Pp. 315. Uc D
Gamboa, Federico. *Santa.* Barcelona. Araluce. 1903. Pp. 394. U-2149 D
Gamboa, Ignacio. *El mundo tabernario.* Hoctún, Yucatán. B. Gamboa. 1910.
　Pp. 204. Uc
Ganivet García, Angel. *Idearium español.* Granada. Sabatel. 1897. Pp. 163.
　U-2682
— *Epistolario.* Ed. F. Navarro y Ledesma. Madrid. Bibl. Nacional y
　Extranjera. 1904. Pp. 292. U-2892
— *Hombres del norte. El porvenir de España.* Madrid. Suárez. 1905. Pp. 111.
　U-3160 B
— *Granada la bella.* Madrid. Suárez. 1905. Pp. 127. U-3159
— *El escultor de su alma.* Pról. F. Seco de Lucena. Granada. El Defensor de
　Granada. 1904. Pp. 112. U-3163
— *La conquista del reino de Maya por el último conquistador español Pío
　Cid.* Madrid. Suárez. 1910. Pp. 383. U-2328 I* C
— *Los trabajos del infatigable creador Pío Cid.* 2 vols. Madrid. Suárez. 1911.
　U-3972-3 I C

Garat, D.J. *Origine des Basques de France et d'Espagne.* Paris. Hachette.
1869. Pp. vi, 294. U-4015

Garate, Justo. *Los estudios de medicina en el país vasco.* San Sebastián.
Diputación de Guipúzcoa. 1929. Pp. 19. U-4946 I D

— *Polémica entre 'El liberal' y 'La gaceta del norte.' El padre Laburu en la
biología.* Bilbao. Dochao. 1930. Pp. 70. U-4117

Garau, Francisco. *La fee triunfante en quatro autos celebrados en Mallorca
por el Santo Oficio de la Inquisición.* Palma de Mallorca. Imp. Colomar.
1931. Pp. 209. U-5487

Garay, Blas. *Compendio elemental de historia del Paraguay.* Madrid. Urbina.
1896. Pp. xvi, 297. U-3624

— *El comunismo de las misiones de la Compañia de Jesús en el Paraguay.*
Madrid. Tello. 1897. Pp. 191. U-610

Garção, Mayer. *A minha paysage.* Coimbra. Amado. 1904. Pp. 76. U-4240

— *Excelsior. (Carteira d'um idealista).* Porto. Chardron. 1907. Pp. 326.
U-3226 n/o D

García, José Jesús. *Quitolis.* Almería. Estrella. 1900. Uc D

— *Tomás I.* Almería. Estrella. 1902. Uc D

García, Juan Agustín, hijo. *La ciudad indiana. Buenos Aires desde 1600 hasta
mediados siglo XVIII.* Buenos Aires. Estrada. 1900. Pp. 375. U-2589 I*

— *Memorias de un sacristán.* Buenos Aires. Moen. 1906. Pp. 182. U-648 I D

— *La chepa leona. Narrajión colonial.* Buenos Aires. Moen. 1910. Pp. 153.
U-2820 D

— *Historia de la Universidad de Buenos Aires y su influencia en la cultura
argentina.* Tomos II, V-VIII. Buenos Aires. Coni. 1921. U-2980-4.
Vols. V, VI, VIII n/o

García, Matías (Azabeño, pseud.). *Mi Salamanca. Fin de una época.*
Salamanca. La Gaceta Regional. 1933. Pp. 222. U-4721

García Al-Deguer, Juan. *Historia de la Argentina. La dominación española.*
Madrid. La España Editorial. [1902]. Pp. vii, 261. U-2019 D

García Blanco, Manuel. *Dialectismos leoneses de un códice del Fuero Juzgo.*
Salamanca. Ferreira. 1927. Pp. 96. (2 copies) U-4970, U-5536 D

García Boiza, Antonio. *Datos para el estudio de la personalidad literaria del
Padre Luís Losada, S.J.* Salamanca. Ateneo. 1915. Pp. 30. U-4102 D

— *Nuevos datos sobre Torres Villarroel.* Salamanca. Calatrava. 1918. Pp. 23.
U-2505

García Calderón, Francisco. *Le Pérou contemporain. Etude sociale.* Préf.
W.G. Séailles. Paris. Dujarric. 1907. Pp. vi, 337. U-720 I* C*

— *Les démocraties latines de l'Amérique.* Préf. M. Raymond Poincaré. Paris.
Flammarion. 1912. Pp. 383. U-2168 I B D

— *La herencia de Lenín y otros artículos.* Paris. Garnier. 1929. Pp. 303.
U-5138 D

- *La creación de un continente.* Paris. Ollendorff. 1914. Pp. xiv, 264.
  U-3881 n/o D
- *Profesores de idealismo.* Paris. Ollendorff. n.d. Pp. 306. U-3440 D
García Calderón, Ventura. *Del romanticismo al modernismo. Prosistas y
  poetas peruanos.* Paris. Ollendorff. 1910. Pp. xvi, 545. U-2137
- *El nuevo idioma castellano.* Tr. León Pacheco. Madrid. Mundo Latino.
  1924. Pp. 109. U-5506 D
- *Si Loti était venu.* Paris. Excelsior. 1927. Pp. 105. U-5239 D
- *Couleur de sang.* Préf. Blasco Ibáñez. Paris. Excelsior. 1931. Pp. 225.
  U-2335 D
- *Frivolamente.* Paris. Garnier. 1908. Pp. vii, 301. U-598 D
García Calderón Rey, Francisco. *De litteris. Crítica.* Pról. J.E. Rodó. Lima.
  Gil. 1904. Pp. viii, 134. U-3694 C
García Camba, Andrés. *Memorias del General García Camba para la historia
  de las armas españolas en el Perú 1809-1821.* 2 vols. Madrid. Edit. América.
  n.d. U-4262-3
García de Diego, Vicente. *Elementos de gramática histórica gallega.* Burgos.
  Rodríguez. 1909. Pp. 200. U-4252 D
- *Elementos de gramática histórica latina.* 1a parte. Burgos. El Castellano.
  1911. Pp. 160. U-905
- *Elementos de gramática histórica castellana.* Burgos. El Monte Carmelo.
  1914. Pp. 324. U-81 D
García Diego, Ramón. *La emoción iluminada. Versos.* Madrid. Prast. 1927.
  Pp. 105. U-5558 n/o D
García Diego de la Huerga, Juan Tomás. *Los cantos de mi primavera.* Madrid.
  Fortanet. 1913. Pp. 190. U-3658 D
García Galdácano, José María. *Pláticas parroquiales.* Bilbao. Múller y
  Zavaleta. 1908. Pp. 226. U-2129 n/o D
García Garófalo Mesa, Manuel. *Los poetas villaclareños.* La Habana. Arroyo.
  1927. Pp. 234. U-5753 I D
García Godoy, Federico. *Rufinito. Sucedido histórico.* Santo Domingo.
  La Cuna de América. 1908. Pp. 207. U-3599 n/o D
- *De aquí y de allá.* Santo Domingo. El Progreso. 1916. Pp. 445.
  U-2891 n/o D
- *La literatura americana de nuestros días.* Madrid. Soc. Española de
  Librería. [1915]. Pp. 304. U-3249
García Hurtado, Saturnino. *Ensayo de patología social.* Madrid. Tordesillas.
  1909. Pp. 222. U-388
García Kohly, Mario. *Gambetta.* Madrid. Pueyo. 1920. Pp. 317. U-2046 D
García Maroto, Gabriel. *La canción interior.* n.p. Imp. de Rogelio de la O.
  1914. Ff. 5. U-3477 D
- *Los senderos. Poemas.* [Barcelona]. [Pedro Ortega]. [1916]. Pp. 89.
  U-1185 D

García Martí, Victoriano. *Del mundo interior. Meditaciones.* Madrid. Tip.
de Archivos. 1911. Pp. 106. U-2897 I C D
— *Del vivir heróico.* Madrid. Sáez. 1915. Pp. 189. U-3868 D
— *El sentimiento de lo eterno.* Madrid. Mundo Latino. 1929. Pp. 179.
U-3141 D
— *El amor. Ensayo.* Pról. G. Marañón. Madrid. Yagues. 1935. Pp. 207.
U-2371 D
— *La muerte. Meditación.* Madrid. Agencia General de Librería y Artes
Gráficas. 1936. Pp. 168. U-275 D
García Mercadal, José. *Del jardín de las Doloras. Impresiones.* Pról. Ramón
de Campoamor. Zaragoza. Escar. 1906. Pp. 105. U-575 D
— *Frente a la vida. Crónicas.* Pról. Rafael Pamplona. Madrid. F. Fé. 1908.
Pp. 202. U-2888 n/o D
— *Los cachorros del león.* Madrid. Alrededor del Mundo. 1912. Pp. 145.
Uc D
García Mérou, Martín. *Juan Bautista Alberdi.* Buenos Aires. Lajouane. 1890.
Pp. 480. U-2225 n/o
García Morales, Pedro. *Gérmenes.* Pról. G. Martínez Sierra. Madrid. Pueyo.
1910. Uc D
García Morente, Manuel. *La filosofía de Kant. Una introducción a la
filosofía.* Madrid. Suárez. 1917. Pp. 361. U-602 D
— *La filosofía de Henri Bergson.* Con el discurso pronunciado por H. Bergson
en la Residencia de Estudiantes el lo de mayo de 1916. Madrid.
Publicaciones de la Residencia de Estudiantes. 1917. Pp. 150. U-147
García Nieto, Juan. *Apuntes sobre el problema religioso.* Madrid. Tip. Rev.
de Arch., Bibl. y Museos. Uc D
García Paladini, Arturo. *Hacia algo más nuevo y humano. Intentos.* Madrid.
Joven América. 1929. Pp. 71. U-5639
García Paz, M. *IV Melodía. Desfíe de Ambente Galego.* Pról. Jacinto Santiago.
Orense. La Industrial. 1935. Pp. 207. U-2690 D
García Sarmiento, Félix Rubén (Rubén Darío, pseud.). *España contemporánea.*
Paris. Garnier. 1901. Pp. 394. U-3335 D
— *Peregrinaciones.* Pról. Justo Sierra. París. Bouret. 1901. Pp. 267. U-2749
— *La caravana pasa.* Paris. Garnier. [1902]. Pp. 296. U-554 D
— *Tierras solares.* Madrid. Bibl. Nacional y Extranjera. 1904. Pp. 230.
U-3202
— *Cantos de vida y esperanza. Los cisnes y otros poemas.* Madrid. Tip. Rev.
de Arch., Bibl. y Museos. 1905. Pp. vi, 175. U-4954 I* D
García Velloso, Juan José. *Lecciones de literatura española y argentina.*
Buenos Aires. Estrada. 1904. Pp. 418. U-2641 D
— *Gramática de la lengua castellana.* Buenos Aires. Estrada. 1906. Pp. 309.
U-3376

García Victoria, J.A. *El servicio militar obligatorio bajo sus diversos aspectos.*
Buenos Aires. La Semana Médica. 1911. Uc D
García y Tassara, Gabriel. *Poesías.* Madrid. Rivadeneyra. 1872. Pp. xiv, 500.
U-78 I
Garcilaso de la Vega. *Obras.* Madrid. La Lectura. 1911. Uc
— *Poesías.* Madrid. Colec. Universal. 1919. Pp. 173. n/n I*
Garibaldi, Carlos Alberto. *Tensiones y alegrías. Poemas.* Montevideo.
Albatros. 1929. Ff. 40. U-5616 n/o D
Garnier, José Fabio. *Perfume de belleza.* Valencia. Sempere. 1909. Pp. 247.
U-3966 D
Garofalo, Pasquale. *Acrisia Vichiana nella 'Scienza Nuova.' Annotazioni
critiche.* Napoli. Detken. 1909. Pp. 540. U-767 D
Garrido, Andrés. *Los abonos en viticultura.* Pról. José Zulueta. Madrid.
Bailly-Baillière. 1909. Pp. xv, 403. U-4199 n/o
Garriga, Francisco J. *Estudios elementales de literatura. Preceptiva especial.*
Barcelona. Libr. Hispano-Americana. n.d. Uc
— *Estudios elementales de literatura. Preceptiva general.* Barcelona. Libr.
Hispano-Americana. Uc D
Garzón, Eugenio. *Una hoja de laurel. La juventud de un libertador de
América.* Paris. Le Livre Libre. 1926. Pp. 126. U-5625 D
— *Jean Orth.* Paris. Belin. [1906]. Pp. 223. U-2068 D
Garzón, Tomás. *Diccionario argentino, ilustrado con numerosos textos.*
Barcelona. Elzeviriana. 1910. Pp. xv, 519. U-798 D
Gascón y Marín, José. *Los sindicatos y la libertad de contratación.* 2 vols.
Barcelona. Henrich. 1907. Uc
Gáscue, Francisco. *Orígen de la música popular vascongada. Boceto de
estudio.* Paris. Chamion. [1913]. Pp. 162. U-1677 D
Gaskell, Elizabeth Cleghorn. *Mi prima Filis.* Tr. P. Martínez Strong. Madrid.
Colec. Universal. 1920. Pp. 173. n/n I
Gaspar Remiro, Mariano. *Gramática hebrea.* Salamanca. Imp. Católica
Salmanticense. 1895. Pp. xi, 252 + 66. U-893 D
Gaspar Rodríguez, Emilio. *Hercules en Yolcos.* Habana. Rambla y Bouza.
1923. Pp. 203. U-2386 n/o D
— *Plática novísima.* La Habana. Montalvo y Cárdenas. 1929. Pp. 271.
U-5618 D
Gassol, Ventura. *Amfora.* Barcelona. [Altés]. [1917]. Pp. 56. U-2586
Gaston, Louis. *Villefranche et le Rouergue. Discours.* Villefranche.
Salingardes. 1901. Pp. 8. U-5275 D
Gatti, Angelo. *Ilia ed Alberto.* Verona. Mondadori. 1923. Pp. 491.
U-2700 I* L D
— *Le Massime e i caratteri.* Milano. Mondadori. [1934]. Pp. 313. U-236 I* D

Gaughin, Paul, et Charles Morice. *Noa Noa.* Paris. De la Plume. n.d. Pp. 239. U-2032

La Gaule et les Gaulois. Paris. Hachette. 1877. Pp. 160. U-4420

La Gaule chrétienne d'après les écrivains et les monuments anciens. Paris. Hachette. 1879. Pp. 145. U-4422

La Gaule romaine d'après les écrivains et les monuments anciens. Paris. Hachette. 1878. Pp. 163. U-4421

Gauna, Dalmiro. *Cantos de adolescencia.* Buenos Aires. La Facultad. n.d. Uc D

Gaztelu, J. *Escepticismo y realidad. Pláticas filosóficas.* San Sebastián. La Voz de Guipúzcoa. 1910. Pp. 115. U-322

— *Estudios sobre la constitución política de Guipúzcoa.* San Sebastián. Baroja. 1913. Pp. 147. U-3582 n/o D

— *Los vascos y sus fueros.* San Sebastián. Martín, Mena. 1915. Pp. 284. U-1140 D

Gebhart, Emile. *L'Italie mystique. Histoire de la Renaissance religieuse au Moyen Âge.* Paris. Hachette. 1893. Pp. vii, 331. U-3112

Geddes, Patrick, and J. Arthur Thomson. *The Evolution of Sex.* London. Walter Scott. 1901. Pp. xx, 342. U-233 I* C B

Geikie, Archibald. *Class-book of Geology.* London. MacMillan. 1893. Pp. xx, 404. U-200 I

Gelm, Robert. *Der Vierte kommt nicht.* Berlin. Ullstein. 1936. Pp. 242. U-5390

Gener, Pompeyo. *La muerte y el diablo. Historia y filosofía de las dos negaciones supremas.* Pról. E. Littré. 2 vols. Barcelona. Cortezo. 1884. U-4159-60

— *Herejías. Estudios de crítica inductiva sobre asuntos españoles.* Madrid. F. Fé. 1887. Pp. 264. U-321

— *Literaturas malsanas. Estudios de patología literaria contemporánea.* Madrid. F. Fé. 1894. Pp. 405. U-1118

— *Amigos y maestros. Contribución al estudio del espíritu humano a fines del siglo XIX.* Madrid. F. Fé. 1897. Pp. 364. U-1117

— *Cosas de España.* Barcelona. Llordachs. 1903. Pp. 360. U-2246 D

— *Pasión y muerte de Miguel Servet. Novela histórica.* Paris. Ollendorff. 1909. Pp. 306. U-1597

Genovese, Blas S. *Canciones de la noche estrellada.* Buenos Aires. Nuestra América. 1927. Pp. 111. U-5514 D

Genta, Edgardo Ubaldo. *El sentido del dolor.* Montevideo. García Morales. 1935. Pp. 176. U-3690

— *El tercio azul. Poemas.* Montevideo. Palacio del Libro. n.d. Pp. 87. U-5144 n/o D

Gentile, Giovanni. *Il modernismo e i rapporti tra religione e filosofía.* Bari. Laterza. 1909. Pp. viii, 289. U-2671

- *I problemi della scolastica e il pensiero italiano.* Bari. Laterza. 1913.
  Pp. 214. U-2670 I C B
- *Sommario di pedagogia generale. Sommario di didattica.* 2 vols. Bari.
  Laterza. 1913-14. U-874, U-4873 I
Geografía universal. Pp. 12-302. U-3703 [Volume incomplete; pages missing]
George, Henry. *Progress and Poverty.* London. Kegan Paul, Trench Trübner
  & Co. 1890. Pp. x, 406. U-2856 I* T*
Geramb, P. José Maria de. *La única cosa necesaria ... seguida de la eternidad
  se acerca y no pensamos en ello.* Barcelona. Libr. Religiosa. 1865.
  Pp. 374. U-286 B
Gerchunoff, Alberto. *Los gauchos judios.* Pról. M. Leguizamón. La Plata.
  Sesé. 1910. Pp. xvi, 186. U-3194 D
- *Nuestro señor Don Quijote.* San José de Costa Rica. Alsina. 1916.
  Pp. 56. U-2811
Germain, André. *De Proust à Dada.* Paris. Ed. du Sagittaire. [1924]. Pp. 307.
  U-5243 I D
- *Chez nos voisins.* Paris. Rieder. 1927. Pp. 230. U-1923 n/o D
Gerundio de Campazas, pseud. *Fray Manolo. 13 años entre frailes.* Madrid.
  Yunque. 1935. Pp. 266. U-1620 I* L D
Getino, O.P., Fr. Luis G. Alonso. *La Summa contra gentes y el pugio fidé.*
  Vergara. El Santísimo Rosario. 1905. Uc
Getzeny, Heinrich. *Vom Reich der Werte.* Habelschwerdt. Frankes
  Buchhandlung. 1925. Pp. 155. U-5399 I*
Gezelle, Guido. *Bloemlezing. Gedichten.* Amsterdam. Veen. [1904]. Pp. 176.
  U-1505 T* L
Ghiraldo, Alberto. *Gesta.* Buenos Aires. 'El Sol.' 1900. Uc D
- *Los nuevos caminos.* Buenos Aires. 'El Sol.' n.d. Pp. 150. U-3355 D
- *El peregrino curioso. Mi viaje a España.* Madrid. Sanz Calleja. 1917.
  Pp. 258. U-3891 D
- *Carne doliente. Cuentos argentinos.* Madrid. Sanz Calleja. n.d. Pp. 249.
  U-3079 D
- *Triunfos nuevos.* Pról. J. Más y Pi. Madrid. América. 1916. Pp. 251.
  U-2423
Ghose, S.N. *The Coulours of a Great City. Two Playlets.* London. Daniel.
  1924. Pp. 35. U-5152 D
Gibbins, H. de B. *The Industrial History of England.* London. Methuen.
  1895. Pp. viii, 240. U-620
Gibbon, Edward. *The History of the Decline and Fall of the Roman Empire.*
  7 vols. Oxford. University Press. 1907. U-452-8 I B
- *Autobiography of Edward Gibbon as Originally Edited by Lord Sheffield.*
  Introd. J.B. Bury. Oxford. University Press. [1907]. Pp. xxxi, 340.
  U-439 I*

Gibson, Percy. *Jornada heroica.* Arequipa. Quiroz. 1916. Pp. 40. U-464 D

Gide, André. *Recuerdos.* Tr. J. García-Monje. Madrid. Ed. América. 1920. Pp. 210. U-5571 [Together with Oscar Wilde's *De Profundis*]

Gide, Charles. *Cours d'economie politique.* Paris. Sirey. 1909. Pp. vii, 795. U-2590 I C D

Gigas, Emil. *Spanien omkring 1789. Kulturhistoriske fragmenter* efter D.G. Moldenhawers Rejsedagbøger. København. Gyldendalske Boghandel. 1904. Pp. 229. U-2092 I T D

Gigli, Giuseppe. *Balzac in Italia. Contributo alla biografia di Onorato di Balzac.* Milano. Treves. 1920. Pp. 236. U-3741

Gil, Martin. *Prosa rural.* Córdoba. Libr. Inglesa. 1900. Pp. 110. U-615 D

– *Agua mansa.* Córdoba. Imp. Argentina. 1906. Uc D

Gil, Pío. *El cabito.* Paris. Cosmopolita. Uc D

Gil Fortoul, José. *Historia constitucional de Venezuela.* 2 vols. Berlin. Haymann. 1907-9. U-1668-9. U-1668 I* C* D. 2a edición Caracas. Leo Hnos. 1930. Tomo I. Pp. 710. U-4215 D

– *Discursos y palabras (1910-1915).* Caracas. Imp. Nacional. 1915. Uc D

Gil y Carrasco, Enrique. *Obras en prosa de Gil y Carrasco.* Coleccionadas J. del Sino y F. de la Vera. Tomo I. Madrid. Aguado. 1883. Uc

Gilson, E. *Por un orden católico.* Tr. J.A. Maravall. Estudio Alfredo Mendizábal. Introd. J. Bergamín. Madrid. Ed. del Arbol. 1936. Pp. xlix, 198. U-2093 I*

Gimena Martínez, Víctor. *Nardos.* Villanueva del Arzobispo. Rojas Martorell. 1915. Pp. 32. U-4423

Giménez Caballero, Ernesto. *Notas marruecas de un soldado.* Madrid. Giménez. 1923. Pp. 254. U-3689 I* D

– *Los toros, las castañuelas y la Virgen.* Madrid. Caro Ragiio. 1927. Pp. 192. U-5012 C D

– *Yo, inspector de alcantarillas. Epiplasmas.* Madrid. Bibl. Nueva. 1928. Pp. 205. U-5534

– *Hércules, jugando a los dados.* Madrid. La Nave. 1928. Pp. 215. U-5118

– *La nueva catolicidad. Teoría general sobre el fascismo en Europa: en España.* Madrid. La Gaceta Literaria. 1933. Pp. 220. U-3503 D

– *Genio de España.* Madrid. La Gaceta Literaria. 1934. Pp. 270. U-3885 D

– *El Belén de Salcillo en Murcia.* Madrid. La Gaceta Literaria. 1934. Pp. 134. U-3147 D

– *Arte y estado.* Madrid. Universal. 1935. Pp. 260. U-2480 D

– *Exaltación del matrimonio. Diálogos de amor entre Laura y Don Juan.* Madrid. Giménez. 1936. Pp. 123. U-1458

Giménez Lomas, Francisco. *Diccionario manual latino-español.* Madrid. Hernando. 1886. Pp. vi, 772 + 332. n/n

Giménez Pastor, Arturo. *Versos de amor*. Buenos Aires. 1912. Ff. 35.
U-4437 n/o D

Giner de los Ríos, Francisco. *Educación y enseñanza*. Madrid. El Tajo. 1889.
Pp. xx, 216. U-1504 D

— *Estudios sobre educación*. Madrid. Bibl. Económica Filosófica. 1892.
Pp. 194. U-4429 n/o D

— *Estudios y fragmentos sobre la teoría de la persona social*. Madrid. Rojas.
1899. Pp. 433. U-2582 D

— *Ensayos sobre educación*. Pról. M.B. Cossío. Madrid. La Lectura. 1902.
Pp. xv, 354. U-853 I

— *Filosofía y sociología. Estudios de exposición y de crítica*. Barcelona.
Henrich. 1904. Uc D

— *Obras completas. I. Principios de derecho natural*. Madrid. Clásica
Española. 1916. Pp. xxii, 319. U-2118

— *La universidad española*. Madrid. 1916. Uc

— y Alfredo Calderón. *Prolegómenos del Derecho. Principios de derecho
natural*. Madrid. 1916. Uc

Gini, Corrado. *I fattori demografici dell'evoluzione delle nazioni*. Torino.
Fratelli Bocca. 1912. Pp. 142. U-2511 D

Giran, Etienne. *Jésus de Nazareth. Notes historiques et critiques*. Paris.
Fischbacher. 1904. Pp. 167. U-3304

— *Le Christianisme progressif*. Paris. Nourry. 1909. Pp. 144. U-3475 D

— *Job, fils de Job. Essai sur le problème du mal*. Paris. Fischbacher. n.d. Uc D

Girón Cerna, Carlos. *Ixquic. Tragedia mitológica Quiché*. La Habana. Hermes.
1935. Pp. 71. U-1547 D

Girondo, Oliverio. *20 Poemas para ser leídos en el tranvía*. Argenteuil.
Coulouma. 1922. Ff. 28. U-3549 D

Gisbert Gosálbez, Antonio. *¡Marcha atrás! Tratado político social*. Madrid.
Bergua. [1935]. Pp. 255. U-2385 D

Giusti, Roberto F. *Nuestros poetas jóvenes*. Buenos Aires. Nosotros. 1911.
Pp. 190. U-3795 D

Givanel y Mas, Juan. *Devocionario poético. Antología sagrada*. Barcelona.
López. n.d. Pp. 162. U-4419

Glaeser, Ernst. *Los que teníamos doce años. Novela de la guerra*. Tr. W. Roces.
Madrid. Cenit. 1929. Pp. 304. U-5098 C

Glosario de voces ibéricas y latinas usadas entre los mozárabes. Estudio sobre
el dialecto hispano-mozárabe por don Francisco Javier Simonet. Madrid.
Fortanet. 1888. Pp. ccxxxvi, 628. U-58

Godoy, Armand. *Laudes*. Paris. Sibi et Paucis. 1927. n/n D

— *Hosanna sur le Sistre*. Paris. Emile-Paul. [1928]. Pp. 216. U-5233 D

— *Páginas escogidas*. Tr. E. Aviles Ramírez. Paris. Excelsior. 1929. Pp. 108.
U-5001

— *Du Cantique des Cantiques au chemin de la Croix.* Paris. Grasset. 1934. Pp. 201. U-3893. n/o

— *Del Cantico dei Cantici alla Via della Croce.* Versione poetica italiana Vincenzo de Simone. Milano. Sicolorum Gymnasium. 1935. Pp. 201. U-5332

— *Le drame de la passion.* Paris. Grasset. 1935. Pp. 121. U-1607 n/o

— *Il dramma della passione.* Versione poetica Salvatore Lo Presti. Milano. Sicolorum Gymnasium. [1935]. Pp. 125. U-2951

Godoy, Juan Silvano. *Monografías históricas.* Buenos Aires. Lajouane. 1893. Uc

— *'Alberdi por el señor Olleros' Comentario crítico.* Asunción. Kraus. 1906. Uc D

Goerres, Johann Joseph von. Vorreden und Epilog zum *Athanasius.* Regensburg. Manz. 1838. Pp. xlv, 156. U-3818

Goethe, Wolfgang. *Gedichte.* Stuttgart. Cotta'schen Buchhandlung. 1871. Uc

— *Faust.* Mit Einleitung von Karl Goedeke. Stuttgart. Cotta. Uc

— *Sämtliche Werke.* Mit einer Einleitung von J.R. Haarhaus. 10 vols. Leipzig. Reclam. n.d. U-1094-103. Vol. I I. vol. V I* B. vols. VI-VII I* C*

— *Poesías de Goethe.* Tr. Eugenio de Castro. Lisboa. Bertrand. 1909. Pp. 102. U-1725

— *La Marguerideta. Escenas del Faust.* Tr. Joan Maragall. Barcelona. L'Avenç. 1904. Pp. 92. U-4452

Gogorza y González, José. *Elementos de biología general.* Madrid. Suárez. 1905. Pp. xiii, 608. U-4849 D

Goiri' tarr Sabin, Arana eta. *Lecciones de ortografía del euskera bizcaino.* Bilbao. Sebastián de Amorrortu. 1896. Pp. 305. U-5697

Goldschmidt, Werner. *Der Linguismus und die Erkenntnistheorie der Verweisungen.* Leipzig. Recht und Gesellschaft. 1936. Pp. 184. U-5401 I D

Goldsmith, Oliver. *The Works of Oliver Goldsmith.* Introd., notes, and a life of O. Goldsmith by J.F. Waller. London. Cassell, Petter and Galpin. n.d. Pp. xliv, 369. U-718 I* T*

— *She Stoops to Conquer* and *The Good-natured Man.* London. Cassell. 1894. Uc

Goll, Claire. *Der Neger Jupiter raubt Europa.* Berlin. Ullstein. [1926]. Pp. 251. U-4723

Gomes de Brito, Bernardo. *Historia trágico-marítima.* 3 vols. Lisboa. Escriptorio. 1904. U-1852-4 I* L

Gómez, Alfonso Javier. *Madre glotona.* Medellín. Imp. Editorial. 1912. Pp. 131. U-1530 n/o D

Gómez, Eusebio. *La mala vida en Buenos Aires.* Pról. J. Ingenieros. Buenos Aires. Roldán. 1908. Pp. 240. U-2159 D

— *Criminología argentina. Reseña bibliográfica.* Buenos Aires. Europea.
   1912. Uc D
Gómez, Jig, pseud. [i.e., Juan Ignacio Gálvez]. *Domingueras. Costumbres*
   Sur-Americanas. Pról. L.E. Escudero. Quito. Gálvez. 1910. Pp. xvi, 255.
   U-2450 D
Gómez, Valentín. *La ley de la fuerza.* Madrid. Montoya. 1886. Pp. 74.
   U-3955
Gómez Carrillo, Enrique. *Maravillas.* Madrid. F. Fe. 1899. Uc
— *El alma encantadora de París.* Pról. A. Cortón. Barcelona. Maucci. 1902.
   Pp. 256. U-3986
— *La Rusia actual.* Pról. D.A. Vicenti. Paris. Garnier. 1906. Pp. xviii, 216.
   U-1146 D
— *En las trincheras.* Madrid. Hernando. 1916. Uc
— *En el corazón de la tragedia.* Madrid. Hernando. 1916. Pp. 289. U-3172
— *Tres novelas inmorales.* Madrid. Mundo Latino. [1919]. Pp. 302. U-2116
— *El libro de las mujeres.* 2 vols. Madrid. Mundo Latino. 1919-21. U-2005-6
— *Primeros estudios cosmopolitas.* Madrid. Mundo Latino. [1921]. Pp. 271.
   U-1927
— *Grecia.* Pról. Jean Moréas. Madrid. Imp. Artística. 1914. Pp. 366. U-4004 I
— *De Marsella a Tokio. Sensaciones de Egipto, la India, la China y el Japón.*
   Pról. Rubén Darío. Paris. Garnier. n.d. Pp. xiii, 269. U-4707 D
— *Jerusalén y la tierra santa.* Paris. Michaud. n.d. Pp. 315. U-158 I* C* D
— *Entre encajes.* Pról. Max Nordan. Barcelona. Sopena. n.d. Uc D
— *El alma japonesa.* Paris. Garnier. n.d. Uc
— *Flores de penitencia.* Paris. Michaud. n.d. Pp. 327. U-889 D
Gómez de Baquero, Eduardo (Andrenio, pseud.). *Novelas y novelistas.*
   Madrid. Calleja. 1918. Pp. 330. U-395
Gómez de la Serna, Javier. *España y sus problemas.* Madrid. El Liberal. n.d.
   Pp. 315. U-1990
Gómez de la Serna, Ramón. *Beatriz. Evocación mística en un acto.* Madrid.
   Soc. de Autores Españoles. 1909. Pp. 31. U-3764
— *El drama del palacio deshabitado.* Madrid. Soc. de Autores Españoles.
   1909. Ff. 20. U-3704
— *Variaciones.* Madrid. Publ. Atenea. 1922. Pp. 256. U-535 D
— *La mujer de ámbar. Novela grande.* Madrid. Bibl. Nueva. [1928]. Pp. 254.
   U-5117 I
— *La utopia.* n.p. n.d. Pp. 36. U-3027
— *El concepto de la nueva literatura.* Madrid. Aurora. n.d. Pp. 32. U-4188
Gómez Hidalgo, F. *Marruecos – la tragedia prevista.* Pról. M. Domingo.
   Madrid. Pueyo. 1921. Pp. 295. U-2640 I*
Gómez Jaime, Alfredo. *Impresiones rápidas. Viajes.* Madrid. Hernando Santos.
   1905. Pp. vii, 88. U-1964 [Vol. incomplete]

— *Rimas del trópico.* Madrid. Imp. de Archivos. 1907. Pp. 146. U-1992 D

Gómez Moreno González, Manuel. *Guía de Granada.* Granada. Ventura. 1892. Pp. 530. U-153

— *Catálogo de la exposición de sus obras, notas críticas y apuntes biográficos.* Granada. Ateneo. 1928. Pp. xv, 34, pl. 17. U-2006

Gómez Pestaña, Luis. *¡Paz!* Habana. Moderna. 1915. Pp. 147. (2 copies) U-3371, U-4694 D

Gómez Redondo, Fernando. *Sindicats d'initiative. Su internacionalización.* Valladolid. Montero. 1908. Uc D

Gómez V., Ernesto. *La hija de la montaña. Novela.* Medellín. Imp. Editorial. 1911. Pp. 287. U-2620 D

Gomila, Sebastián. *Tributo al odio.* Barcelona. Taberner. n.d. Pp. xv, 254. U-1115 D

Goncourt, Edmond et Jules. *Germinie Lacerteux.* Paris. Charpentier. 1887. Pp. xiii, 279. U-3313 C*

Góngora Echenique, Manuel. *El problema de la tierra.* Madrid. Góngora. 1921. Pp. 202. U-5126 n/o D

González, D. *Pulchra leonina.* León. Alvarez, Chamorro. 1913. Uc D

González, Eloy G. *Al margen de la epopeya.* Caracas. Imp. Nacional. 1906. Pp. 253. U-844

González, Fernando. *Las canciones del alba.* Pról. G.G. Puigdeval. Las Palmas. Tip. Canarias Turista. 1918. Pp. 136. U-2353 D

— *Viaje a pie.* Paris. Le Livre Libre. 1929. Pp. 270. U-5565 I D

González, Joaquín V. *Debates constitucionales (1898-1902).* Tomo I. La Plata. Sesé. 1904. Uc

— *La tradición nacional.* Buenos Aires. Lajouane. 1888. Pp. 535. U-1520

— *Educación y gobierno.* Buenos Aires. Lajouane. 1905. Uc

— *Universidades y colegios.* Buenos Aires. Lajouane. 1907. Pp. 501. U-3401

— *Política espiritual.* Buenos Aires. Lajouane. 1910. Uc D

— *El juicio del siglo o Cien años de historia argentina.* Buenos Aires. La Facultad. 1913. Pp. 298. U-3664 D

González, Juan Vicente. *Biografía de José Félix Ribas.* Pref. R. Blanco-Fombona. Paris. Garnier. n.d. Pp. lxxxix, 262. U-3666

González, Julio V. *Significación social de la reforma universitaria.* Buenos Aires. Publ. Centro Estudiantes Derecho. 1924. Pp. 30. U-4928

— *Ensayo histórico sobre el humanismo.* Buenos Aires. Araujo. 1925. Pp. 94. U-5754

— *Tierra fragosa.* Buenos Aires. Roldán. 1926. Pp. 265. U-4998 I D

— *La reforma universitaria.* Pról. A. Ponce. Buenos Aires. Rev. Sagitario. 1927. Pp. 300. U-4867 D

— *La reforma universitaria.* Tomo II. Buenos Aires. Rev. Sagitario. 1927. Pp. 222. U-5567

— *La emancipación de la universidad.* Pról. J.C. Rébora. Buenos Aires. Tall.
    Gráf. Argentinos. 1929. Pp. 366. n/n D
— *Reflexiones de un argentino de la nueva generación.* Buenos Aires. Pueyo.
    1931. Pp. 247. U-1472 I D
González, Luis Felipe. *Historia de la influencia extranjera en el desenvolvi-*
    miento educacional y científico de Costa Rica. San José, C.R. Imp.
    Nacional. 1921. Pp. xi, 317. U-4311 D
González, María Rosa. *Samaritana. Poemas.* Santiago de Chile. Nascimento.
    1924. Pp. 61. U-5230 n/o D
— *Arcoiris. Poemas.* Santiago de Chile. Nascimento. 1925. Pp. 50.
    U-5068 n/o D
González, Pedro A. *Poesías.* Santiago. Miranda. 1905. Pp. 333. U-3294 I D
González, Zeferino. *Filosofía elemental.* 2 vols. Madrid. Policarpo López.
    1876. U-897-8 I C
González Anaya, Salvador. *La sangre de Abel.* Madrid. Renacimiento. 1915.
    Pp. 354. U-3863 I L* D
— *El castillo de irás y no volverás.* Madrid. Pueyo. [1921]. Pp. 435. U-3965
— *Las brujas de la ilusión.* Madrid. Renacimiento. 1923. Pp. 363. n/n D
— *Nido de cigüeñas.* Madrid. Espasa-Calpe. 1927. Pp. 423. n/n D
González Arrili Bernardo. *El pobre afán de vivir.* Buenos Aires. Menéndez.
    1928. Pp. 156. U-5104 D
González Bastías, Jorge. *Misas de primavera.* Santiago. Bellavista. 1911. Uc D
González Blanco, Andrés. *Escritores representativos de América.* Madrid.
    Edit. América. 1917. Pp. ix, 351. U-431 D
González Blanco, Edmundo. *El feminismo en las sociedades modernas.* 3 vols.
    Barcelona. Henrich. 1904. Uc
— *El materialismo combatido en sus principios cosmológicos y psicológicos.*
    Madrid. Suárez. 1906. Pp. 282. U-3072 n/o
— *El hilozoísmo como medio de concebir el mundo.* Barcelona. Henrich.
    1915. Pp. 255. U-490 D
González de Arintero, Fr. Juan T. *La evolución y la filosofía cristiana.*
    Introducción general y libro primero. Madrid. G. del Amo. 1899. Pp. x,
    559. U-4097 n/o
González de la Calle, Pedro Urbano. *Sebastián Fox Morcillo. Estudio*
    histórico-crítico de sus doctrinas. Madrid. Asilo de Huérfanos del S.C. de
    Jesús. 1903. Pp. 381. Uc D
— *Ideas político-morales del P. Juan de Mariana. Apuntes y notas.* Madrid.
    Tip. Rev. de Arch., Bibl. y Museos. 1915. Pp. 101. U-4120
— *Varia. Notas y apuntes sobre temas de letras clásicas.* Madrid. Suárez.
    1916. Pp. 345. U-413 I D
— *Ensayo biográfico. Vida profesional y académica de Francisco Sánchez*
    de las Brozas. Madrid. Suárez. 1922. Pp. 536. U-4318 D

González de la Vega, Francisco. *La reforma de las leyes penales en México.*
México. Secretaría de Relaciones Exteriores. 1935. Pp. 181. U-1709 n/o
González Díaz, Francisco. *Especies.* Las Palmas. Tip. del Diario. 1911. Pp. iv,
308. U-3034 I D
González de Fernández, Clotilde M. *Antología hispano-americana.* Pról. E.
Quesada. Buenos Aires. Peuse. 1906. Uc D
González García, Teodoro. *Liberalismo y renovación.* Gijón. Noroeste. 1921.
Pp. 28. U-5533 D
González Hontoria, Manuel. *El protectorado francés en Marruecos y sus
enseñanzas para la acción española.* Madrid. Publicaciones de la Residencia
de Estudiantes. 1915. Pp. 338. U-3635
González Martínez, Enrique. *Silenter.* Mocorito, México. Voz del Norte.
[1909]. Pp. 143. U-4958 n/o D
González Olmedilla, Juan. *Poemas de Andalucía.* Pról. de Villaespesa. Madrid.
F. Fé. 1912. Pp. 174. U-3647 D
– *La llave de oro. Poesías.* Madrid. Helénica. 1914. Uc D
– *La ofrenda de España a Rubén Darío.* Preliminar de R. Blanco-Fombona.
Madrid. América. 1916. Pp. xii, 266. U-2711
González Prada, Manuel. *Horas de lucha.* Lima. El Progreso Literatio.
1908. Uc D
– *Exóticas. Poesías.* Lima. El Lucero. 1911. Pp. 164, iv. U-2949 D
González Rebollar, Hipólito. *La nueva política. Críticas de actualidad.*
Laguna de Tenerife. Curbelo. 1914. Pp. 350. U-1614 D
González Revilla, Gerardo. *La protección de la infancia abandonada.* Bilbao.
Tip. Popular. 1907. Uc D
González Serrano, Urbano. *Psicología del amor.* Madrid. F. Fé. 1897. Pp. 348.
U-2763 D
– *Preocupaciones sociales.* Madrid. F. Fé. 1899. Uc D
– *Siluetas.* Madrid. Rodríguez Serra. 1899. Pp. 93. U-4040
– *Goethe. Ensayos críticos.* Pról. Leopoldo Alas. Madrid. Libr.
Internacional. 1900. Pp. 495. U-543 n/o D
– *La literatura del día (1900 a 1903).* Barcelona. Henrich. 1903. Pp. 254.
U-4909
González Suárez, Federico. *Memoria histórica sobre Mutis y la expedición
botánica de Bogotá en el siglo decimo octavo (1782-1808).* Quito. Imp.
del Clero. 1905. Pp. xxxi, 127. U-824
González Trilla, Casimiro. *La ciudad octogonal.* Asunción. Edit. Paraguaya.
1927. Pp. 228. U-5759 D
González Vera, J.S. *Alhué. Estampas de una aldea.* Santiago de Chile. Imp.
Universitaria. 1923. Pp. 119. U-5521 C
Gorbea Lemmi, Eusebio de. *Los mil años de Elena Fortún Magerit.* Madrid.
Calleja. 1922. Pp. 282. U-3474 D

Gordon, Charles George. *Reflections in Palestine. 1883.* London. MacMillan.
    1884. Pp. x, 124. U-152 I C
— *The Journals, of Major Gen. C.G. Gordon, at Kartoum.* Introd. and notes
    A. Egmont Hake. 2 vols. Leipzig. Tauchnitz. 1885. U-4767-8. U-4767 I.
    U-4768 B*
Gorgevitch, T.R. See Dordević, Tihomir R.
Gorki, Maksim, pseud. [i.e., Aleksei Maksimovich Peshkov]. *Los tres.* Tr.
    Augusto Riera. Barcelona. Maucci. 1902. Uc
— *La angustia.* Tr. Eusebio Heras. Barcelona. Maucci. 1902. Uc
— *Geld.* Wien und Leipzig. Wiener. 1903. Uc
— *Ricordi su Leone Tolstoi.* Tr. Odoardo Campa. Firenze. La Voce. 1921.
    Pp. 86. U-3869 I*
— *Mein reisegefährte und zwei andere Erzählungen.* Leipzig. Reclam. n.d.
    Pp. 87. U-4551
Gorostarzu, Mario. *Discursos y conferencias.* Pról. O. Magnasco. Buenos Aires.
    Peuser. 1911. Uc D
Gorriti, Fernando. *El 'baldeísmo,' su situación nosográfica y tratamiento.*
    Buenos Aires. La Semana Médica. 1935. Pp. 11. U-2242
— *Consideraciones sobre 'El pozo de balde.' Novela de Rosa Bazán de
    Cámara y su baldeísmo.* Buenos Aires. Tall. Gráf. Argentinos. 1935.
    Pp. 61. U-3078
Gorriti, Juana Manuela. *Sueños y realidades.* 2 vols. Buenos Aires. La Nación.
    1907. U-4462-3
Gortazar, Juan Carlos de. *Bilbao a mediados del siglo XIX, según un
    epistolario de la época.* Bilbao. Bibl. Amigos del País. 1920. Pp. xxi, 261.
    U-1437 I* L
Goti Aguilar, Juan Carlos. *Crítica nuestra.* Buenos Aires. Colombo. 1935.
    Pp. 124. U-2361 D
Goy de Silva, Ramón. *La reina silencio.* Madrid. Vidal. 1911. Uc D
— *La corte del cuervo blanco.* Madrid. Velascor. 1914. Pp. xxii, 127.
    U-3289 D
Gracián y Morales, Baltasar. *El héroe. El discreto.* Estudio crítico A. Farinelli.
    Madrid. Rodríguez Serra. 1900. Pp. 277. U-4619
— *El héroe.* Reimpresión Adolphe Coster. Chartres. Lester. 1911. Pp. 48.
    U-2503
— *Tratados.* Pról. y ed. A. Reyes. Madrid. Calleja. 1918. Pp. 300. n/n I*
— *Pages caractéristiques.* Etude critique A. Rouveyre. Tr. et notices V.
    Bouillier. Paris. Mercure de France. 1925. Pp. 322. U-5318 I L
— *Balthasar Gracian's Hand-Orakel und Kunst der Weltklugheit.* Aus dem
    Spanischen original übersetzt von Arthur Schopenhauer. Leipzig. Reclam.
    n.d. Pp. 178. U-4529

Graell, Guillermo. *La cuestión catalana*. Barcelona. A. López. 1902. Pp. vi, 215. U-1883
- *Conferencias sobre economía política*. Barcelona. Bayer. [1913]. Pp. 331. U-3771 D
- *Historia del fomento del trabajo nacional*. Barcelona. Tasso. 1911. Pp. 506. U-791 n/o

Graetz, H. *Les juifs d'Espagne 945-1205*. Tr. G. Stenne. Paris. Calmann-Lévy. 1872. Pp. vii, 436. U-1838 I

Graham, Gabriela Cunninghame. *Rhymes from a World Unknown*. London. Duckworth. 1908. Pp. 56. U-1304
- *The Christ of Toro and Other Stories*. London. Nash. 1908. Pp. xi, 275. U-1308

Graham, James M. *A World Bewitched*. London. Harper. 1898. Pp. 357. U-2623 D

Graham, María. *Diario de su residencia en Chile (1822) y de su viaje al Brasil (1823)*. Pról. de J. Concha y del traductor José Valenzuela. Madrid. Edit. América. n.d. Pp. 451. U-1776 I

Graham, R.B. Cunninghame. *Success*. London. Duckworth. 1902. Pp. xiv, 196. U-232
- *A Hatchment*. London. Duckworth. 1913. Pp. xv, 254. U-3873 D

Granada, Nicolás. *Cartas gauchas*. Buenos Aires. Kraft. 1910. Pp. 122. U-2044 D

Grand-Carteret, John. *Le jeune premier de l'Europe*. Paris. Michaud. [1910]. Pp. xviii, 263. U-3792

La Grande Revue. Paris (Mars 1931). n/n

Grandmontagne, Francisco. *Teodoro Foronda*. Buenos Aires. La Vasconia. 1896. Pp. 315. U-4456 I C

Granizo, León Martín. *De lo que vió un castellano en Suiza y de lo que apuntó sobre ella*. León. Alvarez, Chamorro. 1913. Pp. 149. (2 copies) U-245. U-3476 D

Gras y de Esteva, Rafael. *Zamora en tiempo de la guerra de la independencia (1808-1814)*. Madrid. Centro de Estudios Históricos. 1913. Pp. 273. U-2470 D
- *La Pahería de Lérida. Organización municipal 1149-1707*. Lérida. Sol y Benet. 1911. Pp. xiv, 363. Uc D

Grau Delgado, Jacinto. *Trasuntos*. Precedidos de una carta de J. Maragall. Barcelona. A. López. 1899. Pp. 419. U-5057 D
- *Don Juan de Carillana*. Madrid. Beltrán. [1913]. Pp. xiv, 117. U-2185 D
- *Entre llamas*. Madrid. Renacimiento. [1915]. Pp. xvii, 150. U-4315 D
- *El conde Alarcos*. Madrid. Minerva. 1917. Uc D
- *El hijo pródigo*. Madrid. Atenea. 1918. Pp. 372. U-3211 I D
- *El señor de Pigmalión*. Madrid. Atenea. 1921. Pp. 254. U-4633 D

Graux, Charles. *L'Université de Salamanque.* Discours MM. G. Paris et E.
Lavisse. Paris. Dupret. 1887. Pp. 84. U-4509

Gray, Thomas. *The Poems of Thomas Gray.* With a selection of Letters and
Essays. Introd. J. Drinkwater. London. Dent. [1912]. Pp. xxiii, 390.
U-1074

Greca, Alcides. *Laureles del pantano.* Buenos Aires. La Baskonia. 1915.
Pp. 220. U-3182 D

— *Viento norte.* Rosario. Inca. 1927. Pp. 235. U-4903 D

— *La torre de los ingleses.* Buenos Aires. Inca. 1929. Pp. 220. U-5678 I* C D

Greef, Guillaume de. *Introduction à la sociologie.* 2 vols. Bruxelles. Mayolez.
1886-9. U-2521-2

— *Las leyes sociológicas.* Tr. P. Umbert. Barcelona. Henrich. 1904. Uc

— *La evolución de las creencias y de las doctrinas políticas.* Tr. P. Umbert.
2 vols. Barcelona. Henrich. 1904. Uc

Green, John Richard. *A Short History of the English People.* London.
MacMillan. 1889. Pp. xlvii, 872. U-3843 I*

Grijalba, Alfonso R. de. *El contrato de trabajo ante la razón y el derecho.*
Preámbulo E. Sanz y Escartín. Pról. Conde de Romanones. Madrid.
Beltrán. [1922]. Pp. 274. U-3036 n/o D

Grijalba y Alcocer, José de. *Poesías.* Madrid. F. Fé. 1905. Uc

Grillo, Max. *Emociones de la guerra.* Bogotá. La Luz. 1903. Pp. 304.
(2 copies) U-3308-9 n/o

— *Ensayos y comentarios.* Paris. Le Livre Libre. 1927. Pp. 346. U-4884 D

Grimberg, Carl. *Svenska folkets underbara öden.* Stockholm. Norstedt.
[1916]. Pp. 584. U-2553 I* B T* D

Grimm, Jacob Ludwig Carl, and Wilhelm Carl. *Aus Grimms Märchen (20 der
schönsten Märchen der Brüder Grimm).* Wien. Konegen. 1925. Pp. 148.
U-5463 T

Grogger, Paula. *Das Gleichnis von der Weberin.* Breslau. Ostdeutsche. 1929.
Pp. 44. U-576

Grondijs, L.-H. *Les Allemands en Belgique.* Paris. Berger-Levrault. n.d.
Pp. 123. U-4634

Grosse, Ernst. *Los comienzos del arte.* Tr. P. Umbert. 2 vols. Barcelona.
Henrich. 1906. Uc

Grossi, Tommaso. *Marco Visconti.* Firenze. Le Monnier. 1889. Pp. 415.
U-533 B

Grote, George. *A History of Greece.* Introd. A.D. Lindsay. 12 vols. London.
Dent. [1907]. U-953-64. Vols. III-V, VII-X I. vols. VII, VIII C. vol. XI B

Groussac, Paul. *Mendoza y Garay.* Buenos Aires. Menéndez. 1916.
Pp. xxxi, 546. Uc

Gual, Adriá. *Llibre d'horas.* Barcelona. Verdaguer. 1899. Ff. 40. U-2580 D

— *L'Emigrant.* Barcelona. Joventut. 1901. Pp. 199. U-3353 D

– *Silenci.* Barcelona. Verdaguer. [1898]. Pp. 113. U-3908 D
– *Misteri de dolor.* Barcelona. Verdaguer. 1904. Pp. 121. U-3907 D
– *La fi de Tomas Reynals.* Barcelona. Verdaguer. [1905]. Pp. 180. U-2718 D
– *Nocturn. Andante moral.* Barcelona. Verdaguer. [1897]. Pp. 71.
   U-2294 D
Guansé, Domènec. *Per Catalunya! Contra una antologia escolar.* Barcelona.
   Bibl. Catalana d'Autors Independentes. 1934. Pp. 140. U-221
Guanyabéns y Jané, Emilio. *Alades. Poesies.* Barcelona. L'Avenç. 1897.
   Pp. 102. U-1856 C D
– *Volianes.* Barcelona. Tobella & Costa. 1903. Pp. 121. U-2895 D
Guardia, José Miguel, et J. Wierzeysky. *Grammaire de la langue latine d'après
   la méthode analytique et historique.* Paris. Durand et Pedone-Lauriel.
   1876. Pp. lxxix, 773, 53. U-2653 I C
Guardiola, Antonio. *La guerra.* Madrid. Bibl. Museo. 1914. Uc D
– *¡¡A la plaza!!* Madrid. Bibl. Museo. 1915. Uc D
Guardiola Valera, Eliseo. *Importancia social del arte.* Pról. A. Bonilla San
   Martín. Tomo I. Madrid. Suárez. 1907. Pp. xv, 306. U-4404 D
Guenne, Jacques. *Prague, ville d'art.* Paris. Libr. Larousse. [1930]. Pp. 186.
   U-59
Guerau de Liost, Micer, pseud. [i.e., Jaume Bofill i Matas]. *La montanya
   d'amethystes; Poesies.* Prol. E. d'Ors. Barcelona. Octavi Viader. 1908.
   Pp. xxii, 276. U-3473
Guerdile, Claudio. *Retorno.* Buenos Aires. Tragant. 1913. Pp. 295. U-627 D
Guérin, George Maurice de. *Le Centaure ... La Bacchante.* Notice E. Pilon.
   Paris. Sansot. 1905. Pp. 84. U-4424
Guerlin, Henri. *Les villes d'art célèbres. Ségovie, Avila et Salamanque.* Paris.
   Renouard, H. Laurens. 1914. Pp. 144. U-1642 D
Gueroco Guero edo arimaren eguitecoen Gueroco utzteac. Bayonan.
   Lamaignère, Alhargunaren Moldequintcan. 1864. Pp. xxiii, 569. U-1567
Guerra, Angel. *Polvo del camino.* Barcelona. López. n.d. Uc
Guerra Gallego, Antonio. *Artefactos explosivos.* Salamanca. Núñez. 1934.
   Pp. 63. U-4654 D
Guerra Junqueiro, Abilio. *Patria.* Porto. Chardron. 1896. Uc D
– *Os simples.* Lisboa. Pereira. 1898. Pp. 126. U-587 T D
– *Oração á Luz.* Porto. Chardron. 1904. Pp. 32. U-1766 D
– *Antologia portuguesa. Junqueiro. Verso e prosa.* Organizada por
   Agostinho de Campos. Paris. Aillaud e Bertrand. 1920. Pp. lxv, 258.
   U-1966
Guerreiro, Candido. *Sonetos.* Porto. Renascença Portuguesa. 1916. Pp. 143.
   U-546 D
Guevara, Fr. Antonio de. *Menosprecio de corte y alabanza de aldea.* Pról., ed.,
   y notas M. Martínez de Burgos. Madrid. La Lectura. 1915. Pp. 261.
   U-936 I L

Guevara, Tomás. *Historia de la civilización de Araucania.* Tomo I.
    Antropología. Santiago de Chile. Anales de la Universidad. 1898. Pp. 309.
    U-3539
Guía de Bilbao y conductor del viajero en Vizcaya. Bilbao. Depont. 1846.
    Pp. 125. U-1575
Guía de Cuenca. Cuenca. Museo Municipal de Arte. 1923. Pp. xviii, 238.
    U-593
Guía-Indicador de los ferrocarriles españoles. Barcelona. Servicio Oficial de
    las Compañías. Julio 1931. Pp. 103. U-1831
Guiard Larrauri, Teófilo. *Historia de la noble villa de Bilbao.* 3 vols. Bilbao.
    Astuy. 1905-8. U-2597-9
—, Manuel Torres López, y Antonio Elías y Suárez. *Las ordenanzas del
    consulado de Bilbao.* Tres conferencias. Bilbao. Academia de Derecho y
    Ciencias Sociales de Bilbao. 1931. Pp. 104. U-2507
Guicciardini, Francesco. *Ricordi politici e civili.* Lanciano. Carabba. 1910.
    Pp. 125. U-1999 I
Guichot, Joaquín. *Don Pedro Primero de Castilla.* Sevilla. Gironés y Orduña.
    1878. Uc
Guichot y Sierra, Alejandro. *La montaña de los ángeles.* Sevilla. La Religión.
    1896. Uc D
— *Ciencia de la mitología. El gran mito chtónico-solar.* Pról. M. Sales Ferré.
    Madrid. Suárez. 1903. Uc D
— *Antropo-sociología.* Sevilla. Artes Gráf. 1911. Pp. 308. U-2999 n/o D
— *Cómo habla Ancián de algunos aspectos de las sociedades civilizadas.*
    Sevilla. 1913. Uc
Guide de Palma et l'île de Majorque. Leipzig. Woerl. n.d. Pp. 66. U-4648
Guido y Spano, Carlos. *Poesías completas.* Buenos Aires. Maucci. 1911.
    Pp. xxi, 434. (2 copies) U-4307 I. U-4812
— *Clásicos y modernos. Poesías.* Apreciaciones preliminares R. Darío y
    J.E. Rodó. San José de Costa Rica. Colec. Ariel. 1914. Pp. 56 + 32.
    U-577
Guignebert, Charles. *L'Evolution des dogmes.* Paris. Flammarion. 1910.
    Pp. 351. U-3342 I B
Guillén, Alberto. *Deucalion.* Pról. V. García Calderón. Madrid. Izquierdo.
    [1921]. Pp. 132. U-5073 D
— *El libro de las parábolas.* Madrid. Nosotros. [1921]. Ff. 60. (2 copies)
    U-4602, U-5022 n/o D
Guillén, Jorge. *Cánticos.* Madrid. Revista de Occidente. 1928. Pp. 171.
    U-5101 C* D
Guillot Muñoz, Gervasio. *Misaine sur l'estuaire.* Montevideo. La Cruz del Sur.
    1926. Pp. 56. U-5274 D

Guimerá, Angel. *Poesías*. Pról. Joseph Yxart. Barcelona. J. Ortega. 1905. Uc
Güiraldes, Ricardo. *Cuentos de muerte y de sangre*. Buenos Aires. La Facultad.
1915. Uc D
— *El cencerro de cristal*. Buenos Aires. Juan Roldán. 1915. Pp. 263.
U-3080 D
— *Don Segundo Sombra*. Buenos Aires. El Ateneo. 1927. Pp. 363. n/n I*
Guirao, Pedro. *Lo oculto. La ciencia de triunfar y de vivir desarrollada en
ejemplos*. Madrid. F. Fé. 1914. Uc
Guiteras y Soto, J. *La paz de la tarde*. Valencia. Pan. 1909. Uc D
Guixé, Juan. *Problemas de España*. Madrid. El Liberal. 1912. Pp. 190.
U-3576 D
— *Idea de España*. Madrid. Soc. General Española de Librería. [1915].
Pp. 247. U-1132 D
— *La nación sin alma*. Madrid. El Liberal. 1917. Pp. 224. U-4292 D
Gumplowicz, Ludwik. *La lutte des races. Recherches sociologiques*. Tr.
Charles Baye. Paris. Guillaumin. 1893. Pp. xi, 381. U-1258 I
Gundolf, Friedrich. *César histoire et légende*. Tr. M. Beaufils. Paris. Rieder.
1933. Pp. 305. QP-23 I
Guthrie, William Norman. *The Relation of the Dance to Religion*. Manhattan.
Stuyvesant Book Guild. n.d. Pp. 36. U-5149
Gutiérrez, Eduardo. *El rastreador*. Buenos Aires. Maucci. 1892. Pp. 319.
U-2442
— *La muerte de un héroe*. Buenos Aires. Maucci. 1892. Uc
— *Hormiga negra*. Buenos Aires. Maucci. 1894. Uc
— *Pastor luna*. Buenos Aires. Maucci. 1895. Uc
— *El chacho*. Buenos Aires. Maucci. 1895. Uc
Gutiérrez, Federico A. *Gérmenes*. Buenos Aires. Rev. Nacional. 1902. Pp. 112.
U-3179 D
Gutiérrez Alfaro, Antonio. *Pobres versos*. Buenos Aires. Ruiz. 1926. Pp. 138.
(2 copies) U-5481, U-5601 n/o D
Gutiérrez Gamero, Emilio. *El ilustre Manguindoy*. Madrid. Velasco. 1899.
Pp. 380. U-1928
— *Andróminas*. Barcelona. Tasso. [1901]. Pp. 177. U-2812 D
— *El conde perico*. Madrid. Hernando. 1906. Pp. 293. U-3787 n/o D
— *La olla grande*. Madrid. F. Fé. 1909. Pp. 294. U-2067 D
— *La piedra de toque*. Madrid. Dossat. 1910. Pp. 350. U-2070 D
— *El placer del peligro*. Madrid. Alrededor del Mundo. 1912. Pp. 224.
U-425 D
Gutiérrez Nájera, Manuel. *Poesías*. 2 vols. Paris. Bouret. 1905. U-4391-2
— *Sus mejores poesías*. Apreciación R. Blanco-Fombona. Madrid. Soc.
Española de Librería. 1915. Pp. 296. U-3460

Gutiérrez Solana, José. *El pintor español (Homenaje)*. Madrid. Espasa Calpe.
    1936. Pp. 46, pl. 104. U-1173 D
Guyau, Jean Marie. *La morale anglaise contemporaine. Morale de l'utilité et*
    de l'évolution. Paris. Alcan. 1885. Pp. xii, 432. U-112 C
— *Esquisse d'une morale sans obligation ni sanction*. Paris. Alcan. 1885.
    Pp. 254. U-840 I*
Guzmán, Alberto. *Elementos de gramática castellana*. Santiago de Chile.
    Universo. 1905. Pp. 152. U-3137 D
Guzmán, Ernesto A. *En pos*. Santiago de Chile. Universitaria. 1906. Pp. 113.
    U-2782 I
— *Los poemas de la serenidad*. Santiago. Universitaria. 1914. Uc D
— *El árbol ilusionado*. Santiago. Universitaria. 1916. Pp. 138. U-2816 D
Guzmán, Eugenio. *El Quijote y los libros de caballerías*. Barcelona. Maucci.
    [1922]. Pp. 190. U-5018 I L*
Guzmán, Martín Luis. *El águila y la serpiente*. Madrid. Aguilar. [1928].
    Pp. 402. U-4913 D
H.A. 'D. Armando Palacio Valdés,' Nagra anteckningar of A.H., *Spansk*
    Nutidslitteratur. Upsala (1895). U-1742 D
Hackett, Francis. *El rey Barba Azul. Enrique VIII y sus seis mujeres*. Tr.
    Isabel de Palencia. Madrid. Edit. España. 1931. Pp. 522. n/n [Volume
    incomplete]
Haeckel, Ernst. *Essais de psychologie cellulaire*. Tr. et préf. Jules Soury.
    Paris. Baillière. 1880. Pp. xxix, 158. U-595
Haggard, Sir Henry Rider. *She and Allan*. Brussels. Collins. 1921. Pp. 284.
    U-3386 T
Halbe, Max. *Lebenswende*. Dresden. Bondi. 1896. Pp. 145. U-3615 I C T
Hale, John Richard. *The Story of the Great Armada*. New York. Nelson.
    [1916]. Pp. vi, 478. U-4746
Halecki, Oskar. *La Pologne de 963 à 1914. Essai de synthèse historique*.
    Préf. Alfred Coville. Paris. Alcan. 1933. Pp. xv, 348. U-5245 I
Halévy, Daniel. *Histoire de quatre ans. 1997-2001*. Paris. Cahiers de la
    Quinzaine. 1903. Pp. xv, 143. U-632 I
Hall, Basil. *El General San Martín en el Perú*. Tr. y pról. Carlos A. Aldao.
    Buenos Aires. Vaccaro. 1920. Pp. 289. U-1797
Hallet, Bernard. *Epaves*. Paris. A la Jeune Parque. 1931. Pp. 184. U-3153 D
Halphen, Louis. *L'Essor de l'Europe. XIe-XIIIe siècles*. Paris. Alcan. 1932.
    Pp. 609. QP-24 I
Hamann, Johann Georg. *Scritti e frammenti del Mago del Nord*. Tr. e introd.
    R.G. Assagioli. Napoli. Perrella. 1908. Pp. lxxxi, 184. U-1527 D
Hamilton, Alexander, J. Jay, and J. Madison. *The Federalist or the New*
    Constitution. Introd. W.J. Ashley. London. Dent. [1911]. Pp. xx, 456.
    U-1026 I*

Hamlet-Gómez. See Sánchez Ruiz, Antonio
Hamsun, Knut. *Sult.* Kristiania. Gyldendalske Boghandel. 1899. Pp. 310.
U-1946 I* T*
Handbuch der Weltliteratur. Zusammengestellt durch L. Goldin. Warsche.
Kunst & Wissenschaft. 1931. Pp. 535. U-2188 [German in Hebrew
characters]
Hanssen, Friedrich. *Spanische Grammatik.* Halle A.S. Niemeyer. 1910.
Pp. xvii, 277. U-1801
Haraneder, M. Joannes de. *Philotea* edo devocioneraco bide erakusçaillea
S. Franses Salescoac, Genevaco Aphespicu eta princeac. Tolosan.
Joannes-Franses Robert. 1749. Uc
Harbottle, T.B., and Martin Hume. *Dictionary of Quotations.* London.
Sonnenschein. 1907. Pp. vii, 462. Uc
Harden, Maximilian. *Apostata.* Berlin. Stilke. 1892. Pp. 209. U-3612 I*
Hardenberg, Friedrich Leopold von (Novalis). *Novalis' Schriften.*
Herausgegeben von J. Minor. 4 vols. Jena. Diederichs. 1907. U-226-9 I T
Hardy, Thomas. *Tess of the D'Urbervilles. A Pure Woman.* 2 vols. Leipzig.
Tauchnitz. 1892. U-5158-9 I
– *Far From the Madding Crowd.* London. Osgood, McIlvaine. 1895.
Pp. xii, 476. U-4798 I T
– *Jude the Obscure.* 2 vols. Leipzig. Tauchnitz. 1896. U-5160-1 I*
Haringer, Jakob. *Die Dichtungen.* Potsdam. Kiepenheuer. 1925. Pp. 240.
U-5378 I
Harnack, Carl Gustav Adolf von. *Lehrbuch der Dogmengeschichte.* 3 vols.
Freiburg i. B. Mohr. 1890-4. U-812-14 I* C*
– *Das Wesen des Christentums.* Leipzig. Hinrichs'sche. 1900. Pp. 189.
U-1277 I C
– *La esencia del cristianismo.* Tr. J. Miró Folguera. 2 vols. Barcelona.
Henrich. 1904. Uc
– *Beiträge zur Einleitung in das neue testament. III. Die Apostelgeschichte.*
Leipzig. Hinrichs'sche. 1908. Pp. 225. U-3829
Harper's Magazine (June 1928). n/n
Harrison, Jane Ellen. *Epilegomena to the Study of Greek Religion.*
Cambridge. University Press. 1921. Pp. 40. U-2214 D
Hartmann, Carl Robert Eduard von. *Philosophie de l'inconscient.* Tr. et
introd. D. Nolen. 2 vols. Paris. Baillière. 1877. U-1803-4 I
Hartmann, Sadakichi. *Passport to Immortality.* Beaumont, Calif. Author's
edition. 1927. Pp. 32. U-5196
Haskin, Frederic J. *The Panama Canal.* New York. Doubleday. 1913. Pp. xi,
386. U-1904
Haslam, Walter T. *From Death into Life.* London. Jarrold. 1904. Pp. xii,
318. U-3996 D

Hasmonaea. Bucarest (1929). n/n

Hatch, Edwin. *The Influence of Greek Ideas and Usages upon the Christian Church.* Ed. A.M. Fairbairn, D.D. Oxford. Williams and Norgate. 1901. Pp. xxiii, 359. U-4180 I B*

Hatzfeld, Adolphe, et Arsène Darmesteter. *Dictionnaire général de la langue française.* 2 vols. Paris. Delagrave. n.d. n/n

Hauff, Wilhelm. *Märchen.* Leipzig. Reclam. n.d. Pp. 372. U-4512 T

Hauptmann, Gerhart. *Fuhrmann Henschel.* Berlin. Fischer. 1899. Pp. 100. U-3613 T L*

Hawthorne, Nathaniel. *The Scarlet Letter.* Leipzig. Tauchnitz. 1852. Pp. vi, 311. U-4772. Chicago. Rand, McNally. n.d. Pp. 292. U-1334 T

Haynes, E.S.P. *The Belief in Personal Immortality.* London. Watts. 1913. Pp. viii, 156. U-2392

Hazlitt, William. *Winterslow, Essays and Characters Written There.* London. Frowde. [1902]. Pp. vii, 213. U-461 I*

– *The Spirit of the Age or Contemporary Portraits.* London. Frowde. [1904]. Pp. 271. U-462 I*

– *Sketches and Essays.* London. Frowde. [1905]. Pp. 244. U-460 I

– *Table-Talk. Essays on Men and Manners.* London. Frowde. [1905]. Pp. vi, 450. U-459 I*

– *Lectures on the English Comic Writers.* Introd. R. Brimley Johnson. Oxford. Frowde. [1907]. Pp. xv, 248. U-463 I

Head, F.B. *Las pampas y los Andes. Notas de viaje.* Tr. y pról. C.A. Aldao. Buenos Aires. Vaccaro. 1920. Pp. 188. U-4183

Hebbel, Christian Friedrich. *Herodes und Marianne.* Leipzig. Reclam. [1850]. Pp. 108. U-4544 B

– *Gyges und sein Ring.* Leipzig. Reclam. [1856]. Pp. 71. U-4543

– *Die Nibelungen.* Leipzig. Reclam. 1862. Pp. 202. U-4541 B

– *Maria Magdalene.* Leipzig. Reclam. n.d. Pp. 88. U-4542 I* T

– *Agnes Bernauer.* Leipzig. Reclam. n.d. Pp. 95. U-4552 T

Hegel, Georg Wilhelm Friedrich. *Wissenschaft der Logik.* Herausgegeben von D. Leopold von Henning. 3 vols. Berlin. Duncker und Humblot. 1841. U-1260 I

Hein. *L'Eté à l'ombre.* Paris. Sansot. 1908. Uc D

– *Cils Mi-Clos.* Paris. Bibliothèque Générale d'Edition. Uc D

Heine, Heinrich. *Heine's Sämtliche Werke.* Leipzig. Reclam. [1887]. U-1091-3. Vol. III I* C* [Vols. I, III, IV]

– *Letzte Gedichte.* Halle. Hendel. 1887. Pp. viii, 118. U-5452 T

– *Intermezzo.* Tr. catalana Apeles Mestres. Barcelona. Llibr. Espanyola. 1895. Pp. 63. U-3269

Helmantica. Buenos Aires (Dic. 1936). n/n

Heltai, Jenö. *Zimmer 111.* Berlin. Ullstein. n.d. Pp. 251. U-4724 T

Helvétius, Claude Adrien. *De l'esprit.* 2 vols. Paris. Chasseriau. 1822. U-4044-5
Henao, P. Gabriel de. *Averiguaciones de las Antigüedades de Cantabria.* 7 vols.
    Tolosa. López. 1894-5. U-3003-9
Henríquez Ureña, Pedro. *Horas de estudio.* Paris. Ollendorff. [1910]. Pp. 304.
    U-1126
 – *En la orilla. Mi España.* México. Cultura. 1922. Pp. 167. U-2171 D
 – *La utopía de América.* La Plata. Estudiantina. 1925. Pp. 22. U-5581 D
Herbert, George. *The Poems of George Herbert.* Introd. Arthur Waugh.
    Oxford. University Press. 1907. Pp. xxviii, 277. U-443 I*
Herculano de Carvalho e Araujo, Alexandre. *Lendas e narrativas.* 2 vols.
    Lisboa. Tavares Cordoso & Irmäo. 1900. U-1577-8 I C
 – *Poesias.* Lisboa. Tavares Cardosso. 1904. Pp. 336. U-265
 – *Opúsculos.* 10 vols. Lisboa. José Bastos. [1907-8]. U-168-77 I C L
 – *Anthologia portuguesa ... Herculano. I. Quadros literários da historia*
    medieval, peninsular e portuguesa. Introd. d'Agostinho Campos. Lisboa.
    Aillaud e Bertrand. 1919. Pp. l, 296. U-298
 – *Scenas de um anno da minha vida e apontamentos de viagem.* Coordenaçao
    e pref. V. Nemésio. Lisboa. Bertrand. 1934. Pp. lv, 323. U-2771 I* L* D
Heredia y Campuzano, José María de. *Les trophées.* Paris. Alphonse Lemerre.
    n.d. Pp. iv, 218. U-1156
 – *Los trofeos.* Tr. y pról. A. de Zayas. Madrid. F. Fé. n.d. Uc
Heredia y Mieses, J.F. *Memorias del Regente Heredia.* Madrid. Edit. América.
    1916. Pp. 301. U-2527
Heredia y Mota, Nicolás. *La sensibilidad en la poesía castellana.* Madrid.
    Soc. Española de Librería. [1915]. Pp. 302. U-5000 I
Hernández, Belisario. *El libro de los madrigales.* Buenos. Aires. Moen. 1914.
    Pp. 145. U-3633 D
Hernández, Eusebio, y Félix Restrepo. *Llave del griego. Colección de trozos*
    clásicos. Friburgo de Brisgovia. Herder. 1912. Pp. xxiii, 566. U-2683 D
Hernández, José. *El gaucho Martín Fierro.* Buenos Aires. La Facultad. 1919.
    Pp. lxxxvii, 230. U-3151 I
Hernández, P. Pablo. *Organización social de las doctrinas guaranies de la*
    Compañía de Jesús. 2 vols. Barcelona. Gili. 1913. U-1215-16 I B
Hernández Cata, A. *Los frutos ácidos.* Madrid. Renacimiento. 1915.
    Pp. 247. n/n D
Hernández González, Luis. *Canciones de la mañana.* Pról. M. Machado.
    Madrid. Edit. Madrid. 1929. Pp. 142. U-5478 D
Hernández Luquero, N. *El ensueño roto.* Madrid. Pueyo. [1910]. Pp. 125.
    U-2039 D
Hernández y Alejandro, Federico. *Lo que siento y lo que pienso.* Pról.
    A. Zozaya. Madrid. 1913. Pp. 154. U-4169 D

Hernansáez, José Ma. *Bocetos agrícolas.* Cartagena. La Cosecha. 1929. Pp. 346.
    U-5009 D
Herodotus. *Herodoti historiarum* libri novem. Curavit F. Palm. Accedit
    libellus de vita Homeri et index historicus. 3 vols. [bound together].
    Lipsiae. Holtze. 1865. U-4047 I* C T
— *Morceaux choisis.* Publiés et annotés Ed. Tournier. Paris. Hachette. 1896.
    Pp. xliii, 292. U-4466 I* T
Heros, Martín de los. *Historia de Valmaseda.* Pról. Sr Marqués de San Juan de
    Piedras Albas ... Bajo la dirección y con notas de D. Gregorio de
    Balgarparda. Bilbao. Echeguren y Zulaica. 1926. Pp. xxxix, 525.
    U-4952 I* C*
— *Privilegios reales de Valmaseda. Apéndice a la historia de Valmaseda.*
    Bilbao. Echeguren y Zulaica. 1926. Pp. 112. U-5760
Herrán, Fermín. *Apuntes para una historia del teatro español antiguo.*
    Madrid. F. Fé. 1887. Pp. ix, 270. U-2702 D
Herrera, Adolfo. *Metodología de la escritura. Teoría y práctica.* Buenos Aires.
    Tragant. 1920. Pp. 200. U-3952 D
Herrera, Ataliva. *El poema nativo.* n.p. Nosotros. 1916. Pp. 201. U-3105 D
Herrera, Lucilo Pedro. *Poesías. Antología hispanoamericana.* Buenos Aires.
    Rosso. 1932. Pp. 414. U-139
Herrera, Luis Alberto de. *La revolución francesa y sud-América.* Paris.
    Dupont. 1910. Pp. 396. U-2193 D
— *El Uruguay internacional.* Paris. Grasset. 1912. Pp. 401. Uc D
Herrera y Obes, Manuel. *Correspondencia del Doctor Manuel Herrera y Obes.*
    Diplomacia de la defensa de Montevideo. 2 vols. Buenos Aires. Martino.
    1913. U-4086-7
Herrera y Reissig, Julio. *El teatro de los humildes. Poesías.* Montevideo.
    Bertani. 1913. Pp. 154. U-4343
— *Los peregrinos de piedra. Poesías.* Montevideo. Bertani. 1913. Pp. 212.
    U-4342
— *Las Pascuas del tiempo.* Montevideo. Bertani. 1913. Pp. 150. U-4344
— *La vida y otros poemas.* Montevideo. Bertani. 1913. Pp. 151. U-3275
— *Las lunas de oro.* Montevideo. Bertani. 1913. Pp. 150. U-2094
— *Ciles alucinada y otras poesías.* San José de Costa Rica. García Monge.
    1916. Pp. 64. U-4689 I
Herrero, Antonio. *Almafuerte, su vida y su obra.* Buenos Aires. Martín García.
    1918. Pp. 194. U-3109 D
— *Imperialismo espiritual. Misión de la Argentina.* La Plata. Edit. Almafuerte.
    1936. Pp. 69. U-3281 D
Herrero, José J. *La mano y su expresión en el arte de Velázquez.* Madrid. Imp.
    Ministerio de Marina. 1927. Pp. 10. U-5774 D

Herrero Ducloux, Enrique. *La ciencia y sus grandes problemas.* Introd.
Joaquín V. González. Buenos Aires. Coni. 1908. Uc
— *Los estudios químicos en la república Argentina (1810-1910).* Buenos
Aires. Coni. 1912. Pp. 431. U-1178 D
Herrero Mayor, Avelino. *Artesanía y prevaricación del castellano.* Buenos
Aires. Gleizer. 1931. Pp. 170. U-1469 L D
Herreros, Pedro. *El libro de los desenfados.* Buenos Aires. Tragant. 1915. Uc D
Herrick, Robert. *The Poems of Robert Herrick.* London. Frowde. [1903].
Pp. 402. U-442 I*
Herrig, Hans. *Gesammelte Aufsätz über Schopenhauer.* Herausgegeben E.
Grisebach. Leipzig. Reclam. n.d. Pp. 115. U-4545 C*
Herrmann, Wilhelm. *Der Verkehr des Christen mit Gott.* Stuttgart.
Cotta'schen Buchhandlung. 1896. Pp. vii, 296. U-1280 I* C*
— *Ethik.* Tübingen. Mohr. 1909. Pp. xv, 229. U-863 I
Hertzka, Theodor. *Eine Reise nach Freiland.* Leipzig. Reclam. n.d. Pp. 64.
U-4557 T L [Volume incomplete]
— *Las leyes de la evolución social.* Versión directa de la última edición
alemana por J. Maciá. Barcelona. Henrich. 1908. Uc
Hesiod. *Hesiodi Carmina.* Recensuit Aloisius Rzach. Editio altera. Accedit
certamen quod dicitur Homeri et Hesiodi. Lipsiae. Teubner. 1908. Pp. v,
263. U-349 I* T*
— *Les travaux et les jours.* Ed. nouvelle P. Mazon. Paris. Hachette. 1914.
Pp. 160. U-5256 I* C
Hesseling, D.C. *Histoire de la littérature grecque moderne.* Tr. N. Pernot.
Paris. Les Belles Lettres. 1924. Pp. xi, 180. U-5310
Hidalgo, Alberto. *España no existe.* Buenos Aires. Agencia General de Libr.
y Publ. 1921. Pp. 115. U-3606 D
— *Tu libro.* Pref. E. González Martínez. Buenos Aires. Mercatali. 1922.
Pp. 134. U-262 D
Hillman, Adolf. 'P. Luis Coloma,' *Spansk Nutidslitteratur.* Nágra antechningar
(1895), 21-31. U-774 D
— 'Juan Valera,' *Spansk Nutidslitteratur.* Nágra antechningar (1894),
485-93. U-771 D
— 'D. Benito Pérez Galdós,' *Spansk Nutidslitteratur.* Nágra antechningar
(1894), 624-36. U-4152
— 'D. José María de Pereda,' *Spansk Nutidslitteratur.* Nágra antechningar
(1895), U-4151 D
— 'Da. E. Pardo Bazán,' *Spansk Nutidslitteratur.* Nágra antechningar (1895).
U-4150 D
— 'Antonio de Trueba,' en *Baskisk Folklifsskildrare,* Skald och Historiker.
1899. Pp. 57. U-772 D

Hilty, C. *Glück.* 3 vols. Frauenfeld. Hubers. 1900-1. U-164-6 I C
Hirschfeld, Georg. *Die Mütter.* Berlin. Fischer. 1896. Pp. 144. U-1881 I*
*Hispanic Anthology. Poems Translated From Spanish by English and North
    American Poets.* Collected Thomas Walsh. New York. Putnam's.
    1920. Pp. 779. U-1411
*Hispanic Notes and Monographs. Essays, Studies and Brief Biographies
    Issued by the Hispanic Society of America.* New York. 1919- :
        List of Wood-Carvings. 1925. U-5151
        Sorolla. 1926. Pl. 32. U-4345. Pp. 2, pl. 32. U-4346
        Jet. Pp. 2, pl. 44. 1930. U-4355
        Ten Panels Probably Executed ... by the Indians of New Mexico. Pp. v,
            25, pl. 11. 1926. U-4739
        Fourteen Spanish Manuscript Documents. Pp. vii, 9. 1926. U-4731
        The Nuns of Santa Clara Sevilla and Juan Guzmán. Ms B 6. Pp. 16.
            1927. U-517
        Inez González, Widow of Alfonso Martínez de las Casas Pintadas. Ms.
            B 11. Pp. 19. 1927. U-4730
        Juan Pérez de Villalvin and his Wife. Ms. B 12. Pp. 13. 1927. U-4729
        Effigies of a Knight of Santiago and his Lady. Pp. v, 10, pl. 2. 1927.
            U-4352
        Pantoja de la Cruz. Pp. v, 10. 1927. U-4735
        Góngora. Pp. v, 4, pl. 4. 1927. U-3387
        Góngora. Delicias del Parnaso. Pp. 14. Ed. of *Todas las obras.* Pp. 42.
            1927. U-4737-8
        Moro. Pp. v, 25, pl. 5. 1927. U-4736
        El Greco. Pp. 2, pl. 37. 1930. U-4351
        *The Tombs of Don Gutierre de la Cueva and Doña Mencia Enríquez de
            Toledo.* Pp. v, 41. 1927. U-4740
        A Privilegio Rodado. King Henry the Second of Castilla. Sevilla.
            26 May 1371. Ms B 8. Pp. 32. 1928. U-4728
        A Privilegio Rodado. Alfonso the Tenth King of Castilla. 8 March 1255.
            Ms. B 13. Pp. 32. 1928. U-4727
        Incunabula ... Arte para bien confesar. Hurus? Zaragoza, 1500? 1928.
            Pp. 3, pl. 2. U-4741
        List of Books Printed Before 1601. Compiled Clara Louisa Penney.
            1929. Pp. xiv, 274. U-2309
        López Mézquita ... Scenes. 1930. Pp. 28. U-2911
        Viladrich. 1930. Pp. 2, pl. 35. (3 copies) U-4347-8, U-2326
        Catalogue of Paintings. 14th and 15th Centuries. By Elizabeth du Gué
            Trapier. 1930. Pp. liii, 256. U-3784
        Catalogue of Sculpture, 16th to 18th Centuries. Compiled Beatrice I.
            Gilman. 1930. Pp. li, 360. U-2408

Catalogue of Paintings, 16th, 17th, and 18th Centuries. Compiled Elizabeth du Gué Trapier. 1929. Pp. xxxvi, 280. U-3880

Daniel Urrabieta Vierge. By Elizabeth du Gué Trapier. 1936. Pp. xl, 186, pl. 24. U-1319

List of Publications. 1926. Ff. 26. U-5658

José Solano. Cannon. 1935. Pp. 23. U-3311

Periodicals in American Libraries for the Study of the Hispanic Languages and Literatures. Compiled Hayward Keniston. 1927. Ff. 32. U-4732

José de Ribera. 1926. Pp. 19, pl. 2. U-4734

Lead-Glazed Pottery From Valencia. 1930. P. 1, pl. 7. U-4349

Modern Glass From Valencia and Cataluña. 1930. Pp. 2, pl. 17. U-4350

Fajalauza Ware. 1930. Pp. 2, pl. 8. U-4353

Unglazed Pottery From Fraga, Lérida. 1930. P. 1, pl. 11. U-4354

Modern Sevillian Pottery. 1930. Pp. 2, pl. 14. U-4356

Modern Pottery From the Basque Provinces. 1930. P. 1, pl. 6. U-4357

Modern Pottery From Muel. 1930. P. 1, pl. 10. U-4358

Modern Pottery From Manises. 1930. Pp. 2, pl. 10. U-4359

Modern Talavera Pottery. 1930. Pp. 2, pl. 13. U-4360

Mudejar Wood-Carvings. 1928. Pp. 63, pl. 16. U-4733

Fourteenth-Century Painting in the Kingdom of Aragón Beyond the Sea. 1929. Pp. 25, pl. 10. U-215

Zuloaga. 1928. Pp. 37, pl. 8. U-4742

Cancionero de Baena. Reproduced in facsimile from the unique manuscript in the Bibliothèque Nationale. Foreword H.R. Lang. 1926. Pp. 33, pl. 2. U-2818

Hispano, Cornelio, pseud. [i.e., Ismael López]. *Leyenda de oro.* Caracas. El Cojo Ilustrado. 1911. Pp. 90. U-3408

— *Colombia en la guerra de independencia. La cuestión venezolana.* Pról. M.F. Suárez. Bogotá. Arboleda y Valencia. 1914. Pp. xiii, 318. U-399 n/o

— *En el país de los dioses.* Bogotá. Edit. de Cromos. 1927. Pp. 279. U-4906 D

Historiadores de Indias. Tomo II. Ed. M. Serrano y Sanz (NBAE, 15). Madrid. Bailly-Baillière. 1909. Pp. 678. U-50 I* L C

Hobbes, Thomas. *Leviathan or the Matter, Form and Power of a Commonwealth, Ecclesiastical and Civil.* London. Routledge. n.d. Pp. x, 501. U-449 I*

Hobson, John A. *Problems of Poverty.* London. Methuen. 1895. Pp. vi, 232. U-606 I* T B

Hoche, Jules. *El emperador Guillermo II Intimo.* Tr. M.R. Blanco Belmonte. Barcelona. La Vida Literaria. 1906. Pp. 286. U-3949

Hoelderlin, Johann Christian Friedrich. *Hölderlins Werke*. Herausgegeben von Manfred Schneider. 4 vols. Stuttgart. Walter Hädecke. 1921. U-5412-15 I*

Hoernes, Moriz. *Prehistoria II. La edad del bronce*. Tr. y anotado en lo relativo a la cultura ibérica Luis Pericot. Buenos Aires. Labor. 1929. Pp. 153. U-5527

Høffding, Harald. *S. Kierkegaard*. Stuttgart. Frommanns. 1896. Pp. 170. U-1300 I*

– *Religionsfilosofi*. København. Gyldendalske Boghandel. 1906. Pp. 368. U-4838 I* C* T

– *La moral*. Tr. P. Umbert. Barcelona. Henrich. 1907. Uc

Hoffman, Gustav. *Schimpfwörter der Griechen und Römer*. Berlin. Gaertners. 1892. Pp. 33. U-5435 I

Holbach, Paul Heinrich Dietrich von, Baron. *Système de la nature, ou des lois du monde physique et du monde moral*. Par M. Mirabaud [or rather by Baron von Holbach]. 6 vols. Leipzig. Guyot-Pelafol. 1780. U-4026-31

Holmes, Oliver Wendell. *The Poet at the Breakfast Table*. London. Dent. 1906. Pp. 343. U-971 I* C* T

– *The Professor at the Breakfast Table*. London. Dent. 1906. Pp. 300. U-972 I* C T

– *The Autocrat of the Breakfast Table*. London. Dent. 1908. Pp. 300. U-973 I*

Holzapfel, Rudolf Maria. *Welterlebnis*. 2 vols. Jena. Eugen Diederich. 1928. (2 copies) U-5434, U-5438-40 I D

– *Panideal. Das Seelenleben und seine soziale Neugestaltung*. 2 vols. Jena. Diederichs. 1923. U-5436-7 I* C

Homen Christo, Francisco Manoel. *Pró-Pátria*. Coimbra. Amado. 1905. Pp. 552. U-2357 D

Homenaje Cruz Roja Italiana. *Del Plata al Tíber*. Buenos Aires. Radaelli. 1915. Pp. 300. U-838 n/o

Homer. *Homer's Werke*. Deutsch von J.H. Voss. 2 vols. Leipsig. Reclam. 1780. U-4032 T

– *Homeri Ilias*. Lipsiae. Tauchnitz. 1839. Pp. 320. U-4059 I* T C

– *Ilias*. 2 vols. Lipsiae. Holtze. 1872-7. U-4585-6

– *Homeri Odyssea*. 2 vols. Lipsiae. Holtze. 1867. U-4060 I* T* C

– *Odyssée*. Texte grec. Introd., arguments analytiques, et notes en français A. Pierron. Paris. Hachette. 1904. Pp. v, 894. U-4670 I* T

– *L'Odissea*. Volum segon (Cants IX-XVI). Tr. Carles Riba. n.p. Ed. Catalana. n.d. Pp. 177. U-1423

– *Himnes Homèrics*. Tr. en vers de J. Maragall y text grec amb la tr. literal de P. Bosch Gimpera. Barcelona. Institut de la Llengua Catalana. [1913]. Pp. 265. (2 copies) U-2140, U-2939

— *Iliade.* Texte grec. Introd., arguments analytiques, et notes en français
    A. Pierron. Paris. Hachette. 1895. Pp. viii, 692. U-4671 I T*
— *Iliade. Chant VI.* Nouvelle éd. argument analytique et notes en français
    A. Pierron. Paris. Hachette. 1892. Pp. 157, 179. U-4475 B
— *La Ilíada.* Tr. Luis Segalá y Estalella. Barcelona. Montaner y Simón. 1908.
    Pp. 443. U-2535
Hoogvliet, J.M. *Elements of Dutch.* The Hague. Nijhoff. 1908. Pp. 335.
    U-4807
Hooker, Richard. *Of the Laws of Ecclesiastical Polity. Books 1 to 5.* 2 vols.
    London. Dent. [1907]. U-994-5 I* C
Hopfen, Hans. *Hexenfang und andere Kleine Stücke.* Berlin. Paetel. 1893.
    Pp. 239. U-3896
Horace. *Quintus Horatius Flaccus. Carmina.* Nitori suo restituta. Paris. Barbou.
    1763. Pp. x, 370. U-4595
— *Horatti Flacci Carmina.* Iterum recognovit Lucianus Mueller. Lipsiae.
    Teubner. 1887. Pp. lxxviii, 295. U-1510 I T* L
— *Horacio.* Versión parafrástica de sus obras por Don Joaquín Arcadio
    Pagaza. Jalapa. El Progreso. 1905. Pp. 476. U-2440 n/o
Hosmer, James Kendall. *Outcome of the Civil War (1863-1865).* New York.
    Harper. 1907. Pp. xiv, 352. U-4801 I
— *The Appeal to Arms 1861-1863.* New York. Harper. 1907. Pp. xvi, 354.
    U-4819 I
Hostos, Eugenio M. de. *Tratado de sociología.* Madrid. Bailly-Baillière. 1904.
    Pp. 272. U-1453
— *Moral social.* Madrid. Bailly-Baillière. 1906. Pp. 262. U-1517
— *Hamlet. Ensayo.* Pról. A.S. Pedreira. Universidad de Puerto Rico. 1929.
    Pp. 112. U-1157
Housman, A.E. *A Shropshire Lad.* London. Grant Richards. 1906. Pp. 95.
    U-2391 I T. 1915. Pp. 101. U-4075
Houtin, Albert. *La question biblique chez les catholiques de France au XIXe*
    siècle. Paris. Picard. 1902. Pp. 324. U-1284 I C B
Hoyer, W.M. *Papiamentoe i su manera di skirbié.* Curaçao. Bethencourt. 1918.
    Pp. 52. U-5666
Hoyos y Vinent, Antonio de. *Mors in vita.* Madrid. Moreno [1904]. Pp. 198.
    U-3303 D
— *Frivolidad.* Madrid. Moreno. 1905. Uc D
— *A flor de piel.* Madrid. Moreno. 1907. Uc D
— *La decadencia. Los emigrantes.* Madrid. Mateu. 1909. Uc D
— *Del huerto del pecado.* Madrid. Fernández. 1910. Pp. 218. U-2778 D
— *El derecho a la vida.* Madrid. Cía. Ibero-Americana de Publicaciones.
    n.d. Pp. 81. U-4445 n/o D

Hsü, Ssu-yüan. *On the Nature and Destiny of Man.* [Nanking]. [1933].
   Pp. 183. U-3583 I
Huarte y Echenique, Amalio. *El archivo universitario de Salamanca.*
   Salamanca. Ateneo de Salamanca. 1916. Pp. 15. U-1705 n/o
— *Guía de Salamanca.* Salamanca. García. 1920. Pp. 200. U-4701 D
Hubert, Lucien. *L'Effort brisé.* Paris. Alcan. 1916. Pp. 152. U-1905
Hubner, Carlos Luis. *Charlas.* Santiago de Chile. Lourdes. 1910. Uc D
Hudson, W.H. *El ombú.* London. Duckworth. [1920]. Pp. 182. U-5211 I
— *The Purple Land: Being the Narrative of One Richard Lamb's Adventures
   in the Banda Oriental in South America, as Told by Himself.* London.
   Duckworth. 1926. Pp. viii, 355. U-5210 I* C
Hügel, Friedrich von. *The Mystical Element of Religion as Studied in Saint
   Catherine of Genoa and Her Friends.* 2 vols. London. Dent. 1908.
   U-710-11. Vol. II I* C*
— *Religione ed illusione.* Tr. A. Crespi. Lugano. Coenobium. 1911. Pp. 61.
   U-1720 D
Hughes, James Langston. *Fine Clothes to the Jew.* New York. Knopf. 1927.
   Pp. 89. U-5213 I* C
Hugo, Victor-Marie. *Oeuvres complètes de Victor Hugo.* (*Les Chatiments.*
   1882. Pp. 468. *Les Contemplations.* 1882. 2 vols. *La Légende des siècles.*
   1883. 4 vols.). Paris. Hetzel. U-208-14 I
Huidobro, Vicente. *Adán. Poema.* Santiago. Universitaria. 1916. Pp. 126.
   U-647 n/o D
— *Mio Cid Campeador. Hazaña.* Madrid. Cía. Ibero-Americana de Publica-
   ciones. 1929. Pp. 433. (2 copies) U-4173, U-4935 D
— *Las pagodas ocultas.* Santiago. Universitaria. n.d. Pp. 213. U-3601 D
— *La gruta del silencio.* Santiago. Universitaria. Uc D
Hume, David. *Essays Moral, Political and Literary.* London. Frowde.'[1904].
   Pp. 616. U-444 I*
— *A Treatise of Human Nature.* Introd. A.D. Lindsay. 2 vols. London. Dent.
   n.d. U-1020-1. Vol. I I B
Hume, Martin A.S. *The Spanish People. Their Origin, Growth and Influence.*
   London. Heinemann. 1901. Pp. xix, 535. U-4797 I D
Huneeus Gana, Jorge. *Cuadro histórico de la producción intelectual de Chile.*
   Santiago de Chile. Biblioteca de Escritores de Chile. [1910]. Pp. xvi,
   880. U-2604
Huneeus Gana, Roberto. *Errante. Poema.* Santiago de Chile. Cervantes. 1898.
   Pp. 162. U-3139 D
— *¡Sursum corda!* 2 vols. Santiago de Chile. Cervantes. 1903. U-3132-3 I C D
Hunt, afterwards Jackson, Helen María. *Ramona, novela americana.* Tr. J.
   Martí. Habana. Rambla, Bouza. 1915. Uc

Hunter, William A. *Introduction to Roman Law.* London. Sweet & Maxwell.
1892. Pp. xii, 235. U-3619 T
Huntington, Archer M. *Sonnets.* New York. 1908. Uc D
Hurtado de Mendoza, Diego. *Obras en prosa de D. Diego Hurtado de Mendoza.*
Madrid. Hernando. 1888. Pp. 438. U-3343
Huvelin, Abbé. *Souvenirs de la Crypte de St Augustin. Quelques directeurs
d'ames au XVIIe siècle – Saint François de Sales. M. Olier. Saint Vincent
de Paul. L'Abbé de Rancé.* Paris. Lecoffre. 1911. Pp. xii, 243. U-3148 I*
Huxley, Aldous. *Contrepoint.* Tr. J. Castier. Préf. A. Maurois. 2 vols. Paris.
Plon. 1930. QP-25-6 I
Huysmans, Joris-Karl. *La cathédrale.* Paris. Stock. 1898. Pp. 488. U-1384 I* T
– *En route.* Paris. Tresse & Stock. 1895. Pp. 458. U-3987
Ibáñez de Ibero. *Commémoration du centenaire de la naissance du Général
Ibáñez de Ibero.* Discours prononcés le 29 Mai 1925, à la Sorbonne. Paris.
Dupont. 1925. Pp. 24. U-5269
Ibarbourou, Juana de. *El cántaro fresco.* San José de Costa Rica. García Monge.
1922. Pp. 54. U-4507
Ibarguren, Carlos. *Una proscripción bajo la dictadura de Syla.* Buenos Aires.
Moen. 1908. Pp. 224. U-4013 D
Iber. *Ami vasco.* Bilbao. Arteche. 1906. Pp. 94. U-4573
Ibérico Rodríguez, Mariano. *El nuevo absoluto.* Lima. Minerva. 1926.
Pp. 229. U-5024 D
Ibsen, Henrick. *Brand. Et Dramatisk Digt.* Kφbenhavn. Gyldendalske
Boghandel. 1898. Pp. 261. U-2120 I* C* T*
– *Peer Gynt. Et Dramatisk Digt.* Kφbenhavn. Gyldendalske Boghandel.
1906. Pp. 238. U-3173 I* C T* L*
Ichaso, Francisco. *Góngora y la nueva poesía.* La Habana. Hermes. 1927.
Pp. 53. U-4914 D
Idea. Atenas, 2, 3, 5 (1933). n/n
Iglesia, Ramón. *Bernal Díaz del Castillo y el popularismo en la historiografía
española.* Madrid. Tierra Firme. 1935. Pp. 18. U-770 D
Iglesia Serrano, Antonio. *Compendios de gramática y ortografía castellana,
con arreglo a las de la Real Academia de la Lengua.* Valladolid. Roldán.
1822. Pp. 131. U-4587
Iglesias, Eugenio Julio. *Ruta de soledad.* Buenos Aires. Gleizer. 1931. Pp. 89.
U-1279 D
Iglesias, Ignaci. *Fructidor.* Barcelona. L'Avenç. 1897. Pp. 177. U-1121 L D
– *Els vells.* Barcelona. L'Avenç. 1903. Pp. 284. U-4019 D
Iglesias Paz, César. *El problema social.* Buenos Aires. Moen. 1907. Uc D
Iglesias y Ejarque, Enrique. *Nociones de química general y descriptiva.*
Valladolid. Martín Sánchez. 1921. Pp. 244. U-2249 C*
Ignacio de Loyola (San). *Exercicios.* Uc

De Imitatione Christi libri quatuor novis curis edidit. J. Gerseníi. Nova editio.
	P. Marietti. Augustae Taurinorum. 1885. Pp. xv, 462. Uc
Imitatio Christi. Jesus-Christoren Imitacionea. M. Chourio. Escararat itçulia.
	Emendatua Meçaz eta Jgandetaco Besperez. Bayonan. Favuet-Duhart.
	1769. Pp. xxiv, 377. U-4426
Inaugural Bulletin. Tucson, University of Arizona (1930). Pp. 54. U-4254
The Independent. New York (25 Aug. 1904). n/n
Individualität. Zürich-Wien, Leipzig (1927). n/n
Infante, Daniel. *Insinuaciones. Serie de conferencias didácticas.* Rosario de
	Santa Fe. Inglesa. 1916. Pp. 63. U-2622
Infante, Juan. *Fechorías, sangre y lágrimas.* Madrid. Renacimiento. 1914. Uc
Infante Ferraguti, Nina. *Nel tempio della luce.* Roma. Formiggini. 1934.
	Pp. 138. U-2667 D
Infante Pérez, Blas. *Ideal andaluz. Varios estudios acerca del Renacimiento
	de Andalucía.* Sevilla. Arévalo. 1915. Pp. 364. U-408
La influencia española en el progreso de la ciencia médica. Con una memoria
	del Instituto de Investigación Wellcome. Londres. 1935. Pp. 121. U-3048
Inge, William Ralph. *Outspoken Essays.* (Second series). New York. Longmans,
	Green, 1922. Pp. vii, 275. U-1332 I* C*
Ingenieros, José. *Dos páginas de psiquiatría criminal.* Buenos Aires. Bredahl.
	1900. Pp. 118. U-1882 D
− *Simulación de la locura.* Buenos Aires. La Semana Médica. 1903. Uc D
− *Los accidentes histéricos y las sugestiones terapeúticas.* Buenos Aires.
	Menéndez. 1904. Uc D
− *La legislation du travail dans la République Argentine.* Paris. Cornély.
	1907. Uc
− *Al margen de la ciencia.* Buenos Aires. Lajouane. 1908. Pp. 428. U-2546
− *Sociología argentina.* Madrid. Jorro. 1913. Uc
− *Principios de psicología biológica.* Madrid. Jorro. 1913. Uc
− *El hombre mediocre.* Madrid. Renacimiento. 1913. Pp. 328. U-3760
− *Criminología.* Madrid. Jorro. 1913. Pp. 386. U-2545
− *Le Dantec, biólogo y filósofo.* Pról. E. Carasa. Buenos Aires. Centro
	Médico Argentino. 1928. Pp. 109. U-5769
− *La simulación de la lucha por la vida.* Valencia. Sempere. n.d. Pp. 254.
	U-3288 D
Ingram, John Kells. *A History of Political Economy.* Edinburgh. Black. 1893.
	Pp. xi, 250. U-2078
− *Outlines of the History of Religion.* London. Black. 1900. Pp. 162. U-287
Inicial. Buenos Aires (Setiembre 1924). n/n
Innes-González, Eduardo. *Teatro.* Caracas. Tip. Americana. 1935. Pp. 47.
	U-5773 D

L'Instantané. Supplément illustré de *La Revue Hebdomadaire.* Vingtième
année. Tome II. Paris (Février 1911). Pp. 140. U-5300
Institut d'Estudis Catalans. *Anuari.* Barcelona. Palau de la Diputació.
1909-10. Uc
Instituto de Reformas Sociales. *La emigración.* Información legislativa y
bibliográfica. Madrid. Minuesa de los Ríos. 1905. Uc
— Sección 1a. *Instituto nacional de previsión y sus relaciones con las
entidades similares.* Madrid. Minuesa de los Ríos. 1906. Uc
— Sección 1a. *Jurisprudencia de los tribunales en materia de accidentes de
trabajo.* Madrid. Minuesa de los Ríos. 1906. Uc
— *Estadística de las huelgas (1904-1905).* Madrid. Minuesa de los Ríos.
1906. Uc
— *Legislación del trabajo.* Madrid. Minuesa de los Ríos. 1906. Uc
— *Legislación del trabajo.* Madrid. Minuesa de los Ríos. 1907. Uc
— *Estadística de la asociación obrera en 1o de noviembre de 1904.* Madrid.
Minuesa de los Ríos. 1907. Uc
— *Preparación de las bases para un proyecto de ley de casas para obreros.
Casas baratas.* Madrid. Minuesa de los Ríos. 1907. Uc
— *Memoria del servicio de inspección en 1907.* Madrid. Minuesa de los Ríos.
1908. Uc
— *Proyecto de reforma de la ley de accidentes del trabajo de 30 de enero de
1900.* Madrid. Minuesa de los Ríos. 1908. Uc
— *Estadística de las huelgas [1906].* Madrid. Minuesa de los Ríos. 1908. Uc
— *Preparación de las bases para un proyecto de ley de accidentes del
trabajo en la agricultura.* Madrid. Minuesa de los Ríos. 1908. Uc
— *Congresos sociales en 1907.* Madrid. Minuesa de los Ríos. 1908. Uc
— *Estadística de las instituciones de ahorro, cooperación y previsión en 1o
de noviembre de 1904.* Madrid. Minuesa de los Ríos. 1908. Uc
— *Legislación del trabajo.* Madrid. Minuesa de los Ríos. 1908. Uc
— *Preparación de las bases para un proyecto de ley de casas para obreros.
Casas baratas.* Madrid. Minuesa de los Ríos. 1910. Uc
— *Memoria general de la inspección del trabajo correspondiente al año 1908.*
Madrid. Minuesa de los Ríos. 1910. Uc
— *Proyecto de ley sobre contrato del trabajo.* Madrid. Minuesa de los Ríos.
1911. Uc
— *Congresos sociales en 1909 y 1910.* Madrid. Minuesa de los Ríos. 1911. Uc
— *Legislación del trabajo. Apéndice sexto.* Madrid. Minuesa de los Ríos.
1911. Uc
— *Legislación del trabajo. Indices de los tomos publicados (1905-1910).*
Madrid. Minuesa de los Ríos. 1912. Uc
— *Legislación del trabajo. Apéndice séptimo. 1911.* Madrid. Minuesa de los
Ríos. 1912. Uc

Instituto Geográfico y Estadístico. *Nomenclator de las ciudades, villas, lugares, aldeas y demás entidades de población de España ... con referencias al 31 diciembre 1900.* 2 vols. Madrid. 1904. Uc
— *Reseña geográfica y estadística de España.* Tomo II. Madrid. Imp. Instituto. 1912. Uc
— *Estadística del suicidio en España.* Sexenio 1906-11. Madrid. Imp. Instituto. 1913. Uc
Instituto Histórico y Geográfico del Uruguay. *Asencio. Informe.* Montevideo. Renacimiento. 1917. Pp. 19. U-4267
Insúa, Alberto. *Don Quijote en los Alpes.* Madrid. Pérez Villavicencio. 1907. Uc D
Internationale Zeitschrift für Individualpsychologie (Sept. 1925). n/n
Ipuche, Pedro Leandro. *Isla patrulla.* Buenos Aires. Amigos del Libro Rioplatense. 1935. Pp. 186. U-428 D
Iraizoz y de Villar, Antonio. *Las ideas pedagógicas de Martí.* Habana. El Siglo XX. 1920. Pp. 30. U-1714 D
Iregui, Antonio José. *El espíritu liberal contemporáneo.* Bogotá. Minerva. 1929. Pp. 143. U-5097 D
Irigoyen, José Francisco de. *Colección alfabética de apellidos bascongados con su significado.* San Sebastián. Baroja. 1881. Pp. viii, 178. U-5709 C
Irrealitá. Catania. Monaco (1911). Uc
Irusta, Hector M. *El mirto quebrado.* Buenos Aires. Smith. 1924. Pp. 120. U-3290 n/o D
Irving, Washington. *A Chronicle of the Conquest of Granada.* From the Mss of Fray Antonio Agapida. Oxford. University Press. [1859]. Pp. xxiii, 458. U-5148
Iscar Peyra, Fernando. *Vestigios.* Madrid. Beltrán. 1914. Pp. 186. U-138 D
— *Literatura salmantina.* Salamanca. Núñez. 1917. Pp. 56. U-3195 D
— *Los peleles.* Pról. M. de Unamuno. Salamanca. Establecimiento Tip. de Calatrava. 1916. Pp. viii, 162. U-3591 [Cover missing]
Isern, Antón. *Esplets d'ánima jove.* Reus. Sugrañés. 1917. Pp. 104. U-3416 I
Isern Dalmau, Eusebio. *Política fiscal de la república.* Barcelona. Bibl. Catalana d'Autors Independients. 1933. Pp. 105. U-224
Ispizua Bajeneta, Segundo de. *Historia de los vascos en el descubrimiento, conquista y civilización de América.* Tomo II. Bilbao. Astuy. 1915. Pp. xv, 354. U-4386
— *Los vascos en América.* Tomo III. Madrid. La Itálica. 1917. Pp. 438. U-4340 D
Iturriza y Zabala, Juan Ramón. *Historia general de Vizcaya.* Pról. P. Fidel Fita, S.J. Barcelona. Subirana. 1884. Pp. 413. U-1910
Izquierdo, Francisco. *Alta plática.* Pról. M. Verdugo. Santa Cruz de Tenerife. Libr. Católica. 1915. Pp. 236. U-4184 n/o

Izquierdo, José Ma. *Divagando por la ciudad de la gracia.* Sevilla. Arévalo.
1914. Uc D

Jaca, Juan S. *Hernandarias y Benalcázar o sea el pasado y presente
económico político y social de la República Argentina.* Buenos Aires.
La Vasconia. 1899. Pp. xiv, 432. (2 copies) U-604, U-3415 D

– *Euskaria. La historia política y social de las naciones al través de la
filosofía.* 2 vols. Buenos Aires. 1910. Uc D

Jacme primer [King of Aragon]. *Cronica o comentaris del gloriosissim e
invictissim Rey en Jacme Primer.* Dictada per aquell en sa llengua natural,
e de nou feta estampar per Marian Aguiló y Fuster. Barcelona. Alvar
Verdaguer. 1905. Pp. xxiii, 535. U-3935 I*

Jacobsen, J.P. *Samlede Skrifter.* Kφbenhavn. Gyldendalske Boghandel. 1918.
Pp. 428. U-5389

– *Niels Lyhne.* Uebersetzung aus dem Dänischen von Theodor Wolff.
Leipzig. Reclam. n.d. Pp. 144. U-4526 I [Incomplete]

Jagadisa-chandra Chattopadhyaya. *La filosofía esotérica de la India.* Tr. y
pról. B. Chamsaur Sicilia. Laguna de Tenerife. Curbelo. 1914. Pp. 162.
U-294

Jahn, Friedrich Ludwig. *Deutsches Volksthum.* Herausgegeben Franz Brümmer.
Leipzig. Reclam. n.d. Pp. 262. U-4527

Jaimes, Julio L. *La villa imperial de Potosí.* Buenos Aires. Rosso. 1905. Pp. xii,
535. U-4157

Jaimes Freyre, Ricardo. *Tucumán en 1810. Noticia histórica y documentos
inéditos.* Tucumán. 1909. Pp. 118. U-3143 D

– *Historia de la república del Tucumán.* Buenos Aires. Coni. 1911. Pp. 198.
U-4000 D

– *Leyes de la versificación castellana.* Buenos Aires. Coni. 1912. Uc D

– *Historia del descubrimiento de Tucumán.* Buenos Aires. Coni. 1916.
Pp. 312. Uc

Jakowenko, Boris. *Vom Wesen des Pluralismus.* Bonn. Cohen. 1928. Pp. 72.
U-5464 C

James, Henry. *Un portrait de femme.* Tr. et préf. P. Noel. Paris. Stock. 1933.
Pp. 702. QP-27 I

James, William. *The Varieties of Religious Experience. A Study in Human
Nature.* London. Longmans, Green. 1902. Pp. xii, 534. U-4237 I C

– *The Will to Believe and Other Essays in Popular Philosophy.* New York.
Longmans, Green. 1902. Pp. xvii, 332. U-4286 I T

– *Los ideales de la vida.* Tr. y pról. C.M. Soldevilla. 2 vols. Barcelona.
Henrich. 1904. Uc

– *Pragmatism. A New Name for Some Old Ways of Thinking.* London.
Longmans, Green. 1907. Pp. xiii, 308. U-3826 I

– *La vida eterna y la fé.* Tr. Santos Rubiano. Barcelona. Henrich. 1909. Uc

Jamin, M.J. *Petit traité de physique.* Paris. Gauthier-Villars. 1870. Uc
Jammes, Francis. *Clairières dans le ciel. 1902-1906.* Paris. Mercure de France.
     1906. Pp. 225. U-1153 I* B
Janés i Duran, Mateo. *Murmuris de corn Marí. Poemes 1929-1932.* Barcelona.
     Altés. 1936. Pp. 58. U-4824 n/o D
Jara, Alfonso. *Fuente y Ovejuna.* Madrid. F. Fé. 1908. Uc D
Jaramillo Meza, J.B. *Bronce latino.* Habana. Studium. n.d. Pp. 106.
     U-2021 n/o D
– *Senderos de otoño.* Manizales, Colombia. Imp. Departamental. 1935.
     Pp. 180. U-4313 D
Jarnés, Benjamín. *Zumalacárregui, el caudillo romántico.* Madrid. Espasa-Calpe.
     1931. Pp. 277. U-5572 D
– *Feria del libro.* Madrid. Espasa-Calpe. 1935. Pp. 249. U-5090 I* C* D
– *Castelar hombre del sinai.* Madrid. Espasa-Calpe. 1935. Pp. 295. U-427 D
– *Libro de Esther.* Madrid. Espasa-Calpe. 1935. Pp. 206. U-2247 D
– *Tántalo.* Madrid. Signo. 1935. Pp. 202. U-3642 I D
– *Viviana y Merlin.* Madrid. Espasa-Calpe. 1936. Pp. 157. U-1632 D
– *Doble agonía de Bécquer.* Madrid. Espasa-Calpe. 1936. Pp. 237. U-918 I D
Jarrín, Francisco. *Religión y moral.* Salamanca. Calatrava. 1897. Pp. vi, 57.
     U-2331
Jaume, Francisco. *El separatismo en Cataluña.* Barcelona. Altés y Alabart.
     1907. Pp. 541. U-3933 n/o
Jaurès, Auguste Marie Joseph Jean. *Acción socialista.* Tr. M. Ciges Aparicio.
     2 vols. Barcelona. Henrich. 1906. Uc
Jefferies, John Richard. *The Story of My Heart. My Autobiography.* London.
     Longmans, Green. 1907. Pp. xiv, 207. U-1417 I
Jeffrey, Francis. *Essays on English Poets and Poetry.* London. Routledge. n.d.
     Pp. 591. U-445 I
Jelinek, H. *Anthologie de la poésie Tchèque.* Paris. Kra. 1930. Pp. xvi, 284.
     (2 copies) U-1975 D. U-4373 n/o
Jenkin, Henry Charles Fleeming. *Elettricità.* Tr. Rinaldo Ferrini. Milano.
     Hoepli. 1897. Uc
Jensen, Chr. *Søren Kierkegaards religiøse Udvikling.* København. Jydsk
     Forlags-Forretning. 1898. Pp. viii, 299. U-2054 I
Jessen, Franz de. *Manuel historique de la question du Slesvig.* Copenhague.
     Nielsen & Lydiche. 1906. Pp. vi, 473. U-1226
Jevons, William Stanley. *Money and the Mechanism of Exchange.* London.
     Kegan Paul, Trench, Trübner. 1893. Pp. xviii, 349. U-142 B*
Jiménez, Juan Ramón. *Almas de violeta.* Madrid. Moderna. 1900. Pp. 52.
     U-2730 C*
– *Ninfeas.* Atrio Rubén Darío. Madrid. Colec. Lux. 1900. Pp. 114.
     U-3267 D

- *Rimas.* Madrid. F. Fé. 1902. Pp. 223. U-3363 D
- *Elegías.* 3 vols. Madrid. Rev. de Archivos. 1908-10. U-3360-2 D
- *Olvidanzas. I. Las hojas verdes. 1906.* Madrid. Rev. de Archivos. 1909. Pp. 74. U-4396 D
- *Baladas de primavera. 1907.* Madrid. Rev. de Archivos. 1910. Pp. 86. U-3268 D
- *La soledad sonora.* Madrid. Rev. de Archivos. 1911. Pp. 240. U-3119 D
- *Poemas mágicos y dolientes. 1909.* Madrid. Rev. de Archivos. 1911. Pp. 214. U-2776 I D
- *Melancolía. 1910-1911.* Madrid. Rev. de Archivos. 1912. Pp. 240. U-3118 D
- *Poesías escogidas (1899-1917).* Madrid. Fortanet. 1917. Pp. 349. U-855 D
Jiménez, Max. *Gleba.* Paris. Le Livre Libre. 1929. Pp. 118. U-5007 D
Jiménez, R. Emilio. *Al amor del Bohio (tradiciones y costumbres dominicanas).* Tomo I. Santo Domingo. Montalvo. 1927. Pp. 301 + 157 + xxv. U-2624 D
Jiménez Arráiz, F. *Del vivac.* Caracas. Herrera Irigoyen. 1900. Uc D
- *Alma criolla.* Caracas. Tip. Americana. 1909. Pp. 199. U-656 D
- *Fragmentos de ilusión y de fé.* Caracas. Tip. Americana. 1920. Pp. xxi, 202. U-3246 D
Jiménez Rueda, Cecilio. *Tratado de las formas geométricas de primera y segunda categoria.* 2 vols. Valencia. Alufre. 1898. U-4223-4. Vol. I C*
Jogos Floraes de Salamanca. Poesias premiadas. Coimbra. Amado. 1910. Pp. 61. U-1745 D
Johannet, René. *La conversion d'un catholique germanophile.* Paris. Bibliothèque des ouvrages documentaires. 1915. Pp. 190. (2 copies) U-1385, U-1922 D
- *Le principe des nationalités.* Paris. Nouvelle Librairie Nationale. 1918. Pp. lvi, 438. U-3960 I* C L* B
- *Eloge du bourgeois français.* Paris. Grasset. 1924. Pp. 348. U-1347 n/o D
- *Joseph de Maistre.* Paris. Flammarion. 1932. Pp. 246. U-5272 I D
- *L'Evolution du roman social au XIXe siècle.* Reims. Action Populaire. [1910]. Pp. 120. U-5235 D
Jókai, Maurus. *Un hombre de oro.* Tr. y pról. P. Umbert. Barcelona. Henrich. 1907. Uc
Jones, Eli Stanley. *El Cristo del camino Hundú.* Tr. E. Hall. Santiago de Chile. Rev. Evangélica. n.d. Pp. 168. U-3280
Jonson, Ben. *The Complete Plays of Ben Jonson.* Introd. F.E. Schelling. 2 vols. London. Dent. [1910]. U-1024-5 I*
Jordán, Luis María. *La túnica del sol.* Buenos Aires. Tragant. 1906. Pp. 149. U-651 D

Jordan, Wilhelm. *Durch's Ohr.* Frankfurt. W. Jordan's Selbftverlag. 1889.
    Pp. xvi, 107. U-653
Jorge, Ricardo. *A margem duma revista alemã.* Lisboa. A Editora Limitada.
    1915. Pp. 13. U-1700 n/o
— *El Greco.* Coimbra. Imp. da Universidade. 1913. Pp. 58. U-744 D
— *A Guerra e o pensamento medico.* Lisboa. Ediçao da Sociedade das
    Sciencias Medicas. 1914. Pp. 63. U-1693 n/o D
Jørgensen, Johannes. *Vor Frue af Danmark.* Kφbenhavn. Det Nordiske Forlag.
    1900. Pp. 306. U-1375 I T
— *Pilgrimsbogen.* Kφbenhavn. Det Nordiske Forlag. 1903. Pp. 271. U-2719 T
— *Den Hellige Frans af Assisi. En Levnedsskildring.* Kφbenhavn. Det Nordisk
    Forlag. 1907. Pp. lxiv, 283. U-4156 T L
— *I det Hφje.* Kφbenhavn. Det Nordisk Forlag. 1908. Pp. 268. U-3860 I T
José de Sigüenza, Fray. *Historia de la Orden de San Gerónimo.* Con un elogio
    de Fr. J. de Sigüenza por Juan Catalina García. 2 vols. Madrid. Bailly-
    Baillière. 1907-9. U-43, U-47 I* L
Jovellanos y Ramírez, Gaspar Melchor de. *Manuscritos inéditos, raros, o
    dispersos.* Dispuestos para la impresión J. Somoza García-Sala. Madrid.
    Gómez Fuentenebro. 1913. Pp. 430. U-697
Juan de Avila, Beato. *Epistolario espiritual.* Ed. y notas V. García de Diego.
    Madrid. La Lectura. 1912. Pp. xxx, 303. U-944 I*
Juan de la Cruz, San. *Obras del místico doctor San Juan de la Cruz.* Ed.
    crítica P. Gerardo de San Juan de la Cruz. Epíl. M. Menéndez y Pelayo y
    J. Vázquez de Mella. 3 vols. Toledo. Peláez. 1912-14. U-71-3
— *Sermones.* Uc
— *The Dark Night of the Soul.* Tr. Gabriela Cunninghame Graham. London.
    Watkins. 1905. Pp. 265. U-1313
Juan de los Angeles, Fray. *Obras místicas del M.R.P. Fr. Juan de los Angeles.*
    Ed. Fr. Jaime Sala. 2 vols. Madrid. Bailly-Baillière. 1912-17. U-55,
    U-57 I* C
Juderias, Julián. *La leyenda negra y la verdad histórica.* Madrid. Tip. Rev. de
    Arch., Bibl. y Museos. 1914. Pp. 227. U-4719 D
Juliá Tolrá, Antonio. *Una opinión más sobre enseñanza secundaria.* Santa Fe.
    1915. Pp. 67. U-2804 D
— 'El alma paraguaya,' Diario *Santa Fe.* n.d. Pp. 15. U-2810 D
Julio, Sylvio. *A Covardia.* Rio de Janeiro. Ribeiro. 1914. Pp. 53. U-2290 D
— *Pampa.* Ceará, Brazil. Jatahy. 1919. Pp. 296. U-3749 D
Junco, Alfonso. *Cristo.* México. Salesiana. 1931. Pp. 70. U-4955 n/o
Jung, Edgar. *Die Herrschaft der Minderwertigen.* Berlin. Deutsche Rundschau.
    1930. Pp. 692. U-5369 I B* T
Jungfer, Johannes. 'Magerit-Madrid,' *Revue Hispanique,* XVIII (1908).
    U-5261 D

– y A. Martínez Pajares. *Estudio sobre apellidos y nombres de lugares hispano-marroquíes*. Pról. F. Rodríguez-Marín. Madrid. Blass. 1918. Pp. 219. U-4484

Junoy, José María. *Arte & artistas*. 1a parte. Barcelona. L'Avenç. 1912. Pp. 97. U-3097

Junta de Iconografía Nacional. *Retratos del museo de la Real Academia de San Fernando*. Nota preliminar J.J. Herrero. Madrid. Aldecoa. 1930. Pp. 41, pl. 33. U-5470

Jurado de la Parra, J. *Antaño y ogaño*. Pról. S. González Anaya. Málaga. Ibérica. [1936]. Pp. 236. U-3217 I

Justo, Juan B. *Teoría y práctica de la historia*. Buenos Aires. Barberis. 1909. Uc D

Juvenalis, Decimus Junius. *D. Iunii Iuvenalis Satirarum libri quinque*. Accedit Sulpiciae satira. Ex recognitione C.F. Hermanni. Lipsiae. Teubner. 1914. Pp. xxxii, 118. U-4495 I* T

Juventud. Santiago de Chile, 14, 15 (1921). n/n

Kaeser, Engelbert. *Los socialistas pintados por sí mismos*. Tr. Domingo Miral. Madrid. Calleja. [1911]. Pp. 246. U-1598

Kaftan, Julius. *Die Wahrheit der christlichen Religion*. Basel. Detloff's Buchhandlung. 1888. Pp. x, 586. U-3770 I

– *Dogmatik*. Tübingen. Mohr. 1909. Pp. viii, 672. U-1806 I*

Kaiser, Georg. *Von Morgens bis Mitternachts*. Potsdam. Kiepenheuer. 1916. Pp. 119. U-5402

– *Der Brand im Opernhaus*. Potsdam. Kiepenheuer. 1922. Pp. 95. U-5377

– *Gas*. Potsdam. Kiepenheuer. 1922. Pp. 117. U-5373 T. Zweiter Teil. Potsdam. Kiepenheuer. 1929. Pp. 67. U-5398 T

Kalevala. The Land of Heroes. Tr. W.F. Kirby. 2 vols. London. Dent. 1915. U-1041-2 I* T*

Kalisch, David. *Ein gebildeter Hausknecht*. Leipzig. Reclam. n.d. Pp. 43. U-4535

Kalthoff, Albert. *Das Christus-Problem*. Leipzig. Diederichs. 1903. Pp. 93. U-3761 I

Kant, Immanuel. *Kritik der reinen Vernunft. Kritik der praktischen Vernunft*. Herausgegeben von J.H. Kirchmann. 2 vols. Heidelberg. Weiss. 1882-4. U-3893 C T

Kardamatis, Ioannis P. *Narki Phyletiki*. Flamma. 1934. Pp. 207. U-2283 D

Katsimpales, Georgios K. *O Palamas ke to Spiti*. Athens. Estia. 1929. Pp. 29. U-2928 D

Kautsky, Karl. *La cuestión agraria*. Tr. Ciro Bayo y revisada y corregida M. de Unamuno. Madrid. Rodríguez Serra. 1903. Pp. 300. U-2613

– *La defensa de los trabajadores y la jornada de ocho horas*. Pról. Santiago Valentí Camp. Barcelona. Henrich. 1904. Uc

Keats, John. *The Poetical Works of John Keats.* Notes F.T. Palgrave. London.
Macmillan. 1899. Pp. 284. U-1419 I* T
Keller, Gottfried. *Der grüne Heinrich.* Berlin-Leipzig. Knaur Nachf. Pp. x, 258.
U-1104 I* C*
Keller, Helen. *Optimism.* New York. Crowell. 1903. Pp. 75. U-3686
Kerr, Alfred. *O Spanien.* Berlin. Fischer. 1924. Pp. 141. U-2209 D
Key, Ellen. *Amor y matrimonio.* Tr. y pról. Magdalena de Santiago-Fuentes.
2 vols. Barcelona. Henrich. 1907. Uc
Keynes, John Maynard. *The Economic Consequences of the Peace.* London.
Macmillan. 1920. Pp. 279. U-1792 I*
Keyserling, Hermann. 'Spannung und Rhythmus,' 'Schlussvortrag,' *Jahrbuch
der Schule der Weisheit* (1923), 5-22, 197-210. U-1968
— *Der Weg zur Vollendung.* Darmstadt. Reich. 1926. Pp. 65. U-5375 I
— *Gesetz und freiheit; veröffentlichung der Schule der weisheit.* Darmstadt.
Reichl. 1926. Pp. 359. U-5458 I* C L*
— *Europe.* Tr. Maurice Samuel. London. Cape. 1928. Pp. 382. U-5190 I T D
— *America Set Free.* London. Cape. 1930. Pp. 489. U-115 I
— *Die Philosophie der Gegenwart in Selbstdarstellungen.* Leipzig. Meiner.
[1924]. Pp. 27. U-1719
Kierkegaard, Søren. *Samlede Vaerker.* Udgivne A.B. Drachmann, J.L. Heibert,
og H.O. Lange. 14 vols. København. Gyldendalske Boghandels Forlag.
1901-6. U-4776-89. Vols. I, II, IV, VI, XII, XIII I* C* T. Vols. VII, IX, XIV
I T. Vol. III I. Vols. X, XI T
— *Il diario del seduttore.* Tr. L. Redaelli. Torino. Bocca. 1910. Pp. xxiii, 187.
U-2672
King, Bolton. *The Life of Mazzini.* London. Dent. 1914. Pp. xv, 380.
U-1078 I*
'The Kingdom of the Serbians, Croats and Slovenes,' *The Central European
Review.* London [1926]. n/n
Kingsley, Charles. *Westward Ho!* London. Dent. 1914. Pp. 635. U-1057 I* T*
Kleist, Bernd Heinrich von. *Penthesilea.* Leipzig. Reclam. n.d. Pp. 103.
U-4519 I T
Klingsor, Tristan. *Essai sur le chapeau.* Paris. Cahiers de Paris. 1926. Pp. 122.
U-5324
Knjizevnik. Zagreb. 1929. n/n
Koeckert, G. *Les idées de mon oncle Robert sur la morale et la religion.* Paris.
Presses Universitaires de France. 1934. Pp. 42. U-386 D
Koerting, Gustav. *Lateinisch-romanisches. Wörterbuch.* Paderborn. Schöningh.
1901. Pp. 1251. U-751
Kolin, Marcel. *Zemlja Srba Hrvata Slovenaca. Territorio de los Serbios
Croatas Eslovanos.* (Map). Buenos Aires. 1918. U-1177 D

Korsi, Demetrio. *Los poemas extraños.* Panamá. Henry. 1920. Pp. 77.
U-2029 D
Kotzebue, August von. *Der häusliche Zwist.* Leipzig. Reclam. n.d. Pp. 48.
U-4514
— *Der Rehbock.* Leipzig. Reclam. n.d. Pp. 62. U-4510 n/o
Kourmoules, Telemachus. *E Paraesthesis the Logokratias.* Athens. Govosti.
1933. Pp. 158. U-2544 D
Kropotkin, Petr Aleksyeevich. *La conquista del pan.* Madrid. Revista Nueva.
1899. Pp. 295. U-1997 C
Krüger, Fritz. *Sprachgeographische Untersuchungen in Languedoc und
Roussillon.* Hamburg. Societé Internationale de Dialectologie Romane.
1913. Pp. 195. U-2541 D
Krupkin, Ilka. *La taza de chocolate.* Buenos Aires. Gleizer. 1926. Pp. 91.
U-5612 D
Kühner, Raphael. *Ausführliche Grammatik der griechischen sprache.* 2 vols.
Hannover. Hahnschen. 1834-5. U-1828-9 C
Kuenen, Abraham. *Volksgodsdienst en Wereldgodsdienst. Vijf Voorlezingen.*
Leiden. S.C. Van Doesburgh. 1882. Pp. xiv, 286. U-2552 I* B T*
Kuhne, Victor. *Les Bulgares peints par eux-mêmes.* Préf. A. Gauvain. Paris.
Payot. 1917. Pp. vii, 314. U-846 I
Kur'an. *Le Koran.* Tr. nouvelle. Faite sur le texte arabe M. Kasimirski avec
notes, commentaires, et préface. Paris. Charpentier. 1847. Pp. 539.
U-5232
L.R.D. *Roteiro illustrado do viajante em Coimbra.* Coimbra. Typ. Auxiliar
d'Escriptorio. 1894. Pp. 138. U-483
Laberthonnière, L'Abbé L. *Positivisme et catholicisme.* Paris. Bloud. 1911.
Pp. 430. U-3231
— *Le catholicisme et la société.* Concours MM. Chevalier ... Legendre. Paris.
Giard & Brière. 1907. Pp. xliv, 307. U-319
Labougle, Eduardo. *La revolución alemana de 1918.* Buenos Aires. Rivadavia.
1921. Pp. 330. U-1848 D
Labra, Rafael M. de. *España y América. 1812-1912. Estudios políticos,
históricos y de derecho internacional.* Madrid. Sindicato de Publicidad.
1913. Uc
Labriola, Antonio. *Saggi intorno alla concezione materialistica della storia. I.
In memoria del manifesto dei communisti.* Milano. Critica Sociale. 1895.
Pp. 96. U-4844
— *Scritti varii. Editi e inediti di filósofia e politica.* Raccolti e pubblicati
B. Croce. Bari. Laterza. 1906. Pp. viii, 507. U-896 I
— *Socrate.* Nuova edicione a cura B. Croce. Bari. Laterza. 1909. Pp. viii, 282.
U-2262

LaBruyère, Jean de. *Les caractères.* Paris. Lemerre. n.d. Pp. 115. U-5299

Lacambra Serena, Vicente. *Yo no mato.* Valencia. Olmos y Luján. 1922. Pp. 78. U-5500 n/o D

Lacor, Pedro. *El estilete de oro.* Valladolid. Bibl. Studium. n.d. Uc

Lacour, Léopold. *Humanismo integral. El duelo de los sexos. La ciudad futura.* Tr. P. Umbert. 2 vols. Barcelona. Henrich. 1908. Uc

Laferrière, Gregorio de. *Los invisibles.* Buenos Aires. Galli. 1912. Pp. 126. U-269 D

La Fontaine, Jean de. *Fables de Jean de La Fontaine.* Nouveau commentaire M. Coste. Toulouse. A. Renault. 1828. Pp. 394. U-4077

— *Fables.* Préf. Jules Claretie. Paris. Crès. [1909]. Pp. xi, 416. U-1507 I

Lafora, Gonzalo R. *Los niños mentalmente anormales.* Madrid. La Lectura. n.d. Pp. 576. U-5512 D

Lafuente Ferrari, Enrique. *Los retratos de Lope de Vega.* Madrid. Junta del Centenario de Lope de Vega. 1935. Pp. 99, pl. 17. U-3739 n/o

Lagarrigue, Juan Enrique. *La religión de la humanidad.* Santiago de Chile. 1907. Uc D

Lagorio, Arturo. *Las tres respuestas.* Buenos Aires. Gleizer. 1925. Ff. 42. U-5591

Lagos Lisboa, J. *Yo iba solo.* Santiago. Imp. Universitaria. 1915. Pp. 139. U-2777 D

Laguardia, Adda. *Sendas contrarias.* Montevideo. Palacio del Libro. 1927. Pp. 171. U-4943 n/o D

Laisant, C.A. *La educación fundada en la ciencia.* Pref. A. Naquet. Tr. E. Heras. Barcelona. Araluce. n.d. Pp. lviii, 240. U-3638

La Lande, Jérôme de. *Tables de logarithmes.* Etendues à sept décimales par F.C.M. Marie. Paris. Mallet-Bachelier. 1856. Pp. xlii, 204. U-4743

Lamarque, Nydia. *Elegía del gran amor.* Buenos Aires. Proa. 1927. Pp. 91. U-5029 D

Lamartine, Marie Louis Alphonse de. *Harmonies poétiques et religieuses.* Bruxelles. Hauman. 1830. Pp. xxix, 268. U-4025

— *Premières méditations et nouvelles méditations.* Bruxelles. Hauman. 1834. Pp. xvi, 324. U-1550

— *Geneviève. Histoire d'une servante.* Paris. Nelson et Calmann-Levy. [1850]. Pp. 384. U-1525 T

— *Rafael.* Tr. F. Lorenzo. Madrid. Colec. Universal. 1920. Pp. 267. n/n I* C

Lamas Carvajal, Valentín. *Espiñas, follas e frores.* Madrid. Tello. 1877. Pp. 226. U-1987

La Mazière, Pierre. *J'aurai un bel enterrement!* Paris. Littérature et Art Française. [1924]. Pp. 220. U-5306 D

Lamb, Charles. *The Essays of Elia.* London. Oxford University Press. 1906. Pp. xii, 382. U-432 I* B T

– *The Letters of Charles Lamb.* 2 vols. London. Dent. [1909].
   U-1081-2 I* C
Lamennais, Felicité R. de. *Paroles d'un croyant. Le livre du peuple.* Paris.
   Garnier. n.d. Pp. 356. U-1382 I*
– *Essai sur l'indifférence en matière de religion.* 4 vols. Paris. Garnier. n.d.
   U-1911-14 I* B
– *Affaires de Rome.* Paris. Garnier. n.d. Pp. 433. U-1935 I*
Landriot, Mgr. J.B.F. *La femme forte.* Paris. Librairie Catholique. 1881.
   Pp. 447. U-5280
Lange, Friedrich Albert. *Die Arbeiterfrage.* Neu bearbeitet und
   herausgegeben von Dr A. Grabowsky. Leipzig. Kröner. n.d. Pp. 92.
   U-2524 B
Langle, Plácido. *Escritores almerienses. Bocetos biográficos.* Almería.
   La Provincia. 1881-2. Pp. 162. U-4196 D
Lanier, Sidney. *Poems of Sidney Lanier.* Ed. his wife. Memorial by W.H.
   Ward. New York. Scribner's. 1929. Pp. xli, 262. U-5220 I* L* T
Lansdell, Henry. *The Sacred Tenth or Studies in Tithe-giving, Ancient and
   Modern.* 2 vols. London. Society for Promoting Christian Knowledge.
   1906. U-105-6 D
Lanson, Gustave. *Histoire de la littérature française.* Paris. Hachette. 1901.
   Pp. xvi, 1166. U-2087 I* C* B
Lapi, Fernando de. *Suma poética 1908-1924.* Madrid. Mundo Latino. 1925.
   Pp. 235. U-4957 C D
Laranjeira, Manuel. *Commigo. Versos d'um solitario.* Coimbra. F. Amado.
   1911. Pp. 61. U-1456 I*
Larasqueta, Pedro. *El país de los gabachos.* Eibar. Nerea. 1928. Pp. 143.
   U-5010
Lardé de Venturino, Alice. *Alma viril.* Santiago. Nascimento. 1925. Pp. 154.
   U-5025 n/o D
– *Belleza salvaje.* Madrid. Espasa-Calpe. 1927. Pp. 125. U-4904 n/o D
– *Las mejores poesías líricas de los mejores poetas.* Barcelona. Cervantes.
   [1926]. Pp. 61. U-5542 D
La Rochefoucauld, François, duc de. *Memorias.* Tr. Cipriano Rivas Cherif.
   Madrid. Universal. 1919. Pp. 304. n/n I
Larrain, Isaac. *Idioma nacional. Curso gradual. Gramática castellana.* Buenos
   Aires. Igón. 1884. Uc D
Larrain, Jacob. *Biografía del Doctor Guillermo Rawson.* La Plata. Solá. 1895.
   Pp. 304. U-2770 D
Larramendi, Manuel de. *El imposible vencido. Arte de la lengua bascongada.*
   Salamanca. Villagordo Alcaráz. 1729. Pp. 404. U-4592
Larrañaga Conget, Pedro de. *Tregua a la honda desventura.* Bilbao. Sociedad
   Bilbaina. n.d. Pp. 47. U-5077 D

Larrazábal, Felipe. *La vida y correspondencia general del libertador Simón Bolívar.* 2 vols. New York. Cassard. 1883. U-708-9 I*

Larrea y Recalde, Jesus. 'El garaixe (hórreo) agregado al caserío,' *Anuario de Eusko-Folklore,* IV (1926). U-4930 D

— 'Garaixe (hórreo). Agregado al caserío,' *Anuario de Eusko-Folklore* (1927), 127-36. U-5779

Larreta, Enrique. *La gloria de don Ramiro.* Madrid. Suárez. 1908. Pp. 446. U-4799 I D. Buenos Aires. Viau y Zona. 1929. Pp. 381. n/n

L'Arronge, Adolf. *Deutsches Theater und deutsche Schauspielkunst.* Berlin. Concordia Deutsche Verlags. 1896. Pp. 152. U-3229

Larsen, J.K. *Studier over Oldspanske Konjunktiver.* Kφbenhavn. Gyldendalske. 1910. Pp. 134. U-2543 D

Larsen, Karl. *Modet og den blanke Klinge.* Kφbenhavn. Bojesen. 1898. Pp. 94. U-1889 T* D

— *I det store hellige Rusland.* Kφbenhavn. Gyldedalske. 1909. Pp. 99. U-2040 I T D

Lartigau Lespada, H. *Corazonadas.* Valencia. Sempere. n.d. Uc D

Lasplaces, Alberto. *El hombre que tuvo una idea.* Montevideo. Cruz del Sur. 1927. Pp. 174. U-5063 D

— *Opiniones literarias.* Pról. V. Pérez Petit. Montevideo. García. 1919. Pp. 200. U-2340 D

Lasserre, Pierre. *Le romantisme français.* Paris. Mercure de France. 1907. Pp. 547. U-5288

Lasso de la Vega, Rafael. *Rimas de silencio y de soledad.* Madrid. Blass. 1910. Uc D

Lasso de la Vega y Cortezo, Javier. *Isaac.* Madrid. F. Fé. 1900. Pp. 468. U-4250 D

Lasswitz, Kurd. *Gustav Theodor Fechner.* Stuttgart. Frommanns. 1902. Pp. viii, 205. U-867 I C B*

Lastarria, José Victorino. *Obras completas de don J.V. Lastarria.* 5 vols. Santiago. Imp. Barcelona. 1907. U-4088-92

Latimer, Hugh. *Sermons.* London. Dent. 1906. Pp. xvi, 379. U-974 I

Latino, Aníbal. *Los factores del progreso de la República argentina.* Buenos Aires. Lajouane. 1910. Uc D

— *Problemas y lecturas.* Madrid. Suárez. 1912. Uc D

— *El concepto de la nacionalidad y de la patria.* Valencia. Prometeo. n.d. Uc D

Latorre, Gabriel. *Kundry.* Medellín. Cano. 1905. Pp. 178. U-4481 I D

Latorre, Henri de. *A la liberté! L'Italie de 1814 à 1848.* Paris. Cornély. 1908. Pp. vii, 665. U-4149 D

Laugel, Auguste. *Les problèmes de l'âme.* Paris. Baillière. 1868. Pp. 164. U-3989

Laurent, Charles. *Su hijo.* Tr. P.S. Pineda. Paris. Ollendorff. n.d. Uc
– *Ocios de emperador.* Tr. J. Rosell. Paris. Ollendorff. n.d. Uc
Laurent, Emile. *La antropología criminal y las nuevas teorías del crimen.*
  Tr. y pról. F. del Río Urruti. Barcelona. Henrich. 1905. Uc
Lauxar. See Acosta, Crispo
Lavalle, Juan Bautista de. *La crisis contemporánea de la filosofía del derecho.*
  Lima. La Opinión Nacional. 1911. Uc D
Lavalle Cobo, Jorge. *Voces perdidas.* Paris. Bouret. 1907. Uc D
Law, William. *A Serious Call to a Devout & Holy Life.* London. Dent. 1906.
  Pp. viii, 355. U-1008 I
The Lay of Kossovo. History and Poetry on Serbia's Past and Present. London.
  Vacher. Pp. 35. U-3723
Lazarillo. *La vida de Lazarillo de Tormes e de sus fortunas e adversidades.*
  Ed. Eudaldo Canibell. Barcelona. La Académica. 1906. Ff. 73. U-2988
Lazcano Colodrero, Godofredo. *El cuerno de oro.* Córdoba. Biffignandi.
  1925. Pp. 104. U-1137 n/o D
– *El cencerro de la madrina.* Buenos Aires. Porter. 1929. Pp. 102.
  U-5683 I D
Lazúrtegui, Julio de. *Un modelo para España.* Bilbao. Revista Bilbao.
  1902-3. Pp. 349. (2 copies) U-1248, U-1754
– *La hulla, el hierro, y el ferrocarril ante la conflagración europea con
  aplicaciones a España.* Bilbao. Rochelt. 1916. Pp. 58. U-4297
Leal Insua, Francisco. *Horas.* Vivero. Fojo. 1935. Pp. 205. U-5088 D
Leante, Eugenio. *Vertiendo ideas.* Cuba. Sardinas. 1917. Uc D
Lebesgue, Philéas. *Les chants féminins serbes.* Préf. M. Miodrag Ibrovac.
  Paris. Sansot. 1920. Pp. 189. U-5311 I
Le Bon, Gustave. *L'Evolution de la matière.* Paris. Flammarion. 1917.
  Pp. 410. U-3351 I* C
– *L'Evolution des forces.* Paris. Flammarion. 1917. Pp. 389. U-2407 I
Le Braz, Anatole. *La chanson de la Bretagne.* Paris. Calmann-Levy. 1898.
  Pp. 224. U-3977
– *La terre du passé.* Paris. Calmann-Levy. [1902]. Pp. 330. U-1149
– *Au pays des pardons.* Paris. Calmann-Levy. [1901]. Pp. xv, 369.
  U-1952 I* C
– *Le sang de la sirène.* Paris. Calmann-Levy. [1901]. Pp. vi, 300. U-599
– *Le théâtre celtique.* Paris. Calmann-Levy. [1905]. Pp. viii, 544. U-2417
– *Ames d'occident.* Paris. Calmann-Levy. [1911]. Pp. 324. U-1915
– *Contes du soleil et de la brume.* Paris. Delagrave. 1919. Pp. 266.
  U-2397 I*
– *Pâques d'Islande.* Paris. Calmann-Levy. 1920. Pp. 312. U-3848
– *Le gardien du feu.* Paris. Calmann-Levy. 1921. Pp. 322. U-3981
Lebrón, Rafael. *Educación regeneradora.* Barcelona. Seix y Barral. 1913. Uc

Leconte de Lisle, Charles Marie René. *Oeuvres de Leconte de Lisle. Poèmes tragiques.* Paris. Lemerre. n.d. Pp. 238. U-484 I* B

Le Dantec, Félix. *L'Athéisme.* Paris. Flammarion. 1906. Pp. iii, 310. U-3341 I*

– *Science et conscience.* Paris. Flammarion. 1908. Pp. 328. U-1984

Ledesma, Angel. *Los vascos en la Universidad de Salamanca.* Bilbao. Editorial Vasca. 1919. Pp. 81. (2 copies) U-3106, U-3673

Ledesma, Dámaso. *Folk-lore o cancionero salmantino.* Madrid. Imp. Alemana. 1907. Uc

Ledesma Miranda, Ramón. *Motivos del viajero imaginario.* Madrid. Ambos Mundos. 1926. Pp. 315. U-5545 D

– *Treinta poemas de transición.* Madrid. Moderna. 1927. Pp. 121. U-4294 D

– *El nuevo prefacio. Hojas literarias.* 2 vols. Madrid. Urdapillera. 1928. U-5680-1 D

– *Viejos personajes.* Madrid. Agencia General de Librería y Artes Gráficas. 1936. Pp. 260. U-1323 I

Lee, Rev. Samuel. *A Grammar of the Hebrew Language.* London. Duncan and Malcom. 1841. Pp. xxiv, 396. U-1287

Legendre, Maurice. *Le problème de l'éducation.* Paris. Bloud. 1911. Pp. 262. U-251 I D

– 'Le coeur de l'Espagne,' *Correspondant.* Paris (1913). U-1702 D

– *Portrait de l'Espagne.* Paris. Revue des Jeunes. [1923]. Pp. x, 304. U-3660

– *Littérature espagnole.* Mayenne. Bloud et Gay. 1930. Pp. 170. U-943

– *En Espagne.* Paris. Hartmann. [1935]. Pp. 13, pl. 158. U-5248 D

Le Gentil, Georges. *Le poète Manuel Bretón de los Herreros et la société espagnole de 1830 à 1860.* Paris. Hachette. 1909. Pp. xxvi, 549. U-1250 I D

– *Estudios literarios. Oliveira Martins. Algumas fontes da sua obra.* Tr. F. Romero. Lisboa. Seara Nova. 1935. Pp. 63. U-3123

Legrain, M. *Degeneración social y alcoholismo.* Tr. R. Castillo. Barcelona. Henrich. 1906. Uc

Legrand, Emile, et Hubert Pernot. *Chrestomatie grecque moderne.* Paris. Garnier. 1899. Pp. xxiv, 492. U-3030 I T* L*

– *Nouveau dictionnaire grec moderne-français.* Paris. Garnier. [1882]. Pp. vii, 920. n/n

Leguizamón, Martiniano. *Recuerdos de la tierra.* Introd. J.V. González. Buenos Aires. Lajouane. 1896. Pp. xxxvii, 302. U-2166

– *Calandria.* Buenos Aires. Ivaldei & Checchi. 1898. Pp. 231. U-2808

– *Montaraz.* Pról. R.J. Payró. Buenos Aires. Peuser. 1900. Pp. xxx, 274. U-1401 I* D

– *Alma nativa.* Buenos Aires. Moen. 1906. Pp. 261. U-3578 D

– *De cepa criolla.* La Plata. Sesé. 1908. Uc D

– *Urquiza y la casa del acuerdo.* La Plata. Sesé. 1909. Pp. xvi, 225. U-2530
– *Rasgos de la vida de Urquiza (1801-1870).* Buenos Aires. Coni. 1920.
 Pp. 208. U-377 I L* D
Leite de Vasconcellos, Jose. *Estudos de philologia mirandesa.* 2 vols. Lisboa.
 Nacional. 1900-1. U-79-80. U-79 I C D
Lemaître, Jules. *Jean-Jacques Rousseau.* Paris. Calmann-Levy. 1907. Pp. 360.
 U-1155 I
– *Al margen de los libros viejos.* Tr. C. de Batlle. Paris. Sociedad de
 Ediciones Literarias y Artísticas. [1910]. Pp. 343. U-2090
Lemoine, Jacques Albert Felix. *Le vitalisme et l'animisme de Stahl.* Paris.
 Baillière. 1864. Pp. vii, 206. U-295
Lemoine, Joaquín de. *Diamantes sud-americanos.* Paris. Michaud. [1910].
 Pp. 280. Uc D
Lemos, Maximiano. *Ribeiro Sanches. A sua vida e a sua obra.* Porto. Tavares
 Martins. 1911. Pp. viii, 369. U-788 n/o D
Lenau, Nikolaus. *Nikolaus Lenaus Sämtliche Werke.* Herausgegeben von A.
 Grün. Stuttgart. Cottas'chen Buchhandlung. 1880. Pp. c, 346 + 379.
 U-3928 I* T
Leneru, Marie. *Journal de Marie Leneru.* Préf. F. de Curel. 2 vols. Paris. Crès.
 1922. U-1380-1 I* C*
Lenz, Maximilian. *Martin Luther.* Berlin. Gaertner. 1897. Pp. 224. U-4314 I* T
Lenz, Rudolf. *Diccionario etimolójico de las voces chilenas derivadas de
 lenguas indijenas americanas.* Santiago de Chile. Cervantes. 1904. Pp. 448.
 U-4081. Santiago de Chile. Cervantes. 1905-10. Pp. xv, 938. U-1667 D
León, Antonio. *Epítome de la Biblioteca Oriental i Occidental, Naútica i
 Geográfica.* Pról. D.L. Molinari. Buenos Aires. Edición Bibliófilos
 Argentinos. [1919]. Pp. xxxiii, 186. U-1816
León, José de la Luz. *Amiel ó la incapacidad de amar.* Pról. S. de Madariaga.
 Madrid. Bibl. Nueva. 1927. Pp. 301. n/n I C D
León, Luis de, Fray. *De los nombres de Cristo.* Barcelona. Salvatella. 1885.
 Pp. xv, 344. U-5538 I L. Ed y notas F. de Onís. 3 vols. Madrid.
 La Lectura. 1914. U-937-9
– *Poésies originales de Frère Luis de León.* Classées pour la première fois
 dans l'ordre chronologique. Tr. et annotées A. Coster. Chartres. Lester.
 1923. Pp. 57. U-4096
– *El poema de Fray Luis.* Salamanca. Núñez de Izquierdo. 1928. Pp. 31.
 U-5114
León-Felipe. *Versos y oraciones de caminante.* Madrid. Imp. Juan Pérez. 1920.
 Pp. 136. n/n D
– *Versos y oraciones de caminante Libro II.* Nueva York. Instituto de las
 Españas. 1930. Pp. 103. U-4369 D
– *Drop a Star.* México. Ortega. 1933. Pp. 27. U-5767 D

— *Antologia.* Madrid. Espasa-Calpe. [1935]. Pp. 138. U-5579 D

León Suárez, José. *Carácter de la Revolución americana.* Buenos Aires.
La Facultad. 1917. Pp. xx, 160. Uc

León y Román, Ricardo. *Alivio de caminantes. Versos.* Madrid.
Renacimiento. 1911. Pp. 246. Uc D

— *La lira de bronce. Poesías.* Málaga. Zambrana. 1901. Uc D

Leonardo. Firenze (agosto 1906, feb. 1907). n/n

Leonardo y Argensola, L. y B. *Unveröffentlichte Gedichte der Brüder
Argensola.* Herausgegeben von L. Pfandl. Extrait de la *Revue Hispanique,*
LV (1922), 1-28. U-1690

Leopardi, Giacomo. *Le prose morali.* Commentate I. della Giovanna. Firenze.
Sansoni. 1905. Pp. xxxii, 408. U-2628 I

— *I canti di Giacomo Leopardi.* Commentati A. Straccali. Firenze. Sansoni.
1908. Pp. xiii, 241. U-2627 I C

— *Le poesie di Giacomo Leopardi.* Nuova edizione a cura Giovanni Mestica.
Firenze. Barbèra. 1919. Pp. xxiv, 569. U-4568

Leopold. E.F. *Lexicon graeco-latinum manuale ex optimis libris concinnatum.*
Nova impressio. Lipsiae. Holtze. 1874. Pp. iii, 895. U-4061

— *Lexicon hebraicum et chaldaicum in libros Veteris Testamenti.* Lipsiae.
Holtze. 1878. Pp. 453. U-4067

Lermina, Jules. *Misterios de la vida y muerte.* Tr. E. Shaiah. Madrid. Pueyo.
[1910]. Pp. 330. U-594

LeRoy, Edouard. *Dogme et critique.* Paris. Bloud. 1907. Pp. xvii, 387.
U-1357 D

Lessing, Gotthold Ephraim. *Lessings Werke.* 3 vols. Leipzig. Reclam. n.d.
U-1430-2 I

Letelier, Valentín. *Filosofía de la educación.* Santiago de Chile. Cervantes.
1912. Pp. xxii, 864. U-796 D

Letras. Revista de Vicente Medina. Rosario de Santa Fé (1916). n/n

Les Lettres. Paris (juin 1925). n/n

Leumann, Carlos Alberto. *El empresario del genio.* Buenos Aires. Agencia
General de Librería y Publicaciones. [1926]. Pp. 290. U-5066 I D

Lévi, Eliphas. *La clef des grands mystères.* Paris. Baillière. 1861. Pp. iv, 498.
U-1842

Levi, Ezio. *Castelli di Spagna.* Milano. Treves. 1931. Pp. viii, 206. U-3604

— *Lope de Vega e l'Italia.* Pref. Luigi Pirandello. Florencia. Sansoni. 1935.
Pp. viii, 172. U-235

— 'La leggenda simbolica del pessimismo. L'Avvento dell'anti-cristo,' *Studi
Critici in Onore di G.A. Cesareo.* Palermo. n.d. Pp. 15. U-1635 D

Levillier, Roberto. *Orígenes argentinos. La formación de un gran pueblo.*
Paris. Fasquelle. 1912. Pp. xii, 324. Uc

- *Les origines argentines. La formation d'un grand peuple.* Paris. Charpentier. 1912. Pp. xii, 327. U-4010 D
- *Publicaciones históricas de la Biblioteca del Congreso argentino.* Madrid. Pueyo. 1919. Pp. lvi. U-4100 I
- *Santiago del Estero en el siglo XVI.* Madrid. Rivadeneyra. 1919. Pp. 15. U-4198
- *La tienda de los espejos.* Madrid. Calleja. 1921. Pp. 240. U-2693 I* C L D
- *Nueva crónica de la conquista del Tucumán.* Buenos Aires. Nosotros. 1926-31. Vol. i. U-4949. I. Vol. iii. U-4116
- *Gobernación de Tucumán. Correspondencia de los Cabildos en el siglo XVI.* Documentos del Archivo de Indias. Publicación dirigida R. Levillier. Pról. A. Rodríguez del Busto. 4 vols. Madrid. Rivadeneyra. 1918-20. U-2976-9. U-2979 n/o
- *Don Francisco de Toledo, supremo organizador del Perú.* Madrid. Espasa-Calpe. 1935. Pp. 494. U-676 D

Lewis, Sinclair. *Elmer Gantry.* London. Cape. [1927]. Pp. 479. U-5204
- *Babbitt.* Leipzig. Tauchnitz. n.d. Pp. 365. U-502

I libri del giorno. Milano (febraio 1919, luglio 1922). n/n

Libros de caballerías. Ed. Bonilla y San Martín. 2 vols. (NBAE, 6, 9). Madrid. Bailly-Baillière. 1907-8. U-41, U-46 I*

Lichtenberg, Georg Christoph. *Georg Christoph Lichtenbergs ausgewählte Schriften.* Herausgegeben von Eugen Reichel. Leipzig. Reclam. n.d. Pp. 566. U-4553 I

Liebmann, Kurt. *Das kosmische Werk.* Dessau. Liebmann & Mette. 1925. Pp. 300. U-5457 D
- *Das kosmische Werk II.* Dessau. Liebmann & Mette. [1927]. Pp. 126. U-5459

Liliencron, Detlev von. *Ausgewählte Gedichte.* Berlin. Schuster und Loeffler. 1900. Pp. 310. U-477 I* T

Lillie, Arthur. *Buddha and Buddhism.* Edinburgh. Clark. 1900. Pp. ix, 223. U-1336 B*

Lillo, Baldomero. *Sub terra. Cuadros mineros.* Santiago de Chile. Moderna. 1904. Pp. 221. U-1571 D
- *Sub sole.* Santiago de Chile. Universitaria. 1907. Pp. 181. U-3188 D

Lillo, Samuel A. *Canciones de Arauco.* Santiago de Chile. Cervantes. 1908. Uc D

Lima, Silvio. *O amor místico. Noção e valor da experiência religiosa.* Coimbra. Universidade. 1935. Pp. xiii, 413. U-2201 I* C D

Limosin, Febo de. *Estrellita de Taboga.* Panamá. Nacional. 1927. Pp. 89. U-5020 D

Lincoln, Abraham. *Speeches and Letters of Abraham Lincoln (1832-1865).* Introd. James Bryce. London. Dent. [1907]. Pp. xxii, 237. U-1056 I*

Lindau, Paul. *Berlin. La marcha hacia el poniente*. Tr. P. Taboada y Oñes. Santiago de Chile. Universitaria. 1906. Pp. 392. U-411 n/o

Linze, Georges. *L'Âme double*. Liége. Groupe Moderne d'Art et Littérature. 1921. Pp. 61. U-5270 D

Liscano, Juan. *Las doctrinas guerreras y el derecho*. Caracas. El Cojo. [1915]. Pp. xvi, 225. U-3098 D

Literatos guatemaltecos. Landívar e Irisarri. Discurso preliminar A. Batres Jáuregui. Guatemala. Nacional. 1896. Pp. 312. U-739

'La littérature espagnole contemporaine,' *L'Ane d'Or. Revue Mensuelle de Littérature et de Critique*. Montpellier (février 1924), 399-440. U-1724

Livius, Titus Patavinus. *Titi Livii Patavini historiarum ab urbe condita libri qui supersunt XXXV*. Recensuit J.N. Lallemand. 7 vols. Paris. Barbou. 1775. U-4637-43 I* C* T

− *Livres XXI et XXII*. Paris. Hachette. n.d. Pp. 549. QP-28 I

Llamazares, Lisandro A. *Besos de quimera*. León. La Democracia. 1913. Uc D

Llanas Aguilaniedo, J. Ma. *Alma contemporánea. Estudio de estética*. Huesca. Pérez. 1899. Uc D

− *Del jardín del amor*. Madrid. F. Fé. 1902. Pp. 134. U-3424 D

Llano, Manuel. *Brañaflor*. Pról. M. Artigas. Santander. Moderna. 1931. Pp. xv, 318. U-2618 I* C L*

− *La braña*. Pról. L. Santa Marina. Santander. Aldus. 1934. Pp. 168. U-3947 I

− *Rabel. Leyendas*. Santander. Aldus. 1934. Pp. 240. U-3861 D

− *Retablo infantil*. Pról. M. de Unamuno. Santander. Tall. Tipográficos Santa Lucia. 1935. Pp. 135. U-4361 D

Llano Roza de Ampudia, Aurelio. *Dialectos jergales asturianos. Vocabularios de la Xiriga y El Brón*. Oviedo. El Correo de Asturias. 1921. Pp. 19. U-3688

− *Del folklore asturiano, mitos, supersticiones, costumbres*. Pról. R. Menéndez Pidal. Madrid. Voluntad. 1922. Pp. xx, 277. U-4281 I* C L D

− *Archivo de tradiciones populares. I. Cuentos asturianos*. Madrid. Centro de Estudios Históricos. 1925. Pp. 316. U-5713 D

− *Pequeños anales de quince días. La revolución de Asturias. Octubre 1934*. Oviedo. Altamirano. 1935. Pp. xiii, 213. U-4951 D

Llano Zapata, José Eusebio. *Memorias histórico-físicas-apologéticas de la América meridional*. Publicadas Ricardo Palma. Lima. S. Pedro. 1904. Pp. xiii, 617. U-773

Llanos y Torriglia, Félix de. *Cómo se hizo la revolución en Portugal*. Madrid. Real Academia de Jurisprudencia y Legislación. 1914. Pp. 103. U-3252 n/o

Lles y Berdayes, Fernando. *La escudilla de Diógenes. Etopeya del cinico*. Habana. Nuestra Novela. 1924. Pp. 119. U-5141 n/o D

Llibre d'or dels jochs florals. Valencia. Domenech. 1895. Pp. 232. U-4708

Llor, Miquel. *Tàntal.* Badalona. Proa. 1929. Pp. 236. U-5330 I D

– *L'Endema del dolor.* Badalona. Proa. 1930. Pp. 220. U-5329 D

– *Laura a la ciutat dels sants.* Badalona. Proa. 1931. Pp. 258. U-5328 I L D.
Badalona. Proa. 1935. U-527

– *L'Oreig al desert.* Barcelona. Catalonia. 1934. Pp. 243. U-2238 I* T D

– *El premi a la virtut.* Barcelona. Verdaguer. 1935. Pp. 101. U-675 D

Llorca, Angel. *El primer año de lenguaje.* Madrid. Jiménez Fraud. 1923.
Pp. 216. (2 copies) U-4017-18 D

– *La escuela primaria.* Madrid. Hernando. 1912. Pp. 215. U-2523 n/o

Loayza, Francisco A. *El Inka piadoso y justiciero.* Barcelona. Maucci. n.d.
Pp. 159. U-5103

Locascio, Santiago. *Juan Bautista Alberdi. Crónica histórica.* Pról. A.R.
Zuñiga. Buenos Aires. Maucci. 1916. Pp. xv, 153. U-2890 D

Lockhart, John Gibson. *Life of Robert Burns.* London. Dent. [1907]. Pp. xiv,
322. U-1049 I C

Lockyer, Sir Joseph Norman. *Elementary Lessons in Astronomy.* London.
Macmillan. 1894. Pp. xvi, 367. U-1416 C

Lodge, Oliver J. *Raymond; or, Life and Death. With Examples of the Evidence
for Survival of Memory and Affection after Death.* London. Methuen.
[1917]. Pp. xi, 403. U-119 I B

Lods, Adolphe. *Israël, des origines au milieu du VIIIe siècle.* Paris. La
Renaissance du Livre. 1930. Pp. xvi, 595. QP-29 I

Loforte-Randi, Andrea. *Sognatori.* Palermo. Reber. 1900. Pp. 324. U-5342 D

Loisy, Alfred. *Autour d'un petit livre.* Paris. Picard. 1903. Pp. xxxvi, 303.
U-201 [Bound with *L'Evangile et l'eglise*]

– *L'Evangile et l'eglise.* [Macon]. [Protat]. 1904. Pp. xxxiv, 279. U-201
[Bound with *Autour d'un petit livre*]

– *La religion.* Paris. Nourry. 1917. Pp. 315. U-2836 I*

Longfellow, Henry Wadsworth. *The Poetical Works of Henry Wadsworth
Longfellow.* London. Nimmo. 1877. Pp. vi, 633. U-4464 I*

Longo, M. *La conciencia criminosa.* Tr. J. Buixó Monserdá. Barcelona.
Henrich. 1905. Uc

Lopes, Francisco Fernandes. *Sobre o poeta João Lúcio.* Conferencia. Faro.
Tip. Uniao. 1921. Pp. 36. U-5717 D

Lopes de Oliveira, José. *A justiça e o homem.* Coimbra. Ensino. 1904.
Pp. 122. U-3215 D

Lopes Praça, J.J. *Historia da philosophia em Portugal.* Coimbra. Imprensa
Litteraria. 1868. Pp. 254. U-4857

Lopes Vieira, Affonso. *Ilhas de bruma.* Coimbra. Amado. 1917. Pp. 133.
U-3409

– *Cancioneiro de Coimbra.* Coimbra. Amado. 1918. Uc

López, Felicísimo. *Virutas o almanaque de pensamientos sinceros.* New York. 1908. Pp. 350. U-4289

López, Julio A. *El terreno de la locura.* Buenos Aires. Universidad Nacional de Buenos Aires. 1909. Uc D

López, Libardo. *La raza antioqueña.* Medellin. La Organización. 1910. Pp. xiv, 258. U-1468 D

López, Luis C. *De mi villorrio.* Pról. M. Cervera. Madrid. Rev. de Archivos. 1908. Uc D

— *Posturas difíciles.* Madrid. Pueyo. n.d. Pp. 114. U-2632 D

López, Nicolás María. *Tristeza andaluza.* Granada. Sabatel. [1898]. Pp. 299. (2 copies) U-4506-7 D

López, Vicente F. *Historia de la República Argentina. Su orígen, su revolución y su desarrollo político hasta 1852.* 10 vols. Buenos Aires. La Facultad. 1911. U-2554-63 I. Vol. VIII I C

López-Abente, Gonzalo. *D'Outono.* n.p. [1924]. Pp. 68. U-5704

López Albo, Wenceslao. *Métodos de selección del profesorado.* Bilbao. Casa Dochao. 1935. Pp. 16. U-5468 D

López Albújar, Enrique. *Cuentos andinos. Vida y costumbres indígenas.* Pról. E.S. Ayllón. Lima. Opinión Nacional. 1920. Pp. xix, 185. (2 copies) U-3957-8

— *De mi casona.* Lima. Castro. 1924. Pp. 159. U-4491 D

— *Matalaché.* Lima. Piura. 1928. Pp. 258. (2 copies) U-2345, U-5706 D

López Ballesteros, Luis. *La cueva de los buhos.* Madrid. Sáenz de Jubera. 1907. Pp. 307. U-3997 D

López de Ayala, Pedro. *Crónica del rey D. Pedro.* Madrid. Ibero-Americana de Public. n.d. Pp. 290. n/n I C

López de Gomara, Justo S. *La ciencia del bien y del mal.* Buenos Aires. Escary. 1891. Uc

— *La nueva doctrina. Ideales y observaciones de moral y filosofía.* Buenos Aires. Escary. 1893. Uc

— *Agraces. Poesías varias.* Valencia. Sempere. n.d. Pp. 169. U-3278

López de Haro, Carlos. *La reforma agraria.* Madrid. Reus. 1931. Pp. 103. U-4897 n/o

López de Mendoza, Iñigo, Marqués de Santillana. *Canciones y decires.* Ed. y notas V. García de Diego. Madrid. La Lectura. 1913. Pp. xxxiv, 288. U-940

López de Mesa, L. *La civilización contemporánea.* Paris. Agencia Mundial de Librería. 1926. Pp. 248. U-4995 n/o D

— *El libro de los apólogos.* Paris. Excelsior. 1926. Pp. 252. U-5549 D

López Ferreiro, Antonio. *El pórtico de la gloria. Estudio sobre este célebre monumento de la basilica compostelana.* Santiago. Seminario Central. 1893. Pp. 155. U-721 I*

López Loayza, Fernando. *Letras de molde*. Iquique. Bini. 1907. Pp. 371.
U-157 D
- *Prosa menuda*. Iquique. Bini. 1908. Uc D
- *Pro-patria*. Iquique. La Académica. 1909. Pp. 311. U-2595 D
López Montenegro, Félix. *Apuntes para la historia de la formación social de los españoles*. Madrid. [Velasco]. 1922. Pp. 491. U-1198
López Núñez, Alvaro. *Ensayo de un vocabulario social*. Madrid. Minuesa de los Ríos. 1911. Pp. xvi, 219. U-597 D
- *Mosaico*. Madrid. Hispano-Alemana. 1916. Pp. 223. U-3157 D
López Peláez, Antolín, Obispo de Jaca. *Injusticias del estado español. Labor parlamentaria de un año*. Barcelona. Gili. [1909]. Pp. 488. U-284
- *El presupuesto del clero*. Madrid. Gómez Fuentenebro. 1910. Pp. 382.
U-895
- *Vida póstuma de un santo. (El culto de San Froilán)*. Madrid. Gómez Fuentenegro. 1911. Pp. 214. U-1324 D
- *Los siete pecados capitales*. Friburgo de Brigovia. Herder. [1902]. Pp. 219.
U-3226 D
- *Las mentiras del alcohol*. Madrid. Patronato Social de Buenas Lecturas.
n.d. Pp. 198. U-4446
López Penha, A.Z. *El libro de las incoherencias*. Madrid. Pueyo. [1909].
Pp. 151. U-1993 D
López Picó, Josep M. Op. i. *Torment-Froment*. Pròl. E. D'Ors. Barcelona.
Horta. 1910. Pp. xviii, 154. U-2866 D
- Op. ii. *Poemes del port*. Barcelona. Altés. 1911. Pp. 74. U-4266 n/o D
- Op. iii. *Amor, Senyor*. Barcelona. Alvar Verdaguer. 1912. Ff. 33.
U-2848 D
- Op. iv. *Espectacles i mitología*. Barcelona. Altés. 1914. Pp. 164.
U-3685 D
- Op. v. *Epigrammata*. Barcelona. Altés. 1915. Pp. 94. U-2952 D
- *Poesies. 1910-1915*. Barcelona. Societat Catalana d'Edicions. 1915.
Pp. 224. U-2716 D
- Op. vi. *L'Ofrena*. Barcelona. Altés. 1915. Pp. 69. U-3878 D
- Op. vii. *Paraules*. Barcelona. Altés. 1916. Pp. 77. U-2293 D
- Op. viii. *Cants i al'legories*. Barcelona. Altés. 1917. Pp. 142. U-2942 D
- Op. ix. *L'Instant, Les noces i El càntic serè*. Barcelona. Altés. 1918.
Pp. 139. U-2825 D
- Op. x. *Les absències paternals*. Barcelona. Altés. 1919. Pp. 97. U-3623 D
- Op. xi. *El meu pare i jo*. Barcelona. 1920. Pp. 60. U-3731 D
- Op. xii. *El retorn*. Barcelona. Altés. 1921. Pp. 106. U-1939 D
- Op. xiii. *Popularitats*. Barcelona. Altés. 1922. Pp. 126. U-1503 D
- Op. xv. *Les enyorances del món*. Barcelona. Altés. 1923. Pp. 70.
U-4407 D

- Op. XVI. *Cinc poemes.* Barcelona. Altés. 1924. Pp. 63. U-2302
- *Antologia lírica.* Pról. C. Riba. Epíl. A. Esclasans. Barcelona. Altés. 1931. Pp. 323. U-1850

López Rocha, Carlos. *Palideces y púrpuras.* Buenos Aires. Galileo. 1905. Pp. 117. U-1651 D

Lorenzana, Maximo. *Diego Velasco.* Bogotá. La Luz. 1905. Pp. 259. U-4477 D

Loria, Achille. *Analisi della proprietà capitalista.* 2 vols. Torino. Bocca. 1889. U-782-3 I
- *La costituzione economica odierna.* Torino. Bocca. 1899. Pp. xv, 822. U-806 I*

Loria, Gino. *Metodi di geometria descrittiva.* Milano. Hoepli. 1919. Pp. xx, 353. U-4684

L'Orim-Unifiée. *Les traîtés à la cause macédonienne.* Paris. Imprimerie d'Editions. 1929. Pp. 274. U-5283

Loti, Pierre. *La muerte de Philae.* Tr. P. Simón Pineda. Paris. Ollendorff. n.d. Uc

Lotze, Rudolf Hermann. *Principes généraux de psychologie physiologique.* Tr. A. Penjon. Paris. Baillière. 1881. Pp. xvi, 168. U-595 I

Lowrie, Donald A. *Masaryk de Tchécoslovaquie.* n.p. Je Sers. n.d. Pp. 302. U-1847 n/o

Loyarte, Adrián de. *Pinceladas de Basconia.* Tolosa. López. 1905. Uc D

Lozano y Ponce de León, Eduardo. *Física.* Barcelona. Soler. n.d. Uc

Lucanus, Marcus Annaeus. *M. Annaei Lucani Pharsalia.* Sive de bello civili Caesaris et Pompeii Lib. x. Additae funt in fine Hugonis Grotii notae. Patavii. Typis Seminarii. 1721. Pp. 430. U-1536 I
- *M. Annaei Lucani Pharsalia,* cum supplemento T. Maii. Paris. Barbou. 1767. Pp. x, 421. U-4700 I T C

Lucas-Dubreton, J. *Le roi sauvage.* Paris. Perrin. 1921. Pp. 301. U-2084 I* D

Lucena, João de. *Vida do Padre Francisco de Xavier.* Introd. A. de Campos. 2 vols. Lisboa. Anuario Comercial. 1921. U-317-18 D

Lucian. *De la manière d'écrire l'histoire.* Ed. A. Lehugeur. Paris. Hachette. 1876. Pp. 80. U-4666 L*
- *Dialogues des morts. Disposés progressivement et annotés à l'usage des classes* par Ed. Tournier. Paris. Hachette. 1894. Uc
- *Luciani samosatensis opera.* Ex recognitione Caroli Iacobitz. 3 vols. Lipsiae. Teubner. 1904-9. U-339-41 I* T L. U-441 B C

Lucifero, Virgilio. *Serraglio di Virgilio Lucifero.* Catania. Mollica. 1895. Pp. 108. U-1998 D

Lucini, Gian Pietro. *Revolverate.* Pref. futurista F.T. Marinetti. Milano. Ed. di Poesia. 1909. Pp. 360. U-2436

Lucio, João. *Descendo.* Coimbra. Amado. 1901. Pp. 147. U-144 n/o D
- *Na aza do Sonho.* Coimbra. Amado. 1913. Pp. 258. U-833 n/o D

Lucretius Carus, Titus. *T. Lucretii Cari de Rerum Natura libri sex.* Lutetiae
Parisiorum. 1754. Pp. xxxv, 288. U-4472 T
- *T. Lucreti Cari de Rerum Natura libri sex.* Revisione del testo, commento,
e studi introduttivi C. Giussani. 2 vols. Torino. Loescher. 1896-7.
U-4810-11 I* L*
Ludwig, Emil. *Goethe.* 2 vols. Berlin. Rowohlt. [1926]. U-3044-5
- *Guillaume II.* Tr. J.P. Samson. Paris. Kra. 1927. Pp. 317. QP-30 I
Lugo, Américo. *A punto largo.* Santo Domingo. La Cuna de América. 1901.
Pp. 222. U-2677 D. Estudio crítico M.A. Garrido. Paris. Ollendorff. n.d.
Pp. xviii, 254. U-3663
Lugones, Leopoldo. *El imperio jesuítico.* Buenos Aires. Cía. Sudamericana de
Billetes de Banco. 1904. Pp. 332. U-2987 I
- *El problema feminista.* San José de Costa Rica. Greñas. 1916. Pp. 69.
U-2803
- *Rubén Darío.* San José de Costa Rica. Alsina. 1916. Pp. 42. U-468 n/o
Luis, de Granada (Fray). *Libro de la oración y meditación en el cual se trata
de la consideración de los principales misterios de nuestra Fé.* Barcelona.
Rosal. 1883. Pp. xii, 514. U-4578
- *Guia de pecadores.* 2 vols. Barcelona. Libr. Religiosa. 1884. U-4078-9.
U-4078 B
Lull, Ramon. *Libre de Amich e Amat.* Proemi, notes, y glosari M. Obrador y
Bennassar ... Palma de Mallorca. Catalunya. 1904. Pp. 213. U-3114
Lumholtz, Carl. *El México desconocido.* 2 vols. New York. Scribner's. 1904.
U-1678-9
Luque Alcardy, Eduardo. *Redención.* Paris. 1927. Pp. 322. U-5600
Luxemburg, Róża. *Rosa Luxemburg Briefe an Karl und Luise Kautsky,
1896-1918.* Herausgegeben von Luise Kautsky. Berlin. Laub'sche
Verlagsbuchhandlung. 1923. Pp. 234. U-5447 I
Luzuriaga, Lorenzo. *El libro del idioma. Lecturas literarias.* Madrid. Publ. de
la Revista de Pedagogia. n.d. Pp. 205. U-5476 D
M.D.L. *De la antiguedad y universalidad del bascuenze en España.* Salamanca.
García de Honorato. 1728. Pp. 170. U-4579
The Mabinogion. Tr. and introd. Lady Charlotte Guest. London. Dent.
[1906]. Pp. 432. U-1070 I* C
Macau, Miguel Angel. *Flores del trópico. Poesías.* Barcelona. Granada.
[1913] Pp. 300. U-1348 D
- *La justicia en la inconsciencia. Julián. La partida.* Matanzas. González.
1913. Pp. 157. U-3437 D
Mach, E. *Die Analyse der Empfindungen und das Verhältniss des Physischen
zum Psychischen.* Jena. Fischer. 1902. Pp. 286. U-1246 I C
Machado, Antonio. *Soledades. Poesías.* Madrid. Alvarez. 1903. Pp. 104.
U-4693 D

— *Soledades. Galerías. Otros poemas.* Madrid. Pueyo. 1907. Pp. 176.
  U-3265 D
— *Campos de Castilla.* Madrid. Renacimiento. 1912. Pp. 198. U-890
— *Poesías completas de Antonio Machado.* Madrid. Residencia de
  Estudiantes. 1917. Pp. 268. U-2182
Machado, Manuel. *Caprichos.* Madrid. Rev. de Archivos. 1905. Pp. 157.
  U-3400 D
— *Alma. Museo. Los cantares.* Pról. M. de Unamuno. Madrid. Pueyo. 1907.
  Pp. xxvii, 159. U-888 I
— *El mal poema.* Madrid. Gutenberg-Castro. 1909. Pp. 155. U-1148 D
— *Apolo. Teatro pictórico.* Madrid. Prieto. 1911. Pp. 124. U-1144 D
— *El amor y la muerte.* Madrid. Helénica. 1913. Pp. 234. U-2061 D
— *La guerra literaria. 1898-1914.* Madrid. Hispano-Alemana. 1913. Pp. 180.
  U-3174 I D
— *Ars moriendi. Poesías.* Madrid. Mundo Latino. 1921. Pp. 98. U-4020 D
— *Alma. Poesías.* Madrid. Marzo. 1902. Pp. 138. U-3266 D
— *Un año de teatro. Ensayos de crítica dramática.* Madrid. Bibl. Nueva.
  1918. Pp. 280. U-3592 D
— *Poesías escogidas.* Pról. M. de Unamuno. Barcelona. Maucci. n.d. Pp. 224.
  U-3171
— y Antonio Machado. *Las adelfas. La Lola se va a los puertos.* Madrid.
  Renacimiento. [1930]. Pp. 282. U-3164 D
— *Desdichas de la fortuna o Julianillo Valcárcel.* Madrid. F. Fé. 1926.
  Pp. 171. U-4900 D
— *Juan de Mañara.* Madrid. Espasa-Calpe. 1927. Pp. 155. U-4901 D
Machado Bonet, Ofelia. *Allegro scherzando.* Montevideo. Peña. 1929. Pp. 69.
  U-5110 n/o D
Machado de Assis, Joaquim. *Dom Casmurro.* Tr. F. de Miomandre. Préf. A.
  Peixoto. Paris. Stock. 1936. Pp. 332. U-2433 I
Machiavelli, Niccolò. *Il principe di Niccolò Macheavelli.* Con commento
  storico, folologico, stilistico a cura di Giuseppe Lisio. Firenze. Sansoni.
  1907. Pp. 160. U-2312 I B
— *Pensieri sugli uomini.* Scelti da tutte le sue opere e ordinati G. Papini.
  Lanciano. Carabba. 1910. Pp. 125. U-237
Macías Picavea, Ricardo. *El problema nacional.* Madrid. Suárez. 1899. Pp. xiv,
  524. U-4279 D
Maciel, Santiago. *Nativos.* Buenos Aires. La Nación. 1901. Pp. 239. U-4704 D
Mackay, Juan A. *Mas yo os digo.* Montevideo. Mundo Nuevo. 1927. Pp. 245.
  U-5134
Mackenna, Juan. *Ensayos psicolójicos y literarios.* Roma. Cuggiani. 1912. Uc D
McMahon, A. Philip. *The Meaning of Art.* New York. W.W. Norton. 1930.
  Pp. 306. U-903 I C

- 'Sextus Empiricus and the arts,' reprinted from *Harvard Studies in Classical Philology*, XLII (1931), U-5195 I

Madariaga, Salvador de. 'Shelley and Calderón,' Transactions *Royal Society of Literature*, XXXVII, Pp. 40. U-5172 D

- *Shelley and Calderón and Other Essays on English and Spanish Poetry*. London. Constable. 1920. Pp. xii, 198. U-1840 I D
- *Romances de ciego. Poesía*. Aról. M. de Unamuno. Madrid. Atenea. 1922. Pp. 120. (3 copies) U-4468, U-4630-1
- *Ensayos angloespañoles*. Madrid. Atenea. 1922. Pp. 202. U-4632
- *El enemigo de Dios*. Madrid. Aguilar. 1936. Pp. 242. U-2380 D

Madinaveitia, Herminio. *El rincón amado*. Madrid. Renacimiento. 1914. Pp. 293. U-2316 D

- *Oro sangriento*. Valencia. Sempere. n.d. Uc

Madrid, Samuel de. *Cesaritis*. Buenos Aires. Suárez. 1913. Pp. 352. U-2995 D

Maeso, Carlos M. *Tierra de promisión*. Montevideo. Escuela Nacional de Artes y Oficios. 1904. Pp. 384. U-1208

- *Pan de bronce. Poemas*. Montevideo. Gaceta Comercial. 1934. Pp. 123. U-2438 D

Maeterlinck, Maurice. *La mort*. Paris. Charpentier. 1913. Uc

Maeztu, Ramiro de. *Authority, Liberty and Function in the Light of the War*. London. George Allen & Unwin. 1916. Pp. 288. U-1161 D

- *La brevedad de la vida en nuestra poesía lírica*. Discurso leído en el acto de su recepción a la Academia Española. Contestación del Ilmo. Sr D. Agustín González de Amezua. 30 junio 1935. Madrid. Universal. 1935. Pp. 77. U-4124
- *La crisis del humanismo*. Barcelona. Minerva. [1919]. Pp. 366. n/n I* C L* B D

Magallanes Moure, M. *La jornada*. Santiago de Chile. La Ilustración. 1910. Uc D

Magnasco, Silvio. *Guerra del Paraguay*. Buenos Aires. Argos. 1906. Pp. 95. U-3037 D

Magnaud, Paul. *Novísimas sentencias del Presidente Magnaud*. Recopiladas y comentadas E. Leyret. Tr. R. Pomés y Soler. Barcelona. Carbonell y Esteva. n.d. Uc

Magnini Tamborino, Maria Luisa. *Frullo d'ali*. Taranto. Lodeserto. 1929. Pp. 123. U-689 D

Magno, Agenore G. *I miei canti (1898-1910)*. Torino. Paravia. 1911. Pp. 254. U-854 D

Magro, Cerqueira. *Matinais do Seixoso. I. Jantar de três felizes condiscípulos*. Lixa. Estância do Seixoso. [1936]. Pp. 61. U-5737 D

Mahaffy, J.P. *Antigüedades griegas*. New York. Appleton. 1884. Pp. xiii, 146. U-4609

Maine, Henry-James. *El derecho antiguo.* Tr. A. Guerra. Vols. i, v. Madrid.
Tip. del Hospicio y A. Alonso. 1893-4. U-2001-2

Maistre, François Xavier de. *Oeuvres.* Paris. Roger et Chernoviz. n.d. Pp. lx,
298. U-1906

Maistre, Joseph de. *Oeuvres choisies de J. de Maistre.* 2 vols. Paris. Chernoviz.
1909. U-4858-9 I* C

Majjhimanikaya. *Die Reden Gotamo Buddhós aus der mittleren Sammlung
Majjhimanikayo des Pàli-Kanons.* Uebertragen von K.E. Neumann. 3 vols.
München. Piper. 1922. U-5419-21 I* C*

Majocchi Plattis, María (Jolanda, pseud.). *El libro de la mujer. Eva Reina.*
Tr. V. Araluce. 2 vols. Barcelona. Araluce. Uc

Malagarriga, Carlos. *Prosa muerta.* Buenos Aires. La Facultad. 1908. Uc D

Malagarriga, Joan. *Passions & somnis.* Barcelona. Tobella. [1911]. Pp. 84.
U-2938 D

– *Aurora. Esparces amorosos.* Barcelona. Artís. [1911]. U-2383 D

– *Al vent de la ciutat. Poemes. 1913-1920.* Barcelona. Llib. Nac. Catalana.
1921. Pp. 77. U-2824 D

Maldonado, Alonso. *Hechos del Maestre de Alcántara don Alonso de Monroy.*
Estudio preliminar A. Rogríguez Moñino. Madrid. Revista de Occidente.
1935. Pp. lxxxiii, 155. U-2769 I* L

Maldonado, Horacio. *Mientras el viento calla.* Montevideo. Serrano. 1916.
Pp. 308. U-3101 D

– *Doña Ilusión en Montevideo.* Montevideo. Peña. 1929. Pp. 294. U-5100 D

Maldonado, Luis. *La montaraza de Olmeda.* Madrid. Sociedad de Autores
Españoles. 1908. Pp. 50. n/n D

– *Don Quijote en los estudios de Salamanca.* Salamanca. Núñez. 1915.
Pp. 32. U-2899

– *Discurso ... con ocasión del doctoramiento 'Honoris Causa' de Santa
Teresa de Jesus por la Universidad de Salamanca.* Salamanca. Calatrava.
1923. Pp. 15. U-4931

Maldonado Macanaz, Joaquín. *Principios generales del arte de la colonización.*
Madrid. Tello. 1875. Pp. xviii, 286. U-4249

Mallarmé, Camille. *La casa seca.* Paris. Calmann-Lévy. 1916. Pp. 336.
U-3850 I D

Mallarmé, Stéphane. *Poésies.* Paris. Nouvelle Revue Française. 1914. Pp. 172.
U-1374

– *Divagations.* Paris. Charpentier. 1922. Pp. 377. QP-31 I

Mallea, Eduardo. *Nocturno europeo.* Buenos Aires. Sur. 1935. Pp. 226.
U-3611 D

Mallet, Christian. *Etapes et combats. Souvenirs d'un cavalier devenu fantassin.
1914-1915.* Paris. Plon. 1916. Pp. iv, 246. U-1112

Malón de Chaide, Fr. Pedro. *Libro de la conversión de la Magdalena.* 2 vols.
Barcelona. Subirana. 1881. U-607-8. U-608 I*
Maluenda, Rafael. *Escenas de la vida campesina.* Santiago de Chile. Cervantes.
1909. Pp. 214. U-2145 n/o D
Mammelis, Ap. *Thalassina.* Athina. 1925. Pp. 125. U-2244 n/o D
– *Stathmoi.* Athina. Gerardos. 1928. Pp. 111. U-2809 D
– *Skopoi.* Athina. 1928. Pp. 75. U-528 D
– *Pera ap' t' anthropina.* Athina. Gerardos. 1930. Pp. 43. U-2457 n/o D
Man, Hendrik de. *Die Intellektuellen und der Socialismus.* Jena. Diederichs.
1926. Pp. 37. U-5382
– *Der Dampf um die Arbeitsfreude.* Jena. Diederichs. 1927. Pp. 289.
U-5370 I* C T D
Mancini, Jules. *Bolívar y la emancipación de las colonias españolas desde los
orígenes hasta 1815.* Tr. Carlos Docteur. Paris. Bouret. 1914. Pp. 591.
U-2569 I*
Mangasarian, M.M. *Sin Dios.* Tr. T. Meabe. Bilbao. Popular. n.d. Pp. 153.
U-393
Manjón, Andrés. *El pensamiento del Ave-María.* Granada. Escuelas del
Ave María. 1903. Uc
Mann, Heinrich. *Der Kopf.* Berlin. Zsolnay. 1925. Pp. 636. U-5424 I* T
Mann, Thomas. *Unordnung und frühes Leid.* Berlin. Fischer. 1926. Pp. 126.
U-5395 I T
– *Tonio Kröger.* Berlin. Fischer. 1926. Pp. 121. U-5411 I T
Manrique, Jorge. *Poesías.* Barcelona. Librería Española. n.d. Uc
Mansilla, Lucio Victorio. *Rozas. Ensayo histórico-psicológico.* Paris. Garnier.
1898. Pp. xxvi, 272. U-186
Mantegazza, Paolo. *Viajes por el Río de la Plata y el interior de la Confedera-
ción argentina.* Tr. y pról. J. Heller. Buenos Aires. Coni. 1916. Pp. 280.
U-671
Le manuscrit autographe. Paris (1927-9). n/n [4 issues]
Manzoni, Alessandro. *I promessi sposi.* Colla vita dell'autore por Giulio
Carcano. Milano. Rechiedei. 1886. Pp. xxiii, 467. U-3929 I* T L*
Mañach, Jorge. *Goya.* La Habana. Revista Avance. 1928. Pp. 57. U-5544 D
Maples Arce, Manuel. *Poemas interdictos.* Jalapa, México. Horizonte. 1927.
Pp. 85. U-4985
Maragall, Joan. *Seqüencias. Poesies.* Barcelona. L'Avenç. 1911. Pp. 51.
U-2303 D
– *Elogios.* Barcelona. Gili. 1913. Pp. 186. U-2366
– *Himnes homèrics.* Barcelona. L'Avenç. 1913. Uc
– *Obras completas de Juan Maragall. Artículos.* Pról. M.S. Oliver. 5 vols.
Barcelona. Gili. 1912. U-1359-63 I*

- *Obres completes d'en Joan Maragall. Serie catalana. Poesies.* Pròl. J. Ruyra. 2 vols. Barcelona. Gili. 1912. U-1364-5
- *Traducciones de Goethe.* Barcelona. Gili. 1912. Pp. 314. U-1366
- *Escrits en prosa.* 2 vols. Barcelona. Gili. 1912. U-1367-8. U-1368 I
- *Las fiestas. Articles. - Problemas del día. Articles.* Pról. J. Estelrich y M. de Unamuno. 2 vols. Barcelona. Parés. 1934. U-355-6. U-1572
  [Another copy of *Problemas del día*]

Marañón, Gregorio. *Tres ensayos sobre la vida sexual.* Ensayo Ramón Pérez de Ayala. Madrid. Bibl. Nueva. 1928. Pp. 250. U-2642 I D
- *Uber das Geschlechtsleben.* Aus dem Spanischen übersetzt von Baron Otto von Taube. Heidelberg. Kampmann. 1928. Pp. 144. U-5380 D
- *Amiel. Un estudio sobre la timidez.* Madrid. Espasa-Calpe. 1932. Pp. xii, 335. U-5608 I* D
- *El Conde-Duque de Olivares. La pasión de mandar.* Madrid. Espasa-Calpe. 1936. Pp. 511. U-758 I D

Marañón. Veinticinco años de labor. Historia y bibliografía de la obra del Prof. Gregorio Marañón y del Instituto de Patología Medica del Hospital de Madrid, por sus discipulos. Madrid. Espasa-Calpe. 1935. Pp. 326. U-3200 D

Marasso Rocca, Arturo. *Bajo los astros.* Buenos Aires. 1911. Pp. 120. U-2841 D
- *El doctor Joaquín V. González. Comentarios e impresiones de sus obras literarias.* Buenos Aires. La Facultad. 1915. Pp. 128. U-2058 D

Marçal, Orlando, y Fernão Côrte-real. *Esfolhadas.* Carta-pref. Abel Botelho. Coimbra. Moura Marques. 1907. Pp. xiii, 114. U-2881 D
- *Asas* (Contos). Coimbra. Amado. 1912. Pp. 250. U-3214 D

March, Auzias. *Les obres d'Auzias March.* Edició crítica Amadeu Pagès. 2 vols. Barcelona. Institut d'Estudis Catalans. 1912-4. U-746-7 I

Marconi, Henri. *Histoire de l'involution naturelle.* Tr. Me Ida Mori-Dupont. Paris. Maloine. 1915. Pp. xii, 505. U-755 D

Marcos, Desiderio. *Páginas de amor.* México. Gil. 1902. Uc D

Marfil García, Mariano. *Relaciones entre España y la Gran Bretaña desde las paces de Utrecht hasta nuestros días.* Madrid. Revista de Derecho Internacional y Política Ext. 1907. Pp. 253. U-1691 n/o

Mari, Giovanni. *In hoc signo, ossia il trionfo del Cristianesimo.* Milano. Manuzio. 1913. Pp. 342. U-1321

Mariana, Juan de. *Historia general de España.* 3 vols. Madrid. Gaspar y Roig. 1852. U-1165-7

Mariategui, José Carlos. *La escena contemporánea.* Lima. Minerva. 1925. Pp. 286. U-5672 n/o D
- *Siete ensayos de interpretación de la realidad peruana.* Lima. Biblioteca Amauta. 1928. Pp. 264. U-4937 C D

Marichalar, Antonio. 'Contemporary Spanish literature,' *The Criterion* (April 1923), 277-92. U-4234 I

Marimar. (Obra anónima). Buenos Aires. Kosmos. 1911. Pp. 389. U-687 I* C

Marín, Andrés. *Civilización (España y América).* Bruselas. Etablissements Généraux d'Imprimerie. 1927. Pp. 250. U-5617 D

Marín del Campo, Rafael. *La política del porvenir.* Madrid. Suárez. 1928. Pp. 186. U-5479 D

Marina y Muñoz, Juan. *Resumen de psicología.* Madrid. Suárez. 1905. Uc D
– *Las direcciones de la psicología contemporánea.* Pról. D.E. Sanz y Escartín. Madrid. F. Fé. 1906. Uc D
– *Etica.* Pról. M. de Unamuno. Madrid. F. Fé. 1908. Uc D

Marinello, Juan. *Sobre la inquietud cubana.* La Habana. Avance. 1930. Pp. 28. U-1457 n/o D

Marinetti, F.T. *La conquête des étoiles. Poème épique.* Paris. Editions de la Plume. 1902. Pp. 190. U-1986 D
– *Le Roi Bombance.* Paris. Mercure de France. 1905. Pp. 268. U-3287 D
– *Enquête internationale sur le vers libre* et *Manifeste du Futurisme.* Milan. Editions de Poesia. 1909. Pp. 153. U-3205
– *Re Baldoria.* Milano. Treves. 1910. Pp. 268. U-2013 D
– *Distruzione. Poema futurista.* Milano. Edizioni Futuriste di Poesia. 1911. Pp. 100. U-2177
– *El futurismo.* Tr. Germán Gómez de la Mata y N. Hernández Luquero. Valencia. Sempere. Uc

Mariño, Cosme. *Disquisiciones. Instantáneas. Pensamientos.* n.p. La Sin Bombo. 1907. Pp. 266. U-145

Marlowe, Christopher. *The Plays of Christopher Marlowe.* London. Dent. n.d. Pp. xv, 488. U-1004 I*
– *Fausto.* Introd. F. Victor Hugo. Tr. J. Aladern. Barcelona. A. López. 1904. Uc

Marmello, Juan. *Juventud y vejez.* La Habana. Avance. 1928. Pp. 23. U-5525 D

Mármol, José. *Amalia. Novela histórica americana.* 2 vols. Paris. Garnier. 1901. U-178-9 I

Marof, Tristán. *El ingenio continente americano.* Barcelona. Maucci. n.d. Pp. 190. U-2783 D

Marone, Gherardo, y Harukichi Shimoi. *Poesie giapponesi* (di Akiko Yosano, Suikei Maeta, Tekkan Yosano, Nobutsuna Sasaki, Isamu Yoshii). Napoli. Ricciardi. 1917. Pp. 78. U-239 D
– *Difesa di Dulcinea.* Napoli. Diana. 1920. Pp. 177. U-3674 D

Marqués Merchán, Juan. *Don Bartolomé José Gallardo. Noticia de su vida y escritos.* Madrid. Perlado, Paez. 1921. Pp. 430. U-3788 I* L D

Márquez (Ex Coronel) y Capo, J.M. *Las juntas militares de defensa*. La Habana.
   Los Rayos x. 1923. Pp. 278. U-3000 I* D
Márquez Sterling, Manuel. *Psicología profana*. Pról. M.S. Pichardo. Habana.
   Avisador Comercial. 1905. Pp. 252. U-650 D
— *Alrededor de nuestra psicología*. Habana. Avisador·Comercial. 1906.
   Pp. 237. U-1461 I
— *Burla burlando*. Habana. Avisador Comercial. 1907. Uc D
— *La diplomacia en nuestra historia*. Habana. Avisador Comercial. 1909.
   Pp. 417. U-2449 n/o D
Marquina Angulo, Eduardo. *Odas*. Barcelona. Serra Hnos. y Russell. 1900.
   Uc D
— *Las vendimias*. Barcelona. Seix. 1901. Pp. 128. U-2849 D
— *Elegías*. Barcelona. Tobella & Costa. 1905. Pp. 173. U-3254 D
— *Vendimión*. Madrid. Hernando. 1909. Uc D
— *Doña María la Brava*. Madrid. Renacimiento. 1910. Uc D
— *Cantiga de serrana*. Madrid. Hispania. 1914. Uc D
— *Juglarías. El último día. Una leyenda*. Barcelona. López. [1920]. Pp. 162.
   (2 copies) U-4503, U-4647
— *Tierras de España*. Madrid. Renacimiento. [1914]. Uc D
Marroquín, Lorenzo. *Pax*. Paris. Ollendorff. n.d. Pp. 498. U-1139
Marryat, Captain Frederick. *Jacob Faithful*. Leipzig. Tauchnitz. 1842.
   Pp. 394. U-4483
Marsillach, Adolfo. *El maleta indulgencias. Catalanistas en adobo*. Barcelona.
   López. 1903. Pp. 125. U-2356 D
Martí, José. *En los Estados Unidos*. 2 vols. Habana. Quesada. 1902-5.
   (2 copies) U-4828-31
— *La edad de oro*. Roma. Casa Editrice Nazionale. 1905. Pp. 258. U-4233
— *Hombres*. Habana. Rambla y Bouza. 1908. Pp. 356. U-4832 I C
— *Nuestra América*. Habana. Quesada. 1909. Pp. 312. U-4833
— *Amistad funesta*. Berlin. Quesada. 1911. Pp. 250. U-2278
— *Ismaelillo. Versos sencillos. Versos libres*. Habana. Rambla y Bouza.
   1913. Pp. 279. U-4834
— *Cuba*. Habana. Rambla y Bouza. 1919. Pp. 572. U-4835 I C
— *Versos*. San José de Costa Rica. Colec. Ariel. 1914. Pp. 160. U-3183
— *Poesías de José Martí*. Estudio preliminar, compilación, y notas Juan
   Marinello. Habana. Cultural. 1928. Pp. xlviii, 350. U-5109 I*
— *Poèmes choisis*. Tr. A. Godoy. Paris. Emile-Paul. 1929. Pp. 47. U-5258 n/o
— *Ideario*. Ordenado Isidro Méndez. Habana. Cultural. 1930. Pp. xxvi, 410.
   U-661
— *Los Estados Unidos*. Madrid. Sociedad Española de Librería. [1915].
   Pp. 350. U-2170

Martí, José Salvador. *La nueva enseñanza de la música*. Valencia. Editorial Mundial Música. 1932. Pp. 52. U-5654 D

Martí Jara, Enrique. *El rey y el pueblo. El constitucionalismo en la postguerra y la propuesta de constitución española*. Madrid. Reus. 1929. Pp. 351. U-5107 D

Martí Orberá, R. *Teatro*. Tomo I. Valencia. López. 1914. Pp. xiii, 275. U-4402 D

– *Vida. Versos*. Toledo. Serrano. n.d. Pp. 132. U-4705 D

Martí y Alpera, Félix. *Joyas literarias para los niños*. Madrid. Hernando. 1907. Pp. 336. U-358

Martín, A. *El campo. Libro de lectura*. Tr. M. Lorenzo Gil. León. Miñón. 1906. Uc

Martín, León. *Italia. Pompeya. Roma. Florencia*. León. Alvarez, Chamorro. 1914. Uc D

Martín, Ramón. *Chinchilla*. Paris. Le Livre Libre. 1929. Pp. 61. U-5539 D

Martín Pérez, Leoncio. *La doncellita de Platino*. Salamanca. Minerva. 1935. Pp. 23. U-5633 D

Martinenche, E. *Propos d'Espagne*. Paris. Hachette. 1905. Uc D

Martínez, Alberto B. *República Argentina. Censo general de educación levantado el 23 de mayo de 1909*. 3 vols. Buenos Aires. Tall. Publ. Oficina Meteorológica. 1910. U-1169-71

Martínez, Alfredo. *Paisajes sentimentales*. Montevideo. Mercurio. 1913. Uc D

Martínez Albín, Homero. *Cántico de mi expresividad*. Montevideo. Palacio del Libro. 1929. Pp. 104. U-5497 D

Martínez Alomía, Salvador. *Nieves*. París. Bouret. 1905. Uc D

Martínez Barrionuevo, M. *Mi infancia*. Barcelona. Henrich. 1906. Pp. 304. U-2261

Martínez Baselga, Pedro. *Las penas del hombre. Patología social española*. Zaragoza. Villagrasa. 1903. Pp. 452. U-1860 D

Martínez Ferrando, Daniel. *Palestina. Sueños y realidades crueles*. Barcelona. Cervantes. 1927. Pp. 222. U-5568 n/o D

– *Guía sentimental de Mallorca*. Pról. G. Alomar. Barcelona. Sintes. [1925]. Pp. xvii, 272. U-5131 D

Martínez Galvez, Julio. *El rosal*. Barcelona. Gili. 1912. Uc D

Martínez Lacuesta, Félix. *Política agraria*. Haro. Viela e Iturre. 1915. Pp. 115. U-2577

Martínez Morás, Andrés. *Siluetas*. Buenos Aires. Arias-Lantero. 1907. Pp. 159. U-2799 D

Martínez Olmedilla, Augusto. *El templo de Talía*. Madrid. Pueyo. 1910. Uc D

Martínez Orozco, José. *El pagano (Vida en la Argentina)*. Buenos Aires. Librería del Colegio. 1935. Pp. 218. U-2018 D

- *Después y otras comedias.* Buenos Aires. Librería del Colegio. 1936.
  Pp. 145. U-4400 n/o D
Martínez Ruiz, José (Azorín). *Soledades.* Madrid. F. Fé. 1898. Pp. 111.
  U-3158 D
- *La evolución de la crítica.* Madrid. F. Fé. 1899. Pp. 72. U-2827 D
- *El alma castellana (1600-1800).* Madrid. Lib. Internacional. 1900. Pp. 213.
  U-481 I
- *La voluntad.* Barcelona. Henrich. 1902. Pp. 301. (2 copies) U-2263,
  U-2288 I
- *Las confesiones de un pequeño filósofo.* Madrid. F. Fé. 1904. Pp. 120.
  U-1963
- *La ruta de Don Quijote.* Madrid. Leonardo Williams. 1905. Uc
- *Los pueblos. Ensayos sobre la vida provinciana.* Madrid. Leonardo
  Williams. 1905. Pp. 207. U-4005
- *La Cierva.* Madrid. Hernando. 1910. Pp. 83. U-537
- *Castilla.* Madrid. Renacimiento. 1912. Pp. 156. U-507 D
- *Un discurso de La Cierva.* Madrid. Renacimiento. 1914. Pp. 176. U-3162
- *Al margen de los clásicos.* Madrid. Residencia de Estudiantes. 1915.
  Pp. 232. (2 copies) U-2062, U-2143 D
- *El licenciado Vidriera visto por Azorín. En el tricentenario de Cervantes,
  1916.* Madrid. Residencia de Estudiantes. 1915. Pp. 161. (2 copies)
  U-2063, U-2066
- *Un pueblecito. Riofrío de Avila.* Madrid. Residencia de Estudiantes. 1916.
  Pp. 168. U-2064
- *Parlamentarismo español (1904-1916).* Madrid. Calleja. 1916. Uc
- *Antonio Azorín. Pequeño libro en que se habla de la vida de este peregrino
  señor.* Madrid. Rodríguez Serra. [1903]. Pp. 231. U-5651 D
- *Il politico.* Tr. di G. Beccari. Firenze. Ferrante Gonnelli. 1910. Pp. 160.
  U-3636 n/o
- *Paa Don Quijotes vei.* Kristiania. Lars Swanström. 1919. Pp. 112. U-1202
- [Martínez Ruiz]. *Fiesta de Aranjuez en honor de Azorín.* Madrid.
  Residencia de Estudiantes. 1915. Pp. 96. U-2065
Martínez Sacristán, Antonio. *El Antecristo y el fin del mundo.* Astorga. López.
  1890. Pp. 402. U-2575 [Bound with Garrote, Alonso]
Martínez Sierra, Gregorio. *Horas de sol.* Madrid. Poveda. 1901. Pp. 95.
  U-4575 D
- *Sol de la tarde.* Madrid. Leonardo Williams. 1904. Pp. 245. U-4001 D
- *Teatro de ensueño.* Melancólica sinfonía de Rubén Darío. Ilustraciones
  líricas Juan R. Jiménez. Madrid. 1905. Pp. 271. U-3680 D
- *La humilde verdad.* Barcelona. Henrich. 1905. Uc
- *La casa de primavera.* Madrid. Pueyo. 1907. Uc D

Martínez y González, Santiago. *La crisis de la agricultura, sus causas y sus remedios.* Salamanca. Imp. Católica Salmanticense. 1893. Uc

Martínez Zuviría, Gustavo A. (Hugo Wast). *Pequeñas grandes almas.* Barcelona. Montaner y Simón. 1907. Uc D
- *La casa de los cuervos.* Buenos Aires. Ateneo Nacional. n.d. Uc D
- *Flor de durazno.* Buenos Aires. Alfa y Omega. n.d. Uc D

Martonne, Emmanuel de. *Traité de géographie physique. Climat hydrographie. Relief du sol. Bio-géographie.* Paris. Colin. 1913. Pp. xi, 922. U-759 I

Martorell, Johanot. *Libre del valeros e strenu caualler Tirant lo Blanch.* Scrites les tres parts per lo magnifich e virtuos caualler Mossen Johanot Martorell e a mort sua acabada la quarta, a pregaries de la senyora dona Isabel de Loric, Mossen Marti Johan de Galba. 4 vols. Barcelona. Alvar Verdaguer. 1873-1905. U-2411-14 I*. Vol. I C

Marvaud, Angel. *L'Espagne au XXe siècle.* Paris. Colin. 1913. Pp. xiv, 515. U-1612 C

Marx, Karl. *Das Kapital. Kritik der politischen Oekonomie.* Herausgegeben von Friedrich Engels. 4 vols. Hamburg. Meissner. 1890-4. U-3822-5. Vol. I I* C

Más, José. *La bruja.* Madrid. F. Fé. 1917. Pp. 351. U-4003 D
- *La locura de un erudito.* 2 vols. Madrid. Renacimiento. 1926. U-4886, U-4917 I* C D
- *La huída.* Madrid. Renacimiento. 1927. Pp. 346. U-4997 D
- *En el país de los Bubis.* Pról. M. de Unamuno. Madrid. Pueyo. 1931. Pp. 236. n/n D

Mas i Jornet, Claudi. *Sátires morals.* Vilafranca. Comas. 1896. Pp. 88. U-2579 D

Mas y Pí, Juan. *Letras españolas.* Buenos Aires. 1911. Pp. 232. U-5143
- *Ideaciones. Letras de América. Ideas de Europa.* Barcelona. Granada. n.d. Pp. 190. U-3801 D

Masaryk, T.G. *La Russia e l'Europa. Studi sulle correnti spirituali in Russia.* Tr. Ettore lo Gatto. Napoli. Ricciardi. 1922. Pp. xv, 400. U-4827 I*
- *T.G. Masaryk, 1850-1925.* Prag. Druck Verlags und Zeitungs. 1925. Pp. 141. U-5279 I
- *The Making of a State. Memories and Observations 1914-1918.* English version, arr. and prep. with introd. H.W. Steed. London. George Allen & Unwin. 1927. Pp. 461. U-804

Maseda, Antonio. *Estudios de crítica literaria.* Bilbao. Editorial Vizcaína. 1915. Pp. 60. U-5505 D

Maseras, Alfons. *Fets y paraules de mestre Blai Martí.* Barcelona. Horta. 1908. Pp. 173. U-2276 D
- *L'Adolescent.* Barcelona. L'Avenç. 1909. Pp. 143. U-2315 D
- *Sota'l cel de París.* Barcelona. L'Avenç. 1910. Pp. 86. U-2945 D

- *Contes fatidics.* Barcelona. L'Avenç. 1911. Pp. 196. U-2280 D
- *Ildaribal.* Barcelona. L'Avenç. 1915. Pp. 296. U-2313
- *A la dériva.* Barcelona. Verdaguer. 1921. Pp. 202. U-3742 D

Masifern, Ramon. *La vida al camp. Poema bucolich popular.* Prol. J. Verdaguer. Barcelona. Giró. 1902. Pp. 94. (2 copies) U-4457, U-4651 D
- *La vida del campo.* Tr. F.J. Garriga y L. Sánchez. n.p. 1906. Pp. 94. U-2377 n/o D
- *Coses de l'Ampurdá.* Barcelona. Castillo. 1918. Pp. xxxii, 176. U-2675 D

Massó-Ventós, Josep. *Arca d'ivori.* Barcelona. L'Avenç. 1912. Pp. 104. U-3388
- *L'Hora tranquila.* Barcelona. L'Avenç. 1914. Pp. 174. U-1133 D

Masson, Malte. *Die autoheilige.* Freiburg. Reichard. n.d. Pp. 72. U-5465 D
Mateus, Jorge. *Por la vida abajo.* n.p. Arboleda. 1912. Pp. 167. U-3948 D
Mathesius, M. Johann. *D. Martin Luthers Leben.* Herausgegeben von Georg Buchwald. Leipzig. Reclam. n.d. Pp. 434. U-4556 I* B*
Matheu, José M. *Carmela rediviva.* Madrid. Juste. 1899. Uc D
Mato, Silvestre. *Cartografía nacional.* Montevideo. El Siglo, la Razón y el Telégrafo. 1917. Pp. 32. U-4365
Matos Fragaso, Juan de. *El ingrato agradecido.* Ed. from the manuscript in the Biblioteca Nacional by Harry Clifton Heaton. New York. Hispanic Society of America. 1926. Pp. lxiii, 180. U-1409
Maturana, José. *Naranjo en flor.* Madrid. Helénica. 1912. Pp. 216. U-2631 D
- *Canción de primavera.* Valencia. Sempere. n.d. Pp. 237. U-263 D

Maupassant, Guy de. *Une vie.* Paris. Ollendorff. 1906. Uc
Maura Gamazo, Gabriel. *Aygo-forts.* Palma. Tous. [1905]. Pp. xviii, 211. U-2828
Maurice, John F.D. *The Kingdom of Christ or Hints on the Principles, Ordinances, Constitution of the Catholic Church. In Letters to a Member of the Society of Friends.* 2 vols. London. Dent. [1906]. U-1017-18 I
Maurois, André. *Edouard VII et son temps.* Paris. Les Editions de France. 1933. Pp. ii, 386. QP-32 I
Maúrtua, Aníbal. *La idea pan-americana y la cuestión del arbitraje.* Lima. La Industria. 1901. Uc D
Maury, Lucien. 'Les étudiants scandinaves à Paris,' *Annales de l'Université* (1934), 223-46. U-2993 D
Mayer Garçao, Francisco de Sande Salema. *A minha paysagem.* Coimbra. Amado. 1904. Uc
- *Excelsior (carteira d'um idealista).* Porto. Chardron. 1907. Uc

Mayo, Francisco de Sales. *El gitanismo. Historia, costumbres y dialecto de los gitanos.* Madrid. Suárez. 1870. Uc
Mayoral Oliver, Fernando. *Un poco de todo.* Madrid. Carrión. 1904. Uc

Mayorga-Rivas, R. *Viejo y nuevo*. San Salvador. Diario del Salvador.
1915. Uc D

Maze-Sencier, G. 'Le socialisme en Espagne,' *Revue Politique et Parlementaire*
(1898), 340-56, 551-76. U-5259

Mazel, Henri. *Le prix du sourire*. Paris. Mercure Universel. 1933. Pp. 146.
U-3154 D

Mazo, Gabriel del. *La reforma universitaria*. 2 vols. Buenos Aires. Ferrari.
1926-7. U-5748-9 D

Mazo, Marcelo del. *Los vencidos*. Buenos Aires. Peuser. 1907. Pp. xvi, 150.
U-2665 n/o D

Mazuranié, Ivan. *La morte di Smail-Aga Cengić*. Versione, pref., e commentario
Vladimiro Bakotić. Split. Hrvatska Knjizara. 1922. Pp. 106. U-5701 I*

Mazzini, Giuseppe. *Scritti scelti di Giuseppe Mazzini*. Firenze. Sansoni. 1901.
Pp. lxiv, 405. U-2304 I* C*

— *Lettere d'amore*. Genova. Libreria Editrice Moderna. 1922. Pp. xv, 297.
U-5340 I*

— *Pagine tratte dall'epistolario* [da] Umberto Zanotti-Bianco. Milano.
Instituto Italiano per el Libro del Popolo. 1926. Pp. 10, 636. U-5339 I*

Medina, José Toribio. *Diccionario biográfico colonial de Chile*. Santiago de
Chile. Elzeviriana. 1906. Pp. viii, 1004. U-30 [Pp. 465-80 missing]

— *La imprenta en México (1539-1821)*. 4 vols. Santiago de Chile. En casa del
autor. 1908-12. U-6-9 n/o

— *El Veneciano Sebastián Caboto al servicio de España*. 2 vols. Santiago de
Chile. Universitaria. 1908. U-3547-8 n/o

— *El descubrimiento del Océano Pacífico. Vasco Núñez de Balboa,
Hernando de Magallanes y sus compañeros. II. Documentos relativos a
Núñez de Balboa*. Santiago de Chile. Universitaria. 1913. Uc

— *Noticias bio-bibliográficas de los Jesuítas expulsos de América en 1767*.
Santiago de Chile. Elzeviriana. 1914. Pp. ix, 327. U-1767 n/o

— *El disfrazado autor del 'Quijote' impreso en Tarragona fue Fray Alonso
Fernández*. Santiago de Chile. Elzeviriana. 1918. Pp. xxii, 140. U-4265

Medina, Sergio. *Poemas de sol y soledad*. Pról. Jesús Semprún. Caracas.
El Cojo. 1912. Pp. xxi, 183. U-3402 D

Medina, Vicente. *La canción de la muerte*. Cartagena. La Tierra. 1904. Uc D

— *La canción de la huerta*. Cartagena. La Tierra. 1905. Pp. 194. U-3772 D

— *El rento. Novela de costumbres murcianas*. Cartagena. La Tierra. 1907.
Pp. 223. (2 copies) U-504 D. U-4718

— *Poesía*. Cartagena. Baut. 1908. Pp. 501. U-140 D

— *Canciones de la guerra*. Rosario. 1914. Pp. 129. U-4168 D

— *Abonico. Nuevos aires murcianos. Las cartas del emigrante*. Montevideo.
Renacimiento. 1917. Pp. 84. U-5075

– *Amaos los unos a los otros.* (Libro de escuela). Rosario. Medina. 1918.
   Pp. 115. U-4973 D
– *Viejo cantar.* Juicio crítico Unamuno. Colección de las obras completas
   de Vicente Medina. Editadas por el propio autor. Rosario de Santa Fé.
   1919. Pp. 101. (2 copies) U-496, U-506
– *¡Padre nuestro! (Breviario).* Colección de las obras completas de Vicente
   Medina. Rosario de Santa Fé. 1920. Pp. 105 (2 copies) U-497, U-4469 D
– *La compañera. El castillo encantado. Poema íntimo.* Colección de las
   obras completas de Vicente Medina. Rosario de Santa Fe. 1921. Pp. 187.
   U-505 D
– *Tribulación. ¿Quién hallará el camino en esta noche?* Rosario de Santa Fé.
   1921. Pp. 410. (3 copies) U-3650, U-3819-20 D
– *Hielos. Versos del ocaso.* Colección de las obras completas de Vicente
   Medina. Rosario de Santa Fé. 1926. Pp. 127, xlviii. U-5522
Medina Bocos, César de. *Espigas y racimos. Poesías.* Pról. L. Maldonado.
   Valladolid. Montero. 1915. Uc
Medina Medinilla, Pedro de. *Egloga en la muerte de doña Isabel de Urbina.*
   Ed. y pról. G. Diego. Santander. La Atalaya. 1924. Pp. 119. (2 copies)
   U-4902, U-5011
Mejías, Laurentino C. *La policia ... por dentro. Mis cuentos.* Barcelona. Tasso.
   1911. Uc D
Melgar, Ramón. *Rivadavia.* Buenos Aires. Cabaut. 1908. Pp. 140. U-1545 n/o D
Melián Lafinur, Luis. *Semblanzas del pasado. Juan Carlos Gómez.* Montevideo.
   El Anticuario. 1915. Pp. 448. U-1196 D
Melis, Pedro Antonio. *Estética del amor. Teoría.* Palma de Mallorca. Crespi y
   Sitjar. 1912. Uc
Melo, Francisco Manuel de. *Auto do fidalgo aprendiz.* Coimbra. Amado. 1898.
   Pp. xvi, 65. U-3244
Melon, Paul. *L'Enseignement supérieur et l'enseignement technique en
   France.* Paris. Colin. 1893. Pp. xliii, 342. U-3762 D
Melot, Auguste. *El martirio del clero belga.* Tr. C. Battle. Paris. Bloud & Gay.
   n.d. Pp. 63. U-2898
Melville, Herman. *Moby Dick or the White Whale.* London. Dent. [1907].
   Pp. viii, 504. U-5208 I* C*
– *Omoo, a Narrative of Adventures in the South Seas.* London. Dent.
   [1908]. Pp. xiv, 328. U-5218 I* T
– *Typee. A Narrative of the Marquesas Islands.* London. Dent. [1907].
   Pp. x, 286. U-5209 T
*Memoria de la Administración del Presidente de la República de Cuba Mayor
   General José Miguel Gómez durante el período comprendido entre el 28
   de enero y el 31 de diciembre de 1909.* Habana. Rambla y Bouza.
   1910. Uc

Memorias de un oficial de la Legión británica. Campañas y cruceros durante la guerra de emancipación hispanoamericana. Tr. Luis de Terán. Madrid. América. [1916]. Pp. 241. U-3020 n/o

Memoria del ejercicio de 1916. Gijón. Junta local para el fomento y mejora de casas baratas. 1917. Pp. 76. U-3058

Memoria del Ministerio de Guerra y Marina. Presentada a la Honorable Asamblea General correspondiente a los años de 1890, 91, 92 y 93. Montevideo. La Nación. 1894. Pp. xvi, 926. U-1179

Memoria presentada por la Comisión Directiva de la Euskal-Echea en la Asamblea ordinaria de junio de 1916. Buenos Aires. La Baskonia. 1916. Pp. 91. U-3643

Menander, the Poet. *Menandrea,* ex papyris et membranis vetustissimis. Ed. Alfredus Koerte. Editio minor. Lipsiae. Teubner. 1910. Pp. vi, 213. U-348 I

Menchaca, Angel. *El fallo.* Buenos Aires. El Comercio. 1903. Pp. 31. U-3144

Mendes dos Remedios, Joaquim. *Os Judeus em Portugal.* Coimbra. Amado. 1895. Pp. 454. U-1245

— *Introducção á historia da litteratura portuguêsa.* Coimbra. Amado. 1898. Pp. 337. U-569

— *Historia da litteratura portuguêsa desde as origens até á actualidade.* Coimbra. Amado. 1908. Pp. xxxi, 696. U-851 D

Méndez, M. Isidro. *José Martí. Estudio biográfico.* Madrid. Agencia Mundial de Librería. [1925]. Pp. 161. U-3729 n/o D

Méndez Bejarano, Mario. *La ciencia del verso.* Buenos Aires. Penitenciaria Nacional. 1906. Uc

Méndez Calzada, Luis. *Desde las aulas.* Pról. E.S. Zeballos. Buenos Aires. Coni. 1911. Uc D

Méndez de Cuenca, Laura. *Simplezas.* Paris. Ollendorff. n.d. Uc

Méndez Pereira, Octavio. *Fuerzas de unificación.* Pref. A. Alvarez. Paris. Le Livre Libre. 1929. Pp. 176. U-5543 D

Méndez Vellido, Matías. *Granadinas. Colección de artículos.* Cartapról. J. España Lledó. Granada. López Guevara. 1896. Pp. xii, 336. U-3404 D

Méndez y Mendoza, J. de D. *Historia de la Universidad central de Venezuela.* Caracas. Tip. Americana. 1911. Pp. 414. U-4217 n/o

Mendieta, Salvador. *La enfermedad de Centro-América.* Barcelona. Maucci. 1910. Pp. 284. U-4334 D. 3 vols. Barcelona. Maucci. [1936]. U-623-5 n/o

— *Cuentos caciquistas centro-americanos.* Managua. Moderna. 1911. Uc D

— *Alrededor del problema unionista de Centro-América.* 2 vols. Barcelona. Maucci. [1934]. U-621-2

Mendilaharsu, Julio Raúl. *Como las nubes. Poesías.* Pról. F. Villaespesa. Madrid. Pueyo. 1909. Pp. 151. U-3866 D

- *Voz de vida. Poesías.* Montevideo. Renacimiento. 1923. Pp. 124.
  U-4275 n/o D
- *Selección de poesías.* Montevideo. Renacimiento. 1926. Pp. 274. U-4983

Mendoza, Diego. *Expedición botánica de José Celestino Mutis al nuevo reino de Granada y memorias inéditas de Francisco José de Caldas.* Madrid. Suárez. 1909. Pp. 150, 296. U-3919 D
- *Apuntes sobre instrucción pública.* Valencia. Sempere. n.d. Uc D

Mendoza, Jaime. *En las tierras del Potosí.* Pról. A. Arguedas. Barcelona. Tasso. [1911]. Pp. 355. U-3124

Mendoza, Juan Antonio. *Centenario de la revolución del 25 de mayo de 1810. Filosofía de la historia.* Buenos Aires. Mena. 1905. Uc D

Menéndez, Miguel Angel. *Otro libro. Poemas.* México. 1932. Pp. 75. U-2233 D

Menéndez Agusty, José. *Marín de Abreda.* Barcelona. Henrich. 1905. Pp. 291. U-129

Menéndez Barriola, Emilio. *La divina locura.* Buenos Aires. Coni. 1926. Pp. 163. U-4959 D

Menéndez Pidal, Ramón. *Poema de Yúçuf. Materiales para su estudio.* Madrid. Tip. Rev. de Arch., Bibl. y Museos. 1902. Pp. 87. U-5761 C
- *Manual elemental de gramática histórica española.* Madrid. Suárez. 1904. Pp. 233. U-908 L*
- *Cantar de mio Cid.* Texto, gramática, y vocabulario R. Menéndez Pidal. 2 vols. Madrid. Bailly-Baillière. 1908. Uc
- *Antología de prosistas castellanos.* Madrid. Centro de Estudios Históricos. 1917. Pp. 384. U-2925 D
- *Manual de gramática histórica española.* Madrid. Suárez. 1918. Pp. 299. U-2576 C* D
- 'Sobre las vocales ibéricas E y O en los nombres toponímicos,' *Revista de Filología Española,* V (1918), 225-55. U-2519 n/o D
- *Un aspecto en la elaboración del 'Quijote.'* Discurso leído en la inauguración del curso 1920-1. Madrid. Ateneo Científico, Literario y Artístico de Madrid. 1920. Pp. 54. U-4125 I D
- *El rey Rodrigo en la literatura.* Madrid. Tip. Rev. de Arch., Bibl. y Museos. 1924. Pp. 247. U-1240 D
- *Homenaje ofrecido a Menéndez Pidal. Miscelánea de estudios lingüísticos, literarios e históricos.* 3 vols. Madrid. Hernando. 1925. U-4921-3. Vol. II I
- *La España del Cid.* Madrid. Plutarco. 1929. Pp. 450. U-4924 I* L D

Menéndez y Pelayo, Marcelino. *Historia de las ideas estéticas en España.* 6 vols. Madrid. Pérez Dubrull. 1883-7. U-1551-6, U-4499 [2 copies, vol. III]
- *Orígenes de la novela.* 3 vols. (NBAE 1, 7, 14). Madrid. Bailly-Baillière. 1905-15. U-36, U-42, U-49 I L

— *Tratado de los romances viejos.* Tomo II. Madrid. Perlado, Páez. 1906.
  Pp. 549. U-4390
— *Juan Boscán. Estudio crítico.* Madrid. Hernando. 1908. Pp. 488. U-2786
— *Historia de los heterodoxos españoles.* 7 vols. Madrid. Suárez. 1911.
  U-2963-9. Vol. IV I*. Vols. V-VII I
— *Monumento a D. José María de Pereda.* Discurso leído en el acto de la
  inauguración. 23 enero 1911. Madrid. Suárez. 1911. Pp. 15. U-3396 D
Menéu y Menéu, Pascual. *Etimologías bíblicas hebreas del antiguo testamento.*
  Universidad de Granada. Discurso leído en la solemne apertura del curso
  académico de 1926 a 1927. Madrid. Voluntad. 1926. Pp. 41. U-5775
Menger, A. *El estado socialista.* Tr. M. Domenge Mir. 2 vols. Barcelona.
  Henrich. 1908. Uc
Mercante, Víctor. *Psicología de la aptitud matemática del niño.* Buenos Aires.
  Cabaut. 1904. Pp. xiii, 391. U-2538 I C*
— *Procedimientos. Enseñanza de la aritmética.* 2 vols. Buenos Aires. Cabaut.
  1904-5. Uc D
— *Cultivo y desarrollo de la aptitud matemática del niño.* Libro II. Buenos
  Aires. Cabaut. 1905. Pp. 726. U-4171
Mercier, Cardenal Desiderio. *Belgiako apezpikuen iardukia.* Etzaiela zillegi
  Alemaniarrci angoak nai eta nai ez urrunerat eramatea. London. Eyre and
  Spottiswoode. 1917. Pp. 14. U-516
Mercure de France [Several issues of 1899, 1900, 1916, 1926]. n/n
El mercurio de América. Buenos Aires (Marzo-junio 1900). n/n
Mercurio peruano [Four issues of 1922, 1923, 1927]. n/n
Meredith, George. *The Ordeal of Richard Feverel. A History of Father and
  Son.* 2 vols. Leipzig. Tauchnitz. 1875. U-4753-4 I T
— *The Tragic Comedians. A Study in a Well-Known Story.* Leipzig.
  Tauchnitz. 1881. Uc
— *The Egoist. A Comedy in Narrative.* 2 vols. Leipzig. Tauchnitz. 1910.
  U-4755-6 I* C T
— *The Poetical Works of George Meredith.* Notes G.M. Trevelyan. London.
  Constable. 1912. Pp. xv, 623. U-4817 I* C T L*
Mérimée, Ernest. *Précis d'histoire de la littérature espagnole.* Paris. Garnier.
  1908. Pp. xix, 525. U-3375 D
Mérimée, Próspero. *Crónica del reinado de Carlos IX.* Tr. Nilo Fabra. Madrid.
  Universal. 1920. Pp. 330. n/n I*
— *Colomba. La Venus d'Ille. Les âmes du purgatoire.* Paris. Calmann-Lévy.
  n.d. Uc
Merlant, Joachim. *Sénancour, poète, penseur, religieux et publiciste.*
  Documents inconnus ou inédits. Paris. 1907. Pp. iv, 346. Uc
Merlos, Salvador R. *América latina ante el peligro.* San José de Costa Rica.
  Matamoros. 1914. Uc

Mesa, Enrique de. *El silencio de la Cartuja.* Madrid. Clásica Española. [1916].
Pp. 110. U-466 D
— *Cancionero castellano.* Ensayo Ramón Pérez de Ayala. Madrid. Clásica
Española. [1917]. Pp. 188. U-467 D
Mesa, Rafael de. *Don Benito Pérez Galdós. Su familia: Sus mocedades. Su
senectud.* Madrid. Pueyo. 1920. Pp. 70. U-5621
Mesquita, Carlos de. *O romantismo inglês.* Coimbra. Universidade. 1911.
Pp. 263. U-778 I B D
Mestres, Apeles. *Liliana. Poema.* Tr. J.M. Arteaga Pereira. Barcelona. Pérez
Bonet. 1907. Pp. 282. U-1203 D
Metge, Bernat. *Lo sommni d'en Bernat Metge.* Text catalá del xive segle
novament publicat ab notes bibliogràfiques y crítiques R. Miquel y
Planas. Barcelona. Giro. 1907. Pp. xxxix, 123. U-3429 I
Le Mexique au début du XXe siècle par M.M. le prince Roland Bonaparte et al.
2 vols. Paris. Delagrave. [1903]. U-31-2
Meyer, Lothar. *Les théories modernes de la chimie et leur application à la
mécanique chimique.* Tr. M. Albert Block et J. Meunier. Paris. Carré.
1887-9. Pp. viii, 452 + xiv, 312. U-82 I C
Meyer-Luebke, Wilhelm. *Romanisches etymologisches Wörterbuch, Sammlung
romanischer Elementarbücher,* etc. Heidelberg. 1911-20. Pp. xxii, 1092.
U-1680 L*. 1914. Pp. 561 + 640. U-4127
— *Introducción al estudio de la lingüística romance.* Tr., revisada por el
autor, de la segunda edición alemana por Américo Castro. Madrid. Tip.
Rev. de Arch., Bibl. y Museos. 1914. Uc
Mez, Adam. *El renacimiento del Islam.* Tr. S. Vila. Madrid. Maestre. 1936.
Pp. 641. U-126 I*
Meza Fuentes, R. *Elogio de la fiesta de la primavera.* Santiago de Chile. Imp.
de la República. 1920. Ff. 7. U-5070 D
Mézan, Saül. *De Gabirol à Abravanel, juifs espagnols promoteurs de la Renais-
sance.* Paris. Lipschutz. [1936]. Pp. 155. U-5236 D
Michaëlis de Vasconcellos, Carolina. *A saudade portuguesa.* Porto.
Renascença Portuguesa. Uc
Michels, Robert. *Sozialismus in Italien. Intellektuelle Strömungen.* München.
Meyer & Jessen. 1925. Pp. xix, 419. U-5448
— *Sozialismus und fascismus in Italien.* München. Meyer & Jessen. 1925.
Pp. vi, 338. U-5372 I*
Micoleta, Rafael. *Modo breve de aprender la lengua vizcayna.* Sevilla. Díaz.
1897. Pp. 36. U-2591 n/o
Mier, Elpidio de. *Pensando en España.* Pról. J. Contreras Ramos y epíl.
V. Casanova. Ponce, P.R. Baldorioty. 1906. Pp. viii, 318. U-3769 n/o
Mier, José Servando de Santa Teresa. *Memorias de Fray Servando Teresa de
Mier.* Pról. Alfonso Reyes. Madrid. América. [1930]. Pp. xxii, 430. U-3024

Mignon, Maurice. *Leçon inaugurale du cours de littératures de l'Europe Méridionale.* Aix-en-Provence. Roubaud. 1923. Pp. 35. U-5271

Miguens Parrado, A. *12 de octubre. Evocaciones. 1910. Canto secular.* Córdoba. Imp. Argentina. 1913. Pp. 75. U-879

Milá de la Roca Díaz, J.M. *Aljaba.* Cumaná, Venezuela. Mila de la Roca. 1907. Pp. 102. U-3625

– *Aristas y facetas.* Cumaná, Venezuela. Mila de la Roca. 1907. Pp. 304. U-3413 D

Mill, John Stuart. *Considerations on Representative Government.* London. Parker. 1861. Pp. viii, 347. U-97 T

– *System of Logic, Ratiocinative and Inductive.* 2 vols. London. Longmans, Green, Reader and Dyer. 1872. U-1799-1800 Vol. I I*

– *L'Utilitarisme.* Tr. P.-L. Le Monnier. Paris. Baillière. 1883. Pp. 134. U-3990

Millares Cubas, Luis, y Agustín Millares Cubas. *De la tierra canaria. Escenas y paisajes.* Madrid. Hernández. 1894. Pp. 265. U-421 n/o

– *Pepe Santana. Santiago Bordón.* Santa Cruz de Tenerife. Benítez. 1898. Pp. 173. U-3087 [Incomplete text]

– *La herencia de Araus.* Las Palmas. Martínez y Franchy. 1903. Pp. 160. U-3883

– *Teatrillo.* Las Palmas. Martínez y Franchy. 1903. Pp. 207. U-3085

– *María del Brial.* Las Palmas. Martínez y Franchy. 1905. Pp. 220. U-3086

– *San Joseph de la Colonia.* Las Palmas. Martínez y Franchy. 1907. Pp. 236. U-3622 I* L

Millares Torres, Agustín. *Historia general de las Islas Canarias.* 10 vols. Las Palmas. Miranda. 1893-5. U-1267-76

Miller, John. *Memorias del General Miller.* Tr. General Torrijos. 2 vols. Madrid. América. [1917]. U-3018-19 n/o

Milosz, O.-W.-L. *Miguel Mañara. Mystère en six tableaux.* Avant-propos d'Armand Godoy. Paris. Grasset. [1935]. Pp. 137. U-3448

Milton, John. *English Poems by John Milton.* Ed. with life, introd., notes R.C. Browne. 2 vols. Oxford. 1875-8. U-640-1 I* C B T

Minelli, Paul. *Todos los caminos.* Montevideo. Renacimiento. 1928. Pp. 99. U-4993 D

Ministerio de Fomento. *Anuario estadístico de Venezuela.* Caracas. Dirección General de Estadística. 1914. Pp. xxvii, 503. U-736

Ministerio de Instrucción Pública y Bellas Artes. Dirección General del Instituto Geográfico y Estadístico. *Movimiento anual de la población de España. Año de 1900.* 2 vols. Madrid. 1901. Uc. *Año de 1901.* 2 vols. Madrid. 1903. Uc

– *Censo de la población de España según el empadronamiento hecho en la península e islas adyacentes el 31 de diciembre de 1900.* 3 vols. Madrid. 1902. Uc

— *Censo escolar de España llevado a efecto el día 7 de marzo de 1903.*
  Madrid. 1904. Uc
— *Movimiento natural de la población de España. Año 1902.* Madrid.
  1906. Uc
Miomandre, Francis de. *Le cabinet chinois.* Paris. Gallimard. [1936]. Pp. 271.
  U-1388 I D
Mir, Jaime. *Mémoires d'un condamné à mort.* Préf. Valère Gille. Paris. Plon.
  [1926]. Pp. 256. U-5240 D
Mirabaud, Jean Baptiste de. *Système de la nature, ou des lois du monde
  physique et du monde moral.* 6 vols. Leipzig. Guyot-Pelafol. 1780.
  U-4026-31
Mirabent, Francisco. *La estética inglesa del siglo XVIII.* Barcelona.
  Cervantes. 1927. Pp. 272. U-5631 D
— *El camino azul.* Madrid. Beltrán. 1913. Uc D
— *Alondra.* Valencia. Sempere. n.d. Uc
Miranda, Arecio. *Hojas al viento.* Maracaibo. Imp. Americana. 1913. Uc D
Miranda, César. *Las leyendas del alma. Poesías.* Montevideo. Bertani. 1907.
  Pp. 158. U-3198 n/o D
Miranda, Francisco de. *The Diary of Francisco de Miranda. Tour of the
  United States 1783-1784.* Ed., introd., and notes W.S. Robertson.
  New York. The Hispanic Society of America. 1928. Pp. xxxvi, 206.
  U-1675
Miró Ferrer, Gabriel. *Hilván de escenas.* Alicante. Esplá. 1903. Pp. 249.
  U-2755 I D
— *Del vivir. Apuntes de parajes leprosos.* Alicante. Esplá. 1904. Pp. 212.
  U-471 I D
— *La novela de mi amigo.* Alicante. Esplá. 1908. Pp. 180. U-486 D
— *El abuelo del rey.* Barcelona. Ibérica. 1915. Pp. 256. U-2158 D
— *Figuras de la pasión del Señor.* Barcelona. Domenech. [1917]. Pp. 314.
  U-4467 D
— *El humo dormido.* Madrid. Atenea. 1919. Pp. 196. U-4622 D
— *El angel, El molino, El caracol del faro.* Estampas rurales y de cuentos.
  Madrid. Atenea. 1921. Pp. 245. n/n D
— *El obispo leproso.* Madrid. Biblioteca Nueva. 1926. Pp. 382. U-2115 I* C D
— *Dentro del cercado. La palma rota.* Barcelona. Domenech. n.d. Uc
— *Libro de Sigüenza.* Barcelona. Domenech. n.d. Pp. 223. n/n
— *Obras completas de Gabriel Miró.* Edicíon conmemorativa emprendida
  por los 'Amigos de Gabriel Miró.' Vols. I-VII, XI, XII. Barcelona. Altés.
  1932. U-1219-25. Vols. I, III, VII I
Miró Quesada, César Alfredo. *Cantos del arado y de las hélices.* Buenos Aires.
  El Inca. 1929. Ff. 46. U-5615 D

Místicos españoles. Sel., pról., y notas biográficas Luis Santullano. Madrid.
    Biblioteca Literaria del Estudiante. 1934. Pp. 214. U-5662

Mistral, Fréderic. *Mireille.* Poème provençal. Paris. Charpentier. 1888.
    Pp. 511. I* C

Mitjana, Rafael. *Estudios sobre algunos músicos españoles del siglo XVI.*
    Madrid. Hernando. 1918. Pp. vii, 247. U-3055 D

Mitre, Bartolomé. *Arengas.* 3 vols. Buenos Aires. La Nación. 1902. U-1533-5
— *Historia de Belgrano y de la independencia argentina.* Vols. II, III, IV.
    Buenos Aires. Biblioteca de La Nación. 1902. U-4612-14. Vol. II I. 4 vols.
    Buenos Aires. Biblioteca Argentina. 1927-8. U-4869-72
— *Historia de San Martín y de la emancipación sudamericana.* 2 vols.
    Buenos Aires. Biblioteca de La Nación. 1903. U-1568-9 I C
— *Memorias de un botón de rosa. Soledad.* Pról. P.P. Figueroa. Buenos Aires.
    Biblioteca de América. 1907. Pp. 157. U-3180

Modern Martyrs. Documents collected by the War Resisters' International.
    Enfield. n.d. Pp. 37. U-5205

Möser, Justus. *Patriotische phantasien.* Leipzig. Reclam. n.d. Pp. 192.
    U-4516 I T

Mogrobejo, Nemesio. *Su vida y sus obras. 1875-1910.* Oración pronunciada
    Miguel de Unamuno. Bilbao. Soc. Bilbaína de Artes Gráficas. 1910.
    Pp. 80, pl. 30. U-1172

Moguel, Juan Antonio de. *El Doctor Peru abarca.* Durango. Eizalde. 1881.
    Pp. 240. U-566

Moguel Faunac, Juan José. *Mayatz-illeraco. Berba-Aldijac.* Tolosan. López.
    1885. Pp. 256. U-2282

Mohr, Luis Alberto. *El hombre. Su interés. Su moral. Su deber. Testamento*
    de un viejo. Buenos Aires. Comp. Sud-Americana de Billetes de Banco.
    1904. Pp. 205. U-556

Le mois. Synthèse de l'activité mondiale. Paris (1 Mai – 1 juin 1935). Pp. 319.
    U-5291

Moledo, Urbano R. *Dolmen. Poemas.* Vigo. La Nueva Prensa. n.d. Pp. 74.
    U-5111 D

Molière, Jean-Baptiste de. *Théâtre. Les précieuses ridicules. Le bourgeois*
    gentilhomme. Les fourberies de Scapin. Paris. Lemerre. 1926. Pp. 1921.
    QP-38 I
— *Tartufo.* Tr. Carlos M. Princivalle. Pról. C. Sabat Ercasty. Montevideo.
    La Facultad. 1932. Pp. 178. U-5546 n/o

Molina, Tirso de. See Téllez, Fray Gabriel

Molina Massey, C. *La musa galante.* Buenos Aires. Peuser. 1919. Pp. 88.
    U-4566 D

Molina y Vedia, Julio. *Señales.* Buenos Aires. Imp. Argentina. 1928. Pp. 78.
    U-5494 D

– *Señales. Libro segundo.* Buenos Aires. 1929. Pp. 71. U-4907 D

Molinari, Víctor Luis. *Pecado de juventud. Poesías.* Buenos Aires. Gleizer. 1928. Pp. 151. U-5509 D

Molinos, Miguel di. *Guida spirituale.* Introd. Giovanni Amendola. Napoli. Perrella. 1908. Pp. xliv, 352. U-1529 I* C D

Molins, W. Jaime. *Bolivia. Crónicas americanas.* Buenos Aires. Mendesky. 1917. Pp. 208. U-184 D

– *Naturaleza. Cuentos y relatos.* Buenos Aires. Oceana. 1922. Pp. 210. U-2384 D

Monasterio. Esther. *Pedazos de alma.* Buenos Aires. Tor. 1926. Pp. 174. U-5627 D

Mondaca C., Carlos R. *Por los caminos.* Barcelona. Imp. Barcelona. 1910. Pp. 121. U-1881 D

Le Monde Nouveau. Paris (Septembre, novembre 1919). n/n

Moneva y Puyol, Juan. *Política de represión.* Madrid. Publicaciones de la Real Academia de Jurisprudencia y Legislación. 1921. Pp. 56. U-3395

– *La educación cristiana de los hijos.* Madrid. Biblioteca Pax. 1936. Pp. 120. U-5501

Monforte, Antonio de, pseud. [i.e., António Sardinha]. *Tronco reverdecido. 1906-1908.* Lisboa. Teixeira. 1910. Pp. 190. U-2710 D

Monner y Sans, Ricardo. *Notas al castellano en la Argentina.* Pról. Estanislao S. Zeballos. Buenos Aires. Parral. 1903. Pp. xxxv, 238. U-3781 I D

– *Ensayos dramáticos.* Buenos Aires. La Sin Bombo. 1910. Pp. 310. Uc

– *Don Guillén de Castro. Ensayo de crítica bio-bibliográfica.* Buenos Aires. Revista de la Universidad de Buenos Aires. 1913. Pp. 116. U-734 n/o D

– *Desde 'La Falda.'* Poesías. Buenos Aires. Martín García. n.d. Uc D

Monroy Ocampo, Benjamín. *Sinónimos castellanos y voces de sentido análogo.* Madrid. Perlado, Páez. 1911. Pp. lxv, 412. U-2896

Monsegur, Sylla J. *Cavilaciones.* Buenos Aires. Peuser. 1928. Pp. 223. U-5502

Montagne, Edmundo. *El fin del mundo.* Buenos Aires. Matalou. 1915. Uc D

Montagne, Víctor. *Cuentos cuyanos.* Buenos Aires. Agencia General de Librería y Publicaciones. [1926]. Pp. 167. U-5093 D

Montaigne, Michel de. *Essais.* Paris. Hachette. 1892. Pp. xii, 334. U-3328

– *Essais de Montaigne.* Nouvelle édition M.J.V. Leclerc. 2 vols. Paris. Garnier. n.d. U-3332-3. Vol. I I* B L. Vol. II I* C*

Montalvo, Juan. *Capítulos que se le olvidaron a Cervantes.* Paris. Garnier. 1921. Pp. clv, 393. U-4918 I C

– *El cosmopolita.* 2 vols. Paris. Garnier. 1923. U-4919-20 I*

Montaner, Joaquín. *Juan Farfán. Poema.* Barcelona. López. 1912-13. Pp. 96. U-2130 D

– *Poemas inmediatos.* Barcelona. 1913-16. Uc D

– *Meditaciones líricas.* Barcelona. Vilanova. 1913-18. Pp. 104. U-4563 D
– *Primer libro de odas.* Barcelona. Altes. 1915. Pp. 148. U-2148 D
Montégut, Maurice. *Los archivos de Guibray.* Tr. M. García Rueda. Paris.
    Ollendorff. Uc
Montenegro, Carlos. *El renuevo y otros cuentos.* Habana. Revista Avance.
    1929. Pp. 227. U-5123 I* D
Montenegro, Ernesto. *Puritania. Fantasías y crónicas norteamericanas.*
    Santiago de Chile. Nascimiento. [1934]. Pp. 288. U-3282 D
Montero, Belisario J. *De mi diario.* Bruselas. Weissenbruch. 1898. Pp. 223.
    U-572 D
– *Estudios sociales.* Barcelona. La Académica. 1910. Pp. 575. U-663 D
Montero, Eloy. *Marruecos. El pueblo moro y el judio.* Salamanca. Tip.
    Popular. 1913. Uc D
Montero Bustamante, Raúl. *El parnaso oriental.* Montevideo. Maucci. 1905.
    Pp. 383. U-3700 D
– *Ensayos. Período romántico.* Montevideo. Arduino. 1928. Pp. 308.
    U-4979 I* D
Montes Viñals, Francisco. *Orillando la vida.* Buenos Aires. Molinari. 1915.
    Pp. 453. Uc D
Montesano, Arturo. *Inquietud.* Pról. S. Fernández. Buenos Aires. Malena.
    1909. Pp. viii, 190. U-2648 I D
– *Los nuevos horizontes de la medicina.* Buenos Aires. Herpig. 1910. Pp. 432.
    U-2460 n/o
Montesquieu, Ch.-L. de. *Oeuvres complètes de Montesquieu.* 2 vols. Paris.
    Hachette. 1865. U-3845-6
– *Lettres persanes.* Tome i. Paris. Didot. 1803. Pp. 234. U-4596
Montherlant, Henri de. *La relève du matin.* Paris. Bloud & Gay. 1922.
    Pp. viii, 269. U-5315 I D
Montoliu, Cebriá. *Institucions de cultura social.* Barcelona. L'Avenç. 1903.
    Pp. viii, 196. U-2153 D
– *Walt Whitman. L'homme i sa tasca.* Barcelona. Societat Catalana
    d'Edicions. [1913]. Pp. 214. U-3508 D
Montoliu, Manuel de. *Pròleg de Manuel de Montoliu al 'Elogi de la paraula i
    altres escrits' de Joan Maragall.* Barcelona. Sala Parés. 1935. Pp. xxviii.
    U-4629 n/o D
Montón Palacios, Clemente. *Una vida al abismo.* Pról. F. Villaespesa. Madrid.
    Bibliófilos Españoles. 1908. Pp. 156. U-3263 D
Montoya, José. *Prosas de amor y dolor.* Medellín. Imp. Editorial. 1912. Uc
Montoya y Flórez, J.B. *Contribución al estudio de la lepra en Colombia.*
    Medellín. Imp. Editorial. 1910. Pp. 453. U-784 D
Moody, William Vaughn. *The Poems and Plays of W.V. Moody.* Introd. J.M.
    Manly. Boston. Houghton Mifflin. [1900]. Pp. xlvi, 448. U-5217 I* C* L* T

— *Poems.* Boston. Houghton Mifflin. 1901. Pp. 106. U-2035 I T

Moore, John F. *Will America Become Catholic?* New York. Harper. 1931.
Pp. x, 252. U-1314 I

Mora, A.H. de. *La iglesia de Jesu-Cristo en España.* Nueva York. Sociedad
Americana de Tratados. n.d. Pp. 190. U-277 I

Morador, Federico. *Poesía.* Montevideo. Los Nuevos. 1920. Pp. 70. U-2362 D

Moraes, Wenceslau de. *O-Yoné e Ko-Haru.* Porto. Renascença Portuguesa.
1923. Pp. 279. U-1958 I*

Morales, Alfredo. *Bosquejo político-social.* Santo Domingo. La Cuna de
América. 1907. Pp. 213. U-2086 D

Morales, Ernesto. *El sayal de mi espíritu.* Impresión J.E. Rodó. Buenos Aires.
Mich. 1914. Pp. 105. U-3039 D

Morales, Tomás. *Poemas de la gloria, del amor y del mar.* Madrid. Gutenberg-
Castro. 1908. Pp. 141. U-2859 D

Morales Lara, Julio. *Savia.* Caracas. Elite. 1930. Pp. 107. U-2794 D

— *Mucura. Poemas.* Caracas. Edit. Cooperativa de Artes Gráficas. 1935.
Pp. 88. U-3385 D

Morales San Martín, Bernardo. *Eva inmortal.* Madrid. Sanz Calleja. Uc D

Morand, Paul. *New York.* Paris. Flammarion. 1930. Pp. 281. QP-33 I

Morato, Juan José. *Historia de la Asociación General del Arte de Imprimir.*
Pról. A. García Quejido y epíl. M. Gómez Latorre. Madrid. 1925. Pp. 622.
U-5137 I* C D

Morato, Octavio. *Problemas sociales.* Montevideo. El Arte. 1911. Pp. 206.
U-2855 D

Moreira, Jayme. *D. Pedro I 'O Crú.' Esboço de estudo nosographico.* Lisboa.
Annuario Comercial. 1914. Pp. 53. U-4095

Moreira de Sá, B.V. *Palestras musicais e pedagogicas.* Porto. Moreira de Sá.
[1916]. Pp. 149. U-4393

Morella, el Marqués de. *El primer acto de la tragedia de los siglos.* Bilbao.
Alvarez. 1916. Uc D

Moreno, Fulgencio R. *Estudio sobre la independencia del Paraguay.* Asunción.
Kraus. 1911. Pp. 256. U-4248

Moreno, Mariano. *Doctrina democrática.* Noticia preliminar R. Rojas. Buenos
Aires. La Facultad. 1915. Pp. 301. U-3659 I

Moreno, Pablo A. *Catecismo.* Madrid. Yagües. n.d. Pp. 172 n/n C

Moreno, Rodolfo. *La ley penal argentina. Estudio crítico.* Buenos Aires.
Abeledo. 1908. Uc D

Moreno, Segundo. *La sangre de Thor.* Buenos Aires. Otero. 1915. Pp. 14.
U-3176 D

Moreno Cantón, Delio. *El sargento primero.* Mérida, México. Revista de
Mérida. 1905. Uc D

Moreno Villa, José. *Garba.* Madrid. Zabala. 1913. Pp. 125. U-887 D

- *El pasajero.* Ensayo J. Ortega y Gasset. Madrid. Clásica Española. 1914. Pp. xlvi, 76. n/n D
- *Evoluciones.* Madrid. Calleja. 1918. Pp. 253. U-2144 D
- *Luchas de 'Pena' y 'Alegría' y su transfiguracion. Alegoría.* Madrid. Clásica Española. [1915]. Pp. 41. U-3716 D

Morera y Galicia, Magí. *De mi viña.* Barcelona. Gili. 1901. Pp. 176. U-3969 D

Morley, John. *Oliver Cromwell.* London. Macmillan. 1913. Pp. viii, 533. U-371 I* C* B
- *On Compromise.* London. Macmillan. 1917. Pp. 284. U-1434 I* C*

Morote, Luis. *La moral de la derrota.* Madrid. Juste. 1900. Pp. xi, 784. U-1851

Mosca, Gaetano. *Elementi di scienza politica.* Torino. Bocca. 1923. Pp. ix, 514. U-4839 C

Moschus. *Theocriti, Bionis et Moschi Idyllia.* Recensuit notasque criticas adjecit C.H. Weise. Lipsiae. Tauchnitz. 1843. Pp. xiii, 182. U-4502 T*

Moses, Bernard. *The Intellectual Background of the Revolution in South America. 1810-1824.* New York. Hispanic Society of America. 1926. Pp. x, 234. U-1407
- *Spain Overseas.* New York. Hispanic Society of America. 1929. Pp. 114. U-2180

Mosqueira, Silvano. *Semblanzas paraguayas.* Asunción. Kraus. 1908. Pp. v, 209. U-4106 D

Motley, John Lothrop. *The Rise of the Dutch Republic. A History.* 3 vols. London. Dent. 1906. U-1083-5 I

Mouriz y Riesgo, José. *Unificaciones en la determinación de la actividad terapéutica de los medicamentos.* Discurso de Recepción. Contestación del Dr Gregorio Marañón. Madrid. Real Academia Nacional de Medicina. 1929. Pp. 126. U-5781

Mourlane Michelena, Pedro. *El discurso de las armas y las letras.* Bilbao. Bibl. de Amigos del País. 1915. Pp. 214. U-418 I* B D

Mousset, Albert. *Le royaume serbe-croate-slovène.* Paris. Bossard. 1926. Pp. 270. U-5255

Mozas, Antonio Alfonso L. de las. *Parodias y glosas.* Pról. C.R. Pinilla. Madrid. F. Fé. 1915. Pp. 100. U-3687 D

Mueller, David. *Geschichte des deutschen Volkes.* Besorgt von Prof. Dr F. Junge. Berlin. Vahlen. 1890. Pp. xxxvi, 512. U-4153 I* C T L

Mueller-Lyer, Franz. *La familia.* Tr. Ramón de la Serna. Madrid. Revista de Occidente. 1930. Pp. 398. n/n I B

Muensterberg, Hugo. *Psicología de la actividad industrial.* Tr. Santos Rubiano. Madrid. Jorro. 1914. Pp. 284. U-2445

Muenzer, Hieronymus. *Itinerarium Hispanicum Hieronymi Monetarii (1494-1495).* Herausgegeben von Ludwig Pfandl. Extrait de la *Revue Hispanique,* XLVIII (1920). U-1689

Mugica y Ortiz de Zárate, Pedro de. *Eco de Madrid. Conversación española moderna.* Stuttgart. Violet. 1906. Uc D

Muhammad ibn Muhammad, al-Ghazzali. *El justo medio en la creencia.* Compendio de teología dogmática de Algazel. Tr. M. Asín Palacios. Madrid. Instituto de Valencia de Don Juan. 1929. Pp. xv, 555. U-809

Mujica, Gregorio de. *Monografía histórica de la Villa de Eibar.* Irún. Valverde. 1910. Pp. 510. U-1665

Mujica, Juan. *El carro de luz.* Bilbao. Grijelmo. 1935. Pp. 203. U-2857 D

Mujika'ko, Gregorio. *Ernani'ar Ospetsuak Iturriaga Lardaberaz Urbieta.* Donostia'n. J. Baroja ta Semearen Etŝean. 1910. Pp. 132. U-2525

Mulder, Elisabeth. *La historia de Java.* Barcelona. Juventud. 1935. Pp. 59. U-1970 D

Mulet de Chambó, Román. *Nomenclator universal de puertos y consulados.* Barcelona. El Anuario de la Exportación. 1906. Uc D

Mulford, Prentice. *Nuestras fuerzas mentales.* Tr. R. Pomés. 2 vols. Barcelona. Carbonell y Esteva. n.d. U-4229-30

Mumford, Lewis. *The Story of Utopias.* Introd. H.W. van Loon. New York. Boni and Liveright. 1923. Pp. 315. U-114 I* C*

Muniagurria, Camilo. *Los herederos.* Rosario de Santa Fé. Imp. Escolar. 1911. Uc D

Muñiz, Narciso. *Estudios de positivismo metafísico.* Bilbao. Casa de Misericordia. 1911. Pp. 517. U-1244

Munizaga Ossandón, Julio. *Las rutas ilusorias.* Santiago. Universitaria. 1914. Pp. 192. U-589 n/o D

Munoa, Manuel. *Esculturas de niebla. Poesías.* San Sebastián. Baroja. 1911. Pp. 213. U-882 D

Muñoz, Isaac. *Libro de las victorias. Diálogos sobre las cosas y sobre el más allá de las cosas.* Madrid. Pueyo. 1908. Uc D

— *La fiesta de la sangre.* Madrid. Pueyo. 1909. Uc D

Muñoz, María Elena. *Lejos. Poemas.* Montevideo. La Cruz del Sur. 1926. Pp. 83. U-5560 D

Muñoz de Diego, Alfonso. *Carnaval.* Madrid. n.d. Uc D

Muñoz García, Emilio. *Por la región azul. Versos.* Pról. M.R. Blanco-Belmonte. Béjar. Muñoz. 1914. Uc D

Muñoz-Orea, Manuel. *Datos para la geografía médica de Salamanca.* Granadilla. Imp. E. Gabañach. 1911. Pp. viii, 92. U-792 D

Muñoz Pérez, Antonio. *A través de París. Crónicas.* Buenos Aires. Hispano-Americana. n.d. Uc

Muntaner, Ramón. *Crónica d'en Ramon Muntaner.* Pref. Joseph Coroleu. Barcelona. Renaixensa. 1886. Pp. xvii, 638. U-2204 I

Munthe, Axel Martin Fredrik. *Le livre de San Michele.* Tr. Paul Rodocanachi. Paris. Albin Michel. [1934]. Pp. 443. U-1837 I

Murga, Gonzalo de. *Poquita cosa ... Amando. Otra cuerda.* México. 1908. Uc D
— *Un epicúreo. Unamuno, poeta.* México. Aguilar Vera. 1918. Pp. 79.
  U-5695
Murray, George Gilbert Aimé. *Historia de la literatura clásica griega.* Tr. E.
  Soms y Castelín. Madrid. La España Moderna. 1899. Pp. 487. U-907 I
Murri, Romolo. *La mia posizione nella Chiesa e nella Democrazia.* Roma.
  Società Nazionale di Cultura. 1909. Pp. 39. U-3682
— *La política clerical y la democracia.* Tr. J. Sánchez-Rojas. Madrid.
  Beltrán. 1911. Pp. 350. U-2381 D
— *La religione nell'insegnamento pubblico in Italia.* Roma. Bilychnis. 1915.
  Pp. 22. U-2510
— *La croce e la spada.* Firenze. I Libri d'Oggi. 1915. Pp. 215. U-2466 D
— *Il partito radicale e il radicalismo italiano.* Roma. Comitato di Azione
  Laica. 1913. Pp. 100. U-1539
Musaeus, the Grammarian. *Hero i Leandre.* Poema atribuit a Museu (Segle v).
  Amb la versió literal en prosa de Lluis Segala i en vers d'Ambrosi Carrión.
  Barcelona. Institut de la Llengua Catalana. n.d. Pp. 72. U-2676
Museo Histórico Nacional. *El clero argentino de 1810 a 1830.* 2 vols. Buenos
  Aires. Rosas. 1907. Uc
Museo Pedagógico Nacional. *El colegio y la universidad en los Estados Unidos.*
  Madrid. Cosano. 1919. Pp. 135. U-1774
— *Las universidades y la enseñanza superior en Francia.* Madrid. Cosano.
  1919. Pp. 123. U-1775
— *Las universidades de Alemania.* Madrid. Cosano. 1919. Pp. 156. U-1772
— *Las universidades, la enseñanza superior y las profesiones en Inglaterra.*
  Madrid. Cosano. 1919. Pp. 139. U-1773 I
Musset, Alfred de. *La confession d'un enfant du siècle.* Vienne. Manz. n.d.
  Pp. 356. U-550 I
Muyden, Arnold van. 'Souvenir conservé de visites à Poblet, Santes Creus,
  Bonmont,' *Journal des Etrangers,* XCIII (1930). U-2574 D
Myers, Frederic W.H. *Human Personality and Its Survival of Bodily Death.*
  2 vols. New York. Longmans. 1903. U-93-4 I B D
Nabuco, Joaquín. *Balmaceda.* Santiago. Universitaria. 1914. Pp. 221.
  U-4895 I
Nakens, José. *Muestras de mi estilo.* Madrid. Blanco. 1906. Pp. 319.
  U-3364 D
— *Cuadros de miseria.* Madrid. Blanco. 1907. Uc D
— *Degradaciones y cobardías.* Madrid. Blanco. 1908. Uc D
Nan de Allariz, Alfredo. *Fume de palla.* La Coruña. Ferrer. 1909. Pp. xvii,
  199. U-2179 D
Napolitano, Leonardo F. *Raza vencida.* Buenos Aires. La Lectura. 1917.
  Pp. 177. U-3699 D

Nascimbeni, Giovanni. *Ricardo Wagner.* Genova. Formiggini. 1914. Pp. 88.
U-1538 D

Navarro, Emidio. *Quatro dias na Serra da Estrela. Notas de um passeio.*
Porto. Libr. Civilisação. 1884. Pp. vii, 194. U-1768

Navarro de Errazquin, Enrique. *Nociones de geometría plana y del espacio.*
Salamanca. La Minerva. 1900. Pp. 102. U-3905 D

Navarro i Ledesma, Francisco, et al. *Angel Ganivet.* Valencia. Serred. 1905.-
Pp. 69. (5 copies) U-470-1 I. U-4644, U-472 n/o. U-1090

Navarro Luna, Manuel. *Surco.* Manzanillo, Cuba. El Arte. 1928. Pp. 108.
U-4905 D

Navas, Federico. *Glosario de un pobre andante. El solitario de la Virreyna.*
Madrid. Peña Cruz. 1916. Pp. 160 + 152. U-376 D

Nāzuinta. Craiova, Rumania (1924). Pp. 92. U-4257 [Issue in honour of
Unamuno]

Nearing, Scott, y Joseph Freeman. *La diplomacia del dólar. Un estudio
acerca del imperialismo americano.* México. Franco-Americana. 1926.
Pp. 391. U-4961 I* C*

Negri, Gaetano. *L'Imperatore Giuliano L'Apostata.* Edizione a cura di M.
Scherillo. Milano. Hoepli. 1914. Pp. xxiii, 533. U-3892 I* L B

Neira Cancela, Juan. *Montaña de Orense.* Pról. Emilia Pardo Bazán. Madrid.
Moreno. 1905. Pp. 144. U-3271 D

Nelson, Ernesto. *Hacia la universidad futura.* Valencia. Sempere. 1913.
Pp. 190. U-3444 D

Nemésio, Vitorino. *Paço do Milhafre. Contos.* Pref. A. Lopez Vieira.
Coimbra. Imp. Universidade. 1924. Pp. xvi, 318. U-5726 I D

— *Varanda de Pilatos.* Paris. Aillaud-Bertrand. [1927]. Pp. 253.
U-4893 I* L* D

— *A mocidade de Herculano.* 2 vols. Lisboa. Bertrand. 1934.
U-1845-6 I* C D

Nepos, Cornelius. *Cornelius Nepos de vita excellentium imperatorum.*
Paris. Barbou. 1784. Pp. 350. U-4702

— *Vidas de los capitanes griegos más famosos.* Notas castellanas Alfonso
Gómez Zapata. Madrid. Aguado. 1825. Pp. 562. U-4681

— *Liber de Excellentibus Ducibus exterarum gentium.* Vol. I. Praefatio et
Miltiadis Themistoclisque vitae. Barcinone. Institut de la Llengua
Catalana. n.d. Pp. 107. U-892

Nerval, Gérard [Labrunie] de. *Oeuvres choisies.* Paris. Larousse. n.d. Pp. 229.
QP-34 I

Nervo, Amado. *La hermana agua.* Madrid. Hernández. 1901. Pp. 11.
U-2617 D

— *El éxodo y las flores del camino. 1900-1902.* México. Oficina Imp. de
Estampillas. 1902. Pp. 167. U-659 I* C* D

- *Almas que pasan. Ultimas prosas.* Madrid. Tip. Rev. de Arch., Bibl. y Museos. 1906. Pp. 144. U-3191 D
- *En voz baja.* Paris. Ollendorff. 1909. Pp. 183. U-3457
- *Ellos.* Paris. Ollendorff. 1909. Uc D
- *Elevación.* Madrid. Tip. Artística. 1917. Pp. 159. U-3407 D
- *Obras completas de Amado Nervo.* 16 vols. Madrid. Biblioteca Nueva. 1920. U-3442-3, U-3483-96. Vols. i-v, xi, xii, xv, xvi I*. Vols. vi, viii, xiv I [Vol. ix is missing; 3 copies of vol. viii]
- *Serenidad. 1909-1912.* Madrid. Renacimiento. 1915. Pp. 253. U-2649 D
- *Otras vidas.* México. Ballesca. n.d. Pp. 222. U-2085 D

Nestroy, Johann. *Der böse Geist Lumpacivagabundus.* Leipzig. Reclam. n.d. Pp. 75. U-4536 I T
- *Hinüber-Herüber.* Herausgegeben von C.F. Wittmann. Leipzig. Reclam. n.d. Pp. 23. U-4547

Neumann, Alfred. *König Haber.* Stuttgart. Engelhorns Nachs. 1927. Pp. 139. U-5397 T

Nevinson, C.R.W. *The Great War: Fourth Year.* Essay J.E. Crawford Flitch. London. Grant Richards. 1918. Pp. 25, pl. 24. U-1207

The New Orient. A Journal of International Fellowship. 1924-6. U-5226-8. U-5227 C* [three issues]

Nicaise, Victor. *Allemands et polonais.* Préf. M. Welschinger. Paris. 1911. Uc

Nicéforo, Alfredo. *Fuerza y riqueza.* Tr. M. Domenge Mir. 2 vols. Barcelona. Henrich. 1907. Uc
- y Escipion Sighele. *La mala vida en Roma.* Tr. J.M. Llanas Aguilaniedo. Madrid. Rodríguez Serra. n.d. Pp. 254. U-2404

Nicolau de Olwer, Luis. *El teatro de Menandro.* Barcelona. L'Avenç. 1911. Pp. 332. U-1252 I D
- *Literatura catalana. Perspectiva general.* Barcelona. La Revista. 1917. Pp. 120. U-2332 D

Nielsen, Christian Ditlef. *Der geschichtliche Jesus.* München. Meyer & Jessen. 1928. Pp. xxvii, 236. U-5426 I* B T

Nielsen, Rasmus. *Regensen. Erindringer fra 1858-62.* København. Hagerups Forlag. 1906. Pp. 128. U-1947 I T

Nieto del Río, Félix. *Crónicas literarias.* Santiago de Chile. Cervantes. 1912. Uc

Nietzsche, Friedrich Wilhelm. *Ainsi parlait Zarathoustra – Un livre pour tous et pour personne.* Tr. Henri Albert. Paris. Mercure de France. 1921. Pp. 511. QP-35 I
- *Ecce homo suivi des poésies.* Tr. Henri Albert. Paris. Mercure de France. 1921. Pp. 299. QP-36 I

Nin, Gastón A. *Las sonatas modernistas.* Montevideo. La Anticuaria. 1904. Uc D

Nin Frías, Alberto. *Ensayos de crítica e historia y otros escritos.* Montevideo.
    Barreiro y Ramos. 1902. Pp. 309. U-2870 D
— *Nuevos ensayos de crítica literaria y filosófica.* Con una carta de J.E. Rodó,
    un estudio sobre el último libro del autor por M. de Unamuno, un
    apéndice con opiniones sobre el autor y bibliografía. Montevideo.
    Dornaleche y Reyes. [1905]. Pp. xxxii, 257. U-1159 D
— *Estudios religiosos.* Carta-pról. M. de Unamuno. Valencia. Sempere.
    [1906]. Pp. vii, 212. U-3140
— *Marcos, amador de la belleza.* Valencia. Sempere. [1913]. Uc D
— *Sordello Andrea, sus ideas y sentires.* Valencia. Sempere. [1910]. Uc
Nin y Silva, Celedonio. *La impureza.* Montevideo. El Siglo Ilustrado. Uc D
Nitobé, Inazo. *Bushido, el alma del Japón.* Tr. G. Jiménez de la Espada.
    Madrid. Jorro. 1909. Pp. 169. U-2004 I C
— *Le Bushido, l'âme du Japon.* Tr. M. Charles Jacob. Préf. M. André
    Bellessort. Paris. Payot. 1927. Pp. 265. U-1956 I
Nobre, António. *Só.* Lisboa. Guillard, Aillaud. 1898. Pp. 172. U-2291
— *Despedidas. 1895-1899.* Pref. J. Pereira de Sampaio. Porto. [1902].
    Pp. 126. U-1855
Noeldeke, Ph. *Historia literaria del Antiguo Testamento.* Tr. Enrique Rouget.
    Madrid. Iravedra. 1879. Pp. v, 412. U-1770
Noguera, Bernardino. *Matheu.* Buenos Aires. 1916. Pp. 144. U-3607 D
Noguera, Vicente. *Cancionero silencioso.* Madrid. Méndez y Altolaguirre.
    1936. Pp. 188. U-724 n/o D
Noma, Seiji. *A New View of Seiji Noma.* Tokyo. Dai Nippon Yubenkwai
    Kodansha. 1933. Pp. 65. U-5206
Nombela Campos, Julio. *Larra (Fígaro).* Madrid. La Ultima Moda. 1906.
    Pp. 290. U-946
— *Labor intelectual.* 2 vols. Madrid. La Ultima Moda. 1911. U-3970-1
Nombela y Tavares, Julio. *El pícaro mundo.* Madrid. Guio. 1884. Pp. 176.
    U-4675 n/o D
— *Obras literarias de Julio Nombela.* Madrid. La Ultima Moda. 1904-11.
    Vols. iii, xix, xx. U-4335-7. Vol. iii n/o D
— *Impresiones y recuerdos.* 4 vols. Madrid. La Ultima Moda. 1909-12.
    U-2842-5 I. U-2845 C
— *El amor propio.* Madrid. [1889]. Pp. 328. U-2916 D
Noronha, Thomás de. *Poesias inéditas de Thomás de Noronha.* Ediçao
    revista e annotada Mendes Dos Remedios. Coimbra. Amado. 1899.
    Pp. xxxiv, 84. U-1976
Nosotros. Buenos Aires (1924-36). n/n [39 issues]
Nothomb, Pierre. *Les barbares en Belgique.* Lettre-préf. M.H. Carton de
    Wiart. Paris. Perrin. 1915. Pp. xxvi, 261. U-3594 I*
— *La barrière Belge.* Paris. Perrin. 1916. Pp. 285. U-1920 D

Nouvelle Revue de Hongrie. Budapest (1936). n/n
La Nouvelle Revue Française. Paris (1 avril 1934, 1 avril 1936, 1 juillet 1936). n/n
Nova Europa. Zagreb (26 March 1926). n/n
Novalis. See Hardenberg, Friedrich Leopold von
Novia de Salcedo, Pedro. *Defensa histórica legislativa y económica del señorío de Vizcaya y provincias de Alava y Guipúzcoa.* 4 vols. Bilbao. Delmas. 1851-2. U-4326-9 n/o
Nucete-Sardi, José. *Aventura y tragedia de D. Francisco de Miranda.* Caracas. Artes Gráficas. 1935. Pp. 415. U-2307 I D
Núcleo Diógenes. *Ideario nuclear.* Buenos Aires. El Ateneo. 1928. Pp. 304. U-5553 D
Nueva Revista Peruana. Lima (1 agosto 1929). n/n
El Nuevo Mercurio (1907). n/n
Núñez, Alvaro L. *De re rustica. Cuentos campesinos.* Valencia. Pascual Aguilar. n.d. Uc D
Núñez Cabeza de Vaca, Alvar. *Naufragios y comentarios.* Madrid. Espasa-Calpe. 1932. Pp. 355. n/n I* L
Núñez Regueiro, Manuel. *Noctámbulos.* Rosario de Santa Fé. La República. 1905. Uc D
Nuova Rassegna di Letterature Moderne. VI, 4 (1908). U-839
Nouveau dictionnaire français-allemand et allemand-français à l'usage des deux nations. Strasbourg. Koenig. 1810. Pp. 1372. U-815
Obligado, Pastor Servando. *Tradiciones argentinas.* Barcelona. Montaner y Simón. 1903. Pp. 392. U-856 C
Obligado, Pedro Miguel. *Gris. Poesías.* Buenos Aires. Soc. Coop. Editorial Limitada. 1918. Pp. 190. U-1918 D
Ocantos, Carlos M. *Don Perfecto.* Barcelona. Montaner y Simón. 1902. Pp. 295. U-1672 I D
— *Fru Jenny. Seis novelas danesas.* Madrid. Tip. Rev. de Arch., Bibl. y Museos. 1923. Pp. 226. U-1341 n/o D
Ochoa, Alvaro Leonor. *Aves en las ruinas. Poesías.* Guadalajara, México. Yguiniz. 1923. Pp. 266. U-807 D
O'Conor, J.F.X. *A Study of Francis Thompson's Hound of Heaven.* New York. John Lane. 1914. Pp. 44. U-5193
Ojetti, Ugo. *I monumenti italiani e la guerra.* Milano. Alfieri e Lacroix. 1917. Pp. 30. U-1206
Olaechea, Bartolomé. *Christinauben doctrinia.* Bilbon. Delmas-Alargunaren Moldateguiyan. 1871. Pp. 264. U-1565
Olascoaga, Laurentino. *Deberismo filosófico-social.* Buenos Aires. La Facultad. 1935. Pp. 414. U-1194 D

Olazabal, Alexandre. *Vers l'émancipation économique*. Paris. Giard. 1921.
   Pp. xv, 87. U-1399 n/o D
O'Leary, General Daniel Florence. *Cartas del Libertador. Memorias del
   General O'Leary*. Publicadas por orden del ilustre americano General
   Guzman Blanco. Caracas. Gobierno Nacional. 1887. Pp. 537, xvii.
   U-4246 I* C*
— *Bolívar y la emancipación de Sur-América*. Memorias del General O'Leary
   traducidas del inglés por su hijo Simón B. O'Leary. Madrid. Soc. Española
   de Librería. [1915]. U-4213-14
— *Ultimos años de la vida pública de Bolívar. Memorias del General O'Leary*.
   Pról. R. Blanco-Fombona. Madrid. Edit. América. [1916]. Pp. 580.
   U-2533 n/o
— *Bolívar y las repúblicas del sur*. Notas R. Blanco-Fombona. Madrid. Edit.
   América. 1919. Pp. 230. U-2321
O'Leary, Rodó. Asunción. La Mundial. 1919. Pp. 648. U-3895 I* L* D
— *El Mariscal López*. Asunción. La Prensa. 1920. Pp. 374. U-259 D
O'Leary, Juan Emiliano. *Nuestra epopeya: Guerra del Paraguay*. Juicio J.E.
   Rodó. Asunción. La Mundial. 1919. Pp. 648. U-3895 I* L* D
Oliva Nogueira, José. *Heliantos*. Barcelona. Cuesta. 1909. Uc D
Olivari, Nicolás. *El gato escaldado*. Buenos Aires. Gleizer. 1929. Pp. 68.
   U-4926 D
Oliveira, Alberto d'. *Pombos-Correios. Notas quotidianas*. Coimbra. Amado.
   1913. Pp. 451. U-271 I C
Oliveira Martins, Joaquim Pedro. *Portugal contemporaneo*. 2 vols. Lisboa.
   Pereira. 1895. U-2625-6 I* C
— *Historia de Portugal*. 2 vols. Lisboa. Pereira. 1901. U-2635-6 I* C* L
— *Os filhos de D. João I*. 2 vols. Lisboa. Pereira. 1901. U-5722 I*. U-4366
— *A vida de Nun'Alvares*. Lisboa. Pereira. 1902. Pp. 472. U-787 I
— *O Brazil e as colonias portuguezas*. Lisboa. Pereira. 1904. Pp. 296.
   U-2634 I C B
— *Historia da civilisação iberica*. Lisboa. Pereira. n.d. Uc
— *Portugal nos mares*. Lisboa. Pereira. n.d. Pp. xvi, 249. U-2633 I
Oliver, Daniel. *Lessons in Elementary Botany*. London. Macmillan. 1891. Uc
Oliver, Francisco. J. *La enseñanza superior en Alemania*. Heidelberg. Hörning.
   1910. Uc D
Oliver, Miguel Santos. *Poesias*. Barcelona. L'Avenç. 1910. Pp. 211. U-2800 D
— *El caso Maura*. (Edición de homenaje popular). Barcelona. Gili. 1914.
   Pp. 187, xxxi. U-3743 D
Oliver Brachfeld, F. *Los sentimientos de inferioridad*. Barcelona. Apolo. 1936.
   Pp. 258. U-5517 D
Oliveros, Antonio L. *Asturias en el resurgimiento español*. Madrid. Juan Bravo.
   1935. Pp. 409. U-127 D
Ollantay. Drama Kjechua en verso, de autor desconocido. Versión castellana
   el P. Miguel A. Mossi. Buenos Aires. Coni. 1916. Uc

Oller Moragas, Narcis. *La papallona.* Barcelona. Renaixensa. 1882. Pp. 224.
U-2305 C T*
- *Figura y Paisatge.* Barcelona. L'Avenç. 1897. Pp. 280. U-4485 T D
- *Le Rapiat.* Tr. du catalan Albert Savine. Barcelona. Gili. n.d. Pp. 225.
U-5327 D
- *La bogeria. Novela de costums del nostre temps.* Barcelona. López. n.d.
Pp. 187. U-2773 T D
Olmedo y Rodríguez, Felipe. *La provincia de Zamora.* Valladolid. Imp.
Castellana. 1905. Pp. 713. U-1858
Olmsted, Everett Ward, and Arthur Gordon. *Gramática castellana. A Spanish
Grammar for Schools and Colleges.* New York. Holt. 1911. Pp. xi, 519.
U-141 D
Olóriz, P. Juan Crisóstomo. *Molestias del trato humano.* Barcelona. Bibl.
Clásica Española. 1887. Pp. 259. n/n I C D
Onieva Santamaria, Antonio Juan. *Entre montañas. La novela de un maestro
rural.* Madrid. El Magisterio Español. 1922. Pp. 420. U-3204 D
Onís, Federico de. 'Sobre la transmisión de la obra literaria de Fray Luis de
León.' *Revista de Filología Española,* ii, 3 (1915), 217-57. U-681 D
- *Disciplina y rebeldía.* Madrid. Residencia de Estudiantes. 1915. Pp. 51.
(2 copies) U-3504. n/n D
Orbe, T. *Redenta.* Sevilla. Francisco de P. Díaz. 1899. Uc D
Orbea, Ramón. *La reconquista de América.* Madrid. Suárez. [1905]. Pp. xii,
202. Uc D
Orchansky, J. *La herencia en las familias enfermas.* Tr. P. Umbert. Barcelona.
Henrich. 1907. Uc
Ordás Avecilla, César. *Para los míos. Entretenimientos literarios.* Madrid.
Cerezo. 1912. Uc D
O'Rell, Max, pseud. [i.e., Leon Paul Blouet]. *John Bull et son ile.* Paris.
Calmann-Lévy. 1885. Pp. vi, 323. U-2026
Orestano, Francesco. *Leonardo da Vinci.* Roma. Edizioni Optima. [1919].
Pp. 218. U-5352 I*
- *Nuovi principi.* Roma. Biblioteca di Filosofia e Scienza. 1925. Pp. 447.
U-5364
Orfer, Léo d'. *Chants de guerre de la Serbie.* Préf. Milenko R. Vesnitch. Paris.
Payot. 1916. Pp. 254. U-5244 I
Orga, Bernabé de la. *Libro del loco amor.* U-2570 D [Typescript]
*Organización de la Iglesia y Ordenes Religiosas en el Virreinato del Perú en el
siglo XVI.* Documentos del Archivo de Indias. Publicación dirigida por
Roberto Levillier. 2 vols. Madrid. Rivadeneyra. 1919. U-1649-50.
Vol. ii n/o
Orgaz, Arturo. *Crítica democrática.* Buenos Aires. Barros. 1926. Pp. 131.
U-4978 D

Orgaz, Raúl A. *La obra de Osvaldo Spengler. Una cultur-psicología mística.*
Córdoba, Argentina. Libr. y Publ. de la Facultad de Derecho y Ciencias
Sociales. Universidad N. de Córdoba. 1924. Pp. 29. U-5637
Oriani, Alfredo. *La lotta politica in Italia. Origini della lotta attuale 476-1887.*
3 vols. Firenze. Libr. della Voce. 1913. U-2451-3 I* C B
Oribe, Emilio. *Alucinaciones de belleza.* Montevideo. 1912. Uc D
 — *Las lejanías extrañas.* Montevideo. Renacimiento. 1915. Pp. 175.
    U-400 n/o D
 — *El halconero astral y otros cantos.* Montevideo. Agencia General de Libr.
    y Publ. 1925. Pp. 146. U-5585 D
 — *La colina del pájaro rojo (Poemas).* Montevideo. Agencia General de Libr.
    y Publ. 1925. Pp. 152. U-5503 D
 — *El castillo interior.* Montevideo. Renacimiento. 1926. Pp. 140. U-5471
 — *El nardo del ánfora. Poesía.* Montevideo. Agencia General de Libr. y Publ.
    1926. Pp. 125. U-5496 D
 — *El nunca usado mar. (Poesías).* Montevideo. García. 1928. Pp. 162.
    U-5091 I D
 — *Los altos mitos.* Montevideo. [1935]. Pp. 27. U-2181 D
 — *El rosal y la esfera.* Montevideo. 1935. Pp. 14. U-5523 D
Orientaciones. Buenos Aires. 1925. Núm. 1. n/n [Issue in honour of Unamuno]
Origen y desenvolvimiento de la sociedad de beneficencia de la capital,
    1823-1912. Buenos Aires. Rodríguez Giles. 1913. Pp. 521, vi. U-24
Oro y plata. Flor de pensamientos de varones ilustres. Barcelona. Comisión
    Provincial de la Cruz Roja. 1912. Uc
Orozco Muñoz, Francisco. *Invasión y conquista de la Bélgica mártir.* Palabras
    de F. Villaespesa. Pról. A. Nervo. Madrid. Beltrán. 1915. Pp. 171. Uc D
Ors, Eugenio d'. *La muerte de Isidro Nonell. Seguida de otras arbitrariedades*
    y de la oración a Madona Blanca María. Tr. E. Diez-Canedo. Madrid.
    Ediciones El Banquete. [1905]. Pp. 115. U-4253 D
 — *Glosari 1906, ab les gloses a la conferencia d'Algeciras y les gloses al viure*
    de Paris. Prol. R. Casellas. Barcelona. Edit. Puig. 1907. Pp. 535. U-822 D
 — 'Religio est libertas,' estratto dalla *Rivista di Filosofia,* I, 2 (1909).
    U-2202 n/o D
 — 'La formule biologique de la logique,' extrait des *Archives de Neurologie*
    (1910). U-2205 D
 — *Discurs presidencial.* Llegit a la festa dels jochs florals de Gerona. Gerona.
    1911. Pp. 16. U-1885
 — *La Ben Plantada de Xenius.* Barcelona. Verdaguer. 1911. Pp. 211. U-2901
 — *La bien plantada.* Tr. R. Marquina. Buenos Aires. Unión Editorial
    Hispano-Americana. n.d. Uc
 — *La filosofía del hombre que trabaja y que juega.* Antología filosófica de
    Eugenio d'Ors por R. Rucabado y J. Farrán. Introd. M. García Morente.

Estudios X. Diego Ruiz, J. Farrán y Mayoral, R. Rucabado, y M. de
Unamuno. Barcelona. López. 1914. Pp. 213. (2 copies) U-2098, U-2122
- *De la amistad y del diálogo.* Madrid. Residencia de Estudiantes. 1914.
Pp. 47. (2 copies) U-2948. U-3914 D
- *Aprendizaje y heroísmo.* Madrid. Residencia de Estudiantes. 1915. Pp. 68.
U-2947 D
- *Grandeza y servidumbre de la inteligencia.* Madrid. Residencia de
Estudiantes. 1919. Pp. 71. U-3916 D
- *El valle de Josafat.* Tr. R. Marquina. Madrid. Atenea. 1921. Pp. 328.
U-4864
Ortega, Canuto Alonso. *Gramática teórica-práctica de la lengua griega.*
Valladolid. Lescano y Roldán. 1853. Uc
Ortega, M.J. *Cartas de la aldea. Artículos de costumbres chilenas.* Santiago de
Chile. Universitaria. n.d. Pp. 184. U-2398
Ortega, Teófilo. *La voz del paisaje.* Burgos. Parábola. 1928. Pp. 240. U-5590 D
- *La muerte es vida.* Madrid. Iberoamericana de Publ. 1929. Pp. 268.
U-5513 I C D
Ortega y Gasset, Eduardo. *España encadenada. La verdad sobre la dictadura.*
Paris. Dura. 1925. Pp. 338. (2 copies) U-1605. U-4889 I* L D
Ortega y Gasset, José. *Meditaciones del Quijote.* Madrid. Residencia de
Estudiantes. 1914. Pp. 207. (2 copies) U-2637-8 D. U-2638 I
- *El espectador.* 3 vols. Madrid. Renacimiento. 1916-21. U-540-2
Ortiz, Daniel (Doys, pseud.). *Chirigotas.* Barcelona. Manent. 1901. Pp. 218.
U-2868 D
- *Chirigotas y epigramas.* Pról. M. de Unamuno. Barcelona. López. [1902].
Pp. 208. U-2647
Ortiz, Fernando. *Hampa afrocubana. Los negros brujos.* Madrid. F. Fé.
1906. Uc D
- *La identificación dactiloscópica. Informe de policiología y de derecho
público.* Habana. La Universal. 1913. Pp. vii, 279. U-1643
- *La reconquista de América. Reflexiones sobre el panhispanismo.* Paris.
Ollendorff. n.d. Uc
Ortiz de la Torre, Elías. *Papeles de Ugarte. Documentos para la historia de
Fernando VII.* Santander. 1934. Pp. 71. U-1706
Ortiz del Barco, Juan, pseud. [i.e., Manuel Rodríguez Martín]. *Propiedad
de la correspondencia privada.* n.p. 1909. Pp. 68. U-1681 D
Ortiz-Lamadria, Rubén. *Alma libre.* Habana. Molina. 1933. Pp. 220.
U-3681 n/o
Ortiz y San Pelayo, Félix. *Boceto histórico de la asociación partriótica
española.* Buenos Aires. La Facultad. 1914. Pp. 304. U-1186 n/o
Ortuño, Emilio. *Reforma de correos.* Pról. A. Maura. Avila. Jiménez. 1911.
Pp. 258. U-2685 D

Orueta, José. *El país vasco*. Madrid. El Mundo. 1907. Pp. 142. U-4975
Orueta y Duarte, Ricardo de. *La vida y obra de Pedro de Mena y Medrano*.
    Madrid. Blass. 1914. Pp. 340. U-1175
— *La escultura funeraria en España. Provincias de Ciudad Real, Cuenca,*
    Guadalajara. Madrid. Centro de Estudios Históricos. 1919. Pp. 384, pl. 111.
    U-4309 D
Ory, Eduardo de. *Amado Nervo. Estudio crítico*. Cadiz. España y América.
    n.d. Pp. 97. U-4714 n/o D
Os Gatos. Publicação mensal d'inquerito á vida portugueza. Porto. 1889-92.
    (No. 1, agosto 1889-No. 41, 23 abril 1892). U-180-3. U-180 I* C T
Osorio de Castro, Alberto. *A cinza dos Myrtos*. Nova Goa. Imp. Nacional.
    1906. Pp. viii, 212. U-130 D
Osorio de Oliveira, José. *Psicología de Portugal, e outros ensaios*. Lisboa.
    Descobrimento. 1934. Pp. 193. U-3220 I* C* D
Ossorio, Angel. *Historia del pensamiento político catalán durante la guerra de*
    España con la República Francesa (1793-1795). Madrid. Oliva. 1913.
    Pp. xx, 271. U-1227 D
— *El contrato de opción. Boceto de una monografía jurídica*. Madrid. Rojas.
    1915. Pp. 118. U-3321
— 'Un jurista mártir. Episodio de la guerra en Cataluña en tiempos de Felipe
    IV,' *Revista General de Legislación y Jurisprudencia*, XXXVIII (1928).
    U-4927
— *Una posición conservadora ante la república*. Madrid. Pueyo. 1931. Pp. 30.
    U-4896
— *Un libro del abate Sturzo*. Madrid. Pueyo. 1928. Pp. 258. (2 copies)
    U-5006, U-5041
Ostwald, Wilhelm. *L'Energie*. Tr. E. Philippi. Paris. Alcan. 1910. Pp. x, 238.
    U-618 I*
Otaegui, Tomás. *Derecho de gentes argentino*. Buenos Aires. Amorrortu.
    [1926]. Pp. 339. U-4878
Oteriño, Felipe A. *Prosas heterogéneas*. Buenos Aires. Martín García. 1914.
    Pp. 212. Uc D
Otero, Clemencia, y Eugenio Fernández Leis. *Almas gemelas. Cartas*. Vigo.
    Heraldo de Vigo. 1914. Pp. 48. U-5655
Otero Pedrayo, Ramón. *A Romeiria de Gelmirez*. Santiago. Nós. 1934.
    Pp. 294. U-5739 I C D
Oteyza, Luis de. *Baladas*. Madrid. Pueyo. 1908. Pp. 123. U-3712 D
Othón, Manuel José. *Poemas rústicos de Manuel José Othón. 1890-1902*.
    México. Aguilar Vera. 1902. Pp. iv, 152. U-3522 I
Otto, Rudolf. *Lo santo*. Tr. Fernando Vela. Madrid. Revista de Occidente.
    1925. Pp. 220 n/n C* D
Ouranis, Costas. *Sol y sombra*. Flamma. 1934. Pp. 281. U-2612 I* C* D

Oyhanarte, Horacio B. *El hombre.* Buenos Aires. Mendesky. 1916. Pp. 342.
U-1604 D
– *Breviario de la haraganería.* Buenos Aires. Oliveiri y Domínguez. 1928.
Ff. 188. U-5035 C
Oyhanarte, Raúl F. *Al ras de los ensueños. Poesías.* La Plata. Sesé. 1912. Uc D
P., Mr de. *Défense des recherches philosophiques sur les Américains.* n.p.
1770. Pp. 256. U-4627
– *Recherches philosophiques sur les Egyptiens et les Chinois.* Tôme II.
Amsterdam. Leyde, Barth, Vlam & Murray. 1773. Pp. 320. U-4458
P.V.C. *La fórmula guerra (Algunas consideraciones militares y filosóficas
de la guerra).* Madrid. Horno. 1915. Pp. 143. U-574 D
Paço D'Arcos, Anrique. *Divina tristeza.* Porto. Gráfica do Porto. 1925. Pp. 108.
U-5731 D
– *Peregrino da noite.* Lisboa. Seara Nova. 1931. Pp. 163. U-312 n/o
Padilla, Rafael. *Sangre argentina.* Madrid. San Bernardo. 1910. Uc D
Padilla, Salvador. *Gramática histórica de la lengua castellana.* Madrid. Jubera.
1903. Pp. 380. U-4185 D
La palabra de Dios. (Evangelio de Colomb.) Córdoba, Argentina. Liendo.
1920. Pp. 27. (2 copies) U-5670-1 D
Palacios, Alfredo L. *El nuevo derecho. Legislación del trabajo.* Pról. M.B.
Gonnet. Buenos Aires. Lajouane. 1920. Pp. xxii, 390. U-1242
– *La universidad nueva.* Buenos Aires. Gleizer. 1925. Pp. 257. U-5756 D
– *Universidad y democracia.* Buenos Aires. Claridad. 1928. Pp. 269.
U-5632 D
– y Carlos N. Caminos. *Derecho de asilo (Caso Maciá-Gassol).* Buenos Aires.
Claridad. 1928. Pp. 118. U-5132 D
Palacios, Pedro Bonifacio (Almafuerte, pseud.). *Obras. I. Lamentaciones.*
La Plata. 1906. Pp. 87. U-3065 D
– *Apóstrofe para la nota del poeta argentino Almafuerte.* La Plata. 1915.
Ff. 4. U-2239
– *Almafuerte y la guerra.* Buenos Aires. Otero. 1916. Pp. 81. U-3316
Palamas, Kostis. *Iambi ke Anapesti.* Athina. Zikakis. 1920. Pp. 58. U-2863 T
– *E Phlogera tou Vasilia me tin Iroïki Trilogia.* Athina. Kollaros. 1920.
Pp. 161. U-2476 I* C* T*
– *Dodekalogos tou Giftou.* Athina. Estia. 1921. Pp. 187.
U-2475 I* C* T* B D
– *Oi Kaïmi tis Limnothalassas.* Athina. Estia. 1925. Pp. 117. U-5750 I* T*
– *Poems by Kostes Palamas.* Sel. and tr. T. Ph. Stephanides and G.C.
Katsimbalis. London. Hazell, Watson & Viney. 1925. Pp. 143. U-5171 C
– *E Asalefti Zoï.* Athina. Kollaros. 1926. Pp. 214. U-2585 I* T* D
– *O Taphos.* Athina. Kollaros. 1928. Pp. 77. U-2285 C* T*

Palamas, Leandros. *E phinikia. Analytiko simioma.* Athina. 1912. Pp. 19.
U-5778
Palazzeschi, Aldo. *L'Incendiario.* Milano. Edizioni Futuriste di Poesia. 1910.
Pp. 292. U-2055
Palcos, Alberto. *Sarmiento. La vida, la obra, las ideas, el genio.* Buenos Aires.
El Ateneo. 1929. Pp. 445. U-5634 I* C D
— *El 'Facundo.' Rasgos de Sarmiento.* Buenos Aires. El Ateneo. 1934.
Pp. 174. U-3310 D
Palma, Angélica. *Ricardo Palma.* Buenos Aires. Tor. 1933. Pp. 156. U-5079 D
Palma, Clemente. *Cuentos malévolos.* Pról. M. de Unamuno. Barcelona. Salvat.
1904. Pp. xvi, 169. U-4505 D
Palma, Ricardo. *Recuerdos de España ... La bohemia de mi tiempo.* Lima.
La Industria. 1899. Pp. 309. U-3250 I B D
— *Cachivaches.* Lima. Torres Aguirre. 1900. Pp. xxiv, 252. U-4226 D
— *Mis últimas tradiciones peruanas.* Barcelona. Maucci. 1906. Pp. 604. n/n D
— *Apéndice a mis últimas tradiciones peruanas.* Barcelona. Maucci. [1911].
Pp. 538. n/n D
Palomeque, Alberto. *Guerra de la Argentina y el Brasil. El general Rivera y la
Campaña de Misiones (1828).* Buenos Aires. López. 1914. Pp. 532. U-1718
Paludan, Hans Aage. 'Spanske Romancer i Danmark og paa Island.' Pp. 85-112.
U-5266 D [Offprint with no identification]
Paludan-Müller, Fr. *Ungdomsarbeider.* Kφbenhavn. Reikels. 1847. Pp. 476.
U-4593
Pamplona Escudero, Rafael. *Cuartel de inválidos.* Barcelona. Henrich. 1904. Uc
— *Juego de damas.* Madrid. 1906. Uc D
Panagiotopoulos, I.M. *To Poetiko Ergo tou K. Palama.* Athina. Potamianos.
1921. Pp. 39. U-2742 n/o
Pantaleoni, Matteo. *Principii di economia pura.* Firenze. Barbèra. 1894.
Pp. 376. U-1576 B
Pànteo, Tullio. *Il poeta Marinetti.* Milano. Soc. Edit. Milanese. 1908. Pp. 215.
U-3446
Pantoja, Domingo de. *Los Estados Unidos y la América del Sur.* Buenos Aires.
Peuser. 1893. Pp. xviii, 374. (2 copies) U-3411, U-4016
Paparrhegopulos, K. *Istoria tou Ellinikou Ethnous Apo tis Aloseos tis
Konstantinoupoleos.* Athina. Issari. 1874. Pp. 523. U-2619 T
Papini, Giovanni. *Il crepuscolo dei filosofi.* Milano. Lombarda. 1906. Pp. xi,
293. U-2121 I
— *L'Altra metà. Saggio di filosofia mefistofelica.* Ancona. Puccini. 1911.
Pp. 191. U-872
— *Cento pagine di poesia.* Firenze. Libr. della Voce. 1915. Uc
— *Storia di Cristo.* Firenze. Vallecchi. 1921. Pp. xxix, 638. U-3793 I D

Paradas del Cerro, Enrique. *Impresiones. Cantares.* Madrid. Helénica. 1913.
  Pp. 187. Uc
Paraire, V., et G. Rimey. *La patria española. El país y los habitantes pintados
  por escritores españoles modernos.* Paris. Colin. 1913. Pp. 336. U-3918
Pardo Bazán, Emilia. *San Francisco de Asís (Siglo XIII).* 2 vols. Madrid.
  Olamendi. 1882. n/n
– *La sirena negra.* Madrid. Pérez Villaricercio. 1908. Uc D
– *Dulce dueño.* Madrid. Prieto. 1911. Uc
– *Porvenir de la literatura después de la guerra.* Madrid. Residencia de
  Estudiantes. 1917. Pp. 48. U-3088
– *Los poetas épicos cristianos.* Madrid. Avrial. [1895]. Pp. 330. U-261 I
– *Novelas ejemplares. Los tres arcos de Cirilo. Un drama. Mujer.* Madrid.
  Avrial. [1895]. Pp. 272. U-3176 I
– *Retratos y apuntes literarios.* Madrid. [1909]. Pp. 371. U-2319 I* D
– *La literatura francesa moderna. I. El romanticismo.* Madrid. Renacimiento.
  [1910]. Pp. 331. U-4370 D
– *Cuentos de Navidad y Reyes. Cuentos de la patria. Cuentos antiguos.*
  Madrid. [1902]. Pp. 278. U-1350 D
– *De siglo a siglo (1896-1901).* Madrid. [1902]. Pp. 272. U-2324 D
– *La España de ayer y la de hoy.* Madrid. [1899]. Pp. 107. U-2318 D
– *Cuentos sacro-profanos.* Madrid. [1899]. Pp. 318. U-2317 D
– *Una cristiana.* Madrid. La España Editorial. [1900]. Uc
– *La prueba.* 2a parte de *Una cristiana.* Madrid. La España Editorial.
  [1900]. Uc
Paredes Guillén, Vicente. *Historia de los framontanos celtíberos desde los
  más remotos tiempos hasta nuestros días.* Plasencia. El Cantón Extremeño.
  1888. Pp. 205. U-2621 D
– *Orígenes históricos de la leyenda La serrana de la vera.* Plasencia. Montero.
  1915. Pp. 414 + 112. U-582 D
Pareto, Vilfredo. *Manuel d'economie politique.* Tr. A. Bonnet. Paris. Giard et
  Brière. 1909. Pp. 695. U-109 I* B
Parkman, Francis. *The Conspiracy of Pontiac and the Indian War after the
  Conquest of Canada.* Introd. Thomas Seccombe. 2 vols. London. Dent.
  [1908]. U-965-6 I*
Parnaso Panameño. Pról. y biografías O. Méndez Pereira. Panamá. El Istmo.
  1916. Pp. ix, 392. U-600
Parra, Pedro María. *Lugareña.* Caracas. Bolívar. 1908. Pp. 227. Uc D
Parra, Porfirio. *Nuevo sistema de lógica inductiva y deductiva.* México. Tip.
  Económica. 1903. Uc D
Parra, Teresa de la. *Las memorias de Mamá Blanca.* Paris. Le Livre Libre.
  1929. Pp. 285. U-4915 I L D

Parreira, Carlos. *A esmeralda de Nero*. Porto. Renascença Portuguesa.
[1915]. Pp. 214. U-1977 D

Pascal, Blaise. *Pensées sur la religion et sur quelques autres sujets*. Paris.
Charpentier. 1847. Pp. 520. U-2788. Préf. Emile Boutroux. Introd.
Victor Giraud. London. Dent. 1913. Pp. x, 405. U-1506 I* C*

— *Les provinciales ou lettres écrites pour Louis de Montalte*. Edition
accompagnée des notes et précédés d'un précis historique sur le Jansénisme
par Ch. Louandre. Paris. Charpentier. 1880. Pp. 444. U-1951 I

Pascal, Ernesto. *Lezioni di calcolo infinitesimale*. 2 vols. Milano. Hoepli.
1918-19. U-4682-3

Pascarella, Luis. *Cuervos caseros. Las dos esclavas*. Buenos Aires. Apolo. 1915.
Pp. 100. U-2873 n/o D

Pascoaes, Teixeira de. See Pereira Teixeira de Vasconcellos, Joaquin

Pascoli, Giovanni. *Poemi conviviali*. Bologna. Zanichelli. 1904. Pp. xii, 214.
U-1786 I T

Pascual Español, Mariano. *Socialismo y democracia cristiana*. Madrid.
Ambrosio Pérez. 1904. Pp. xlvii, 433. (2 copies) U-2954, U-3514 D

Passos, João. *Diogenes de Medeiros*. Rio de Janeiro. Manzolillo, Tossi. 1931.
Pp. 40. U-2419 D

Pastor, Antonio R. *The Theology of Plotinus*. London. Balliol College, Oxford.
1919. Pp. 289. U-800 I D [Typescript]

Pater. See Paterson, Roberto G.

Pater, Walter. *La Renaissance*. Tr. F. Roger-Cornaz. Paris. Payot. 1917.
Pp. 365. QP-37 I

Paterson, Roberto G. *Solos de flauta*. Buenos Aires. Menéndez. 1905. Pp. 141.
U-4474 D

— *La ruta del sol*. Buenos Aires. Pellerano. 1915. Pp. 300. U-1615 n/o D

— *Chispazos*. Buenos Aires. Moen. n.d. Uc D

Patmore, Coventry. *The Angel in the House* and *The Victories of Love*.
Introd. Alice Meynell. London. Routledge. [1905]. Pp. xvi, 336.
U-451 I* T

Patrikiou Iakovidi, Lili. *E Chaeretismi tis Heliogennitis*. Athina. Estia. 1929.
Pp. 23. U-3791

Patrum apostolicorum opera. Recensuerunt Oscar de Gebhardt, Adolfus
Harnack, Theodorus Zahn. Lipsiae. Heinrichs. 1900. Pp. 226. U-3737 I T

Paul, Herman. *Prinzipien der Sprachgeschichte*. Halle A.S. Niemeyer. 1898.
Pp. x, 396. U-2985 I C*

Paulsen, Friedrich. *Einleitung in die Philosophie*. Berlin. Hertz. 1901. Pp. xvi,
464. U-3827 I C

Paulucci di Calboli, R. 'Il fallimento delle teorie delle razze,' *Nuova Antologia*
(1905). U-1239

Payró, Roberto J. *La Australia argentina.* Carta-pról. general B. Mitre. Buenos
    Aires. La Nación. 1898. Pp. viii, 448. U-2600
Paz, Felipe S. *Cantos de primavera.* Pról. Gabriel E. O'Byrne. Barcelona.
    Taberner. 1909. Uc D
Paz, José María. *Memorias póstumas del General José María Paz.* Madrid.
    Edit. América. 1917. Pp. 491. U-3023. 3 vols. La Plata. La Discusión.
    1892. U-1180-2 I
Pedraza, P.A. *República de Colombia. Excursiones presidenciales. Apuntes de
    un diario de viaje.* Norwood, Mass. Plimpton Press. 1909. Pp. x, 275.
    U-3542
Pedreira, Antonio S. *Aristas. Ensayos.* San Juan de Puerto Rico. Campos.
    1930. Pp. 272. U-2425 D
Pedrell, Felipe. *Orientaciones (1892-1902).* Paris. Ollendorff. [1903]. Pp. vii,
    300, U-3509
 — *Jornadas de arte (1841-1891).* Paris. Ollendorff. [1894]. Pp. ix, 336.
    U-1599
Pegaso (Rassegna de lettere e arti). Firenze (March 1930). n/n
Péguy, Charles. *Notre patrie.* Paris. Cahiers de la Quinzaine. 1905. Pp. 81.
    U-630
 — *De la situation faite à l'histoire et à la sociologie dans les temps modernes.*
    Paris. Cahiers de la Quinzaine. 1906. Pp. 64. U-629 n/o
 — *De la situation faite au parti intellectuel dans le monde moderne.* Paris.
    Cahiers de la Quinzaine. 1906. Pp. 72. U-628 C*
 — *Victor-Marie, comte Hugo.* Paris. Cahiers de la Quinzaine. 1910. Pp. 264.
    U-633 n/o
 — *Notre jeunesse.* Paris. Ollendorff. 1910. Pp. 222. U-1371
 — *Oeuvres choisies. 1900-1910.* Paris. Grasset. 1911. Pp. 412. U-3976 I
 — *Le mystère de la charité de Jeanne d'Arc.* Paris. Plon et Nourrit. [1912].
    Pp. 250. U-1392
Pel & Ploma. Barcelona, III, 77-88 (juny 1901–maig 1902). Uc
Péladan, Josephin Aimé. *La décadence latine. Ethopée.* Paris. Flammarion.
    1899. Uc
Peláez Cueto, Andrés. *Criticrónicas (1916-1919).* Madrid. Reus. 1920.
    Pp. 145. U-407 n/o D
Pelegrin Falcon, J. *Necesidad y constitucionalidad de la ley de moratoria
    hipotecaria.* Buenos Aires. López. 1934. Pp. 212. U-1285
Pella y Forgas, J. *La crisis del catalanisme.* Barcelona. Henrich. 1906. Pp. 104.
    U-3906
Pellicer, Julio. *Tierra andaluza.* Pról. S. Rueda. Madrid. El Trabajo. 1900.
    Pp. 135. U-4709
 — *A la sombra de la mezquita.* Madrid. Moreno. 1902. Uc D

Pellico, Silvio. *Le mie prigioni.* Firenze. Le Monnier. 1890. Pp. 201. U-1450
- *Prose e tragedie scelte.* A cura di Michele Scherillo. Milano. Hoepli. 1910.
 Pp. xliv, 416. U-3931
Pelliza, Mariano A. *Historia de la organización nacional.* Buenos Aires.
 Lajouane. 1897. Pp. 410. U-4179
Pellizzon, Ettore. *Trilogie.* Treviso. Pietrobon. 1916. Pp. 55. U-785 D
Pena, Leonardo. *Las puertas.* Santiago de Chile. Imp. Santiago. 1911. Vol. II.
 Pp. 215. U-4395 n/o
- *Yo.* Santiago de Chile. Universitaria. 1907. Pp. 324. U-4002
- *Los héroes moribundos.* Santiago de Chile. Imp. Santiago. 1910. Uc D
Pendola, Tommaso. *Curso de lecciones de pedagogía especial para uso de los
 maestros que se dediquen a la enseñanza oral de los sordo-mudos.* Versión
 de A.J. Torcell. La Plata. Sesé. 1896. Uc
Pensamiento del Ave María. 3a parte. *Modos de enseñar.* Granada. Escuelas
 del Ave María. 1902. Pp. 248. U-3069 n/o
Peña, David. *Juan Facundo Quiroga.* Buenos Aires. Coni. 1906. Pp. xii, 445.
 U-3016 D
Peña, Enrique. *Don Jacinto de Lariz. Turbulencias de su gobierno en el Río
 de la Plata. 1646-1653.* Madrid. Suárez. 1911. Pp. 171. U-2498
Peralta, José M. *Doctor Gonorreitigorrea. Cuadro de costumbres.* El Salvador.
 Biblioteca Cuscatlania. 1926. Pp. 151. U-4890 D
Percy, Thomas. *Reliques of Ancient English Poetry.* 2 vols. London. Dent.
 [1906]. U-1065-6 I T
Perea, Martín. *Este sabor amargo!* Buenos Aires. Romero. n.d. Pp. 104.
 U-5557 D
Pereda, José María de. *Tipos trashumantes.* Barcelona. Henrich. 1897. Pp. 261.
 U-74 D
- *La novela en el teatro. Cartas.* Aclaraciones y comentarios de L. Ruiz y
 Contreras. Barcelona. Granada 1910. Pp. 165. U-3595
Pereda, Setembrino E. *Liberalismo práctico. Ser o no ser.* Montevideo. El
 Siglo Ilustrado. 1910. Pp. 372. U-4306 D
- *Artigas. 1784-1850.* 3 vols. Montevideo. El Siglo Ilustrado. 1930. U-702-4
Pereira da Fonseca e Aragão, Maximiano. *Vizeu (Apontamentos historicos).*
 Vizeu. Popular. 1894. Pp. 218. U-4845 n/o D
Pereira da Silva, Luciano. *Astronomia dos Luisiadas.* Coimbra. Imp.
 Universidade. 1915. Pp. xv, 228. U-1633 D
Pereira de Sampaio, José (Bruno, pseud.). *A Geração nova. Ensaios criticos.
 Os novellistas.* Porto. Magalhães & Moniz. 1886. Pp. 359. U-2629 I D
- *Notas de exilio. 1891-1893.* Porto. Chardron. 1893. Pp. 347. U-2703 n/o D
- *O Brazil mental. Esboço critico.* Porto. Chardron. 1898. Pp. xxxvii, 470.
 U-2011 I D
- *A idéa de Deus.* Porto. Chardron. 1902. Pp. lxiv, 483. U-2785 D

– *O encoberto.* Porto. Moreira. 1904. Pp. xx, 381. U-2704 L D
Pereira Teixeira de Vasconcellos, Joaquin (Teixeira de Pascoaes, pseud.).
   Sempre. Coimbra. Amado. 1902. Pp. 326. U-1741 D. Porto. Renascença
   Portuguesa. [1915]. Pp. 168. U-499 D
– *Jesus e Pan.* Porto. Figueirinhas. 1903. Pp. 67. U-3279 D
– *Para a luz.* Porto. Universal. 1904. Pp. 168. U-1903 D
– *Vida etérea.* Coimbra. Amado. 1906. Pp. 192. U-1784 D
– *As sombras.* Lisboa. Ferreira. 1907. Pp. 210. U-2708 I D
– *Senhora da noite.* Porto. Magalhães & Moniz. 1909. Pp. 54. U-2014 D
– *Maranos.* Porto. Magalhães & Moniz. 1911. Pp. 298. U-2279 I D
– *Regresso ao paraíso.* Porto. Renascença Portuguesa. 1912. Pp. 218.
   U-2097 I D
– *O espíritu lusitano ou o saudosismo.* Porto. Renascença Portuguesa. 1912.
   Pp. 19. U-777 D
– *O doido e a morte.* Porto. Renascença Portuguesa. 1913. Pp. 31. U-2339 D
– *Elegias.* Porto. Costa Corregal. 1913. Pp. 80. U-524 D
– *Verbo escuro.* Porto. Renascença Portuguesa. 1914. Pp. 171. U-498 D
– *A era Lusíada. (Duas conferencias).* Porto. Renascença Portuguesa.
   [1914]. Pp. 49. U-2872 D
– *Arte de ser português.* Porto. Renascença Portuguesa. [1915]. Pp. 186.
   U-4588 D
– *Terra proíbida.* Porto. Renascença Portuguesa. 1917. Pp. 214. U-476 D
– *Os poetas lusíadas.* Porto. Costa Carregal. 1919. Pp. xi, 314. U-2390 C D
– *O pobre Tolo.* Porto. Renascença Portuguesa. 1924. Pp. 207. U-3257 n/o.
   Paris. Aillaud e Bertrand. n.d. Pp. 143. U-3307 D
– *São Paulo.* Porto. Tavares Martins. 1934. Pp. 427. U-160 I* C*
– *San Pablo (São Paulo).* Pról. M. de Unamuno. Tr. R. Martínez López.
   Barcelona. Apolo. 1935. Pp. xi, 327. U-128
– *São Jerónimo e a trovoada.* Lisboa. Lello & Irmao. 1936. Pp. 306.
   U-5730 I D
Perés, Ramón Domingo. *Cantos modernos.* Barcelona. Jepús. 1888. Pp. 214.
   U-562
– *A dos vientos. Críticas y semblanzas.* Barcelona. L'Avenç. 1892. Pp. 317.
   U-3223 D
– *Norte y sur. Poema cíclico.* Barcelona. L:Avenç. 1893. Pp. 151. U-1611
– *Bocetos ingleses.* Barcelona. L'Avenç. 1895. Pp. 268. U-4414
– *Musgo.* Barcelona. L'Avenç. 1903. Pp. 158. U-279 D
Pereyra, Carlos. *Bolívar y Washington. Un paralelo imposible.* Madrid.
   América. [1917]. Pp. 444. U-3589
– *El General Sucre.* Madrid. América. [1918]. Pp. 303. U-638 I
– *Historia del pueblo mejicano.* 2 vols. Méjico. Ballescá. n.d. U-2024-5

Pérez, Enrique. *Causa y efecto*. Pról. E. Olaya Herrera. Bogotá. 1910. Pp. xxv,
153. U-2223
— *Vida de Felipe Pérez*. Bogotá. La Luz. 1911. Pp. 336. Uc D
Pérez, Enrique. *Cirugía política*. Pról. M. de Unamuno. Paris. Garnier. [1913].
Pp. xii, 227. U-1519
Pérez, Fausto. *Fundamento histórico y filosófico del esoterismo griego*.
Montevideo. Campo. 1934. Pp. 208. U-5032
Pérez, Manuel. *Tucumán intelectual*. Tucumán. La Argentina. 1904. Uc D
Pérez Cabello, Rafael. *Rápidas. Colección de rimas*. Pról. J. de Lara y E.J.
Varona. Habana. Avisador Comercial. 1907. Pp. 207. U-3993 D
Pérez Canto, Julio. *Economical and Social Progress of the Republic of Chile*.
Santiago de Chile. Imp. Barcelona. 1906. Uc
Pérez-Cardenal Olivera, Andrés. *Alpinismo castellano. Guía y crónicas de
excursiones. Sierras de Gredos, Béja y Francia*. Bilbao. 1914. Uc
Pérez de Ayala, Ramón. *La paz del sendero*. Madrid. F. Fé. 1904. Pp. 153.
U-2780 D
— *La paz del sendero. El sendero innumerable*. A manera de prólogo
palabras de Rubén Darío. Madrid. Soc. Gral. Española de Libr. 1916.
Pp. 214. U-591 D
— *Troteras y danzaderas*. Madrid. Renacimiento. [1913]. Pp. 384.
U-2053 I D
— *Las máscaras. Ensayos de crítica teatral*. Madrid. Clásica Española. 1917.
Uc D
— *Política y toros. Ensayos*. Madrid. Calleja. 1918. Pp. 291. U-429 I
— *El sendero andante. Momentos. Modos. Ditirambos. Doctrinal de vida y
naturaleza. Poemas*. Madrid. Calleja. 1921. Pp. 204. U-1370 n/o D
— *Los trabajos de Urbano y Simona*. Madrid. Mundo Latino. 1923. Pp. 283.
n/n D
— *El ombligo del mundo*. Madrid. Renacimiento. 1924. Pp. 279. U-430 D
— *La pata de la raposa*. Madrid. Renacimiento. 1912. Uc D
Pérez Díaz, Pedro. *El socialismo*. Madrid. Hernando. 1910. Pp. vii, 512.
U-5646 n/o D
— *El problema social y el socialismo. Una solución*. Pról. A.A. Buylla. Madrid.
Renacimiento. 1915. Pp. xxv, 180. U-3655 D
Pérez Galdós, Benito. *Zumalacárregui. Mendizábal. De oñate a la Granja.
Luchana. La campaña del maestrazgo. La estafeta romántica. (Episodios
Nacionales,* Tercera serie). Madrid. 1898-9. U-2830-5. U-2833 I D
— *Fortunata y Jacinta*. 4 vols. Madrid. Hernando. 1929-32. n/n I D
Pérez Gutierrez, Dionisio. *La juncalera*. Barcelona. Henrich. 1902. Pp. 239. Uc
Pérez-Jorba, J. *Poemes*. Barcelona. L'Avenç. 1913. Pp. 263. U-1403 D
Pérez Petit, Víctor. *Los modernistas*. Montevideo. Dornaleche y Reyes. 1903.
Pp. 333 (2 copies) U-2325 D. U-3120

– *Gil. Acuarelas. Aquafuertes.* Montevideo. Dornaleche y Reyes. 1905. Uc D
– *Rodó. Su vida, su obra.* Montevideo. Imp. Latina. 1918. Pp. 325.
U-3077 I D

Pérez Rosales, Vicente. *Recuerdos del pasado. 1814-1860.* Santiago de Chile.
Gutenberg. 1886. Pp. xxiv, 432. n/n I. Santiago de Chile. Imp. Barcelona.
1910. Pp. xxiv, 507. U-2606

Pérez Solís, Oscar. *Memorias de mi amigo Oscar Perea.* Madrid. Renacimiento.
1931. Pp. 346. U-3646 I D

Pérez Triana, Santiago. *De Bogotá al Atlántico por la vía de los ríos Meta,
Vichada y Orinoco.* Paris. Sudamericana. 1897. Pp. 358. U-3452 I* C
– *Reminiscencias tudescas.* Pról. J. Valera. Madrid. F. Fé. 1902. Pp. 148.
U-3392 I D
– *Down the Orinoco in a Canoe.* Introd. R.B. Cunninghame Graham.
London. Heinemann. 1902. Pp. xv, 253. U-3669 D
– *Cuentos a Sonny.* Versión castellana de T.O. Eastman. Madrid. F. Fé.
1907. Pp. 109. U-1474 n/o
– *The Pan-American Financial Conference of 1915.* London. Heinemann.
1915. Uc
– *Aspectos de la guerra.* Londres. Hispania. 1915. Uc

Perojo y Figueras, José de. *Ensayos sobre educación.* Madrid. Nuevo Mundo.
1907. Pp. 313. Uc D

Perrini, Carlo. *El mundo y el hombre.* Tr. Jaime Barceló. Barcelona. Henrich.
1906. Uc

Perrotta, Antonio. *The Modernist Movement in Italy and Its Relation to the
Spread of Protestant Christianity.* Boston. Badger. [1929]. Pp. 116.
U-3654
– *Inni e pensieri.* Utica. Amitrano. n.d. Pp. 88. (2 copies) U-4442,
U-4494 n/o
– *Inni in lode e gloria del nostro Signore Gesu' Cristo.* Utica. Amitrano. n.d.
Pp. 43. (2 copies) U-4443-4

Perseus, Journal for den speculative Idee. Udgiven af J.L. Heiberg. København.
Reitzels. 1837-8. Pp. 264 + 181. U-2286

Persius Flaccus. *Les Satires de Perse.* Texte établi et tr. A. Cartault. Paris.
Les Belles Lettres. 1920. Pp. 56. U-891 I* L*

Persona. *A New Gospel.* New York. Privately printed. 1908. Pp. vi, 88.
U-4287

Perticone, Giacomo. *L'Eredità del mondo antico nella filosofia politica.*
Torino. Paravia. n.d. Pp. 105. U-5336

Peru de Lacroix, Louis. *Diario de Bucaramanga o vida pública y privada del
libertador Simón Bolívar.* Introd. y notas C. Hispano. Paris. Ollendorff.
1912. Pp. 267. U-3676 I*

Peschkau, Emil. *Moderne probleme.* Leipzig. Reclam. n.d. Pp. 94. U-4549

Petermann, Julius Henr. *Brevis linguae arabicae. Grammatica litteratura, chrestomathia cum glossario.* Scriptsit J.H. Petermann. Lipsiae. Reuther. 1867. Pp. 136 + 112. U-646 C*

Petit Muñoz, Eugenio. *El camino. Etapas de una política educacional vivida.* Montevideo. La Cruz del Sur. 1932. Pp. 553. U-5048 D

Petit-Senn, J. *Chispas y caprichos.* Tr. V. Figueredo-Lora. San José de Costa Rica. Imp. Universal. n.d. Pp. xvi, 109. U-5656

Petrarca, Francesco. *Le rime di Messer Francesco Petrarca.* 2 vols. Firenze. Nella Stamperia Gran-Ducale. 1815. U-4057-8

— *François Pétrarque. Oeuvres choisies.* Préf. et tr. H. Cochin. Paris. La Renaissance du Livre. n.d. Pp. 208. U-4698 I

— *Rime di Francesco Petrarca.* Interpretazione Giacomo Leopardi e note inedite Eugenio Camerini. Milano. Sonzogno. 1876. Pp. 454. U-2840

Pettazzoni, Raffaele. *Svolgimento e carattere della storia delle religioni.* Bari. Laterza. 1924. Pp. 31. U-3708 n/o

Pezoa Véliz, Carlos. *Alma chilena. Poesías líricas, poemas, prosa escogida.* Valparaiso. Scherrer y Herrmann. 1912. Pp. 181. U-1233

Pfandl, Ludwig. 'Ein Romance en títulos de comedias,' extrait de la *Revue Hispanique,* LV (1922), U-1707

Pfleiderer, Otto. *Religionsphilosophie auf geschichtlicher Grundlage.* Berlin. Reimer. 1896. Pp. x, 761. U-811

— *Die Entstehung des Christentums.* München. Lehmann. 1905. Pp. vi, 255. U-1900 I C*

La Phalange. Paris (20 mars 1914, 15 février 1936, 15 mars 1936). n/n

Philippe, Charles-Louis. *Charles Blanchard.* Préf. L.P. Fargue. Paris. Nouvelle Revue Française. 1913. Pp. 240. U-391 I*

— *La mère et l'enfant.* Paris. Nouvelle Revue Française. 1911. Uc

Philippi, Felix. *Daniela.* Leipzig. Reclam. n.d. Pp. 75. U-4522

Phillips, Stephen. *Poems.* London. John Lane. 1904. Pp. vii, 108. U-1333 I* T

— *The New Inferno.* New York. John Lane. 1910. Pp. 151. U-3598

Phöbus. Ein Journal für die Kunst. Herausgegeben von Heinrich v. Kleist und Adam H. Müller. Dresden. Gärtner. 1808. U-5443

Phoutrides, Aristides. *Palamas ke Isiodos.* Athina. Estia. 1929. Pp. 17. (2 copies) U-2715, U-5751

Pi, Wifredo Francisco. *Antología gauchesca.* Montevideo. García. 1917. Pp. 204. U-601 D

Pí y Margall, Francisco. *Las nacionalidades.* Madrid. Eduardo Martínez. 1877. Pp. viii, 380. U-2822

Pi y Suñer, August, y L. Ródrigo Lavin. *Tratado de fisiología. Fisiología general.* Barcelona. Gili. 1909. Pp. viii, 810. U-766 I C*

Piazzi, G. *El arte en la muchedumbre.* Tr. M. Domenge Mir. 2 vols. Barcelona. Henrich. 1905. Uc

Picabia, Juan Héctor. *Lirismos*. Madrid. Sanz Calleja. 1918. Pp. 83. U-3276 D
Picarel, F. Julio. *La verdadera felicidad del pueblo. Conferencia*. Buenos Aires.
    Peuser. 1915. Pp. 31. U-3653
Picatoste Rodríguez, Felipe. *El universo en la ciencia antigua*. Madrid. 1881. Uc
Piccione, Enrico. *Il genio latino nella historia. Conferenza*. Valparaiso. Soc.
    Editrice Italiana. 1897. Pp. 16. U-2003
  — *Estudios filosóficos y sociales*. 2 vols. Santiago de Chile. Patria. 1898.
    U-2838-9. U-2838 n/o
Picón, Jacinto Octavio. *La honrada. Novela de costumbres contemporáneas*.
    Barcelona. Henrich. 1890. Pp. 351. U-2996
Picón Febres, Gonzalo. *Notas y opiniones*. Caracas. Herrera Irigoyen. 1898.
    Pp. 256. U-3374 D
  — *El sargento Felipe*. Caracas. Herrera Irigoyen. 1899. Pp. 187. U-1398 D
  — *La literatura venezolana en el siglo diez y nueve. Ensayo de historia
    crítica*. Caracas. El Cojo. 1906. Pp. 429. U-3531
  — *Libro raro. Voces, locuciones y otras cosas de uso frecuente en Venezuela*.
    Curazao. Bethencourt. 1912. Pp. 404. U-1670 n/o
  — *Teatro crítico venezolano*. Curazao. Bethencourt. 1912. Uc
Pidal Bernardo de Quirás, Pedro. *Instrucción pública*. Madrid. Beltrán. 1913.
    Pp. 533. (2 copies) U-1830, U-4251
  — *Segundo y símbolo, no sustituto*. Madrid. Comp. Iber. Amer. de Publ.
    1930. Pp. 182. U-5467 D
Piernas Hurtado, José María. *Vocabulario de la economía*. Barcelona. Soler.
    n.d. Pp. 185. U-1526
Pierron, Alexis. *Histoire de la littérature romaine*. Paris. Hachette. 1869.
    Pp. 654. U-2645 C
Pijoan, Joseph. *El cançoner d'en Joseph Pijoan*. n.p. Vilanova y Geltrú. 1905.
    Pp. 52. U-4247
  — *El meu Don Joan Maragall*. Barcelona. Llibr. Catalonia. [1915]. Pp. 120.
    U-5326 D
Pillepich, Pietro. 'Wenceslao Fernández Flórez,' estratto della rivista
    La Lucerna, fasc. v-vi (Giugno 1927). U-5460
  — 'L'ultimo liberatore d'America José Martí,' estratto dalla *Rivista Colombo*,
    iv, fasc. xx (1929). U-5362 I D
Pin y Soler, Joseph. *Varia*. 3 vols. Barcelona. Verdaguer. 1903-6. U-1734-6
  — *Orient*. Barcelona. Verdaguer. 1906. Uc D
Pina, Ruy de. *Chronica d'el rei D. Duarte*. Estudo crítico, notas, e glossario
    A. Coelho de Magalhães. Porto. Renascença Portuguesa. [1914]. Pp. 237.
    U-3368 I L
Pindar. *Pindari Carmina cum fragmentis selectis*. Ed. Otto Schroeder. Lipsiae.
    Teubner. 1908. Pp. xii, 360. U-350 I* T*

– *Pythiques. Néméennes. Isthmiques et fragments.* 3 vols. Texte établi et
   tr. Aimé Puech. Paris. Les Belles Lettres. 1922-3. U-3921-3
Pineda, Luis Felipe. *Oro de Guaca.* Bogotá. Mundo al Día. 1936. Pp. 115.
   U-1459 D
Pinilla Sánchez, Antonio. *El palacio del sueño.* Lima. Moya. [1930]. Pp. 60.
   U-2211 n/o
Pino, Fernando del. *La gran decisión.* Pról. L. Araujo Costa. Madrid. Fax.
   [1936]. Pp. xv, 231. U-3445 n/o D
Pinta Llorente, Miguel de la. 'Una investigación inquisitorial sobre Pedro
   Ramos en Salamanca,' *Religión y Cultura,* xxiv (1933). U-4099 D
– *La 'Confesión' del maestro Martín Martínez de Cantalapiedra.*
   Aportaciones inéditas para la cultura española del siglo XVI. Madrid.
   Huelves. [1932]. Pp. 27. U-4098 D
Pinto, Alvaro. *O Brasil actual (Duas conferências).* Lisboa. Edição do Autor.
   1935. Pp. 58. U-5720 D
Pinzón Uzcátegui, M. *Crítica histórica sobre el 'Diario de Bucaramanga.'*
   Caracas. Tip. de Comercio. 1914. Pp. 225. U-2299 D
Piquer, Constantino. *Cuentos aristocráticos.* Valencia. Pascual. 1907. Uc D
– *Sangre azul.* Valencia. López. [1911]. Pp. 108, xxiv. U-217 n/o D
– *Siluetas de príncipes.* Pról. A. Renda. Valencia. López. [1911]. Pp. 104,
   xv. U-216 D
Piquet, Julio. *Tiros al aire.* Buenos Aires. Rodríguez Giles. 1910. Pp. 209.
   U-4713 D
Pirandello, Luigi. *Il fu Mattia Pascal.* 2 vols. Milano. Treves. 1910. U-5333-4
– *El difunto Matías Pascal.* Tr. R. Cansinos Assons. Madrid. Biblioteca
   Nueva. 1924. Pp. 375. U-3894
Pistrack, E. *Les problèmes fondamentaux de l'Ecole du Travail.* Préf. Van de
   Moortel. Paris. Internationale des Travailleurs de l'Enseignement. n.d.
   Pp. 157. U-5229
Pitollet, Camille. *V. Blasco Ibáñez. Sus novelas y la novela de su vida.* Tr.
   Tulio Moncada. Valencia. Prometeo. [1921]. Pp. 307. U-3315
Pittaluga, Gustavo. *Enfermedad del sueño.* Madrid. 1910. Uc
– *Il canzoniere.* Roma. Modes e Mendel. 1898. Pp. 123. U-1537 D
Pittard, Eugène. *La Roumanie.* Paris. Bossard. 1917. Pp. 327. U-1263 I B
Piuma Schmid, Alfredo. *El derecho de morir.* Buenos Aires. Libr. las Ciencias.
   1920. Pp. 171. U-672 D
Pius X. *Syllabus Pius X Aliaque nuperrima documenta Sanctae Sedis, Sacrarum
   Cong. Rom. ac Commissionis Biblicae Pontificalis in usum Sacerdotum et
   Seminaristarum.* Pampilone. Bescansa. 1907. Pp. 165. U-2743
Pivert de Sénancour, Etienne Jean Baptiste Pierre Ignace. See Sénancour
Plá, Josep. *Madrid. L'Adveniment de la republica.* Barcelona. Bibl. Catalana
   d'Autors Independents. 1933. Pp. 197. U-218

- *Viatge a Catalunya.* Barcelona. Bibl. Catalana d'Autors Independents. 1934. Pp. 240. U-219
Plana, Alexandre. *Antología de poetes catalans moderns.* Barcelona. Societat Catalana d'Edicions. 1914. Pp. xxiii, 310. U-3168 I T D
- *Sol en el llindar. Poesies.* Barcelona. Societat Catalana d'Edicions. 1915. Pp. 201. U-2333 D
- *Contrabaedecker.* Barcelona. Publ. de la Revista. 1918. Pp. 89. U-2320 D
Plana y Dorca, Joseph. *Curtas ... y més curtas.* Barcelona. Giró. 1901. Pp. 102. U-4498 D
- *Bastides y Pedruscall.* Barcelona. Giró. 1904. Pp. 208. U-3071 D
- *Papellones.* Barcelona. Giró. 1907. Pp. 195. U-2245
Planes Mundet, J. *Lliure existir. I. Refracciones de una vida.* Barcelona. Llibr. Catalonia. [1933]. Pp. 247. U-2059 I D
- *Superestat.* Barcelona. Llibr. Catalonia. 1936. Pp. 180. U-3782 D
Plange, Th. J. *Christus-ein Inder?* Stuttgart. Schmidt. 1906. Pp. xvi, 250. U-790
Plato. *Platonis dialogi secundum Thrasylli tetralogias dispositi.* Ex recognitione C.F. Hermanii. 6 vols. Lipsiae. Teubner. 1905. U-327-31 I* L C [Vol. I is missing]
- *Dialogues de Platon.* Première et deuxième série. 4 vols. Paris. Charpentier. 1861-2. U-1512-15
- *Ion.* Texte grec publié avec une introduction des notes critiques et des notes L. Mertz. Paris. Hachette. 1889. Pp. xxii, 43. U-4662 I
- *Phédon.* Texte grec ... publié avec une introduction et des notes P. Couvreur. Paris. Hachette. 1893. Pp. li, 144. U-4663 I T
- *Criton, ou le devoir du citoyen.* Texte grec accompagné d'une introduction, d'un argument analytique et des notes Ch. Waddington. Paris. Hachette. 1902. Pp. 56 + 8. U-4665 T
- *Oeuvres complètes.* Tome I. Texte établi et tr. M. Croiset. Paris. Les Belles Lettres. 1920. Pp. 233. U-3924
- *Apología de Sócrates.* Versão, introdução, e notas Angelo Ribeiro. Porto. Renascença Portuguesa. 1923. Pp. 115. U-4069
- *O banquete. Elogio do amor.* Versão e notas Angelo Ribeiro. Porto. Renascença Portuguesa. 1924. Pp. 197. U-4062
Plötz, J. v. *Dumm und gelehrt.* Durchgesehen und herausgegeben von C.F. Wittmann. Leipzig. Reclam. n.d. Pp. 35. U-4524
Plotinus. *Plotini Enneades.* Praemisso Porphyrii de vita Plotini deque ordine librorum eius libello. Ed. Ricardus Volkmann. 2 vols. Lipsiae. Teubner. 1883-4. U-337-8. U-337 I T. U-338 B
La pluma. Montevideo (abril 1929). n/n
Plummer, Henry C. *An Introductory Treatise on Dynamical Astronomy.* Cambridge. University Press. 1918. Pp. xix, 343. U-1168

Plutarch. *Plutarchi vitae parallelae*. Iterum recognovit C. Sintenis. 5 vols.
  Lipsiae. Teubner. 1902-8. U-332-6 I* T L
- *Vie de Démosthène*. Texte grec. Notes Ch. Graux. Paris. Hachette. 1886.
  Pp. xxv, 95. U-4661 I
- *Vie de Périclès*. Texte grec. Notice sur les sources de la vie de Périclès, un
  argument, et des notes en français Alfred Jacob. Paris. Hachette. 1893.
  Pp. xxxv, 110. U-4667 B
Poal Aregall, Miquel. *Gloses femenines*. Sabadell. Sallent i Prat. 1914. Pp. 154.
  U-1793 n/o D
Pocaterra, José Rafael. *Memorias de un venezolano de la decadencia 1898-1908;
  Castro; 1908-1919 Gómez*. 2 vols. Bogotá. Ediciones Colombia. 1927.
  U-5127-8 I* C L D
Podesta Costa, Luis A. *El extranjero en la guerra civil*. Buenos Aires. Coni.
  1913. Pp. 272. U-1726 D
Poe, Edgar Allan. *Tales by Edgar Allan Poe*. Ed. J.H. Ingram. Leipzig.
  Tauchnitz. 1884. Pp. vi, 328 + 31. (2 copies) U-4774 B. U-5222 T
- *The Poems of Edgar Allan Poe With Selected Essays*. Introd. A. Lang.
  London. Dent. 1927. Pp. xx, 340. U-5221 I* T L* C
- *Le corbeau*. Tr. A. Godoy. Paris. Emile-Paul. 1929. Pp. 18. n/n n/o
Poema de Mio Cid. Ed. y notas R. Menéndez Pidal. Madrid. La Lectura. 1913.
  Pp. 358. U-933 C
Poèmes nationaux du peuple serbe. Tr. A. Al Yarchitch et M. Robert. Préf.
  J. Cvijic. Paris. Bloud & Gay. 1918. Pp. vii, 78. U-5267
Poems from the Portuguese. (With the Portuguese text.) Tr. A.F.G. Bell.
  Oxford. Blackwell. 1913. Pp. viii, 131. U-552
*Poesías inéditas de Herrera el Divino, Quevedo, Lope de Vega, L. Argensola,
  Góngora*. Madrid. Edit. América. 1917. Pp. 198. U-1134
Pohl, Emil. *Vasantasena*. Stuttgart. 1893. Pp. 128. U-3617 T
Poincaré, Jules Henri. *La valeur de la science*. Paris. Flammarion. 1917.
  Pp. 278. U-2375 I*. 1925. U-394 I
- *El valor de la ciencia*. Tr. E. González Llana. Madrid. Gutenberg. 1906.
  Pp. 262. U-1446
- *La science et l'hypothèse*. Paris. Flammarion. 1917. Pp. 292. U-3152 I C.
  1925. U-380 I
- *Science et méthode*. Paris. Flammarion. 1918. Pp. 314. U-2900 I*
Poincaré, Lucien. *La physique moderne. Son évolution*. Paris. Flammarion.
  1916. Pp. 311. U-3352 I* B
- *L'Electricité*. Paris. Flammarion. 1917. Pp. 297. U-1967
Poirier, Eduardo. *Chile en 1908*. Santiago de Chile. Imp. Barcelona. 1909.
  Pp. ix, 453 + 287. U-1184 D
Polar, Jorge. *Arequipa. Descripción y estudio social*. Arequipa, 1891. Pp. 302.
  U-4282 [Cover missing]

Polavieja, Camilo García de (Marqués de). *Hernán Cortés. Estudio de un carácter.* Toledo. 1909. Uc

Pombo, Manuel Antonio, y José Joaquín Guerra. *Constituciones de Colombia.* 2 vols. Bogotá. La Luz. 1911. U-4082-3 n/o

Pomés Soler, Ramón. *La riallera.* Barcelona. Badia. 1903. Pp. 151. U-4408 D

Ponce de la Fuente, Constantino. *Confesión de un pecador escrita por el Doctor Constantino Ponce de la Fuente en el siglo XVI.* Reimpresa L. Usoz y Río. Nashville, Tenn. Iglesia Metodista Episcopal del Sur. 1902. Pp. xiv, 52. U-5605

Poncel y de Cardenas, Carolina. *El romance en Cuba.* Habana. Revista de la Facultad. 1914. Pp. 132. U-745 n/o D

Pons, Silvio. *Saggi pascaliani.* Roma. Tip. dell'Unione Editrice. 1914. Pp. 30. U-5359

Pons y Meri, José. *Reseña de la Escuela Superior de Comercio de Bilbao.* Bilbao. Salvador. 1893. Pp. 198. Uc

Pons y Umbert, Adolfo. *El salón de conferencias.* Madrid. Real Academia de Jurisprudencia y Legislación. 1916. Pp. 39. U-3042

Pontoppidan, Henrik. *Det Forjaettede land.* København. Bojesen. 1898. Pp. 565. U-1973 T

Popol-Vuh. Los dioses, los héroes y los hombres de Guatemala antigua o El libro del Consejo Popol-Vuh de los Indios Quichés. Tr. de la versión francesa del Profesor Georges Raynaud por M.A. Asturias y J.M. González de Mendoza. Paris. Ed. Paris-América. 1927. Pp. xlviii, 147. U-4947 I*

Popper, José. *El derecho a vivir y el deber de morir.* Tr. A. González Blanco. Barcelona. Carbonell. 1907. Pp. 182. Uc

Porcioles, Joan de. *Notes folk-lóriques de la Vall d'Ager.* Barcelona. L'Avenç. 1899. Pp. xxiv, 54. U-4406

Porras Márquez, Antonio. *País de ensueño.* Madrid. Prieto. 1911. Pp. 187. U-3468 n/o D

Portela, Marcos d'a. *Catecismo d'a doutrina labrega.* Orense. El Eco de Orense. 1898. Pp. 40. U-2802

Porter, Arthur Kingsley. *La sculpture du XIIe siècle en Bourgogne.* Paris. Gazette des Beaux-Arts. 1921. Pp. 22. U-733

Porzhezinsky, Victor. *Einleitung in die Sprachwissenschaft.* Leipzig. Teubner. 1910. Pp. 229. U-3091

Posada, Adolfo. *Para América desde España.* Paris. Ollendorff. 1910. Pp. ix, 334. Uc

— *Ciencia política.* Barcelona. Soler. n.d. Pp. 182. Uc

Posada, Andrés. *Estudios científicos.* Medellín, Colombia. Molina. 1909. Uc

Posada, Guillermo. *Quimeras.* Madrid. Ricardo Fé. 1906. Pp. 86. U-530 D

Posada, R. Julio. *Jacillas.* Bogotá. Equis. [1926]. Pp. 135. U-5076 D

Pott, August Friedrich. *Sobre los apellidos vascongados publicado en 1875 en Detmold.* Tr. Eliano de Ugarte. Bilbao. Pérez. 1887. Pp. 43. U-3713

Potter, John. *Archaeología Graeca or the Antiquities of Greece.* Appendix and account G. Dunbar. 2 vols. Edinburgh. Doig & Stirling. 1813. U-1808-9

Pound, Ezra. *Quia pauper amavi.* London. The Egoist Ltd. [1919]. Pp. 51. U-4142 I D

Pous Pagès, J. *Per la vida.* Barcelona. L'Avenç. 1903. Pp. 118. U-4451

— *La vida y la mort d'en Jordi Fraginals.* Barcelona. Soc. Catalana d'Edicions. 1912. Pp. 576. U-3169 I L D

Praag, J.A. van. *La comedia espagnole aux Pays-Bas au XVIIe et au XVIIIe siècle.* Amsterdam. H.J. Paris. 1922. Pp. 292. U-5247 I

Prack, Enrique B. *Los grandes problemas de la actualidad.* La Plata. Imp. la Nueva. 1905. Pp. 131. U-4460 D

Prado, Pedro. *Flores de cardo.* Santiago. Imp. Universitaria. 1908. Pp. 126. Uc D

— *La casa abandonada.* Santiago. Imp. Universitaria. 1912. Uc D

— *El llamado del mundo.* Santiago. Imp. Universitaria. 1913. Pp. 126. U-2699 D

Precioso, Artemio. *Flores de pasión.* Madrid. Atlántida. n.d. Pp. 235. U-4881 D

Prescott, William H. *Historia del reinado de los Reyes Católicos D. Fernando y Da. Isabel.* Tr. P. Sabau y Larroya. 2 vols. México. Rafael. 1854. U-76-7

— *History of the Reign of Philip the Second, King of Spain.* Vols. I and II. London. Richard Bentley. 1855. Pp. xvi, 500. U-1310

— *History of the Conquest of Peru.* Introd. Thomas Seccombe. London. Dent. 1907. Pp. xlii, 649. U-1043 I

— *The Conquest of Mexico.* 2 vols. London. Dent. [1909]. U-1044-5 I

— *Unpublished Letters to Gayangos.* Ed. Clara Louisa Penney. New York. Hispanic Society of America. 1927. Pp. xxi, 215. U-1408

Presenzini-Mattoli, A. *Segni nel cielo. Maditazioni.* Foligno. Campitelli. 1922. Pp. 130. U-3570

Prevelaki, P. *Stratiotes.* Athina. Kallergi. 1928. Pp. 22. U-2488 C* T D

Prevost, (Antoine François) Abbé. *Histoire de Manon Lescaut et du chevalier Des Grieux.* Nouvelle édition précédée d'une notice sur la vie et les ouvrages de Prévost par M. Sainte-Beuve. Suivie d'une appréciation de Manon Lescaut par M. Gustave Planche. Paris. Charpentier. n.d. Pp. 291. U-1386

Prezzolini, Giuseppe. *Benedetto Croce.* Napoli. Ricciardi. 1909. Pp. 118. (2 copies) U-1302 I. U-3302

— *Discorso su Giovanni Papini.* Firenze. Libr. della Voce. 1915. Pp. 139. U-3728

— *Dopo Caporetto.* Roma. La Voce. 1919. Pp. 65. U-3239

Price, W.H. Crawfurd. *Serbia's Part in the War.* Vol. I. *The Rampart Against Pan-Germanism Being the Political and Military Story of the Austro-Serbian Campaigns.* London. Simpkin, Marshall, Hamilton, Kent & Co. 1918. Pp. ix, 250. U-111

Priestley, J.B. *The Good Companions.* London. Heinemann. [1934]. Pp. viii, 646. U-4288 I* T

Prince, John Dyneley. *Grammaire pratique de la langue latvienne.* [Tr. J.D. Prince. Adaptations C. Barret and E. Blese]. Riga, Bruxelles. 1928. Pp. 130. U-810

Proceso de Nariño. Fiel copia del original que existe en el Archivo General de Indias de Sevilla, cuidadosamente confrontada y publicada por José Manuel Pérez-Sarmiento. Tomo I. Cadiz. Alvarez. 1914. Pp. xi, 238. U-722

Il progresso religioso. Genova, IV, VI (1925). n/n

Prokes, Jaroslav. *Histoire tchécoslovaque.* Prague. Orbis. 1927. Pp. 374. U-757 I L

Propertius. *Catulli. Tibulli et Propertii Carmina* ad Praestantium Librorum lectiones accurate recensuit C.H. Weise. Lipsiae. Tauchnitz. 1843. Pp. 272. U-4589 T*

Prose. Roma, IV, V (1907). n/n

Proudhon, P.J. *El principio federativo.* Tr. y pról. F. Pí y Margall. Madrid. Duran. 1868. Pp. 184. U-3568

Proust, Marcel. *Correspondance générale. Lettres à Robert de Montesquiou. 1893-1921.* Paris. Plon. 1930. Pp. iv, 291. QP-39 I

Provenzal, Dino. *Una vittima del dubbio: Leonida Andreief.* Appendice Ettore lo Gatto. Roma. Bilychnis. 1921. Pp. 64. U-1722

Prudhomme, René François Armand. See Sully Prudhomme

Prüm, Emilio. *Alemania en Bélgica a la luz de las doctrinas de la iglesia.* Tr. y pról. P. Sangro y Ros de Olano. Notas de la edición francesa René Johannat. Madrid. Tip. Rev. de Arch., Bibl. y Museos. 1915. Pp. 230. U-389

Przybyszewski, Stanislaw. *Satans Kinder.* München. Müller. 1919. Pp. 261. U-5400 I

Publications of the Modern Language Association of America (June 1934). n/n

Puccini, Mario. *Faville.* Milano. Lombardo. 1914. Pp. 162. U-1303 I D

— *Dove è il peccato è Dio.* Foligno. Campitelli. 1922. Pp. 300. U-2088

— *Uomini deboli e uomini forti.* Milano. Treves. 1922. Pp. 190. (2 copies) U-509 D. U-5337

— *Racconti cupi.* Foligno. Campitelli. 1922. Pp. 260. U-2049 D

— *La vera colpevole.* Aquila. Vecchioni. 1926. Pp. 240. U-5344 I* D

— *Davanti a Trieste.* Milano. 1919. Pp. 261. U-1936

— *La vergine e la mondana.* Milano. Sonzogno. 1919. Pp. 339. U-3926 I

Puente, José Félix de la. *La visión redentora.* Trujillo, Perú. Olaya. 1917.
Pp. 288. U-2358 D

Puente, P. Luis de la. *Vida del V.P. Baltasar Alvarez, de la Compañía de Jesús.*
Madrid. Aguado. 1880. Pp. 648. U-2571 I C

Puerto Rico. Revista mensual (Junio 1935). n/n

Pufendorf, Samuel von. *Konung Carl X. Gustafs Bragder.* Ofversatta af Adolf
Hillman. 7 vols. Stockholm. Wahlström & Widstrand. [1913]. U-3549-55.
Vols. II-VII n/o

Puig, Juan B. *Tratado de tecnicismos.* Gerona. Dalmau Carles. 1906. Uc D

Pujol, Juan. *Jaculatorias y otros poemas compuestos.* Cartagena. Imp. de J.
Palacios. 1908. Pp. 106. U-3453 n/o D

Pujols, Francesc. *Llibre que conté les poesíes d'en Francesc Pujols.* Prol. Joan
Maragall, Barcelona. Tobella & Costa. 1904. Pp. 167. U-2907 D

Pulgar, Hernando de. *Claros Varones de Castilla y letras de Hernando de Pulgar,
consejero, secretario y cronista de los reyes católicos Don Fernando y
Doña Isabel.* Madrid. G. Ortega e Hijos de Ibarra. 1789. Pp. 328. U-2795 I

Pulido Fernández, Angel. *Los Israelitas españoles y el idioma castellano.*
Madrid. Rivadeneyra. 1904. Pp. 244. U-161 D

— *Intereses nacionales. Españoles sin patria y la raza sefardí.* Madrid.
Teodoro. 1905. Pp. 659. U-680 D

Puyol y Alonso, Julio. *La vida política en España.* Madrid. Minuesa de los Ríos.
1892. Uc D

Pyrenaica, núm. 11 (1928), núm. 14 (1929). n/n

Pythagoras. *La vie sage. Commentaires sur les vers d'or des Pythagoriciens.*
Revisée Paul Carton. Paris. Maloine. n.d. Pp. 208. U-5246 I D

Quaderns d'estudi. (Barcelona. Consell de pedagogía), I, 2 (1916), U-4865

Quadra Salcedo, Fernando de la. *Libros raros y curiosos de la imprenta en
Bilbao. 1800-1830.* Bilbao. Ambos Mundos. 1920. Pp. 94. U-1190 D

Le quatrième evangile. Tr., introd., notes, et commentaires Henri Delafosse.
Paris. Rieder. 1925. Pp. 234. U-5320

Queipo de Llano, José Ma. (Conde de Toreno). *Historia del levantamiento,
guerra y revolución de España.* 5 vols. Madrid. Jordan. 1835-7.
U-2564-8 I* C*

Queiros Veloso, J.M. de. *Gil Vicente e a sua obra.* Lisboa. Teixeira. 1913.
Pp. 80. U-1790 D

— *D. Sebastiao. 1554-1578.* Lisboa. Emprêsa Nacional de Publicidade. 1935.
Pp. 450. U-900 I* C L D

Quental, Anthero de. *Primaveras románticas.* Pôrto. Imp. Portuguesa. 1872.
Pp. vii, 202. U-1892

— *Sonetos completos de Anthero de Quental.* Publicados J.P. Oliveira
Martins. Pôrto. Livr. Portuense. 1890. Pp. 51, 184, vi. U-2701

— *Odes modernas.* Pôrto. Chardron. 1898. Pp. 190. U-3297 I

- *Prosas.* Vol. i. Coimbra. Imp. da Universidade. 1923. Pp. vi, 398. U-1902 I
- *Los sonetos completos de Anthero de Quental.* Pref. J.P. Oliveira Martins. Tr. Emilia Bernal. Madrid. Hernández y Galo Sáez. 1926. Pp. 235. U-2871

Quental, P. Bertholameu do. *Meditaçoens da gloriosa resurreyçam de Christo Senhor nosso.* Lisboa. Deslandes. 1683. Pp. 318. U-4580
- *Sermoens do Padre Bertholameu do Quental.* 2 vols. Lisboa. Deslandes. 1692-4. U-1345-6. U-1345 I*

Quer Boule, Luis. *La embajada de Saavedra Fajardo en Suiza. Apuntes históricos 1639-1642.* Madrid. Velasco. 1931. Pp. 96. U-2030 D

Querol, Vicente W. *Rimas.* Pról. T. Llorente. Madrid. Tello. 1891. Pp. xliv, 365. U-536

Der Querschnitt. Berlin (April 1926, Mai 1928, Oktober 1928). n/n. U-780 n/n

Quesada, Ernesto. *Dos novelas sociológicas.* Buenos Aires. Peuser. 1892. Pp. 223. U-3862 n/o
- *Reseñas y críticas.* Buenos Aires. Lajouane. 1893. Pp. 531. Uc
- *La política chilena en el Plata.* Buenos Aires. Moen. 1895. Pp. 382. Uc
- *La época de Rosas.* Buenos Aires. Moen. 1898. Pp. 392. (2 copies) U-3336, U-3421
- *La política argentina respecto de Chile (1895-1898).* Buenos Aires. Moen. 1898. Pp. 239. U-825
- *El problema del idioma nacional.* Buenos Aires. Revista Nacional. 1900. Pp. viii, 157. U-1214
- *Las reliquias de San Martín.* Buenos Aires. Revista Nacional. 1900. Pp. 176. U-1462
- *Comprobación de la reincidencia. Proyecto de ley.* Buenos Aires. Coni. 1901. Pp. 190. U-2456 D
- *La política argentino-paraguaya.* Buenos Aires. Brédahl. 1902. Uc
- *La propiedad intelectual en el derecho argentino.* Buenos Aires. Menéndez. 1904. Uc
- *La Facultad de Derecho de Paris.* Buenos Aires. Coni. 1906. Uc

Quesada, Gonzalo de. *La patria alemana.* Leipzig. Weber. 1913. Pp. 382. U-35 D

Quesada, Héctor C. *Bases de estudio sobre la matanza de vacas.* La Plata. Taller de Impresiones Oficiales. 1907. Uc D

Quesada, Vicente G. *Recuerdos de mi vida diplómatica. Misión en Estados Unidos (1885-1892).* Buenos Aires. Menéndez. 1904. Uc

Quevedo, José María. *La tierra triste.* La Plata. El Día. 1903. Pp. 93. U-2768 n/o D

Quevedo Hijosa, Manuel. *Variedades científico-literarias.* La Plata. Gasparini. 1907. Pp. 270. Uc

Quevedo y Villegas, Francisco de. *Obras satíricas y festivas.* Tomo XXXIII. Madrid. Biblioteca Clásica. 1904. Pp. 566. U-948 I

- *Historia de la vida del Buscón.* Introd. y notas Américo Castro. Madrid. La Lectura. 1911. Pp. xxii, 273. U-952 I* C
- *Obras completas.* Textos descubiertos, clasificados, y anotados D.L. Astrana Marín. 2 vols. Madrid. Aguilar. 1932 n/n I

Quicherat, L. *Chrestomathie* ou premiers exercisses de traduction grecque, extraits des auteurs classiques avec un lexique. Paris. Hachette. 1893. Uc

Quidde, L. *Caligula. Eine Studie über römischen Cäsarenwahnsinn.* Leipzig. Wilhelm Friedrich. [1894]. Pp. 20. U-5386 I*

Quintero Alvarez, Alberto. *Saludo de alba. Cuatro años de poesía.* Presentación E. González Martínez. México. Diana. 1936. Ff. 64. U-2254 D

Quintilianus, Marcus Fabius. *M. Fabii Quintiliani de Institutione Oratoria. Libri XII.* 2 vols. Lipsiae. Tauchnitz. 1829. U-4036-7

Quiroga, Carlos. *Timideces de sol.* La Plata. La Nacional. 1911. Pp. 180. U-2444 n/o D

Rabelais, François. *Les cinq livres.* Avec une notice par le bibliophile Jacob. Variantes et glossaire P. Chéron. Tome I. Paris. Libr. des Bibliophiles. n.d. Pp. xx, 333. QP-40 I

Racine, Jean. *Théâtre complet de J. Racine.* Avec des remarques littéraires et un choix de notes classiques par M. Félix Lemaistre. Paris. Garnier. n.d. Pp. xii, 740. U-3116 I

Rahavánez, Rodrigo de. *Contrastes.* Bogotá. Forero Franco. 1905. Pp. xxv, 274. U-1532

Rahola, Federico. *L'Oasis. Poesíes.* Barcelona. Ilustració Catalana. n.d. Pp. 179. U-1405 D
- *Los ingleses vistos por un latino. Impresiones de viaje.* Barcelona. Antonio López. Uc

Raleigh, Thomas. *Política elemental.* Tr. A. Guerra. Madrid. Suárez. 1893. Pp. 114. U-544

Ramacharaka, Yogi, pseud. [i.e., Wm. Walker Atkinson]. *Advanced Course in Yogi Philosophy and Oriental Occultism.* Chicago. Yogi Publ. Soc. 1905. Pp. 337. U-4805
- *Hatha Yoga o Filosofía Yogi del bienestar físico.* Buenos Aires. Centro de Publ. Yogis. 1907. Pp. 291. U-131
- *Catorce lecciones sobre filosofía Yogi y ocultismo oriental. Lección primera.* Buenos Aires. Centro de Publ. Yogis. 1907. Pp. 320. U-1305

Ramakrishna Paramahamsa. *El evangelio de Râmakrishna.* Traducción autorizada del inglés. Buenos Aires. Soc. Vedanta. 1912. Pp. xi, 466. U-1415 I L

Ramalho Ortigão, José Duarte. *O culto da arte em Portugal.* Lisboa. Pereira. 1896. Pp. 176. U-1782 D
- *Rei D. Carlos o martirisado.* Lisboa. 1908. Pp. 18. U-1699

Ramasso, Ambrosio L. *El estadista.* Montevideo. Editor, El Anticuario. 1909. Uc

Rambaud, Alfred. *Histoire de la civilisation française.* 2 vols. Paris. Colin. 1893-4. U-3982-3

Ramírez, Alfonso Francisco. *Discursos parlamentarios.* México. 1926. Pp. 114. U-4934 D

– *Canciones de amor y olvido.* México. 1927. Pp. 127 + 30. U-4940 D

Ramírez Angel, Emiliano. *Cabalgata de horas.* Madrid. Gutenberg-Castro. 1908. Pp. 204. Uc D

Ramoedo, Luis. *Libro iris.* Madrid. Imp. Española. 1916. Pp. 131. U-3610 n/o D

Ramón y Cajal, Santiago. *Reglas y consejos sobre investigación biológica.* 3a ed. Madrid. Moya. 1913. Pp. xv, 279. U-603 D. 4a ed. Madrid. Fortanet. 1916. Pp. xviii, 297. U-2775 D

– *Recuerdos de mi vida.* 2 vols. Madrid. Moya. 1917. U-4841-2 I* D

Ramos, José Antonio. *Manual del perfecto fulanista.* Habana. Montero. 1916. Pp. 363. U-2172 D

Ramos, Juan P. *Historia de la instrucción primaria en la República Argentina (1810-1910).* 2 vols. Buenos Aires. Peuser. 1910. U-753-4 D

Ramos i Duarte, Félix. *Diccionario de mejicanismos.* Pról. R. Gómez. Méjico. Herrero. 1898. Pp. 584. U-1777

Ramos Mejía, Francisco. *Historia de la evolución argentina.* (Obra póstuma). Buenos Aires. La Facultad. 1921. Pp. xv, 415. U-91

Ramos Sanguino, Joaquín. *Historia cómica de Trujillo desde los tiempos más remotos hasta el final del siglo XVIII.* Trujillo. La Minerva. 1913. Uc

Ramos y Loscertales, José Ma. *La formación del dominio y los privilegios del Monasterio de San Juan de la Peña entre 1035 y 1094.* Madrid. Tip. de Archivos. 1929. Pp. 107. U-775 D

Ranke, Leopold von. *Weltgeschichte.* 8 vols. München-Leipzig. Duncker und Humblot. 1921. U-4107-14 I* C*

Rapisardi, Mario. *Poesie religiose.* Catania. Tropea. 1887. Pp. 174. U-3939

– *L'Ascéta.* Catania. Giannota. 1902. Pp. 222. U-3941

Raposo, Hipólito. *Coimbra doutora.* Pref. J. Dantas. Coimbra. Amado. 1910. Pp. xvi, 162. U-3216 D

– *Boa gente.* Coimbra. Amado. 1911. Pp. 230. U-3243 D

– *Livro de horas (1908-1911).* Coimbra. Amado. 1913. Pp. xii, 262. U-2694 I* D

– *Outro mundo.* Coimbra. Amado. 1917. Pp. 195. U-2709 D

Rappoport, Anatole. *Die marxistische Rechtsauffassung.* Riga. Selbstverlage. 1927. Pp. 53. U-5387 I

Ras, Aureli. *Discurs.* Barcelona. Soc. d'Estudis Económics. 1911. Pp. 14. U-4284

Rasch, Gustav. *Das heutige Spanien.* Stuttgart. Kötzle. 1871. Pp. 269. U-3842

Rashdall, Hastings. *The Universities of Europe in the Middle Ages.* Ed. F.M.
Powicke and A.B. Emden. 3 vols. Oxford. Clarendon Press. 1936.
U-5199-5201 I. U-5199 B

Ratti, F.V. *Bruto.* Firenze. Vallecchi. 1925. Pp. 162. U-5346

Rauh, Frédéric. *De la méthode dans la psychologie des sentiments.* Paris.
Alcan. 1899. Pp. 305. U-1785

Raupach, Ernst. *Die Schleichhändler.* Leipzig. Reclam. n.d. Pp. 55. U-4520

Ravaisson, Félix. *De l'habitude.* Introd. J. Baruzi. Paris. Alcan. 1927. Pp. 62.
U-5301

Ravegnani, Giuseppe. *Io e il mio cuore.* Ferrara. Taddei. 1916. Pp. 215.
U-875 D

Ravīndranātha Thākura, Sir. *Gitanjali (Song Offerings).* Introd. W.B. Yeats.
London. Macmillan. 1913. Pp. xxii, 101. U-3865

— *Obras de Rabindranath Tagore. El cartero del rey. Poema dramático.*
Tr. Zenobia Camprubí de Jiménez. Con un poema de Juan Ramón
Jiménez. Madrid. Alcoy. 1917. Pp. 99. U-3515

— *El jardinero.* Tr. Zenobia Camprubí de Jiménez. Con un poema de Juan
Ramón Jiménez. Madrid. 1917. Uc

Raza chilena. Libro escrito por un chileno para los chilenos. Valparaiso.
Schäfer. 1904. Pp. xiii, 743. U-4848 I

Razetti, Luis. *La cruzada moderna.* Tomo I. Caracas. Universal. 1907. Uc D

Reade, Charles. *Peg Woffington and Christie Johnstone.* London. Dent.
[1908]. Pp. ix, 330. U-1071 I*

— *The Cloister and the Hearth, A Tale of the Middle Ages.* Introd. A.C.
Swinburne, London. Dent. [1906]. Pp. 703. U-1072 I* C T

Readings From Modern Spanish Novelists. Sel. and ed. M. Stephenson.
London. Harrap. [1929]. Pp. 139. U-549

Real Academia Española. *Diccionario de la lengua castellana.* Madrid.
Hernando. 1899. Pp. xviii, 1054. n/n

Rebaudi, A. *Guerra del Paraguay. Un episodio. ¡Vencer o morir!* [Tucumán].
Imp. Constancia. 1918. Pp. 188. U-742

Rebaudi, Ovidio. *Elementos de magnetología.* Madrid. Bibl. de la Irradiación.
[1909]. Pp. 448. Uc

Rebolledo, Efrén. *Joyeles.* Paris. Bouret. 1907. Pp. iii, 134. U-649

Rébora, Juan Carlos. *La familia (boceto sociológico y jurídico).* 2 vols.
Buenos Aires. Roldán. 1926. U-4945, U-5766

Reboux, Paul. *La maison de danses.* Paris. Calmann-Lévy. 1904. Pp. 347.
U-3978

— et Charles Muller. *A la manière de ...* Paris. Grasset. 1913. Pp. 330.
U-2382

Recaséns Siches, Luis. *Direcciones contemporáneas del pensamiento jurídico.*
Barcelona. Labor. 1929. Pp. 238. U-5004 D

Récéjac, E. *Essai sur les fondements de la connaissance mystique.* Paris. Alcan.
1897. Pp. 306. U-1283

'Recital poético de Mony Hermelo.' Buenos Aires. Porter. 1935. Ff. 4. U-5776
[Programa]

Reclus, Elisée. *La montaña.* Tr. A. López Rodrigo. Valencia. Sempere. n.d.
Pp. 216. U-3206

Réconciliation. Préf. L. Ragaz. n.p. Editions de 'La Réconciliation.' 1929.
Pp. vi, 194. U-5278

*Reconstitución y europeización de España. Programa para un partido
nacional.* Madrid. Directorio de la Liga Nacional de Productores. 1900.
Pp. xxvi, 366. U-4134

Recueil de dissertations. Sur les apparitions, les visions & les songes. Tome II,
part II, n.p. n.d. Pp. 312. U-488

La reforma. Buenos Aires (enero 1907). n/n

*Reformas a la Ley Constitutiva de la República de Guatemala decretadas por
la asamblea constituyente el 11 de marzo de 1921.* Guatemala. Tip.
Nacional. 1921. Pp. 76. U-2814

Reformas Sociales (Instituto de). Sección la. *Legislación del trabajo. Apéndice
cuarto. Julio 1908–Junio 1909.* Madrid. 1909. Uc. *Apéndice octavo. 1912.*
Madrid. 1913. Uc

— Sección 2a. *Memoria general de la inspección del trabajo correspondiente
al año 1911.* Madrid. Minuesa de los Ríos. 1913. Uc

— *Memoria redactada por la comisión nombrada por el instituto para
estudiar las condiciones del trabajo en las minas de Riotinto.* Madrid.
Minuesa de los Ríos. 1913. Uc

— Sección 3a. *Conflicto de obreros y empleados de las compañías de
ferrocarriles. Septiembre-octubre de 1912.* Madrid. 1913. Uc

Rega Molina, Horacio. *Domingos dibujados desde una ventana.* Buenos Aires.
El Inca. [1928]. Pp. 75. U-4892 D

Rega Molina, Mary. *Canto llano.* Buenos Aires. Ricordi. 1928. Pp. 109.
U-5765

Régio, José. *Jôgo da cabra cega. Romance.* Coimbra. Ediçoes Presença.
1934. Pp. 367. U-255 D

Reglamento General de los Colegios Universitarios de Salamanca. n.d. Ff. 16.
U-5780 [Typescript]

*Reglamento aprobado por el Excmo. Ayuntamiento en sesión del día 28 de
agosto de 1907, para el servicio de carruajes y coches de alquiler con las
reformas acordadas en 23 de octubre siguiente.* Salamanca. Almaráz. 1913.
Pp. 15. U-4726

Reglamento para el régimen del Cuerpo de Guardia municipal de Policia urbana de la ciudad de Salamanca. Salamanca. Almaráz. 1915. Pp. 23. U-4560

Reglamento para el régimen interior del mercado en esta capital. Salamanca. Almaráz. 1909. Pp. 20. U-4508

Reglamento para las corridas de toros en la provincia de Salamanca. Salamanca. Almaráz. 1915. Pp. 36. U-4561

Reich, Emil. *Success Among Nations.* New York. Harper. 1904. Pp. 292. U-4803 I C

Reichls Verlagsbericht. Darmstadt (1923). U-5406

Reid, Whitelaw. *American and English Studies.* 2 vols. New York. Scribner's. 1913. U-3816-17 I C

Reissig, José Luis. *La campaña del General Bulcle.* Buenos Aires. Tall. Gráf. Radio-Revista. 1928. Pp. 159. U-5689

Relgis, Eugen. *L'Internationale pacifiste.* Lettre et message Romain Rolland. Paris. Delpeuch. 1929. Pp. 151. U-5238 D

Rembao, Alberto. *Lupita: A Story of Mexico in Revolution.* Foreword J.A. Mackay. New York. Friendship Press. 1935. Pp. 180. U-1318 I D

La Renaissance Latine. Paris (15 mai 1905). n/n

Renard, Jules. *Journal.* 4 vols. Paris. Bernauard. 1927. QP-41-4 I* C

Rendón, Francisco de P. *Inocencia.* Medellín. Restrepo. 1904. Uc D

Rendón, Victor Manuel. *Olmedo.* Paris. Nilsson. 1904. Pp. 285. U-1890

René-Moreno, Gabriel. *Bolivia y Perú. Nuevas notas históricas y bibliográficas.* Santiago de Chile. Universo. 1907. Pp. xii, 676. U-2336

Rensi, Giuseppe. *Lineamenti di filosofia scettica.* Bologna. Zanichelli. 1921. Pp. 442. U-823 I* C

Reparaz, Gonzalo de. *Política de España en Africa.* Barcelona. Imp. Barcelonesa. 1907. Pp. 469. U-4189 D

– *Aventuras de un geógrafo errante.* 2 vols. Barcelona. Imp. Moderna-Sintes. 1921-2. U-4363-4 I*

Repertorio. San José de Costa Rica, núm. 54 (marzo de 1915). U-4492

Répide, Pedro de. *La negra.* Madrid. Hispania. 1914. Uc D

Representación Nacional en Santa Fé. *1828-29, Actas y otros documentos.* Santa Fé. Imp. de la Provincia. 1928. Pp. liv, 353. U-5745

Resende, García de. *Miscellanea.* Pref. e notas Mendes dos Remedios. Coimbra. Amado. 1917. Pp. xxviii, 165. U-2722

Restrepo, Antonio José. *Poesías originales y traducciones poéticas.* Pról. J. de D. Uribe y carta-pref. Ed. Haraucourt. Lausana. Bridel. 1899. Pp. cxlii, 422. U-257

– *Fuego graneado.* Madrid. Rev. de Arch. 1903. Pp. xxxviii, 866. U-4362

Retamoso, Conde de. *Memoria que eleva al gobierno de S.M. en cumplimiento de lo dispuesto por la ley del 23 de enero de 1906 el delegado regio.* Madrid. Alvarez. 1909. Uc

Retana y Gamboa, Wenceslao Emilio. *Archivo del bibliófilo filipino.*
Recopilación de documentos históricos, científicos, literarios y políticos
y estudios bibliográficos. Vols. IV, V. Madrid. Minuesa de los Ríos. 1898.
U-4388-9
— *La tristeza errante.* Madrid. R. Fé. 1903. Pp. xx, 388. U-1541 I* C D
— *Vida y escritos del Dr José Rizal.* Pról. y epíl. J. Gómez de la Serna y M.
de Unamuno. Madrid. Suárez. 1907. Pp. xvi, 515. U-1712 D
Reuscher, Max. *Der Kampf gegen den Geburtenrückgang in Deutschland*
früher und heute. Stettin. 1935. Pp. 47. U-3732
Revilla, Manuel de la, y Pedro de Alcántara García. *Principios generales de*
literatura e historia de la literatura Española. 2 vols. Madrid. Iravedra y
Novo. 1877. U-4235-6
Revilla, Manuel G. *El arte en México.* México. Porrua. 1923. Pp. 165. U-3540
Réville, Albert. *Jésus de Nazareth. Etudes critiques sur les antécédents de*
l'histoire évangélique et de la vie de Jésus. 2 vols. Paris. Fischbacher. 1897.
U-827-8 I
Revista Blanca. Barcelona (junio 1923). n/n
Revista Contemporánea. Santiago de Chile (enero 1911). n/n
Revista de Avance. La Habana, núms. 17-18 (1927-8). n/n
Revista de Estudios Hispánicos. Nueva York (enero-marzo 1928). n/n
Revista de Filología Española. Madrid (1925-9, 1935-6). n/n [Diverse issues]
Revista de la Facultad de Letras y Ciencias. La Habana (jul.-dic. 1924). n/n
Revista de la Habana, I, 9 (sept. 1930). n/n
Revista del Círculo Médico Argentino y Centro Estudiantes de Medicina
(enero 1915). n/n
Revista del Grupo Minorista de Matanzas, I, 1 (junio 1927). n/n
Revista de Letras y Ciencias Sociales. Tucumán (octubre 1905). U-4080
Revista de Oriente. Buenos Aires. (agosto 1925). n/n
Revista de Pedagogía. Madrid (sept. 1935). n/n
Revista de Vizcaya. Bilbao (1 nov. 1885-15 abril 1886). Uc
Revista Hispanoamericana de Ciencias, Letras y Artes. Madrid.
(enero 1930). n/n
Revista Internacional. Portugal, tomo I. n/n
Revista Jurídica y de Ciencias Sociales, XLIV (nov. 1926-mayo 1927). n/n
Revista Nueva. Madrid (25 mayo, 5 junio, 5 oct. 1899). n/n
Revista Socialista Internacional. Buenos Aires, I, 1-7 (1909). U-1619
Revista Universitaria. Lima, I, 1-4 (1927). n/n
Revue de Dialectologie Romane. Bruxelles, Núms. 1-4 (1909). U-4850.
U-4851-2 n/o
La Revue de France. Paris (15 janvier 1926). n/n
La Revue de Genève (janvier 1923). n/n
La Revue de Paris (1 juin 1925, 1 déc. 1927). n/n
Revue d'Italie. Rome (juine 1917). n/n

La Revue Européenne. Paris (avril 1925). n/n
La Revue Nouvelle, II, 14, 20-4; III, 26-34. n/n
Reyes, Alfonso. *Cuestiones estéticas.* Paris. Ollendorff. [1911]. Pp. 292.
   (2 copies) U-410 D. U-3961
— 'Un tema de "La vida es sueño,"' *Revista de Filología Española* (1917).
   U-1704
— *El suicida. Libro de ensayos.* Madrid. García y Sáez. 1917. Pp. 183.
   U-2737 D
— *Retratos reales e imaginarios.* México. Lectura Selecta. 1920. Pp. 212.
   U-2790 D
— *El plano oblicuo. Cuentos y diálogos.* Madrid. Tip. Europa. 1920. Pp. 128.
   U-2650 D
— *Simpatías y diferencias.* Madrid. Teodoro. 1922. Pp. 199. U-381 D
— *Reloj de sol.* Madrid. Tip. Artística. 1926. Pp. 207. U-4876 I D
— *Pausa.* Paris. Génér. 1926. Pp. 80. U-4936 D
— *El testimonio de Juan Peña.* Rio de Janeiro. Villas Boas. 1930. Ff. 25.
   U-1634 D
— *La saeta.* Trazos José Moreno Villa. Rio de Janeiro. Villas Boas. 1931.
   Pp. 51. U-1663
— *5 Casi sonetos.* París. Poesía. 1931. Ff. 6. U-2497 D
— *Discurso por Virgilio.* México. Contemporáneos. 1931. Ff. 20. U-2235 D
— *Horas de Burgos.* Rio de Janeiro. Villas Boas. 1932. Pp. 91. U-1641 D
— *Tren de ondas. (1924-1932).* Rio de Janeiro. Villas Boas. 1932. Pp. 182.
   U-4877 D
— *Atenea política.* Rio de Janeiro. Fernandez & Irmao. 1932. Pp. 42.
   U-4834 D
Reyes, Arturo. *Las de Pinto.* Madrid. Velasco. 1908. Pp. 215. Uc D
— *Béticas. Poesías.* Madrid. Velasco. 1910. Pp. 205. Uc D
— *Del crepúsculo. Poesías póstumas.* Málaga. Zambrana. 1914. Pp. xxvii,
   250. Uc
Reyes, César. *La sociedad argentina.* Córdoba. La Minerva. 1913. Pp. 642.
   U-725 n/o D
— *Vista fiscal en el proceso Alvaro Carrizo Rueda y Aníbal González.*
   La Rioja. Giraud. 1914. Pp. 303. U-3349
Reyes, Rodolfo. *El juicio de amparo de garantías en el derecho constitucional
   mexicano.* (Conferencia.) Madrid. Ratés. 1916. Pp. 40. U-842 D
— *Benito Juárez. Ensayo sobre un carácter.* Madrid. Ed. Nuestra Raza.
   [1935]. Pp. 217. U-2402 I D
Reyles, Carlos. *La raza de Caín.* Montevideo. Dornaleche y Reyes. 1900.
   Pp. 440. U-1433 D
— *La muerte del cisne.* Paris. Ollendorff. [1910]. Pp. 286. U-3300 D

– *El terruño.* Pról. J.E. Rodó. Montevideo. Renacimiento. 1916. Pp. viii, 373.
    U-3964 I D
– *Diálogos olímpicos.* 1o. *Apolo y Dionisos.* 2o. *Cristo y Mammon.* 2 vols.
    Buenos Aires. Peuser. 1918-19. U-28-9 D [2nd copy of vol. I, U-34]
– *Panoramas del mundo actual.* Montevideo. Imp. Uruguaya. 1932. Pp. 99.
    U-5477 D
Reyna Almandos, Luis. *Poesías.* La Plata. Imp. Oficiales de la Provincia de
    Buenos Aires. 1906. Pp. 203. U-2227 D
– *Dactiloscopia argentina; su historia e influencia en la legislación.* La Plata.
    Sesé. 1909. Pp. lv, 271. Uc
Reynal O'Connor, Arturo. *Los poetas argentinos.* Buenos Aires. Tragant.
    1904. Pp. 379. U-4847 D
– *Noches blancas.* Buenos Aires. Tommasi. 1909. Uc D
Riba Bracons, Carles. *Les bucóliques de Virgili.* Barcelona. Altés Albert.
    [1911]. Pp. 71. U-1136 D
Ribadeneyra, Pedro de. *Vida del Bienaventurado Padre Ignacio de Loyola
    fundador de la religión de la Compañia de Jesús.* Madrid. Apostolado de
    la Prensa. 1900. Pp. 555. U-2724 I C B
– *Tratado de la tribulación.* Madrid. Apostolado de la Prensa. n.d. Pp. 272.
    U-2807
Ribeiro, Bernardim. *Eclogas ... Introdução a psicologia portuguêsa na
    literatura.* Lisboa. 1923. Pp. xxiii, 166. U-2616
Ribeiro, Thomaz. *D. Jayme. Poema.* Porto. Chardron. 1901. Pp. 296.
    U-523 I
Riber, Llorenç. *A sol ixent.* Palma de Mallorca. Amengual y Muntaner. 1912.
    Pp. xiii, 139. U-3649 D
Ribera i Rovira, Ignaci. *Atlantiques. Antologia de poetes portuguesos.*
    Barcelona. L'Avenç. 1913. Pp. 139. U-4447 D
– *Solitaris.* Barcelona. Rafols. 1918. Pp. 80. U-2823 D
Ribera Llovet, Ramón. *Ecloga.* Sabadell. Sallent. 1915. Pp. 47. U-3748 D
Ribera y Tarragó, Julian. *La supresión de los exámenes.* Zaragoza. Comas.
    1900. Pp. 138. U-4454
Ribot, Théodule Armand. *La psychologie allemande contemporaine (ecole
    expérimentale).* Paris. Baillière. 1879. Pp. xxxiv, 368. U-113
– *Les maladies de la mémoire.* Paris. Baillière. 1881. Pp. 170. U-609
– *Psychologie de l'attention.* Paris. Alcan. 1889. Pp. 182. U-3450
– *Les maladies de la volonté.* Paris. Alcan. 1894. Pp. 184. U-2010
Ricardo, David. *The Principles of Political Economy & Taxation.* Introd.
    F.W. Kolthammer. London. Dent. [1911]. Pp. xvi, 300. U-5179 I* C*
Riccardi, Giuseppe. *Casa di Savoja e la rivoluzione italiana. Storia popolare
    degli ultimi trent'anni.* Firenze. Le Monnier. 1889. Pp. 457. U-534

Ricca-Salerno, Giuseppe. *La teoria del valore nella storia delle dottrine e dei fatti economici.* Roma. R. Accademia dei Lincei. 1894. Pp. 173. U-1205 I* C*

Ricci, Clemente. *La significación histórica del cristianismo. La historia de Europa y la segunda Roma.* 2 vols. Buenos Aires. Kidd. 1909. U-749-50 D

Richardson, Samuel. *Pamela.* Introd. G. Saintsbury. 2 vols. London. Dent. [1914]. U-1005-6 I C T

Richet, Charles. *Essai de psychologie générale.* Paris. Alcan. 1887. Pp. xiv, 193. U-363 I

— *Los venenos de la inteligencia.* Buenos Aires. Maucci. n.d. Pp. 135. U-2429

Richter, Jean Paul Friedrich. *Levana oder Erziehlehre.* Leipzig. Reclam. n.d. Pp. 388. U-4513 C

— *Leben des Quintus Fixlein.* Leipzig. Reclam. n.d. Pp. 261. U-4609 T

Rictus, Jehan. *Les soliloques du pauvre.* Paris. Eugène Rey. 1913. Pp. 256. U-1866 I

Rieu-Vernet, A., y J. Ruiz-Conejo. *¡Voz suprema!* Madrid. Velasco. 1915. Pp. 59. U-135 n/o

Rilke, Rainer Maria. *Gedichte.* Leipzig. Insel. n.d. Pp. 79. U-5446.

Il rinnovamento. Milano (feb. 1907). n/n

Río, Angel del. 'Quijotismo y Cervantismo,' *Revista de Estudios Hispánicos,* I, 3 (jul-sept. 1928), 241-67. U-5764 D

Río Joan, Francisco del. *La prevención de los accidentes del trabajo y la higiene industrial.* Madrid. Instituto de Reformas Sociales. 1913. Uc

Río Sainz, José del. *La amazona de Estella.* Santander. La Atalaya. 1926. Pp. 246. U-5052 D

Ríos, Blanca de los. *La rondeña. Cuentos andaluces. El Salvador. Cuentos varios.* Madrid. Moreno. 1902. Pp. 274. U-2165

— *Romancero de Don Jaime El Conquistador.* Madrid. Rubiños. 1891. Pp. 257. U-3038 D

— *Esperanzas y recuerdos. Poesías.* (Obras completas, IV). Madrid. Bernardo Rodríguez. 1912. Pp. 200. U-3579 D

— *Madrid Goyesco* (Obras completas, V). Madrid. Bernardo Rodríguez. 1912. Pp. 283. U-3129 D

— *El tesoro de Sorbas (cuentos)* (Obras completas, VI). Madrid. Bernardo Rodríguez. 1914. Pp. 296. U-877 D

— *Sangre española.* Madrid. Valero Díaz. n.d. Uc D

Ríos Urruti, Fernando de los. *La filosofía del derecho en Don Francisco Giner y su relación con el pensamiento contemporáneo.* Madrid. Bibl. Corona. 1916. Pp. 229. U-1475 D

Ríos y Ríos, Max. *La bella intrusa.* Toulouse. Maurin. 1930. Pp. 315. U-612 n/o

Riou, Gaston. *Aux écoutes de la France qui vient.* Introd. Emile Faguet. Paris.
Grasset. 1913. Pp. 334. U-1151 I* D
— *Journal d'un simple soldat. Guerre. Captivité. 1914-1915.* Préf. Ed. Herriot.
Paris. Hachette. 1916. Pp. xxvii, 249. (2 copies) U-2079, U-3852 n/o D
— *La ciudad doliente. Diario de un soldado raso.* Prefs. M. de Unamuno y
Ed. Herriot. Paris. Ediciones Literarias. [1916]. Pp. 303. U-3273
Ripa Alberdi, Héctor. 'Sor Juana Inés de la Cruz,' *Humanidades,* v (1923).
U-1696 n/o D
Riquer, Alexandre de. *Quan jo era noy.* Barcelona. L'Avenç. 1897. Pp. 192.
U-555 D
— *Crisantemes.* Barcelona. Verdaguer. 1899. Pp. 117. U-3227 D
— *Anyoranses.* Barcelona. Verdaguer. 1902. Pp. 70. U-3228
— *Aplech de sonets. Les cullites.* Barcelona. Verdaguer. 1906. Pp. 154.
U-2337 D
— *Poema del Bosch.* Barcelona. Verdaguer. 1910. Pp. 161. U-1652 D
Ritschl, Albrecht. *Die christliche Lehre von der Rechtfertigung und
Versöhnung.* 2 vols. Bonn. Adolph Marcus. 1870-4. U-107-8 I* C
Ritter, Albert. *Die Religion.* Berlin. Engel und Toeche. 1930. Pp. 100.
U-1989 I B
Riu, Francisco Aníbal. *Por la cultura. Discursos.* Buenos Aires. Tragant. 1916.
Pp. 37. U-4679
Riu i Dalmau, Fidel. *El cant geórgic.* Manresa. Esperbé. 1918. Pp. 136.
U-2428 D
Riva Agüero, José de la. *Carácter de la literatura del Perú independiente.*
Lima. Galland. 1905. Pp. 299. U-4323 I C D
— *La historia en el Perú.* Lima. Barrionuevo. 1910. Pp. 558. U-1841 D
Rivadeneira, P. Pedro de. See Ribadeneyra, Pedro de
Rivarola, Enrique E. *Meñique.* La Plata. Solá y Franco. 1906. Uc D
— *Ritmos.* La Plata. Sesé. 1913. Uc
Rivarola, Rodolfo. *Fernando en el colegio.* Buenos Aires. Revista Argentina
de Ciencias Políticas. 1913. Uc
Rivas, Duque de. See Saavedra, Angel de
Rivas Moreno, Francisco. *Lecherías y queserías cooperativas. Seguro del
ganado.* Pról. V. Alvarado. Valencia. Vives Mora. 1905. Uc
Rivero Astengo, Agustín P. *Anfora llena.* Buenos Aires. Mercatali. 1920.
Ff. 45. U-2882 D
— *Hombres de la organización nacional. Retratos literarios.* Buenos Aires.
Coni. 1936. Pp. 170. U-2192 I D
Rivière, Jacques, et Paul Claudel. *Correspondance 1907-1914.* Paris. Plon.
1926. Pp. xxi, 264. QP-45 I
Rivista di Roma (1 gennaio 1924). n/n

Rivodó, Baldomero. *Entretenimientos filosóficos y literarios.* Caracas. Herrera
    Irigoyen. 1902. Pp. xi, 354. U-2301 D
Rizal, José. *Noli me tangere. Novela tagala.* Barcelona. Maucci. 1903. Uc
— *El filibústerismo. Novela filipina.* Barcelona. Henrich. 1908. Uc
Rizzi, Miguel Angel. *Tratado de derecho privado romano.* Pról. H.C. Rivarola.
    Buenos Aires. Menéndez. 1936. Pp. xiv, 1191. U-761 n/o D
Roberts, Alexander von. *Satisfaktion.* Leipzig. Reclam. n.d. Pp. 90. U-4533
Robertson, Frederick W. *Sermons Preached at Trinity Chapel, Brighton.*
    2 vols. Leipzig. Tauchnitz. 1861. U-4687-8 I*
Robertson, Ricardo. *Diccionario inglés-español y español-inglés.* Barcelona.
    Sopena. 1929. Pp. xxiii, 657 + 535. U-4658
Robertson, William P., y John P. Robertson. *La Argentina en la época de la
    revolución.* Tr. y pról. C.A. Aldao. Buenos Aires. Vaccaro. 1920. Pp. 269.
    U-4231
Robinson, Rev. Wade. *The Philosophy of the Atonement and Other Sermons.*
    Introd. Rev. F.B. Meyer. London. Dent. n.d. Pp. xv, 215. (2 copies)
    U-975 I C. U-5182
Robledo, Alfonso. *Don Miguel Antonio Caro y su obra en el tercer aniversario
    de su muerte.* n.p. 1912. Pp. 133. U-2924 D
Roby, Henry John. *A Grammar of the Latin Language From Plautus to
    Suetonius.* 2 vols. London. Macmillan. 1881-2. U-196-7 I* L* B
Rocuant, Miguel Luis. *Poemas.* Santiago de Chile. Imp. Barcelona. 1905. Uc D
Rodó, José Enrique. *Ariel.* Montevideo. Dornaleche y Reyes. 1900. Pp. 141.
    U-2762 D
— *Liberalismo y Jacobinismo.* Montevideo. La Anticuaria. 1906. Pp. 92.
    U-3945 I D
— *Motivos de Proteo.* Montevideo. Serrano. 1909. Pp. 462. n/n I C* D
— *El mirador de Próspero.* Montevideo. Serrano. 1913. Pp. 570. U-1402 I D
— *Homenaje a Rodó. Selección de motivos de Proteo.* Santiago. Los Diez.
    1917. Pp. 126. U-2869
— *Cinco ensayos. Montalvo. Ariel. Bolívar. Rubén Darío. Liberalismo y
    Jacobinismo.* Madrid. Soc. Española de Libr. [1915]. Pp. 414. U-3264
Rodrigo Lavín, L., y A. Pí y Suñer. *Tratado de fisiología. Fisiología general.*
    Barcelona. Gili. 1900. Pp. viii, 810. U-766 I C*
Rodríguez, Alonso. *Ejercicio de perfección y virtudes cristianas.* 4 vols.
    Madrid. Apostolado de la Prensa. 1898. U-2725-7, U-4439. Vol. I I I
Rodríguez, Gregorio F. *Historia de Alvear. Con la acción de Artigas en el
    período evolutivo de la revolución argentina de 1812 a 1816.* 2 vols.
    Buenos Aires. Mendesky. 1913. U-4238-9 D
— *La patria vieja. Cuadros históricos.* Buenos Aires. Cía. Sud-Americana de
    Billetes de Banco. 1916. Pp. viii, 476. U-3062

Rodríguez, Miguel. *Organización municipal de Buenos Aires. ¿Qué sistema conviene adoptar?* Buenos Aires. Biedma. 1903. Uc D

Rodríguez, Miguel F. *De mi carpeta.* Buenos Aires. Hall. 1910. Uc D

Rodríguez Alcalde, Leopoldo. *Tapices y miniaturas.* Santander. J. Martínez. 1935. Pp. 221. U-4497 D

Rodríguez Avecilla, C. *Los crepúsculos.* Madrid. López del Arco. 1905. Uc D

Rodríguez Bravo, Joaquín. *Estudios constitucionales.* Santiago de Chile. Imp. Victoria. 1888. Pp. xx, 341. U-1174 n/o

– *Balmaceda y el conflicto entre el Congreso y el Ejecutivo.* 2 vols. Santiago de Chile. Gutenberg y Cervantes. 1921-5. U-5743-4 I*

Rodríguez Carracido, José. *Compendio de química orgánica.* Barcelona. Soler. n.d. Uc

Rodríguez Cerna, José. *El libro de las crónijas.* Guatemala. El Jardín. 1914. Pp. 275. Uc D

Rodríguez de la Torre, Walfrido. *El cráneo y la locura.* Buenos Aires. 1887. Pp. 223. U-2578

Rodríguez del Busto, Antonio. *El sistema del gobierno dual de Argentina y su origen.* Buenos Aires. Cía. Sud-Americana de Billetes de Banco. 1906. Pp. 205. Uc

Rodríguez del Busto, Francisco. *El proteccionismo en la República Argentina.* Buenos Aires. Peuser. 1904. Pp. 239, xv. U-1662

– *Problemas económicos y financieros.* Córdoba. La Moderna. 1905. Pp. 219, xv. U-2236

– *Impresiones.* Córdoba. La Moderna. 1905. Pp. 214. U-2614 D

Rodríguez del Busto, N. *Colaboraciones.* Buenos Aires. La Facultad. 1917. Pp. 113. U-2355 D

Rodríguez-Embil, Luis. *Gil Luna, artista.* Madrid. Pérez Villavicencio. 1908. Uc D

– *La insurrección.* Paris. Ollendorff. [1911] Uc

Rodríguez Etchart, Carlos. *La ilusión.* Buenos Aires. Coni. 1912. Pp. 253. U-3462 D

Rodríguez Marín, Francisco. *Varios juegos infantiles del siglo XVI.* Madrid. Tip. de Arch. 1932. Pp. 102. U-4967 D

Rodríguez Mateo, Juan. *Flora. Poemas del campo.* Sevilla. Tall. Gráf. Colectivos. 1934. Pp. 126. U-2846 n/o D

Rodríguez Mendoza, Emilio. *Cuesta arriba.* Paris. Ollendorff. [1909]. Pp. xviii, 295. U-1114

Rodríguez Pereira, Eladio. *Tinta de colores.* Astorga. López. 1912. Uc D

Rodríguez Pinilla, Cándido. *Cantos de la noche.* Pról. J.O. Picón. Madrid. Avrial. 1899. Pp. xiii, 128. (2 copies) U-423. U-3104 D

– *El poema de la tierra.* Pról. M. de Unamuno. Salamanca. Almaráz. 1914. Pp. xix, 132. n/n D

- *Heroísmo y no quijotismo. Conferencia.* Salamanca. Núñez. 1916. Pp. 16. U-4187
- y H. Rodríguez Pinilla. *Un hombre de antaño. Tomás Rodríguez Pinilla (1814-1886). Remembranza.* Salamanca. Núñez. 1926. Pp. 30. U-5768

Rodríguez Pinilla, Hipólito. *Diccionario general hidrológico.* Madrid. Cosano. 1916. Pp. 408. U-5507

Rodríguez Sanjurjo, Primitivo. *Las mesetas ideales. Poesías.* Madrid. A. Marzo. 1910. Uc D

Rodríguez Villa, Antonio. *Crónicas del Gran Capitán.* Madrid. Bailly-Baillière. 1908. Pp. lxx, 612. (NBAE, 10). U-45 I* L

Rodríguez y Rodríguez, Manuel, auxiliado por Angel Longa. *Origen filológico del romance castellano.* Santiago. Escuela Tip. Municipal. 1905. Pp. xxiii, 586. U-4190 D

Rohde, Erwin. *Psyche. Seelencult und Unsterblichkeitsglaube der Griechen.* Tübingen. Mohr. 1907. Pp. 448. U-700 I

Roig i Llop, Tomás, Salvi Valenti, i Ernest Albert Galter. *L'Obra de la B.C.A.I. Tres conferències.* Barcelona. Bibl. Catalana d'Autors Independents. 1934. Pp. 139. U-2879

Rojas, Fernando de. *La Celestina. Tragi-comedia de Calisto y Melibea.* Madrid. Bibl. Universal, 1878. Uc

Rojas, Nerio A. *Psicología de Sarmiento.* Buenos Aires. La Facultad. 1916. Pp. 171. U-1455 D

Rojas, Ricardo. *La victoria del hombre.* Buenos Aires. Imp. Europea. 1903. Pp. xvi, 150. U-2367 D

- *El país de la selva.* Paris. Garnier. 1907. Pp. xii, 268. U-1436 D
- *Cartas de Europa.* Barcelona. Sopena. 1908. Pp. 269. U-2142 n/o
- *Los lises del blasón.* Buenos Aires. Martín García. 1911. Pp. 202. U-2045 D
- *Blasón de plata. Meditaciones y evocaciones ... sobre el abolengo de los argentinos.* Buenos Aires. Martín García. 1912. Pp. 249. U-2932 D
- 'La literatura argentina,' *Revista de la Universidad de Buenos Aires,* XXI (1913). U-1697 D
- *La Universidad de Tucumán.* Buenos Aires. Lib. de E. García. 1915. Pp. 160. (2 copies) U-383, U-2399 n/o D
- *La literatura argentina.* 3 vols. Buenos Aires. Coni. 1917-20. U-4243-5. Vols. II-III I* C B. Vols. I-II L*
- *El Cristo invisible.* Buenos Aires. La Facultad. 1928. Pp. 378. U-1322 n/o
- *La obra de Ricardo Rojas. XXV años de labor literaria. Homenaje.* Pról. A. Chiappori. Buenos Aires. La Facultad. 1928. Pp. 591. U-4976
- *Elelín.* Buenos Aires. La Facultad. 1929. Pp. 216. U-5675 I C D
- *Cervantes.* Buenos Aires. La Facultad. 1935. Pp. xvii, 424. U-2943 D
- *El alma española.* Valencia. Sempere. n.d. Uc D

Rojas Vincenzi, Ricardo. *Flores de almendro.* Pról. M. Ugarte. San José,
C.R. Trejos. 1927. Pp. 46. U-5142 D
— *Crítica literaria.* Pról. Gabriela Mistral. San José, C.R. Borrasé. 1929.
Pp. 63. U-4899 I D
Rolán, Feliciano. *De mar a mar.* Madrid. Aguirre. 1934. Pp. 71. U-2296 D
Roldán, Esteban. *Francia y los católicos españoles.* Barcelona. Borrás. 1915.
Pp. 106. U-120 n/o
Rolla, Giuseppe. *Pensiero e realtà.* Genova. Formiggini. 1913. Pp. 42. U-690 D
Rolland, Romain. *Jean Christophe.* 4 vols. Paris. Ollendorff. 1907-8.
U-2110-13 I
— *Jean Christophe à Paris.* 3 vols. Paris. Ollendorff. 1908-9. U-2107-9 I C
— *Vida de Beethoven.* Tr. J.R. Jiménez. Con unas palabras de Romain
Rolland a la Residencia de Estudiantes. Madrid. Residencia de Estudiantes.
1915. Pp. 182. U-3165
Román y Calvet, Juan. *Los nombres e importancia arqueológica de las Islas
Pythiusas.* Barcelona. L'Avenç. 1906. Pp. viii, 342. U-3529 D
Romano, Julio. *Cabrera, el tigre del maestrazgo.* Madrid. Pueyo. 1936. Pp. 258.
U-384 D
Romano, Luis. *De la vida.* Salamanca. Iglesias. 1904. Pp. 93. U-2801 D
— *Tardes de otoño.* Salamanca. Calón. 1908. Pp. 125. Uc D
Romanones, Conde de. See Figueroa y Torres, Alvaro de
Romera Navarro, Miguel. *Ensayo de una filosofía feminista (refutación a
Moebius).* Pról. Segismundo Moret. Madrid. Revista Técnica de Infantería
y Caballería. 1909. Pp. xiv, 244. U-3757 I
— *El hispanismo en Norte-América.* Madrid. Renacimiento. 1917. Pp. xii,
451. U-1971
Romero, Rafael (Alonso Quesada, pseud.). *El lino de los sueños.* Pról. M. de
Unamuno y epístola en versos castellanos T. Morales. Madrid. 1915.
Pp. xvii, 145. n/n D
— *La umbría. Poema dramático.* Madrid. Atenas. 1922. Pp. 222. U-4628 D
Romero, Rómulo A. *Voces de mi vergel.* Buenos Aires. Caras y Caretas. 1914.
Pp. 197. Uc D
— *Néctar de hipocrene.* Buenos Aires. Caras y Caretas. 1915. Uc D
— *Confidencias. Poesías.* Buenos Aires. Agencia General de Libr. y Publ. n.d.
Pp. 246. U-3627 D
Romero de Terreros, Manuel. *Historia sintética del arte colonial de México.
(1521-1821).* México. Porrúa. 1922. Pp. 89. U-4720
Romero Flores, H.R. *Perfil moral de nuestra hora.* Madrid. Yunque. 1935.
Pp. 273. U-4285 D
Romero y Rizo, José María. *Muñoz Torrero. Apuntes histó ricos-biográficos.*
Cádiz. Alvárez. 1911. Pp. 143. Uc D

Ronsard, Pierre de. *Poésies choicies.* Paris. Payot. 1924. Pp. xiv, 302.
QP-46 I* C*

Roosevelt, Theodore. *The Strenuous Life. Essays and Addresses.* New York.
The Century Co. 1901. Pp. 225. U-1160 I*

— *La guerra mundial. Norte-América y la situación mexicana.* Tr. J. Lara.
Barcelona. Maucci. 1915. Pp. 321. Uc

Ros, Francisco J. *Discurso inaugural del Instituto Histórico y Geográfico
del Uruguay.* Montevideo. Renacimiento. 1917. Pp. 19. U-4260

Rosales, José Miguel. *Historias y paisajes.* Pról. A. Gómez Restrepo. Barcelona.
Henrich. 1909. Pp. 242. U-2104 D

Rosales, Ramón. *El 20 de noviembre de 1910 y el patriota ciudadano Dr
Francisco Vázquez Gómez.* San Antonio, Texas. Rosales. 1920. Pp. 45.
U-3377 D

Rosenkranz, Hans. *El Greco and Cervantes in the Rhythm of Experience.*
Tr. Marcel Aurousseau. London. Peter Davies. 1932. Pp. 204. U-5203 I C

Roso de Luna, Mario. *Preparación al estudio de la fantasía humana bajo el
doble aspecto de la realidad y del enseueño.* 2 vols. Mahón. Fábregas.
1902. Uc D

— *Hacia la gnosis. Ciencia y teosofía.* Madrid. Pueyo. 1909. Pp. 236.
U-3090 D

Ross, Agustín. *La question du pacifique. A qui doivent revenir Tacna et
Arica? Au Chili, au Pérou ou à la Bolivie?* Paris. Desfossés. 1919. Pp. 40.
U-385 I

Ross Múgica, Luis. *Más allá del Atlántico.* Pról. M. de Unamuno. Epíl.
C. Bernaldo de Quirós. Valencia. Sempere. [1909]. Pp. xxi, 209.
U-2421

Rosselló de Son Forteza, Joan. *Manyoc de fruita mallorquina.* Prol. Mn.
Miquel Costa y Llobera. Barcelona. Publ. Catalunya. 1903. Pp. 242.
U-3384 I D

Rossetti, Christina. *Poems of Christina Rossetti.* Chosen and ed. William M.
Rossetti. London. Macmillan. 1905. Pp. xxvi, 332. U-1422 I* B T

Rossetti, Dante Gabriel. *Poems.* Memoir of the author by Franz Hüffer.
Leipzig. Tauchnitz. 1873. Pp. xxvi, 282. U-4770 I T

Rossi, Ecio. *Ingenuidades.* Rosario de Santa Fé. Bitetti. 1935. Pp. 76.
U-583 D

Rossi, Pasquale. *Místicos y sectarios.* Tr. J. Buixó Monserdá. 2 vols. Barcelona.
Henrich. 1905. Uc

— *El alma de la muchedumbre.* Tr. R. Carreras. 2 vols. Barcelona. 1906. Uc

— *Los sugestionadores y la muchedumbre.* Tr. Félix Limendoux. Barcelona.
Henrich. 1906. Pp. 146. Uc

— *Psicología colectiva morbosa.* Tr. M. y C. Santiago-Fuentes. 2 vols.
Barcelona. Carbonell y Esteva. 1908. Uc

Rossi Denevi, Alfredo C. *Ritmos heróicos (Poesías).* Pról. A.P. Rivero Astengo. Buenos Aires. 1921. Pp. 80. U-1965 n/o D

Rouff, Marcel. *Les devoirs de l'amitié.* Paris. Les Cahiers de Paris. 1926. Pp. 91. U-5307 D

Rougemont, Denis de. *Politique de la personne.* Paris. Ed. 'Je Sers.' 1934. Pp. 255. U-1383 I* D

Roule, Louis. *L'Embryologie générale.* Paris. Reinwald. 1893. Pp. xiv, 510. U-1400

Roure y Figueras, Narciso. *Las ideas de Balmes.* Madrid. Perlado, Páez. 1910. Pp. 338. U-2083 D

— *La vida y las obras de Balmes.* Madrid. Perlado, Páez. 1910. Pp. xii, 352. U-278 D

Rousseau, Jean Jacques. *Emile ou l'éducation.* 3 vols. Paris. Didot. 1817. U-4581-3 I

— *Rêveries d'un promeneur solitaire.* Uc

Roussel, Louis. *Palamas et Mistral.* Montpellier. Hestia. 1930. Pp. 16. U-4277

Rousselot, Paul. *Los místicos españoles.* Versión española precedida de una advertencia preliminar por P. Umbert. 2 vols. Barcelona. Henrich. 1907. U-919-20 I

Rovira i Virgili, Antoni. *Diccionari Catalá-Castellá & Castellá-Catalá.* Barcelona. López. 1914. Pp. xiv, 840. n/n D

— *Historia dels moviments nacionalistes.* Pròl. Pere Corominas. 3 vols. Barcelona. Soc. Catalana d'Edicions. 1912-14. U-3902-4 D

Royère, Jean. *Masques et idées. Frontons.* Paris. Seheur. [1932]. Pp. 221. U-4022 D

Royo, F.C. *Flores y lágrimas.* Barcelona. Taberner. n.d. Pp. 48. U-2174 D

Royo Villanova, Antonio. *La descentralización y el regionalismo. (Apuntes de actualidad).* Pról. Joaquín Costa. Zaragoza. Gasca. 1900. Pp. xix, 121. U-4653

— *Ciencia política.* Barcelona. Gili. 1903. Pp. 185. U-1573

— *El problema catalán. Impresiones de un viaje a Barcelona.* Madrid. Suárez. 1908. Pp. xi, 286. U-3874 D

— *Cuestiones obreras.* Pról. Gumersindo de Azcárate. Valladolid. Imp. Castellana. 1910. Pp. 247. U-4175 n/o

— *El nacionalismo regionalista y la política internacional de España.* Conferencia. Madrid. Justo Martínez. 1918. Pp. 39. U-3954

Royo Villanova, Luis. *Manchas de tinta.* Pról. S. y A. Alvarez Quintero. Madrid. Bergne. 1935. Pp. 509. U-3870

Royo Villanova, Ricardo. *La locura de D. Quixote.* Zaragoza. Casañal. 1905. Pp. 30. U-1701

Roz, Firmin. *L'Energie américaine.* Paris. Flammarion. 1911. Uc

Rubio, David. *Los Agustinos en el Perú.* Lima. Torres. 1912. Pp. 101.
  U-4264 D
— *Cantos de mi juventud. Poesías.* Pról. P.M. Vélez. Lima. Moreno. [1911].
  Pp. lxiv, 128. Uc D
Rubio, Laura. *Libro de horas.* Guatemala. Ritmo. [1929]. Pp. 91.
  U-5046 n/o D
Rubio y Galí, Federico. *La mujer gaditana. Apuntes de economía social.*
  Pról. Luis Marco. Madrid. Moreno. 1902. Pp. xxx, 344. U-1666 I
Rubió y Lluch, Antonio. *Catalunya a Grecia. Estudis historics i literaris.*
  Barcelona. L'Avenç. 1906. Pp. 102. U-4453
Rubris, Marcus de. *L'Eterno viandante. Favola umana.* Milano. Sandron. 1911.
  Pp. 186 + 16. U-3301
Rucabado, Ramón. *Tres apòlegs.* Barcelona. Vives. 1914. Pp. 26. U-3523 D
Rueda Santos, Salvador. *El ritmo.* Madrid. Hernández. 1894. Pp. 152. Uc D
— *Fuente de salud. Poesías.* Pról. M. de Unamuno. Madrid. Rueda. 1906.
  Pp. iii, 256. U-3358 D
— *Trompetas de órgano.* Pról. M. Ugarte. Madrid. Fernández. 1907. Pp. xxxii,
  172. U-3347 D
Ruimar, Cándido. See Ruiz Martínez, Cándido
Ruiz, Diego. *Genealogio de los símbolos.* 2 vols. Barcelona. Henrich. 1905. Uc
— *Teoría del acto entusiasta.* Pról. Dorado Montero. Barcelona. Serra y
  Russell. 1906. Pp. xiv, 139. U-3574 D
— 'Los orígenes de la interpretación psiquiátrica de la historia humana.
  ¿Qué es el genio de la interpretación psiquiátrica de la historia?'
  La Semana Médica. Buenos Aires (1914). U-4105
Ruiz, Eduardo B. *Versos.* Buenos Aires. Rosas. 1906. Uc D
Ruiz, Gustavo A. *Epistolario fragante. Poesías.* Buenos Aires. Mercatali.
  1916. Pp. 136. U-403 n/o D
Ruiz, Juan, Arcipreste de Hita. *Libro de buen amor.* Ed. y notas J. Cejador
  y Frauca. 2 vols. Madrid. La Lectura. 1913. U-930-1 I* L*
Ruiz Almansa, Javier. *Sensaciones de residencia y de camino.* Madrid.
  Hércules. 1921. Pp. xv, 189. U-3391 D
Ruiz Carnero, C., y José Mora Guarnido. *El libro de Granada.* la parte.
  Los hombres. Granada. Traveset. 1915. Pp. 126. U-4341
Ruiz de Obregón y Retortillo, Angel. *Vasco Núñez de Balboa. Historia del
  descubrimiento del océano pacífico escrita con motivo del cuarto
  centenario de su fecha, 1913.* Barcelona. Maucci. [1913]. Pp. 191.
  U-1955
Ruiz de Villa, Manuel. *Sobre el corazón del silencio.* Le saluda: A. Casanueva.
  Le presenta: W. Roces. Santander. J. Martínez. 1925. Pp. xviii, 197.
  U-5635 D

Ruiz Guiñazú, Alejandro. *Andrómeda*. Buenos Aires. La Facultad. 1936. Pp. 207. U-5047 D

Ruiz Gutiérrez, A. *Tesoro del viajero*. Buenos Aires. Kraft. 1898. Pp. 357. U-3373 D

Ruiz López, Rafael. *La verdadera redención*. Barcelona. Maucci. 1907. Uc D

Ruiz Martínez, Cándido. *España colonizadora*. Madrid. Helénica. 1921. Pp. 95. U-1574 n/o

Ruiz y Contreras, Luis. *El pedestal*. Madrid. Imp. Marzo. 1898. Pp. 92. Uc D

Ruiz y Pablo, Angel. *Clara sombra*. Barcelona. Estudio. 1915. Pp. 184. U-3672 D

Rusiñol, Santiago. *Anant pel món*. Barcelona. L'Avenç. 1896. Pp. 256. U-3735 T D

– *Fulls de la vida*. Barcelona. L'Avenç. 1898. Pp. 269. U-2250 D

– *El jardí abandonat*. Barcelona. L'Avenç. 1900. Pp. 89. U-2160

– *El pueblo gris*. Madrid. Williams. 1904. Uc

– *El mistic*. Barcelona. L'Avenç. 1904. Pp. 256. U-3993 D

– *El català de 'La Mancha.'* Barcelona. López. [1914]. Pp. 293. U-3934 D

Ruskin, John. *Unto This Last. Four Essays on the First Principles of Political Economy*. London. Ballentyne, Hansor and Co. 1895. Pp. xx, 199. U-359 T

– *Fragments*. Tr. de l'anglés amb un assaig introd. Cebrià Montoliu. Barcelona. L'Avenç. 1901. Pp. 201. U-573

– *Natura*. Aplech d'estudis y descripcions de sas bellesas, triats d'entre las obras de J. Ruskin. Tr. y ordenats Cebrià Montoliu. Barcelona. Joventut. 1903. Pp. xxxii, 246. U-3234

– *The Stones of Venice*. 2 vols. Leipzig. Tauchnitz. 1906. U-4765-6. Vol. ɪ I

La Russie. Rapport officiel de la Délégation Britannique des Trades-Unions en Russie et au Caucase. Novembre et Décembre 1924. Paris. L'Humanité. 1925. Pp. 233. U-5254

Der Russische Gedanke. Bonn (1929). n/n

Russo, Andrea. *In memoria del Cav. Marcellino Pizzarelli*. Catania. Pastore. 1907. Pp. 24. U-4131 n/o D

Ryner, Han. *L'Individualisme dans l'antiquité. Histoire et critique*. Paris. Le Fauconnier. 1924. Pp. 74. U-5237 D

Saavedra, Alberto. *A linguagem médica popular de Fiahlo*. Porto. Renascença Portuguesa. 1916. Pp. 73. U-526 D

Saavedra, Angel de, Duque de Rivas. *Romances*. 2 vols. Madrid. La Lectura. 1912. U-914-15

Saavedra, Osvaldo. *Grandezas chicas*. Buenos Aires. Moen. 1901. Uc D

Saavedra de Cervantes, M., pseud. [i.e., Manuel Lugilde Huerta]. *Panquijote*. Madrid. Tebares. 1906. Uc D

Sabat Ercasty, Carlos. *Poemas del hombre.* Montevideo. La Joya Literaria.
    1921. Pp. 151. (2 copies) U-3095, U-5472
— *Poemas del hombre. Libro del mar.* Montevideo. Escuela Industrial. 1922.
    Pp. 91. U-5499 D
— *Vidas. Poemas.* Montevideo. Escuela Industrial. 1923. Pp. 118. U-5146 D
— *El vuelo de la noche. Poemas.* Montevideo. Escuela Industrial. 1925.
    Pp. 157. U-5473 D
Sabatier, Louis Auguste. *Esquisse d'une philosophie de la religion d'après la
    psychologie et l'histoire.* Paris. Fischbacher. 1897. Pp. xvi, 415. U-3170
Sabatier, Paul. *Vie de S. François d'Assise.* Paris. Fischbacher. 1894. Pp. cxxvi,
    418. U-1796 I
Sá-Carneiro, Mario de. *A confissão de Lucio.* Lisboa. Casa do Autor. 1914.
    Pp. xvii, 206. U-2141 D
Sacchi, Filippo. *Citta'.* Milano. Alpes. 1923. Pp. 211. U-3584 I D
Sachsel Lichtenstein, Olga. *Spanische novellen.* Dresden. Aurora. 1918.
    Pp. 124. U-1995 D
Sacs, Joàn, pseud. [i.e., Felíu Elias]. *La pintura francesa moderna fins el
    cubisme.* Pròl. Joaquim Folguera. Barcelona. La Revista. 1917. Pp. 192.
    U-3224 I D
Sáenz, Raquel. *La almohada de los sueños. Poemas.* Pról. L. Ruiz Contreras.
    Madrid. Helénica. [1926]. Pp. 160. U-5649
Sáenz Hayes, Ricardo. *Almas de crepúsculo.* Pról. M. Ugarte. Paris. Garnier.
    [1909]. Pp. viii, 161. U-568 D
— *Las ideas actuales.* Valencia. Sempere. 1910. Pp. 237. U-3186 D
— *La polémica de Alberdi con Sarmiento y otras páginas.* Buenos Aires.
    Gleizer. 1926. Pp. 174. U-5491 I* D
— *Los amigos dilectos.* Buenos Aires. Gleizer. 1927. Pp. 177. U-5622 D
— *Antiguos y modernos.* Buenos Aires. Agencia General de Libr. y Publ.
    1927. Pp. 180. U-5611 D
Sáenz Peña, Roque. *Escritos y discursos.* Tomo I. *Actuación internacional.*
    Buenos Aires. Peuser. 1914. Pp. 476. U-3537
Saetas populares. Recogidas, ordenadas, y anotadas Agustín Aguilar Tejera.
    Madrid. Cía. Ibero Americana de Publ. 1928. Pp. xxvi, 263. U-5056
Sagarmínaga, Fidel de. *Memorias históricas de Vizcaya.* Bilbao. Delmas.
    1880. Pp. lxxv, 511. U-1106 n/o
Sagarra, Josep M. *Primer llibre de poemes.* Barcelona. La Neotipia. 1914.
    Pp. 101. U-674 D
— *El mal caçador.* Barcelona. Altés. [1916]. Pp. 141. U-673 D
Sagastume, José Pío. *Bocetos criollos.* La Plata. Larrañaga y Cía. 1908.
    Pp. viii, 267. Uc D
— *La Sarmiento. Viaje mundial. Memorias de un conscripto.* Buenos Aires.
    Martín García. 1910. Pp. 190. U-4800 D

– *Los vascos en la Argentina. Psicología del inmigrante.* La Plata. Gasparini.
  n.d. Pp. 126. U-3192 n/o D
Sage, M. *La yoga ou le chemin de l'union divine.* Paris. Nourry. 1915. Pp. 118.
  U-1356 I D
Sagitario. La Plata, núms. 1, 2 (1925); núms. 8-12 (1927). n/n
Said Armesto, Víctor. *La leyenda de Don Juan. Orígenes poéticos de 'El
  burlador de Sevilla y el convidado de piedra.'* Madrid. Hernando. 1908.
  Pp. 302. U-2691 I C D
Saint Martin, Louis Claude de. *Il filósofo sconosciuto.* Tr., introd., e note
  Aldo de Rinaldis. Napoli. Perrella. 1908. Pp. lviii, 216. U-1528
Saint-Sulpice, M. le Curé de. *Vie de Saint François de Sales d'après les
  manuscrits et les auteurs contemporains.* 2 vols. Paris. Lecoffre. 1856. n/n
Saint-Victor, Paul de. *Las dos carátulas. Sófocles, Eurípides, Aristófanes,
  Calidasa.* Tr. M.R. Blanco-Belmonte. Paris. Ollendorff. Uc
Saintine, Xavier-Boniface. *Picciola.* Paris. Hachette. 1883. Pp. xxxi, 341.
  U-2654 T*
Saintyves, P. *Les responsabilités de l'Allemagne dans la guerre de 1914.* Paris.
  Nourry. 1915. Pp. 551. U-3628 I* D
Sáinz Rodríguez, Pedro. *Introducción a la historia de la literatura mística en
  España.* Madrid. Voluntad. 1927. Pp. 310. U-3714 I B D
Sáiz, Concepción. *Lecturas escolares.* Notas históricas y páginas selectas de
  literatura castellana. 2 vols. Madrid. Suárez. 1913-14. Uc
Sáiz de la Mora, Jesús. *Por caminos de España* (Castilla, Andalucía, Cataluña).
  Habana. La Propagandista. 1929. Pp. 191. U-5040 D
Sáiz y Otero, Concepción, y Urbano González Serrano. *Cartas ... ¿Pedagógicas?
  Ensayos de psicología pedagógica.* Pról. Adolfo Posada. Madrid. Suárez.
  1895. Pp. 383. U-148 I C D
Salado, Luis. *En marcha.* Madrid. F. Fé. 1905. Uc D
Salamanca, Octavio. *Nuestra vida republicana.* Cochabamba. Ponce de León.
  1916. Pp. 289. U-660 I
Salas, Carlos P. *El periodismo en la provincia de Buenos Aires. Año 1907.*
  La Plata. Taller de Impresiones Oficiales. 1908. Uc
Salas, Luis M. *Ensayo de psicología celular.* Mérida, Venezuela. El Posta
  Andino. n.d. Pp. 28. U-5485
Salaverría, José Ma. *Vieja España. Impresión de Castilla.* Pról. B. Pérez Galdós.
  Madrid. Hernando. 1907. Pp. xxxvi, 189. U-3348 I D
– *La Virgen de Aránzazu.* Madrid. Pueyo. 1909. Uc D
– *Nicéforo el bueno.* Madrid. Pueyo. 1909. Pp. 202. U-655 D
– *Tierra argentina.* Madrid. F. Fé. 1910. Pp. 229. U-2430 D
– *Cuadros europeos.* Madrid. Pueyo. 1916. Pp. 319. U-3433 D
Salcedo Ruiz, Angel. *Historia de España. Resumen crítico e historia gráfica de
  la civilización española.* Madrid. Calleja. [1914]. Pp. 969. U-1264 I*

- *La literatura española. Resumen de historia crítica.* 3 vols. Madrid. Calleja. 1915-16. U-1757-9

Saldaña, Quintiliano. *Las corridas. Novela de pasión y entendimiento.* Madrid. Pérez Torres. 1914. Pp. 190. U-3260 D

Saldías, Adolfo. *Historia de la confederación argentina. Rozas y su época.* 5 vols. Buenos Aires. Lajouane. 1892. U-2195-9

- *Cervantes y El Quijote.* Buenos Aires. Lajouane. 1893. Pp. 277. U-2950
- *La evolución republicana durante la revolución argentina.* Buenos Aires. Moen. 1906. Pp. 503. U-2194
- *Vida y escritos del P. Casteñeda.* Buenos Aires. Moen. 1907. Uc

Salinas, Pedro. *Seguro azar.* Madrid. Revista de Occidente. [1929]. Pp. 129. U-5039 D

Salinas, Wérfield A. *Sarmiento.* Buenos Aires. La Industrial. 1910. Pp. 322. U-1937 I* D

Sallustius Crispus. *Bellum Catilinarium et Iugurthinum.* Commentariis Joannis Min-Ellii. Matriti. Apud Michaelem Escribano. 1775. Pp. 408. (2 copies) U-1566. U-1523 L

- *De conjuratione Catilinae.* Texte latin. Publié R. Lallier. Paris. Hachette. n.d. Pp. iv, 190. U-5281 I
- *Jugurtha.* Expliqué littéralement, tr. en français et annoté M. Croiset. Paris. Hachette. n.d. Pp. 398. QP-47 I

Salom Solbes, José. *Solución racional, positiva, práctica y estable al llamado problema social.* Madrid. R. Fé. 1904. Pp. 578. U-1832 D

Salterain Herrera, Eduardo de. *La casa grande.* Montevideo. Palacio del Libro. 1928. Pp. 216. U-5130 D

- *Fuga.* Montevideo. Palacio del Libro. 1929. Pp. 183. U-5055 D

Salvá, Vicente. *Gramática de la lengua castellana segun ahora se habla.* Paris. Salvá. 1844. Pp. xxxix, 471. U-2821

Salvat Ciurana, Ramón. *Desde Berlín. Cartas y artículos científicos, literarios y artísticos.* Barcelona. Jepús. 1892. Pp. 162. Uc

Salvemini, Gaetano. *Mazzini.* Roma. La Voce. 1920. Pp. 174. U-1320 I* C

- *The Fascist Dictatorship in Italy.* New York. Holt. [1927]. Pp. 319. U-5187 I

Samadhy, Allan, pseud. [i.e., Higinio Espíndola]. *Horas perdidas.* Santiago de Chile. Miranda. 1908. Pp. 185. U-3199 I D

- *Poesías, libamen, humos y otras.* Hamburgo. Bitter. 1928. Pp. 159. U-5038

Sammartino, Victor. *Verdad desnuda. Poesías.* Buenos Aires. Fueyo. 1910. Pp. 144. U-3882 n/o D

Sánchez, Luis Alberto. *Don Ricardo Palma y Lima.* Lima. Torres Aguirre. 1927. Pp. xx, 144. U-4898 D

Sánchez-Albornoz y Menduiña, Claudio. *Estampas de la vida en León durante el siglo X.* Pról. R. Menéndez Pidal. Madrid. Espasa-Calpe. 1934. Pp. xvi, 199. U-1644 I L

Sánchez Alonso, Benito. *Fuentes de la historia española.* Pról. Rafael Altamira. Madrid. Centro de Estudios Históricos. 1919. Pp. xxi, 448. U-686 D

Sánchez de Castro, Manuel. *La gracia. Apuntes para una filosofía del arte.* Sevilla. María Auxiliadora. 1903. Pp. viii, 510. Uc

Sánchez de Toca, Joaquín. *Reconstitución de España en vida de economía política actual.* Madrid. Ratés Martín. [1911]. Pp. lx, 393. U-1297

— *Las cardinales directivas del pensamiento contemporáneo en la filosofía de la historia.* Madrid. La Lectura. [1918]. Pp. 205. U-409

Sánchez Días, Ramón. *Amores.* Madrid. Hernández. 1901. Pp. 136. U-4427 D

— *Mis viajes.* Madrid. F. Fé. 1901. Pp. 133. U-4673

— *Odios.* Madrid. F. Fé. 1903. Pp. 171. U-250 L

Sánchez Jara, Diego. *Libro de las gestas españolas.* Murcia. Casa del Niño. 1933. Pp. 162. U-4863 D

Sánchez Lustrino, Ricardo V. *Cosas del terruño y cosas mías.* Santo Domingo, R.D. Bernier. 1912. Pp. 176. Uc D

— *Pro-psiquis.* Valencia. Sempere. Uc D

Sánchez Mazas, Rafael. *Pequeñas memorias de Tarin.* Bilbao. Bibl. de Amigos del País. 1915. Pp. xix, 339. U-859 I* C

— *XV Sonetos de Rafael Sánchez Mazas para XV esculturas de Moisés de Huerta.* Bilbao. Lux. 1917. Ff. 16. U-3406 D

Sánchez Moguel, Antonio. *Reparaciones históricas. Estudios peninsulares.* Primera Serie. Madrid. Imp. y Lit. de los Huérfanos. 1894. Pp. xvi, 302. U-942

Sánchez Rojas, José. *Paisajes y cosas de Castilla.* Madrid. Edit. América. 1919. Pp. 232. U-2043 D

— *Castilla y Cataluña. Madrid y Barcelona. Conferencia.* Valladolid. Montero y Ferrari. 1919. Pp. 28. U-5698 D

— *Elogio de José María Gabriel y Galan.* Madrid. Mundo Latino. 1926. Pp. 42. U-5113

Sánchez Ruiz, Antonio [Hamlet-Gómez, pseud.]. *Inri. El pantano.* Madrid. Rev. de Archivos. 1908. Pp. 178. U-2917 D

— *Del alma de Andalucía.* Madrid. Alvarez. 1909. Pp. 184. U-256 D

— *Verdes, negros, azules, rojos.* Madrid. 1910. Uc D

Sánchez Sorondo, Matías Guillermo. *La instrucción obligatoria.* Buenos Aires. Coni. 1915. Pp. 116. U-843 D

Sánchez Viamonte, Carlos. *El derecho de juzgar y otros discursos.* La Plata. Imp. El Libro. 1922. Pp. 122. U-3899 D

Sánchez Villalba, Anselmo. *Nieblas al amanecer.* Buenos Aires. López. 1936. Pp. 377 n/n D

Sancho, Antonio. *Análisis social.* Madrid. F. Marqués. 1908. Uc D

Sanctis, Gaetano de. *Storia dei Romani.* Vol. IV. *La fondazione dell'imperio.*
Torino. Bocca. 1923. Pp. 616. U-4823

Sandburg, Carl. *Selected Poems of Carl Sandburg.* Ed. Rebecca West. New
York. Harcourt, Brace and Co. 1926. Pp. 289. U-5219 I* L* T

Sanders, Daniel. *Handwörterbuch der deutschen Sprache.* Leipzig. Wigand.
1878. Pp. 1067. U-1255

Sandoval, Lisandro. *Diccionario de raíces griegas y latinas y de otros orígines
del idioma español.* Tomo I. *Raíces griegas.* Guatemala. Tip. Nacional.
1930. Pp. lxxii, 932. U-3535 D

Sandoval, Manuel. *El abogado del diablo.* Valladolid. Bibl. Studium. 1915.
Pp. 239. U-4695 D

San Jordi, Jordi de. See Sant Jordi, Jordi de

San Martín, José de. *Mis profetas locos.* Buenos Aires. Tommasi. 1909. Uc D

Sanmartin, Olyntho. *Bento Manoel Ribeiro. Ensáio histórico.* Pôrto Alegre.
1935. Pp. 261. U-693 D

Sanson, Henry. *Tagebuecher der Henker von Paris 1685 bis 1847.* Potsdam.
Kiepenheuer. 1924. Pp. viii, 822. U-5455 I* C

Sant Jordi, Jordi de. *Obres poetiques de Jordi de Sant Jordi (Segles XIV-XV).*
Recullides i publicades J. Massó Torrents. Barcelona. L'Avenç. 1902.
Pp. xiv, 56. Uc

Santacruz, Pascual. *Ciencia antigua y ciencia nueva. Polémica filosófica con el
P. Domínico Fr. Casto Paradís.* Boceto biográfico del autor por P. Langle.
Almería. Estrella. 1902. Uc D

Santamaría i Monné, Joan. *Narraciones extraordinaries.* Barcelona. Casanovas.
1915. Pp. 256. U-1617 D

Sant'Ana Dionísio, José Augusto de. *Antero. Algumas notas sôbre o seu drama
e a sua cultura.* Lisboa. Seara Nova. 1933. Pp. 228. U-301 I* C D

Santander, Federico. *Charlas.* Valladolid. Imp. Castellana. 1916. Uc D

― *Alma mater.* Madrid. Bibl. Patria. n.d. Pp. 136 + 25. U-4699 D

Santayana, George. *The Life of Reason.* New York. Scribner's. 1914. Pp. 205.
U-2069 I

― *Egotism in German Philosophy.* London. Dent. [1916]. Pp. 171. U-894 I*

Santiago-Fuentes, Magdalena de. *Emprendamos nueva vida.* Barcelona. Henrich.
1905. Uc

Santibáñez Puga, Fernando [Santivan, pseud.]. *Palpitaciones de vida.* Santiago
de Chile. Imp. Universitaria. 1909. Pp. 233. Uc D

― *La hechizada.* Santiago. Imp. Universitaria. 1916. Pp. 114. U-564 n/o

Santillana, Marqués de. See López de Mendoza, Iñigo

Santillana, Roque de. *El último héroe. Maravillosa novela del porvenir.*
Madrid. Beltrán. Uc D

Santísimo Sacramento, Wenceslao del. *Fisonomía de un doctor.* (Ensayo crítico.) 2 vols. Salamanca. Calatrava. 1913. U-2920-1 I

Santivan, F. See Santibáñez Puga, Fernando

Santos Chocano, José. *El fin de Satán y otros poemas.* Guatemala. Tip. Nacional. 1901. Pp. 142. U-4691 I D

— *Alma América. Poemas indo-españoles.* Pról. M. de Unamuno. Madrid. Suárez. 1906. Pp. xxii, 346. U-4178 D

— [Homenaje]. *La coronación de José Santos Chocano.* Lima. 1922. Pp. 187. U-4966 I

Santullano, Luis. *Bartolo o La vocación.* Madrid. Espasa-Calpe. 1936. Pp. 212. U-5015 D

Saponaro, Michele. *Peccato. Sette mesi di vita rústica.* Milano. Treves. 1919. Pp. 304. U-3836 I

Sarasola, Luis de. *San Francisco de Asís.* Madrid. Espasa-Calpe. 1929. Pp. 603. n/n

Sardá y Salvany, Félix. *El liberalismo es pecado. Cuestiones candentes.* Barcelona. Libr. y Tip. Católica. 1887. Pp. 183. Uc

Sarmiento, A. Belin. *Sarmiento anecdótico.* Buenos Aires. Soria. 1905. Pp. xiv, 386. U-1783 I

Sarmiento, Domingo Faustino. *Obras de D.F. Sarmiento.* Buenos Aires, Santiago de Chile. Moreno-Gutenberg. 1886-96. Vols. III, V. U-83-4 I*

— *Civilización y barbarie. Vidas de Quiroga, Aldao i el Chacho.* Buenos Aires. Lajouane. 1889. Pp. vi, 376. U-1661 I

— *Educación popular.* Noticia preliminar R. Rojas. Buenos Aires. La Facultad. 1915. Pp. vi, 456. U-3235

— *Condición del extranjero en América.* Buenos Aires. Bibl. Argentina 28. 1928. Pp. 549. U-4874 I* C B

— *Facundo.* Tr. Marcel Bataillon. Préf. A. Ponce. Paris. Institut International de Coopération Intellectuelle. 1934. Pp. 317. U-2155

Sarret, Cecilio S. *Tierra.* Habana. Alfa. 1935. Ff. 121. U-2253 D

Sarriá, Jesús de. *Vibraciones de la patria.* Bilbao. Edit. Vasca. 1918. Pp. 19. U-3586

— *En defensa nacional.* Bilbao. Edit. Vasca. 1919. Pp. 21. U-5081

Sarriomandia, Pedro H. *Gramática de la lengua rifeña.* Tánger. Imp. Hispano-Arábiga. 1905. Pp. xx, 458. U-4804

Satorres, Esteban. *Cigarra de otoño.* Cartagena. Carreño. 1935. Pp. 158. U-2034 D

Saura Mascaró, Santiago Angel. *Dicionario manual ó vocabulario completo de las lenguas castellana-catalana.* Barcelona. Estévan Pujol. 1862. Pp. 592 + 383. n/n

Saurí, Manuel I. *Dios no existe.* Barcelona. F. Granada. Uc D

Savage, Minot J. *Psychics: Facts and Theories.* Boston. Ellis. 1899. Pp. x, 153.
   U-2953
Savj-López, Paolo. 'Una cavalcata con Don Chisciotte,' estratto dalla
   Miscellanea in Onore di R. Renier. Torino (1912), 447-52. U-2573
— 'Romanticismo antiromantico,' estratto dagli *Atti R. Accademia di*
   Archeologia, Lettere e Belle Arti, II (1910), 212-39. U-4255 D
— *Cervantes.* Tr. A.G. Solalinde. Madrid. Calleja. 1917. Pp. 260. U-5643 I D
Sayce, A.H. *Principes de philologie comparée.* Tr. Ernest Jovy et précédés d'un
   avant-propos par Michel Bréal. Paris. Delagrave. 1884. Pp. xxii, 310.
   U-567 C
Scanno, Alfredo di. *Mitis aura.* Bari. Ed. Barese. 1916. Pp. 102. U-3041 D
Scardin, Francisco. *La estancia argentina.* Buenos Aires. Cía. Sud-Americana
   de Billetes de Banco. 1908. Uc D
Schack, Adolf Friedrich von. *Historia de la literatura y del arte dramático en*
   España. Tr. Eduardo de Mier. 5 vols. Madrid. Tello. 1885-7. U-1557-61
Scheffler, Johann, Angelus Silesius. *Selections From the Cherubinic Wanderer.*
   Tr. and introd. J.E. Crawford Flitch. London. George Allen & Unwin.
   1932. Pp. 253. U-4806 I
— *Aus der Angelus Silesius Cherubinischer Wandersmann.* Leipzig.
   Breitkopf und Haitel. n.d. Pp. 45. U-586 I
Schell, Herman. *Christus. Das Evangelium und seine weltgeschichtliche*
   Bedeutung. Mainz. Kirchheim. 1906. Pp. 242. U-3831
Schenkel, Daniel. *Jésus, portrait historique.* Tr. de l'allemand sur la 3ème
   édition. Paris. Reinwald. 1865. Pp. xvi, 292. U-1231
Schevill, Rudolph. 'Studies in Cervantes, Part II. "Persiles y Sigismunda,"'
   Modern Philology, IV, 4 (April 1907). U-5194 D
— 'Studies in Cervantes – Persiles y Sigismunda III,' reprinted from *Trans.*
   Conn. Acad., XIII (May 1908), 475-548. U-2474 D
Schiller, F.C.S. *Humanism. Philosophical Essays.* London. Macmillan. 1912.
   Pp. xxxi, 381. U-5192
Schiller, Johann Christoph Friedrich von. *Schillers sämtliche Werke.* Mit einer
   biographischen Einleitung von Prof. Dr J. Wychgram. 4 vols. Leipzig.
   Reclam. n.d. U-1426-9. Vols. I-III I
— *Don Carlos, Infant von Spanien.* Leipzig. Reclam. n.d. Pp. 192. U-4511
Schinca, Francisco Alberto. *Oriflamas. Discursos y críticas literarias.*
   Montevideo. Mercurio. 1914. Uc D
Schleiermacher, Friedrich. *Monologen.* Leipzig. Reclam. n.d. Pp. 79.
   U-4608 T
— *Die Weihnachtsfeier.* Leipzig. Reclam. n.d. Pp. 68. U-4605
Schlüter, Willy. *Deutsches Tat-Denken.* Dresden. Laube. 1919. Pp. 260.
   U-2487
— *Empor Menschlichung.* Dresden. Laube. 1919. Pp. 43. U-1241

Schmidt, Johann Caspar [Max Stirner, pseud.]. *Der Einzige und sein Eigentum.*
  Leipzig. Reclam. n.d. Pp. 429. U-4501 I T
Schmoller, Gustav Friedrich von. *Política social y economía política.* Tr.
  Lorenzo Benito. 2 vols. Barcelona. Henrich. 1905. Uc
Schnitzler, Arthur. *Anatol.* Berlin. Fischer. 1896. Pp. 138. U-881
— *Liebelei.* Berlin. Fischer. 1896. Pp. 142. U-3501 I
Schopenhauer, Arthur. *Sämmtliche Werke.* Herausgegeben von Eduard
  Grisebach. 6 vols. Leipzig. Reclam. [1892]. U-4048-53. Vols. II-IV I.
  Vol. I I* T
— *Schopenhauer's Briefe.* Herausgegeben von Eduard Grisebach. Leipzig.
  Reclam. n.d. Pp. 504. U-4546
— *Anmerkungen zu Platon, Locke, Kant und nachkantischen Philosophen.*
  Leipzig. Reclam. n.d. Pp. 210. U-4531
— *Einleitung zur Philosophie nebst Abhandlungen zur Dialektik –*
  Aesthetik und über die deutsche Sprachverhunzung. Leipzig. Reclam.
  n.d. Pp. 197. U-4530
— *Neue Paralipomena.* Leipzig. Reclam. n.d. Pp. 510. U-4532
— *Dores do mundo.* Tr. y pref. A. Forjaz de Sampayo. Lisboa. Santos &
  Vieira. n.d. Pp. 24. U-3573
— *Sobre la voluntad en la naturaleza.* Tr. M. de Unamuno. Madrid.
  Rodríguez Serra. 1900. Pp. 244. Uc
Schug, Howard Lesher. *Latin Sources of Berceo's 'Sacrificio de Misa.'*
  Nashville, Tenn. George Peabody College for Teachers. 1936. Pp. 112.
  U-2542 D
Schulten, Adolf. *Tannenberg und Cannae.* Erlangen. Grub der Universität.
  1917. Pp. 11. U-2471
Schultzky, O. *Modernismus.* II Band: *Die Selbsterlösung.* Potsdam. Stein.
  1913. Pp. 235. U-4222
Schulz, Hans, und Wilhelm Sundermeyer. *Deutsche Sprachlehre für*
  Ausländer. Grammatik und Uebungsbuch. Berlin. Verlag des Deutsches
  Instituts für Ausländer. 1936. Pp. 228. U-5381
Schuré, Edouard. *Les grands initiés. Esquisse de l'histoire secrète des*
  religions. Paris. Perrin. 1907. Pp. xxxii, 554. U-313 I
Schweisthal, Martin. *Drames & Comédies.* Paris. Flammarion. Uc D
Schweitzer, Albert. *Aus meiner Kindheit und Jugendzeit.* München.
  C.H. Beck. [1924]. Pp. 63. U-5379 I* T
Schwietz, Lorenz. *Das Tagebuch des Scharfrichters Lorenz Schwietz.*
  Bearbeitet von Helmuth Kionka. Breslau. Kulturspiegel Verlag. 1925.
  Pp. 110. U-5394
La science française. Exposition universelle et internationale de San
  Francisco. 2 vols. Paris. Ministère de l'Instruction Publique et des
  Beaux-Arts. 1915. Uc

Scott, James Brown. *El progreso del derecho de gentes. Conferencias y estudios internacionales.* Introd. A. de la Pradelle. Madrid. Espasa-Calpe. 1936. Pp. 319. U-4182

Scott, Sir Walter. *Waverley or 't Is Sixty Years Since.* Leipzig. Tauchnitz. 1845. Pp. 483. U-511 B* T*

— *Quentin Durwald.* Leipzig. Tauchnitz. 1845. Pp. 514. U-4482

Scottish Ballads. A Selection. Note J.E. Crawford Flitch. London. Grant Richards. [1912]. Pp. 94. U-4076

Secchi, Angelo. *L'Unità delle forze fisiche. Saggio di filosofia naturale.* Milano. Treves. 1885. Pp. xxiii, 381. U-1896

Seeley, Sir J.R. *Ecce Homo. A Survey of the Life and Work of Jesus Christ.* Introd. Sir Oliver Lodge. London. Dent. [1908]. Pp. xvii, 264. U-5176 I* C

Segarra, José. *Vocación.* Barcelona. Henrich. 1905. Pp. 270. U-2322

— y Joaquín Juliá. *Excursión por América. Costa Rica.* San José, C.R. Alsina. 1907. Pp. 655. Uc D

Seignobos, Charles. *Histoire narrative et descriptive des anciens peuples de l'Orient.* Paris. Colin. n.d. Pp. 435. U-5285

Seillière, Ernest. *Les origines romanesques de la morale et de la politique romantiques.* Paris. La Renaissance du Livre. 1920. Pp. 176. U-396 I B D

Sela, Aniceto. *La educación nacional. Hechos é ideas.* Madrid. Suárez. 1910. Pp. 456. U-2272

Selph, Julio. *Diseños.* Santiago de Chile. Nascimento. 1932. Pp. 86. U-1135 D

Selva, Josep. *La llum i l'ombra.* Badalona. Edicions Proa. 1931. Pp. 254. U-614 D

Sénancour, Etienne Jean Baptiste Pierre Ignace Pivert de. *Obermann.* Préf. George Sand. Paris. Charpentier. n.d. Pp. 432. U-644 I* C*

— *Aldomen ou le bonheur dans l'obscurité.* Etude sur ce premier Obermann inconnu André Monglond. Paris. Les Presses Françaises. 1925. Pp. xxxix, 89. U-5282 I* C

Sencourt, Robert. *La vie de Meredith.* Tr. Georges Luciani. Préf. André Maurois. Paris. Gallimard. 1931. Pp. 263. QP-48 I

Seneca, Lucius Annaeus. *Medea.* Deutsch von Max Schmitt-Hartlieb. Leipzig. Kurt Vieweg. 1929. Pp. 39. U-2095

— *Hercules.* Deutsch von Max Schmitt-Hartlieb. Saarbrücken. Hofer. 1931. Pp. 58. U-3057

Senet, Rodolfo. *Evolución y educación.* La Plata. Sesé y Larrañaga. 1901. Pp. viii, 662. U-3014 D

— *Apuntes de pedagogía, adaptados al programa del primer año normal.* Buenos Aires. Cabaut. 1905. Uc

— *Patología del instinto de conservación.* Buenos Aires. Bibl. Científica Argentina. 1906. Pp. viii, 266. U-3017 D

- *Las estoglosias.* Madrid. Jorro. 1911. Pp. 255. U-3155
Serantes, Marta. *La ofrenda de la vida.* Buenos Aires. Rosso. 1926. Pp. 174.
U-5641 D
Sergi, Giuseppe. *La decadencia de las naciones latinas.* Tr. S. Valentí Camp y
Vicente Gay. Barcelona. López. 1901. Pp. 296. U-4320
- *Leopardi a la luz de la ciencia.* Tr. J. Buixó Monserdá. 2 vols. Barcelona.
Henrich. 1904. Uc
- *La evolución humana individual y social. Hechos e ideas.* Tr. S. Valentí
Camp. 2 vols. Barcelona. Henrich. 1905. Uc
Sérgio de Sousa, Antonio. *Ensaios.* Tomo II. Lisboa. Seara Nova. 1928.
Pp. 267. U-5728 C D
Serna, José S. *Cuaderno sentimental (Estampas albacetenses).* Albacete.
Guirado y González. 1928. Pp. 84. U-5559 D
Serrano y Sanz, Manuel. *Noticias y documentos históricos del Condado de
Ribagorza hasta la muerte de Sancho Garcés III (Año 1035).* Madrid.
Centro de Estudios Históricos. 1912. Pp. 508. U-1688
Sesto, Julio. *A través de América. El México de Porfirio Díaz.* Valencia.
Sempere. [1909]. Pp. 261. U-3145 I D
Seuse (Suso), Heinrich. *Schriften.* Herausg. nhd. von H.S. Denifle. München.
Literarisches Institut v. Dr M. Zuttler. 1876. Pp. xxx, 644. U-4792 I T
Severino, Agostino. *Il sentimento religioso di Federico Amiel.* Roma.
Bilychnis. 1921. Pp. 51. U-1721
Sforza, Angel E. *El ideal de Lilia. La voz del amor.* Buenos Aires. Agencia
General de Libr. y Publ. 1917. Pp. 254. U-2733 D
Shakespeare, William. *The Works of William Shakespeare.* Ed. Howard
Staunton. 4 vols. London. Routledge, Warne. 1864. U-4206-9 I* T*
- *Enrique IV de Shakespeare.* Tr. Miguel Cané. Buenos Aires. Moen. 1900.
Pp. lvi, 256. U-392
- *Hámlet, principe de Dinamarca.* Tr. J. Roviralta Borrell. Barcelona.
López. 1906. Uc
- *XXIV Sonets de Shakespeare.* Tr. ab breus notes d'introd. M. Morera y
Galicia. Barcelona. Vilanova y Geltrú. 1912. Pp. xv, 24. U-1732
- *Lo Rei Lear.* Tragedia de Guillem Shakespeare feelment arromançacada
en estil de catalana prosa per Anfós Par. Barcelona. Associació Wagneriana.
1912. Pp. xv, 447. U-121
- *Selecta de sonets de William Shakespeare.* Tr. M. Morera i Galicia.
Barcelona. Vilanova i Geltrú. 1913. Pp. 94. U-2867
- *Homenaje a William Shakespeare (1564-1616).* Habana. Alma Cubana.
1924. U-4256
Shaw, Albert. *El gobierno municipal en la Europa continental.* Tr. Julio Carrié.
2 vols. Buenos Aires. Peuser. 1902. U-2462-3. Vol. I I

— *El gobierno municipal en la Gran Bretaña.* Tr. Julio Carrié. Buenos Aires.
    Peuser. 1902. Pp. xi, 498. U-2461 I
Shaw, George Bernard. *Plays: Pleasant and Unpleasant.* 2 vols. London.
    Constable. 1905. U-365-6 I
— *Man and Superman. A Comedy and a Philosophy.* London. Constable.
    1906. Pp. xxxviii, 244. U-364 I*
— *John Bull's Other Island* and *Major Barbara.* London. Constable. 1907.
    Pp. lix, 293. U-1435 I
— *Santa Juana.* Tr. Julio Broutá. Madrid. Aguilar. 1927. Pp. 250. U-3722
Shelley, Percy Bysshe. *The Poetical Works of Percy Bysshe Shelley.* Ed. and
    introductory memory William B. Scott. London. Routledge. [1880].
    Pp. xxxi, 603. U-230 I* T*
Showerman, Grant. *With the Professor.* New York. Holt. 1910. Pp. x, 360.
    U-3900 D
Shu, Seyuan. See Hsü, Ssu-yüan
Sicardi, Francisco A. *Libro extraño.* 4 vols. Buenos Aires. Libr. Científica de
    A. Etchepareborda. 1894-9. U-1463-6. Vols. III, IV n/o. 2 vols. Barcelona.
    Granada. n.d. U-2186-7 D
Siciliani, Luigi. *Rime della Lontananza (1900-1906).* Roma. Modes. 1906.
    Pp. 150. U-2946 D
— *Corona.* Roma. Modes. 1907. Pp. 79. U-5345 D
— *Poesie per Ridere (1907-1908).* Milano. Quintieri. 1909. Pp. 152, xiii.
    U-1961 D
— *Studi e Saggi.* Milano. Quintieri. 1913. Pp. 363. U-3898 D
Siciliani, Pietro. *Prolégomènes à la psychogénie moderne.* Tr. A. Herzen.
    Paris. Baillière. 1880. Pp. 176. U-595
Sienkievicz, Henryk. *Quo vadis. Racconto storico.* Versione italiana Federigo
    Verdinois. Napoli. 1899. Uc
— *Oltre il mistero (Bez Dogmatu).* Tr. Dominico Ciàmpoli. Milano. Treves.
    1900. Pp. xx, 380. U-3463 I
— *La famiglia Polaniecki.* Milano. Baldini, Castoldi. 1900. Uc
Sienra Carranza, José. *Cuestiones americanas.* Montevideo. El Siglo Ilustrado.
    1907. Pp. 98. U-4319 D
Sierra, Adolfo M. 'Breve ensayo de psicopatología literaria,' extracto de la
    Revista de Criminología, Psiquiatría y Medicina Legal. Buenos Aires
    (1922). U-4956 D
— *Los caminos del Parnaso.* Buenos Aires. C. García. Uc D
Sierra, Justo y Santiago Ballescá. *México. Su evolución social.* 3 vols. México.
    Ballescá. 1900-2. U-3563-5
Sievers, Eduard. *Grundzüge der Lautphysiologie zur Einführung in das
    Studium der Lautlehre der Indogermanischen Sprachen.* Leipzig.
    Breitkopf und Härtel. 1876. Pp. x, 156. U-2532 T

Silió, Evaristo. *Poesías*. Pról. M. Menéndez y Pelayo. Valladolid. Imp.
Castellana. 1897. Pp. xliii, 183. U-187
Silió y Cortés, César. *Problemas del día*. Pról. G. Tarde. Madrid. Suárez. 1900.
Pp. ix, 295. U-1601 D
Silva, Arturo S. *La fuente inagotable*. Montevideo. El Pueblo. 1920. Pp. 163.
U-136 D
Silva, J. Francisco V. *El libertador Bolívar y el Deán Funes en la política
argentina*. Madrid. Ed. América. 1918. Pp. 421. U-2240 D
Silva, José Asunción. *Poesías*. Pról. M. de Unamuno. Barcelona. Maucci.
1908. Pp. xiv, 159. U-3668. Notas B. Sanín Cano. Paris. Michaud. [1923].
Pp. 251. U-4009
Silva, Víctor Domingo. *Hacia allá*. Santiago de Chile. Imp. Universitaria.
1905. Pp. 234. U-3331
– *El derrotero*. Poema nacional constituído por un prólogo, diez episodios
y un epílogo original de V.D. Silva (1905-6). Valparaiso. Universo. 1908.
Pp. 115. U-2176 D
Silva Gayo, Manuel da. *Os novos*. I. *Moniz Barreto*. Coimbra. Amado. 1894.
Pp. xii, 101. U-829
– *Mondego*. Coimbra. Amado. 1900. Pp. 94. U-3245 D
– *A dama de Ribadalva*. Lisboa. Tavares Cardoso & Irmao. 1903. Pp. 195.
U-3296 D
– *Novos poemas*. Coimbra. Imp. da Universidade. 1906. Pp. 117. U-551 D
– *Eugénio de Castro. Traços biográficos e literários*. Conferência. Coimbra.
Imp. da Universidade. 1928. Pp. 31. U-5721 D
Silva-Passos, Francisco da. *O evangelho novo*. Lisboa. Tavares Cardoso. 1905.
Pp. 296. U-3232 D
Silvano Godoi, Juan. *Monografías históricas*. Buenos Aires. Lajouane. 1893.
Pp. xvi, 216. U-1695 n/o
Silvela, E. *Vida picaresca*. Madrid. F. Fé. 1910. Uc D
– *Aventuras contemporáneas*. Madrid. Bernardo Rodríguez. 1912.
Pp. 172. Uc D
Silvela Corral, Eugenio. *Ensayos de política y administración*. Madrid. Imp. de
la Rev. de Legislación. 1904. Pp. vii, 288. U-272 D
Silvestre. *El proyecto de ley de asociaciones. Semblanza (Cuento pardo)*.
Madrid. Tip. Terceño. 1907. Pp. 20. U-3937 n/o D
Simmel, Georg. *Einleitung in die Moralwissenschaft. Eine Kritik der Ehischen
Grundbegriffe*. 2 vols. Stuttgart-Berlin. Cotta. 1904. U-861-2
– *Die Religion*. Frankfurt. Rutten & Leonig. 1906. Pp. 79. U-2100 I
Simon, Francisco. *Partido colorado. El ejecutivo colegiado*. Montevideo.
Peña. 1916. Pp. 273. Uc
Simonet, Francisco Javier. *Glosario de voces ibéricas y latinas usadas entre los
mozárabes precedido de un estudio sobre el dialecto hispano-mozárabe*.
Madrid. Fortanet. 1888. Pp. ccxxxvi, 628. U-58

Sinner, Louis de. *Choix de discours tirés des pères grecs*. Notes E. Sommer.
Paris. Hachette. 1893. Uc
Síntesis, i, 1, 6, 10; ii, 17-19, 21-3; iv, 37. Buenos Aires (1927, 1928,
1930). n/n
Sitio de Bilbao. Reseña histórica. Pp. 218. U-5708 [Cover missing]
Sitio de Bilbao en 1874 (El). Por un testigo ocular. Pról. don Gumersindo
Vicuña. Madrid. Medina y Navarro. [1874]. Pp. xv, 152. U-5710
Skowronnek, Richard. *Im Forsthause*. Leipzig. Reclam. n.d. Pp. 64. U-4538
Slabý, Rudolf J., y Rudolf Grossmann. *Diccionario de las lenguas española y
alemana*. Tomo i. Leipzig. Tauchnitz. 1932. Pp. lxiv, 740. U-75
Slataper, Scipio. *Ibsen*. Con un cenno du Scipio Slataper di Arturo Farinelli.
Torino. Bocca. 1916. Pp. xxv, 331. U-3068 I*
Sloane, William Milligan. *The Life of Napoleon Bonaparte*. 4 vols. New York.
The Century Co. 1915. U-3051-4 I*. Vol. i B. Vol. iii C
Smith, Egbert Watson. *The Creed of Presbyterians*. New York. Baker and
Taylor. [1901]. Pp. viii, 223. U-3083 I B
Smith, George. *The Life of William Carey. Shoemaker & Missionary.* London.
Dent. [1909]. Pp. viii, 326. U-5178 I*
Smith, Goldwin. *Guesses at the Riddle of Existence and Other Essays on
Kindred Subjects*. New York. Macmillan. 1897. Pp. viii, 244. U-1309 I
— *A Trip to England*. New York. Macmillan. 1906. Pp. 136. U-1511 I
Smith, Léon. *Nouveau dictionnaire français-anglais et anglais-français*. Paris.
Ch. Fouraut et Fils. 1876. Pp. xvii, 320 + xxxii, 478. n/n
Soiza Reilly, Juan José de. *Cien hombres célebres. Confesiones literarias.*
Barcelona. Maucci. 1909. Pp. iv, 433. Uc
— *Hombres y mujeres de Italia*. Valencia. Sempere. n.d. Uc
— *El alma de los perros*. Pról. M. Ugarte. Valencia. Sempere. n.d. Pp. xii,
233. U-3430
Solá, Alfonso de. *Un estadista argentino. Nicolás Avellaneda*. Pról. E. Gómez
Carrillo. Madrid. Santos González. [1915]. Pp. xvi, 335. Uc
Solá, Juan d'. *La parroquia*. Habana. Avisador Comercial. 1906. Pp. 101.
U-1884 D
Solana y Gutiérrez, Mateo. *La esencia de Teresa de Jesús*. Pról. A. Caso.
Oaxaca, México. Colección María Bettina. 1935. Pp. 266. U-2016 D
Solano, Armando. *La melancolía de la raza indígena*. Bogotá. Rev. Universidad.
1929. Pp. vi, 166. U-4932 D
Solano Asta-Buruaga, Francisco. *Diccionario geográfico de la República de
Chile*. Santiago de Chile. Brockhaus. 1899. Pp. 903. U-1235
Soldevila, Carles. *Lletaníes profanes*. Barcelona. L'Avelí Artís. 1913. Pp. 35.
U-1919 D
Soldevila, Ferrán. *Exili (Poesies)*. Barcelona. La Revista. 1918. Pp. 60.
U-2117 D

Solé Rodríguez, Oriol. *Leyendas guaraníes.* Montevideo. Dornaleche y Reyes. 1902. Pp. xvi, 179. U-3286 D

Soler, Cayetano. *La iglesia separada del estado. Cuestiones político-religiosas.* Barcelona. Gili. 1911. Pp. 125. U-489 D

Soler, Mariano. *La iglesia y la civilización.* Montevideo. Martínez. 1905. Pp. lxxix, 288. U-4007 D

Soler y Miquel, José. *Escritos de José Soler y Miquel.* Nota-pról. Juan Maragall. Barcelona. L'Avenç. 1898. Pp. ix, 234. U-2583

Solis, Abelardo. *Ante el problema agrario peruano.* Lima. Editorial Perú. 1928. Pp. 228. U-5540 D

Solov'ev, Vladimir Sergyeevich. *Tre discorsi in memoria di F. Dostojevskij.* Tr. Ettore Lo Gatto. Roma. Bilychnis. 1923. Pp. 74. U-670

Somonte Ibarreta, Miguel D. *Correrías por la América del Sur. Exploración del río Pilcomayo en Bolivia y Paraguay.* San Esteban de Pravia. Pueyo. 1912. Pp. 174. U-362

Sonderéguer, Pedro. *Los fragmentarios.* Buenos Aires. Nosotros. 1909. Pp. 129. U-5552 D

Sophocles. *Sophoclis tragoediae.* Accurate recensuit C.H. Weise. 2 vols. Lipsiae. Tauchnitz. 1841. U-4056 I* T* C

— *Antigone.* Texte grec. Annoté à l'usage des classes Ed. Tournier. Revu A.M. Desrousseaux. Paris. Hachette. 1903. Pp. xvi, 92. U-4669 I* T*

— *Oedipe à Colone.* Texte grec. Annoté Ed. Tournier. Revu A.M. Desrousseaux. Paris. Hachette. 1900. Pp. xvi, 122. U-4660 B T

— *Oedipe-Roi.* Texte grec. Annoté Ed. Tournier. Revu A.M. Desrousseaux. Paris. Hachette. 1905. Pp. xvi, 106. U-4668 I*

Sorel, Georges. *Considerazioni sulla violenza.* Tr. Antonio Sarno y introd. B. Croce. Bari. Laterza. 1909. Pp. xxvii, 307. U-2265 I*

Sorgues, Maurice de. *Les catholiques espagnols et la guerre.* Paris. Bloud et Gay. 1915. Pp. 79. U-302 D

Soriano, Rodrigo. *Moros y cristianos. Notas de viaje (1893-1894).* Madrid. F. Fé. 1895. Uc D

— *Darío de Regoyos (Historia de una rebeldía).* Madrid. Peña Cruz. 1921. Pp. 200. U-2684 I C D

Sosa, Juan B., y Enrique J. Arce. *Compendio de historia de Panamá.* Panamá. Diario de Panamá. 1911. Pp. vii, 322. U-3718

Sosa, Raúl. *Amiclas. Tragedia eleusina.* Paris. Le Livre Libre. 1928. Pp. 105. U-4887 D

Sota y Aburto, Manuel de la. *Pedro Ignacio. Leyenda dramática en tres actos.* Bilbao. Edit. Vasca. 1925. Pp. 168. U-5650 D

Sotela, Rogelio. *Recogimiento (apuntes, comentarios, reflexiones).* Madrid. Reus. 1925. Pp. 170. U-5609 C D

Soto y Calvo, Edelina. *Afectos.* Paris. Durant. 1907. Pp. 166. U-3356

Soto y Calvo, Francisco. *Cuentos de mi padre.* Buenos Aires. Coni. 1897.
Pp. 357. U-2874
— *Nastasio.* Chartres. Durand. 1899. Pp. x, 165. (2 copies) U-1454,
U-2815 D
— *Nostalgia.* Chartres. Durand. 1901. Pp. 617. U-2388 I D
— *El demiurgo.* Paris. 1908. Uc D
— *Antología de poetas líricos brasileños.* Buenos Aires. Agencia General de
Libr. y Publ. 1922. Pp. 390. U-3121 D
Sotomayor Valdés, Ramón. *Historia de Chile bajo el gobierno del General D.
Joaquín Prieto.* 4 vols. Santiago de Chile. Imp. Esmeralda. 1900-3.
U-2481-4 I C
Sousa, António de. *Caminhos. Poemas.* Lisboa. Seara Nova. 1933. Pp. 46.
U-2184 D
Souviron, José Ma. *Amarilis (un amor de Lope de Vega).* Santiago de Chile.
Edit. Ercilla. 1935. Pp. xi, 121. U-3076 D
Souza Dias, Gastäo. *No planalto da Huíla.* Porto. Renascença Portuguesa.
1923. Pp. 230. U-2343 n/o
A Spanish Poetry Book, for School and Home. Compiled E. Allison Peers.
London. Methuen. [1924]. Pp. 87. U-4480
Spaventa, Bertrando. *La filosofía italiana nelle sue relazioni con la filosofia
europea.* Note e appendice di documenti a cura di Giovanni Gentile. Bari.
Laterza. 1908. Pp. xxii, 317. U-2264 I
Spaventa, Silvio. *La politica della destra.* Scritti e discorsi raccolti B. Croce.
Bari. Laterza. 1910. Pp. viii, 486. U-3525 I*
Spencer, Herbert. *Les premiers principes.* Tr. M.E. Cazelles. Paris. Baillière.
1871. Pp. cxxix, 604. U-866
— *Principes de psychologie.* Tr. Th. Ribot et A. Espinas. 2 vols. Paris.
Baillière. 1875. U-122-3
— *Classification des sciences.* Tr. F. Réthoré. Paris. Baillière. 1881. Pp. ii,
171. U-297
— *Essays: Scientific, Political & Speculative.* 3 vols. London. Williams and
Norgate. 1891. U-2548-50 I* T
— *La beneficencia.* Tr. M. de Unamuno. Madrid. La España Moderna. Uc
Spengler, Oswald. *Der Untergang des Abendlandes. Umrisse einer Merphologie
der Weltgeschichte.* 2 vols. Munich. Oskar Beck. 1921-2. U-85-6 I* C* B
— *El hombre y la técnica. Contribución a una filosofía de la vida.* Tr. M.
García Morente. Bilbao. Espasa-Calpe. 1932. Pp. 125. U-5529
Spielhagen, Friedrich. *Ein neuer Pharao.* Leipzig. Staackmann. 1889. Pp. 513.
U-5425 T L
Spingarn, J.E. *Creative Criticism. Essays on the Unity of Genius and Taste.*
New York. Holt. 1917. Pp. 138. U-291 I C

Spinoza, Benedictus de. *Benedicti de Spinoza opera quae supersunt omnia.*
Ex editionibus principibus denuo edidit et praefatus est Carolus
Hermannus Bruder. 3 vols. Lipsiae. Tauchnitz. 1843-6. U-492-4 I* C*
Spir, Afrikan Aleksandrovich. *Saggi di filosofia critica.* Tr. Odoardo Campa.
Introd. Piero Martinetti. Milano. Libr. Editrice Milanese. 1913. Pp. xlviii,
150. U-2269 B
– *Esquisses de philosophie critique.* Introd. L. Brunschvicg. Paris. Alcan.
1930. Pp. xvi, 167. U-3991
Spitzer, Leo. 'Die klassische Dämpung in Racines Stil,' Sonderabdruck aus
Archivum Romanicum, xii, 4 (1928), 362-472. U-5368 D
– *Stilstudien II. Stilsprachen.* München. Max Hueber. 1928. Pp. 592.
U-5416 I* C B
Staël-Holstein, Anne Louise Germaine de. *Diez años de destierro. Memorias.*
Tr. Manuel Azaña. Madrid. Colec. Universal. 1919. Pp. 279. n/n I
Stahl, Francis. *Der rechte Schlüssel.* Leipzig. Reclam. n.d. Pp. 104. U-4534
Stambolis, G. *Analambes.* Athina. 1925. Pp. 80. U-1933
– *Idonika Sonetta.* Athina. Rallis. 1928. Pp. 38. U-1962 D
Stanley, Arthur P. *Historical Memorials of Canterbury.* London. Dent. [1906].
Pp. x, 295. U-969 I*
– *Lectures on the History of the Eastern Church.* Prefatory note A.J.
Grieve. London. Dent. [1907]. Pp. xx, 396. U-970 I* C
Stapfer, Paul. *Des réputations littéraires. Essais de morale et d'histoire.* Paris.
Hachette. 1893. Pp. xii, 388. U-3840 I*
Starkie, W.J.M. 'An Aristotelian analysis of "The Comic," illustrated from
Aristophanes, Rabelais, Shakespeare, and Molière,' reprinted from
Hermathena, xix (1920), 26-51. U-3711 D
Starkweather, William E.B. *Paintings and Drawings by Francisco Goya in the
Collection of the Hispanic Society of America.* New York. Hispanic Society
of America. 1916. Pp. 231. U-2297
Stearns, Harold E. *Civilization in the United States.* Ed. H.E. Stearns. New
York. Harcourt, Brace and Co. 1922. Pp. 577. U-852 I*
Stein, Ludwig. *Die Soziale Frage im Lichte der Philosophie.* Stuttgart. Enke.
1897. Pp. xx, 791. U-760 I*
Stempf, V. *La langue basque possède-t-elle, oui ou non, un vêrbe transitif?*
Tr. de l'allemand. Bordeaux. 1890. Pp. 15. U-5265
Stendhal. See Beyle, Marie Henri
Sterne, Laurence. *A Sentimental Journey Through France and Italy.* London.
Printed for T. Cadell. 1794. Pp. 311. U-1452. Paris. Baudry's European
Library. 1851. Pp. viii, 210. U-4070
– *Voyage sentimental suivi des Amours de mon Oncle Tobie, du Voyage de
Tristam Shandy en France, de l'Histoire de l'abbesse des Andouillettes.*
Paris. Dentu. 1883. Uc

— *The Life and Opinions of Tristam Shandy, Gentleman.* Introd. G. Saints
   Saintsbury. London. Dent. n.d. Pp. xxvi, 478. U-993 I
Stevenson, Robert Louis. *Across the Plains. With Other Memories and Essays.*
   Leipzig. Tauchnitz. 1892. Pp. 286. U-5168 I* B*
— *Familiar Studies of Men and Books.* London. Chatto & Windus. 1903.
   Pp. xxviii, 397. U-1315 I
— *An Inland Voyage, Travels with a Donkey in the Cévennes. The Silverado
   Squatters.* London. Dent. [1925]. Pp. xviii, 277. U-1050 I* T
— *Treasure Island* and *Kidnapped.* Introd. Sir A.T. Quiller-Couch. London.
   Dent. [1925]. Pp. xxiv, 370. U-5223 T
— *The Strange Case of Dr Jekyll and Mr Hyde* and *Prince Otto.* New York.
   Burt. n.d. Pp. 350. U-1316 I*
Stevenson, William Bennet. *Memorias de William Bennet Stevenson sobre las
   campañas de San Martín y Cochrane en el Perú.* Tr. Luis de Terán. Noticia
   sobre Stevenson por Diego Barros Arana. Madrid. Editorial América.
   [1917]. Pp. 300. U-3022
Stinde, Julius. *Die familie Buchholz.* Berlin. Freund & Jeckel. 1897. Pp. vi,
   210. U-4232 T
Stock, Guillermo. *Fragmentos de una vida.* Buenos Aires. Lantés. 1910.
   Pp. 249. U-529
— *Palabras que no son parolas.* Buenos Aires. Lantés. 1911. Pp. 188.
   U-2644 n/o D
— *El regreso del bosque.* Buenos Aires. 1915. Pp. 15. U-1980 D
Stoll, Otto. *Zur Ethnographie der Republik Guatemala.* Zurich. Orell Füssli.
   1884. Pp. x, 175. U-1836
— *Guatemala.* Leipzig. F.A. Brockhaus. 1886. Pp. xii, 518. U-2206 D
Storni, Alfonsina. *La inquietud del rosal.* Pról. Juan Julián Lastra. Buenos
   Aires. La Facultad. 1916. Pp. 126. U-3203 D
— *El dulce daño.* Buenos Aires. Coop. Editorial Limitada. 1918. Pp. 157.
   U-3128 D
— *Irremediablemente.* Buenos Aires. Coop. Editora Limitada. 1919. Pp. 165.
   U-2910 I* D
Storni, Segundo. *Intereses argentinos en el mar.* Buenos Aires. Moen. 1916.
   Pp. 110. U-2210 D
Strabo. *Strabonis rerum geographicarum libri XVII,* etc. 3 vols. Lipsiae.
   Tauchnitz. 1829. U-4041-3 I T
Strauss, David Friedrich. *Vie de Jésus ou examen critique de son histoire.*
   Tr. E. Littré. 2 vols. Paris. Ladrange. 1864. U-901-2
Street, Cecil J.C. *President Masaryk.* London. Geoffrey Bles. 1930. Pp. 256.
   U-2231 I
Strich, Fritz. *Dichtung und Zivilisation.* München. Meyer & Jessen. 1928.
   Pp. vii, 248. U-5466 I*

Strich, Walter. *Die Dioskuren.* München. Meyer & Jessen. 1924. Pp. 305.
U-5433 I* C
Stromer, Theodor. *Das zweite Gesicht und andere Novellen.* München.
Callwey. 1891. Pp. 368. U-1438 D
Stuart-Menteath, P.W. 'The Alpine paradoxes,' part 1, *Pyrenean Geology.*
London. Dulau. 1903. Pp. 16. U-4276 D
Studien zur griechischen und lateinischen Grammatik. Num. 1-2 (1868,
1870-1, 1873-5, 1877), num. 1 (1869, 1872). n/n
Suarès, André. *Tolstoi vivant.* Paris. Cahiers de la Quinzaine. [1911].
Pp. 183. U-634 I
− *Péguy.* Paris. Emile-Paul. 1915. Pp. 94. U-2074 I D
− *Cervantes.* Paris. Emile-Paul. 1916. Pp. 121. U-2126 I* C D
− *Don Quijote en Francia.* Tr. y palabras preliminares Ricardo Baeza.
Madrid. Minerva. 1916. Pp. 153. U-1128
− *La nation contre la race.* 2 vols. Paris. Emile-Paul. 1916-17. (2 copies
vol. ɪ) U-2071-3 I* D
− *Poète tragique. Portrait de Prospéro.* Paris. Emile-Paul. 1921. Pp. 396.
U-4815 I C D
− *Sur la vie. Essais.* Paris. Emile-Paul. 1925. Pp. 416. U-5242 I* C D
Suárez, Bernardo F. *El ideal del condor.* Jujuy. Sarmiento-Salta. 1920.
Ff. 6. U-5469 D
− *América.* Buenos Aires. Díaz y Pelligrini. 1921. Ff. 7 (2 copies)
U-5687-8 D
Suárez, José León. *Carácter de la revolución americana.* Con un apéndice
conteniendo juicios sobre estas obras. Buenos Aires. La Facultad. 1917.
Pp. xx, 160. (2 copies) U-273, U-1916
Suárez, Marco Fidel. *Estudios gramaticales. Introducción a las obras
filológicas de D. Andrés Bello.* Advertencia y noticia bibliográfica M.A.
Caro. Madrid. Pérez Dubrull. 1885. Pp. xvi, 382. U-512 C
Subirá, José. *Su virginal pureza.* Madrid. Pueyo. Uc D
Subirana, Luis. *La salud por la instrucción. Una lanza en pro de una
pedagogía biológica.* Madrid. F. Fé. 1915. Pp. 337. U-3656 D
Sucre, Josep Ma. de. *L'Ocell Daurat.* Barcelona. Libr. Nacional Catalana.
1921. Pp. 60. U-3414 D
− *Joan Maragall.* Barcelona. Libr. Nacional Catalana. 1921. Pp. 71.
(2 copies) U-570, U-3417 n/o D
− *Poema barbre de Serrallonga.* Barcelona. Libr. Nacional Catalana. 1922.
Pp. 36. U-3910 n/o D
− *Poemas de abril y mayo.* Barcelona. Omega. 1922. Pp. 51. U-4504 D
− *Apol-noi.* Barcelona. Llibreri Espanyola. n.d. Pp. 79. U-2935 D
Sudermann, Hermann. *Die Ehre.* Berlin. Lehmann. 1891. Pp. 156. U-5391 T

— *Iolanthes hochzeit.* Stuttgart. Union Deutsche Verlagsgesellschaft. 1892.
  Pp. 110. U-151 C* T*
— *Heimat.* Stuttgart. Cotta. 1893. Pp. 168. U-3593 T L
— *El deseo.* Tr. y pról. Ramiro de Maeztu. Madrid. La España Moderna. n.d.
  Pp. 203. U-831 I C
Suero de Quiñones. *Tanto va el cántaro a la fuente ... Diatriba contra el
  modernismo literario.* Madrid. Primitivo Fernández. 1910. Pp. 70. U-4717
Suess, Wilhelm. *Aristophanes und die Nachwelt.* Leipzig. Dieterich. 1911.
  Pp. 226. U-4854
Sully Prudhomme, René François Armand. *Oeuvres de Sully Prudhomme.
  Poésies. 1866-1872.* Paris. Lemerre. n.d. Pp. 245. U-469
Sundby, Thor, og Euch. Baruël. *Dictionnaire dano-norvegien-français.* 2 vols.
  København. Gyldendal. 1883-4. n/n
Supervielle, Jules. *Débarcadères.* Paris. Revue de l'Amérique Latine. 1922.
  Pp. 115. U-5294 D
Sureda y Massanet, José. *Del positivismo vigente, en medicina, y la necesidad
  de su reforma.* Discurso leído en la Real Academia de Medicina de Palma
  de Mallorca en el acto de su recepción. Discurso de contestación José
  Sampol y Vidal. Palma. La Esperanza. 1923. Pp. 64. U-3015 D
Suríguez y Acha, Carlos. *Despertar.* 2 vols. Buenos Aires. Tommasi. 1908.
  U-416, U-4339 n/o D
— *En la pampa. Narraciones gauchescas de la República argentina.* Buenos
  Aires. Tommasi. 1908. Pp. 255. U-3569 n/o
Sutta-Pitaka. *Die Reden Gotamo Buddhos aus der Sammlung der Bruchstuecke/
  Suttanipâto/des Pali-Kanons* übersetzt von Karl Eugen Neumann. München.
  Piper. 1924. Pp. xxi, 599. U-5422 I*
— *Die letzten Tage Gotamo Buddhos.* Aus dem grossen Verhör über die
  Erlöschung Mahâparinibbânasuttam des Pali-Kanons übersetzt von K.E.
  Neumann. München. Piper. 1923. Pp. xxvii, 278. U-5417 I T
— *Der Wahrheitpfad. Dhammapadam.* Ein buddhistisches Denkmal ...
  Übersetzt K.E. Neumann. München. Piper. 1921. Pp. xi, 156. U-5423 I
— *Die Lieder der Mönche und Nonnen Gotamo Buddhos.* Übersetzt von
  K.E. Neumann. München. Piper. 1923. Pp. xxvii, 634. U-5418
Swedenborg, Emanuel. *Heaven and Its Wonders, and Hell: From Things
  Heard Seen.* Introd. J. Howard Spalding. Tr. and rev. Mr F. Bayley.
  London. Dent. [1909]. Pp. xviii, 340. U-1068 I
— *The Divine Love and Wisdom.* Introd. Oliver Lodge. Tr. and rev. Mr F.
  Bayley. London. Dent. [1912]. Pp. xxiii, 216. U-1069
Swift, Jonathan. *Gulliver's Travels.* London. Dent. [1906]. Pp. xx, 279.
  U-1019 I
— *A Tale of a Tub, the Battle of the Books and Other Satires.* Introd. Lewis
  Melville. London. Dent. [1909]. Pp. xix, 325. U-1007 I* C T

– *Journal to Stella.* Ed. J.K. Moorhead. Introd. Sir Walter Scott. London.
Dent. [1924]. Pp. xxx, 445. U-5173 I

Swinburne, Algernon Charles. *Atalanta in Calydon. A Tragedy.* London.
Chatto & Windus. 1905. Pp. xvi, 98 + 32. U-1338 I B*

– *Poems and Ballads.* London. Chatto & Windus. 1906. Pp. ix, 338.
U-1895 I

E Synchroni Skepsi. Panellinia Epitheorisi. Chicago. 1928-9. Pp. 352.
U-2490 C T*

Systematische christliche Religion von E. Troeltsch, J. Pohle, J. Mausbach,
C. Krieg, W. Herrmann, R. Seeberg, W. Faber, H.J. Holtzmann. Berlin.
Teubner. 1909. Pp. viii, 286. U-1636 I

Tablanca, Luis. *Cuentos sencillos.* Comentario a modo de epíl. E. Ramírez
Angel. Madrid. Pueyo. [1909]. Pp. 120. U-414 D

Taboada, Gaspar. *Los Taboada; Luchas de la organización nacional.*
Documentos seleccionados y comentados. Vol. I. Buenos Aires. López.
1929. Pp. 479. U-5599 I D

Taboadela, José Antonio. *Notas ligeras.* Pról. R. Montoro. Habana.
Casanova. 1913. Pp. xv, 139. U-3397 n/o D

Taborda, Saul Alejandro. *La sombra de Satán. Episodio de la vida colonial.*
Córdoba. Cubas. 1916. Pp. 167. U-3108 n/o

– *Investigaciones pedagógicas.* I. Córdoba. Universidad Nacional. 1932.
Pp. 256. U-619 D

Tacitus. *Cornelii Taciti libri qui supersunt.* Quartum recognovit Carolus Halm.
2 vols. Lipsiae. Teubner. 1909-11. U-353-4 I* C T L

Tagopoulos, D.P. *O Prophitikos.* Athina. Estia. 1929. Pp. 19. (2 copies)
U-2713-14

Tagore, Sir Rabindranath. See Ravindraantha Thakura, Sir

Taine, Hippolyte-Adolphe. *L'Idéalisme anglais, étude sur Carlyle.* Paris.
Baillière. 1864. Pp. 187. U-314

– *Philosophie de l'art.* 2 vols. Paris. Hachette. 1885. U-308-9 I

– *Notas sobre Inglaterra.* Tr. León Sánchez Cuesta. 2 vols. Madrid.
Universal. 1920. n/n I

– *Les origines de la France contemporaine.* Uc

Talero, Eduardo. *Voz del desierto.* Buenos Aires. Rodríguez Giles. 1907.
Pp. 271. U-2779

Tamayo, Franz. *Creación de la pedagogía nacional.* La Paz. Editoriales de
El Diario. 1910. Pp. viii, 220. U-92

– *Proverbios sobre la vida, el arte y la ciencia.* La Paz. Velarde. 1905. Uc

– *La prometheida o las oceanides.* La Paz. Imp. y Lit. Artística. 1917. Uc

Tannenberg, Boris de. *L'Espagne littéraire. Portraits d'hier et d'aujourd'hui.*
Paris. Picard. 1903. Pp. xvi, 316. U-2406 D

Tapia, Luis de. *Coplas del año.* Madrid. Renacimiento. 1917. Uc D

Tapia Aubá, José. *Gramática francesa* ... *Primer curso.* Barcelona. Ortega.
    1916. Pp. 254. U-5593 I D
Tapia Bolivar, Daniel. *San Juan.* Madrid. Bibl. Nueva. 1935. Pp. 209.
    U-4016 D
Taracena, Blas, y José Tudela. *Soria. Guia artística de la ciudad y su provincia.*
    Soria. Las Heras. 1928. Pp. 244. U-514 D
Tarnassi, José. *Los poetas del siglo VI de Roma, estudiados en los escritores*
    latinos. Buenos Aires. Peuser. 1903. Pp. xxiv, 263. U-3536 I D
— *Vida de Cicerón. Lecciones de literatura latina.* Buenos Aires. Estrada.
    1897. Uc
Tasin, N. *La revolución rusa. Sus orígenes, caída del Zarismo, la revolución*
    de marzo. Madrid. Bibl. Nueva. n.d. Pp. 288. U-4861 I D
Tassara, Gabriel García y. *Poesías.* Madrid. Rivadeneyra. 1872. Uc
Tasso, Torquato. *Gerusalemme liberata.* Note Pio Spagnotti e proemio
    Michele Scherillo. Milano. Hoepli. 1918. Pp. xxxviii, 488. U-2364 I* C
Tavera-Acosta, B. *Anales de Guayana.* Ciudad Bolívar. La Empresa. 1905.
    Pp. 362. U-4305 D
Taylor, A.H.E. *The Future of the Southern Slavs.* London. Fisher Unwin.
    [1917]. Pp. 326. U-3032 I B
Taylor, Henry U. *The Mediaeval Mind. A History of the Development of*
    Thought and Emotion in the Middle Ages. 2 vols. London. Macmillan.
    1914. U-816-17 I* B*
Teixeira de Pascoaes. See Pereira Teixeira de Vasconcellos, Joaquin
Teixeira de Vasconcellos, Maria da Gloria. *Horas de Deus.* Porto. Porto Medico.
    1921. Pp. 70. U-4038 D
Teja Zabre, Alfonso. *Historia de México. Una moderna interpretación.*
    México. Secr. de Relaciones Exteriores. 1935. Pp. xii, 399. U-832
Tejeda, Luis José de. *Coronas líricas. Prosa y verso.* Noticia histórica y
    crítica E. Martínez Paz. Córdoba, Argentina. Bautista Cobas. 1917.
    Pp. lv, 340. U-1163
Téllez, Fray Gabriel (Tirso de Molina). *Comedias.* Colección ordenada e
    ilustrada E. Cotarelo y Mori. 2 vols. (NBAE, 4, 9). Madrid. Bailly-Baillière.
    1906-7. U-39, U-44 I
— *El vergonzoso en palacio. El burlador de Sevilla.* Ed. Américo Castro.
    Madrid. La Lectura. 1910. Pp. xxiv, 292. U-935
Téllez y López, Juan. *Cuentos para Mimí.* Madrid. F. Fé. 1903. Pp. 122.
    U-4676 D
— *Manual de fisiología e higiene.* Madrid. Bailly-Baillière. 1904. Pp. 288.
    U-4398 D
— *Enciclopedia de la cultura general.* Madrid. Bailly-Baillière. 1909. Pp. 788.
    U-729 n/o
— *Vidas sin vida. Novela.* Madrid. Renacimiento. 1915. Pp. 250. U-3798

– *De espaldas al sol.* Madrid. Uc D

Tello, Wenceslao. *El espíritu universitario mundial.* Buenos Aires. Cía.
Sud-Americana de Billetes de Banco. 1909. Pp. 26. U-2455 D

Temperley, Harold William V. *History of Serbia.* London. Bell. 1917. Pp. x,
359. U-3828 I* B

Temple, Charles Lindsay. *Native Races and Their Rulers.* Cape Town. Argus.
1918. Pp. xi, 252. U-2663 I* C B

Tena, Alberto. *La otra Alemania.* Buenos Aires. Moen. 1915. Pp. 109.
U-1127 D

– *El pájaro sin alas.* Buenos Aires. Nosotros. 1916. Pp. 259. U-2886 D

Tennemann, Wilhelm Gottlieb. *Geschichte der Philosophie.* 11 vols. Leipzig.
Barth. 1798-1819. U-3804-15. Vols. IV, VIII I C

Tennyson, Alfred. *The Works of Alfred Tennyson. Poet Laureate.* London.
Macmillan. 1900. Pp. 900. U-2958 I* C* T

Tenorio, Oscar. *México revolucionario.* Rio de Janeiro. Folha Academica.
1928. Pp. 232. U-4974 D

Tenreiro, Ramón María. *La ley del pecado.* Madrid. Renacimiento. 1930.
Pp. 348. U-2341 D

Terán, Juan B. *Estudios y notas.* Tucumán. Rev. Letras y Ciencias Sociales.
1908. Pp. 287. (2 copies) U-1925, U-3142 D

– *Tucumán, y el Norte Argentino (1820-1840).* Buenos Aires. Coni. 1910.
Pp. 252. U-3428 D

– *El descubrimiento de América en la historia de Europa.* Buenos Aires.
Coni. 1916. Pp. 196. U-1613 D

– *La salud de la América española.* Paris. Ed. Franco-Ibero-Americana.
1926. Pp. 206. U-4986

Terán, Luis de. *Violetas.* Pról. Jacinto Benavente. Madrid. Asilo de Huérfanos.
1900. Uc D

Terentius Afer, Publius. *Publii Terentii comoediae.* Interpretatione et notis
illustravit J. Juvencius. Venetiis. Haeredis Nicolai Pezzana. 1768. Pp. 500.
U-4657

– *Publii Terentii Afri. Comoediae.* Notis Joh. Min-Elli. Illustratae
accurante D. Roderico ab Oviedo. Madrid. Antonio de Sancha. 1775.
Pp. 624. U-645

Teresa de Jesús, Santa. *Obras de Santa Teresa de Jesús.* Novísima edición
corregida y aumentada Vicente de la Fuente. 6 vols. Madrid. Impresores
y Libreros del Reino. 1881. U-1748-53

– *Vida de la santa madre ... y Camino de perfección por la misma santa
madre.* Madrid. Apostolado de la Prensa. Uc

– *Colección de las principales obras de la insigne fundadora de la reforma de
la Orden de Nuestra Señora del Carmen.* Ed. ilustrada, precedida de un
artículo 'Santa Teresa en la literatura patria' de Angel Lasso de la Vega.
Barcelona. Bibl. Salvatella. Uc

Terzakis, Anghelos. *Desmotes. Mythistorima.* n.p. Ekdotis Ar. N. Mauridis.
    n.d. Pp. 255. U-2744-5 D
Teweles, Heinrich. *Der Ring des Polykrates.* Leipzig. Reclam. n.d. Pp. 23.
    U-4525
Thackeray, William Makepeace. *Vanity Fair. A Novel Without a Hero.* New
    York. Burt. [1848]. Pp. 617. U-234 I* T
— *The History of Pendennis.* Introd. Edmund Grosse. 2 vols. London.
    Oxford University Press. [1907]. U-440-1 I* T
— *The History of Henry Esmond.* London. Dent. [1906]. Pp. xxix, 601.
    U-996 I*
— *The Newcomes.* Introd. Walter Jerrold. 2 vols. London. Dent. [1910].
    U-999-1000 I* T
— *The English Humourists. The Four Georges.* Introd. Walter Jerrold.
    London. Dent. [1912]. Pp. xviii, 423. U-1001 I* T
— *The Virginians.* Introd. Walter Jerrold. 2 vols. London. Dent. [1911].
    U-997-8 I C
Tharaud, Jérome et Jean. *Les hobereaux. Histoire vraie.* Paris. Cahiers de la
    Quinzaine. Juillet 1904. Uc
Thayer Ojeda, Tomás. *Las antiguas ciudades de Chile.* Santiago de Chile.
    Cervantes. 1911. Uc
Theocritus. *Theocriti, Bionis et Moschi Idyllia.* Recensuit notasque criticas
    adjecit C.H. Weise. Lipsiae. Tauchnitz. 1843. Pp. xiii, 182. U-4502 T*
Theologia deutsch. Herausgegeben von Franz Pfeiffer. Gütersloh.
    Bertelsmann. 1900. Pp. xxxii, 239. U-1606 I
Theophrastus. *Les caractères.* Texte établi et tr. Octave Navarre. Paris. Les
    Belles Lettres. 1920. Pp. 74. U-4291
Theotokas, Giorgos. *Argo. Mythistorima.* Athina. Pyrsos. 1936. Pp. 482.
    U-2753 D
Thibaudet, Albert. *Gustave Flaubert 1821-1880. Sa vie, ses romans, son style.*
    Paris. Plon. 1922. Pp. 339. QP-49 I*
Thirlmere, Rowland. *Polyclitus and Other Poems.* London. Elkin Mathews.
    1916. Pp. 76. U-3855 I C T D
Thomas Aquinas, Saint. *Divi Thomae Aquinatis ... Summa Theologica,* ad
    Mss Codices a F. Garcia, G. Donato, J. Nicolai, ac T. Madalena ... collata:
    Secundis curis, ac dissertationibus in singulos Tomos à B.M. de Rubeis
    illustrata. 6 vols. Matriti. Doblado. 1782-3. U-60-5
Thomas, Lowell, and Frank Schoonmaker. *The American Travellers' Guide
    Book: Spain.* New York. Simon and Schuster. 1932. Pp. 260. U-3590
Thomè de Jesus, Fr. *Trabalhos de Jesus.* Lisboa. Fernandes Lopes. 1865.
    Pp. xxx, 351. U-1756 I
Thompson, Francis. *The Hound of Heaven.* London. Burns & Oates. [1914].
    Pp. 17. U-4692

Thompson, George. *La guerra del Paraguay.* Tr. Diego Lewis y Angel Estrada. Nuevas notas José Arturo Scotto. 2 vols. Buenos Aires. Rosso. 1911. U-1175-6

Thompson, Silvanus P. *The Quest for Truth.* Kingsway. Headley Bros. 1917. Pp. 128. U-2431 I C

Thomson, James. 'B.V.' *The City of Dreadful Night and Other Poems.* London. Bertram Dobell. 1899. Pp. xx, 256. U-4626

Thoreau, Henry David. *Walden.* Introd. Bradford Torrey. Boston. Houghton, Mifflin. 1902. Pp. xliii, 522. U-3502 I* C* T L

Thucydides. *Thucydidis de Bello Peloponnesiaco libri octo.* Recognovit G. Boehme. 2 vols. Lipsiae. Teubner. 1851. U-2022-3 I* C* L* T

Thury, M. *El paro forzoso. Causas y remedios.* Tr. M. Domenge Mir. Barcelona. Henrich. 1906. Uc

La tia fingida. Anotaciones a su texto y estudio crítico acerca de quien fue su autor por J.T. Medina. Pról. J. Vicuña Cifuentes. Santiago de Chile. Elzeviriana. 1919. Pp. xxx, 493. U-2114 n/o

Tiberghien, Guillerme. *La science de l'âme dans les limites de l'observation.* Bruxelles. Decq. 1868. Pp. v, 525. U-2601

— *Teoría de lo infinito.* Tr. G. Lizárraga. Madrid. Suárez. 1872. Pp. xviii, 239. U-293

Tiberio, Oscar. *Palingenesia. Florilegio de muerte, de galantería, de amor.* n.p. González. 1912. Pp. 249. U-2986 D

Tibullus. *Catulli, Tibulli et Propertii Carmina* ad Praestantium Librorum lectiones accurate recensuit C.H. Weise. Lipsiae. Tauchnitz. 1843. Pp. 272. U-4589 T*

Ticknor, George. *Letters to Pascual de Gayangos From Originals in the Collection of the Hispanic Society of America.* Ed. Clara Louisa Penney. New York. Hispanic Society of America. 1927. Pp. xliv, 578. U-1410

Tiempo, César, pseud. [i.e., Israel Zeitlin]. *Sebatión argentino.* Buenos Aires. Soc. Amigos del Libro Rioplatense. 1933. Pp. 185. U-2689 D

Tilgher, Adriano. *La visione greca della vita.* Roma. Libr. di Scienze e Lettere. 1926. Pp. 171. U-5347 I C D

Tillier, Claude. *Mon oncle Benjamin.* Berlin. Internationale Bibliothek G.M.B.H. n.d. Pp. 260. U-5241

Timoneda, Juan de. *La oveja perdida. Auto sacramental.* Introd., notas, y glosario A. García Boiza. Salamanca. Pérez Criado. 1921. Pp. 86. U-5606 n/o

Tinayre, Marcelle. *La maison du péché.* Paris. Calmann-Lévy. n.d. Uc

Tinoco, Juan C. *Album de viajero.* Maracaibo. Imp. Americana. 1903. Pp. 126. U-2817 D

Tissi, Silvio. *La tragedia di un'X.* Milano. Audace. 1923. Pp. 83. U-3585 D

Tobal, Gastón Federico. *Comenzar de un camino.* Buenos Aires. Moen.
     1909. Uc D
Tocco, Felice. *L'Eresia nel medio evo.* Firenze. Sansoni. 1884. Pp. viii, 564.
     U-307 I
Todd, Alpheus. *Gobierno parlamentario en Inglaterra.* Ed. revisada y
     abreviada Spencer Walpole. Tr. Julio Carrié. 2 vols. Buenos Aires. Peuser.
     1902. U-4135-6
Todi, Jacopone da. See Benedetti, Giacopone de' da Todi
Toepffer, Rodolphe. *La bibliothèque de mon oncle.* Paris. Nilsson. [1914].
     Pp. 242. U-3399
Tojal, Leoncio. *Carta de Benedicto XV al genio humano.* Pp. 41. U-1629
     [Typescript]
Toller, Ernst. *Hinkemann.* Potsdam. Kiepenheuer. 1924. Pp. 60. U-5409
— *Das Schwalbenbuch.* Potsdam. Kiepenheuer. 1924. Pp. 54. U-5408
— *Masse-Mensch.* Potsdam. Kiepenheuer. 1925. Pp. 82. U-5376
Tolstoi, Lev Nikolaevich. *La guerre et la paix.* Roman historique tr. avec
     l'autorisation de l'auteur par une Russe. 3 vols. Paris. Hachette. 1891.
     U-1376-8
Tomaselli, Alfio. *Il minotauro.* Catania. Vena & Martínez. 1896. Pp. 14.
     U-3435 D
— *Inni sacri.* Catania. Battiato. 1900. Pp. 30. U-422 D
Toreno, Conde de. See Queipo de Llano, José Ma
Toro y Gisbert, Miguel. *Ortología castellana de nombres propios.* Carta-pról.
     José Cuervo. Paris. Ollendorff. 1911. Pp. xxi, 491. U-912
— *Apuntaciones lexicográficas.* Paris. Ollendorff. n.d. Uc
Toro y Gómez, Miguel de. *Por la cultura y por la raza.* Paris. Ollendorff.
     1908. Pp. vii, 308. U-1369 D
Torón, Saulo. *Las monedas de cobre. Poemas.* Poesía preliminar Pedro Salinas.
     Madrid. Clásica Española. 1919. Pp. 147. U-3580 D
— *Canciones de la orilla.* Pról. E. Díez-Canedo. Madrid. Pueyo. 1932.
     Pp. 156. U-3652 D
Torras y Báges, José. *El rosario y su mística filosofía.* Barcelona. Tip. Católica.
     1886. Pp. 331. U-4435
— *El estadismo y la libertad religiosa.* Vich. Anglada. 1912. Uc
Torre, Claudio de la. *El canto diverso.* Pról. E. Díez-Canedo. Madrid. Clásica
     Española. 1918. Pp. 60. U-3405 D
Torre-Isunza, Ramón de. *La enseñanza religiosa y el discurso del Sr Mella.*
     Madrid. Fortanet. 1913. Uc
Torre Ruiz, A. *Federico Nietzsche.* Valladolid. Imp. Castellana. 1907. Pp. 147.
     U-2712 D
— *Poemas.* Valladolid. Montero. 1917. Pp. 121. U-1546 D

– *Dos ensayos.* I. *Escultura helenística o helenismo y barroquismo.*
II. *Poesía humana y poesía deshumanizada.* Valladolid. Imp. Castellana.
1928. Pp. vii, 148. U-4963 D

Torrendell, Juan. *La república española en su primer hervor. Diario de un
periodista residente en Buenos Aires.* Buenos Aires. Tor. [1935]. Pp. 268.
U-3872 n/o D

– *El año literario 1918.* Pról. Constancio C. Vigil. Buenos Aires. Tor.
[1918]. Pp. 222. U-3236 n/o D

Torres, Carlos Arturo. *Estudios ingleses. Estudios varios.* Madrid. Angel de
San Martín. [1907]. Pp. 325. (2 copies) U-2678 n/o. U-3736 D

– *Idola Fori. Ensayo sobre supersticiones políticas.* Valencia. Sempere. n.d.
Pp. 217. U-2735 L D

– *Obra poética.* Madrid. Angel de San Martín. [1906]. Pp. 224. U-4283

– *Poemas fantásticos.* Paris. Roger et Chernoviz. n.d. Pp. 101. U-3156 n/o D

Torres, Sagunto. *Prismas. Poesías.* Buenos Aires. Mercatali. 1920. Pp. 57.
U-2883 n/o D

Torres Frías, Domingo. *Argentinas.* Pról. R. Obligado. Buenos Aires. Peuser.
1908. Pp. xxiv, 152. U-2738 D

Torres Frías, María. *Aurora boreal.* Buenos Aires. Portel. 1934. Pp. 151.
U-4280 D

Torres García, José. *Notes sobre art.* Girona. Masó. [1913]. Pp. 135.
U-4440 D

Torres Hernández, Rodrigo. *Por la senda sonora.* México. 1914. Pp. 148.
U-3864 n/o D

Torres Pinzon, C.A. *Prosas y esbozos.* Bogotá. Minerva. n.d. Uc D

Torres Rioseco, Arturo. *Poetas norteamericanos. I. Walt Whitman.* San José
de Costa Rica. García Monge. 1922. Pp. 129. U-4655

Torres Villarroel, Diego de. *Anatomía de todo lo visible e invisible.* Madrid.
Ibarra. 1794. Pp. 315. U-4610

– *Sueños morales, visiones y visitas con D. Francisco de Quevedo por
Madrid.* Vol. II. Madrid. Ibarra. 1794. Pp. 379. U-4611

– *Vida, ascendencia, nacimiento, crianza y aventuras del Dr D. de T.V.,
escrita por él mismo.* Ed., introd., y notas F. de Onís. Madrid. La Lectura.
1912. Pp. xxx, 294. U-934 I*

Torres y Gómez, Enrique. *Gramática histórica-comparada de la lengua
castellana.* Madrid. Sáenz de Jubera. 1899. Pp. xvi, 490. U-1105

Tovar, Antonio. *El imperio de España.* Valladolid. Aguado. n.d. Pp. 73. n/n D

Tovar, Enrique D. *Ventura Gracía Calderón y su obra literaria.* Paris. Agencia
General de Librería. [1920]. Pp. 64. U-3190 D

Towiański, Andrzéj. *Testimonianze di Italiani su Andrea Towianśki.* Roma.
Tip. del Senato. 1903. Pp. 292. U-696

Traducciones poéticas. Por Ismael-Enrique Arciniegas. Paris. Excelsior. 1925.
    Pp. 253. U-5099
Trafelli, Luigi. *Nous, citoyens du royaume de Satan.* Tr. Maxime Formont.
    Paris. Hachette. n.d. Pp. 135. U-2127 D
Tralles, Alexandre de. *Crónicas y siluetas.* Paris. Ollendorff. 1912. Pp. 267.
    U-2363 I D
Trasplantades. Poesies franceses contemporanies. Tr. E. Guanyabéns. Proleg-
    estudi J. Pérez-Jorba. Barcelona. L'Avenç. 1910. Pp. xlviii, 119. U-4650 B
Treitschke, Heinrich von. *Politik.* 2 vols. Leipzig. Hirzel. 1911-13.
    U-3832-3 I*. Vol. ɪ C
Trelawny, Edward John. *Records of Shelley, Byron and the Author.* London.
    Routledge. n.d. Pp. xxiv, 264. U-446 I*
Trend, J.B. *A Picture of Modern Spain.* London. Constable. 1921. Pp. viii, 271.
    U-1746
Trentin, Silvio. *L'Aventure italienne. Légendes et réalités.* Préf. M.A. Aulard.
    Paris. Les Presses Universitaires de France. 1928. Pp. 332. U-5321 I
— *Antidémocratie.* Paris. Valois. 1930. Pp. 278. U-3329 D
Trigo, Felipe. *Socialismo individualista.* Madrid. F. Fé. 1904. Pp. 206.
    U-2829 D
— *El amor en la vida y en los libros. Mi ética y mi estética.* Madrid.
    Pueyo. Uc D
Trilles, Ramón. *Amores.* Valencia. Domenech Mar. n.d. Pp. 93. U-2896 D
Trindade Coelho, José Francisco de. *Os meus amores.* Lisboa. Aillaud. 1901.
    Pp. 423. U-2426 I
Tristan. *Le roman de Tristan et Iseut.* Tr. et restauré J. Bédier. Préf. Gaston
    Paris. Paris. [1900]. Pp. 284. U-588
El triunfo del Ave María de 'Un ingenio de esta corte.' Pról. D. Francisco de
    Pa. Vallador. Granada. El Defensor de Granada. 1899. Pp. 199. U-5638
Troeltsch, Ernest, et al. *Systematische christliche Religion.* Berlin. Teubner.
    1909. Pp. viii, 286. U-1636 I
Trofeos. Bogotá (1 febrero 1907). n/n
Trotsky, Lev. *Mi vida. Ensayo autobiográfico.* Tr. W. Roces. Madrid. Cenit.
    1930. Pp. 612. U-4205 I*
— *Où va l'Angleterre?* Tr. Victor Serge. Paris. L'Humanité. [1926]. Pp. 246.
    U-5295 n/o
Troward, T. *Bible Mystery and Bible Meaning.* London. The Edinburgh
    Lecture Series. [1905]. Pp. 245. U-3684
Trueba, Antonio de. *Leyendas genealógicas de España.* 2 vols. Barcelona.
    Cortezo. 1887. U-3102-3
— *En honor de Antonio de Trueba.* Bilbao. Biblioteca Bascongada. 1896.
    Pp. 211. U-3920 n/o

Trujillo Molina, Rafael Leonidas. *La nueva patria dominicana. Recopilación de discursos, mensajes y memorias.* (1930-4). 2 vols. Santo Domingo. 1934-5. U-2218-19

El Tucumán colonial (Documentos y mapas del Archivo de Indias). Introd. y notas R. Jaimes Freyre. Tomo I. Buenos Aires. Coni. 1915. Pp. 193, pl. 4. U-4820

Tudela, Ricardo. *El inquilino de la soledad.* Buenos Aires. Gleizer. 1929. Pp. 168. U-5135 D

Turchi, Nicola. *La civiltà bizantina.* Torino. Bocca. 1915. Pp. vii, 327. U-2300 I

Turcios, Froylán. *Cuentos del amor y de la muerte.* Paris. Le Livre Libre. 1930. Pp. 351. U-5086 D

Turell, Gabriel. *Recort.* Barcelona. L'Avenç. 1894. Pp. xv, 171. U-2887

Turini, Ernesto P., hijo. *Líricas.* Buenos Aires. Sarramea y Lajous. 1907. Pp. 96. U-3189 D

Turmo Baselga, Mariano. *Miguelón.* Barcelona. Henrich. 1904. Pp. 315. U-3692 I D

Turró, R. *Les origines de la connaissance.* Paris. Alcan. 1914. Pp. 274. U-857 I* C

− *La base trófica de la inteligencia.* Madrid. Residencia de Estudiantes. 1918. Pp. 139. U-657 D

− *Filosofía crítica.* Barcelona. Editorial Catalana. 1918. Pp. 241. U-4486 D. Versión castellana por Gabriel Miró. Madrid. Atenea. 1919. Pp. 359. U-1414 D

Turull, Paul M. *La societat de les nacions, la moral internacionalista i Catalunya.* Barcelona. Verdaguer. 1917. Uc D

Tusquets, Francisco. *La hembra. (Historia de un hombre).* Barcelona. Henrich. 1893. Pp. 299. U-4129

Tyler, Royall. *Spain, a Study of Her Life and Arts.* London. Grant Richards. 1909. Pp. 620. U-4242 D

Tyrrell, George. *Lex Credendi − a Sequel to Lex Orandi.* London. Longmans, Green. 1906. Pp. xviii, 256. U-2106 I

− *A Much-Abused Letter.* London. Longmans, Green. 1906. Pp. 104 + 12. U-3889

− *Essays on Faith and Immortality.* Arr. M.D. Petre. London. Arnold. 1914. Pp. xv, 277. (2 copies) U-292 I. U-1893

Tzara, Tristan. *Vingt-cinq poèmes.* Zurich. Heuberger. 1918. Pp. 34. U-3510 n/o D

Ueberweg, Friedrich. *Grundriss der Geschichte der Philosophie.* Herausgegeben von Dr Max Heinze. Berlin. Mittler. 1905. Pp. viii, 402. U-4228 I* C* B

Uexküll, Jakob von. *Ideas para una concepción biológica del mundo.* Tr. R.M. Tenreiro. Madrid. Calpe. 1922. Pp. 268. U-5592 I C. 2a ed. 1934. U-4960

Ugarte, Manuel. *Paisajes parisienses.* Pról. M. de Unamuno. Paris. Imp. Réunies.
    1901. Pp. xvi, 244. U-243 D. Epíl. F. de Nión. Paris. Garnier. 1903.
    Pp. xvi, 248. U-249 D
— *Crónicas del bulevar.* Pról. Rubén Darío. Paris. Garnier. 1903. Pp. x, 320.
    U-2880 I* C D
— *La joven literatura hispanoamericana. Antología de prosistas y poetas.*
    Paris. Colin. 1906. Pp. xlvii, 320. U-3207 C D
— *Una tarde de otoño ... pequeña sinfonía sentimental.* Paris. Garnier. 1906.
    Pp. 220. U-2418 D
— *Las nuevas tendencias literarias.* Valencia. Sempere. [1909]. Pp. 227.
    U-398 n/o D
— *Los problemas contemporáneos. Enfermedades sociales.* Barcelona.
    Sopena. [1906]. Pp. 207. U-3427 D
— *Visiones de España. Apuntes de un viajero argentino.* Valencia. Sempere.
    [1904]. Pp. 194. U-404 D
— *El porvenir de la América latina.* Valencia. Sempere. Uc D
— *Vendimias juveniles.* Preludio Floro M. Ugarte. Paris. Garnier. Uc D
Ugarte Revenga, Angel de. *Desde la sombra.* Bilbao. Celorrio. [1923]. Pp. 114.
    U-513 D
Uhland, Ludwig. *Uhlands gesammelte Werke.* Herausgegeben von Friedrich
    Brandes. 2 vols. Leipzig. Reclam. n.d. U-1420-1 I B T
Ulacia, Francisco de. *El caudillo.* Bilbao. Rojas. 1910. Pp. 312. U-2369
Ulenspiegel. 6 Anvers (1934). n/n
Unamuno, Miguel de. *Paz en la guerra.* Madrid. F. Fé. 1897. Uc
— *De la enseñanza superior en España.* Madrid. Revista Nueva. 1899. Uc
— *Tres ensayos. ¡Adentro! La ideocracia. La fé.* Madrid. Rodríguez Serra.
    1900. Uc
— *Paisajes.* Salamanca. Calón. 1902. Uc
— *En torno al casticismo.* Madrid. F. Fé. 1902. Uc
— *De mi país.* Madrid. F. Fé. 1903. Uc
— *Vida de D. Quijote y Sancho.* Madrid. F. Fé. 1905. Uc
— *Poesías.* Bilbao. Rojas. 1907. Uc
— *Recuerdos de niñez y de mocedad.* Madrid. V. Suárez-F. Fé. 1908. Uc
— *Mi religión y otros ensayos breves.* Madrid. Renacimiento. 1910. Uc
— *Soliloquios y conversaciones.* Madrid. Renacimiento. 1911. Uc
— *Niebla (nivola).* Madrid. Renacimiento. 1914. Uc
— *Rosario de sonetos líricos.* Madrid. Uc
— *El Cristo de Velázquez. Poema.* Madrid. Calpe. 1920. Pp. 170. U-4383
— *Contra esto y aquello.* 2a ed. Madrid. Renacimiento. [1928]. Pp. 251.
    U-4374
— *Andanzas y visiones españolas.* 2a ed. Madrid. Renacimiento. [1929].
    Pp. 306. U-4376

- *El espejo de la muerte.* Novelas cortas. Madrid. F. Fé. [1930]. Pp. 157. U-2132
- *Por tierras de Portugal y de España.* Madrid. Renacimiento. [1930]. Pp. 296. U-4375
- *Amor y pedagogía.* 2a ed. Madrid. Espasa-Calpe. 1934. Pp. 285. U-4378
- *El hermano Juan o el mundo es teatro. Vieja comedia nueva.* Madrid. Espasa-Calpe. 1934. Pp. 205. U-4380
- *The Other One.* Pp. 105. U-1516 [Translation in manuscript]
- *Tres novelas ejemplares y un prólogo.* 3a ed. Madrid. Espasa-Calpe. n.d. Pp. 213. U-4379
- 'La foi Pascalienne,' *Revue de Métaphysique et de Morale.* Paris (1923), 345-9. U-2514
- [Many of Unamuno's first editions are missing from this list due to the fact that his own catalogue only goes up to c. 1917, and the present collection has undoubtedly suffered losses over the years]

Uncal, José María. *Diez velas sobre el mar.* Madrid. Yunque. 1935. Pp. 126. U-3366 D

Underhill, Evelyn. *Practical Mysticism. A Little Book for Normal People.* London. Dent. 1914. Pp. xiii, 163. U-3603 I

Unión Interparlamentaria sobre Seguridad y Desarme. *Cómo sería una nueva guerra.* Ed. española con los últimos acuerdos de la UISD y pref. Juan Estelrich. Barcelona. Montaner y Simón. [1934]. Pp. 410. U-4925 I* D

The Universal Standard. Longbeach, USA, III, 3, 4 (June 1923). U-5155-6

Universidad de Nuevo León. *Documentos y datos relativos a su creación.* Monterrey, México. 1933. U-3557

Universidad de Salamanca. *Estatuto para el régimen autonómico de la Universidad de Salamanca.* Salamanca. Núñez. 1919. Pp. 39. U-1687

Universidad Nacional de Buenos Aires. Facultad de Ciencias Económicas. *Cursos de Seminario. Años 1915-1916.* Buenos Aires. Ministerio de Agricultura de la Nación. 1916. Pp. 73. U-1467

Universidad Nacional de la Plata. [10 ff. of photographs and plans of the various colleges] U-3533

Unruh, Fritz von. *Nouvel empire.* Tr., préf., et notes Benoist-Méchin. Paris. Sagittaire. 1925. Pp. 179. U-5302 I

Urales, Federico. *Sembrando flores.* Barcelona. Escuela Moderna. 1906. Pp. 161. U-375 n/o D
- *Mi vida.* 2 vols. Barcelona. Revista Blanca. n.d. U-5082-3 I* D

Urbano, Rafael. *Manual del perfecto enfermo.* Pról. J. Francos Rodríguez. Madrid. Beltrán. 1911. Pp. 138. U-2359 D

Urbina, Luis G. *Ingenuas.* Paris. Bouret. 1902. Pp. 182. U-3422 I
- *Puestas de sol.* Paris. Bouret. 1910. Pp. 211. U-1909 B D
- *El glosario de la vida vulgar.* Madrid. Pueyo. 1916. Pp. 172. U-2919 D

– *Bajo el sol y frente al mar.* Madrid. García y Galo Sáez. 1916. Pp. 258.
U-3113 D

Urdaneta, Rafael. *Memorias del General Rafael Urdaneta.* Pról. R. Blanco-Fombona. Madrid. Editorial América. n.d. Pp. xxxi, 444. U-1744

Urdeval, Rafael. *Crímenes literarios y meras tentativas escriturales y delictuosas.* Oviedo. 1906. Uc D

Ureta, Alberto J. *Rumor de almas.* Lima. La Revista. 1911. Pp. 121.
U-2927 D

Uriarte, Gregorio. *Problemas de política internacional americana.* Buenos Aires. Perrotti. 1915. Pp. 71. U-3709 D

Uribe, Diego. *Margarita.* Paris. Imp. Sudamericana. 1906. Uc D

– *Hielos.* Paris. Roger y Chernoviz. n.d. Pp. 148. U-2885 D

Urien, Carlos M. *Quiroga. Estudio histórico constitucional.* Buenos Aires. Tall. Gráf. de la Cía. General de Fósforos. 1907. Pp. 403. U-2528 D

– *Revelaciones de un manuscrito.* Buenos Aires. Mendesky. 1915. Pp. 260.
U-2791 D

– *Mitre. Contribución al estudio de la vida pública del teniente general Bartolomé Mitre.* 2 vols. Buenos Aires. Molinari. 1919. U-3724-5 D

– y Ezio Colombo. *Geografía argentina.* Buenos Aires. Tip. de la Penitenciaría Nacional. 1905. Pp. xxxi, 688. U-1197 D

Urquia, Delfino. *San Martín.* Paris. Jouve. 1916. Pp. 113. U-3324 D

Urquieta, Miguel A. *Caleidoscopio. Prosas ingenuas.* Arequipa, Perú. Quiroz. 1915. Pp. 280. U-491 D

Urquijo e Ibarra, Julio de. *Menéndez Pelayo y los caballeros de Azcoitia.* San Sebastián. Martín y Mena. 1925. Pp. 152. U-4969

Urquinaona y Pardo, Pedro. *Memorias de Urquinaona.* Madrid. Editorial América. [1917]. Pp. 383. U-2529

Urrutia, Alejandro. *Versos.* Córdoba. Giménez. 1915. Pp. 256. U-2918 D

Urueta, Jesús. *Alma poesía.* México. Escalante. 1904. Pp. 138. U-3035 I D

Usque, Samuel. *Consolaçam ás tribulaçoens de Israel.* Rev. e pref. Mendes dos Remédios. 3 vols. Coimbra. Amado. 1906. U-2681

Utrilla y Calvo, Francisco. *Morriones, sotanas y boinas.* Madrid. F. Fé. 1897. Pp. 598. U-2761 D

Vaccaro, Eduardo. *Signos y símbolos. Versos.* Buenos Aires. Samet. 1929. Pp. 80. U-5092 D

Vaccaro, Michele Angelo. *Génesis y función de las leyes penales.* Tr. M. Domenge Mir. 2 vols. Barcelona. Henrich. 1907. Uc

Vacherot, Etienne. *La science et la conscience.* Paris. Baillière. 1870. Pp. 184.
U-3988

Val, Mariano Miguel de. *Edad dorada.* Madrid. Rodríguez. 1905. Uc D

– *Los novelistas en el teatro. Tentativas dramáticas de Da. Emilia Pardo Bazán.* Madrid. Rodríguez. 1906. Pp. 181. U-635 D

– *Alfredo Vicente, poeta.* Madrid. 1907. Pp. 73. U-4409 D

Valderrama, Adolfo. *Obras escogidas en prosa de don Adolfo Valderrama.* Colección hecha por don Enrique Nercasseau y Morán y precedida de una biografía del autor. Santiago de Chile. Bibl. de Escritores de Chile. 1912. Pp. xvii, 544. U-2611

Valderrama, Pilar de. *Huerto cerrado.* Madrid. Caro Raggio. n.d. Pp. 189. U-5013 D

Valdés, Juan de. *Diálogo de doctrina cristiana.* Reproduction en facsimile de l'exemplaire de la Bibliothèque Nationale de Lisbonne, avec introd. et notes M. Bataillon. Coimbra. Imp. da Universidade. 1925. Pp. 319, ff. cvii. U-5486 I*

Valdés, Ramón M. *Geografía de Panamá.* Panamá. Benedetti. 1914. Pp. 191. U-658

Valdés Cange, J., pseud. [i.e., Alejandro Venegas]. *Sinceridad. Chile íntimo en 1910.* n.p. Imp. Universitaria. 1910. Uc D

Valdés Vergara, Francisco. *Historia de Chile para le enseñanza primaria.* Valparaiso. Babra. 1904. Pp. 376. U-3210 I*

Valdivia, Victor de. *El imperio Iberoamericano.* Paris. Hispanoamericana. 1929. Pp. 302. U-5030 I* C* D

Valencia, Miguel Santiago. *Madame Adela.* Bogotá. 1913. Uc D

– *La gitana.* Bogotá. Arboleda y Valencia. 1914. Uc D

Valentí Camp, Santiago. *Bosquejos sociológicos.* Pról. Alfredo Calderón. Madrid. F. Fé. 1899. Uc D

– *Premoniciones y reminiscencias.* Pról. A. Bonilla y San Martín. Barcelona. Henrich. 1907. Uc

– *Vicisitudes y anhelos del pueblo español.* Pról. P. Dorado Montero. Barcelona. Virgili. 1911. Pp. xv, 301. U-4192 D

Valentí Vivó, I. *La sanidad social y los obreros.* 2 vols. Barcelona. Henrich. 1905. Uc

Valentinis, Gualtiero. *In Friuli.* Udine. Tosolini. 1903. Pp. 92, viii + 84. U-133

Valenzuela, Jesús. E. *Almas.* México. Escalante. 1904. Pp. vii, 276. U-1301

– *Lira libre.* México. Escalante. 1906. Pp. xxxvi, 212. U-4166 n/o

Valenzuela Olivos, Eduardo. *Infantiles.* Santiago de Chile. Universo. 1909. Pp. 134. U-2374 D

Valera, Juan. *Cartas americanas.* Madrid. Fuentes y Capdeville. 1889. Pp. xii, 278. U-4646

– *Nuevas cartas americanas.* Madrid. F. Fé. 1890. Pp. viii, 295. U-584

– *Pepita Jiménez.* Ed. y pról. Manuel Azaña. Madrid. La Lectura. 1927. Pp. lxxii, 255. U-932 I* C* L

Valero Martín, Alberto. *La moza del mesón.* Madrid. Editorial de España. 1915. Pp. 206. U-1609 D

— *Castilla Madre. Salamanca (de la tierra, de las piedras y de los hombres).*
Versos de don Miguel de Unamuno, de Gregorio Martínez Sierra, de
Francisco Villaespesa, de Salvador Rueda, y de Eduardo Marquina. Madrid.
Renacimiento. 1916. Pp. 254. U-412 D

— *Los perros de la alquería y Juicios críticos sobre 'Ninón.'* Pról. M. Bueno.
Madrid. Beltrán. [1912]. Pp. 262 + 40. U-3632 D

— *Campo y hogar.* Salamanca. Bibl. Salmantina. n.d. Pp. 178. U-3778 D

Valéry, Paul. *Monsieur Teste.* Paris. Gallimard. 1929. Pp. 138. QP-50 I

— *Variété II.* Paris. Gallimard. 1930. Pp. 269. QP-51 I

— *Regards sur le monde actuel.* Paris. Stock. 1931. Pp. 214. QP-52 I

— *Choses tues.* Paris. Gallimard. 1932. Pp. 211. QP-53 I*

— *El cementerio marino.* Tr. Mariano Brull. Edición bilingüe. Paris. Sánchez
Cuesta. 1930. Pp. xxix, U-3605

Valle Arizpe, Artemio de. *Vidas milagrosas.* Madrid. Cervantes. 1920. Pp. 256.
U-3478 D

Valle Caviedes, Juan del, et al. *Flor de academias y Diente del Parnaso.* Lima.
El Tiempo. 1899. Uc

Valle Iberlucea, E. de. *La crisis y el presupuesto.* Buenos Aires. García. 1915.
Pp. 464. U-3061

— *La cuestión internacional y el partido socialista.* Buenos Aires. García.
1917. Pp. 256. U-3634

Valle-Inclán, Ramón del. *La lámpara maravillosa. Ejercicios espirituales.*
Madrid. Helénica. [1916]. Pp. 258. U-2852 I D

Vallejo, José Joaquín. *Obras de D. José Joaquín Vallejo.* Estudio crítico y
biográfico Alberto Edwards. Santiago de Chile. Bibl. Escritores Chilenos.
1911. Pp. liii, 567. U-2609

Vallenilla Lanz, Laureano. *El libertador juzgado por los miopes.* Caracas.
Lit. y Tip. del Comercio. 1914. Pp. 16. U-4123 D

Vallmitjana, Julio. *Criminalidad típica local.* Barcelona. L'Avenç. 1910.
Pp. 81. U-2940 D

— *La Xava.* Barcelona. L'Avenç. 1910. Pp. 359. U-1887 D

— *Fent memoria.* Barcelona. Renaixensa. 1906. Pp. 167. U-1932 D

— *Els oposats.* Drama en tres actes. Barcelona. Bibl. Orientalista. 1906.
Pp. 69. U-2929 D

— *De la ciutat vella.* Barcelona. Universal. 1907. Pp. 227. U-2687 D

— *Cóm comencèm à patir.* Barcelona. Duran y Bori. 1908. Pp. 124.
(2 copies) U-1861, U-2584 n/o D

— *Sota Montjuic. Novela.* Barcelona. L'Avenç. 1908. Pp. 276. U-2692 n/o D

Vallotton, Benjamín. *Au pays de la mort.* Paris. Attinger. [1917]. Pp. 63.
U-264

Valoraciones. La Plata (Sept. 1923, agosto 1926). n/n

Van Caenegem, F. *Los comerciantes del siglo XX.* Introd. C. van Oberbergh. Tr. E. Dieste. Pról. R. Rucabado. Barcelona. Horta. 1912. Pp. xxvii, 196. U-794

Vandellós, Josep A. *Catalunya, poble decadent.* Barcelona. Bibl. Catalana d'Autors Independents. 1935. Pp. 236. U-220

Vanderborght, Paul. *Hommage à Rupert Brooke. 1887-1915.* Poèmes de Rupert Brooke tr. Roland Hérelle. Bruxelles. L'Eglantine. 1931. Pp. 218. U-1217

Van Duinen, R. *Nouveau dictionnaire français-hollandais.* Amsterdam. [1900]. n/n

Varela, Benigno. *Senda de tortura.* Madrid. Pueyo. n.d. Uc D

Varela, Juan Cruz. *Poesías ... y las tragedias Dido y Argia.* Buenos Aires. La Tribuna. 1879. Pp. 486. U-705

— *Seis tragedias.* Buenos Aires. La Facultad. 1915. Uc

Vargas, Moisés. *Bosquejo de la instrucción pública en Chile.* Santiago de Chile. Imp. Barcelona. 1908. Pp. 453. U-728 D

Vargas Vila, J.M. *Del opio.* Caracas. Herrera Irigoyen. 1904. Uc D

— *La voz de las horas.* Barcelona. Maucci. n.d. Uc

Varios a varios. Manuel Cervera, Luis C. López, y A.Z. López-Penha. Pról. F. Ramos González. Madrid. Pueyo. [1910]. Pp. 144. U-2125 D

Varisco, Bernardino. *I massimi problemi.* Milano. Libr. Editrice Milanese. 1910. Pp. xi, 331. U-1243 I* C

Varney, León. *El sentido de una vida.* Bogotá. Eléctrica. 1906. Uc D

Varsi, Tomás. *Los grandes problemas nacionales.* Rosario de Santa Fé. Peuser. 1914. Uc D

Vasilakaki, Chr. *Pliges ke Frangelion.* Athina. O Koraïs. 1930. Pp. 400. U-2741 T* D

Vasseur, Alvaro Armando. *Hacia el gran silencio.* Montevideo. García. 1924. Pp. 126. U-2913 n/o D

Vayreda, Marián. *Sanch nova.* Olot. Planadevall. 1900. Pp. 501. U-2695

— *La punyalada.* Barcelona. Ilustració Catalana. 1904. Pp. 392. U-2784

Vaz Ferreira, Carlos. *Los problemas de la libertad.* Montevideo. El Siglo Ilustrado. 1907. Pp. 92. (2 copies) U-1684-5 D

— *El pragmatismo. Exposición y crítica.* Montevideo. Escuela Nac. de Artes y Oficios. 1909. Pp. 117. U-826 D

— *Lógica viva.* Montevideo. Escuela Nac. de Artes y Oficios. 1910. Uc D

— *Sobre los problemas sociales.* Montevideo. El Siglo Ilustrado. 1922. Pp. 121. U-2905 D

— *Estudios pedagógicos.* Serie III. *Un proyecto sobre escuelas y liceos.* Montevideo. El Siglo Ilustrado. 1922. Pp. 77. U-3968 D

— *Enero de 1908. I. Conocimiento y acción.* Montevideo. Mariño y Caballero. n.d. Pp. 110. U-1686 D

Vázquez Cey, Arturo. *La doble angustia.* Buenos Aires. Martín García.
　　1914. Uc D
— *Invocación a Don Quijote (Poema).* Buenos Aires. Martín García. 1916.
　　Pp. 18. U-2051 D
Vázquez de Aldana, Enrique. *Del jardín de la Murta.* Madrid. Velasco.
　　1912. Uc D
Vecchio, Giorgio del. *Filosofía del derecho.* Tr., pról., y extensas ediciones
　　L. Recaséns Siches. Barcelona. Bosch. 1929. Pp. 531. U-4855 D
Vedia, Agustín de. *Constitución argentina.* Buenos Aires. Coni. 1907. Uc D
Vedia, Enrique de. *Transfusión.* Buenos Aires. Mendesky. n.d. Pp. 303.
　　U-3070 n/o D
Vedia y Mitre, Mariano de. *Cuestiones de educación y de crítica.* Pról.
　　O. Magnasco. Buenos Aires. Moen. 1907. Uc D
Vega, Carlos. *Campo.* Buenos Aires. La Facultad. 1927. Pp. 94. U-5660 D
Vega, José de la. *La federación de Colombia (1810-1912).* Madrid. Editorial
　　América. n.d. Pp. 325. U-3744 D
Vega, Lope de. *La Dorotea.* Ed. Américo Castro. Madrid. Renacimiento.
　　1913. Pp. xxiii, 305. n/n I*
— *Semblanza y selección poética* por Andrés Ochando. Valencia. Miguel Juan.
　　1935. Pp. 72. U-5080
— *Catálogo de la exposición bibliográfica de Lope de Vega organizada por la
　　Biblioteca nacional.* Pról. M. Artigas. Madrid. Junta del Centenario de
　　Lope de Vega. 1935. Pp. viii, 245. U-797 n/o
Vega de Mina, Juana. *Apuntes para la historia por la Excma. Sra. Da. Juana
　　Vega de Mina, Condesa de Espoz y Mina.* Revisados por el Excmo. Sr D.M.J.
　　Quintana. Pról. Exmo. Sr D.J. Pérez de Guzmán y Gallo. Madrid.
　　Hernández. 1910. Pp. clxx, 752. U-805 I*
— *Memorias de la Excma. Sra Condesa de Espoz y Mina.* Madrid.
　　Hernández. 1910. Uc
Vega de Rivera, José. *Rutas, momentos, lejanías.* Madrid. Pueyo. 1925.
　　Pp. 84. U-5574 n/o D
Velao, Darío. *El conde Ansúrez.* Valladolid. Imp. Castellana. [1912]. Pp. 141.
　　U-1111 D
Velarde, César Augusto. *Patología indolatina. Sociología Latino-Americana.*
　　Pról. C. Camargo y Marín. Madrid. Góngora. 1933. Pp. 248. U-426 D
Velasco y Arias, María. *Dramaturgia argentina.* Buenos Aires. Molinari.
　　1912. Pp. 302. U-3779 D
[Velázquez, Diego de Silva]. *The Masterpieces of Velázquez.* London.
　　Gowans Gray. 1907. Pl. 64. U-4572
Vélez, José Ma. *Montes y maravillas.* Córdoba. Mitre. 1906. Uc D
Vélez de Guevara, Luis. *El diablo cojuelo.* Ed. y notas F. Rodríguez Marín.
　　Madrid. La Lectura. 1918. Pp. xl, 295. U-941 I* L*

Venturino, Agustín. *Sociología primitiva chileindiana. La conquista de América y la guerra secular austral.* Tomo II. Barcelona. Cervantes. 1928. Pp. 458. U-5530 D

Verdaguer, Jacinto. *Patria. Poesíes.* Pról. J. Collell. Barcelona. Verdaguer. 1888. Pp. xiii, 204. U-3516 I T

— *Idilis y cants místichs.* Pról. D.M. Milá y Fontanals. Barcelona. Libr. Católica. 1891. Pp. xii, 215. U-4697 T

— *Jesús Infant.* Barcelona. Bastinos. 1896. Pp. 288. U-1509

— *Flors del Calvari. Llibre de consols.* Barcelona. López. 1902. Pp. 208. U-2275

— *La Atlántida.* Ab la traducció castellana per Melchor de Palau. Barcelona. López. 1902. Pp. 293. U-3126 L

— *Dietari d'un pelegrí a Terra Santa.* Barcelona. L'Avenç. 1906. Pp. 129. U-4450

— *Obres completes de Mossen Jacinto Verdaguer.* 27 vols. Barcelona. Ilustració Catalana. n.d. U-1477-1502. Vols. II, VIII, IX, XVI I L

Verdaguer, Mario. *La isla de oro.* Barcelona. Lux. [1926]. Pp. 300. U-5027 D

— *Canigo. Llegenda pirenayca del temps de la reconquista.* Barcelona. Llibr. Católica. Uc

Verga, Giovanni. *Novelle.* Milano. Treves. [1920]. Pp. 240. U-2048 I C L

— *Per le vie.* Milano. Treves. [1899]. Pp. 97-243 [incomplete]. U-4716 I

Vergara, Carlos N. *Revolución pacífica.* Buenos Aires. Perrotti. 1911. Pp. 853. U-4856 D

Verlaine, Paul. *Choix de poésies.* Paris. Charpentier. 1900. Pp. vi, 360. U-3844 I*

Verwey, Albert. *De Honderd Beste Gedichten (lyriek) in de nederlandsche taal.* Gekozen door A. Verwey. Amsterdam. Kerberger & Kesper. 1910. Uc

Vesanis, Demetrius. *O palamas philosophos.* n.p. Rallis. 1930. Pp. 294. U-2746 C

Veyga, Francisco de. *Estudios médico-legales sobre el código civil argentino.* Buenos Aires. Etchepareborda. 1900. Uc D

Viale, César. *Hojas sueltas.* Buenos Aires. Tall. Gráf. de la Penitenciaría Nacional. 1914. Pp. 145. U-274 n/o D

Vic, Jean. *La littérature de guerre. Manuel méthodique et critique des publications de langue française. (Août 1914-août 1916).* Préf. G. Lanson. 2 vols. Paris. Payot. U-246-7 D

Vicent, P. Antonio. *Socialismo y anarquismo.* Valencia. Ortega. 1895. Pp. 672. U-3953 [Incomplete text]

Vicent y Portillo, Gregorio. *Biblioteca histórica de Cartagena.* Tomo I. Madrid. Montegrifo. 1889. Uc

Vicente, Angeles. *Sombras. Cuentos psíquicos.* Madrid. F. Fé. n.d. Pp. 212. U-378 D

– *Los buitres.* Madrid. Pueyo. n.d. Uc

Vicente, Gil. *Obras de Gil Vicente.* Revisão, pref., e notas Mendes dos
Remédios. 3 vols. Coimbra. Amado. 1907-14. U-4301-3 I* C L* T B

– *Poesías de Gil Vicente.* Publicadas Dámaso Alonso. Madrid. Cruz y Raya.
1934. Pp. 46. U-1729

Vicente Concha, José. *Tratado del derecho penal y comentarios al Código
Penal Colombiano.* Paris. Ollendorff. n.d. Pp. 416. U-3911

Victor, Eduardo. *As vozes.* Porto. Costa. 1935. Pp. 81. U-1130 D

Vicuña Cifuentes, Julio. *Coa. Jerga de los delincuentes chilenos.* Santiago.
Imp. Universitaria. 1910. Pp. 144. U-3193 n/o D

– *Romances populares y vulgares. Recogidos de la tradición oral chilena.*
Santiago de Chile. Bibl. de Escritores de Chile. 1912. Pp. xxxiii, 581.
U-2610

Vicuña Solar, Benjamín. *Recuerdos.* Santiago de Chile. Imp. Barcelona. 1906.
Pp. xlix, 232. U-3380 D

Vicuña Subercaseaux, B. *Un país nuevo. (Cartas sobre Chile).* Paris. Eyméoud.
1903. Pp. 280. U-3134 I

– *La ciudad de las ciudades. (Correspondencias de París).* Santiago de Chile.
Universo. 1905. Pp. 608. U-4862 I

– *Gobernantes i literatos.* Santiago de Chile. Universo. 1907. Pp. 299.
U-1974

– *El socialismo revolucionario y la cuestión social en Europa y Chile.*
Santiago de Chile. Universo. 1908. Uc

– *Crónicas del centenario. La colonia. La patria vieja.* Santiago de Chile.
Universo. 1910. Uc

Vida Intelectual. Madrid (jun., sept., oct. 1907). n/n

Vidal, Plácido. *Las grans accions. Las soletats.* Barcelona. Imp. Catalana.
1904. Pp. 101. U-3994 n/o D

– *L'Assaig de la vida.* Barcelona. Estel. 1934. Pp. 507. U-3637 I* C* T L D

– *La cançó dels hèroes.* Barcelona. Giro. n.d. Pp. 399. U-2933 D

Vidal de La Blache, Paul. *La terre. Géographie physique et économique.*
Paris. Delagrave. 1891. Pp. 304. U-5305

Vidal Tolosana, Mariano. *Cuerpo y alma de España (ensayos políticos).*
México. La Ideal. 1935. Pp. 147. (2 copies) U-2387. U-5653 D

Vidal y Díaz, Alejandro. *Memoria histórica de la Universidad de Salamanca.*
Salamanca. Oliva. 1869. Pp. 616. U-4324

La Vie des Peuples. Paris (Juillet 1924). n/n

Vieira de S. Guimarães, J. *A ordem de Christo.* Lisboa. Empreza da Historia
de Portugal. 1901. Pp. xi, 373. U-834 D

Vignale, Pedro Juan. *Sentimiento de germana.* Buenos Aires. El Inca. 1927.
Pp. 36. U-4968 n/o D

– y César Tiempo. *Exposición de la actual poesía argentina (1922-1927)*.
Buenos Aires. Minerva. 1927. Pp. xviii, 256. U-5614 I* D

Vigny, Alfred de. *Oeuvres complètes de Alfred de Vigny. Poésies*. Paris.
Delagrave. n.d. Pp. 274. U-1379 I*

Vikelas, Demetrio. *Lukis Laras*. Athina. Anesti Konstantinidou. 1891. Pp. 198.
U-2739 T*

Vilariño Ugarte, Remigio. *Vida de Nuestro Señor Jesucristo*. Bilbao. El
Mensajero del Corazón de Jesús. 1912. Pp. 710. U-4808

Villa, Guido. *La psicologia contemporanea*. Torino. Bocca. 1899. Pp. 660.
U-708 I* C

Villa de Fon, Miguel. *El humanismo*. Paris. Colon. n.d. Pp. 122. U-5596 D

Villaespesa, Francisco. *El mirador de Lindaraza*. Madrid. Fernández. 1908.
Pp. 152. U-2329 D

– *El jardín de las quimeras*. Barcelona. Granada y Cía. 1909. Pp. 160.
U-3521 D

– *Viaje sentimental. Elogio de Vargas Vila*. Madrid. Pueyo. 1909. Pp. 169.
U-2314 D

– *Bajo la lluvia*. Madrid. Renacimiento. 1910. Pp. 186. U-3130 D

– *Saudades*. Madrid. Pueyo. 1910. Pp. 186. U-2756 D

– *Torre de marfil*. Pról. Pedro César Dominici. Paris. Ollendorff. 1911.
Pp. ix, 208. U-2178

– *El libro de Job*. Madrid. Pueyo. n.d. Pp. 146. U-2757 D

– *Las horas que pasan*. Barcelona. Granada y Cía. n.d. Pp. 169. U-3651 D

Villaespesa Calvache, Vicente. *El funesto caciquismo y algo de su terapéutica*.
Madrid. Fernández Murcia. 1908. Pp. 272. U-3059 n/o D

Villafrañé, Benjamín. *Irigoyen, el último dictador*. Buenos Aires. Moro, Tello.
1922. Pp. 416. U-3423

– *Degenerados*. Buenos Aires. 1928. Pp. 280. U-5682 I C

– *La miseria de un país rico*. Buenos Aires. El Ateneo. 1927. Pp. 260.
U-4888

Villalobos, Rosendo. *Ocios crueles*. Paris. Ollendorff. [1912]. Pp. 299.
U-1138 D

Villalobos Domínguez, C. *Nuestro feudalismo y la salvadora doctrina
georgista*. Córdoba. Imp. Argentina. 1919. Pp. 23. U-5668 n/o

– 'Que la tierra debe ser confiscada y otros conceptos actuales y genuinos
del georgismo,' *Revista Argentina de Ciencias Políticas,* CXV-CXVII
(1920). U-5714

Villa-Moura, Visconde de. *Nova Sapho. Tragedia extranha*. Lisboa. Ferreira.
1912. Pp. 272. U-3213 I D

– *Doentes da belleza*. Porto. Renascença Portuguesa. [1913]. Pp. 150.
U-2289 D

– *Bohemios*. Porto. Renascença Portuguesa. [1914]. Pp. 147. U-3507 D

– *Antonio Nobre. Seu genio e sua obra.* Porto. Renascença Portuguesa.
   1915. Pp. 145. U-3454 D
– *Pão Vermelho. Sombras da grande guerra.* Porto. Renascença Portuguesa.
   1923. Pp. 62. U-3258 n/o
– *Cristo de Alcácer.* Porto. Renascença Portuguesa. 1924. Pp. 30. U-3259 n/o
– *Almas do mar.* Porto. Renascença Portuguesa. 1924. Pp. 205. U-5725 I C D
– *Um homem de treze anos.* Porto. Renascença Portuguesa. 1924. Pp. 59.
   U-3441 n/o
– *Novos mitos.* Porto. Imprensa Portuguesa. 1934. Pp. 257. U-1131 D
Villanúa, León. *Peral, marino de España.* Madrid. Col. Europea. 1934. Pp. 251.
   U-2017 D
Villanueva, Carlos A. *La monarquía en América.* 4 vols. Paris. Ollendorff.
   1911-13. (2 copies vol. I: U-2150, U-3639). U-2443, U-3511, U-1908
Villanueva, Francisco. *Pluma al viento. Diario de un testigo.* Madrid.
   A. Marzo. 1909. Pp. 258. U-3630
– *El momento constitucional.* Madrid. Morata. 1929. Pp. 391. U-5563
Villar, Lino. *El precipicio.* Habana. Bibl. Studium. n.d. Pp. 229. U-3184 D
Villari, Luigi Antonio. *Memorie di Oliviero Oliverio.* Catania. Giannotta.
   1900. Pp. vi, 534. U-244 D
– *Le chiese cristiane. Considerazioni di un libero credente non modernista.*
   Lugano. Coenobium. 1912. Pp. 128. U-1232 I D
– 'Dai "Miei Ricordi,"' *Aprutium,* Anno III, Fasc. III (1914). U-5361
Villari, Pasquale. *Discussioni critiche e discorsi.* Bologna. Zanichelli. 1905.
   Pp. 598. U-3847 I* C
– *Scritti vari.* Bologna. Zanichelli. 1912. Pp. 395. U-420 I
– *Niccolò Machiavelli e i suoi tempi.* 3 vols. Milano. Hoepli. 1912-13.
   U-3479-81 I* C* B
– *Le invasioni barbariche in Italia.* Milano. Hoepli. 1920. Pp. xv, 490.
   U-2060 I
Villaronga, Luis. *Alas victoriosas.* San Juan, P.R. Real. 1925. Pp. 219.
   U-5060 D
Villatte, Césaire, und Karl Sachs. *Encyklopädisches Französisch-Deutsches
   und Deutsch-Französisches Wörterbuch.* Berlin. Langenscheidtsche
   Verlags Buchhandlung. 1895. Pp. 2132. U-748
Villavaso, Camilo de. *La cuestión del Puerto de la Paz y La Zamacolada.*
   Bilbao. Delmas. 1887. Pp. iv, 75 + 271. U-4278
Villegas, Baldomero. *Libro patriótico. Estudio psicológico de las novelas
   ejemplares del sin par Cervantes.* Valladolid. Colegio Santiago. 1911.
   Pp. xxxii, 261. U-3780 D
Villon, François. *Oeuvres.* Editées par un ancien archiviste. Avec un index des
   noms propres. Paris. Champion. 1911. Pp. xvi, 123. U-2008 I

Vincenzi, Moisés. *La señorita Rodiet. Caracteres humanos.* San José,
C.R. Trejos. 1936. Pp. 192. U-280 D
Vinet, Alexandre-Rodolphe. *Etudes sur Blaise Pascal.* Paris. Fischbacher.
1904. Pp. vii, 387. U-242 I
Vinyals, F. *Cuentos verosímiles.* Madrid. Juste. 1896. Uc D
Virgilius Maro, Publius. *Oeuvres de Virgile.* Tr. française M.F. Lemaistre.
Étude sur Virgile par M. Sainte-Beuve. Paris. Garnier. 1859. Uc
– *Las Bucólicas de Virgilio.* Tr. J.D. Casasus. México. Escalante. 1903.
Pp. xviii, 444. U-4802
– *La Eneida en la República argentina.* Tr. Dr D. Velez Sarsfield y J.C. Varela.
Buenos Aires. Lajouane. 1888. Pp. 395. U-2458 n/o
Viscardini, Mario. *Collane d'Ambra.* Milano. 1922. Ff. 41. U-4073
Viscasillas y Urriza, Mariano. *Gramática hebrea.* Barcelona. Subirana. 1872.
Pp. xii, 324. U-4308 C
Viteri Lafronte, Homero. *Un libro autógrafo de espejo.* Quito, Ecuador.
Salesianas. 1920. Pp. 113. U-1630 D
Vitoria, Eduardo. *Manual de química moderna.* Barcelona. Tip. Católica
Casals. 1929. Pp. 480. U-2248 C*
Vitoria, Francisco de. *De Justitia.* Ed. R.P. V. Beltrán de Heredia, O.P. Tomo II.
Madrid. Publ. de la Asoc. F. de Vitoria. 1934.
Pp. 428. U-4115
– *Relecciones teológicas del Maestro Fray Francisco de Vitoria.* Edición
crítica, con facsimil de códices y ediciones príncipes, variantes, versión
castellana, notas, e introd. el P. Mtro. Fr. Luis G. Alonso Getino. Tomo II.
Madrid. La Rafa. 1934. Pp. 538. U-4203
Vitureira, Cipriano Santiago. *La siega del musgo.* Montevideo. Gutenberg.
1927. Pp. 85. U-5495 D
Vivekānanda, Svami. *Filosofía Yoga. Conferencias dadas en Nueva York en el
invierno de 1895 y 96 ... sobre el Râja Yoga o conquista de la naturaleza
interna.* Tr. J. Granés. Barcelona. Bibl. Orientalista R. Maynadé. 1904.
Pp. 260. U-3082
Vivero, Augusto. *El derrumbamiento. La verdad sobre el desastre del Rif.*
Pról. R. Gasset. Madrid. Caro Raggio. 1922. Pp. 238. U-4011 I* D
Vives, Joannes Ludovicus. *Opera omnia.* Distributa et ordinata in argumen-
torum classes praecipuas a G. Majansio. Vols. II-V. Valentiae Edetanorum.
1782-4. U-3543-6
– *Tratado de la enseñanza.* Tr. J. Ontañón. Pról. Foster Watson. Madrid.
La Lectura. [1923]. Pp. xlvi + vii, 268. U-2268
Vives-Guerra, Julio. *Volanderas y tal.* Medellín. Imp. Editorial. 1911. Pp. xiv,
282. U-2662 n/o
Viviani, Alberto. *Il mio cuore.* Firenze. Gaileiana. 1914. Pp. 61. U-678 D
– *Le ville silenziose.* Firenze. Ferrante Connelli. 1915. Pp. 82. U-2124 D

Vizcarrondo, Carmelina. *Pregón en llamas.* San Juan, P.R. Imp. Venezuela.
[1935]. Pp. 170. U-3470 D
La Voce. Firenze (10, 17, 24 oct. 1912). n/n
Vogel, Eberhard. *Diccionari portàtil de les lléngues catalana y alemanya.*
Berlin. Langenscheidt. 1911. Pp. lii, 586. n/n D
– *Einführung in das spanische für lateinkundige.* Mit erläutertem
lektüretext und vokabular. Paderborn. Druckerei. 1914. Pp. 267. U-508 D
– *Diccionario manual de las lenguas española y alemana.* Berlin. Langenscheidt.
1927. Pp. xliv, 552. n/n
Voltaire, François-Marie Arouet. *Oeuvres choisies.* Edition du Centenaire.
Paris. Bureaux du Comité Central. 1878. Pp. 1000. U-1387 I
Voltoire. *Anciens proverbes Basques et Gascons,* recueillis par V. et remis au
jour par G.B [runet]. Bayonne. Cazals. 1873. Pp. 29. U-4299
Vondel, Joost van den. *De Werken van J. van den Vondel.* Uitgegeven door
Mr J. van Lennep. Herzien en bijgewerkt door J.H.W. Unger. 1646. Publius
Virgilius Maroos Wercken. Leiden. A.W. Sijthoff. Pp. 276. U-581
– *Lucifer.* Gent. Siffer. n.d. Pp. viii, 95. U-561. Opnieuw uitgegeven door
J.H.W. Unger. Leiden. Sijthoff. n.d. Pp. 127. U-579
– *Palamedes, oft Vermoorde Onnooselheyd.* Ponieuw uitgegeven door
J.H.W. Unger. Leiden. Sijthoff. n.d. Pp. 137. U-580
Vontade, Jacques. *L'Ame des anglais.* Paris. Grasset. 1910. Pp. 327. U-1938 I
Voss, Johann Heinrich. *Luise.* Berlin. Hempel. n.d. Pp. 120. U-5392 I* T*
Voutieridi, Ilia P. *Kostis Palamas, to poetiko ergo tou.* Athina. Zikaki. 1923.
Pp. 49. U-3785
Vovard, P. *Kathaline.* Paris. Jeune Académie. 1930. Pp. 90. U-3237 D
Vuillemin, Paul. *La biologie végétale.* Paris. Baillière. 1888. Pp. 380. U-316 I*
Wackenroder, Wilhelm Heinrich. *Herzensergieszungen eines kunstliebenden*
Klosterbruders. Phantasien über die Kunst für Freunde der Kunst.
Potsdam. Kiepenheuer. 1925. Pp. 205. U-5385 I* C
Wätjen, Hermann. *Das Judentum und die Anfänge der modernen Kolonisation.*
Berlin. Kohlhammer. 1914. Pp. 72. U-4128 I* C
Wahl, Fritz. *Spanien unter der Diktatur 1926.* Frankfurt. Druck der
Frankfurter Societäts. n.d. Pp. 46. U-5184 I C D
Waley, Arthur. *The No Plays of Japan.* With letters by Oswald Sickert.
London. George Allen & Unwin. 1921. Pp. 319. U-2200 I
Walker, Francis A. *Political Economy.* London. Macmillan. 1892. Pp. 537.
U-2592 C I
Walker, Richard Johnson B. *AntimiaΣ: An Essay in Isometry.* 2 vols. London.
Macmillan. 1910. U-124-5 B
Walker Martínez, Carlos. *Portales.* Paris. Lahure. 1879. Pp. 466. U-3011 I D
Wallace, Sir Donald Mackenzie. *Russia.* 2 vols. Leipzig. Tauchnitz. 1878.
U-500-1 T

Walpole, Sir Hugh Seymour. *Jeremy.* Bruxelles. Collins. 1921. Pp. 269.
U-4745

Walton, Izaac. *The Compleat Angler.* London. Dent. 1902. Pp. 248. U-4415

— *The Lives of Dr John Donne, Sir Henry Wotton, Mr Richard Hooker,
Mr George Herbert, and Dr Robert Sanderson.* Ed. C.H. Dick. London.
Walter Scott. [1899]. Pp. xiv, 320. U-1404 I*

Wandlung. Blätter für panidealistischen Aufbau. Heft 1 (Mai-Juni 1936).
Pp. 32. U-5384

Wapnir, Salomon. *Crítica positiva.* Buenos Aires. Tor. [1926]. Pp. 124.
U-5661 D

Ward, Mary Augusta (Mrs Humphry Ward). *Robert Elsmere.* 3 vols. Leipzig.
Tauchnitz. 1888. U-4757-9 I

Wassermann, Carl Jacob. *Christoph Columbus.* Berlin. Fischer. 1930. Pp. 263.
U-5451 I* C

Watson, Foster. *Les relations de Joan Lluís Vives.* Barcelona. Institut d'Estudis
Catalans. 1918. Pp. 327. U-1737 I* C L*

— *Luis Vives, el gran valenciano. (1492-1540).* Oxford University Press.
1922. Pp. 126. U-1406

Weaver, Raymond M. *Herman Melville, Mariner and Mystic.* New York. Doran.
[1921]. Pp. xi, 399. U-110 I* C* T B D

Webster, John. *La duquesa de Malfi.* Tr. E. Díez-Canedo. Madrid. Calpe. 1920.
Pp. 191. U-4431

Webster, Noah. *Webster's International Dictionary of the English Language.*
London. Bell. 1890. Pp. xcviii, 2011. n/n

Wedel, V. *Die Carlistische Armee u. Kriegführung.* Hannover. Helwing. 1876.
Pp. 206. U-4259 [Incomplete text]

Weibel, Walther. *Frühlingsfahrt in Spanien 1933.* Sonderabdruck aus der
Neuen Zürcher Zeitung. n.d. Pp. 127. U-652 I

Weizsaecker, Carl von. *Das apostolische Zeitalter der christlichen Kirche.*
Freiburg. Mohr. 1892. Pp. viii, 698. U-701 T I

Wellhausen, Julius. *Einleitung in die drei ersten Evangelien.* Berlin. Reimer.
1905. Pp. 115. U-1739

— et al. *Geschichte der christlichen Religion.* Berlin. Teubner. 1909. Pp. 792.
U-1211 I* C

Wells, Herbert G. *Anticipations of the Reaction of Mechanical and Scientific
Progress Upon Human Life and Thought.* Leipzig. Tauchnitz. 1902.
Pp. 286. U-4769 I*

Werfel, Franz. *Verdi.* Berlin. Zsolnay. 1928. Pp. 569. U-5454 I* T

Wertheimer, Emanuel. *Pensées et maximes.* Tr. Marcellin, Bon. Grivot de
Grandcourt. Lettre-préf. F. Coppée. Paris. Ollendorff. 1895. Uc

— *Paradojas y verdades.* Tr. Julio Broutá. Carta-pról. J. Echegaray. Madrid.
Rivadeneyra. 1898. Uc

Wesley, John. *The Journal of the Rev. John Wesley*. Introd. Rev. F.W. Macdonald. 4 vols. London. Dent. [1906]. U-1009-12 I* C

Wharton, Edith Newbold. *Ethan Frome*. New York. Scribner's. 1929. Pp. 195. U-5207 I* T

Where are the Dead? London. Cassell. [1928]. Pp. ix, 136. U-5215

White, Andrew D. *A History of the Warfare of Science With Theology in Christendom*. 2 vols. New York. Appleton. 1910. U-117-18 I*

— *Historia de la guerra de la ciencia con la teología en la cristiandad*. Tr. A.E. Salazar. U-3526 [Typescript]

— *Seven Great Statesmen in the Warfare of Humanity With Unreason*. New York. The Century Co. 1910. Pp. xi, 552. U-2537 I D

White, Gilbert. *The Natural History of Selborne*. London. Dent. [1906]. Pp. xvi, 255. U-5174 I* C*

Whitman, Walt. *Leaves of Grass*. Including a facsimile autobiography, variorum readings of the poems and a department of *Gathered Leaves*. Ed. David McKay. Philadelphia. [1900]. Pp. xi, 516. U-4816 I* C T

— *Feuilles d'herbe*. Tr. León Bazalgette. 2 vols. Paris. Mercure de France. 1909. U-2409-10

Whitney, W.D. *La vie du langage*. Paris. Baillière. 1880. Pp. 264. U-4258

Wiechert, Ernst. *Die Bekenntnisse einer armen Seele*. Leipzig. Reclam. n.d. Pp. 47. U-4521

— *Die Realisten*. Leipzig. Reclam. n.d. Pp. 93. U-4515 T

— *Ein Schritt vom Wege*. Leipzig. Reclam. n.d. Pp. 94. U-4517

— *Der Freund des Fürsten*. Leipzig. Reclam. n.d. Pp. 86. U-4518

— *Die glückliche Insel*. Leipzig. Reclam. n.d. Pp. 59. U-4550

Wihgrabs, Georg. *Das lettische Schrifttum*. Riga. Rigna. 1924. Pp. 51. U-1447 I

Wilamowitz-Moellendorff, U. v. und B. Niese. *Staat und Gesellschaft der Griechen und Römer*. Berlin-Leipzig. Teubner. 1910. Pp. vi, 280. U-799 I* C*

— et al. *Die griechische und lateinische Literatur und Sprache*. Berlin. Teubner. 1912. Pp. viii, 582. U-1212 I* C*

Wilde, Oscar. *De profundis*. London. Methuen. 1905. Pp. 151. U-3857 B

— *De profundis. El alma del hombre. Máximas*. Tr. A.A. Vasseur. Preceden unos recuerdos de A. Gide. Tr. J. García Monje. Madrid. Ed. América. 1920. Pp. 210. U-5571

— *La casa de las granadas*. Tr. E. Mazorriaga. Pról. E. Díez-Canedo. Madrid. Gómez Fuentenebro. 1909. Uc

Wildenbruch, Ernest von. *Die Haubenlerche*. Berlin. Freund & Jeckel. 1891. Pp. 179. U-3858

— *Meister Balzer*. Berlin. Freund & Jeckel. 1893. Pp. 160. U-1954

Wildik, Vizconde de. *Nuevo diccionario portugués-español y español-portugués*. Paris. Garnier. 1899. Pp. vi, 889. n/n

Wilkins, Lawrence A. *La enseñanza de lenguas modernas en los Estados Unidos*. New York. Instituto de las Españas en los Estados Unidos. 1922. Pp. 160. U-1247

Wille, Bruno. *Offenbarungen des wacholderbaums*. 2 vols. Leipzig. Diederich. 1901. U-3758-9 T I

Williams, Alberto. *Poesías musicales*. Buenos Aires. Coni. 1901. Uc D

Williman, Claudio. *Memoria Universitaria correspondiente a los años 1909-1914*. Montevideo. Universidad de la Rep. O. del Uruguay. 1915. Pp. 621. U-752 n/o

Wilson, Woodrow. *El estado. Elementos de política histórica y práctica*. Introd. O. Brownin. Tr. y estudio preliminar Adolfo Posada. 2 vols. Madrid. Suárez. 1904. U-3802-3

— *El gobierno del congreso. Estudio sobre la organización política americana*. Tr. Julio Carrié. Buenos Aires. Peuser. 1902. Pp. 359. U-2459

Windelband, Wilhelm. *Präludien*. 2 vols. Tübingen. Mohr. 1911. U-3775-6 I*

Winther, Rasmus Villads Christian F. *Digte, gamle og nye*. København. Bianco Lunos. 1846. Pp. iv, 284. U-478

Wissen und Leben. Zürich (Feb. 1921, August 1925). n/n

Wissenschaftliche Neuerscheinungen 1923 aus dem Verlage der Weidmannschen Buchhandlung in Berlin. Pp. 16. U-5453

Wobbermin, Georg. *Theologie und Metaphysik*. Berlin. Duncker. 1901. Pp. xii, 291. U-1730 I

Wolff, J. *La democracia en la iglesia*. Barcelona. Codina. 1875. Pp. 272. U-1543 C

Wolston, W.T.P. *The Church: What is it?* Edinburgh. Gospel Messenger. 1905. Pp. viii, 265. U-2853

Wolzogen, Ernst Ludwig von. *Das Lumpengesindel*. Berlin. Fontane. 1892. Pp. 80. U-880

— und William Schumann. *Die Kinder der Excellenz*. Leipzig. Reclam. n.d. Pp. 88. U-4537

Woolman, John. *The Journal with other Writings of John Woolman*. Introd. Vida D. Scudder. London. Dent. [1910]. Pp. xix, 250. U-1013 I

Wordsworth, William. *The Poetical Works of William Wordsworth*. London. Warne. n.d. Pp. xxxix, 530. U-3841 I* C T*

The World Tomorrow. New York (May 1930). n/n

Wundt, Wilhelm. *Grundzüge der physiologischen Psychologie*. 2 vols. Leipzig. Engelmann. 1893. U-2243

Xenes, Nieves. *Poesías*. Pról. Aurelia Castillo de González. Habana. El Siglo XX de A. Miranda. 1915. Pp. xxiii, 224. U-2156

Xenofon, I. *Filarmonica della 1833.* Bucuresti. Munca Literara. 1934. Pp. 62. U-2216

Xenophon. *Xenophontis Commentarii.* Recognovit Walther Gilbert. Editio minor. Lipsiae. Teubner. 1907. Pp. 150. U-346 I T

- *Xenophontis historia graeca.* Recensuit Otto Keller. Editio minor. Lipsiae. Teubner. 1908. Pp. xvii, 295. U-347 T

- *Anabasis. Expeditio Cyri.* Recensuit Guilelmus Gemoll. Editio minor. Lipsiae. Teubner. 1910. Pp. x, 266. U-345 I T*

- *Economique.* Texte grec accompagné d'une introd., d'une analyse de l'ouvrage complet, et de notes en français par Ch. Graux et A. Jacob. Paris. Hachette. 1896. Pp. 174. U-4664 I* L* T*

Ximénez, Ximeno. *¡Muera el presidente!* Madrid. R. Fé. 1909. Uc D

Xirau, Antoni. *Safreu.* Barcelona. Verdaguer. 1934. Pp. 130. U-4293 D

Xuriguera, Ramón. *L'Aportació de l'occident Català a l'obra de la Renaixença.* Barcelona. Bibl. Catalana d'Autors Independents. 1936. Pp. 179. U-225

Yeats, W.B. *Poems.* London. Fisher Unwin. 1899. Pp. 298. U-1894

- *Selected Poems. Lyrical and Narrative.* London. Macmillan. 1932. Pp. x, 202. U-3500 I* L*

Ylera, Zacarías. *De la vida a la estrofa.* Valladolid. Bibl. Studium. 1913. Uc D

Ylla Moreno, J.J. *Rubies y amatistas.* Montevideo. Bertani. 1907. Pp. 155. U-2729 D

Yo acuso por un alemán. Valencia. Vives Mora. 1915. Pp. 308. U-1618 C

La Yougoslavie avec illustrations. Belgrade. Association des Professeurs Yougoslaves. 1925. Pp. 208. U-5290 n/o

Yunque, Alvaro, pseud. [i.e., Aristides Gandolfi Herrero]. *Zancadillas.* Buenos Aires. La Campana de Palo. 1926. Pp. 149. U-5636 D

- *Barrett.* San José, C.R. Claridad. n.d. Pp. 54. U-5573 D

- *Bicho feo (Escenas para una sirvientita de diez años).* Buenos Aires. Claridad. n.d. Pp. 61. U-5526 D

- *Nudo corredizo.* Buenos Aires. Claridad. n.d. Pp. 62. U-5541 D

- *ta-te-ti (Otros barcos de papel).* Buenos Aires. Editorial Hoy. n.d. Pp. 183. U-5690 D

Yuste y la Sierra de Gredos. Madrid. Comisaria Regia del Turismo y Cultura Artística. 1919. Pp. xxiii, 125. U-4636

Yxart, Joseph. *Obres catalanes de Joseph Yxart.* Barcelona. L'Avenç. 1895. Pp. 424. U-2376 T

Zabala, Angel de. *Defensa del libro 'Historia de Bizkaya' de Zaba eta Otzamis-Tremoya condenado por el señor Obispo de Vitoria y dispuesta por el autor para la Sagrada Congregación Romana del Indice.* Bilbao. Soc. Bilbaína de Artes Gráficas. 1910. Pp. 205. U-2526 D

Zaldumbide, Gonzalo. *La evolución de Gabriel d'Annunzio.* Madrid. Editorial América. [1916]. Pp. 373. U-311 D

Zaleski, Z.L. *Attitudes et destinées. Faces et profils d'écrivains polonais.*
Paris. Les Belles Lettres. 1932. Pp. 374. U-5296 I* C

Zamacois, Eduardo. *Las raices.* Madrid. Renacimiento. [1923]. Pp. 409.
U-5051 I* L D

— *Los vivos muertos.* Madrid. Renacimiento. 1929. Pp. 400. U-4912 C D

Zamora Elizondo, Hernán. *Aguja y ensueño.* San José, C.R. Lines. 1927.
Pp. 125. U-5629 D

Zamorano, Mario. *Dos almas fuertes.* San José, C.R. Imp. Alsina. 1912. Uc D

Zanfrognini, Pietro. *Itinerario di uno spirito che si cerca (1912-1919).*
Modena. Vincenzi e Nipoti. 1922. Pp. vii, 252. U-3093 D

Zangwill, Israel. *Dreamers of the Ghetto.* Vol. ii. Leipzig. Tauchnitz. 1898.
Pp. 270. U-5157 I*

— *Ghetto Comedies.* 2 vols. Leipzig. Tauchnitz. 1907. U-5164-5 I T

— *Ghetto Tragedies.* 2 vols. Leipzig. Tauchnitz. 1908. U-5169-70 I

Zanotti-Bianco, Umberto. *La basilicata.* Roma. Coll. Meridionale. 1926.
Pp. xl, 412. U-5335

Zaragoza. *Real Junta del Centenario de los sitios de 1808-1809. Exposición
retrospectiva de arte.* Zaragoza. Edición Oficial. 1908. Uc

Zaragüeta, Juan. *Introducción general a la filosofía.* Madrid. Tip. Rev. de
Arch., Bibl. y Museos. 1909. Pp. 86. U-2241

— *El problema del alma ante la psicología experimental.* Madrid. Tip. Rev.
de Arch., Bibl. y Museos. 1910. Pp. 112. U-2992 n/o D

— *Modernas orientaciones de la psicología experimental.* Madrid. Asilo de
Huérfanos del S.C. de Jesús. 1910. Pp. 101. U-741

— *Teoría psico-genética de la voluntad.* Madrid. Ungría. 1914. Pp. ix, 263.
U-789

— *La filosofía de Jaime Balmes.* Madrid. Gran Imprenta Católica. 1915.
Pp. 41. U-1727

— *Caracteres fundamentales de la enseñanza superior o universitaria.* Madrid.
Gran Imprenta Católica. 1915. Pp. 20. U-4195

— *Contribución del lenguaje a la filosofía de los valores.* Discurso leído por el
Ilmo. Sr D.J. Zaragüeta Bengoechea en el acto de su recepción como
académico de número. Contestación del Sr D.E. Sanz y Escartín. Madrid.
Ratés. 1920. Pp. 221. U-1266

— *El concepto católico de la vida según el cardenal Mercier.* Tomo ii.
Madrid. Espasa-Calpe. 1930. Pp. 495. U-4221

Zarante, José Dolores. Reminiscencias históricas. Lorica, Colombia. Imp.
Departamental. 1933. Pp. xv, 445. U-4140 D

Zardain, Claudio. *Remembranzas de antaño y hogaño de la villa de Tineo.*
Salamanca. Imp. Comercial Salmantina. 1930. Pp. 274. U-4298

Zas, Enrique. *Galicia patria de Colón.* La Habana. Fernández. 1923. Pp. 291.
U-4268

Zavala Muñiz, Justino. *Crónica de Muñiz.* Montevideo. El Siglo Ilustrado.
1921. Pp. 414. U-2922 I* C D
- *Crónica de un crimen.* Montevideo. Ed. Teseo. 1925. Pp. 325. n/n I D
- *Crónica de la reja.* Montevideo. Imp. Uruguaya. 1930. Pp. 302. U-1660 D
Zayas, Antonio de. *Joyeles bizantinos.* n.p. A. Marzo. 1902. Uc D
- *Retratos antiguos.* Madrid. A. Marzo. 1902. Uc D
- *Paisajes.* n.p. 1903. Uc D
- *Noches blancas.* n.p. 1905. Uc D
- *Leyenda.* Madrid. A. Marzo. 1906. Pp. 215. U-143 D
Zhabotinskii, Vladimir E. (Altalena, pseud.). *Richter und Narr.* München.
Meyer & Jessen. [1928]. Pp. 382. U-5450 I* T L
Ziegler, Leopold. *Gestaltwandel der Götter.* 2 vols. Darmstadt. Reichl. 1922.
U-5428-9 I* T
- *Der ewige Buddho.* Darmstadt. Reich. 1922. Pp. 433. U-5427 I* T
- [in] *Die Philosophie der Gegenwart in Selbstdarstellungen,* IV (1923).
U-4139 I T
- *Das Heilige Reich der Deutschen.* 2 vols. Darmstadt. Reichl. 1925.
U-5430-1 I* C* B T
Ziegler, Theobald. *Die soziale Frage eine sittliche Frage.* Stuttgart.
Goschen'sche Verlagshandlung. 1891. Pp. 182. U-2327 T
- *La cuestión social es una cuestión moral.* 2 vols. Barcelona. Henrich.
1904. Uc
Zimmern, Alfred E. *Nationality & Government.* London. Chatto & Windus.
1918. Pp. xxiv, 364. U-1261 I* C* B
- *The Greek Commonwealth. Politics and Economics in Fifth Century
Athens.* Oxford. University Press. 1922. Pp. 462. U-818
Zittel, Emil. *Die Entstenhung der Bibel.* Leipzig. Reclam. n.d. Uc
Zobeltitz, Fedor von. *Ohne Geläut.* Dresden. Pierfon. 1895. Pp. 97. U-2028
Zola, Emile. *L'Assomoir.* Paris. Charpentier. 1888. Pp. vii, 568. U-1396
- *Germinal.* Paris. Charpentier. 1890. Uc
- *Le Docteur Pascal.* Paris. Charpentier. 1893. Pp. 390. U-3233
Zoraida. *El Hadits de la Princesa Zoraida, del Emir Abulhasan y del
caballero Aceja.* Relación romancesca del siglo XV o principios del XVI
en que se declara el origen de las pinturas de la Alhambra. Sácala a luz
L. de Eguilaz Yánguas. Sabatel. 1892. Pp. 361. U-4616
Zorrilla, José. *Treinta y tres cartas inéditas de Zorrilla al poeta Emilio
Ferrari.* Ed. e introd. M. de la Pinta Llorente. Madrid. Monasterio de
El Escorial. 1934. Pp. 34. U-765
Zorrilla, José M. *Veraneo en Mar del Plata.* Buenos Aires. 1913. Uc D
Zorrilla, Oscar Alberto. *De mi raza. Males y remedios.* Pról. J. Piquet.
Montevideo. Barreiro y Ramos. 1904. Pp. 64. U-3621 D

Zorrilla de San Martín, Juan. *Tabaré.* Montevideo. Barreiro y Ramos. 1889.
Pp. xix, 300. U-795 I
— *Resonancias del camino.* Paris. Imp. Nouvelle. 1896. Pp. 361. U-1945
— *Huerto cerrado.* Montevideo. Dornaleche y Reyes. 1900. Pp. 179. U-1570
— *Conferencias y discursos.* Pról. B. Fernández y Medina. Montevideo.
Barreiro y Ramos. 1905. Pp. xxvii, 431. U-2539
— *La epopeya de Artigas. Historia de los tiempos heróicos del Uruguay.*
2 vols. Montevideo. Barreiro y Ramos. 1910. U-1292-3 I*. 2a ed.
Barcelona. Gili. 1916-17. U-4330-1
— *Detalles de la historia rioplatense.* Montevideo. Claudio García. 1917.
Pp. 138. U-3456 n/o D
— *Address delivered for the reception of the US Pacific Fleet – July 15, 1917.*
Montevideo. 1917. Pp. 6. U-4690
— *Discurso del monumento.* Pronunciado en la inauguración del erguido a
Artigas en Montevideo el 28 de febrero de 1923. Montevideo. Claudio
García. 1923. Pp. 19. U-4014 n/o D
— *El libro de Ruth. Ensayos.* Montevideo. Arduino. 1928. Pp. 226.
U-5045 C D
Zozaya, Antonio. *La dictadora.* Barcelona. Henrich. 1902. Uc
— *Por los cauces serenos.* Pról. A. Guardiola. Valencia. Sempere. n.d.
Pp. xii, 256. U-3241
Zuazagoitia, Joaquín de. *La criolla. Episodio familiar en la costa vascongada.*
Bilbao. Echeguren y Zulaica. n.d. Pp. 104. U-4744 I
Zubiaur, J.B. *La enseñanza en Norte América.* Buenos Aires. Canter. 1904.
Pp. 335. U-4846 D
— *Surcos y semillas escolares.* Buenos Aires. La Sin Bombo. 1907. Uc D
Zubillaga, Juan Antonio. *Sátiras e ironías. Páginas de periodismo.*
Montevideo. Serrano. 1913. Pp. 176. U-3662 n/o
— *Crítica literaria.* Montevideo. Monteverde. 1914. Pp. 315. U-1944 D
Zucca, Antioco. *Roberto Ardigò e il Vescovo di Mantova.* Roma. Ferri. 1922.
Pp. 36. U-5343 D
Zugazagoitia, Julián. *Una vida heróica: Pablo Iglesias.* Madrid. Morato Pedreño.
1925. Pp. 198. U-5657 I D
— *Una vida anónima.* Madrid. Morato. 1927. Pp. 239. U-4994 I*
— *Pedernales.* Bilbao. Edición de la Caja de Ahorros y Monte de Piedad
Municipal. 1929. Pp. 218. U-5630 I D
— *El botín.* Madrid. Historia Nueva. 1929. Pp. 294. U-5034 D
Zulen, Pedro S. *La filosofía de lo inexpresable: bosquejo de una interpretación
y una crítica de la filosofía de Bergson.* Lima. Sanmartin. 1920. Pp. 62.
U-2441 D
Zuleta, Eduardo. *Tierra virgen.* Medellín. Molina. n.d. Pp. 403. U-3346 D

Zuloaga, Manuel A. *Nuestra raza y la condición del extranjero en la Argentina.*
    Buenos Aires. Ferrari. 1931. Pp. 214. U-5049 D
Zulueta, Luis de. *La edad heróica.* Madrid. Residencia de Estudiantes. 1916.
    Pp. 150. U-2081 D
— y Eduardo Marquina. *Jesús y el diablo. Poema en forma dramática.*
    Barcelona. Verdaguer. 1899. Pp. 40. U-3693 D
Zum Felde, Alberto. *Proceso intelectual del Uruguay y crítica de su*
    literatura. 3 vols. Montevideo. Imp. Nac. Colorada. 1930. U-1228-30 D
Zuñiga, Antonio R. *Cristiana.* Buenos Aires. Landreau. 1908. Pp. 174.
    U-4703 D
Zunzunegui, Juan Antonio. *Vida y paisaje de Bilbao.* Bilbao. Comercial. 1926.
    Pp. 205. U-4984 I* D
Zweig, Arnold. *Der streit um den sergeanten Grischa.* Potsdam. Keipenheuer.
    1928. Pp. 552. U-1317 I* T
Zweig, Stephan. *La guérison par l'esprit. La fantastique existence de Mary*
    Baker-Eddy. Tr. Alzir Hella et Juliette Pary. Paris. Stock. 1932. Pp. 253.
    QP-54 I
— *Marie-Antoinette.* Tr. Alzir Hella. Paris. Grasset. 1933. Pp. 505. QP-55 I

Appendix I

Titles and authors cited by Unamuno in his collected works and not
included in the catalogue

In each case where the specific edition could not be ascertained the volume
and page number of the citation from the *Obras completas* is given following
the author and/or title. Only one representative entry from the *Obras
completas* is given in each case.

Abbadie, Antoine Thompson d', and J. Augustine Chaho. *Etudes grammaticales sur la langue Euskarienne*. Paris. 1836

Abbagnano, Nicola. *Le sorgenti irrazionali del pensiero*. *OC*, x, 907

Abeille, Luciano. *OC*, vi, 829 ff.

Acuña, Hernando ed. *OC*, iii, 245

Adelung, Friedrich von. *Mithridates*. *OC*, iii, 562

Aeschylus. *Las siete tragedias de Eschylo puestas del griego en lengua castellana*. Notas, introd. Fernando Segundo Brieva Salvatierra. Madrid. 1880. Pp. xcvii, 523

Aesop. *OC*, v, 958

Aguirre, Adolfo. *Excursiones y recuerdos*. *OC*, i, 897

Agustini, Delmira. *Cantos de la mañana*. *OC*, xiv, 97

Aizquíbel, D.J. Francisco de. *Diccionario Basco-Español, titulado: Euskeratik Erderara Biurtzeco Iztegia*. Tolosa. [1882-4]. Pp. 1257

Alarcón, Pedro Antonio. *Diario de un testigo de la guerra de Africa*. *OC*, i, 829

– *El sombrero de tres picos*. *OC*, viii, 459

– *El escándalo*. *OC*, x, 430

Alas, Leopoldo (Clarín). *La regenta*. *OC*, x, 430

– 'Zurita.' *OC*, viii, 719⁻

Alcalá Galiano, Antonio. *Recuerdos de un anciano*. *OC*, v, 382

Alcázar, Cayetano. *La juerga de la estudiantina*. Pról. M. de Unamuno. Madrid. La Itálica. 1916. Pp. 95

Alcoforado, Marianna, de Beja, Sor. *Cartas de una religiosa portuguesa*. *OC*, xii, 876

Alcover, Antoni Maria. 'Dietari de l'exida de Mn. Antoni Ma. Alcover a Alemania y altres nacions l'any del Senyor 1907,' *Bolleti del Diccionari de la Llengua Catalana*, v. Ciutat de Mallorca. 1908

Aldrete, Bernardo de. *Del origen y principio de la lengua castellana y romance que oi se habla en España*. *OC*, vi, 98

Alexander, Aphrodisaeus. *OC*, xvi, 215

Almagro San Martín, Melchor. *OC*, v, 519

Alphonso vii. *Chronica adefonsi imperatoris*. *OC*, vi, 963

Alphonso x. *Cantigas*. *OC*, iii, 290

– *Siete partidas*. *OC*, vi, 973

– *Código de las partidas y tablas astronómicas*. *OC*, vii, 508

Alvarez Quintero, Serafín y Joaquín. *El genio alegre*. *OC*, iv, 479

Amador de los Ríos, José. *Historia de la literatura española*. *OC*, iii, 916

El amigo de los niños. *OC*, i, 257

Ampère, J.Q. *Histoire littéraire de la France avant le douzième siècle*. *OC*, iii, 563

Anaxagoras, Clazomenius. *Anaxagorae fragmenta*. *OC*, xvi, 271

Angela de Foligno. *OC,* XVI, 412

Angilbert. *OC,* VI, 169

Antonio, de Lebrixa, The Elder. *Reglas de ortografía en la lengua castellana.* *OC,* III, 392

Antonio de Leyva. OC, I, 285

Año cristiano. OC, II, 454

Aparisi y Guijarro, Antonio. *OC,* II, 109

Arana, Sabino. *OC,* V, 618-9

Arana, Vicente de. *Oro y Oropel. OC,* V, 537

- *Los últimos iberos. OC,* V, 537

Araquistain, Juan V. *OC,* I, 342

Araquistain, Luis. 'El complejo sindicalista.' *OC,* V, 57

- 'Los escritores y la política,' *España,* CCLVIII (10 abril 1920)

- 'Sobre hispanoamericanismo.' *OC,* VI, 898-902

Arbois de Jubainville, Marie Henri d'. *OC,* VI, 304-5

Ardigo, Roberto. *OC,* XVI, 364

Arenas, Pedro. 'La novia de Don Quijote,' *Estampa* (19 noviembre 1932)

Aretino, [Pietro?] *OC,* V, 155

Argelliés, Mr. *OC,* VI, 92

Argente, Baldomero. 'Los escritores y el pueblo,' *Nuevo Mundo. OC,* IV, 433-40

Aribau, Buenaventura Carlos. *OC,* I, 809

Arlincourt, Charles Victor Prévôt d'. *OC,* V, 783

Arndt, Christian Gottlieb. *Ueber den Ursprung und die verschiedenartige Verwandtschaft der europäeschen Sprachen.* Frankfurt am Main. 1818

Arte de hacer maridos. OC, IX, 344

Arte de ser buenos y felices. OC, IX, 343

Arvers, Félix. *OC,* IX, 909

Ascasubi, Hilario. *Abiceto el Gallo. Oc,* VIII, 89

Ashley [Sir William James?]. *OC,* VIII, 124

Astete, Gaspar de. *Catecismo de la doctrina cristiana. OC,* V, 869

Astrain, P. Antonio. *Historia de la Compañía de Jesús en la asistencia de España. OC,* V, 190

Astur, Eugenia. *Riego.* Pról. Miguel de Unamuno. Oviedo. 1933. Pp. 350

Athanasius, Saint, Patriarch of Alexandria. *OC,* XVI, 190

Augustine, Saint, Bishop of Hippo. *De Civitate Dei. OC,* VI, 130

d'Avezac, M. 'Basque,' *Encyclopédie Nouvelle. OC,* VI, 106

Baedeker, Carl. *Espagne et Portugal. OC,* I, 641

Baena, Juan Alfonso de. *Cancionero de Baena. OC,* III, 334

Bailey, Cyril. *OC,* VIII, 836

Bain, Alexander. *System of Logic. OC,* VII, 148

- *Mind and Body. OC,* VII, 148

Balzac, Honoré de. *Peau de chagrin. OC,* x, 860
- *Le Curé de Tours. OC,* xvi, 504
Bannerman, David A. *OC,* x, 661
Barco, Juan. *OC,* xi, 71
Baroja, Pío. *Discurso leído ante la Academia Española el 12 de mayo de 1935. Contestación de Gregorio Marañón. OC,* v, 265
- *El tablado de Arlequín. OC,* iii, 1112
Barré, Louis. *Herculaneum et Poempéi. OC,* viii, 570
Barrès, Maurice. *La colina inspirada. OC,* v, 401
Un Barrido hacia fuera en la Compañía de Jesús. OC, iv, 355
Bartrina, Joaquín María. *OC,* iii, 1069
Baruzi, Jean. *Saint Jean de la Croix et le problème de l'expérience mystique.* Paris. Alcan. 1924. Pp. vii, 772
Bashkirtseva, Mariya Konstantinovna. *OC,* viii, 99
Basileiades, Spuridon N. *Galatea. OC,* iv, 769
Basterra, Ramón de. *La obra de Trajano. OC,* x, 1066
Bastiat, Claude Frédéric. *OC,* ii, 88
Baudrimont, Alexandre Edouard. *Histoire des Basques ou Escualdunais primitifs restaurée d'après la langue, les caractères ethnologiques et les moeurs des Basques actuels. OC,* vi, 117
Baur, Ferdinand Christian. *OC,* iii, 99
Beccari, Gilberto. *Un ángolo d'America inesplorata. OC,* viii, 452
- *I Guaraní. OC,* viii, 452
- 'L'Argentine poetica,' *Nuova Rassegna di Letterature Moderne. OC,* viii, 453
Benavente, Jacinto. *Los intereses creados. OC,* iii, 1127
- *Los malhechores del bien. OC,* xi, 509
Benítez Caballero. Rafael. *El Barquero de Cantillana. OC,* i, 709
Benot, Eduardo. *OC,* v, 190
Bension, Ariel. *El 'Zohar' en la España musulmana y cristiana.* Versión castellana del Dr Ariel Bension. Pról. M. de Unamuno. Madrid. c.i.a.p. [1931]. Pp. 327
Bérard, Victor. 'Los orígenes de la Odisea,' *Revue des Deux Mondes* (15 May 1902). *OC,* v, 935
Berceo, Gonzalo de. *II. Berceo. Colección de poesías castellanas anteriores al siglo XV.* Pról. don Tomás Antonio Sánchez. Madrid. 1780
- *Vida de Santo Domingo de Silos. OC,* vi, 970
- *Milagros. OC,* vi, 972
Berganza y Arce, Francisco. *Antigüedades de España propugnadas. OC,* vi, 962
Berkeley, George. *A Treatise Concerning the Principles of Human Knowledge. OC,* xvi, 214
Bernard, Saint, Abbot of Clairvaux. *De diligendo Deo. OC,* xvi, 502

Bernardy, Amy A. 'Americanismo,' *Nuova Antologia.* Roma (16 Sept. [1906?]). *OC,* iv, 408

Bernat y Baldoví, José. *OC,* v, 678

Berni, Francesco. *OC,* v, 150

Bertillon [Louis Adolphe?]. *OC,* xi, 256

Bertoldo. OC, v, 780

Bertrand, Louis. 'Mes Espagnes,' *Revue des Deux Mondes.* (10 Dec. [1913?]). *OC,* viii, 922-30

- 'Nietzsche y el Mediterráneo,' *Revue des Deux Mondes. OC,* viii, 940-5

- 'Nietzsche y la guerra,' *Revue des Deux Mondes* (15 Dec. [1914]). *OC,* viii, 1100-7

- 'Goethe et le germanisme,' *Revue des Deux Mondes* (15 Avril [1915]). *OC,* viii, 1110-20

Besant, Annie. *Autobiografía. OC,* xvi, 414

Betarn, W. *De l'identité de l'etrusque et du basque. OC,* vi, 115

Bethmann-Hollweg, Theovald von. *OC,* v, 122

Beuter, Pero Anton. *Crónica general de toda España y especialmente del Reyno de Valencia.* Valencia. 1604. *OC,* vi, 98

Biblioteca de Autores Españoles de Rivadeneyra. OC, vi, 1013

Biblioteca Moderna de Ciencias Sociales. OC, iii, 157

Bjørnson, Bjørnstjerne. *OC,* x, 176

Bladé, Jean François. *Etudes sur l'origine des peuples basques. OC,* vi, 114

Blanc Saint-Hilaire, Marie Jean. *Les Euskariens ou Basques. OC,* vi, 139

Blanco Belmonte, Marcos Rafael. *Por la España desconocida. OC,* i, 694

Blanco White, José María. *OC,* x, 671

Blasco, Eusebio. 'Escuela lógica,' *Revista Política y Parlamentaria,* núm. 2. *OC,* xi, 702

Blasco Ibáñez, Vicente. *La barraca. OC,* i, 811

- *La tierra de todos. OC,* v, 911

- *El intruso. OC,* xi, 557

Blatchford, Roberto. *Merry England. OC,* viii, 657

Boccalini, Traiano. *OC,* v, 152

Bocharti, Samuelis. *Geographia sacra. OC,* vi, 115

Bodley, J.E.C. *Cardinal Manning, and Other Essays. OC,* viii, 912

Boileau-Despréaux, Nicolas. *OC,* iv, 940

Bonaparte, Luis Luciano. *Langue basque et langues finoises. OC,* vi, 111

Bonaventura, Saint, Cardinal, Bishop of Albano [Giovanni Fidanza]. *OC,* xvi, 346

Bosch de la Trinxería, Carlos. *OC,* v, 609

Bossuet, Jacques Bénigne. *Discurso sobre la historia universal. OC,* xvi, 896

- *Traité de la concupiscence. OC,* xvi, 356

- 'Culte [qui est] dû à Dieu.' *OC,* xvi, 352

Bourget, Paul Charles Joseph. *Le disciple. OC,* VIII, 99
- *Outre-mer. OC,* III, 1048
Braga, Theophilo. *OC,* I, 731
Brandão, Antonio. *Monarchia Lusytana* (pt. 3, 4, A. Brandão). See Brito,
    Bernardo de. *OC,* I, 461
Bremond, Marie Joseph François. *Historia literaria del sentimiento religioso
    en Francia. OC,* XI, 988
Brenner, Anita. *Idolos detrás de los altares. OC,* VI, 946
Bretón de los Herreros, Manuel. *OC,* V, 307
Breviarium romanum ex decreto S.S. Concilii Tridentini. OC, XI, 805
Brito, Bernardo de. *Monarchia Lusytana.* Parte primeira (segunda). *OC,* I, 461
Brizeux, Julien Auguste. *Histoires poétiques. OC,* VI, 377
Broca, Paul. *OC,* VI, 92
Brooks, Van Wyck. 'Henry James: The American Scene.' *OC,* X, 529
Brulart de Genlis, Stéphanie Félicité. *Les Battuécas. OC,* I, 711
Brunetière, Ferdinand. *OC,* XVI, 231
Bruzen de la Martinière, Antoine Augustin. *Le Grand dictionnaire
    géographique et critique. OC,* VI, 114
Bryce, James. *The American Commonwealth.* Tr. Adolfo Posada. *OC,* VIII,
    1170
Buechner, Friedrich Carl Christian Ludwig. *Fuerza y materia. OC,* IV, 850
Bullet, Jean Baptiste. *Mémoires sur la langue celtique. OC,* VI, 115
Burton, Robert. *The Anatomy of Melancholy. OC,* IX, 792
Byron, George Gordon. *Cain, a Mystery. OC,* VIII, 1010
- *Heaven and Earth. OC,* X, 585
- *Sardanapulus. OC,* IV, 650
Cabanyes, Manuel de. *Spanish Texts and Studies. The Poems of Manuel de
    Cabanyes.* Ed. with introd. notes, and bibl. E. Allison Peers. 1923. *OC,*
    XIV, 441
Cabezon, Cárlos. *Neógrafos kontemporáneos. Tentativa bibliográfika. OC,*
    III, 388
Cabrera, Fray Alonso de. *Sermones.* NBAE. *OC,* IV, 505
Caignart de Saulcy, Louis-Félicien-Joseph. [*Essai de classification des
    monnaies autonomes d'Espagne?*] *OC,* VI, 170
Calvete de la Estrella, Juan Cristóbal. *Rebelión de Pizarro en el Perú y vida
    de don Pedro Gasca. OC,* V, 1066
Calvin, Jean. *Institutio Christianae religionis. OC,* IV, 847
Cambó y Batllé, Francisco de Asis. *OC,* V, 617
Campanella, Tommaso. *OC,* XVI, 424
Campión, Arturo. *Don Garcia Almorabid, crónica del siglo XIII. OC,* VI, 315
- *Blancos y Negros (Guerra en la paz).* Pamplona. 1898. Pp. 382
Canale, Martino da. *Historia de Venecia. OC,* VI, 971

Cano, Leopoldo. *La pasionaria. OC,* III, 357

Cánovas del Castillo, Antonio. *Ilusiones y desengaños. Obras poéticas.*
   Madrid. 1887. Pp. 284

– El solitario y su tiempo. OC, v, 461

– Reminiscencias. OC, v, 464

Canto de Altobiscar. OC, I, 344

Capdevila, Arturo. *Córdoba del recuerdo. OC,* xv, 854

Capmany y Montpalau, Antonio de. *OC,* III, 491

Capus, Alfred, and Emmanuel Arene. *El adversario. OC,* xI, 522

La carcajada. OC, v, 293

Carrasquilla, Tomás. *Salve, Regina. OC,* VIII, 311

Carvalho da Costa, Antonio. *Chorographia portugueza e descripçam
   topographica do famoso Reyno de Portugal. OC,* I, 412

Casares y Sánchez, Julio. *Crítica profana. Valle inclán, 'Azorin,' Ricardo León.*
   Madrid. 1916. Pp. 365

Castiglione, Baldassare. *Il cortegiano. OC,* v, 164

Castilho, Antonio Feliciano de. *OC,* I, 730

Castillo y Ocsiero, Mariano. *El firmamento. Calendario zaragozano para
   1929. OC,* xv, 340

Castro, Eugenio de. *Crystallisacoes da morte. OC,* I, 351

Castro, Rosalía de. *En las orillas del Sar. OC,* I, 653

Catalá, Víctor, pseud. [i.e., Caterina Albert i Paradis]. *OC,* v, 634

Cauchy, Augustin Louis. *Mémoire sur la dispersion de la lumiére. OC,* xvI, 361

Cavia, Mariano de. *OC,* v, 470

Cénac-Moncaut, Justin Edouard Mathieu. *OC,* III, 574

Cervantes, Miguel de. *El Licenciado Vidriera. OC,* v, 43

Chagas, João. 'Justiça militar.' *OC,* III, 977

Chaho, Augustin. *Histoire primitive des Euskariens-Basques, langue, poésie,
   moeurs, et caractères de ce peuple. Introduction à son histoire ancienne et
   moderne.* 1847. *OC,* vI, 108

*– Lettre à Mr Xavier Raymond sur les analogies qui existent entre la langue
   basque et le sanscrit.* Paris. 1836.

Chamberlain, Houston Stewart. *OC,* IV, 1122

Chamfort, Sebastien Roch Nicolas. *OC,* xI, 461

Chandler, Frank Wadleigh. *Romances of Roguery. OC,* v, 735

Charencey, H. *La langue basque et les idiomes de l'Oural. OC,* vI, 111

– 'Etymologies basquaises,' Le Museón, 4. *OC,* vI, 137

Chartier, Emile Auguste (Alain, pseud.). *Propos sur le christianisme. OC,*
   xvI, 536

Chateaubriand, François René. *René. OC,* v, 990

– Le génie du christianisme. OC, III, 447

– De Buonaparte et des Bourbons. OC, xv, 361

Cueva, Juan de la. *OC*, III, 335
Curtius, Georg. *OC*, VI, 492
Cuvier, Georges. *OC*, V, 999
Cyrano de Bergerac, Savinien. *OC*, I, 684
Dante, Alighieri. *De monarchia*. *OC*, XVI, 179
Darrigol, Jean Pierre. *Dissertation critique et apologétique sur la langue basque. Par un ecclésiastique du diocèse de Bayonne*. Bayonne. [1829]. Pp. 163
Darwin, Charles Robert. *Origen de las especies*. *OC*, IV, 539
Daudet, Alphonse. *OC*, V, 577
Davies, [Edward?]. *OC*, VI, 143
De la sangre, de la voluptuosidad y de la muerte. *OC*, VIII, 172
Dechepare, Bernard. *Poésies basques*. *OC*, VI, 145
De Quincey, Thomas. *Sobre el asesinato considerado como una de las bellas artes*. *OC*, XI, 443
Derrotero del Mediterráneo. *OC*, V, 937
Dewey, John. *German Philosophy and Politics*. *OC*, VII, 354
Díaz del Castillo, Bernal. *Verdadera historia de los sucesos de la conquista de la Nueva España*. *OC*, I, 571
Díaz Mirón, Salvador. *OC*, XI, 486
Diccionario de galicismos. *OC*, III, 172
Diccionario geográfico histórico de España. 'Sección I relativa a Navarra y las Provincias Vascongadas' por Joaqúín Traggia. *OC*, III, 560
Dicenta, Joaquín. *Juan José*. *OC*, III, 1135
Diderot, Denis. *OC*, XVI, 227
Diego de Estella, Fray. *Vanidad del mundo*. *OC*, XVI, 425
Diez, Federico. *OC*, VI, 496
Diharce de Bidassouet, Pierre. *Histoire des cantabres, ou des premiers colons de toute l'Europe. I. OC*, VI, 113
Dionysius, Saint, called the Areopagite. *OC*, XVI, 288
Dobson, Henry Austin. *OC*, XV, 519
Domingo de Guzmán, Saint. *OC*, XVI, 412
Domínguez Berrueta, Mariano. *Alma charra*. *OC*, V, 315
Los dos virreyes. *OC*, I, 630
Dozy, Reinhart Pieter Anne. *OC*, VI, 962
Du Bellay, Joachim. *OC*, I, 1097
Dubreton, Lucas. *Le roi sauvage*. *OC*, IX, 90
Dumas, Alexandre. *Los tres mosqueteros*. *OC*, XI, 533
Du Mège, Alexandre Louis Charles André. *OC*, VI, 106
Duns, Joannes Scotus. *OC*, XVI, 288
Durkheim, Emile. *De la division du travail social*. *OC*, III, 447
Duvoisin, J. 'Antigüedades ibéricas,' *Revista Euskara*, núm. 27. *OC*, VI, 106

Fernández Almagro, Melchor. *Orígenes del régimen constitucional en España.*
   OC, xv, 872
Fernández de Córdoba, Fernando. *Mis memorias íntimas. OC,* v, 383
Fernández de Moratín, Nicolás. *Desengaños al teatro español. OC,* v, 505
Fernández de Navarrete, Pedro. *OC,* iii, 238
Fernández Guerra, Aureliano. *El libro de Santoña. OC,* vi, 109
– *Discursos leídos en la recepción de don Eduardo Saavedra ante la*
   R. Academia de la Historia. OC, vi, 93
– 'La cantabria,' *Boletín de la Sociedad Geográfica,* iv. *OC,* vi, 127-8
Fernández Iparraguirre, Francisco, y Tomás Escriche. *Nociones de gramática*
   general. OC, vi, 189
Fernández Moratín, Leandro. *El sí de las niñas. OC,* xi, 505
Fernández y González, Manuel. *OC,* v, 889
Ferrán, Augusto. *OC,* v, 392
Ferrero, [?]. *OC,* iv, 726
Ferrero, Guillermo. *OC,* i, 534
Feuerbach, Ludwig Andreas. *OC,* viii, 658
Fichte, Johann Gottlieb. *OC,* iii, 510
Figueiredo, Fidelino de. *Las dos Españas. OC,* viii, 1073
Figueroa y Torres, Alvaro de. *Espartero, el general del pueblo. OC,* v, 509
– *Sagasta o el político. OC,* v, 519
Fita y Colomé, Fidel. *El gerundense y la España primitiva. OC,* vi, 109
Florez, Henrique. *La cantabria. OC,* vi, 93
Florus, Publius Annius. *Epítome de historia romana, libro IV. OC,* vi, 173
Fourier, François Charles Marie. *OC,* xvi, 401
France, Anatole. *El anillo de amatista. OC,* x, 798
Franchetti, Leopoldo. *Condizioni politiche e amministrative della Sicilia.*
   OC, viii, 663
Francke, August Hermann. *OC,* xvi, 248
Frank, Waldo. *Virgin Spain: Scenes from the Spiritual Drama of a Great*
   People. London. Jonathan Cape. 1926
Fredegarius, Scholasticus. *OC,* vi, 169
Frederick ii, called the Great, King of Prussia. *Anti-Machiavel. OC,* ix, 823
Freiligrath, Ferdinand. *OC,* iii, 355
Fresne, Charles du, sieur Du Cange. *Glossarium ad scriptores mediae et*
   infimae latinitatis. OC, iii, 588
Frontaura, Carlos. *OC,* v, 386
Fuero juzgo. OC, vi, 973
Fustel de Coulanges, Numa Denis. *La cité antique. OC,* viii, 124
Gallardo, Bartolomé José. *Opúsculos gramáticos y satíricos. OC,* v, 227
Garat de Montglave, Mr. *OC,* vi, 207

Gracián, Baltasar. *El criticón. OC*, v, 197
- *Agudeza y arte del ingenio. OC*, v, 202
Grammar of Science. OC, vi, 642
Grandgagnage, [François Charles Joseph?]. *OC*, vi, 123
Grandmontagne, Francisco. *La maldonada. OC*, viii, 64
- *Vivos, tilingos y locos lindos.* Buenos Aires. 1901
Gratry, [Auguste Joseph Alphonse?]. *OC*, xvi, 361
Gregory, of Nazianzus, Saint. *Cristo paciente. OC*, iii, 332
Gregory, Saint, Bishop of Tours. *OC*, vi, 169
Grimmelshausen, Hans Jacob Christoffel von. *Simplicisimus. OC*, viii, 1131
Groussac, Paul. *Del Plata al Niágara.* Buenos Aires. 1897
Guarini, Giovanni Battista. *Pastor Fido. OC*, vii, 239
Guerra Junqueiro, Abilio. *Morte de D. João. OC*, i, 364
- *Velhice do Padre Eterno. OC*, i, 364
Guevara, Antonio de. *Arte de marear. OC*, v, 105
Gui de Bourgogne. OC, iii, 252
Guiches, Gustave. 'Por qué los literatos no escriben para el cine.' *OC*, xi, 531
Guillén, Nicolás. *Sóngoro cosongo. OC*, xv, 882
Guimerá, Angel. *Tierra baja. OC*, xi, 518
Gutiérrez, Eduardo. *Juan Moreira. OC*, iv, 912
Gutiérrez Abascal, Ricardo (Juan de la Encina, pseud.). 'Lazaro el payador.'
  OC, viii, 564
Gutiérrez Somoza, Pedro. *OC*, xvi, 796
Guyon, Jeanne Marie. *OC*, xvi, 501
Guzmán, Ernesto A. *Vida interna. OC*, xiii, 89
Haeckel, Ernst. *Los enigmas del universo. OC*, iv, 836
Haemmerlin, Thomas a Kempis. *Imitación de Cristo. OC*, ii, 352
Hanotaux, G. *Historia ilustrada de la guerra.* Tr. Luis Contreras. Pról.
  M. de Unamuno. 1915
- 'De l'histoire et des historiens,' *Revue des Deux Mondes* (15 Sept. 1913).
  OC, i, 683
Hapfer, Paul. *Des reputations litteraries. OC*, iv, 628
Hartzenbusch, Juan Eugenio. *OC*, v, 386
Hatch, Edwin. *The Influence of Greek Ideas and Usages upon the Christian
  Church.* Oxford. 1901
Hauptmann, Gerhart. *Die Weber. OC*, iii, 355
- *La campana sumergida. OC*, iv, 675
Hegel, Georg Wilhelm Friedrich. *Fenomenología del espíritu. OC*, xi, 674
Heraclitus. *OC*, v, 98
Herbart, Johann Friedrich. *OC*, iii, 591
Herculano de Carvalho e Araujo, Alejandro. *O Bobo. OC*, i, 438
- *Eurico el presbítero. OC*, v, 784

Herder, Johann Gottfried von. *OC*, vi, 769

Hermann, Wolfgang. *Der Verkehr des Christen mit Gott, im Anschluss an Luther dargestellt.* Dritte auflage. Stuttgart. 1866

– in *Systematische Christliche Religion. OC*, xvi, 196

Hernández, José. *La vuelta de Martín Fierro. OC*, viii, 53

Hero y Leandro. OC, i, 746

Herriot, M. Edouard. *OC*, v, 63

Hervás y Panduro, Lorenzo. *OC*, vi, 143

Hessen, Johannes. *Gotteskindschaft. OC*, x, 906

Hippocrates. *OC*, xvi, 271

Hitzig, Eduard. *OC*, xx, 325

Hobson, John Atkinson. *The Evolution of Modern Capitalism. OC*, iii, 101

– *The Nation and the Athenaeum. OC*, x, 804

Hodgson, Shadworth H. *Time and Space, a Metaphysical Essay. OC*, xvi, 157

Höffding, Harald. *Historia de la filosofía moderna. OC*, iv, 686

Holberg, Ludwig. *OC*, xvi, 238

Holtzmann, Oscar. *Leben Jesu. OC*, iii, 546

Houtin, Albert. *Le Père Hyacinthe dans l'Eglise romaine, 1827-1869. Le Père Hyacinthe, réformateur catholique, 1869-1893. Le Père Hyacinthe, prêtre solitaire, 1893-1912.* Paris. Librairie Emile Nourry. 1924

Hovelacque, Abel. *La linguistique. OC*, vi, 103

Huarte de San Juan, Juan. *Examen de ingenios para las ciencias. OC*, iii, 236

Huerta y Vega, Francisco Javier Manuel de. *OC*, vi, 100

Hugo, de Sancto Victore. *OC*, x, 918

Humboldt, Carl Wilhelm von. *Prüfung der Untersuchungen über die Urbervohner hispaniens, vermittelst der Vaskischen sprache.* Berlin. 1821

– *Wilhelm von Humboldt's gesammelte Werke.* Berlin. 1841-52

– *Correcciones i adiciones al Mithridates de Adelung sobre la lengua cantábrica o vasca.* Tr. Justo Garate. San Sebastián. Rev. Internacional de los Estudios Vascos. 1933. Pp. 83

– 'Reiseskizzen aus Biscaya.' *OC*, vi, 246

Humboldt, Friedrich Heinrich Alexander. *Kosmos. OC*, vi, 247

Hunter, William A. *A Systematic and Historical Exposition of Roman Law in the Order of a Code. OC*, vii, 148

Huon de Bordeaux. OC, iii, 252

Huysmans, Joris-Karl. *Sainte Lydwine de Schiedam. OC*, xvi, 577

Ibarbourou, Juana de. *Las lenguas de diamante. OC*, vi, 918

Ibsen, Henrick. *Kongs-Aemnerne. OC*, ii, 469

– *Los espectros. OC*, xi, 511

Ignatius, Saint, of Loyola. *Cartas. OC*, xvi, 527

Inchauspe, Emmanuel. *Le verbe basque. OC*, vi, 96

Inocencia [de Tonay]. *OC*, iv, 917

Instrucciones náuticas y derroteros. OC, v, 936

Iñiguez de Ibargüen, Juan. *OC*, vi, 136

Iparraguirre, José María de. *OC*, vi, 207

Irizar y Moya, Joaquín. *OC*, iii, 563

Isaacs, Jorge. *María. OC*, vii, 218

Isidore, Saint, Archbishop of Seville. *Orígenes. OC*, vi, 964

Iturribarría, Francisco de. *OC*, i, 342

Izasti, Lope de. *Compendio historial de la M.N. y M.L. provincia de Guipúzcoa. OC*, vi, 100

Jacobo Ortis. OC, viii, 99

Jaloux, Edmond. 'La actitud de los neutros,' *Le Soleil du Midi. OC*, x, 357

James, Henry. *The Jolly Corner. OC*, x, 529

Jansenius, Cornelius, Bishop of Ypres. *OC*, xvi, 249

Jarnés, Benjamín. *El convidado de papel. OC*, xv, 315

- 'Oro trillado y néctar exprimido,' *La Gaceta Literaria. OC*, x, 891

Jiménez de Rada, Rodrigo. *De Rebus Hisp.*, vii, 13. *OC*, v, 209

Johnson, James. 'La ciudad de la noche terrible.' [*sic*; see Thomson, James.] *OC*, v, 492

Johnson, James. 'La ciudad de la noche terrible.' *OC*, v, 492

Joly, Edmundo. *L'Œillet de Seville: impressions d'Espagne. OC*, ix, 90

Joseph, Saint, Husband of Virgin Mary. *Vida de San José, patriarca. OC*, vi, 390

Juana Inés, de la Cruz, Sor. *OC*, iv, 708

Juanito. OC, i, 266

Justi, Carl. *OC*, i, 642

Justin, Martyr, Saint. *OC*, xvi, 190

Kaplan, Julio. *Dogmatik. OC*, xvi, 21

Kastner, Ioannes Nicolaus. *OC*, vi, 201

Keyserling, Hermann. *Diario de viaje de un filósofo. OC*, x, 721

Kidd, Benjamin. *Principles of the Western Civilization. OC*, v, 327

Kipling, Rudyard. *OC*, v, 650

Kock, Paul de. *OC*, v, 783

Krause, Christian Friedrich. *OC*, xvi, 417

La Bastide. *Dissertation sur les basques.* Paris. 1876. *OC*, vi, 112

Labayru y Goicoechea, Estanislao Jaime de. *Historia general del Señorío de Bizcaya.* Bilbao. 1895

Laborde, Jules. *Il y a toujours des Pyrénées. OC*, i, 799

Lactantius, Lucius Coelius Firmianus. *OC*, xvi, 292

Lafuente, Modesto. *Historia general de España. OC*, v, 766

Lagrange, Fernand. *Fisiología de los ejercicios corporales. OC*, viii, 216

Lamartine, Alphonse de. *Jocelyn. OC*, x, 638

Landa, Dr. 'Cranía euskara,' *Revista Euskara*, i, 3 (abril 1878). *OC*, vi, 92

Lang, Andrew. *Angling Sketches. OC*, iii, 788

Marañón, Gregorio. *Contestación al discurso de Baroja leído ante la Academia Española el 12 de mayo de 1935*. *OC*, v, 265

- *Las ideas biológicas del padre Feijóo*. *OC*, xi, 1027

Marco, Luis. *Sonetos y poesías varias*. *OC*, v, 304

Marden, Orison Swett. *Pushing to the Front*. *OC*, iv, 1036

Mariátegui, E. de. 'Los toros de Guisando,' *El Arte en España*, iv (1865). *OC*, vi, 93

Marineus, Lucius. *Obra compuesta por L. Marineo ... de las cosas memorables de España*. *OC*, vi, 98

Marrast, A. *OC*, vi, 135

Martel, Edouard. *OC*, i, 757

Martin de Moussy, v. *Description de la Confederation Argentine*. *OC*, viii, 340

Martínez de Isasti, Lope. *OC*, vi, 136

Martínez Marina, Francisco. *OC*, iii, 173

Martínez Ruiz, José. *Lecturas españolas*. *OC*, v, 363

Martínez Zuviria, G.A. (Hugo Wast, pseud.). *Valle negro. Ciudad turbulenta, ciudad alegre*. *OC*, vi, 918

Martini, Raymundus. *Pugio fidei*. *OC*, xvi, 527

Marx, Karl. *OC*, v, 89

Mas, Sinibaldo de. *OC*, v, 1107

Más y Prat, Benito. *La tierra de María Santísima*. *OC*, v, 486

Masdeu, Juan Francisco. *OC*, vi, 100

Massip, Paulino. 'El problema de la juventud.' *OC*, x, 1028

Maurois, André. *Byron*. *OC*, xv, 845

Maurras, Charles. *Enquête sur la monarchie suivi d'une campagne royaliste au Figaro et si le coup de force est possible*. Paris. 1924

Maury, Alfred. *OC*, vi, 115

Mauthner, Fritz. *Beiträge zu einer Kritik der Sprache*. *OC*, xv, 960

May, Thomas. *OC*, v, 140

Mayans y Siscar, Gregorio. *OC*, iii, 559

Maybon, Albert. 'La malaise japonais,' *Mercure de France* (10 May 1907). *OC*, v, 338

Mazel, Henri. *OC*, viii, 659

Medina, Pedro de. *Grandezas de España*. *OC*, vi, 222

Medina, Vicente. *OC*, v, 84

Meigret, Louis. *OC*, iii, 391

Mela, Pomponio. *OC*, vi, 172

Melanchthon, Philipp. *Loci communes*. *OC*, xvi, 196

Mele, Eugenio. *OC*, v, 148

Melo, Francisco Manuel de. *Historia de los movimientos, separación y guerra de Cataluña en tiempo de Felipe IV*. *OC*, v, 901

Oihenart u Oyenarte, Arnaldo. *Notitia utriusque Vasconiae*. Paris. 1637.
   OC, VI, 98
Olavarría y Duarte, Eugenio de. 'Cómo se forman los mitos. La historia por el
   pueblo,' *El Folklore de Madrid. Biblioteca de las Tradiciones Populares
   Españolas*, II. *OC*, XI, 543
Oller, Narciso. *La febre d'or. OC*, V, 600
- *L'Escanya-pobres. OC*, V, 600
Ollivier, Emilio. *OC*, VII, 317
'Omar Khaiyâm. *OC*, V, 495
Origen. *OC*, XVI, 370
Orlani, Alfredo. *La lotta politica in Italia. OC*, V, 157
Orosius, Paulus. *OC*, XVI, 896
Ortega y Frías, Ramón. *OC*, V, 389
Ortíz, Fernando. *Entre cubanos. Rasgos de psicología criolla*. Paris.
   Ollendorf. *OC*, XVI, 788
Ortiz de Zárate, Ramón. *OC*, VI, 304
Ossorio y Gallardo. *OC*, XI, 1040
Otálora y Guisasa, Gonzalo de. *Micrología geográfica de la merindad de
   Durango. OC*, VI, 93
Ovejero, Fray Esteban Ginés. *Guadalupe. OC*, I, 473
Overstone, Samuel Jones Loyd. *OC*, IV, 1038
Owen. *OC*, VI, 143
Pacheco, E.H. 'Las mesetas de moda,' *Revista Nueva*, núm. 9 (1899?).
   OC, IV, 1052
Palacio Valdés, Armando. *Maximina. OC*, V, 317
- *Los majos de Cádiz. OC*, VI, 846
- *La hermana San Sulpicio. OC*, XIV, 281
Paley, William. *OC*, V, 1018
Palma, Ricardo. *Dos mil setecientas voces que hacen falta en el Diccionario
   Académico*. Lima. 1903
- *Neologismos y americanismos. OC*, VI, 841
El pan del pobre. OC, III, 357
Papini, Giovanni. *Maschilità. OC*, X, 340
Pardo Bazán, Emilia. *La quimera. OC*, X, 483
- *Los tres arcos de Cirilo. OC*, X, 485
- *La cuestión palpitante. OC*, X, 486
Pascoli, Giovanni. 'La buona novella.' *OC*, IX, 82
Pastor Díaz, Nicomedes. *OC*, I, 880
Paul IV, Pope. *OC*, V, 156
Pellegrini, Carlos. *OC*, VI, 828
Pellot, Etienne. *El almirante cojo. OC*, X, 789

Pereda, José María de. *Peñas arriba. OC,* I, 869
– *Sotileza. OC,* V, 473
Pérez Cardenal, Andrés. *Alpinismo castellano.* Epíl. M. de Unamuno. Bilbao. 1914
Pérez de Hita, Ginés. *Historia de los bandos de Cegríes. OC,* V, 493
Pérez Escrich, Enrique. *Historia de un beso. OC,* I, 438
– *Las obras de misericordia. OC,* V, 389
Pérez Galdós, Benito. *Gerona. OC,* III, 357
– *Realidad. OC,* III, 357
– *La de San Quintín. OC,* III, 357
– *León Roch. OC,* III, 357
– *Doña Perfecta. OC,* III, 357
– *Gloria. OC,* III, 357
– *La loca de la casa. OC,* XI, 515
– *Electra. OC,* VIII, 647
– *Torquemada en el purgatorio. OC,* XI, 836
– *Torquemada y San Pedro. OC,* XI, 841
– *El amigo manso. OC,* XI, 845
– *Casandra. OC,* XII, 166
Pérez Lugín, Alejandro. *La casa de la Troya. OC,* X, 451
Pérez Martín, Héctor. *OC,* VI, 956
Los perfumes de Barcelona. OC, XI, 1057
Pericles, of Athens. *OC,* V, 151
Perrucci, Andrea. *Dell'arte rappresentativa. OC,* V, 152
Petronius Arbiter, Titus. *Satyricon. OC,* XVI, 500
Pezron, Paul Yves. *OC,* VI, 114
Philips. *Ueber das lateinisch und romanisch Element in der baskischen Sprache. OC,* VI, 121
Pi y Margall, Francisco. *OC,* V, 58
Pichardo, Juan Nepomuceno. *OC,* XVI, 793
Pichet, Mr. *OC,* VI, 159
Piferrer, P. *OC,* V, 577
Pina, Ruy de. *Chronica de el Rey Dom Afonso o Quarto. OC,* I, 461
Pinilla, Cándido Rodríguez. *Cantos de la noche.* Madrid. 1899
Pitrè, Giuseppe. *OC,* V, 157
Pius IX. *OC,* XVI, 199
Plautus, Titus Maccius. *Poenulus. OC,* VI, 112
Plinius Secundus, Caius. *Naturalis historiae. OC,* VI, 967
– *C. Plinii panegyricus trajano. OC,* XVI, 292
Pohle, Joseph. 'Christliche katolische Dogmatik,' *Systematische Christliche Religion.* Berlin. 1909. *OC,* XVI, 203

– *L'Avenir de la science. Pensées de 1848. OC,* VIII, 979
– *Cahiers de jeunesse. OC,* VIII, 989
– *Palabras de un creyente. OC,* IX, 63
– *Feuilles détachées. OC,* XVI, 485
– *Choses passées. OC,* XVI, 485
– *Souvenirs d'enfance et de jeunesse. OC,* XVI, 512
Retzius, Andrés. *OC,* VI, 92
Reuter. *OC,* III, 99
Revilla, Angel. *José María Gabriel y Galán. Su vida y sus obras.* Pról. M. de Unamuno. Madrid. Rivadeneyra. 1923. Pp. 210
Reynal O'Connor, Arturo. *Mi año literario, I.* 2a ed. Buenos Aires. 1903. *OC,* VIII, 241
Ribadeneira, Pedro de. *OC,* VI, 912
Ricardus, Prior S. Victoris Parisiensis. *OC,* III, 258
Rioja, Francisco de. *OC,* I, 110
Ríos, José Amador de los. *Estudios monumentales y arqueológicos sobre las provincias vascongadas. OC,* VI, 93
Riquetti, Honoré Gabriel, comte de Mirabeau. *Cartas a Sofía. OC,* XI, 631
Risco, Manuel. 'La Vasconia,' *España Sagrada. OC,* VI, 130
Ritschl, Albrecht. *Geschichte des Pietismus, II.* Bonn. 1884
Rivarola, Rodolfo. 'Discurso de apertura del curso.' Universidad de la Plata. *OC,* VIII, 555
Robertson, William D.D., the Historian. *OC,* V, 215
Rodenbach, Georges Raymond. *Brujas la muerta. OC,* I, 498
Rodríguez de la Cámara o del Padrón, Juan. *El siervo libre de amor. OC,* I, 652
Rodríguez Ferrer, Miguel. *Los vascongados; su país, su lengua y el príncipe L.L. Bonaparte.* Introd. A. Cánovas del Castillo. *OC,* III, 563
Rodríguez Mendoza, Emilio. *Vida nueva.* Santiago de Chile. 1902. Pp. 355
Rogers, James Edwin Thorold. *OC,* VIII, 124
Rogers, Samuel. *OC,* V, 905
Rojas, Arístides. *Leyendas históricas. OC,* X, 597
Rojas, Ricardo. *La restauración nacionalista. Informe sobre educación. OC,* IV, 801
– *Los arquetipos. OC,* XI, 830
Rojas Zorrilla, Francisco de. *Del rey abajo, ninguno. OC,* III, 241
Roland. *Chanson de Roland. OC,* III, 249
Rolph, W.H. *Problemas biológicos. OC,* III, 691
Romano, Luis. *Horas grises.* Pról. M. de Unamuno. Salamanca. 1902. Pp. 76
Romero Alpuente, Juan. *OC,* XVI, 873
Roscellinus. *OC,* VI, 198

Roscher, Wilhelm Georg Friedrich. *Grundlagen der Nationalökonomie.*
  Stuttgart. 1877
Rostand, Edmond. *Cyrano de Bergerac. OC,* iv, 629
Rousseau, Jean Jacques. *Contrato social. OC,* iv, 742
– *Confessions. OC,* ix, 96
Rousselot, P. Jean Abbé. *OC,* vi, 496
Royce, Josiah. 'El pesimismo y el pensamiento moderno.' *OC,* xiv, 286
Royer, Clémence Auguste. *OC,* vi, 194
Rueda, Lope de. *OC,* iii, 334
Ruhland, Gustav. *OC,* iv, 1060
Ruiz Aguilera, Ventura. *La gaita gallega. OC,* i, 664
Rullán, Idelfonso. *OC,* i, 762
Rumano, Mihail Tican. *La España de hoy.* Pról. M. de Unamuno. *OC,* xvi, 805
Rusiñol, Santiago. *Oracions. OC,* v, 587
Ruskin, John. *Mornings in Florence. OC,* iii, 381
Russell, Bertrand Arthur William. *OC,* viii, 830
Ruysbroeck, Jan van. *OC,* iii, 510
Saavedra, Angel de (Duque de Rivas). *Documentos inéditos. OC,* iii, 236
– *Don Alvaro. OC,* iii, 357
Sabunde, Raymundus de. *OC,* xvi, 527
Saint-Simon, H.J.V. de. *Memorias. OC,* iii, 801
Sainte-Beuve, Charles Augustin. *Port Royal. OC,* iv, 587
Sainte-Claire Deville, Etienne Henri. *OC,* i, 558
Saintsbury, George. *A History of Criticism and Literary Taste in Europe.*
  OC, v, 1167
Salaverría, José María. 'El protocolo,' *ABC* de Madrid. *OC,* v, 897
– 'Intelectualismo y propaganda.' *OC,* v, 917
Salazar y Torres, Agustín de. *Elegir al enemigo. OC,* xvi, 445
Salignac de la Mothe Fénelon, François. *Telémaco. OC,* xvi, 350
Salillas, Rafael. *Hampa. OC,* iii, 158
Salimbene, Minorite. *Crónica. OC,* iii, 801
Sallaberry, J.D.J. *OC,* vi, 207
Salmerón, Nicolás. *OC,* iv, 581
Samain, Albert Victor. *OC,* v, 863
Samaniego, Félix María de. 'La barca de Simón.' *OC,* x, 1054
Samosata, Luciano de. *Diálogos de los muertos. OC,* xi, 874
Sánchez, Florencio. *Los derechos de la salud. OC,* iv, 676
Sánchez Mármol, M. *Las letras patrias. OC,* iii, 1087
Sánchez y Casado, Félix. *Elementos de historia de España. OC,* vi, 304
Sanctis, Francesco de. *Storia della litteratura italiana. OC,* xvi, 346
Sanctis, G. de. *Historia de los romanos. OC,* v, 48
Sand, George, pseud. [i.e., Amore Dupin]. *Un hiver à Majorque. OC,* i, 781

Sandoval, Fr. Prudencio de. *Vida y hechos del emperador Carlos V.*
   OC, III, 203
- *Fundaciones de San Benito. OC,* VI, 962
Sanín Cano, B. 'La race incomprise,' *Hispania* (Londres). *OC,* IV, 1098
San Pedro, Diego de. *Cárcel de amor. OC,* XIV, 284
Sanz, Eulogio Florentino. *Epístola a Pedro. OC,* I, 987
- *Don Francisco de Quevedo. OC,* XI, 503
Sanz del Río, Julián. *Analítica. OC,* III, 593
Saulcy. See Caignart de Saulcy, Louis-Félicien-Joseph
Savigny, Friedrich Carl von. *OC,* III, 313
Say, Jean Baptiste. *OC,* II, 88
Sbarbi y Osuna, José María. In 'El averiguador universal.' *OC,* IX, 1058
Scala (Scaligero), José de la. *Opúscula.* Parisiis. Apud Hadrianum Beys. 1610.
   OC, VI, 1060
Schaeffle, Albert Eberhard Friedrich. *OC,* IV, 1060
Schelling, Friedrich Wilhelm Joseph von. *OC,* III, 510
Schleicher, August. *Die Sprachen Europas in systematischer Uebersicht.*
   Bonn. 1850
Schmoller, Gustav Friedrich von. *Manual de economía general popular.*
   OC, VIII, 381
Schneider, Reinhold. *La pasión de Camoens. OC,* VIII, 1077
- *Religión y poder. OC,* VIII, 1077
Scotus, subtilis Doctor. See Duns, Joannes Scotus
Seeberg, Reinhold. 'Christliche-protestantische Ethik,' *Systematische*
   Christliche Religion. OC, XVI, 315
Seeley, Sir John Robert. *Expansion of England. OC,* VI, 729
Selgas, José. *OC,* V, 563
Senador Gómez, Julio. *Castilla, en escombros. OC,* I, 823
- *La ciudad castellana. OC,* I, 823
- *La canción del Duero. OC,* I, 823
Seneca, Lucius Annaeus. *De consolatione ad Helviam. OC,* VI, 105
- *De ira. OC,* VIII, 683
- 'A Sereno: de la constancia del sabio. XIV.' *OC,* IX, 773
Seoane, Juan Antonio de, Marquis. *Ensayo de filosofía elíptica. OC,* III, 294
Sepúlveda, Juan Ginés de. *De convenientia militaris disciplinae cum*
   Christiana religione. OC, III, 272
Serafí Pitarra. See Soler y Hubert, Federico
Sering, Max. *OC,* IV, 1060
Servetus, Michael. *OC,* V, 74
Sévigné, Marie de Rabutin-Chantel, Marquise de. *OC,* IV, 713
Shestov, Lev Isaakovich, pseud. (i.e., Lev Isaakovich Shvartsman). *La Nuit de*
   Gethsémani, essai sur la philosophie de Pascal. OC, XVI, 496

Sierra, Justo. *Historia de México. OC*, III, 1094

Simonena, Antonio. *OC*, XI, 106

Sinués, María del Pilar. *OC*, V, 387

Smith, Adam. *OC*, II, 88

Smith, William Robertson. *The Prophets of Israel. OC*, XVI, 287

Soler y Hubert, Federico (Serafí Pitarra, pseud.). *OC*, V, 609

Sorel, Albert. *Europa y la revolución francesa. OC*, VIII, 836

Soto y Calvo, Francisco. *El genio de la raza. OC*, IV, 912

– 'De la falta de carácter en la literatura argentina.' *OC*, VI, 829

– *El jurado de las sombras. OC*, VIII, 186

Sousa, Francisco de. *Tratado das ilhas novas. OC*, I, 412

Southey, Robert. In *Quarterly Review*, XII (1814), 64. *OC*, VI, 963

Souvestre, Emile. *El mundo en el año 2000. OC*, XI, 81

Spencer, Herbert. *El individuo contra el estado. OC*, XI, 980

Spencer, Philipp Jacob. *OC*, XVI, 378

Staël, Madame de. *De l'Allemagne. OC*, V, 164

Stead, W.T. *OC*, III, 109

Stecchetti, Lorenzo, pseud. [i.e., Olindo Guerrini]. *OC*, XIV, 270

Stein, Lorenz von. *Die drei Fragen des Grundbesitzes und seiner Zukunft.* Stuttgart. 1881. *OC*, IV, 1062

Steinthal, Heymann. *OC*, VI, 194

Stewart, Dugald. *OC*, III, 101

Stirner, Max. *Der Einzige und sein Eigentum. OC*, VIII, 1101

Stowe, Harriet Elizabeth. *La cabaña del tío Tom. OC*, V, 353

Sudermann, Hermann. *Magda. OC*, XI, 513

Sué, Eugène. *OC*, V, 783

Sulzer. *OC*, VI, 201

Supervielle, Jules. *Gravitations. OC*, XIV, 631

Surius, Laurentius. *De probatis sanctorum. OC*, VI, 130

Symonds, John A. *OC*, I, 1001

Symons, Arthur. *OC*, IV, 947

Tacitus, Publius Cornelius. *C. Cornelii Taciti ab excessu divi Augusti annalium. OC*, XVI, 343

– *Historias. OC*, XVI, 343

– *Germanía. OC*, IX, 900

Taine, Hippolyte-Adolphe. *De l'intelligence. OC*, IV, 882

Tárrago y Mateos, Torcuato. *OC*, V, 389

Tasso, Torquato. Aminta. *OC*, IV, 21

Tauler, Johann. *OC*, III, 510

Tertullianus, Quintus Septimus Florens. *Tertulliani ... adversus Marcionem libri V. OC*, XVI, 234

Thales, of Miletus. *OC*, XVI, 271

Thierry, Amédée-Simon-Dominique. *Histoire des Gaulois. OC*, VI, 170

Thierry, Jacques Nicolas Augustin. *Récits des Temps Mérovingiens.*
  OC, III, 190
Thomas, de Celano. *OC,* XVI, 179
Thomas [More], Saint. *Utopía. OC,* IV, 1041
Thomson, James. *Estaciones. OC,* VIII, 439
Thomson, James (poet, 19th century). 'La ciudad de la noche terrible.'
  OC, V, 492
Thorold, A.L. *The Life of Henry Labouchere. OC,* VIII, 739
Thorold Rogers. See Rogers, James Edwin Thorold
Toledano, Rodrigo. See Jiménez de Rada, Rodrigo
Tolstoi, Leon. *La sonata a Kreutzer. OC,* XI, 168
Torre, Guillermo de. 'Las últimas versiones de España (Waldo Frank,
  Keyserling, Jean Cassou),' *Síntesis. OC,* XV, 919
Traggia, Joaquín. 'Navarra,' *Diccionario Geográfico-Histórico de España.*
  1802. *OC,* VI, 100
Trueba, Antonio de. *Libro de los cantares. OC,* I, 965
– *Marisanta. OC,* I, 299
– *Bosquejo. OC,* VI, 286
– *Cuentos de color de rosa. OC,* XV, 275
Tubino. *Recherches d'anthropologie sociale. OC,* VI, 92
Turgenev, Ivan. *OC,* VI, 196
Los ultimos fueros. OC, I, 343
Unamuno, Miguel de. *Commento al Don Chisciotte.* Tr. Gilberto Beccari.
  Pról. M. de Unamuno. *OC,* VII, 238
Urani, Costa. *Sol y sombra. Figuras y paisajes de España. OC,* XI, 1010
– *Spleen. OC,* XI, 1011
Vailati, Giovanni. *El papel de la paradoja en el desarrollo de las teorías*
  filosóficas. OC, IV, 823
Valbuena, Antonio de. *OC,* XIV, 448
Valdegamas, Marqués de. See Donoso Cortés, Juan
Valdés, Juan de. *Diálogo de la lengua. OC,* III, 386
– *Ziento i diez consideraziones. OC,* III, 776
Valéry, Paul. *Variété, I. OC,* XI, 855
Valle Arizpe, Artemio de. *La muy noble y leal ciudad de México. OC,* XI, 871
Valle-Inclán, Ramón María del. *Sonatas. OC,* V, 423
Vallenilla Lanz, Laureano. *Cesarismo democrático. OC,* VI, 934
Valmīki. *Rāmāyana. OC,* XI, 764
Van Eys, W.J. *Dictionnaire basque-français.* Amsterdam. 1873
Vaz Ferreira, Carlos. *Moral para intelectuales. OC,* IV, 667
– *Ideas y observaciones. OC,* VIII, 400
– *Sobre la propiedad de la tierra. OC,* VIII, 585
– *Lecciones sobre pedagogía y cuestiones de enseñanza. OC,* VIII, 585
Vega, Lope de. *Santiago el Verde. OC,* I, 964

Willy, pseud. (i.e., Henry Gauthier Villars). *Las Claudinas. OC,* iv, 480

Winteler, J. *OC,* vi, 494

Wittelshofer. *Archiv für Soziale Gesetzgebung. OC,* iv, 1061

Wolff, F. *Historia de las literaturas castellana y portuguesa.* Tr. M. de
     Unamuno. *OC,* x, 283

Yeats, W.B. *Per amica silentia lunae. OC,* ix, 76

Young, Arthur. *OC,* xi, 75

Zapata, Antonio Lupián de. *Pseudo-chronicon de Auberto. OC,* vi, 130

Zeballos, Estanislao S. *OC,* viii, 296

Zielinski. *La Sibylle. OC,* xvi, 482

Zóbel de Zangróniz, Jacobo. *OC,* vi, 107

Zola, Emile Edouard Charles Antoine. *Les Rougon-Macquart. OC,* v, 835

- *Lourdes. OC,* xvi, 514

Zorrilla, José. *Don Juan Tenorio. OC,* i, 301

- *A buen juez, mejor testigo. OC,* viii, 764

- *Margarita la Tornera. OC,* viii, 764

- 'Granada.' *OC,* viii, 764

- *Cantos del trovador. OC,* x, 1037

- 'Las nubes.' *OC,* xi, 824

Zulueta, Luis de. 'La educación moral,' *La Publicidad* (9 July 1908).
     OC, iv, 441

Appendix II

Newspapers and journals not included in the catalogue but cited by Unamuno in his collected works and/or newspapers and journals in which he published articles. Only one representative entry from the *Obras Completas* is given in each case.

Los Lunes de El Imparcial (Madrid).
   OC, I, 554
Madrid Científico. *OC*, XI, 295
Madrid Cómico. *OC*, II, 721
Magisterio Salmantino. *OC*, VII, 546
La Mañana (Las Palmas). *OC*, X, 213
*El Mensajero del Sagrado Corazón de
   Jesús*. *OC*, XI, 904
El Mercantil Valenciano (Valencia).
   OC, V, 47
Mercure de France. *OC*, I, 356
Mercurio (New Orleans). *OC*, VI, 869
El Mercurio (Rosario, Argentina).
   OC, VIII, 48
El Mercurio (Santiago de Chile).
   OC, III, 1084
La Moda Elegante e Ilustrada. *OC*, XI,
   903-4
El Mundo (Madrid). *OC*, VII, 785
El Mundo Cómico. *OC*, II, 715
Mundo Gráfico (Madrid). *OC*, II, 784
El Mundo Latino (Madrid). *OC*, VIII,
   361
Le Museon. *OC*, VI, 137
La Nación (Buenos Aires). *OC*, I, 877
El Nacional (Madrid). *OC*, XI, 74
The Nation. *OC*, V, 914
La Nazione (Florence). *OC*, VIII, 452
El Nervión (Bilbao). *OC*, I, 140
La Noche (Madrid). *OC*, V, 352
El Noroeste (La Coruña). *OC*, VII,
   562
El Norte (Bilbao). *OC*, VI, 234
El Norte de Castilla (Valladolid).
   OC, IV, 1051
Las Noticias (Barcelona). *OC*, III,
   791
El Noticiero Bilbaíno. *OC*, I, 163
El Noticiero Salmantino. *OC*, IV,
   1075
El Noticioso (Corrientes, Argentina).
   OC, VIII, 48

Les Nouvelles Littéraires. *OC*, X, 845
Nuestro Tiempo (Madrid). *OC*, III, 34
Nueva Antologia (Roma). *OC*, VI, 589
Nuevo Mundo (Madrid). *OC*, I, 847
El Nuevo Tiempo (Colombia). *OC*,
   VIII, 317
Nuova Parola. *OC*, VII, 240
Orden y Progreso (México). *OC*, IV,
   522
El Oriental (Paysandu, Uruguay).
   OC, VIII, 48
El Pais (Buenos Aires). *OC*, IV, 912
O Paiz (Portugal). *OC*, I, 424
La Pampa (Buenos Aires). *OC*, VIII,
   48
La Pluma (Madrid). *OC*, XIV, 898
Plus Ultra (Buenos Aires). *OC*, V,
   1012
El Poble Catalá. *OC*, V, 878
El Porvenir (Sevilla). *OC*, X, 97
La Prensa (Belgrano, Argentina).
   OC, VIII, 48
La Prensa (Buenos Aires). *OC*, IV,
   1099
O Primeiro de Janeiro (Oporto).
   OC, I, 385
El Progreso (Madrid). *OC*, V, 720
El Progreso (Pontevedra). *OC*, VII,
   823
El Progreso Latino (México). *OC*, IV,
   433
La Publicitat (Barcelona). *OC*, IV,
   441
El Pueblo (San Nicolas, Argentina).
   OC, VIII, 48
El Pueblo (Valencia). *OC*, VII, 985
El Pueblo Gallego (Vigo). *OC*, VI,
   947
The Puerto Rico Herald. *OC*, V, 115
Quarterly Review. *OC*, VI, 963
La Quincena (Sevilla). *OC*, V, 829
Le Quotidien. *OC*, XIV, 543

Vida Nueva (Madrid). *OC*, III, 428

La Voz de Guipúzcoa (San Sebastian).
  OC, XI, 688

La Voz del Interior (Cordoba,
  Argentina). *OC*, VI, 882

A Voz Publica (Portugal). *OC*, I, 414

*Zeitschrift für Romanische
  Philologie*. *OC*, VI, 278